THE ANGLO-SAXON POETIC RECORDS

A COLLECTIVE EDITION

VI

THE ANGLO-SAXON MINOR POEMS

THE
ANGLO-SAXON
MINOR POEMS

EDITED BY

ELLIOTT VAN KIRK DOBBIE

PROFESSOR OF ENGLISH
IN COLUMBIA UNIVERSITY

NEW YORK: COLUMBIA UNIVERSITY PRESS

LONDON: ROUTLEDGE AND KEGAN PAUL

PREFACE

THIS VOLUME, numbered Volume VI of the *Anglo-Saxon Poetic Records*, contains the many verse texts, most of them short, which are scattered here and there in manuscripts not primarily devoted to Anglo-Saxon poetry. The title, *The Anglo-Saxon Minor Poems*, seems the most convenient one available, although a number of the poems, notably the BATTLE OF MALDON and SOLOMON AND SATURN, are not "minor" in the ordinary sense of that word. As a general rule, only those poems have been admitted which are written in the regular alliterative verse; but the DEATH OF ALFRED, which has rime instead of alliteration, is included with the five other Chronicle poems, following the practice of earlier editors, and the metrical charms are printed in their entirety, though most of them are only partly in verse and their metrical structure is often far from regular. The only poem included here which has not previously been published is the SEASONS FOR FASTING, discovered not many years ago in a British Museum manuscript. With the publication of this volume only the two poems in MS. Cotton Vitellius A.xv, BEOWULF and JUDITH, remain to be edited; they will appear together in Volume IV, now in preparation.

In its general arrangement, this volume is intended to conform as closely as possible to the earlier volumes of the series. But with fifty-three poems to be edited, from seventy-two separate manuscripts and several other sources, it was necessary to modify the plan to some extent. The Introduction has become a series of introductions to the several poems, with descriptions of the manuscripts; these, though placed together, are more or less independent of each other. These introductions are necessarily much compressed, and problems of selection of material have been difficult; but it is hoped that nothing of importance has been omitted. Wherever possible, poems from the same manuscript are discussed

v

as a unit. In a few cases, however, this was not feasible; for example, the poems in MS. 41 of Corpus Christi College, Cambridge, have been dealt with at three different places in the book. The Bibliography, which follows the Introduction, is presented in a more compact form than in the earlier volumes; to save unnecessary repetition, editions and periodicals frequently cited are abbreviated according to the list of abbreviations on pp. cxlix–cl. The texts and notes are printed in the usual way. A list of the accent marks in the manuscripts is given on pp. cxxxix–cxlv, immediately after the Introduction. The contents of the folios in the manuscripts are listed in the footnotes to the Introduction, instead of being placed together at the end; the list of small capitals, a feature of the earlier volumes, is omitted here, as impracticable for so many different manuscripts. Attention is called to the analytical Table of Contents on pp. ix–x, which will facilitate the finding of material on any desired poem.

No special virtue is claimed for the order in which the poems are printed in this volume. All that can be said is that the order adopted seemed a natural one from the beginning, and that no better order suggested itself. The texts, except those of the LEIDEN RIDDLE and the Hague manuscript of BEDE'S DEATH SONG, are based on photostats, supplemented in each case by a first-hand examination of the manuscript. For reasons stated in the introduction to the LEIDEN RIDDLE, it seemed best to base the text of that poem on the readings of earlier editors. As in *The Exeter Book*, words or letters which are illegible or lost from the manuscript are indicated by points within brackets; no attempt has been made to restore such losses in the text, but the suggested restorations are recorded in the notes.

It is a pleasure to acknowledge my gratitude to Professor Robert J. Menner, of Yale University, for his generous help on the introduction and text of SOLOMON AND SATURN; to Professor Francis P. Magoun, Jr., of Harvard University, for the loan of some materials illustrative of the RUNE POEM; to Professor Philip W. Souers, of Newcomb College, Tulane University, for lending me the photographs of the Franks Casket which are reproduced in this volume, and for criticizing my introduction to the Franks Casket; to Professor Harry Morgan Ayres of Columbia University, for reading the

Introduction and making a number of very helpful comments; and to all those who, at one time or another, have expressed the conviction that this volume would some day be finished. I wish also to thank Messrs. Methuen and Co., Ltd., for permitting me to reproduce the drawing of the Ruthwell Cross, and the Trustees of the British Museum, for authorizing the reproduction of the two photographs of the Franks Casket.

E. V. K. D.

January 30, 1942

CONTENTS

INTRODUCTION

INTRODUCTION

THE BATTLE OF FINNSBURH

THE FRAGMENTARY text of the BATTLE OF FINNS-
BURH was first printed in George Hickes' *Thesaurus* in
1705, from a "singulare folium, in codice MS. homiliarum
Semi-Saxonicarum qui extat in Bibliotheca Lambethana."[1] In
spite of repeated search no trace of the original leaf has since been
found. Hickes' word "Semi-Saxonicarum" seems to point to
Lambeth Palace MS. 487, a thirteenth-century collection of Anglo-
Saxon homilies, as the manuscript from which he took the fragment.[2] Lambeth Palace MS. 489, an Anglo-Saxon homily book of
the eleventh century, is also a possibility; but the language of this
manuscript is hardly what we should call "semi-Saxon." At any
rate, the BATTLE OF FINNSBURH is no longer to be found in either
of these manuscripts; and consequently Hickes' printed transcript
is our only source for the poem.

Hickes' text of the BATTLE OF FINNSBURH, like the other Anglo-
Saxon verse texts printed in his *Thesaurus*, is arranged (not always
correctly) by half-lines, and provided with a capital letter at the
beginning of each half-line and a period at the end of each half-line.
All proper names, and the common nouns *Eastun*, l. 3, *Nama*,
l. 24, and *Celæs*, l. 29, are also capitalized. Except for the capitalization and punctuation of the half-lines, we may presume that
Hickes intended to provide an accurate copy of the manuscript.
Unfortunately, Hickes' reputation for accuracy, according to

[1] Part 1, pp. 192–193. See also Wanley, *Catalogus historico-criticus* (Oxford,
1705), p. 269.

[2] See M. R. James and C. Jenkins, *A Descriptive Catalogue of the Manuscripts
in the Library of Lambeth Palace* (Cambridge, 1930ff.), pp. 680–681; the authors
point out that the "cod. MS homil. Semi-Sax." referred to by Hickes, p. 222,
note, is undoubtedly MS. 487.

modern standards, is not very high,[1] and it is likely that many of
the corruptions in the extant text are to be imputed to him rather
than to the scribe of the original manuscript.   The very unusual
spellings *Eastun*, l. 3, and *weuna*, l. 25, are probably the result of
his having misread *a*'s in the manuscript as *u*'s; the exclusive use
of capital *Đ* (for both *þ* and *Đ*) at the beginnings of half-lines is in
accordance with his practice elsewhere in the *Thesaurus*, and it is
probable that some of the *Đ*'s were *þ*'s in the original text.[2]   Under
the circumstances, therefore, it is impossible to have any great
confidence in the authority of Hickes' readings, and scholars have
been inclined to emend the text of this poem more readily than
most other Anglo-Saxon verse texts.

The relationship between the BATTLE OF FINNSBURH (often
called simply the "Finnsburh Fragment") and the so-called "Finnsburh Episode" of BEOWULF (ll. 1063–1159) has been the subject
of widespread controversy.   No other versions of the story are
preserved, in either English or Scandinavian literature.[3]   The
Fragment by itself is certainly not clear; it opens at the beginning
of the fight at Finn's hall and closes before the fight is over, and the
internal indications of the action are not very definite.   It is only
by placing the Fragment within the framework of the Episode, as
told in BEOWULF, that it is possible to reconstruct the entire story
and to estimate the original length and contents of the complete
poem.

The story in BEOWULF 1063–1159 concerns the death of the
Danish prince Hnæf in a fight against the retainers of Finn Folc-
walding, at Finn's hall in Friesland, and the revenge subsequently

[1] See the comment by R. W. Chambers, *Beowulf: an Introduction* (revised
ed., Cambridge, 1932), p. 245.

[2] Hickes very often prints *ð* for *þ*, or *þ* for *ð*, as a collation of any of his texts
will show; but he invariably uses *Đ* as the capital letter, using the capital *þ* as
one of his forms for the runic capital *W*.

[3] The names of Hnæf (as ruler of the Hocings) and Finn are found in WID-
SITH, ll. 27, 29.   The O.H.G. forms *Huochingus* (= *Hocing*) and *Nebi* (=
Hnæf) appear in an Alemannic genealogy of the eighth century; for these and
other German occurrences of the names, see K. Müllenhoff, *Zeitschrift für
deutsches Altertum* XI (1859), 282; XII (1865), 285–287.   Proper names from
the Finn story in Anglo-Saxon documents and place-names are discussed by G.
Binz, *Beiträge* XX (1895), 179–186.

taken by his men. The narrative is condensed and allusive; but
we gather from it that Hildeburh, a princess of the Danish royal
blood and probably Hnæf's sister,[1] has been married to Finn; that
during a visit of the Danes to Finn's court a conflict breaks out
between Danes and Frisians, in which Hnæf is killed. After both
parties have fought to the point of exhaustion, a truce is arranged
between Finn and Hengest, the leader of the surviving Danes.
By the terms of this truce Finn becomes the protector of the Danes;
they are to share equally with the Frisians in the possession of the
high hall and in the distribution of treasure. Hengest and his men
remain with Finn during the remainder of the winter, but their
duty of revenge to their fallen lord—prescribed by the spirit of
the *comitatus*—finally outweighs in Hengest's mind the pledges
which he has made to Finn. In the spring two of the Danes,
Guthlaf and Oslaf, egg Hengest on to action. Another battle
results, in which Finn and his men are slain.

There is considerable difference of opinion among scholars as to
the precise details of the narrative, but the bare outline given above
would probably command general acceptance.[2] Now we may ask,
where does the Finnsburh Fragment fit into this story? The
situation presented in the Fragment is a night battle between two
opposing forces, one of them sheltered in Finn's hall (*Finnsburuh*,
l. 36), the other attacking from without. Among the defenders of
the hall are several of the Danish heroes mentioned in the Episode:
Hengest (l. 17) and Guthlaf (l. 16) take part in the defence of one
of the doors, and the Ordlaf who helps them (l. 16) is quite possibly
the same man as the Oslaf mentioned along with Guthlaf in BEO-
WULF 1148. Hnæf, the Danish prince, must be presumed from
l. 40 to be the leader of the hall-defenders, and in l. 2 Trautmann's
emendation *Hnæf*, for the meaningless *Næfre* printed by Hickes,[3]
is convincing. Since Hnæf is represented as still alive, the action
of the Fragment must be the earlier of the two fights referred to in

[1] On the evidence of BEOWULF 1076, where she is described as *Hoces dohtor*,
and of WIDSITH 29, *Hnæf [weold] Hocingum*.

[2] The problems raised by the Finnsburh Episode will be discussed in more
detail in Volume IV of this series.

[3] See the note on this line, p. 131, below.

the Episode, the one which results in Hnæf's death.[1] But since this fight is not described at all in the Episode, there is no possibility of clearing up the textual obscurities in the Fragment by a comparison of the two poems. A careful study of the Fragment, however, yields a fairly clear picture of the action. The letters -nas byrnað, l. 1 (to be restored to read [hor]nas byrnað) are all that remains of a speech by one of the Danes, possibly Hengest. And in view of the repetition of the phrase in l. 4b, hornas ne byrnað, it is best to take l. 1 as the end of a question put to Hnæf, the "battle-young king," by one of his followers;[2] then ll. 3–12 are Hnæf's answer, repeating the several clauses of the question. In anticipation of an attack, the Danes arm themselves and take up positions at the doors of the hall—Sigeferth and Eaha at one door, Ordlaf and Guthlaf at the other.[3] The meaning of l. 17 is open to question. Do the words hwearf him on laste mean simply that Hengest followed the others into the hall,[4] or do they mean that he took up a position near Ordlaf and Guthlaf, so as to be able to reinforce them in case of need?[5]

The phraseology of ll. 19–20 makes it clear that the Garulf and Guthere mentioned in l. 18 are Frisians. One of them[6] cautions the other not to be too hasty in attacking, and at the same time calls out to Sigeferth, who is guarding one of the doors, to learn

---

[1] Möller's old theory (Das altenglische Volksepos I, 46ff.) that the Fragment describes a later fight (to be placed between l. 1145 and l. 1146 of the Episode), the heaþogeong cyning of l. 2 being Hengest, is not supported by the evidence. The accepted interpretation of the Fragment, which in general is followed here, goes back to Bugge, Beiträge XII, 20–28.

[2] Chambers in his edition also treats l. 1 as a question; see the note on this line, p. 131, below.

[3] In l. 16, durum is probably to be translated as a singular.

[4] But the Danes are probably in the hall when the Fragment begins.

[5] The phrase Hengest sylf, which has caused difficulty for some commentators, is perhaps merely an indication that in the later part of the poem, as in the Episode, Hengest is to play the leading role.

[6] Just which one, is not quite certain; see the note on this line, p. 133, below. R. W. Chambers (in Wyatt and Chambers, Beowulf, 2d ed., p. 160) believes that Guthere is cautioning Garulf; according to him, the death of Garulf in l. 31 is the result of his having neglected Guthere's advice. Klaeber, Englische Studien XXXIX, 307f., suggests that Guthere and Garulf are uncle and nephew—a common epic motive.

his identity. That the Frisian Garulf is called "Guthlaf's son" in
l. 33 does not necessarily mean that he is the son of the Danish
Guthlaf who is stationed at the other door, since the name Guthlaf
must have been fairly common in Germanic antiquity.[1] The
wund hæleð of l. 43 is generally taken to be a Frisian, and the
folces hyrde, l. 46, to be Finn, who is inquiring about the state of
the Danish resistance.[2] The last line of the Fragment is very
difficult to interpret, and in the absence of the context it is perhaps
better not to interpret it at all.

From l. 41 of the Fragment, we learn that the battle has already
lasted five days, but that none of the Danish defenders has fallen.
On the other hand, a line in the Episode (*syþðan morgen com*, l.
1077) suggests that the battle was over and done in a single night.
This seems to be the only serious discrepancy between the Fragment and the Episode, and whether the fight lasted one night or
five is immaterial to the course of the story. When the Fragment
breaks off, Hnæf has not yet been killed, but we know from the
Episode that both he and the son of Finn fall before the end of the
battle. Rieger's suggestion[3] that the Frisians later set the hall on
fire—a frequent practice in Old Germanic warfare—seems unlikely,
since if the Danes had been driven into the open by the burning of
their shelter, the stalemate described in the Episode could hardly
have come about.

This, then, is the situation described in the Fragment. Unlike
the Episode, which concentrates the entire story of Hnæf's death
and Hengest's revenge within the limits of a hall recitation of only
ninety-one lines, the Fragment is strongly dramatic, with extensive use of direct discourse.[4] Characteristic of this text, as contrasted with the generality of Anglo-Saxon poetry, are the high

[1] To be sure, W. G. Searle, *Onomasticon Anglo-Saxonicum* (Cambridge, 1897),
p. 273, lists the Anglo-Saxon name only from the present text; but for the Old
Norse form *Gunnleifr*, see E. H. Lind, *Norsk-isländska dopnamn och fingerade
namn fra medeltiden* (Uppsala, 1905–1915), col. 415.

[2] For the contrary opinion, see especially Bugge, *Beiträge* XII, 28; Trautmann, *Finn und Hildebrand*, pp. 61–62.

[3] *Zeitschrift für deutsches Altertum* XLVIII, 12.

[4] Of the five speeches indicated in the text of the Fragment, three (the question ending in l. 1*b*, Hnæf's answer, ll. 3–12, and the speech of Sigeferth in ll.
24–27) are in direct, and two (ll. 18–23, 46–48*a*) in indirect discourse.

frequency of end-stopped lines and the regular use of the adverb
Ða (in ll. 13, 14, 18, 28, 43, 46) to introduce the rather abrupt
transitions in the narrative. Although there are a number of
verbal resemblances between the Fragment and other Anglo-Saxon
poems,[1] the usual ornaments of the more leisurely epic style are
conspicuously absent. The closest stylistic parallel in Germanic
literature is to be found in the Old High German *Hildebrandslied*,
the extant lines of which show the same abruptness of manner and
the same economy of diction as the Fragment.[2] These two poems,
the BATTLE OF FINNSBURH and the *Hildebrandslied*, are the only
surviving examples from the Old Germanic period of the short
epic lay, the most primitive form of Germanic narrative poetry.[3]
The *Hildebrandslied*, of which nearly seventy lines remain, is incomplete at the end, but it is not likely to have run to more than
twice its present length. It is probable that the BATTLE OF
FINNSBURH, in its complete state, was somewhat longer, say two or
three hundred lines in all, and that it treated within this space the
entire story of the Danish-Frisian relationships from the arrival of
Hnæf and his men in Friesland to the death of Finn.

The date of composition of the BATTLE OF FINNSBURH is difficult
to determine. Metrical criteria suggest a fairly late date; for
example, the irregular placing of the alliteration in ll. 22*a*, 28*b*,
41*b*, and 46*a* can be paralleled in the BATTLE OF MALDON and other
poems of the late Anglo-Saxon period, but is very infrequent in the
older poetry. On the other hand, the subject matter belongs with
that of BEOWULF and the other heroic poetry, and may point to an

---

[1] See Klaeber, *Beowulf* (3d ed.), p. 238.

[2] The comparison between the Finnsburh Fragment and the *Hildebrandslied*
is fairly obvious, and has been made by many commentators. An interesting
parallel is to be found in the use of the introductory *dô* in the *Hildebrandslied*,
ll. 33, 63, 65, corresponding to the use of *Ða*, noted above, in the Fragment.
A similarity to the style of the later popular ballads has also been suggested;
see Brandl, in Paul's *Grundriss der germanischen Philologie* (2d ed.), II, 1, 985;
Schücking, *Kleines angelsächsisches Dichterbuch*, p. 36.

[3] For discussions of the characteristics of the epic lay, as contrasted with the
full-length book epic, see A. Heusler, *Die altgermanische Dichtung* (Berlin-
Neubabelsberg, 1923), pp. 147–149; G. Ehrismann, *Geschichte der deutschen
Literatur bis zum Ausgange des Mittelalters* I (2d ed., Munich, 1932), 134–135.
A much later example of the lay is the Middle Low German poem *Von Koninc
Ermenrîkes dôt*.

early date for the poem, say the eighth century, or about the same period as the *Hildebrandslied*. If the BATTLE OF FINNSBURH was written as early as the eighth century, then the various late spellings in the extant text (such as *buruhðelu*, l. 30, *Finnsburuh*, l. 36, both with the intrusive vowel; *sword*, l. 15, *Heordra*, l. 26, *fǽla*, l. 33, and so forth) must[1] be the work of the scribe of the Lambeth manuscript or of one of his immediate predecessors.

WALDERE

The two leaves of Anglo-Saxon verse dealing with the legend of Walter of Aquitaine, first published in 1860 by George Stephens, were discovered in January of that year by Dr. E. C. Werlauff, Chief Librarian of the Royal Library at Copenhagen, among some miscellaneous bundles of loose paper and parchment leaves. They are still preserved in the Royal Library under the number Ny kgl. saml. 167b. The earlier history of the fragments is completely unknown, but Stephens' suggestion that they were brought to Denmark by Grímur Thorkelin, the pioneer editor of BEOWULF, in the closing years of the eighteenth century is as good a guess as any.

One of the two leaves is somewhat taller than the other, but 8 by 5 inches (or about 20 by 13 cm.) would be a fair approximation of size for both. Each leaf contains two consecutive pages of text, together with a half-inch or so of the conjugate leaf, the rest of which has in each case been trimmed away. The two leaves are usually referred to, for the sake of convenience, as Fragment I (beginning *hyrde hyne georne*)[2] and Fragment II (beginning *-ce bæteran*).[3] Fragment I was originally the left half of a folded sheet; Fragment II was originally the right half of a sheet. Whether the two sheets originally belonged to the same gathering of the

---

[1] That is, in so far as they are not to be ascribed to Hickes; see p. xiii, above.

[2] Most editors take this fragment as preceding the other in the order of the narrative, but the sequence of the fragments is not undisputed; see below, p. xxv.

[3] The contents of the four pages in the line numbering of this edition are as follows: Fragment I*a*, *hyrde*, I, 1, to *byrn-*, I, 17; Fragment I*b*, *-homon*, I, 17, to *ða*, I, 32; Fragment II*a*, *-ce bæteran*, II, 1, to *dyrre*, II, 16; Fragment II*b*, *æt*, II, 17, to *is*, II, 31.

manuscript or to two different gatherings, it is naturally impossible to tell, and consequently we cannot estimate, except on internal evidence, the amount of text which originally stood in the manuscript between the two fragments. On the narrow edges remaining from the conjugate leaves, a few letters belonging to the inner edge of the text can still be read, especially on the leaf belonging to Fragment I.[1] Of the last line on the page opposite Fragment I*a*, the letters *swil* still remain, and it has been proposed[2] to attach these letters to the -*ce* at the beginning of Fragment II*a*; then *swilce bæteran* would be the proper restoration of l. 1*b* of Fragment II. According to Norman, the only arrangement of the two fragments which will give the reading *swilce bæteran* is the one with Fragment I preceding Fragment II, and with the two fragments belonging to adjacent folds of the same gathering; in this case, also, not more than about 150 lines can have been lost between the two fragments. But the possible reading *swilce* may be merely a coincidence,[3] and we therefore cannot draw any positive conclusions from it.

Both of the fragments are written in a single large and angular, occasionally somewhat awkward, hand, which is probably to be assigned to the year 1000, perhaps a little earlier or a little later.[4]

Since the two fragments are so short, it is not easy to fit them into their proper place in the story of Walter and Hildegund, but a comparison with other medieval texts dealing with the Walter legend throws some light on this problem. The longest and best known version of the story is found in the Latin epic variously known as *Waltharii poesis* or *Waltharius manu fortis*, or simply as *Waltharius*, consisting of 1456 hexameter lines, written by Ekke-

[1] A list of these remnants of text is given by Norman, *Waldere*, p. 2.

[2] By Leitzmann, *Walther und Hiltgunt bei den Angelsachsen*, p. 7, and Norman, *Waldere*, p. 3. Norman's complete discussion of this point is instructive and should be consulted.

[3] See Holthausen, *Die altenglischen Waldere-Bruchstücke*, pp. 2–3.

[4] According to Förster, *Englische Studien* XXIX, 107f., the hand cannot be earlier than the second half of the tenth century. Keller, *Angelsächsische Palaeographie*, p. 42, would date it "after 1000." See also Norman, *Waldere*, pp. 4–5. Holthausen's facsimiles, in his *Die altenglischen Waldere-Bruchstücke*, give a good idea of the state of the text.

hard I of St. Gall, who died in 973.[1]   Other important texts dealing
with the Walter story are: (1) Book II, Chapters 7–13, of the
Chronicon Novaliciense, a Latin chronicle of the Benedictine abbey
at Novalesa, in Piedmont, compiled at some time in the latter part
of the eleventh century;[2] (2) two short fragments[3] of a Middle
High German epic, written in the first half of the thirteenth century
in a variant form of the *Nibelungenlied* strophe; (3) a rather lengthy
passage (Chapters 241–244)[4] in the Norwegian *þiðriks saga*, also
of the thirteenth century; (4) the Polish story of a hero by the
name of Walter (called *wdały Walter*, "Walterus robustus"), the
earliest form of which is found in the Latin *Chronicon Poloniae*,
ascribed to Boguphal II, bishop of Poznan, who died in 1253, but
more probably a fourteenth-century compilation.[5]   To these may
be added a large number of references to Walter in the *Nibelungenlied* and other Middle High German poems.[6]

In the study of the Walter legend, Ekkehard's *Waltharius* is of
fundamental importance.   The main points of the narrative are
briefly indicated in the following summary.

Hagano, a young Frankish nobleman, Hiltgunt, only daughter
of the Burgundian king Heririeus, and Waltharius, son of King
Alphere of Aquitania, are sent as hostages to Attila, king of the
Huns.   In Attila's wars Waltharius and Hagano, who have sworn

[1] The standard edition of the poem is by H. Althof, 2 vols., Leipzig, 1899–
1905.   A convenient text for students, with a Modern German translation, is
the edition by H. Ronge, Munich, 1934.

[2] Edited by L. C. Bethmann in *Mon. Germ. hist.*, Scriptores, VII (Berlin,
1846), 73–133, and by C. Cipolla, *Monumenta Novaliciensia vetustiora* (Rome,
1898ff.) II, 97–305.   See also J. Bédier, *Les Légendes épiques* II (3d ed., Paris,
1926), 158–164.

[3] Preserved at Graz and Vienna; see Althof, *Waltharii poesis* I, 17–18.

[4] H. Bertelsen, *þiðriks Saga af Bern* (Copenhagen, 1905 ff.) II, 105–109.

[5] Edited by A. Bielowski, *Monumenta Poloniæ historica* II (Lwów, 1872),
510–515.   See also Heinzel, *Über die Walthersage*, pp. 27–36; Althof, *Waltharii
poesis* I, 21–23.

[6] All the known texts relating to the Walter legend are printed by M. D.
Learned, *The Saga of Walther of Aquitaine*, and may conveniently be consulted
there.   The Latin versions are translated by H. M. Smyser and F. P. Magoun,
Jr., *Survivals in Old Norwegian of Medieval English, French, and German Litera-
ture, together with the Latin Versions of the Heroic Legend of Walter of Aquitaine*
(Baltimore, 1941), pp. 111–152.

brotherhood, distinguish themselves by their military prowess. Gibicho, the Frankish king, dies and is succeeded by Guntharius, who renounces the Frankish alliance with Attila. Hagano flees by night from the Hunnish court.

To avoid a proposed marriage of Waltharius to a Hunnish princess, Waltharius and Hiltgunt, who have been betrothed since childhood, flee secretly, carrying with them two chests filled with treasure. None of the Hunnish warriors dares to pursue the fugitives, who make their way to the Rhine and cross it at Worms. King Guntharius, learning of their flight, hopes to capture their treasure as a return for the tribute paid by his father to Attila. He sets out with twelve warriors, including Hagano, and overtakes the fugitives. Waltharius refuses Guntharius' demand for Hiltgunt and the treasure, but offers gold rings in tribute. In spite of Hagano's warnings, the king determines to attack Waltharius. Hagano at first refuses to take part in the fighting.

Waltharius, protected by overhanging rocks, kills eight of the Frankish warriors, one after another, in single combat. A simultaneous onslaught by three other warriors also ends in their defeat and death. Finally Hagano, whose nephew is among those slain, agrees to assist Guntharius in a final attack. The next morning he and the king waylay Waltharius and Hiltgunt in the open. In the ensuing fight Guntharius loses a leg and Waltharius his right hand. Hagano loses his right eye and six of his teeth. With this the fight ends, and the three heroes converse amicably together while Hiltgunt binds their wounds. Guntharius and Hagano return to Worms; Waltharius proceeds with Hiltgunt to Aquitania, where he reigns as king for thirty years.

The other versions of the story differ variously from Ekkehard's narrative. In the *Chronicon Novaliciense*, the Walter legend is attached to an eighth-century local hero, Waltharius or Waltarius, who after a very active life spent his last years in the monastery at Novalesa. This version is of interest to us only because the compiler knew and used at least part of Ekkehard's poem, quoting extensively from it down to the beginning of the fight with Guntharius and his men. The Polish story deals not with the Aquitanian Walter, but with a Polish hero of the same name who is attacked by a German prince while conveying his bride Helgunda

from France back to Poland; its derivation from the Germanic
Walter legend is, however, beyond question. The narrative in the
þiðriks saga is perhaps closest of all to Ekkehard's poem, but here
Walter's fight is not with the Frankish king, but with Attila's men,
led by Högni (Hagano), who are pursuing him. The two Middle
High German fragments by themselves tell us very little about the
thirteenth-century epic poem from which they come,[1] but from
scattered clues derived from other Middle High German texts,
especially from *Biterolf und Dietleib*, Schneider has reconstructed
the most probable form of the German poem.[2] Except for the
adaptation of the story to a later medieval setting and the introduction of characters from the *Nibelungenlied*, the Middle High
German *Walther* seems to have differed little in its essential features
from the form of the legend used by Ekkehard three hundred years
earlier. In this version, according to Schneider, Hagene is the
first of the Burgundians to attack Walter, but he withdraws from
the combat as soon as he has recognized his old comrade.

We have, then, two independent versions of the Walter legend,
the *Waltharius* from the tenth century and the *Walther* from the
thirteenth, which, in spite of their differences in detail, go back to
the same original story of the flight of Walter and Hildegund from
Attila's court, Walter's fight with the Burgundian king Gunther
and his men, and the final return of the fugitives to Walter's
kingdom.[3] And it seems equally clear that in the two fragments
of the Anglo-Saxon WALDERE we have the remains of a long Anglo-
Saxon epic poem based on the same materials. Just as Walter's
father is called Alphere in Ekkehard's poem, and Alker (or Alpker)
in the Middle High German fragments, so in the Anglo-Saxon text

[1] In the Graz fragment Walther, Hiltegunt, and Hagene are still at the Hunnish court; in the Vienna fragment Walther and Hiltegunt are being escorted
home from Worms by Volker, presumably after the fight with Gunther.

[2] H. Schneider, *Germanisch-romanische Monatsschrift* XIII (1925), 14–32,
119–130, and *Germanische Heldensage* I (Berlin, 1928), 331–344.

[3] That the Middle High German poet derived his materials from sources
independent of Ekkehard is beyond doubt. For example, he identifies Gunther
correctly as king of the Burgundians, whereas Ekkehard, adapting the story to
the geography of his own time, makes Guntharius a Frank and Hiltgunt a
Burgundian princess. On this point see especially B. Dickins, *Runic and Heroic
Poems*, pp. 41–43.

Waldere is described as *Ælfheres sunu*, I, 11, and his corselet as
Ælfheres laf, "the heirloom of Ælfhere," II, 18. His military
prowess among the Huns is reflected in the phrase *Ætlan ordwyga*,
"champion of Attila," I, 6.[1] Guthhere (Guntharius and Gunther
in the other versions) is correctly described as *wine Burgenda*, II,
14, and Hagano's reluctance to do battle with Waltharius in
Ekkehard's poem is reflected in Waldere's words *Hwæt! Đu huru
wendest...þæt me Hagenan hand hilde gefremede*, II, 14–15. The
name of the heroine unfortunately does not appear in the Anglo-
Saxon fragments, but the proper Anglo-Saxon form would be
Hildegȳð,[2] and it may be that, as Cosijn suggested,[3] this name stood
in the half-line lost before *hyrde hyne georne*, I, 1, and alliterated
with *hyrde*.

It remains to determine the situation presented in the WALDERE
fragments, and to identify the speakers. With regard to the
identity of the speakers, there can be no doubt whatever that
Hildegyth is the speaker of I, 2–32, although her name does not
appear in the text. That Waldere is the speaker of II, 14–31 is
expressly stated. But the identity of the speaker of II, 1–10 is
difficult to determine. This speech is incomplete at the beginning,
and consequently there is no indication of the speaker in the manuscript. From Müllenhoff's time until comparatively recently,
editors and commentators were agreed that Guthhere is the speaker
here, ll. 14ff. (addressed to the *wine Burgenda*) then being Waldere's
reply. But in 1925 Wolff proposed to take II, 1–10 as the concluding lines of Hagena's refusal to take part in the combat.[4]
More recently Norman has suggested that Waldere is the speaker
of II, 1–10 as well as of what follows, ll. 11–13 being merely a re-
introduction of the same speaker.[5] The problem presented by this

---

[1] Waldere's sword Mimming is called *Welande[s] worc*, I, 2; in the *Waltharius*
it is his coat of armor which is *Wielandia fabrica* (l. 965).

[2] Not *Hildegūð*, as assumed by many commentators. The name *Hildegȳð*
appears twice in the *Liber vitae Dunelmensis* (Sweet, *Oldest English Texts*, p.
155, l. 40; p. 166, l. 445); compare also other feminine names with the same
suffix, *Ælfgȳð, Eadgȳð, Heregȳð*, etc.

[3] *Verslagen en Mededeelingen der k. Akademie van Wetenschappen, Afd.
Letterkunde*, 3d Series, XII, 68.

[4] *Zeitschrift für deutsches Altertum* LXII, 81–86. See also Klaeber, *Englische
Studien* LXX, 333f.

[5] *Waldere*, pp. 16ff.

passage is very difficult, but after all is said, probability still favors Guthhere as the speaker of II, 1–10.

The proper order of the two fragments also presents considerable difficulty. Most commentators have placed the action of Fragment I before that of Fragment II; but Fischer[1] and some later commentators[2] have preferred for various reasons to arrange the fragments in the reverse order. Fragment I, Hildegyth's speech of encouragement to Waldere, must come shortly after Guthhere's rejection of the offered tribute (*Forsoc he ðam swurde and ðam syncfatum*, I, 28), whether or not before the actual beginning of hostilities.[3] In Fragment II, on the other hand, Waldere has been fighting for some time (*æt ðus heaðuwerigan*, II, 17). In this second fragment, we may judge from ll. 14ff. that Hagena has either refused to fight with Waldere at all, as in the early battle scenes of the *Waltharius*, or has fought with him only until he has recognized him, as seems to have been the case in the Middle High German epic. At any rate, it seems certain that both fragments describe the early part of the fight, before anything resembling a final assault has taken place; though, since we do not know which of the continental versions the Anglo-Saxon poet followed, internal evidence hardly suffices to settle the order of events. If, however, the reading [*swit*]*ce* in II, 1 (with *swil-* taken from the edge of the page opposite Fragment I*a*)[4] be adopted, then Fragment I must be taken as preceding Fragment II, and the order of events proceeds most naturally as follows: 1. Guthhere's refusal of the sword and rings offered by Waldere; 2. Hildegyth's speech of encouragement (I, 2–32); 3. Hagena's refusal to attack his old comrade (or, Hagena's attack on Waldere, the recognition, and his withdrawal from the fight);[5] 4. Guthhere's (?) speech, praising a famous sword

---

[1] *Zu den Waldere-Fragmenten*, pp. 17ff.

[2] See Leitzmann, *Walther und Hiltgunt bei den Angelsachsen*, pp. 17ff.; Brandl, in Paul's *Grundriss der germanischen Philologie* (2d ed.), II, 1, 986ff.; Schücking, *Kleines angelsächsisches Dichterbuch*, pp. 54ff.

[3] Lines 4*b*–5 of this fragment may refer to previous encounters with Guthhere's men on the same day, but more probably to Waldere's victories in the service of Attila.

[4] See above, p. xx.

[5] The latter alternative seems preferable; the word *heaðuwerigan*, II, 17, implies that some fighting had taken place between the action of Fragments I and II.

which he has (II, 1–10); 5. Waldere's speech, in which he defies Guthhere to attack him without Hagena's help (II, 14–31).

Concerning the original length of the poem it is impossible to be very definite; but judging from what we know of the continental Walter legend and from the rather deliberate manner of the two fragments, it must have been an epic of considerable magnitude, at least a thousand lines long, perhaps even as long as BEOWULF. The date of composition of WALDERE, like that of most Anglo-Saxon epic poetry, is likely to have been early, say in the eighth century, but any date up to the writing of the manuscript, about 1000, is not excluded by the evidence. The language of the fragments is, in general, late West Saxon, but there are a few forms (*worc*, I, 2, *hworfan*, I, 30,[1] and *hafa*, II, 2) which are most plausibly explained as late Northumbrian. The usual assumption of an early Northumbrian original copied by a late West Saxon scribe is not necessarily contradicted by the presence of a few late Northumbrian forms in the text; it may be that, as Norman suggests,[2] we have an attempt by a late tenth-century Northumbrian to write "Standard" Anglo-Saxon, whether or not from an early Northumbrian original.

THE BATTLE OF MALDON

Among the manuscript treasures destroyed by fire in the Cottonian Library at Westminster in 1731 was the fragmentary text of the BATTLE OF MALDON in MS. Cotton Otho A.xii, fol. 57*a*–62*b*. Five years earlier, however, the text of the poem had been printed as one of the illustrative appendices in Thomas Hearne's edition of the Chronicle of John of Glastonbury, with the following caption, based in part upon the descriptions of the manuscript already published by Smith and Wanley:[3] "Fragmentum quoddam historicum de Eadrico &c. vel Fragmentum historicum, capite & calce mutilum, sex foliis constans, quo Poetice & Stylo Cæd-

---

[1] See Bülbring, *Altenglisches Elementarbuch* I, §265.

[2] *Waldere*, pp. 6f.

[3] T. Smith, *Catalogus librorum manuscriptorum bibliothecae Cottonianae* (Oxford, 1696), p. 67; H. Wanley, *Catalogus historico-criticus* (Oxford, 1705), pp. 232–233.

moniano celebratur virtus bellica Beorhtnothi Ealdormanni &
aliorum Anglo-Saxonum, in prælio cum Danis."

After the destruction of the original manuscript, Hearne's printed
text became, and remained until recently, the only known source
for the text of the poem. But it was discovered a few years ago[1]
that MS. Rawlinson B 203, in the Bodleian Library, contains the
transcript of the poem from which Hearne's printed text was set
up. This transcript consists of six paper leaves (fol. 7–12 of the
manuscript), or twelve pages, written in a large hand closely
imitative of Anglo-Saxon script. From a note in Hearne's handwriting at the head of the first page (later crossed out when the
copy was sent to the printer) we learn that the transcript was made
by John Elphinston, of the Cottonian Library, and was given to
Hearne in 1725 by Richard Graves, the antiquary of Mickleton in
Gloucestershire.[2] This transcript by Elphinston, as affording a
more immediate record of the original manuscript than Hearne's
printed text, was made the basis of E. V. Gordon's edition of the
poem, published in 1937, and has been followed in the present text.
In several places (ll. 7, 86, 122) we find that incorrect readings in
Hearne, which have been emended by modern editors, are nothing
more than printer's errors for correct forms which appear in the
transcript. Unfortunately, however, the total gain is not large,
and the more difficult passages in the poem are unaffected. The
deviations of Hearne's printed text from the transcript are: *leofre*
Hearne, *leofne* MS., l. 7; *luðe* Hearne, *laðe* MS., l. 86; *pest* Hearne,
west (or possibly *pest*) MS., l. 97; *stið hugende* Hearne, *stið hicgende*
MS., l. 122; *wræce* Hearne, *wręce* MS., l. 257; *gearc* Hearne, *gearo*
MS., l. 274; *læge* Hearne, *lęge* MS., l. 279; *Da* Hearne, *þa* MS., ll.
162, 202, 273, 277.

The theme of the BATTLE OF MALDON is sufficiently well known;
the poem describes, in 325 verse lines, the heroic resistance offered
to a band of Danish raiders by Byrhtnoth, alderman of the East
Saxons, and his followers at Maldon, in Essex, on August 10th or

[1] By Mr. N. R. Ker of Magdalen College, who called my attention to this
manuscript in 1935.

[2] See also Hearne, *Johannis . . . Glastoniensis chronica*, p. li, where, however,
Elphinston's name is incorrectly given as "Elphinson."

11th, 991.[1] Not all of the text has been preserved, matter having been lost both at the beginning and at the end. But the extant fragment begins with Byrhtnoth's preparations for the battle, and ends some time after the death of Byrhtnoth; it is therefore likely that not a great deal has been lost in either place, and the assumption of a single leaf lost from the manuscript before and after the extant text would be enough to account for both the missing portions.

The battle at Maldon does not appear to have been a very important event in English history of the tenth century; except for the death of Byrhtnoth, it would probably have received no more attention from contemporary writers than half a dozen other forays by the Danes which are duly recorded in the Anglo-Saxon Chronicle. In fact, it is very briefly treated in the Chronicle manuscripts. The most complete of the Chronicle entries dealing with it is that in A, which under the year 993 reports: "Her on ðissum geare com Unlaf mid þrim and hund nigentigon scipum to Stane, and forhergedon þæt on ytan, and for ða ðanon to Sandwic, and swa ðanon to Gipeswic, and þæt eall ofereode, and swa to Mældune; and him þær com togeanes Byrhtnoð ealdorman mid his fyrde, and him wið gefeaht, and hy þone ealdorman þær ofslogon, and wælstowe geweald ahtan." The earlier part of this annal seems to be the result of a lumping together, under the year 993, of two separate Danish campaigns, a raid along the Suffolk and Essex coasts, in 991, and the invasion of southern England by Anlaf and Swegen, reported in the other manuscripts under the year 994.[2] The campaign of 991 was apparently confined to the plundering of Ipswich and the battle of Maldon, and is correctly reported under the year 991 by Chronicle E: "Her wæs Gypeswic gehergod, and æfter þam swiðe raðe wæs Brihtnoð ealdorman ofslægen æt Mældune."

---

[1] August 11th has been generally accepted as the date of the battle, on the evidence of the eleventh-century Newminster calendar in MS. Cotton Titus D.xxvii (see W. de G. Birch, *Transactions of the Royal Society of Literature*, 2d Series, XI, 496ff.), which lists Byrhtnoth's death under that day; but the twelfth-century Ely calendar in MS. O.2.1, Trinity College, Cambridge, gives Byrhtnoth's obit under August 10th; see B. Dickins, *Leeds Studies in English* VI (1937), 14ff.

[2] See Plummer, *Two of the Saxon Chronicles Parallel* II (Oxford, 1899), 173.

Such short entries do not speak much for the historical significance of Byrhtnoth's death as viewed by contemporary annalists.
And yet we have detailed accounts of the battle and of Byrhtnoth's
bravery, not only from the poem, but also from the anonymous
Vita S. Oswaldi, written not long after the battle,[1] and from the
semi-fictional treatments of the subject in the monastic histories
of Ely and Ramsey.[2] It is clear that these writers, like the author
of our poem, were attracted to the theme of Byrhtnoth's death by
the great contemporary fame of the man himself. His name is
found, both as grantee and as witness, in a number of royal charters
of the period 956–990,[3] and he was related by marriage to several
of the Anglo-Saxon royal houses. After the battle he was buried
at Ely Minster, of which his widow was later a benefactor.

Under the circumstances, therefore, it is not surprising that
a contemporary poet in the east of England should have desired
to immortalize Byrhtnoth's heroism in verse. Who this poet may
have been, there is naturally no direct evidence to show. It has
frequently been pointed out that the author of the poem knows
most of the English leaders by name, but is completely ignorant of,
or unconcerned with, the identity of the Danish leaders. From
this it may be inferred that he must either have been a participant
in the battle or else have derived his information directly from
someone who fought in Byrhtnoth's army. The phrase *Gehyrde ic*,
l. 117, does not necessarily imply that the poet was not an eye-
witness of the battle, since this is an old rhetorical formula which
can be paralleled elsewhere;[4] neither does his condemnation of the
cowardly fugitives in ll. 195–197 rule out the possibility that he
himself was a survivor of the fighting, since surely there must have
been some of the English who deemed it expedient to withdraw
after the battle had been lost, to whom the stigma of cowardice
did not attach. It is in the immediateness of the author's knowl-

[1] See J. Raine, *The Historians of the Church of York* (London, 1879ff.) I, 456.
[2] These passages may conveniently be consulted, in Modern English translation, in Sedgefield, *The Battle of Maldon and Short Poems from the Saxon Chronicle*, pp. xvii–xx.
[3] On the historical sources for Byrhtnoth's life, see Liebermann, *Archiv* CI,
15–28; Laborde, *Byrhtnoth and Maldon*, pp. 9–28.
[4] Compare the use of *hyrde* in BEOWULF 62, 2163, 2172.

edge of the battle, and his keen interest in minor details of the action, that the BATTLE OF MALDON differs so widely from the BATTLE OF BRUNANBURH, in the Anglo-Saxon Chronicle for 937, which was written from a more remote, though no less patriotic, point of view by one who understood the larger political issues involved. The poet of the BATTLE OF MALDON seems to have cared only that there was a battle to be commemorated—a battle in which Byrhtnoth and other English leaders displayed the traditional Germanic heroic virtues which were so conspicuously lacking in England at the end of the tenth century. It is of course unwise to draw highly positive conclusions from internal evidence, since part of the poem is lost; but it is probable that the missing beginning and end of the poem, if they were available to us, would be too short to alter our conclusions materially. It is most likely that the author of the BATTLE OF MALDON was a layman, but a well educated man, perhaps of noble blood, who had read widely in the heroic poetry of earlier times. The tone of the poem throughout is so thoroughly Germanic, with few definitely Christian allusions, that we can hardly attribute it to a cleric.[1] The vividness of the poet's memories suggests further that the poem was written very shortly after the battle, and it is generally agreed by scholars that such was the case.

A few words may be said here concerning the probable site of the battlefield.[2] The town of Maldon is at the head of the estuary of the Blackwater River (the *Pante* of Anglo-Saxon times), some nine miles due east of Chelmsford. The town stands on a low hill, at the base of which the River Chelmer, flowing from the west, is joined by the old stream of the Blackwater, which curves around

---

[1] An excellent illustration of what the BATTLE OF MALDON might have become in the hands of a religiously-minded author is to be found in the *Vita S. Oswaldi*, in which Byrhtnoth's valor is described in these terms: "Stabat ipse, statura procerus, eminens super cæteros, cujus manum non Aaron et Hur sustentabant, sed multimoda pietas Domini fulciebat, quoniam ipse dignus erat. Percutjebat quoque a dextris, non reminiscens cigneam canitiem sui capitis, quoniam elemosinæ [*sic*] et sacræ Missæ eum confortabant" (Raine, *Historians of the Church of York* I, 456).

[2] A useful map of Maldon and its vicinity is given by Laborde, *Byrhtnoth and Maldon*, p. 3. The Ordnance Survey map, Large Sheet Series, Sheet 109, may also be used.

from the northwest past Heybridge. According to Freeman,[1] whose identification of the battle site was accepted for many years, the Danes occupied the short peninsula between the two streams, to the north of Maldon, while Byrhtnoth and his men, having come from the direction of Colchester, confronted them from the north on the other side of the Blackwater. But Laborde has recently shown, by a careful study of the topographical allusions in the poem, that the Danes were probably camped on Northey, a triangular island in the shallow part of the estuary two or three miles below Maldon, while the English were on the southern bank opposite. A very old causeway, submerged at high tide, connects the southwest corner of Northey with the mainland, and it is here at the causeway, according to Laborde, that the action described in the poem took place. Laborde's arguments are not easy to summarize, and it is naturally impossible to restate them here at length; but his findings are now generally regarded as correct.[2]

In style and vocabulary the BATTLE OF MALDON, despite its late date, clearly belongs to the traditional heroic poetry. The kenning appears less frequently than, say, in BEOWULF, but there are still sufficient examples (*wælwulfas*, l. 96, *sincgyfan*, l. 278, *feorhhus*, l. 297, *hæleða hleo*, l. 74) to illustrate the type. We also find the ornamental epithets characteristic of the older poetry, such as *har hilderinc*, l. 169, *wiga wintrum geong*, l. 210, besides the phrase *cafne mid his cynne*, l. 76, which recalls similar expressions in BEOWULF (ll. 13, 77). The poet makes good use of stock descriptions of weapons, such as *feolhearde speru*, l. 108, *fealohilte swurd*, l. 166, and *brad and bruneccg*, l. 163 (compare BEOWULF 1546), and of conventional pictures of warfare, as *hremmas wundon, earn æses georn*, ll. 106–107 (which recalls older allusions to birds and beasts of prey in BEOWULF 3021ff., EXODUS 162ff., and ELENE 27ff.), and *seo byrne sang gryreleoða sum*, ll. 284–285. Beyond a couple of loan-words from the Scandinavian, *grið*, "truce" (O.N. *grið*), l. 35, and *dreng*, "warrior" (O.N. *drengr*), l. 149, there are no very striking innovations of vocabulary.[3]

---

[1] E. A. Freeman, *The Norman Conquest* I (2d ed., London, 1870), 268ff.

[2] See Laborde, *English Historical Review* XL, 161–173; also *Byrhtnoth and Maldon*, pp. 39–43.

[3] The verb *ceallian*, l. 91, has been called a loan-word from O.N. *kalla*, but the compound noun *hildecalla*, EXODUS 252, seems to prove its existence in the earlier period of the language.

The metrical structure of the half-lines also follows the older poetry with some degree of regularity, but there are noticeable irregularities in the use of alliteration. For example, the second stress of a second half-line occasionally bears the alliteration instead of the first stress (ll. 45, 75, 288), and sometimes there is double alliteration in the second half-line (ll. 29, 32, 192). In l. 271 and l. 282 we have end-rime in addition to the alliteration; in the first of these two lines *st-* alliterates with *s-*, and it may be that this line was not intended to have alliteration at all, but only the end-rime. Other less important irregularities are the occasional alliteration of a verb in preference to a noun (ll. 7*a*, 127*b*, 240*b*, 242*a*), the alliteration of the adjective *min*, l. 224*b*, instead of the noun *hlaford*, and the apparent alliteration of the second element of a compound in l. 239*a* (*formoni*) and l. 266*a* (*Norðhymbron*). Such a weakening of the older rules of alliteration at the end of the tenth century is in striking contrast to the rigorous observance of rule in the BATTLE OF BRUNANBURH, in the first half of the same century, and points in the direction of the further relaxing of technique in Middle English alliterative verse. The poet of the BATTLE OF MALDON was well grounded in the style and subject matter of the early heroic poetry, but was evidently unable to understand, or at least to follow perfectly, the metrical conventions of his predecessors.

THE POEMS OF THE ANGLO-SAXON CHRONICLE

In the various manuscripts of the Anglo-Saxon Chronicle, from the year 937 to the end, there are six annals, or parts of annals, which are in sufficiently regular meter to be included in a collective edition of Anglo-Saxon poetry. These six poems are the BATTLE OF BRUNANBURH (937), the CAPTURE OF THE FIVE BOROUGHS (942). the CORONATION OF EDGAR (973), the DEATH OF EDGAR (975), the DEATH OF ALFRED (1036), and the DEATH OF EDWARD (1065) The DEATH OF ALFRED is not regularly alliterative, like the other five poems, but is partly prose and partly irregular rimed verse. It is, however, included here, following the practice of earlier editors.[1] A number of other passages in irregular meter, in the

[1] Wülker, *Bibliothek* I, 384–385; Sedgefield, *The Battle of Maldon and Short Poems from the Saxon Chronicle*, pp. 24–26.

later years of the Chronicle, have been omitted from this edition. Since these texts are all to be found in Plummer's edition of the Chronicle, their omission here will be no hardship to scholars.[1]

The six Chronicle poems to be considered here are found in four manuscripts, MS. 173 of Corpus Christi College, Cambridge (A),[2] and three manuscripts of the British Museum, MS. Cotton Tiberius A.vi (B), MS. Cotton Tiberius B.i (C), and MS. Cotton Tiberius B.iv (D). The so-called "Peterborough Chronicle," MS. Laud Misc. 636 of the Bodleian Library (E), and the Latin-English epitome of E, MS. Cotton Domitian A.viii (F), do not contain any of the poems printed in the present edition.

The manuscripts may be described briefly as follows:[3]

MS. 173, CORPUS CHRISTI COLLEGE, CAMBRIDGE (A), the famous "Parker Manuscript" of the Chronicle. The text of the Chronicle, which runs to the year 1070, occupies fol. 1a–32a. Up to the year 891 (at the end of fol. 16a), it is written in a single hand; but from this point on, Plummer distinguishes the work of thirteen different scribes, besides a number of insertions in other hands. The manuscript, judging from internal evidence, was at first a Winchester book but was moved to Canterbury about the year 1001. It cannot have been the original manuscript of the Chronicle, but was copied from the original manuscript about 891 or 892 and then

---

[1] It is not always easy to draw the line between irregular meter and rhythmical prose. A list of the passages which are arranged as verse by Plummer, though not in regular metrical form, follows: "On his dagum hit godode georne" (King Edgar), 959 DE; "Her Eadgar gefor," 975 DE; "On his dagum for his iugoðe," 975 D; "Ne wearð Angelcynne nan wærsa dæd gedon" (the murder of Edward), 979 E; "Wæs ða ræpling," 1011 E; "Her com Eadward æþeling to Englalande," 1057 D; "and cwæð þæt heo hine ne nanne habban wolde" (Malcolm's wooing of Margaret), 1067 D; "Þær wes þæt brydeala mannum to beala," 1075 DE; "Sume hy wurdon ablænde," 1075 DE; "Castelas he let wyrcean" (William the Conqueror), 1086 E; "Eall þis wæs god mid to gremienne," 1104 E. The letter symbols which represent the several MSS. are explained in the next paragraph.

[2] These letter symbols are based on Plummer's, and differ from those used by Wülker and Sedgefield.

[3] For further descriptions of MS. A, see Plummer, *Two of the Saxon Chronicles Parallel* II, xxiii–xxvii; M. R. James, *Descriptive Catalogue of the Manuscripts in the Library of Corpus Christi College* I (Cambridge, 1912), 395–401. For descriptions of the other MSS., see British Museum, *Catalogue of the Manuscripts in the Cottonian Library* (1802), pp. 33–35; Plummer, *Two of the Saxon Chronicles Parallel* II, xxviii–xxxiv.

continued from that date by the monks at Winchester and Canterbury. MS. Cotton Otho B.xi, almost entirely destroyed by the Cottonian fire of 1731, was a Winchester copy of A to the year 1001.[1]

MS. COTTON TIBERIUS A.VI (B). This chronicle, which occupies fol. 1a–34a of the manuscript, runs only to the year 977. The entire text is written in a single hand, of about the year 1000. The manuscript is traditionally associated with St. Augustine's Abbey, Canterbury, but there is no real evidence for its provenience. It must, however, have been copied from an Abingdon text of the Chronicle, on which C, next to be described, is also based.

MS. COTTON TIBERIUS B.I (C). Here the Chronicle occupies fol. 115b–164a, following the Alfredian translation of Orosius (fol. 3a–111b), the MENOLOGIUM (fol. 112a–114b), and MAXIMS II (fol. 115a–115b). The text of the Chronicle, which extends to the year 1066, is in several hands, all of about the middle part of the eleventh century. From internal evidence the manuscript appears to have originated in Abingdon.

MS. COTTON TIBERIUS B.IV (D). The Chronicle is on fol. 3a–86a[2] and runs to the year 1079. The manuscript is written in a number of hands, all to be assigned to the period 1050–1100. It is generally known as the "Worcester Chronicle," but Plummer suggests that it more probably came from Evesham;[3] at any rate, its place of origin must have been somewhere in the West Midlands. Throughout, D is very carelessly written, with many omissions and

[1] Since this MS. was only a copy of A, and is of no independent value for the establishment of the Chronicle text, it is not edited here, although a transcript made by Laurence Nowell in 1562 is extant in Add. MS. 43,703 of the British Museum (see p. xcii, below), and a copy of Nowell's transcript, made by William Lambarde in 1564, is preserved as MS. E.5.19 of Trinity College, Dublin. MS. Cotton Otho B.xi was also used by Wheloc as the basis for his edition of the Chronicle in 1643. For a discussion of this MS. and the transcripts, see Campbell, *The Battle of Brunanburh*, pp. 133–144.

[2] Plus a much later entry on fol. 86b, dated 1080, but describing the rebellion of the Earl of Moray in 1130.

[3] For evidence in favor of Worcester, see W. Keller, *Die litterarischen Bestrebungen von Worcester* (Strassburg, 1900), pp. 53–59. M. Ångström, *Studies in Old English MSS* (Uppsala, 1937), pp. 46–48, thinks the MS. was "written at Worcester, but not by Worcester scribes exclusively."

corruptions, and is a much less dependable basis for the text than the other three manuscripts.[1]

The history and development of the various texts of the Chronicle are presented in great detail by Plummer, primarily from the internal evidence of the texts themselves. Copies of the original compilation, to the year 891, must have been sent, in accordance with King Alfred's custom, to various monasteries of the realm. Our present MS. A, the first hand of which ends at 891, is evidently a transcript of the Winchester copy of the Chronicle. Another copy, sent to Abingdon, is represented by the late copies B and C. With some few exceptions, A, B, and C present almost identical texts up to 891. Following this original Chronicle, we find in A, B, and C: (1) a continuation of the original Chronicle from 894 to 925, called by Plummer the "official" continuation, which is found in its most complete form in A, but in part also (up to 915) in B and C; (2) the so-called "Mercian Register," from 902 to 924, appearing only in B and C, and used in these manuscripts to supplement the "official" continuation; (3) a second continuation from 925 to the death of Edgar in 975, found in all three manuscripts but filled out in each manuscript by the insertion of local items. In B and C the second continuation is extended to 977, at which point B ends.

The other two English manuscripts of the Chronicle, D and E, present up to 891 a northern recension of the original Chronicle, perhaps made at Ripon,[2] incorporating into the text some materials

---

[1] The folio references to the Chronicle poems in the several MSS. are best given together. MS. A: BATTLE OF BRUNANBURH, fol. 26a, l. 18, to fol. 27a, l. 10; CAPTURE OF THE FIVE BOROUGHS, fol. 27a, ll. 18–25; CORONATION OF EDGAR, fol. 28b, ll. 6–17; DEATH OF EDGAR, fol. 28b, l. 18, to fol. 29a, l. 16.   MS. B: BATTLE OF BRUNANBURH, fol. 31a, l. 22, to fol. 32a, l. 21; CAPTURE OF THE FIVE BOROUGHS, fol. 32b, ll. 4–11; CORONATION OF EDGAR, fol. 33a, l. 22, to fol. 33b, l. 11; DEATH OF EDGAR, fol. 33b, l. 12, to fol. 34a, l. 13.   MS. C: BATTLE OF BRUNANBURH, fol. 141a, l. 8, to fol. 141b, l. 23; CAPTURE OF THE FIVE BOROUGHS, fol. 142a, ll. 1–8; CORONATION OF EDGAR, fol. 142b, ll. 11–23; DEATH OF EDGAR, fol. 142b, l. 24, to fol. 143a, l. 20; DEATH OF ALFRED, fol. 156a, ll. 5–25; DEATH OF EDWARD, fol. 160b, ll. 1–20.   MS. D: BATTLE OF BRUNANBURH, fol. 49a, l. 3, to fol. 50a, l. 7; CAPTURE OF THE FIVE BOROUGHS, fol. 50a, l. 19, to fol. 50b, l. 4; DEATH OF ALFRED, fol. 70a, ll. 6–23; DEATH OF EDWARD, fol. 78b, l. 23, to fol. 79a, l. 15.

[2] As suggested by Plummer, *Two of the Saxon Chronicles Parallel* II, lxxi.

from Bede's History and from an independent Northumbrian chronicle. From 891 on, D incorporates the same portions of the "official" continuation as B and C, that is, from 894 to 915, then parts of the "Mercian Register," a further group of fragments from Northumbrian sources, and a much expanded version of the second continuation (925–975). The second continuation is also found in E, in a still different form.

The first four of the Chronicle poems, the BATTLE OF BRUNAN-BURH (937), the CAPTURE OF THE FIVE BOROUGHS (942), the CORONATION OF EDGAR (973), and the DEATH OF EDGAR (975), are all part of the second continuation (925–975), which, as we have seen, is common in one form or another to all the five English manuscripts of the Chronicle. In each case, however, E omits the poem, usually substituting a prose summary. We may, therefore, exclude E from further consideration here. Under 973 (dated 972) and 975, D, like E, substitutes for the poems short passages on the same subjects in prose or irregular meter. The two poems on Edgar, then, are found only in A, B, and C.

As we should expect, B and C, both transcribed at a late date from the Abingdon copy of the Chronicle, are much more like each other than they are like A, the Winchester text, or D, based on a northern copy of the second continuation. For example, in the BATTLE OF BRUNANBURH the spellings of B and C frequently agree as against A and D, as in *cing*, ll. 1, 58, *embe*, l. 5, *bordweall*, l. 5, *hamera*, l. 6, *dennade*, l. 12, and *upp*, l. 13. In a number of cases B, C, and D agree in spelling as against A, as in *drihten*, l. 1, *lafum*, l. 6, *fram*, l. 8, *crungon*, l. 10, *leode*, l. 11. In l. 13, B, C, and D agree on *secga swate*, where A has the corrupt reading *secgas hwate*; and in l. 49, A's reading *culbodgehnades* is clearly impossible, a later attempt having been made to emend it to the proper form *cum-bolgehnastes* found in B, C, and D. Other places in which B, C, and D show a more correct reading than A are *heardes*, l. 25 (A, *he eardes*), *þara* (*þæra*) *þe*, l. 26 (A, *þæ*), *Iraland* (*Yraland*), l. 56 (A, *hira land*), and *Wealas*, l. 72 (A, *weealles*). The other poems of the second continuation show the same agreement of B and C as against A and D, and frequently (as in CAPTURE OF THE FIVE BOROUGHS 8, 9) the agreement of B, C, and D as against A.[1]

---

[1] Except, of course, in the Edgar poems (973, 975), which are not in D.

The last two of the Chronicle poems, the DEATH OF ALFRED (1036) and the DEATH OF EDWARD (1065), are found only in C and D. As we have seen, B was not continued after 977; and A after 975, the end of the second continuation, seems to have gone its own way independently of the other Chronicle texts.

In the present edition, MS. A has been made the basis of the text for the four poems which it contains;[1] the text of the other two poems has been based on MS. C.

The battle of Brunanburh, commemorated in the earliest of the Chronicle poems, was only one episode in the struggle between King Æthelstan and the Norse kings of Dublin for the control of Northumbria. From 920 until his death in 927, Sihtric (Sigtryggr), king of Dublin, had ruled as king at York, but in the latter year his brother and successor, Guthfrith, was expelled from Northumbria by Æthelstan. In 934 Æthelstan, wishing to consolidate his power in the North, led an expedition into Scotland against King Constantine II and overran a large part of that country. In retaliation for this invasion, a coalition was formed in 937 by Anlaf, the son of Guthfrith and then king of Dublin,[2] Constantine, king of Scotland, and Eugenius (or Owen), king of the Strathclyde Britons. The combined armies, under Anlaf, entered England but were met by Æthelstan and his brother, Prince Edmund, at Brunanburh and were put to flight with very heavy losses. According to the poem, five young kings and seven earls of Anlaf's army were slain, besides a countless number of others, with a greater slaughter than had ever been known in English history. King Constantine, whose son was among the killed, fled to his Scottish kingdom, while Anlaf and the survivors of his Irish-Norse army escaped by sea to Dublin.

In MS. A the original scribe, following the dislocated chronology of that manuscript,[3] gave the date of the battle of Brunanburh as 938, but a corrector changed it, together with the other annals

[1] For a justification of this choice, see Campbell, *The Battle of Brunanburh*, p. 13.

[2] Another Anlaf, the son of Sihtric, called Óláfr Kvaran in the Norse sources, was also prominent in English history at this time; see p. xli, below. But the Anlaf of our poem is generally believed to be Anlaf the son of Guthfrith.

[3] See Plummer, *Two of the Saxon Chronicles Parallel* I, 85, note 1.

from 931 to 942, by the subtraction of one year, making it 937. In MS. B the date of the annal is not given, but C and D agree on 937, and the evidence from other sources points to 937, and probably to August or September of that year, as the date of the battle.[1] The spelling of the name *Brunanburh* also varies in the several manuscripts. A and D have *brunan burh* in l. 5 (though in A a later hand has added a second *n* in *brunan*); C has *brun nanburh*, with two *n*'s; the reading of B is almost illegible, but seems to have two *n*'s like C.[2] On the evidence of the manuscripts, therefore, we might postulate either *Brunanburh* or *Brunnanburh* as the proper form. But the personal name *Brunna* does not appear in any of the extant Anglo-Saxon records, whereas *Brūna* is known to have been in actual use at the time.[3] It seems almost certain, then, that we should read *Brūnanburh* as the name of the place where the battle was fought.[4]

The question of the site of the battle, that is, the location of Brunanburh, has never been satisfactorily settled, since none of the medieval authorities on the history of this period tells us much more than the name.[5] According to Florence of Worcester, Anlaf's

[1] See Campbell, *The Battle of Brunanburh*, p. 47, note 3.

[2] See the note on this line, p. 147, below.

[3] See Searle, *Onomasticon Anglo-Saxonicum*, p. 117.

[4] See Malone, *Modern Language Notes* XLII, 238–239; he translates the name as "Brown's castle." Magoun, *Zeitschrift für deutsches Altertum* LXXVII, 65–66, would read *Brūnan burh* as two words. For the names *Brūn, Brūna*, see M. Redin, *Studies on Uncompounded Personal Names in Old English* (Uppsala, 1919), pp. 11–12, 45. The place-name *Brunanhyll* is found in a charter of King Edward the Elder, A.D. 909 (Birch, *Cartularium Saxonicum* II, 297–298, no. 625).

[5] The forms of the name in the Chronicle MSS. have been discussed above. But Æthelweard, in the tenth century, gives the name as *Brunandune* (dat. sing.), and the twelfth-century chroniclers provide a variety of forms: Symeon of Durham, *Hist. eccl. Dunelmensis*, Book II, Chapter 18, "apud Weondune, quod alio nomine Etbrunnanwerc, vel Brunnanbyrig appellatur"; *Hist. regum*, §83, "apud Wendune" (Arnold II, 93); William of Malmesbury, *Gesta regum Anglorum*, §131, "apud Brunefeld" (with the variant "Bruneford" in some MSS.); Henry of Huntington, *Hist. Anglorum*, Book V, §18, "ad Bruneburh"; Florence of Worcester, *Chronicon ex chronicis* (ed. Thorpe, p. 132), "Brunanburh"; Gaimar, *Lestorie des Engles*, l. 3524, "a Bruneswerce." The names for the battlefield in the Celtic sources, as, for example, "Duinbrunde" in the Pictish Chronicle and "the plaines of Othlynn" in the Annals of Clonmacnoise, are of little help.

army entered England by way of the Humber, but there is no other evidence to support this statement, and it seems more natural that such a combination of Irish, Scots, and Strathclyde Britons would operate from a base in Scotland or on the west coast of England. It is also evident from ll. 32–36 of the poem that the battle must have taken place near the sea. If we knew what body of water the phrase *Dinges mere*, l. 54, refers to, we should perhaps be in a better position to identify the site of the battle. The most commonly accepted identification of Brunanburh is Burnswork (or Birrenswark) Hill, near Ecclefechan in Dumfriesshire.[1] Recently A. H. Smith has argued, chiefly on philological grounds, for Bromborough, in Cheshire, close to the estuary of the Mersey.[2] Other identifications which have been proposed, all on insufficient grounds, are Bourne and Burnham, in Lincolnshire, Burnley, in Lancashire, and Aldborough and Kirkburn in Yorkshire.[3] These possibilities cover a rather large area, and the Lincolnshire and Yorkshire sites involve the acceptance of Florence of Worcester's statement that the invading army entered England by way of the Humber. There is good reason to believe that the battle fought "á Vínheiði við Vínuskóga" between Æthelstan and one Olaf the Red (Anlaf?), as described in the *Egils saga*, Chapters 52–55,[4] is the same as the battle of Brunanburh, but here again the saga text does not give us any definite indication of the site.[5] The battle of Brunanburh was fought, we may assume, somewhere along the west coast of England, roughly in the area between Chester and

---

[1] T. Hodgkin, *Athenæum*, August 22, 1885, p. 239; G. Neilson, *Annals of the Solway* (Glasgow, 1899), p. 34, and *Scottish Historical Review* VII, 37–55, 435–436; W. S. Angus, *Antiquity* XI, 283–293. The name Burnswork is very close to the forms *Bruneswerce*, given by Gaimar, and *Etbrunnanwerc*, given by Symeon. For objections to Burnswork, see Law, *Scottish Historical Review* VII, 431–435; Campbell, *The Battle of Brunanburh*, pp. 66ff.

[2] *London Mediæval Studies* I, 56–59. Smith points out that the older spellings of the name Bromborough point to an original form *Brunanburh*. The Bromborough site had previously been suggested by R. F. Weymouth, *Athenæum*, August 15, 1885, p. 207.

[3] For bibliographical references see Campbell, *The Battle of Brunanburh*, p. 58, note 4.

[4] F. Jónsson, *Egils Saga Skallagrimssonar* (Halle, 1894), pp. 146–164.

[5] The element *Vín-* in the two names may be related to the form *Weondune*, used by Symeon of Durham.

Dumfries, but the available evidence does not enable us to determine the exact place.[1]

From the point of view of literary history, the poem is most naturally compared with the BATTLE OF MALDON, written a little more than fifty years later. Both poems are animated by the spirit of English patriotism, but in temper they are markedly different. The BATTLE OF MALDON is a sober, highly detailed narrative, which may well have been written by an eye-witness of the battle.[2] The BATTLE OF BRUNANBURH, on the other hand, is an unrestrained song of triumph, in which the poet seems to know little, and care less, of the actual course of events, but gives full play to his feelings of exultation at the victory over a foreign foe. In style and diction the BATTLE OF BRUNANBURH follows the older poetry rather closely, and yet it is not quite in the old heroic tradition. Biblical influence has been suggested, especially of the story of Joshua's victory over the five kings of the Amorites in Joshua x.1–27.[3] Other parallels to the triumphant tone of the BATTLE OF BRUNANBURH may be sought in the Norse poem *The Battle of Hafrsfjord*, celebrating the final victory of King Harold Fairhair in 872, and in Laurence Minot's poems on the victories of King Edward III in the fourteenth century.[4] Whether the poet of the BATTLE OF BRUNANBURH was a cleric or a layman seems immaterial; he is perhaps best described, in Klaeber's words,[5] as a "gifted and well trained publicist" of the West Saxon court, who took the opportunity to commemorate Æthelstan's victory in a more vigorous and striking way than would be possible in a prose annal.

Of the other poems in the Anglo-Saxon Chronicle there is much less to be said. But the fact that the BATTLE OF BRUNANBURH has been much more frequently edited than the other Chronicle

[1] These problems are admirably treated by Campbell, *The Battle of Brunanburh*, pp. 43–80, to which the student should refer for a more complete statement than is possible here.

[2] See above, p. xxix.

[3] Brandl, in Paul's *Grundriss der germanischen Philologie* (2d ed.), II, 1, 1077; Klaeber, in *Anglica* II, 1–7.

[4] As suggested by Kershaw, *Anglo-Saxon and Norse Poems*, pp. 64–65. The *Battle of Hafrsfjord* is edited by Kershaw, pp. 88–91, Minot's poems by J. Hall (Oxford, 1897).

[5] *Anglica* II, 7.

poems must not cause us to overlook the essential unity of thought and purpose which is common to all of them. The CAPTURE OF THE FIVE BOROUGHS, like the earlier poem, commemorates an English victory, this time the freeing of the Five Boroughs of the Danelaw, Leicester, Lincoln, Nottingham, Stamford, and Derby, from the Norsemen of York by King Edmund in 942. The Five Boroughs had submitted to Edward the Elder in 924 and had remained under English rule until the death of Æthelstan in 940. After Æthelstan's death, Anlaf the son of Guthfrith, who had been so badly defeated at the battle of Brunanburh, returned from Ireland and was again received as king at York. Apparently he marched south soon after his arrival in England and made himself master of the Mercian Danelaw. But in 941 Anlaf died and was succeeded by his cousin Anlaf the son of Sihtric.[1] Taking advantage of the confusion which ensued, Edmund entered Mercia with an army and restored English rule over the Five Boroughs. This phase of Anglo-Saxon history ended with the baptism of Anlaf.[2]

The only difficult point of interpretation in this poem arises in l. 8, where MS. B reads *denum*, but A and D *dæne* and C *dene*. Reading *Dæne* or *Dene* with Mawer,[3] we seem to parallel the actual political situation at the time; that is, the Danes of the Five Boroughs were ruled over by the heathen Norsemen[4] (*under Norðmannum...on hæþenra hæfteclommum*, ll. 9–10) under the two Anlafs until the freeing of the boroughs by Edmund. The reading *Denum*, which makes the Danes (of the Danelaw) and the Norse-

---

[1] See above, p. xxxvii, note 2.

[2] For the political history of this period, see especially Beaven, *English Historical Review* XXXIII, 1–9.

[3] *Saga-Book of the Viking Society* VII, 61–62; *English Historical Review* XXXVIII, 551ff.

[4] Whether the Scandinavians of York were Norwegians or Danes is a difficult question, but it is probable that, like the Scandinavians of Dublin, they were a mixture of both races. Sihtric and the two Anlafs, as descendants of Ivarr Beinlauss, were, however, probably Norwegians. The important point of difference is that the Danes of Mercia, unlike Anlaf's Norsemen in York, were undoubtedly Christianized by this time. The best treatment of the Scandinavian kingdom at York is that by Mawer, *Saga-Book of the Viking Society* VII, 38–64.

men (of Northumbria) the same people, is unsatisfactory.[1] The
two place-names in ll. 3–4, *Dor* and *Hwitanwyllesgeat*,[2] together
with the River Humber, evidently marked the western and northern
limits of Edmund's campaign.

The third of the Chronicle poems, found in MSS. A, B, and C
under the year 973, describes the coronation of King Edgar in that
year. The ceremony, at which both the English archbishops,
Dunstan and Oswald, officiated, took place at Acemannesceaster,
or Bath, on Whitsunday, May 11th. Why Edgar was crowned at
this time, fourteen years after his accession, is not clear, unless the
coronation was intended as a manifestation of English political
unity and of the imperial status which Edgar, almost alone of all
the Anglo-Saxon kings, enjoyed.[3]

The DEATH OF EDGAR (975, A, B, and C) is unlike the preceding
Chronicle poems in that it deals not with a single event of national
significance, but with all the important happenings of the year
975. In its lack of structural unity it is very similar to the typical
prose annals in the Chronicle. The events narrated are: (1) the
death of the king, and the accession of the young Edward, ll. 1–12;
(2) the departure from Britain[4] of Cyneweard, bishop of Wells, ll.
13–15; (3) the anti-monastic reaction in Mercia under Ælfhere,
ll. 16–23; (4) the expulsion of Oslac, earl of Northumbria, ll. 24–28;
(5) the comet seen in the autumn of the year, ll. 29–33a; and (6)
the great famine, ll. 33b–37.

The DEATH OF ALFRED (1036, C and D), partly in prose, partly
in verse, deals with the imprisonment and murder of the unfortunate Prince Alfred, one of the sons of Æthelred, at the hands of
Earl Godwine. The DEATH OF EDWARD (1065, C and D), the last
of the regularly metrical passages in the Chronicle, eulogizes King
Edward the Confessor to the extent of nearly thirty lines, and
closes briefly with the alleged bequest of the crown to Harold.

In the consideration of the Chronicle poems, the question of
date does not cause much difficulty, since, like the prose annals of

[1] See the note on this line, p. 150, below.
[2] Probably the modern Dore (5 miles SW. of Sheffield) and Whitwell (5 miles
W. of Worksop), both on the northeastern edge of Derbyshire.
[3] See Plummer, *Two of the Saxon Chronicles Parallel* II, 160–161.
[4] His death, or only a journey to Rome? See the note on l. 14.

the Chronicle, they must all have been written shortly after the events they describe. The problem of authorship, however, is as impossible of solution here as it is for most other Anglo-Saxon poems. What has been said above regarding the unknown author of the BATTLE OF BRUNANBURH applies also, in general, to the authors of the other poems. There is no reason why the two Edgar poems, coming so close together in date, may not have been written by the same man;[1] but beyond this there is little we can say.

DURHAM

The latest of the extant Anglo-Saxon poems in the regular alliterative meter is a verse description of the city of Durham and of the relics preserved there, written in the early years of the twelfth century. For the text of this poem, we have two independent sources, MS. Ff.i.27 of the University Library, Cambridge (C), and a text (H) printed by Hickes in his *Thesaurus*[2] from MS. Cotton Vitellius D.xx, later burned in the Cottonian fire of 1731.

The Cambridge manuscript is a rather miscellaneous volume, made up of a number of historical texts, written at various dates, and comprising altogether 321 folios. The text of DURHAM, headed by the rubric "De situ Dunelmi et de sanctorum reliquiis quae ibidem continentur carmen compositum," is on page 202 (fol. 101*b*); it is the last item in the fourth section of the manuscript, which also contains Symeon's *Historia Dunelmensis ecclesiae* (pages 122–186), a number of shorter articles relating to Durham (pages 186–194), and the *Historia de sancto Cuthberto* (pages 195–202).[3] This part of the manuscript is written in several hands of the late twelfth century.

[1] Campbell, *The Battle of Brunanburh*, p. 36, suggests that the DEATH OF EDGAR originally ran only to l. 12, the remaining lines, which are obviously inferior, being the work of the chronicler.

[2] Part 1, pp. 178–179.

[3] A detailed list of the contents of the entire MS. is given in *A Catalogue of the Manuscripts Preserved in the Library of the University of Cambridge* II (Cambridge, 1857), 318–329. MS. Harley 533, in the British Museum, is a transcript of this MS. The *Historia de sancto Cuthberto* is edited by Arnold, *Symeonis monachi opera omnia* I, 196–214, the shorter items on pages 186–194 of the MS. by Twysden, *Historiae anglicanae scriptores decem*, col. 58–68.

The lost Cotton manuscript, from which Hickes took his text, is dated by Wanley[1] at about the beginning of the thirteenth century, not long therefore after the Cambridge manuscript.

The two texts of the poem agree very closely in their readings, and together present a typical English work of the transition period, with a number of spellings characteristic of that time: *eo* for *ē*, as in *breome*, l. 1, *breoma*, l. 15; the loss of initial *h-* before a consonant, in *leo*, l. 12; the confusion of *e* and *a* in end-syllables, as in *steppa* C, *steopa* H (for *stēape*), l. 2, *ymbeornad* C, *ymb eornað* H, l. 3, *wilda* (perhaps for *wildu?*), l. 7, *deopa* H (but *deope* C), l. 8, *Engla* H (but *Engle* C), l. 12, *bocera*, l. 15, *monia* C (but *monige* H), l. 20; the loss of an inflectional final *-n* in *deope*, l. 8, *clene*, l. 11, *eadige*, l. 18; and the substitution of the *-s* plural for an originally weak ending, in *geferes*, l. 13. Obvious errors on which the two manuscripts agree are *wunað* (for *wuniað*), l. 4, *reliquia* (perhaps intended as the plural of a neuter *reliquium*), l. 19, the omission of the article in l. 15, and the complete loss of the inflectional ending in *eadig*, l. 10. The chief differences between the two versions are: *ea* C, *ean* H, l. 4; *stronge* C, *strong* H, l. 4; *fcola* (for *feola*) *fisca* C, *fisca feola* H, l. 5; *gemonge* C, *gemong* H, l. 5; *is* C, omitted in H, l. 6; *wis* C, *his* H, l. 17; *ðe* C, *ðær* H, l. 20; *ðes* C, omitted in H, l. 20; *writ* C, *writa* H, l. 20. Any attempt to emend these readings systematically, or to substitute the linguistic forms of the pre-Conquest period, would result in a mixture of forms of various dates, and the text of the poem in this edition has therefore been based on the actual readings of C, but with the substitution of H's reading in two places (*his*, l. 17, *ðær*, l. 20) to improve the sense.

The date of composition of the poem can be established within a few years. It cannot have been written before 1104, when the translation of St. Cuthbert to the new cathedral at Durham took place. The posterior limit for the writing of the poem is provided by the mention of it in Symeon's *Historia Dunelmensis ecclesiae*,[2]

---

[1] *Catalogus historico-criticus* (Oxford, 1705), p. 240. On this MS. see also T. Smith, *Catalogus librorum manuscriptorum bibliothecae Cottonianae* (Oxford, 1696), pp. 94–95.

[2] Book III, Chapter 7 (ed. Arnold, 89, 23ff.): "Cujus [i.e. the priest Alfred, who stole the bones of the Venerable Bede from Jarrow and brought them to Durham] de Beda sententiæ concordat etiam illud Anglico sermone compositum carmen, ubi cum de statu hujus loci, et de sanctorum reliquiis quæ in eo con-

which appears to have been finished by the year 1109.[1] It is possible, therefore, to say that the poem was written during the years 1104–1109, and probably not long after 1104, for the translation of the relics and the splendor of the new cathedral seem to have been still fresh in the poet's mind. The enumeration of the relics in the last chapter of the *Capitula de miraculis et translationibus sancti Cuthberti*,[2] possibly Symeon's own work, but written after 1122, corresponds closely to the order of the proper names in the poem, and it may well be that the poem served as a source for the Latin account of the translation.

Considering its late date, the poem is surprisingly regular in its conformity to the Anglo-Saxon verse types, and in its use of alliteration, having usually double alliteration in the first half-line (ll. 1, 2, 3, 4, 5, 7, 8, 12, etc.). There are no traces of the end-rime which we find more than a century earlier in two lines of the BATTLE OF MALDON (ll. 271, 282) and regularly in several of the eleventh-century pieces in the Anglo-Saxon Chronicle (1036 C, 1086 E).

The literary relationships of DURHAM have recently been clarified by Margaret Schlauch,[3] who points out that the poem is the only extant example in Anglo-Saxon of the *encomium urbis*, a form of literary exercise which came down to the Middle Ages from the rhetorical schools of ancient times. A famous Latin example of this type is the long poem by Alcuin (written about 780–782) in praise of the city and church of York.[4]

---

tinentur agitur, etiam reliquiarum Bedæ una cum cæteris ibidem mentio habetur."

[1] Arnold, *Symeonis monachi opera omnia* I, xix. J. M. Lappenberg is sometimes cited (as by Wülker, *Grundriss zur Geschichte der angelsächsischen Litteratur*, p. 516, and Schlauch, *Journal of English and Germanic Philology* XL, 15) as authority for the statement that the *Historia Dunelmensis ecclesiae* was completed in 1129. But the "chronicle of events from the year 848 to 1129" which Lappenberg mentions (*History of England under the Anglo-Saxon Kings*, transl. by B. Thorpe, 2d ed., London, 1884, I, xlviii) is not the *Historia Dunelmensis ecclesiae*; it is the second part (§§ 88–124 in Arnold's edition) of Symeon's *Historia regum*. Lappenberg does not offer any precise dating of the *Historia Dunelmensis ecclesiae*.

[2] Arnold, *Symeonis monachi opera omnia* I, 252. On the dating of this text, see Arnold I, xxx.

[3] *Journal of English and Germanic Philology* XL, 14–28.

[4] Edited by E. Dümmler, *Poetae latini aevi Carolini* I (Berlin, 1881), 169–206.

THE RUNE POEM

The RUNE POEM was formerly preserved in MS. Cotton Otho B.x, fol. 165*a*–165*b*, but this manuscript, like so many of the other manuscripts in the Cottonian Library, was destroyed by the fire of 1731.[1] Fortunately, the text of the poem had already been printed by George Hickes in 1705.[2] Hickes' text has necessarily formed the basis of all later editions.

The RUNE POEM consists of ninety-four lines, which fall naturally into twenty-nine short stanzas, of from two to five lines each, corresponding to the twenty-nine runes which the poem explains. In justification of the arrangement of the text in the present edition, it will be necessary to describe Hickes' printed copy of the poem in some detail. Hickes printed the text as prose, but divided it into the proper twenty-nine stanzas, with hanging indention, so that each of the rune passages begins a new line. The runes were not printed from type, like the rest of the text, but were engraved separately on a copper plate, impressed in the left-hand margin in such a way that each rune stands immediately in front of the stanza to which it belongs. Each of the runes is preceded by its phonetic equivalent in Anglo-Saxon minuscule script, and is marked further by its Anglo-Saxon name (*feoh, ur, ðorn, os,* etc.), likewise in minuscule. For five of the runes, *wen, hægl, nyd, eoh,* and *Ing* (ll. 22, 25, 27, 35, 67), variant forms are given, and at the foot of the column are added two more runes, *cweorð* and an unnamed rune (*calc*), which are not dealt with in the poem. A second copper plate across the foot of the page contains still two more runes, *stan* and *gar*. This tremendous apparatus of runic erudition is not likely to have been present in the original text of the Cotton manuscript, and Hempl[3] has shown conclusively that Hickes took the phonetic equivalents of the runes, together with the variant forms and the extra runes which are not treated in the poem, from a runic alphabet in MS. Cotton Domitian A.ix, fol. 10*a*,

---

[1] For descriptions of this MS. as it was before the fire, see T. Smith, *Catalogus librorum manuscriptorum bibliothecae Cottonianae* (Oxford, 1696), pp. 70–71; H. Wanley, *Catalogus historico-criticus* (Oxford, 1705), pp. 190–193.

[2] *Thesaurus*, Part 1, p. 135.

[3] *Modern Philology* I, 135–141.

reproduced in the *Thesaurus* on the page following the RUNE POEM. The rune names given by Hickes were not taken from MS. Domitian A.ix, but that they came from a different source than MS. Otho B.x may perhaps be inferred from the Kentish form *wen*, l. 22.[1] It is in fact probable that only the runic letters themselves were present at the beginning of each stanza in the original manuscript; if so, the form of our RUNE POEM in the manuscript would have been similar, with respect to the arrangement of runes and text, to that of the Old Norwegian and Old Icelandic rune poems.[2]

With these facts in mind, the text of the RUNE POEM in this edition has been arranged in the following way: the rune is printed at the beginning of the stanza, in the form which it appears to have had in the original text;[3] then follows, in parentheses, the name of the rune, as given by Hickes, and finally the rest of the stanza, following Hickes' printed text. Hickes' variant runes, as well as the extra runes which he added at the foot of the page, are omitted.

In its general character and contents the RUNE POEM is not markedly different from the Norwegian and Icelandic rune poems. The Norwegian poem, written in couplets of six-syllabled lines, with both end-rime and alliteration, is usually ascribed to the late twelfth or early thirteenth century; the Icelandic poem, of the fifteenth century, is written in three-line stanzas, with alliteration, each of the three lines of a stanza containing a kenning for the name of the rune. Each of these Scandinavian rune poems deals only with the sixteen runes of the shorter Scandinavian alphabet.[4] The greater length of the Anglo-Saxon poem (twenty-nine runes in all) is of course due to the extension of the older alphabet of twenty-four runes to take account of the new Anglo-Saxon sounds, the runes for *O*, *A*, *Y*, *IA* (*IO*), and *EA* (ll. 10, 77, 84, 87, and 90 in

---

[1] Elsewhere the text of the RUNE POEM has the West Saxon forms *wyn*, *wynnum*, *wynna;* see the note on l. 22, p. 155, below. There is, however, one other form in the poem which is possibly Kentish, *breneð*, l. 43; see the note on this line.

[2] See L. Wimmer, *Die Runenschrift* (Berlin, 1887), pp. 275ff.

[3] For typographical reasons, no effort is made to reproduce the exact form which the runes have on Hickes' copper plate.

[4] They are most adequately edited, with German translations, by L. Wimmer, *Die Runenschrift*, pp. 275–288; also, with English translations, by B. Dickins, *Runic and Heroic Poems*, pp. 24–33.

the RUNE POEM) being added.[1] All the other twenty-four runes
treated in the RUNE POEM belonged to the original Germanic runic
alphabet, though the forms which they take in the earliest inscriptions are often quite different from the later Anglo-Saxon forms.
In Scandinavia, on the other hand, the development was in the
contrary direction, the earlier alphabet of twenty-four letters being
gradually reduced to the sixteen which we find in the Scandinavian
rune poems.

In detail, also, there are numerous similarities between the Anglo-
Saxon RUNE POEM and the two Scandinavian poems. For example, the comparison of hail and grain in *Hægl byþ hwitust corna*,
l. 25 of the Anglo-Saxon poem, appears also in the phrases *Hagall er
kaldastr korna*, "hail is the coldest of grains," in the Norwegian
poem, and *Hagall er kaldakorn*, "hail is a cold grain," in the Icelandic poem; similarly, *Ger byþ gumena hiht*, l. 32, is closely echoed
by *Ár er gumna góði (góðe)*, "the year (or produce, plenty?) is a
boon to men," in the Scandinavian poems; and *Man byþ on myrgþe
his magan leof*, l. 59, is strikingly like *Maðr er manns gaman*,
"man is the delight of man," in the Icelandic poem (there being,
however, no corresponding phrase in the Norwegian). The exact
significance of these resemblances is open to question. It may be,
as Brandl seems to imply in his discussion of the RUNE POEM,[2]
that the three poets all drew material from some earlier Germanic
rune poem dating from heathen times; but it is far more likely that
the similarities which have been noted rest upon the independent
use of traditional popular material. The Anglo-Saxon poem, in
particular, gives the impression of being a miscellaneous compilation from all kinds of sources, both literary and popular. A number of the stanzas are remarkably like riddles, and may originally

---

[1] The full Anglo-Saxon alphabet, with all additions, seems to have contained
thirty-three runes, the last four being *cweorð, calc, stan,* and *gar,* mentioned
above as additions made by Hickes to the text of the poem. A complete discussion of the history of the runic alphabet in England would be irrelevant here;
the most intelligible treatment of the subject is by O. von Friesen in the *Reallexi-
kon der germanischen Altertumskunde* IV (Strassburg, 1918–1919), 5–51, especially pp. 20–26. Keller in a very important article, *Anglia* LX, 141ff., points
out a number of apparent examples of mutual influence between the Anglo-
Saxon and continental rune names.

[2] Paul's *Grundriss der germanischen Philologie* (2d ed.), II, 1, 964f.

have been written as such, the proper rune being written at the beginning of each stanza as a clue for the solver; among these riddle-like stanzas are ll. 25–26 (*hægl*), 29–31 (*is*), 48–50 (*Tir*), and 51–54 (*beorc*). Other stanzas, such as ll. 1–3 (*feoh*), 27–28 (*nyd*), 59–62 (*man*), and 90–94 (*ear*), are clearly in the tradition of the proverbs or sententious sayings so popular in Old Germanic poetry. The *Ing* stanza, ll. 67–70, contains material from Germanic mythology which is not exactly duplicated anywhere else and which may be contrasted with the mention of the Christian deity in the stanzas dealing with *feoh, ger, man*, and *dæg* (ll. 1–3, 32–34, 59–62, 74–76). The *hægl* and *nyd* stanzas (ll. 25–28), which are written in expanded (three-stress) lines, may have been derived from some other source than the stanzas written in normal verse. All these considerations argue for a diversity of sources for the various parts of the RUNE POEM, but the exact nature of the sources and the way in which they were combined to form the extant text remain obscure. It is of course possible that the poem grew by accretion, as a result of the activity of several poets or compilers. But in the form in which we now have it, it gives the impression of a complete and unified work by a single compiler, who drew from a variety of materials but adapted and revised these materials to suit his artistic purposes. Evidence of such unity is easily discoverable; for example, in the almost uniform use of the *biþ* formula in the first line of each stanza, a device which is neglected only in ll. 22, 41, and 67; in the general conformity of length between the stanzas;[1] and in the clever arrangement of the verbs to give an effect of finality in ll. 90–95.

The date of the RUNE POEM in its present form is best placed fairly early, say in the eighth or early ninth century. There are a number of late spellings in the text, such as the frequent use of *-un* for final *-um* (*miclun*, l. 2, *ungemetun*, l. 8, etc.), and of *y* as the vowel of unstressed syllables (*yfyl*, l. 8, *recyde*, l. 13, *underwreþyd*, l. 37, etc.), and the Cotton manuscript, therefore, can hardly have been written earlier than the end of the tenth century. But here,

---

[1] All but three of the stanzas contain either three or four lines; the two two-line stanzas (ll. 25–28) are written in expanded lines, and the use of five lines in the last stanza is justified by the effect of climax for which the poet seems to have been striving.

as elsewhere, the date of the manuscript is no evidence for date of composition; and the regularity of the meter, together with the poet's general adherence to the style and diction of the older poetry, places a pre-Alfredian date of composition almost beyond question.

The rune names recorded by Hickes, although they may have been taken from a source other than MS. Otho B.x, seem, on the whole, to be quite accurate, and conform closely to the rune names given in the tenth-century Salzburg runic alphabet in MS. 795 of the Nationalbibliothek in Vienna,[1] as well as in the other Anglo-Saxon runic alphabets. There is therefore no difficulty in identifying the words or names for which the runes stand in our text, and in this respect the RUNE POEM presents fewer problems than, for example, the Cynewulfian runic signatures. There is, however, considerable doubt as to the meaning of certain of the rune names (*os*, l. 10, *peorð*, l. 38, *eolhx-*, l. 41, *yr*, l. 84, *iar*, l. 87, and others). The various interpretations which have been suggested are recorded in the notes at the end of the volume.

SOLOMON AND SATURN

The Anglo-Saxon poetical dialogues known by the name of SOLOMON AND SATURN are now represented by two fragmentary texts, contained in MS. 41 and MS. 422 of Corpus Christi College, Cambridge.

MS. 422 (A) contains 294 folios, about 7.6 by 5.1 inches (19.25 by 13 cm.) in size. All but a small part of the volume is taken up by a calendar and missal, fol. 14–294,[2] written in several eleventh-century (and twelfth-century?) hands. This part of the manuscript is of some considerable importance for the history of the Anglo-Saxon liturgy,[3] but since it was quite unconnected in its origins with the text of SOLOMON AND SATURN, it will not be necessary to consider it in detail here.[4]

---

[1] A reproduction of this alphabet is given by Wimmer, *Die Runenschrift*, p. 85.

[2] Numbered by pages from 27 to 585; fol. 127 is omitted in the pagination.

[3] See, for example, B. Fehr, "Altenglische Ritualtexte," in *Texte und Forschungen zur englischen Kulturgeschichte* (Halle, 1921), pp. 20–67.

[4] It is traditionally known as the "Red Book of Derby," from a note on the last page; but James reads this note as "The rede boke of darleye," that is, the parish of Darley, near the Peak in Derbyshire. The appearance of the names

The text of SOLOMON AND SATURN, on pages 1–26 (fol. 1–13) of the manuscript, is written in a single hand, very small and precise, probably of the late tenth century.[1] It is composed of three separate fragments: (a) The first verse dialogue, ll. 1–169, begins at the head of page 1 and extends to about the middle of page 6, where it breaks off with the words ðonne his feond cyme. (b) A fragment of a prose dialogue of Solomon and Saturn[2] follows immediately, with no indication of a break in the manuscript, and extends to the foot of page 12, where it ends abruptly in the middle of a sentence. A leaf has been lost from the manuscript at this point. (c) At the head of page 13, immediately after the lost leaf, are the nine lines of verse numbered ll. 170–178, which occupy about a third of the page. Then follows the second verse dialogue (ll. 179–506), with l. 179a written in large capitals, HWÆT·IC ·FLI·TAN·GEFRÆGN. The extant text ends in the middle of a sentence at the foot of page 26.

Not only are the verse dialogues broken up by the insertion of the prose dialogue and the loss of several passages, but the extant portions are in very poor condition. The first leaf has been damaged by the action of damp, which has faded the writing and made several holes in the parchment. Page 1 (ll. 1–30) is almost entirely illegible, only a few words being recoverable here and there.[3] Page 2 (ll. 30–60), except for a few letters, is legible throughout, though difficult to read except under good light conditions. There are also several holes in the parchment on pages 3 to 6. Later pages of the text have been rendered partially

---

of Grimbald, Swithun, Æthelwold, and Ælfeah in the calendar (page 29) and the Litany (page 378) suggests that this part of the MS. originated in Winchester; for its contents, see M. R. James, Descriptive Catalogue of the Manuscripts in the Library of Corpus Christi College II (Cambridge, 1912), 317ff.

[1] James, Catalogue II, 315, ascribes it doubtfully to the tenth century. Kemble, The Dialogue of Salomon and Saturnus, p. 132, applying (one fears) nineteenth-century standards, thought the handwriting was a woman's.

[2] Not edited here, but available in Menner, The Poetical Dialogues of Solomon and Saturn, pp. 168–171.

[3] Vincenti's list of the legible parts of page 1 (Die altenglischen Dialoge von Salomon und Saturn, Part 1, pp. 44–45) is now superseded by the report of page 1 given by Menner in his critical apparatus (The Poetical Dialogues of Solomon and Saturn, pp. 80–81).

obscure by the application of galls and other reagents.   There is a
gap of about thirty lines between l. 201 and l. 202, the original text
of page 14 having been erased to permit the writing of a Latin
formula of excommunication,[1] in two rather crude hands of the
twelfth century.   Ultraviolet prints of pages 1 and 14 would
probably reveal extensive portions of the text which are now illegible, but the manuscript has never been photographed in this
manner.   The loss of page 1 is not so serious as it might be, since
the text of ll. 1–30 can be supplied from MS. B.[2]

MS. 41 (B) is a copy of the Alfredian translation of Bede's
Ecclesiastical History, written about the middle of the eleventh
century.[3]   It contains 244 folios, about 13.8 by 8.3 inches (35 by
21 cm.) in size.   In the margins are written a great number of
short texts, in Latin and Anglo-Saxon, all in the same rather small
and unusual hand, also of the eleventh century.   This was one of
the manuscripts given by Bishop Leofric to Exeter Cathedral,[4] and
it may have been written in Exeter or the vicinity.[5]   The text of
SOLOMON AND SATURN, in the margins of pages 196–198 (fol. 98b–
99b), runs only from the beginning to the letter T. in l. 94; it

[1] Edited by F. Liebermann, *Die Gesetze der Angelsachsen* I (Halle, 1903),
435–436.

[2] The contents of the pages of A in terms of the line-numbering of this edition are: page 1, *Saturnus*, l. 1, to *bið*, l. 30; page 2, *leofre*, l. 30, to *hæleða*, l. 60;
page 3, *under*, l. 60, to g[...]*man*, l. 91; page 4, *feond*, l. 91, to *wyrnað*, l. 121;
page 5, *deorra*, l. 122, to *str*[.]*nges*, l. 153; page 6, *and*, l. 153, to *cyme*, l. 169
(followed by the prose dialogue); page 13, *swice*, l. 170, to *Hierusa-*, l. 201; page
15, *oððe*, l. 202, to *meahta*, l. 229; page 16, *Saturnus*, l. 230, to *ic*, l. 253; page 17,
ðe, l. 253, to *geond*, l. 282; page 18, *ðas*, l. 282, to *reafað*, l. 308; page 19, *swiðor*,
l. 309, to *ðu*, l. 331; page 20, *in*, l. 331, to *fracoðast*, l. 352; page 21, *Saturnus*,
l. 353, to *earfoðu*, l. 376; page 22, *orlegstunde*, l. 376, to *neahtes*, l. 399; page 23,
his, l. 400, to *fyrn*, l. 426; page 24, *gehyrde*, l. 426, to *dryht-*, l. 453; page 25, *-ne
hierde*, l. 453, to *foldan*, l. 477; page 26, *fira*, l. 477, to *middes*, l. 506.

[3] See T. Miller, *The Old English Version of Bede's Ecclesiastical History* (London, 1890ff.) I, xvi-xvii; II, ix-x; M. R. James, *Descriptive Catalogue of the
Manuscripts in the Library of Corpus Christi College* I, 81–85.

[4] See *Records III*, *The Exeter Book*, pp. ix-x.

[5] So M. Ångström, *Studies in Old English MSS* (Uppsala, 1937), pp. 55–56.
T. Miller, *Place Names in the English Bede* (Strassburg, 1896), p. 5, concluded
from the forms of place-names in the text of Bede that the MS. was written in
Wessex, "not far from Abingdon and Winchester."

contains altogether less than one-fifth of the extant text.[1] But it
gives the passages at the beginning which are illegible in A, and by
putting the evidence of the two manuscripts together, we have a
fairly complete text. Lines 1–30, which are so largely obliterated
in A, can be supplied from B, and for ll. 30–94 we have the evidence
of both manuscripts.

In the present edition, the text of SOLOMON AND SATURN as far
as *biᵹ*, l. 30, is based on B, with the legible variant readings of A
recorded at the foot of the page. From *leofre*, l. 30, to the end the
text is based on A. Readings of A which are reported by Menner
in his edition are marked "A (M)" in the apparatus below the text;
all readings of A which are not specifically credited to Menner in
this way are from my own collations. As in earlier editions, the
indications of speaker (*Saturnus cwæᵹ*, etc.) are printed as separate
lines of the text but are not included in the line-numbering. Before
ll. 212, 230, 238, 245, 292, 334, 344, 351, and 372 (that is, wherever
the indication of speaker is written with capital letters in the
manuscript), the spelling is *CVÆÐ* (i.e. *cuæᵹ*) instead of the usual
cwæᵹ. Wherever the word *cwæᵹ* is abbreviated (as before ll. 253,
302, 327, etc.), it is expanded to *cwæᵹ* in the text, regardless of the
capitalization.

In considering the subject matter of this text, it is necessary to
bear in mind the existence of the two separate verse fragments
(ll. 1–169 and ll. 170–506), with the prose fragment inserted
between them. In the first of the verse fragments (ll. 1–169)
Saturn, who is learned in all the books of pre-Christian wisdom,
asks a series of questions concerning the nature of the "palm-
twigged"[2] Pater Noster, to each of which Solomon replies in the
light of Christian doctrine. It is important to notice that the
Saturn represented here is not the pagan divinity of that name or

[1] The contents of the pages of B in terms of the line-numbering of this edition
are: page 196, *Saturnus*, l. 1, to *fremde*, l. 34; page 197, *frean*, l. 34, to *se*, l. 63;
page 198, *godes*, l. 63, to *T.*, l. 94.

[2] On the palm as a symbol of victory, Vincenti, p. 59, cites the homily for
Palm Sunday in the *Blickling Homilies* (ed. R. Morris), p. 67, l. 7. See also
C. Mackay, "The Sign of the Palm Tree," *Church Quarterly Review* CXXVI
(1938), 187–212, for a discussion of the palm as a symbol of life and the resurrection in Old Testament usage.

(as some scholars have thought) a native Germanic god, but a "prince of the Chaldeans" (*Caldea eorl*, l. 176), a people traditionally associated with the practice of oriental astrology and magic.[1] In the longest speech of this fragment (ll. 63–169), Solomon describes the virtues of the separate letters of which the text of the Pater Noster is composed. The poet's intention must have been to give the nineteen letters which are required for writing the Pater Noster in the Vulgate text of Matthew vi.9–13,[2] in the order in which they appear (*P A T E R N O S Q U I C L F M D G B H*). But only sixteen of these letters appear in the text of SOLOMON AND SATURN, in the order *P A T E R N S Q U L C F M G D H*. Of the three missing letters, it is probable (as Grein suggested) that *O* and *I* are to be inserted in l. 108*a* and l. 123*a*, but the problem of *B* is more difficult. The proper place for *B* (judging from the order of the letters in the Latin text) would be immediately before *H*, and Grein suggested that *B* is mentioned indirectly in ll. 136*b*-137. It is difficult to see why *B* should be referred to as *se ðridda*, but there does not seem to be any other place for it in ll. 89–140.[3]

The prose dialogue which follows (on pages 6–12 of the manuscript) contains an account of the various likenesses in which the devil and the Pater Noster will fight with each other, together with a rather lengthy and detailed description of the Pater Noster itself. Then follow, at the head of page 13, ll. 170–178, which may or may not be the conclusion of the verse dialogue in ll. 1–169.[4] In this passage we are told that the wise son of David has overcome and surpassed in knowledge (*forcumen and forcyðed*) the Chaldean prince but has nevertheless pleased him with his wisdom.

At this point we come to a new section of the text, marked in

[1] For the term "Chaldeans" as applied to practitioners of the Babylonian occult sciences in biblical (post-exilic) usage, see Daniel ii. 2, ii. 10, iv. 7, v. 7, v. 11; also, S. R. Driver, *The Book of Daniel* (Cambridge, 1900), pp. 12–16; R. H. Charles, *A Critical and Exegetical Commentary on the Book of Daniel* (Oxford, 1929), pp. 14–16.

[2] Or, as Menner suggests (*The Poetical Dialogues of Solomon and Saturn*, p. 36), in the familiar form of the liturgy, which has *panem nostrum quotidianum* instead of *panem nostrum supersubstantialem*. The order of the letters would, however, be the same in either text.

[3] See the notes on this passage, pp. 162–163, below.

[4] See below, p. lviii.

the manuscript by the capitalization of the entire first line. It is apparent, in view of the capitalization and the use of the epic formula *Hwæt! Ic...gefrægn*, that we have here, if not a separate dialogue, at least a second main division of the text. That ll. 179–506 form a new and distinct poem is strongly indicated by the repetition of the same sort of material which has already been given in the earlier part of the text; that is, the statement in ll. 182–185*a* that Saturn had studied in many lands and the list of countries in ll. 185*b*-201 remind us of Saturn's own remark in ll. 1–4 of the first fragment, *ic iglanda ealra hæbbe boca onbyrged*, etc. The beginning of this second section seems in every respect to be independent of ll. 1–169, and the most likely conclusion is that we have here not merely a continuation of what has preceded, but a separate literary effort, probably in imitation of the first.

The dialogue part of this second poem, which begins in the middle of a sentence (l. 202) at the head of page 15,[1] is a rather miscellaneous collection of proverbial wisdom, in which one sage asks riddling questions and the other answers them, much in the style of the Old Norse *Vafþrúðnismál*. Usually, as in the first poem, Saturn is the inquirer; but at the very beginning, ll. 202–224, it is Solomon who asks the question and Saturn who furnishes the reply. Solomon's replies to Saturn are sometimes in the form of questions (as in ll. 338–339, 344–347), the answers to which are perhaps supposed to be obvious. In ll. 238–246, Saturn's riddle of the book leads to a series of observations by both parties concerning the usefulness of literature; and occasionally (as in ll. 225–229, 312–331) we have sententious utterances by one or the other which bear little or no apparent relationship to the questions which have been asked.

In view of the difficulties which arise in the interpretation of this second poem, it is tempting to assume gaps in the text, even where no loss is evident in the manuscript. In two places we may be sure that matter is lost,[2] after *reafað*, l. 308 (at the end of page 18 of A), and again after *neahtes*, l. 399 (at the end of page 22). In l. 308, Saturn is inquiring why the snow falls, but ll. 309–311 have

---

[1] After the gap in the text caused by the erasure of page 14; see above, p. lii.

[2] As was pointed out by Vincenti, *Die altenglischen Dialoge von Salomon und Saturn*, Part 1, pp. 71, 75.

INTRODUCTION

nothing to do with this question and must in any case be taken as part of a speech by Solomon, since they are immediately followed by the indication *Saturnus cwæð* before l. 312.   Similarly, after l. 399, the end of Saturn's question about water, we are immediately plunged into the middle of a rather long discourse by Solomon on light and fire.   It is very likely that leaves have been lost from the manuscript in both these places.[1]

Of all the extant dialogue texts on the Solomon and Saturn theme in western literature, our poems are the oldest.   There are two other dialogues of the same sort in Anglo-Saxon, the prose *Solomon and Saturn* in MS. Cotton Vitellius A.xv, fol. 86*b*-93*b*, and the prose *Adrianus and Ritheus* in MS. Cotton Julius A.ii, fol. 137*b*-140*a*.[2]   But although these two prose dialogues are very similar and are perhaps related, they have little in common with the verse dialogues.   In other western European versions Solomon's opponent bears various forms of the name Marcolf; as, for example, Marcolfus in the Latin dialogue,[3] Morolf and Markolf in the Middle High German poems,[4] and Marcoul, Marcoux, Marcon in medieval French sources.[5]   In most of the later texts Marcolf appears as a lively and somewhat ribald jester, in strong contrast with the seriousness of Saturn in the Anglo-Saxon poems.

The historical relationship between Saturn and Marcolf, in the development of the dialogue, presents a difficult problem.   Although the texts in which Marcolf's name appears are all later than our SOLOMON AND SATURN, it is generally believed that he is an older figure in the history of the dialogue than Saturn.   That

---

[1] Such leaves would be conjugate and would therefore leave no trace; see Menner, *The Poetical Dialogues of Solomon and Saturn*, p. 2.

[2] Both of these texts are printed by Kemble, *The Dialogue of Salomon and Saturnus*, pp. 178–206.

[3] Edited by W. Benary, *Salomon et Marcolfus* (Heidelberg, 1914).

[4] A popular epic, *Salman und Morolf*, of the late thirteenth or early fourteenth century (the original redaction is assigned to the end of the twelfth century), dealing with the old story of the abduction of Solomon's wife; and a verse dialogue, *Salomon und Markolf*, of the fourteenth century, based in large part on the Latin dialogue.   On these German versions, see especially G. Ehrismann, *Geschichte der deutschen Literatur bis zum Ausgange des Mittelalters* II, 1 (Munich, 1922), 313–328.

[5] Described in detail by Kemble, *The Dialogue of Salomon and Saturnus*, pp. 73–83.

Marcolf was known in this connection in Germany as early as the
end of the tenth century is shown by a frequently quoted passage
in Notker Labeo's paraphrase of the Psalms.[1] The name *Marculf*
is also found in SOLOMON AND SATURN 189, in the phrase *Marculfes
eard*, one of the places visited by Saturn in the course of his travels.
The origin and significance of the name Marcolf are, however, not
definitely known.   Kemble[2] suggested that it was a form of Anglo-
Saxon *Mearcwulf*, "wolf of the marches"; but, while Marcolf may
be a Germanic name-form, most scholars have assumed that it is
derived from an oriental original.   It has been suggested, for
example,[3] that it comes, through a Hebrew form *Markolis*, from the
name of the Roman god Mercurius.   But the history of the name
Marcolf, though it is important for the interpretation of the continental dialogues, is of less value in the study of SOLOMON AND
SATURN.   The origin of the whole tradition of Solomon's trials of
wit with an oriental sage seems to lie in the Talmudic and Arabic
legends of Solomon's conversations with demons, who revealed to
him the mysteries of the universe.[4]   A direct source for some, if
not all, of the western versions may perhaps be sought in the "Salomonis contradictio," listed as a forbidden text by the so-called
Decretum Gelasii de libris recipiendis et non recipiendis,[5] but since
we know nothing about the "Salomonis contradictio" except its
name, it does not help us very much.   The frequent use of Latin
words in both of the Anglo-Saxon poems[6] seems to indicate a Latin

[1] On Psalm cxviii. 85 (cxix. 85 in the English Bible): *Vuaz ist ioh anderes
daz man Marcholfum saget sih éllenon uuider proverbiis Salomonis*, "What else is
it, then, that they say of Marcolf that he contended against the proverbs of
Solomon?" (ed. P. Piper, Freiburg, 1883, II, 522).

[2] *The Dialogue of Salomon and Saturnus*, p. 118.

[3] See Schaumberg, *Beiträge* II, 52; Vogt, *Salman und Morolf*, pp. lv–lvii.

[4] For a general survey of these oriental legends, see Vincenti, *Die altenglischen
Dialoge von Salomon und Saturn*, Part 1, pp. 1–13; Menner, *The Poetical Dialogues of Solomon and Saturn*, pp. 22–23.

[5] Traditionally ascribed to Gelasius, who was pope from 492 to 496, but
probably not earlier than the first half of the sixth century; see E. von Dob-
schütz, *Das Decretum Gelasianum de libris recipiendis et non recipiendis* (Leipzig,
1912), p. 345.

[6] As, for example, *Greca*, l. 3 (for the usual Anglo-Saxon form *Creca*), *istoriam*,
l. 4, *cantic*, ll. 24, 49 (and *cantices*, l. 17), *organ*, l. 53 (and *organes*, l. 33), *prologa prima*, l. 89, *uasa mortis*, l. 281, etc.

source or sources, but whatever Latin sources were used have not come down to us, or at least have not been identified.

Unquestionably the most difficult parts of the second poem, from the point of view of literary history, are Saturn's statement about Nimrod and the *weallende Wulf* (ll. 212–224) and Solomon's description of the bird called *uasa mortis* (ll. 255–281). Both of these passages have been explained in detail by Menner.[1] According to him, the poet in ll. 212–224 follows the Hebrew and Christian tradition which makes Nimrod the builder of the Tower of Babel, in the land of Shinar. Veiled references to the building of the tower are to be found in ll. 209–210 (the warning which befell the Chaldeans on the field of Shinar) and in ll. 328*b*–331 (the work which Saturn's people began against God's will and failed to accomplish). The connection between Nimrod and the wolf (or a proper name, *Wulf?*) may be explained by a confusion between Nimrod and the Babylonian myth of Bel the dragon-slayer, on the one hand, and on the other hand by a transference of the legend of Bel to Saturn and through him to Marculf (taken as the equivalent of *Mearcwulf*).[2] Solomon's binding of the *uasa mortis* (ll. 255–281) is to be interpreted as a reflection of the binding of the demon Ashmedai (Asmodeus), treated in the Talmudic writings. The Philistine god Dagon was also probably confused with the legend of Asmodeus, and for this reason the *uasa mortis* is represented by the poet as dwelling *on Filistina middelgemærum*. The name *uasa mortis* (a plural taken by the poet as a singular) must go back to some Latin commentary in which the phrase *uasa mortis* ("the instruments of death," Psalm vii.13) was applied to an order of demons.

It is necessary to say a few words about the proper place of ll. 170–178. Vincenti and Menner are of the opinion[3] that these lines formed the end of the second poem; that is, that they followed after l. 506, with some intervening material which was contained on the leaf lost between pages 12 and 13. Support for this view

---

[1] *Journal of English and Germanic Philology* XXXVII, 332–354; *Studies in English Philology*, pp. 240–253.

[2] See above, p. lvii. *Mearcwulf* might then be rendered as *weallende wulf*, "wandering wolf"; Menner compares the phrase *mære mearcstapa*, applied to Grendel.

[3] Vincenti, *Die altenglischen Dialoge von Salomon und Saturn*, Part 1, p. 64; Menner, *The Poetical Dialogues of Solomon and Saturn*, pp. 10–11.

may be found in the double occurrence of the phrase *forcumen and forcyð(ð)ed* in l. 176 and l. 207, and the general similarity of phraseology between ll. 171–172 and ll. 505–506.[1] It is also true, as Menner suggests, that the unity of the second poem would be considerably increased by putting ll. 170–178 after l. 506. In the present edition, the arrangement in the manuscript has been followed; but it is not impossible that ll. 170–178 were displaced in an earlier copy of the poems.[2]

Whether we put ll. 170–178 after l. 506 or leave them where they are, it seems reasonably certain that ll. 1–169 and ll. 179–506 are parts of two separate poems, by two different authors. It is most likely that the rather fanciful description of the Pater Noster, presented in dialogue form in ll. 1–169 and in the prose fragment, inspired a second poet to put together, in the form of the riddle contest elsewhere widely known in Old Germanic tradition, the miscellaneous material of ll. 179–506, derived in part from traditional gnomic literature, in part from Latin works on theology and demonology.

For the date of composition of the two poems there is little direct evidence. Certain metrical and syntactical irregularities in the second poem, pointed out by Brandl,[3] might argue for a date in the latter half of the tenth century, or not much before the writing of MS. A. But, as Sweet pointed out,[4] there are a number of spellings in both poems which are characteristic of the early West Saxon of Alfred's time and are probably vestiges of an older copy.[5]

---

[1] Vincenti also claims that there is linguistic evidence for placing ll. 170–178 with the second poem; but his study of the phonology of SOLOMON AND SATURN (in the projected second part of his book) was never published.

[2] The argument from parallel passages proves less than, at first sight, it may appear to prove; the occurrence of the same phraseology in two different poems or fragments may indicate common authorship, or it may be merely the result of deliberate imitation of one poet by another. This problem is a commonplace of Cynewulf criticism; see, for example, the remarks by A. S. Cook, *The Christ of Cynewulf* (Boston, 1900), p. xxi.

[3] Paul's *Grundriss der germanischen Philologie* (2d ed.), II, 1, 1092.

[4] *Anglia* I, 152–153.

[5] Menner, *The Poetical Dialogues of Solomon and Saturn*, pp. 16–17, notes especially the back-spelling *ie* (as in *sienful, brieceð, hieltas, siemle*) in MS. A, and the spelling *sð* for *st* (in *wesðe, eaðusð, gesemesð*) in MS. B; both these spellings are characteristic of the late ninth-century copy of the *Pastoral Care* in MS. Hatton 20.

All things considered, the end of the ninth century (or at least the beginning of the tenth century) seems the most probable date for the poems in their present state. Certain Anglian forms, pointed out by Menner,[1] suggest that the original text was in the Anglian dialect rather than in West Saxon.

THE MENOLOGIUM AND MAXIMS II

In addition to the poems of the Anglo-Saxon Chronicle, MS. Cotton Tiberius B.i[2] contains two other Anglo-Saxon verse texts, the MENOLOGIUM and MAXIMS II, on fol. 112a-115b. Both of these poems are written in the same hand as the beginning of the Chronicle, fol. 115b-118b, which is dated by Plummer about the middle of the eleventh century.[3] The practice of editors has been to treat the two poems as independent of the Chronicle text, but the evidence of the capitalization in the manuscript makes it probable that the scribe, at least, regarded the MENOLOGIUM and MAXIMS II as preliminary matter to the Chronicle. The MENO-LOGIUM begins at the head of fol. 112a,[4] with a very large and orna-mental capital C, built around the picture of a bird; the rest of l. 1 of the poem, except for the letters -dor of wuldor, is also written in two lines of large capitals. In contrast to this impressive be-ginning of the MENOLOGIUM, the beginning of the Chronicle proper (Ær Cristes geflæscnesse, etc.), near the foot of fol. 115b, has a considerably smaller, though still highly ornamented, capital Æ, and only one line of large capitals (through æ of geflæscnesse). The beginning of MAXIMS II, at the head of fol. 115a, has only a plain large capital C (in Cyning), with small capitals for the rest of l. 1a. But even though the scribe may have intended his text of the Chronicle to begin with the MENOLOGIUM and MAXIMS II, there can be little doubt that the two poems were originally separate pieces. The MENOLOGIUM, to be sure, has some connection with the subject matter of the Chronicle, being itself an account of the

---

[1] In his complete discussion of the language of the two poems, *ibid.*, pp. 18–21.

[2] For a brief description of this MS., see p. xxxiv, above.

[3] *Two of the Saxon Chronicles Parallel* II, xxx f.

[4] At the very top of the page a modern (sixteenth-century?) hand has written: "Cronica Saxonica Abbingdoniæ ad annum 1066."

seasons and festal days of the Christian year; but MAXIMS II, like MAXIMS I in the Exeter Book, has no relationship in subject matter to either the MENOLOGIUM or the Chronicle.[1]

The MENOLOGIUM is only one of many medieval texts, in Latin and in the vernacular languages, which deal in one way or another with the chronology of the Christian year. Besides the simple tabular calendars which were prefixed to many kinds of liturgical books (and which still survive, in essentially the same form, in the Roman Missal and Breviary and in the Anglican Book of Common Prayer), there were a considerable number of calendars and martyrologies in more extended form, verse or prose, which made some pretensions to literary worth. Among the extant examples of this type of literature may be mentioned, in addition to our Anglo-Saxon poem, the Latin *Martyrologium poeticum* formerly ascribed to the Venerable Bede;[2] a longer verse martyrology, also in Latin, composed by Wandalbert of Prüm in the middle of the ninth century;[3] and the so-called Calendar of Oengus the Culdee, in Irish verse, probably written about the end of the tenth century.[4] These three poems are all similar to the MENOLOGIUM in subject matter and in the chronological arrangement of the materials handled; but they vary widely in scope. The pseudo-Bedan martyrology, like the MENOLOGIUM, gives only a limited selection of saints' festivals, and runs to only 113 hexameter lines; Wandalbert's martyrology is much fuller, giving at least a line, usually more, to each day in the year; while the Calendar of Oengus is still longer, containing 365 quatrains, one for each day, besides Prologue and Epilogue.

[1] The contents of fol. 112a–115b, in terms of the line-numbering of this edition, are: fol. 112a, *Crist*, MEN. 1, to *ymb III*, MEN. 30; fol. 112b, *and twa*, MEN. 30, to *martira*, MEN. 69; fol. 113a, *gemynd*, MEN. 69, to *agrynt*, MEN. 111; fol. 113b, *to*, MEN. 112, to *neorxnawange*, MEN. 151; fol. 114a, *hæfde*, MEN. 151, to *Simon*, MEN. 191; fol. 114b, *and*, MEN. 191, to *tiid*, MEN. 231; fol. 115a, *Cyning*, MAX. II, 1, to *gebeorh*, MAX. II, 38; fol. 115b, *Fugel*, MAX. II, 38, to *wunað*, MAX. II, 66.

[2] Printed by J. A. Giles, *Venerabilis Bedæ opera quæ supersunt omnia* I (London, 1843), 50–53. This poem cannot be by Bede, since it mentions Wilfrid II of York, who died about 744–745; see C. Plummer, *Bedae opera historica* I (Oxford, 1896), clviii.

[3] Edited by E. Dümmler, *Poetae latini aevi Carolini* II (Berlin, 1884), 578–602.

[4] See Whitley Stokes, "On the Calendar of Oengus," *Transactions of the Royal Irish Academy*, Irish Manuscript Series, I (Dublin, 1880).

The Anglo-Saxon prose martyrology[1] need not be discussed in this connection, since it is merely a collection of short prose narratives of saints' lives, with little unity of content and form except such as derives from the chronological arrangement. The poem on the SEASONS FOR FASTING, printed at a later place in this volume, treats of only the Ember weeks and Lent and is therefore not a calendar at all. But the prose menologium, recently edited by Henel,[2] is remarkably similar in content to the verse MENOLOGIUM. It is naturally much shorter, without the stylistic amplifications of the poem; it omits the names of the months and some of the holy days which the poem includes, but it adds St. Cuthbert's Day (March 20th), which the poem does not mention. It is most probable[3] that the two texts represent independent compilations from missals or from ecclesiastical calendars, the purpose of both compilers being to furnish readable accounts of the chronology of the Christian year in the vernacular language, for the benefit of those who could not read Latin.[4]

It is necessary to say a few words here concerning the reckoning of dates in the MENOLOGIUM. The usual method of indicating dates is by counting the number of days (sometimes weeks and days) elapsed since the beginning of the month or since the last date previously mentioned; for example, the phrase *And þæs embe fif niht*, l. 11, immediately following the mention of January 1st (ll. 7–10), indicates January 6th as the date of the Epiphany. But occasionally the number of days elapsed is stated as the sum or difference of two periods of time, as in *Swylce . . . ymb III and twa* (three plus two days, i.e. five days), ll. 29–30; *emb feower wucan . . . butan twam nihtum* (four weeks less two days, i.e. twenty-six days), ll. 15–17.[5] The dates as given in the poem are usually correct;

---

[1] Edited by G. Herzfeld, *An Old English Martyrology* (London, 1900).

[2] *Studien zum altenglischen Computus*, pp. 71–77; from MS. Harley 3271, in the British Museum, and MS. 422 of Corpus Christi College, Cambridge.

[3] See Henel, *Studien*, pp. 87ff.

[4] The word "menologium" is, strictly speaking, not quite appropriate, since it denotes primarily the calendars of saints' festivals used in the Eastern Church; but it has been in general use among Anglo-Saxon scholars for a hundred years or more, and it would be confusing to abandon it now.

[5] The count is always noninclusive, according to the modern method of computation; that is, from January 1st to January 6th counts as five days, not as six.

but there are a few cases in which the poet or the scribe seems to be in error, and which have been emended in the text.[1] In l. 107, the manuscript reading *ymb twa and þreo* is wrong, since the count is from May 26th to June 1st; the proper reading is *ymb twa and feower*. In ll. 187–188, *ymb twentig þæs ... and fif nihtum*, the proper count of days is not twenty-five, but twenty-seven, from October 1st to October 28th; here the alliteration confirms the emendation of *fif* to *seofon*. In l. 71 and l. 76, both of which are incomplete in the manuscript, the number of days to be counted indicates in each case the matter to be supplied.[2] The only real difficulty of interpretation arises in ll. 1–4, where the date indicated for the Nativity of Christ, eight days before January 1st, seems to be December 24th rather than December 25th, the date given in ll. 226–228a. The correctness of *eahteoðan*, l. 3b, is confirmed by the alliteration; it is then possible either that the poet was wrong in his counting, or that we are really to take December 24th, the vigil of the Nativity, as the date indicated in ll. 1–3a. Whether *on midne winter*, l. 2a, refers specifically to "Midwinter Day" (corresponding to Midsummer Day, June 24th), or to the middle of the winter in general, is uncertain; if the former, then December 25th, rather than December 24th, is probably the day indicated.[3]

With these interpretations of the text in mind, a list of the seasons, months, and days enumerated in the MENOLOGIUM may be drawn up, as follows:[4]

December 25 (or December 24?). Nativity of Christ (ll. 1–2a)
January (ll. 7–10)
   1. Circumcision; beginning of the year (ll. 2b–6)
   6. Epiphany (ll. 11–15a)
February (ll. 15b–19a)

---

[1] Emendation seems justified in these cases, since we have more definite evidence to work on than is usual where suspicion of error arises in Anglo-Saxon texts.

[2] See the notes on these lines, pp. 171–172, below.

[3] Henel, *Studien zum altenglischen Computus*, p. 73, note 3, points out that Midwinter Day is December 21st in the Julian reckoning, but December 25th in the ecclesiastical calendar. The prose menologium gives December 25th as Midwinter Day.

[4] This list is based to some extent on the one given by Piper, *Die Kalendarien und Martyrologien der Angelsachsen*, pp. 71–73.

2. Purification of the Virgin Mary (ll. 19*b*–22)
7. End of Winter (ll. 23–24*a*)
24. St. Matthias (ll. 24*b*–29*a*)
29. Bissextile Day (ll. 32–34)
March (ll. 29*b*–31, 35–37*a*)
12. St. Gregory the Great (ll. 37*b*–40*a*)
21. St. Benedict; Vernal Equinox (ll. 40*b*–47)
25. Annunciation of the Virgin Mary (ll. 48–54*a*)
April; most frequent occurrence of Easter (ll. 54*b*–68*a*)
25. Greater Litany (ll. 68*b*–75*a*)
May (ll. 75*b*–79)
1. St. Philip and St. James (ll. 80–82)
3. Invention of the Cross (ll. 83–87*a*)
9. Beginning of Summer (ll. 87*b*–95*a*)
26. St. Augustine of Canterbury (ll. 95*b*–106*a*)
June (ll. 106*b*–115*a*)
24. Nativity of St. John the Baptist; Midsummer Day (ll. 115*b*–119)
29. St. Peter and St. Paul (ll. 120–130*a*)
July (ll. 130*b*–132*a*)
25. St. James the Greater (ll. 132*b*–136*a*)
August (ll. 136*b*–138*a*)
1. Lammas Day (ll. 138*b*–140*a*)
7. Beginning of Autumn (ll. 140*b*–143*a*)
10. St. Laurence (ll. 143*b*–147)
15. Assumption of the Virgin Mary (ll. 148–153*a*)
25. St. Bartholomew (ll. 153*b*–156*a*)
29. Martyrdom of St. John the Baptist (ll. 156*b*–162)
September (ll. 163–167*a*)
8. Nativity of the Virgin Mary (ll. 167*b*–169*a*)
21. St. Matthew (ll. 169*b*–173*a*)
24. Autumnal Equinox (ll. 173*b*–175)
29. St. Michael (ll. 176–180)
October (ll. 181–186*a*)
28. St. Ṣimon and St. Jude (ll. 186*b*–193*a*)
November (ll. 193*b*–198)
1. All Saints' Day (ll. 199–201)
7. Beginning of Winter (ll. 202–207*a*)

11. St. Martin of Tours (ll. 207*b*–210*a*)
23. St. Clement (ll. 210*b*–214)
30. St. Andrew (ll. 215–218*a*)
December (ll. 218*b*–221*a*)
21. St. Thomas (ll. 221*b*–225)
25. Nativity of Christ (ll. 226–228*a*)

As we have seen, it is unlikely that the poet of the MENOLOGIUM used any sources beyond the ecclesiastical calendars in missals and other liturgical books readily available to him.[1] Imelmann[2] believed that he had found a main source in the Gregorian Sacramentary, but his arguments have been refuted by Sokoll[3] and Henel. For the date of composition, there is little evidence. As Bouterwek pointed out as long ago as 1857,[4] the poet appears to have taken ll. 60–62, with minor modifications, from PSALM 117,22 in the Paris Psalter, and the MENOLOGIUM must therefore have been written after the Anglo-Saxon verse translation of the Psalter came into circulation. Imelmann[5] finds a further limit of date in the reference to the observance of the Benedictine Rule, ll. 42*b*–44*a*, which he thinks could have been written only after the Benedictine reform came into full swing in England, in 963, the year of Æthelwold's consecration as bishop of Winchester, and the years following. These indications are not very precise, but such as they are they point toward the latter half of the tenth century, or more definitely the years 965–1000, as the probable time of writing.[6] The manuscript is believed to have come originally from Abingdon,[7] and the MENOLOGIUM may have been written there;[8] but on the evidence of the poet's local knowledge of Canterbury (ll. 104*b*–106*a*) and his omission of any mention of Abingdon in connection

---

[1] See p. lxii, above.   [2] *Das altenglische Menologium*, pp. 43–44.

[3] *Anglia*, Beiblatt XIV, 308–309.

[4] *Calendcwide*, p. 23.

[5] *Das altenglische Menologium*, pp. 52–53.

[6] Imelmann, *ibid.*, pp. 39–40, further suggests that the provisions for the observance of feast days contained in a decree of Æthelred of the year 1008 (printed by Liebermann, *Die Gesetze der Angelsachsen* I, 253) provided the motiv for writing. This is possible and, if true, would place the date of the poem some what later than the limits suggested in the text.

[7] See above, p. xxxiv.

[8] As suggested by Imelmann, *Das altenglische Menologium*, p. 54.

with St. Helen (ll. 83–87*a*), Liebermann[1] would place the origin of
the poem in Canterbury. At any rate, it made its way to Abingdon
at some time before the middle of the eleventh century, and was
there inserted in an Abingdon copy of the Anglo-Saxon Chronicle.

The study of MAXIMS II, the second of the poems, is best begun
by a comparison with the similar collection of gnomic verses in the
Exeter Book, called MAXIMS I in this edition.[2] Like MAXIMS I,
the present text is characterized by lack of unity in content and
arrangement, and gives the impression of a purely mechanical
juxtaposition of ideas gathered from a great diversity of sources.
But in contrast to MAXIMS I, the greater part of MAXIMS II divides
readily into a number of short sentences, frequently (as in ll. 20*b*–
40*a*) only two half-lines in length, which are bound together by
alliteration and by very little else. One is tempted to make a rough
division into parts on the basis of phraseology, the *bið* and *sceal*
formulas in the early part of the poem being then contrasted with
the less rigid forms of expression which we find toward the end.
Following the opening half-line, *Cyning sceal rice healdan*, we have
a series of miscellaneous maxims, ll. 1*b*–13*a*, in all of which the
verb *bið*, *byð* (or the plural forms *beoð*, *syndan*) is used or is at least
to be supplied in sense. At l. 14 begins a similar series in which
sceal (or *sceolan*, l. 14) is repeated as the verb of each sentence.
The *sceal* group fades out gradually, at about ll. 54ff., into some
general reflections on the Judgment Day and the life after death.
But such a purely formal division does not tell us anything about
the origins of the various component parts of the poem, and an
attempt to classify according to subject matter tells us very little
more. In ll. 20*b*–40*a*, stylistically the most homogeneous part of
the poem, the poet refers successively to a good man, a spear, a
precious stone, a stream, the mast of a ship, a sword, a dragon, a
fish, a king, and so on. Clearly such analysis is useless, and it is
evident that the poet had no definite idea in mind beyond putting
a number of unrelated ideas into alliterative form. It is possible
that the expanded (three-stress) meter of ll. 1–4, 42–45, and 47*a*
points to a more or less homogeneous and separate origin for these
portions of the poem. It is also possible that, as Miss Williams

[1] *Archiv* CX, 98f.
[2] See *Records III, The Exeter Book*, pp. xlv-xlvii, 156–163.

suggests,[1] ll. 54*b*–66 are a later and Christian addition to the original poem. These lines, as a statement of the Christian doctrine of the future life, differ considerably in content and style from what precedes; but here, as elsewhere in Anglo-Saxon poetry (for example, in the WANDERER and the SEAFARER), lack of unity in style and content does not necessarily indicate diversity of origin. As in MAXIMS I, the attempt to divide the heathen from the Christian elements in the poem does not add much to our understanding of the text, and certainly does not prove that we have here a heathen text reworked by a Christian poet.[2] The author of MAXIMS II, whether a cleric or a layman, evidently worked, not very skilfully, from the materials at hand, without looking too closely into their philosophical and cultural origins. It is of course possible that, as Strobl suggested,[3] ll. 1–41 were "school exercises" in versification; but if all Anglo-Saxon poetry of similarly uninspired and mechanical form were to be classed as school exercises, then a great deal of other late Anglo-Saxon verse would have to be put into the same category.

Concerning the date of composition of MAXIMS II, it is impossible to be any more specific than for MAXIMS I.[4] Whether or not we assume that certain parts of our text are survivals of "pre-Christian" gnomic verse, it is reasonably certain that the poem as a whole was put into its present form at some time in the tenth century, or perhaps a little earlier.

A PROVERB FROM WINFRID'S TIME

The oldest extant verse proverb in English is the one customarily known as the PROVERB FROM WINFRID'S TIME ("Spruch aus Winfrid's Zeit"), preserved in the Vienna manuscript of the letters of St. Boniface (or St. Winfrid, his Anglo-Saxon name).[5] The

---

[1] *Gnomic Poetry in Anglo-Saxon*, p. 110.

[2] As Brandl would assume, in Paul's *Grundriss der germanischen Philologie* (2d ed.), II, 1, 960. He distinguishes a "heidnisch-höfischer Kern" and "christlich-fromme Zutaten eines Überarbeiters."

[3] *Zeitschrift für deutsches Altertum* XXXI, 63.

[4] See *Records III, The Exeter Book*, p. xlvii.

[5] Wülker, *Grundriss zur Geschichte der angelsächsischen Litteratur*, p. 145, also mentions a Mainz MS., but this MS., now MS. 8112 of the Staatsbibliothek

INTRODUCTION

manuscript, MS. 751 of the Nationalbibliothek in Vienna, is a
volume of 188 folios, 11.8 by 7.9 inches (30 by 20 cm.) in size,
written in a number of hands of the first half of the tenth century.
It formerly belonged to the Cologne Cathedral Library, but came
to Vienna in the sixteenth century, probably through the agency
of the imperial councilor Caspar von Neidbruck.[1] The collection
of St. Boniface's letters, which occupies fol. 1a–77a, includes also
a number of letters written by and to other eighth-century eccle-
siastics and some anonymous letters. It is in one of the anonymous letters, on fol. 34b–35a of the manuscript, that our proverb
appears. A certain monk, *nomine latito*, is writing to one "N,"
who is described as *reverentissimus atque sanctissimus* and consequently appears to have been a church dignitary of some importance,[2] exhorting him not to desist from the course of action he
has chosen. Remember, he says, the Saxon proverb (*Memento
saxonicum uerbum*), *Oft daedlata*, and so forth, as in the text. The
letter is assigned by Dümmler[3] to the period 757–786. Of the
origin of the proverb nothing is known; it may have been taken
from a longer Anglo-Saxon poem which is no longer extant, as suggested by Wülker,[4] or it may have been an independent composition. In the latter case, it may be compared with the highly
sententious tone of BEDE'S DEATH SONG, composed only a few
years earlier.

The orthography of this proverb is continental, showing the same
treatment of historical *þ* (spelled *th* initially and medially, *t* finally)
as the early continental texts of BEDE'S DEATH SONG.[5] In view of

---

in Munich, does not contain the proverb. On the Vienna MS., see *Tabulae
codicum manuscriptorum...in Bibliotheca Palatina Vindobonensi asservatorum*
I (Vienna, 1864), 126.

[1] See Dümmler, *S. Bonifatii et Lulli epistolae*, p. 221; also P. Lehmann,
Quellen und Untersuchungen zur lateinischen Philologie des Mittelalters II, Part 1
(Munich, 1908), p. 92.

[2] The entire salutation is: *Reuerentissimo atque sanctissimo .N. ego minimus
nomine latito sine fine salutem in domino.*

[3] *S. Bonifatii et Lulli epistolae*, pp. 427–428.

[4] *Grundriss zur Geschichte der angelsächsischen Litteratur*, p. 145.

[5] See Dobbie, *The Manuscripts of Cædmon's Hymn and Bede's Death Song*
(New York, 1937), p. 110.

the continental origin of this text, the spelling ę (in domę and foręldit) has not been normalized.

THE JUDGMENT DAY II, AN EXHORTATION TO CHRISTIAN LIVING, A SUMMONS TO PRAYER, THE LORD'S PRAYER II, THE GLORIA I

One of the most important manuscripts containing poetical texts from the later part of the Anglo-Saxon period is MS. 201 of Corpus Christi College, Cambridge. Viewed as a whole, this manuscript is a miscellaneous collection of homilies, laws, and other ecclesiastical and legal documents. It consists of 131 folios, 11 by 6.7 inches (28 by 16.7 cm.) in size, and is written in a number of hands of the latter part of the eleventh century.[1] The manuscript is perhaps best known as containing the only extant copy of the Anglo-Saxon *Apollonius of Tyre*;[2] it was also one of the two principal manuscripts used by Napier for his edition of Wulfstan's homilies,[3] containing, like MS. Hatton 113 (formerly MS. Junius 99) in the Bodleian Library, all of the eight homilies accepted by Napier as the work of Wulfstan himself.[4]

Like most of the other manuscripts of Corpus Christi College, MS. 201 was presented to the college by Archbishop Matthew Parker, the eminent sixteenth-century Saxonist. For the earlier history of the manuscript we are dependent upon conjecture. Wanley, the first scholar to study it, assigned it to Worcester on the evidence of its contents.[5] The homilies of Wulfstan which it con-

---

[1] The contents of the MS. are described by M. R. James, *Descriptive Catalogue of the Manuscripts in the Library of Corpus Christi College* I (Cambridge, 1912), 485–491; also, more briefly but in some respects more clearly, by F. Liebermann, *Die Gesetze der Angelsachsen* I (Halle, 1903), xxii-xxiii. Liebermann ascribes the MS. to the years 1050–1080.

[2] Edited by J. Zupitza, *Archiv* XCVII (1896), 17–34.

[3] A. S. Napier, *Wulfstan, Sammlung der ihm zugeschriebenen Homilien nebst Untersuchungen über ihre Echtheit*, Part 1 (Berlin, 1883).

[4] *Über die Werke des altenglischen Erzbischofs Wulfstan* (Weimar, 1882), pp. 7, 18–19. In Napier's edition these homilies are numbered 2, 3, 19, 20, 21, 22, 33, and 34.

[5] *Catalogus historico-criticus* (Oxford, 1705), p. 141.

tains would not in themselves be sufficient to place the origin of the manuscript in Worcester; but there are two other texts, the poem GLORIA I, on pages 169–170, and the prose fragments of the Benedictine Office, on pages 112–115, which are elsewhere preserved only in the Worcester MS. Junius 121.[1] Feiler, the editor of the Benedictine Office, came to a conclusion similar to Wanley's, that MS. 201 was copied either in Worcester or in a scriptorium closely connected with Worcester.[2] Fehr, from a study of the language of one of the scribes, was inclined to place the origin of the manuscript in the South-English speech area, and most probably in Kent.[3] The linguistic criteria employed by Fehr are, however, open to question,[4] and for the present we may say that the manuscript is in all likelihood a Worcester book, though precise indications to that effect are lacking.

The five verse texts of the manuscript are found on pages 161–170. They are the work of two different scribes, the first of whom wrote the JUDGMENT DAY II, the EXHORTATION TO CHRISTIAN LIVING, and the SUMMONS TO PRAYER (pages 161–167); the remaining two poems, the LORD'S PRAYER II and the GLORIA I (pages 167–170) are the work of the second scribe.[5]

The text of the JUDGMENT DAY II[6] begins at the top of page 161 of the manuscript, with a heading in red, as follows: "Incipit versus

---

[1] See below, p. lxxv.

[2] *Das Benediktiner-Offizium* (Heidelberg, 1901), p. 8, note 2. Doubts that the MS. was written in Worcester are expressed by W. Keller, *Die litterarischen Bestrebungen von Worcester* (Strassburg, 1900), p. 65, and M. Ångström, *Studies in Old English MSS* (Uppsala, 1937), pp. 114–115.

[3] *Die Hirtenbriefe Ælfrics* (Hamburg, 1914), pp. xv-xvi.

[4] The Kentish features which he finds may possibly be due to an earlier copy of the text.

[5] The contents of pages 161–170, in terms of the line-numbering of this edition, are: page 161, *Hwæt*, J. D. II, 1, to *la*, J. D. II, 65; page 162, *earme*, J. D. II, 65, to *þære*, J. D. II, 136; page 163, *dægtide*, J. D. II, 136, to *magon*, J. D. II, 207; page 164, *naht*, J. D. II, 207, to *glædlice*, J. D. II, 273; page 165, *ðenað*, J. D. II, 273, to *god*, EXHORT. 28; page 166, *ece*, EXHORT. 29, to *clænan*, SUMMONS 16; page 167, *clara*, SUMMONS 16, to *fyrde*, L. P. II, 47; page 168, *fægere*, L. P. II, 47, to *bodu*, L. P. II, 109; page 169, *bræcon*, L. P. II, 109, to *haligdomes*, GLORIA I, 47; page 170, *heofonas*, GLORIA I, 47, to *miht*, GLORIA I, 57.

[6] So called in this edition to distinguish it from the poem on the same subject in the Exeter Book (see *Records III, The Exeter Book*, pp. 212–215).

Bede presbiter [*sic*]. De die iudicii. Inter florígeras fecundi cespites herbas flamine uentorum resonantibus undique ramis." At the end of the poem is a further rubric: "Her endað þeos boc þe hatte inter florigeras. ðæt is on englisc betwyx blowende þe to godes rice farað. 7 hu ða þrowiað. þe to helle farað."[1] The reference in these rubrics is to Bede's Latin poem *De die iudicii*,[2] of which the Anglo-Saxon poem is a rather close translation. The difference in length of the two versions, 157 lines in the Latin[3] as against 306 lines in the Anglo-Saxon text, is somewhat misleading as a guide to the Anglo-Saxon poet's treatment of his original, since much of this difference is due to the substitution of the Anglo-Saxon metrical form, with its alliterative and rhetorical embellish- ments, for the more terse Latin hexameters. The additions made by the Anglo-Saxon translator are very slight and, for the most part, seem to have been intended to increase the vividness of the narra- tive and to give it a more popular tone. In contrast with the scholarly but uninspiring Latin in the original, the vigorous ver- nacular style of the Anglo-Saxon poem provides abundant evidence of the translator's skill.[4]

With regard to the metrical form of the JUDGMENT DAY II, it may be said that although the verse types of the older poetry are reproduced with tolerable accuracy (except in a few cases, as, for example, ll. 89*a*, 167*b*), the technique of alliteration shows many traces of decay. Some of the lines which show no alliteration at all (such as ll. 42, 152, 190, 251, 255) may have resulted from cor- ruption of the text; but there are other lines in which end-rime is substituted for alliteration (ll. 3, 28, 266, and perhaps also l. 4,

---

[1] This rubric is not quite complete in sense unless we supply something after *blowende*, e.g. "how happy those are," parallel to *hu ða þrowiað*. See Holthau- sen, *Anglia*, Beiblatt V, 197.

[2] For Bede's authorship of this poem, which has been called into question, see M. Manitius, *Geschichte der lateinischen Literatur des Mittelalters* I (Munich, 1911), 86. In particular, Symeon of Durham, *Historia regum*, §25 (Arnold, *Symeonis monachi opera* II, 23), ascribes the poem to Bede. It is printed by Migne, *Patrol. lat.* XCIV, 633–638, and by Lumby and Löhe in their editions of the JUDGMENT DAY II.

[3] The Latin poem contains 166 lines in all, but the last nine lines, which form a prayer, are not translated.

[4] Löhe, *Be Domes Dæge*, pp. 53–62, gives a detailed analysis of the relation- ships of the two versions.

gehæge : *secge*), and two lines (ll. 6, 82) in which we find both alliteration and end-rime.[1] The alliterative technique, then, argues for a rather late date of composition for the poem, probably the late tenth century.[2]

The text of the JUDGMENT DAY II was used as a source by the unknown author of a homily on the terrors of the Last Judgment, preserved in MS. Hatton 113 in the Bodleian Library.[3] A large part of this homily shows a very close verbal dependence upon ll. 92–271 of the poem; the chief difference between the two texts lies in the omission by the homilist of a number of lines of the poem which did not serve his immediate purpose, and a substitution in many places of the freer style and syntax suitable to prose. The value of the homily for the present edition lies in the fact that by its aid a number of corruptions in the text of the poem can be emended, as, for example, in ll. 112, 125, 154, 178, and 229.[4]

The EXHORTATION TO CHRISTIAN LIVING is a poem of eighty-two lines, in which the poet urges the full observance of Christian morality, especially the abundant bestowal of alms, as a safeguard against the perils of the approaching Judgment. The poem is homiletic in tone throughout (*Nu lære ic þe swa man leofne sceal*, l. 1) and is addressed to a hypothetical reader or hearer (*Gif þu wille . . . þænne beo þu*, etc., ll. 2–3). In general style it resembles most closely the poem called PRECEPTS, in the Exeter Book, especially in the direct address to the reader or hearer, but it differs from that poem in its emphasis upon the religious side of human conduct. The words *har hilderinc*, l. 57, are best explained as an archaizing conceit on the part of the poet,[5] rather than, as Brandl

---

[1] Compare the use of rime in MALDON 271, 282, at the end of the tenth century.

[2] Löhe, *Be Domes Dæge*, p. 47, would assign the poem to about the year 950, but this seems rather early.

[3] Printed by Napier, *Wulfstan*, pp. 134–143. The parts of the homily which are based on the poem are also printed by Wülker and Löhe in their editions of the JUDGMENT DAY II, opposite the corresponding lines of the poem. See Löhe, *Be Domes Dæge*, pp. 47–52, for a discussion of the homilist's use of his source.

[4] See the notes on these lines, pp. 179–181, below.

[5] The same half-line occurs in BEOWULF 1307, 3136, MALDON 169, BRUNANBURH 39.

takes them,[1] as a reference to a specific "gray-haired warrior" to whom the poem is addressed. The reference to the approaching millennium (*þeos woruld is æt ende*, l. 20*a*) has been taken as indicating that the EXHORTATION was written shortly before the end of the tenth century; but its application is perhaps more general, since recent historical research has tended to minimize the tenth-century expectation of the end of the world.[2]

The SUMMONS TO PRAYER consists of thirty-one lines written in alternating Anglo-Saxon and Latin half-lines, the first half of each line being in Anglo-Saxon, the second half in Latin. A similar alternation of the two languages is to be found in the concluding lines (ll. 667–677) of the PHOENIX, in the Exeter Book. The second halves of l. 3 and l. 4 are not in the manuscript, which reads only *a butan ende saule þine* for the two lines; but it is probable that the Latin portions of these lines once stood in their proper place in the text, though they are not absolutely necessary for the sense of the passage.[3] The poet's knowledge of Latin inflectional endings and syntax was not always adequate (as, for example, in ll. 2, 14, 20, 21, etc.); but, unless we are prepared to emend so extensively as to approximate a reconstructed text, it seems best to retain the manuscript forms of the Latin words, and this procedure has been followed in the text of the present edition.[4]

The LORD'S PRAYER II, the next poem in the manuscript, is ostensibly a verse paraphrase of the Latin text, but in view of its length it is perhaps better regarded as an original poem on the theme of the Lord's Prayer. It extends to no less than 123 lines, and is consequently much longer than either the LORD'S PRAYER I, in the Exeter Book,[5] or the LORD'S PRAYER III, in MS. Junius 121,

[1] Paul's *Grundriss der germanischen Philologie* (2d ed.), II, 1, 1095.

[2] A convenient survey of this subject is given by G. L. Burr, "The Year 1000 and the Antecedents of the Crusades," *American Historical Review* VI (1901), 429–439.

[3] See the note on these lines, p. 184, below.

[4] In the text of PHOENIX 667–677 (*Records III, The Exeter Book*, pp. 112–113), the errors in the Latin have been corrected; but the inconsistency in this respect is only apparent, since the errors in the PHOENIX appear to be the result of scribal inaccuracy, while it is the editor's conviction that the faulty Latin which we have here is due to the poet himself.

[5] See *Records III, The Exeter Book*, pp. 223–224.

which will be edited on a later page of this volume.[1]   The fact that both Corpus Christi College MS. 201 and MS. Junius 121 contain the GLORIA I, the next poem to be discussed, might suggest a similarity of origin for the translations of the Lord's Prayer contained in these two manuscripts; but that the LORD's PRAYER II and the LORD's PRAYER III were from the beginning two separate translations is shown not only by the difference in length, but also by definite criteria of subject matter and style.   The poet of the LORD's PRAYER II, for example, not only asserts the identity of the Father and the Son (l. 42b), but in several places (*swa þin fæder worhte*, l. 40; *þines fæder rice*, l. 72; and apparently also in l. 42, where the emendation to *sinre* seems unavoidable) he makes the poem a prayer to the Son as well as to the Father, without regard for its dominical origin.

The GLORIA I, a fifty-seven-line version of the *Gloria patri*, is also preserved as a part of the Benedictine Office in MS. Junius 121. Like the LORD's PRAYER II, it rather transcends the limits of a verse paraphrase; but, except for the great expansion of the original which resulted from the translator's efforts, there is little in the GLORIA I which is distinctive.   The two texts of the poem are substantially alike.   Aside from the expected vagaries of orthography, the chief differences lie in the omission by the Corpus manuscript of the words *and halig gast*, l. 13b, *and on þone*, l. 23b, and the second *and* in l. 31a, and by the Junius manuscript of *word*, l. 48a.   All of these omissions are obviously the result of scribal carelessness.[2]

THE BENEDICTINE OFFICE: THE LORD'S PRAYER III, THE CREED, FRAGMENTS OF PSALMS

Besides the second text of the GLORIA I, MS. Junius 121 in the Bodleian Library also contains Anglo-Saxon verse translations of the Lord's Prayer and the Apostles' Creed, similar in style to the

[1] See below, pp. 77–78.

[2] The Latin texts which accompany the LORD's PRAYER II and the GLORIA I in the MS. are printed in italics, with expansion of abbreviations but without further editorial changes; they are not included in the line-numbering.

LORD'S PRAYER II, and a number of fragments of the Anglo-Saxon
metrical Psalter.

MS. Junius 121 is an eleventh-century manuscript of 160 folios,
measuring 10.4 by 6.2 inches (26.5 by 15 cm.) in size.[1] The greater
part of the volume, fol. 5a–101a, is taken up by a collection of
canons and constitutions of the English church, in Anglo-Saxon,
compiled for the most part in the late tenth century.[2] Fol. 9a–
101a, or nearly the whole of this part of the manuscript, were written by a Worcester scribe named Wulfgeat, as is indicated by a note
at the foot of fol. 101a.[3] That the manuscript remained in Worcester for some time after it was written we know from the presence
of glosses by the thirteenth-century glossator with the "tremulous"
hand whose work is found in so many Worcester manuscripts.[4]
The poetical texts preserved in the manuscript are all part of a
Benedictine Office, or collection of daily services for the canonical
hours, which occupies fol. 42a–53b.

This text is traditionally called a "Benedictine Office," even
though, like numerous other liturgical books of its time, it is rather
uneven in its content. It begins at fol. 42a, l. 18, with the rubric
"De officiis diurnalium [et] nocturnalium horarum." The most
significant part of the office is perhaps the series of symbolic interpretations of the canonical hours, in Anglo-Saxon, which, together
with a general preface beginning "Godcund þeowdom is gesett on

[1] For descriptions of this MS., see H. Wanley, *Catalogus historico-criticus*
(Oxford, 1705), pp. 45–59; W. Keller, *Die litterarischen Bestrebungen von Worcester in angelsächsischer Zeit* (Strassburg, 1900), pp. 64, 67; Feiler, *Das Benediktiner-Offizium*, pp. 6–8; F. Liebermann, *Die Gesetze der Angelsachsen* I (Halle,
1903), xlii; B. Fehr, *Die Hirtenbriefe Ælfrics* (Hamburg, 1914), pp. xx–xxii; *Summary Catalogue of Western Manuscripts in the Bodleian Library* II, Part 2
(Oxford, 1937), pp. 989–990.

[2] On fol. 17b is a reference to King Edgar which suggests that Edgar had
recently died: "Ac nu hit is geworden ealles to swyðe, syððan Eadgar geendode
swa swa god wolde." Edgar died in 975.

[3] "Me scripsit Wulfgeatus scriptor Wigornensis," etc. The MS. must have
been written after 1076, since it contains, on fol. 4a–4b, a Latin account of the
proceedings of Lanfranc's council at Winchester in that year; see Feiler, *Das
Benediktiner-Offizium*, p. 6.

[4] See Keller, *Die litterarischen Bestrebungen von Worcester*, p. 20, who ascribes
the hand to the late twelfth century. But that this glossator was active as late
as 1225–1250 is shown by N. R. Ker, *Leeds Studies in English* VI (1937), 28–29.

cyriclicum þenungum æfter canoneclican gewunan to nydrihte
eallum gehadedum mannum," are ultimately based on the Latin
De institutione clericorum of Hrabanus Maurus.[1] These symbolic
interpretations are also preserved in MS. 201 of Corpus Christi
College, Cambridge, pages 112–115, but without the rest of the
Benedictine Office.

Of the services for the several hours of the Benedictine Office, only
prime is given in full, with Anglo-Saxon translations of the important prayers and Psalm verses. For the other hours the services
are much briefer, with short indications in Latin of the proper
prayers and responses; the only two of these hours which contain
any Anglo-Saxon translations are tierce, with verse renderings of
PSALMS 40,4 and 89,15, and vespers, with PSALM 140,2. A detailed
analysis of the contents of the Benedictine Office would be out of
place here; but such analyses are given by Bouterwek[2] and
Feiler[3] in the introductions to their editions.

For information concerning the authorship and probable date
of the Benedictine Office we are dependent upon conjecture.
Feiler, citing the many resemblances in style between the prose
parts of the office and the genuine homilies of Wulfstan, suggests
that the great bishop of Worcester, perhaps following out a suggestion by Ælfric in his first pastoral letter, compiled the Benedictine Office at some time during the years 1006–1016.[4] Such
evidence does not, of course, amount to proof, but it is clearly impossible to go further in the present state of our knowledge.

The verse texts contained in the Benedictine Office are the following:

fol. 43b, ll. 8–12, PSALM 69,1
fol. 43b, l. 13, to fol. 44b, l. 18, the GLORIA I[5]
fol. 44b, ll. 20–23, PSALM 53,1
fol. 45a, ll. 5–8, PSALM 43,27.
fol. 45a, l. 10, to fol. 45b, l. 23, the LORD'S PRAYER III[6]

[1] Feiler, *Das Benediktiner-Offizium*, p. 20. On possible intermediate texts
between Hrabanus' work and the Benedictine Office, see Fehr, *Englische Studien* XLVI, 337–346.
[2] *Cædmon's des Angelsachsen biblische Dichtungen* I, clxxix–cxciii.
[3] *Das Benediktiner-Offizium*, pp. 28–42.
[4] *Ibid.*, pp. 43–46.
[5] Fol. 43b ends at *beald*, l. 12, fol. 44a at *eall*, l. 38.
[6] Fol. 45a ends at *forð*, l. 13.

fol. 45*b*, l. 23, to fol. 46*a*, l. 9, PSALM 118,175–176
fol. 46*a*, l. 10, to fol. 47*a*, l. 18, the CREED[1]
fol. 47*a*, l. 18, to fol. 50*b*, l. 16, PSALMS 87,13; 5,1–3; 24,3–6;
  34,1–3; 70,7; 50,10–13; 139,1 (ll. 1–2); 58,1–2; 60,6 (ll. 2–4);
  64,6; 102,1–5; 84,4 (ll. 1–2); 32,18; 19,9; 27,10; 121,7; 101,1;
  50,1; 79,18[2]
fol. 51*a*, ll. 4–8, PSALM 69,1
fol. 51*a*, ll. 10–19, PSALM 89,18–19
fol. 52*a*, ll.8–17, PSALMS 40,4; 89,15
fol. 53*b*, ll. 11–15, PSALM 140,2.

Of the three long poems contained in the Benedictine Office, the GLORIA I has already been discussed.[3] The other two poems, the LORD'S PRAYER III and the CREED, have few distinctive characteristics as compared with other religious paraphrases of the late Anglo-Saxon period. The CREED, in which the Latin text is enlarged upon to the extent of fifty-eight lines, is occasionally rather disjointed in style and logic, and in several places (as, for example, in ll. 38–40, 44–48) it introduces homiletic and explanatory material for which there is no warrant in the original text. The LORD'S PRAYER III, on the other hand, is a clear, straightforward paraphrase, and is probably to be regarded as the best of all the Anglo-Saxon verse translations of Latin liturgical texts.[4]

The Psalm fragments in the Benedictine Office were taken from a complete Anglo-Saxon verse translation of the Psalter, from which PSALMS 51,6–150,3 of the Paris Psalter, that is, all the metrical portions of the Paris Psalter, were also taken. The Psalm passages which appear in both manuscripts show so complete an agreement between the two texts that no other conclusion is possible.[5] Our Benedictine Office, then, preserves the only remains of the Anglo-Saxon verse translation of the first fifty

[1] Fol. 46*a* ends at *unmæne*, l. 14, fol. 46*b* at *gelæsten*, l. 40.
[2] Fol. 47*a* ends at *becume*, 87,13,4; fol. 47*b* at *lyfige*, 24,4,2; fol. 48*a* at *syððan*, 34,3,4; fol. 48*b* at *wyrðe*, 50,12,4; fol. 49*a* at *wese*, 60,6,3; fol. 49*b* at *mild-*, 102,5,2; fol. 50*a* at *lifigen*, 27,10,4.
[3] See above, p. lxxiv.
[4] The Latin passages which accompany these two poems in the MS. are handled in the same way as those which accompany the LORD'S PRAYER II and the GLORIA I; see p. lxxiv, note 2.
[5] See *Records V, The Paris Psalter and the Meters of Boethius*, pp. xix–xx.

Psalms.[1] The Latin Psalm verses which appear in the manuscript usually follow the Roman Psalter, St. Jerome's earlier revision of the Old Latin, rather than the Gallican Psalter, the later revision which is found in the Vulgate Bible. A few of the Latin verses, however, are closer to the Gallican Psalter than to the Roman; these are PSALMS 5,3; 27,10; 32,18; 60,6,2–4; 69,1; 89,15; and 89,19.[2]

The literary and historical problems raised by the Anglo-Saxon metrical Psalms are discussed at length in Volume V of this edition.[3] Here it will be sufficient to say that the translation was most probably made at some time during the monastic revival of learning in the latter part of the tenth century, perhaps in Worcester, where MS. Junius 121 was written, although there is no direct evidence for any specific place of origin.

To conform more closely to the text of the Paris Psalter in this edition, the Psalm fragments are printed below in numerical order, following the numbering of the Vulgate Bible, rather than of the English Authorized Version.[4]

THE KENTISH HYMN AND PSALM 50

Among the few and scattered Kentish texts written during the Anglo-Saxon period, a place of high importance must be accorded to the two poems contained in MS. Cotton Vespasian D.vi, the so-called KENTISH HYMN and a rather lengthy paraphrase of the fiftieth Psalm.[5] The manuscript, the greater part of which was written in the late tenth century, is a small quarto of 125 folios,

[1] The prose portions of the Paris Psalter, translating Psalms i. 1–l. 9, are edited by J. W. Bright and R. L. Ramsay, *The West-Saxon Psalms* (Boston and London, 1907).

[2] In this edition no attempt is made to normalize the Latin Psalm verses; abbreviations have been expanded without comment, and omitted letters have been supplied where they are necessary for the sense.

[3] See *Records V, The Paris Psalter and the Meters of Boethius*, pp. xvii–xxi.

[4] Those verses which also appear in the Paris Psalter are numbered according to the numbering of the Paris Psalter, in order to facilitate comparison. In a few cases, therefore, the numbering of the verses does not agree with the standard editions of the Vulgate.

[5] That is, Psalm l in the numbering of the Vulgate, corresponding to Psalm li in the English Authorized Version.

measuring 7.4 by 5.3 inches (19 by 11.3 cm.) in size.[1]   The KENT-
ISH HYMN is on fol. 68b–69b, PSALM 50 on fol. 70a–73b.   Between
these two verse texts is a short chronology of the Old Testament,
also in Anglo-Saxon, beginning with the words, "Fram adame þam
ærestan mænn 7 frā fræmðe middangeardes oð ðane flod wæs
gergerimes twa hund wintra 7 twa ðusenda 7 twa 7 fiowertig."
The other contents of the manuscript are rather miscellaneous: a
Latin text of the book of Proverbs, fol. 2a–37b, followed by a
Latin glossary of difficult words in the text, fol. 37b–38a, Alcuin's
Exhortatio ad Guidonem comitem, fol. 38b–66b, and a Latin life of
the abbot Macharias, fol. 67a–68b, occupy the part of the manuscript preceding the Anglo-Saxon texts; after PSALM 50 follow the
Distichs of Cato, in Latin, and a few shorter Latin texts, fol.
73b–77b.   The last and longest item in the manuscript is the Latin
life of St. Wilfrid, written about 710 by Eddi Stephanus, fol. 78a–
125a.   The life of St. Wilfrid was once a separate book, the original
foliation from 1 to 48 being still preserved on a number of pages.

This manuscript is of importance to the Anglo-Saxon scholar not
only for the two Kentish poems, but also for a great number of
interlinear Kentish glosses, which run through most of the Latin
texts as far as fol. 66b.[2]   The Latin texts on fol. 2a–37b and fol.
38b–68b, together with the Kentish glosses and the three Anglo-
Saxon texts on fol. 68b–73b, are all written by the same scribe, in a
neat, rather square hand, which, however, varies surprisingly in
size.   The earlier editors, following Dietrich,[3] dated this hand in
the early ninth century, but Zupitza in 1878[4] correctly ascribed it
to the late tenth century, or about the same time as the Exeter
Book and the Vercelli Book.[5]

[1] The MS. is described by H. Wanley, *Catalogus historico-criticus* (Oxford,
1705), p. 243; and British Museum, *Catalogue of the Manuscripts in the Cottonian Library* (1802), p. 475.

[2] These glosses were first edited by J. Zupitza, *Zeitschrift für deutsches Altertum* XXI (1877), 1–59, with a supplementary collation, *ibid.* XXII (1878),
223–226; also by T. Wright and R. P. Wülker, *Anglo-Saxon and Old English
Vocabularies* I (London, 1884), 55–87, and by H. Sweet, *Second Anglo-Saxon
Reader* (Oxford, 1887), pp. 152–175.

[3] "Anglosaxonica," pp. iv–v.

[4] *Zeitschrift für deutsches Altertum* XXII, 226.

[5] The contents of fol. 68b–73b, in terms of the line-numbering of this edition

The KENTISH HYMN, forty-three lines in length, divides naturally into two parts: (1) a brief exhortation to Christian people to praise and love God, ll. 1–6, and (2) an extended apostrophe addressed to God, praising Him and beseeching His mercy and forgiveness, ll. 7–43. No single source for the hymn is known, but a great deal of scriptural and liturgical material has been woven together to form a tolerably unified whole. Scriptural reminiscences are to be found in ll. 4–6 (Luke ii.14) and in the allusion to the *Agnus Dei* (John i.29) in ll. 22–24; in ll. 29–31 there is an obvious borrowing from the Apostles' Creed. Brandl[1] also notes resemblances (especially apparent in ll. 7ff.) to the Song of the Three Children (DANIEL 362ff., AZARIAS 73ff.).

The other poem in the manuscript, PSALM 50, begins with a thirty-line introduction, which in general follows the patristic interpretation[2] of this Psalm as David's expression of penitence for his sin against Uriah and Bathsheba (2 Samuel xi–xii). At the end of the Psalm is a brief epilogue (ll. 146–157), in which the poet prays that, like David, he and others may obtain God's forgiveness. The text of the Psalm itself occupies no less than 115 lines of verse, or an average of nearly six lines for each verse of the Latin text. It therefore represents a much freer and more diffuse type of translation than we find in the Paris Psalter, though, since the translation of the fiftieth Psalm is not preserved in the Paris Psalter, a direct comparison is impossible. Before each section of the text, the corresponding Latin verse is quoted, sometimes in full but generally in a more or less abbreviated form.[3] These

---

(and disregarding the Latin verses in the text of PSALM 50), are: fol. 68*b*, *Wuton*, HYMN 1, to *cyninga*, HYMN 15; fol. 69*a*, *cyningc*, HYMN 15, to *ðrinesse*, HYMN 40; fol. 69*b*, *and*, HYMN 41, to *wuldre*, HYMN 43 (here follows the Anglo-Saxon prose text); fol. 70*a*, *Dauid*, PSALM 50,1, to *þonne*, PSALM 50,11; fol. 70*b*, *cumbulgebrec*, PSALM 50,11, to *manna*, PSALM 50,31; fol. 71*a*, *geðohtas*, PSALM 50,31, to *blisse*, PSALM 50,46; fol. 71*b*, *Nu*, PSALM 50,47, to *beeode*, PSALM 50,66; fol. 72*a*, *Ac*, PSALM 50,67, to *adilga*, PSALM 50, 87; fol. 72*b*, *Æc*, PSALM 50,88, to *ðurh*, PSALM 50,109; fol. 73*a*, *sibbe*, PSALM 50,109, to *lifiende*, PSALM 50,134; fol. 73*b*, *Swa*, PSALM 50,135, to *Amen*, PSALM 50,157.

[1] Paul's *Grundriss der germanischen Philologie* (2d ed.), II, 1, 1049.

[2] As given, for example, by St. Jerome and St. Augustine, and still found as the heading of this Psalm in the Vulgate Bible: "In finem, Psalmum David, cum venit ad eum Nathan propheta, quando intravit ad Bethsabee."

[3] No attempt has been made to normalize the Latin Psalm verses, which contain some errors in case endings.

Latin Psalm passages follow the Roman Psalter, St. Jerome's earlier revision of the Latin text, rather than the Gallican Psalter which appears in the Vulgate.

Much of the earlier criticism of PSALM 50, as well as of the KENTISH HYMN, was influenced by the ninth-century date assigned to the manuscript by Dietrich and other early scholars; Zupitza's date for the manuscript, the late tenth century, permits much wider limits of date for the original composition of the two poems. In fact, both the hymn and PSALM 50 seem closer in style and content to the religious poetry of the tenth century, such as the LORD'S PRAYER II, the GLORIA I, and the PRAYER, than to anything which we possess from the ninth century or earlier. But the problems of date and authorship of these poems are somewhat complicated by the dialect in which they are written, which is not pure Kentish but a mixture of Kentish and West Saxon.

Among the characteristically Kentish spellings in the two poems are: (1) *io* for regular West Saxon *ĕo*, as in *hiofen*, HYMN 13, and *hiortan*, PSALM 50,88, and for *ēo*, as in *hlioðor-*, HYMN 2, *liof-*, HYMN 3, and *geiode*, PSALM 50,13; (2) *e* for *ǣ* (*i*-umlaut of West Germanic *ai*), as in *lene*, PSALM 50,15, and *helende*, PSALM 50,50; (3) *e* for *ў*, as in *senna*, HYMN 28, *gefelled*, HYMN 43, *geltas*, PSALM 50,39, and *wenne*, PSALM 50, 80, and for *ӯ*, in *gerena*, HYMN 11, and *ontende*, PSALM 50,28.[1] But the corresponding West Saxon vowels are also frequently found, as in *heofenlic*, HYMN 22, *beeode*, PSALM 50,66, *hleoðor*, PSALM 50,77, *synna*, PSALM 50,28, *gyltas*, PSALM 50,29, and *ontyn*, PSALM 50,77. The *u-*, *a*-umlaut of *ĕ* to *eo* before a velar consonant, not found in West Saxon and very infrequent in Anglian, appears twice, in *breogo*, PSALM 50,49, and *weogas*, PSALM 50,105. Another characteristic spelling which is probably to be regarded as Kentish is *æ* for *ē* (*i*-umlaut of *ō*) and for *īe* (*i*-umlaut of *ēa*), as in *blætsiað*, HYMN 8, *sigehræmig*, HYMN 30, and *hænðum*, PSALM 50,82. The symbol *ę*, frequent in most Kentish texts,[2] is found in both poems, usually for Kentish *ĕ* (West Saxon *ǣ*, *ĕ*, *ĕa*), as in *fęder*, HYMN 8, *Hwęðere*, PSALM 50,13, *sigefęst*, HYMN 4, *gefręmed*, PSALM 50,143, *lifęs*, HYMN 3, and *gescęft*, HYMN 17, but

---

[1] The spelling *e* for *ǣ* (as in *feder, fegere, heleða*, etc.) is of course Mercian as well as Kentish.

[2] See I. F. Williams, "The Significance of the Symbol *ę* in the Kentish Glosses," *Otia Merseiana* IV (1904), 81–83.

lxxxii   INTRODUCTION

also for Kentish ē, as in *hēlend*, HYMN 16, *begēton*, PSALM 50,57, and
clēne, PSALM 50,88. But here again, the West Saxon spellings are
frequent, as in *mægena*, HYMN 11, *fæder*, HYMN 21, *hæleð*, PSALM
50,1, and *ceastre*, HYMN 19. In view of the peculiar dialectal
features of these poems, the spellings with ę have been retained in
the text, instead of being treated as manuscript variants of spellings
in *æ*.

Such a mixture of West Saxon and Kentish dialect features
might result from the copying of a Kentish text by a West Saxon
scribe,[1] or of a West Saxon text by a Kentish scribe; or, in the late
tenth century, the date of our manuscript, it might represent a
normal phase in the spread of West Saxon as the common English
literary language in former non-West-Saxon areas. That the
manuscript was written at Canterbury is highly probable. We
know that in the late fifteenth century it belonged to St. Augustine's
abbey in Canterbury;[2] another piece of evidence, pointed out by
Dietrich, which serves to connect the manuscript with St.
Augustine's abbey is the invocation to the saint in one of the Latin
verses[3] on fol. 77*a*, which certainly gives the impression that the
writer was a member of Augustine's own monastery. If, then, the
manuscript was written at Canterbury, the West Saxon forms in
the text were probably not introduced by a West Saxon scribe
copying a Kentish original. It is then possible that both the
poems were composed in Kent in essentially their present form,
with the mixture of West Saxon and local dialect characteristics
which is found in Kentish charters of that time.[4] Since, however,
the Kentish glosses in the same manuscript display a purer form
of Kentish than the poems, with a slighter admixture of West
Saxon forms, it seems likely that the poems, unlike the glosses,

---

[1] As suggested by Cook, *A First Book in Old English*, p. 266.

[2] See M. R. James, *The Ancient Libraries of Canterbury and Dover* (Cambridge,
1903), pp. 204 (no. 131), 516.

[3] "Gemma sacerdotum, rutilans lux alma priorum,
    Anglorum doctor, pariter prothe nec ne sacerdos,
    Augustine, tuis fer opem, flagitamus, alumnis
    Et munda culpis ornas quos ossibus almis." (Quoted
    by Dietrich, "Anglosaxonica," p. iv.)

[4] See, for example, the charter of Æthelwyrd printed by Birch, *Cartularium
saxonicum* III, 213–214 (no. 1010), from Stowe Charter 26.

were originally written in West Saxon.[1]   Parallels for a Kentish
copy of a West Saxon text may be found in the two complete
manuscripts of the Alfredian Boethius, MS. Cotton Otho A.vi, of
about the same date as our manuscript, and MS. Bodley 180 in
the Bodleian Library, of the early twelfth century.[2]

The probabilities, then, are that both the KENTISH HYMN and
PSALM 50 were originally written in West Saxon, but were later
copied by a Kentish scribe at St. Augustine's in Canterbury, the
Kentish forms of the present text being introduced at that time.
The original date of composition of these poems is more open to
question, but, as has been previously pointed out, they are much
more similar in content and style to the literature of the monastic
revival in the middle tenth century than to the earlier, Alfredian
or pre-Alfredian, poetry.

THE GLORIA II

This three-line poetical version of the *Gloria patri* is one of a
series of Anglo-Saxon sentences of uncertain significance.   The
text is preserved in MS. Cotton Titus D.xxvii in the British
Museum, fol. 55*b*–56*b*, with no title or other heading; it is described
by the catalogue of the Cotton manuscripts as "Alphabetum cum
significatione uniuscujusque literæ, Saxonice."[3]

The manuscript contains 92 parchment leaves, measuring only
5 by 3.8 inches (12.8 by 9.4 cm.).   With its companion volume,
MS. Cotton Titus D.xxvi, to which it was probably once joined,
it is an extremely miscellaneous collection of calendars and compu-
tations, ecclesiastical offices, prayers, and other religious texts,
written in several hands of the first half of the eleventh century.

[1] As is implied by Bülbring, *Altenglisches Elementarbuch* I, §26.

[2] Perhaps also MS. Cotton Julius A.ii of Ælfric's Grammar and Glossary
(cited by Bülbring, §26), though the variants from this MS. given by Zupitza,
Ælfrics Grammatik und Glossar (Berlin, 1880), show very little evidence of
Kentish dialect.

[3] British Museum, *Catalogue of the Manuscripts in the Cottonian Library*
(1802), p. 567.   Fuller descriptions of the MS. are given by W. de G. Birch,
Transactions of the Royal Society of Literature, 2d Series, XI, 495–512, and
Palaeographical Society, *Facsimiles of Manuscripts and Inscriptions* (London,
1873–1883), Plate 60 and the accompanying letterpress.

There are numerous bits of internal evidence which serve to connect these two manuscripts with New Minster, in Winchester, and several allusions to Ælfwine, abbot of New Minster from 1035 to 1057, suggest that he was the person for whom the collections were made, if not the actual compiler.[1] It seems likely that the compilation was carried out before Ælfwine became abbot, since in the calendar in MS. Titus D.xxvii, fol. 3a–8b, Ælfwine is referred to several times as *monachus* (or the genitive *monachi*), the title *abbas* (or the genitive *abbatis*) being added later in a different hand.[2] In any case, Birch's description of the two manuscripts as "the Religious and Scientific commonplace books of Ælfwine, the Abbot of Newminster,"[3] is sufficiently accurate for all practical purposes.

Since the entire alphabet has been published twice, by Sievers and by Birch, it seems unnecessary to print the prose portions here. Precisely what the purpose of such an alphabetical compilation may have been is by no means clear. The several letters of the alphabet, written down the left-hand margin of the page, are followed by sentences which are quite independent of each other and which usually have no apparent relation to the letters which they follow; for example, the first two entries are: "A. He gangeð 7 biþ his siðfæt gesund.   B. God þu fintst gyf ðu hit onginst 7 þe bið wel." The short verse text, the GLORIA II, is the last of these sentences, following the letter Z. Birch's explanation of the sentences as "descriptive of a set of illustrations which had been prepared for an alphabet of illuminated initial letters"[4] has little to commend it, and it is more likely that (as Steinmeyer suggested for the similar Middle High German alphabet in the twelfth-century Vienna MS. 2245)[5] they were intended for fortune-telling,

[1] In MS. Titus D.xxvii, fol. 65b, a drawing of Christ on the cross, with St. Mary and St. Joseph standing beside him, has the inscription:
"Hec crux consignat Ælfwinum corpore mente,
in qua suspendens trax[it] deus omnia secum."
[2] A later date might be indicated by the fact that this calendar contains the obits of Cnut (November 12, 1035) and Harthacnut (June 8, 1042). Unfortunately Birch does not make it clear whether these obits are in the original hand of the calendar or in later hands.
[3] *Transactions of the Royal Society of Literature*, 2d Series, XI, 512.
[4] *Ibid.*, p. 507.
[5] E. Steinmeyer, "Bedeutung der Buchstaben," *Zeitschrift für deutsches Al-*

probably by the casting or drawing of lots inscribed with the letters of the alphabet.

A PRAYER

The metrical PRAYER is preserved in two copies, one of them a fragment:

MS. COTTON JULIUS A.II, BRITISH MUSEUM (J). A parchment manuscript of 144 folios, measuring about 9 by 6 inches (22.8 by 15.3 cm.) in size.[1] The principal item in the manuscript is an eleventh-century text of Ælfric's Grammar and Glossary, fol. 10a–135b. On the last few folios, immediately after the end of the Glossary, follow the PRAYER, fol. 136a–137a, and three short prose texts: the dialogue of *Adrian and Ritheus*,[2] fol. 137b–140a; a number of short sentences on various topics, perhaps supplementary to the preceding text,[3] fol. 140b; and the Anglo-Saxon version of the Distichs of Cato,[4] fol. 141a–144b.

The PRAYER and the three prose texts which follow it are all written in a single hand of the early part of the twelfth century.[5] This part of the manuscript (fol. 136–144) was somewhat damaged by the Cottonian fire of 1731, the edges of the parchment being somewhat shrunk, and torn in places; but the only loss in the text of the PRAYER is the large capital *D* at the beginning of l. 51. The several folios have been preserved from further damage by being mounted on parchment trimmed to the size of fol. 10–135.

The text of the PRAYER is divided into sections by the use of colored large capitals in the words *Æla*, l. 1, *Æla*, l. 8, *Se*, l. 11, *Se*,

tertum XVII (1874), 84. A similar Latin alphabet, intended for the interpretation of dreams, was printed by E. Sievers, *Zeitschrift für deutsches Altertum* XXII (1878), 297, from a Gotha MS.

[1] The only published descriptions of this MS. are the old ones by H. Wanley, *Catalogus historico-criticus* (Oxford, 1705), p. 183, and British Museum, *Catalogue of the Manuscripts in the Cottonian Library* (1802), p. 1.

[2] Edited by J. M. Kemble, *The Dialogue of Salomon and Saturnus* (London, 1848), pp. 198–211.

[3] See M. Förster, *Englische Studien* XXIII (1897), 433–434.

[4] Edited by J. Nehab, *Der altenglische Cato* (Berlin, 1879).

[5] On the dating of this hand, see A. S. Napier, *Academy* XXXVII (1890), 133.

l. 16, *Æla*, l. 21, *Đu*, l. 27, *Ne*, l. 30, *ne*, l. 33*a*, *Ne*, l. 35, *Đu*, l. 45, [*Đ*]*yn*,[1] l. 51, *Ic*, l. 56, *Ac*, l. 67, and *Ne*, l. 74. These sectional divisions correspond in general to the natural divisions of thought, except for the eighth section, which begins with *ne*, l. 33*a*, in the middle of a sentence.[2]

MS. 427, LAMBETH PALACE LIBRARY (L). A parchment manuscript of 211 folios, measuring 8.25 by 6.3 inches (21 by 16 cm.).[3] This manuscript, the so-called "Lambeth Psalter," is a Latin Psalter text with an interlinear Anglo-Saxon gloss, of the first quarter of the eleventh century. Following the Psalter, on fol. 182*a*–211*b*, are a number of short texts. The PRAYER, in a hand of about the end of the eleventh century, fills the lower half of fol. 183*b*. This copy of the PRAYER is, however, incomplete, containing only ll. 1–15. It is probable that the manuscript once contained a complete text of the PRAYER, corresponding to the one in MS. Julius A.ii, but that a folio or more, containing the missing matter, has been lost after fol. 183. Beginning on fol. 184 are a series of fifteen Latin hymns, in the same hand as the Psalter, and likewise accompanied by an Anglo-Saxon gloss.[4] All of these hymns have titles in red except the first, the *Canticum Isaiae prophetae* (Isaiah xii), which begins with the words "Confitebor tibi," without any rubric, at the head of fol. 184*a*. The rubric which we expect here may have been on a folio lost after fol. 183.

There are no sectional divisions in the fifteen lines of this text, though there is a colored large capital in *Eala*, l. 1, and smaller capitals in *Gehæl*, l. 4, *Eala*, l. 8, *Syle*, l. 10, and *Se*, l. 11.

The textual differences between L and the corresponding parts of J (ll. 1–15) are chiefly orthographical, consisting usually in the

---

[1] The initial large capital in this word has been torn away.

[2] The contents of fol. 136*a*-137*a* in MS. J, in terms of the line-numbering of this edition, are: fol. 136*a*, *Æla*, l. 1, to *god*, l. 29; fol. 136*b*, *Ne*, l. 30, to *and*, l. 60; fol. 137*a*, *se*, l. 60, to *Amen*, l. 79.

[3] For descriptions of this MS., see H. Wanley, *Catalogus historico-criticus* (Oxford, 1705), pp. 268–269 (no. 188); U. Lindelöf, *Der Lambeth-Psalter* II (Acta societatis scientiarum Fennicae, XLIII, 3, Helsingfors, 1914), 1–15; M. R. James and C. Jenkins, *Descriptive Catalogue of the Manuscripts in the Library of Lambeth Palace* (Cambridge, 1930–1932), pp. 588–590.

[4] Other copies of these hymns are noted in *Records V, The Paris Psalter and the Meters of Boethius*, p. xii.

variation between *y* and *i* or in the reduction of unstressed syllables in one or the other of the texts. Both versions of the poem are unusually accurate, considering their late date. In a few places, L seems to preserve the better reading, as for instance in *Eala*, ll. 1*a*, 1*b*, 8 (where J has the late spelling *Æla*), *þynum*, l. 10*b* (where J has *þyne*), *þe*, l. 11 (where J has *þeo*), and *dæges*, l. 12 (*dæiges* in J). In l. 14, however, L omits the words *he ða*, which are required by the sense. In l. 9, J has *Gemilsa*, L has *gemilda*; either of these readings is possible. In l. 12, both texts have the dative plural forms *deoflon* J, *deoflum* L, where the dative singular is to be expected.[1] As we have seen, the text of L is somewhat earlier than J; but since L is not noticeably better than J, and J is complete, the text of the PRAYER in the present edition has been based on J.

In previous editions it has been customary to print this text as three separate prayers or poems, each beginning with the word *Æla*. In this arrangement, the first prayer includes ll. 1–7, the second prayer ll. 8–20, and the third prayer the remainder of the text, ll. 21–79. But, as Förster has pointed out,[2] there is no internal evidence which would justify such a division. The large capitals in the word *Æla* in l. 8 and l. 21 of J are no larger or more prominent than the other large capitals in this text; the only large capital in the text of J for which special provision has been made is the initial capital of *Æla*, l. 1, which occupies a space left vacant at the beginning of each of the first two lines of the poem. Similarly, in L the initial capital of *Eala*, l. 8, is not set off in any way from the other capital letters in this text (ll. 4, 10, 11), and is much less prominent than the colored capital of *Eala*, l. 1. Furthermore, the concluding formula *Amen* is found only in l. 79, and not in l. 7 and l. 20, where we would expect also to find it if ll. 1–7 and ll. 8–20 were really separate prayers. Finally, the rhetorical form of ll. 1–2, 8–9, and 21–22, in each of which passages the *Eala* formula is immediately followed by an exhortation (*Geara me*, l. 2; *Gemilsa þyn mod me to gode*, l. 9; *Getiþa me*, l. 22), gives an effect of studied unity to the whole composition and makes it very unlikely that a division into three separate prayers was part of the poet's intention.

[1] See the note on this line, p. 193, below.
[2] *Archiv* CXXXII, 331–332.

In the present edition, therefore, the text is treated as a single prayer.

THURETH

A short poem of intercession for a certain Thureth is preserved in MS. Cotton Claudius A.iii in the British Museum, fol. 31*b*. This manuscript, according to the official foliation, contains 150 folios, about 9.5 by 6.3 inches (24.1 by 16 cm.) in size.[1] It appears to have been made up of texts taken from several liturgical books, of various dates, rather miscellaneously put together and with several parts misplaced; the principal items are: (1) a fragment of a Canterbury gospel book, in which some Latin and Anglo-Saxon charters and papal letters have been written in various hands of the eleventh and early twelfth century, fol. 2*a*–7*b*; (2) fragments of an order of coronation and pontifical, preceded in the manuscript by an illuminated portrait of St. Dunstan, all of the early eleventh century, fol. 8*a*–18*b*, 87*a*–105*b*,[2] (3) an order of coronation of the time of Henry I, fol. 19*a*–29*b*; (4) the Anglo-Saxon poem THURETH, in a hand of the early eleventh century, fol. 31*b*; (5) the canons of the Council of Enham (near Andover), 1008–1011, in Latin and Anglo-Saxon, in two hands of the early eleventh century,[3] fol. 32*a*–38*b*; (6) fragments of a pontifical, of the end of the eleventh century, fol. 39*a*–86*b*, 106*a*–136*b*; (7) a benedictional, of the late tenth or early eleventh century, fol. 137*a*–150*b*.

The first question which requires consideration is the relationship of THURETH to the other texts in the manuscript. The one part of the manuscript to which we can confidently attach the poem is the text of the canons of the Council of Enham, which immediately follows it in the manuscript. That these canons and THURETH have always belonged together is shown by the evidence of the

---

[1] For a description of this MS., see British Museum, *Catalogue of the Manuscripts in the Cottonian Library* (1802), pp. 188–189.

[2] The order of coronation is edited from the present manuscript by A. Taylor, *Glory of Regality* (London, 1820), Appendix, pp. 393–405; more correctly, from this and other manuscripts, by W. G. Henderson, *Liber pontificalis Chr. Bainbridge archiepiscopi Eboracensis* (Surtees Society, LXI, 1875), pp. 267–277.

[3] Printed by F. Liebermann, *Die Gesetze der Angelsachsen* (Halle, 1903ff.) I, 246–258; see also III, 166–171.

gatherings. But exactly which of the other texts in the present manuscript were contained in the original volume for which the poem was written, it is more difficult to tell. The order of coronation on fol. 19a–29b and the pontifical on fol. 39a–86b, 106a–136b, are both of later date than the poem, and cannot have belonged to the original manuscript; but either the pontifical on fol. 8a–18b, 87a–105b, or the benedictional at the end of the manuscript may have been the *halgungboc* referred to in l. 1 of the poem. This word *halgungboc*, which is not elsewhere recorded, is usually translated as "benedictional."[1] The proper meaning of the noun *halgung*, however, is not "benediction," but "consecration, hallowing," especially with reference to the consecration of a bishop or the dedication of a church.[2] It may also refer to the coronation of a king, as in the Chronicle, MS. C, for the year 979.[3] The usual word for "benedictional" (Latin *benedictionalis*) was *bletsungboc*,[4] and we may suppose that if a benedictional were referred to in the poem, this word would have been used. It seems likely, therefore, that the word *halgungboc* refers to the eleventh-century coronation liturgy which begins on fol. 8a, rather than to the benedictional at the end of the manuscript. We have, then, as the parts probably remaining from Thureth's *halgungboc*: (1) the early eleventh-century coronation order and pontifical; (2) the poem; (3) the canons of the Council of Enham. Whether the benedictional was a part of this manuscript, we have no way of telling. At any rate, at some later time the two sections of the eleventh-century coronation

[1] See Bosworth-Toller, *Anglo-Saxon Dictionary*, Supplement, p. 502; Napier, *Transactions of the Philological Society*, 1903–1906, p. 299.

[2] See the examples given by Bosworth-Toller, *Anglo-Saxon Dictionary*, p. 504, and Supplement, p. 502.

[3] "On þys geare wæs Æþelred to cininge gehalgod . . . and þær wæron æt his halgunge twegen ercebisceopas" (Plummer, *Two of the Saxon Chronicles Parallel* I, 122,21–23). For further examples of the verb *halgian*, see Chronicle 973A, "Her Eadgar wæs . . . to cyninge gehalgod" (Plummer I, 118,5–6); 978C, "and he [i.e. Æþelred] wæs on þam ylcan geare to cinge gehalgod" (Plummer I, 122, 17–18); 979E, "and he wæs . . . gehalgod to cyninge æt Cyningestun" (Plummer I, 123, 34–36). In Chronicle 853A (Plummer I, 64,30), the verb *halgian* is used of Alfred's confirmation by the pope, but evidently in error, the compiler of the Chronicle mistaking the rite for a royal unction; see Plummer II,79.

[4] See Bosworth-Toller, *Anglo-Saxon Dictionary*, Supplement, p. 97, for examples of this word.

order and pontifical were misplaced while binding, probably at the
time when the later pontifical (also with parts misplaced) and the
twelfth-century coronation order were added to the manuscript.
The Thureth by whose command the early eleventh-century
portions of the manuscript were put together is undoubtedly to
be identified with the Thored who, by a charter preserved on fol. 6a
of the same manuscript,[1] granted land at Horsley (Surrey) to
Christ Church in Canterbury. Lines 8–9 of the poem may be a
reference to this benefaction. He is possibly also the *þorod eorl*
who is mentioned in the Anglo-Saxon Chronicle (MS. E), under
the year 992, as one of the commanders of the English fleet against
the Danes.[2] A *Ðureð* (or *Ðuræð*) *dux* is also found among the
witnesses to three charters of King Æthelred, of the years 983 and
985, preserved in the Winton Codex (Add. MS. 15,350).[3] That
these three were all one and the same man cannot be regarded as
certain, but it seems at least highly probable. But that the Thored,
presumably a Northumbrian, who is mentioned by Chronicle E
as having ravaged Westmoreland in the year 966[4] is the same as
the Thureth of our poem is much less likely, for chronological
reasons.[5]

ALDHELM

MS. 326 of Corpus Christi College, Cambridge, in which this
poem in praise of Aldhelm is preserved, is a manuscript of Aldhelm's prose treatise *De virginitate*. It contains 71 parchment
leaves, 9.2 by 6.3 inches (23.2 by 16 cm.) in size, numbered by
pages from 1 to 139.[6] The Anglo-Saxon poem begins at page 5,

---

[1] Kemble, *Codex diplomaticus aevi saxonici* IV (London, 1846), 294 (no. 958).

[2] Plummer, *Two of the Saxon Chronicles Parallel* I, 127.

[3] Kemble, *Codex diplomaticus aevi saxonici* III (London, 1845), 197, 210, 213 (nos. 639, 648, 650).

[4] Plummer, *Two of the Saxon Chronicles Parallel* I, 119; see also his note, II, 159. The name Thureth is also found in the *Liber vitae Dunelmensis*, fol. 43b, in a twelfth-century hand.

[5] The forms *þūreð*, *þōrod*, *þōred* are English adaptations of O.N. *þórvarðr*, *þórðr*; see Holthausen, *Anglia* XLI, 404, and for *ú* instead of *ó* in the Scandinavian forms, see A. Kock, *Arkiv för nordisk filologi* XV (1899), 327–330.

[6] For a description of the MS., see M. R. James, *Descriptive Catalogue of the Manuscripts in the Library of Corpus Christi College* II (Cambridge, 1912), 143–146.

l. 18, immediately following the list of chapters of the *De virginitate*, and breaks off in an incomplete condition at page 6, l. 5. Aldhelm's prologue (*Reverentissimis Christi virginibus*, etc.) fills the remainder of page 6, being followed on page 7 by the text of the *De virginitate*. The entire manuscript, the Anglo-Saxon as well as the Latin text, is the work of a single scribe of the tenth century.[1] It formerly belonged to Christ Church, Canterbury, and was probably written there.[2]

The poem is unique in Anglo-Saxon literature in having a great number of Latin and Greek words scattered through the text. In the closing lines of the PHOENIX, in the Exeter Book, and throughout the SUMMONS TO PRAYER,[3] we find a regular alternation of Anglo-Saxon and Latin half-lines, but nowhere else do we find Greek words mixed in with Latin and Anglo-Saxon, or so irregular an occurrence of the foreign words as here. The school at Canterbury, where the poem was probably composed, is the place where, if anywhere in England, we might expect to find such an interest in Greek; for the tradition of Greek learning, established in Canterbury by Theodore and Hadrian in the late seventh century, came down at least to the time of Archbishop Odo (942–959). At Odo's request, at about the middle of the tenth century, Fridegod, a monk of Canterbury, wrote a Latin life of Wilfrid, a chief characteristic of which is the great number of Greek words used. But that Canterbury was not the only place in England where such Latin-Greek works could be produced is shown by the example of the *Vita Ethelwoldi*, written in the late tenth century by Wulfstan of Winchester, and of the *Vita S. Dunstani*, of uncertain origin but doubtfully ascribed to Byrhtnoth, the author of the *Handboc*.[4] There is, then, nothing surprising in the Greek words scattered through our poem; nor is there any need to assume that the poet had an extensive knowledge of the Greek language, since, like the authors of the Latin works which have been mentioned, he may

[1] So Napier, *Old English Glosses*, p. xiv, and Ehwald, *Aldhelmi opera*, p. 219. James says the tenth or eleventh century.
[2] See M. R. James, *The Sources of Archbishop Parker's Collection of Manuscripts at Corpus Christi College* (Cambridge, 1899), p. 58.
[3] See below, pp. 69–70.
[4] On these Latin works see M. Manitius, *Geschichte der lateinischen Literatur des Mittelalters* II (Munich, 1923), 442–446, 704–705.

have taken the words from a Greek-Latin glossary. In any case, the literary value of the poem is small, and it is probably to be regarded simply as an exercise in metrical and linguistic ingenuity.

THE SEASONS FOR FASTING

Among the more important of the recent additions to the manuscript collections of the British Museum is Additional MS. 43,703, formerly the property of Laurence Nowell, the famous antiquary. It is a paper transcript of MS. Cotton Otho B.xi, made by Nowell while the latter manuscript was in the possession of Sir William Cecil in 1562.[1] Since the Cotton manuscript was destroyed in large part by the fire of 1731, surviving only in small fragments, the transcript is of great value.[2] Its chief contribution to a collective edition of Anglo-Saxon poetry is the poem here called the SEASONS FOR FASTING, hitherto known only from the transcript of the opening lines (ll. 1–7a) given by Wanley in his description of the Cotton manuscript.

The poem itself is an exhortation to fasting, especially on Ember days and during Lent. It is incomplete at the end. The 230 lines of the extant text are divided into twenty-nine stanzas, normally of eight lines each.[3] A regular stanzaic division in so long a poem is not elsewhere found in Anglo-Saxon literature.

After a somewhat disorganized introduction (ll. 1–38), dealing with the Jewish people under Moses and with the Crucifixion and Resurrection of Christ, the poet proceeds to a detailed discussion of the Ember fasts (ll. 39–102). Here the Ember seasons are placed in the first week of Lent (ll. 48–50), the week after Whitsunday (ll. 58–62), the week before the autumnal equinox (ll. 67–70), and the week before Christmas (ll. 72–73). This arrange-

---

[1] At the foot of the last page, fol. 264b, is the note: "Hæc scripsit Laurentius Nowellus propria manu in ædibus Cecillianis. anno dni. 1562. Londini."

[2] The Cotton MS. was described before the fire by H. Wanley, *Catalogus historico-criticus* (Oxford, 1705), p. 219. Besides the poem here edited, it contained the Alfredian translation of Bede's Ecclesiastical History, the Anglo-Saxon Chronicle, and some laws and medical recipes. On the text of the Anglo-Saxon Chronicle, itself a copy of the Parker MS., see above, p. xxxiv, note 1.

[3] The fourth stanza (ll. 25–30) has only six lines; the fifteenth (ll. 111–119) has nine lines. The last stanza (ll. 224–230) is incomplete.

ment, which makes the dates of the first two Ember weeks depend on the date of Easter, is very similar to present-day usage;[1] it is also found in St. Egbert's dialogue *De institutione Catholica*[2] and in some Anglo-Saxon liturgical texts.[3] Like Egbert's dialogue, our poem (ll. 92–94) attributes the establishment of these dates for the Ember fasts to St. Gregory the Great. A different, and presumably older, usage places the Ember days in the first week of March, the second week of June, the third week of September, and the week before Christmas.[4] The somewhat obscure protest against "Frankish" usage in ll. 87–94 of our poem may well refer to this other dating of the Ember days.

In his discussion of the Lenten fast (ll. 103–183), the poet cites the example of Moses and Elijah as well as of Jesus Christ.[5] The poem closes with some injunctions against sin on the part of the priesthood (ll. 192–207) and against the practice of breaking one's fast by drinking wine or eating oysters and other fish immediately after mass on fast days (ll. 208–230).

[1] Since the Council of Piacenza in 1095, the Ember fasts have been fixed in the first week of Lent, the week after Whitsunday, the week after Holy-Cross Day (September 14th), and the week after St. Lucy's Day (December 13th). On the dates of observance of the Ember weeks in Anglo-Saxon times, see F. Tupper, *Publications of the Modern Language Association of America* X (1895), 235–236, and H. Henel, *Studien zum altenglischen Computus* (Leipzig, 1934), pp. 60–64.

[2] Migne, *Patrol. lat.* LXXXIX, 440–442.

[3] A short Latin account of the Ember fasts, in which the same dates are prescribed, is found in the Leofric Missal (edited by F. E. Warren, Oxford, 1883, p. 53) and in some other MSS.; see Henel, *Studien*, pp. 28, 63. An Anglo-Saxon passage in MS. 422 of Corpus Christi College, Cambridge, pages 46–47 (printed by Henel, p. 61), differs only in putting the third Ember fast in the week before "octaua kalendas Octobris," i.e. September 24th.

[4] See, for example, Ælfric's *De ecclesiastica consuetudine* (printed by B. Fehr, *Die Hirtenbriefe Ælfrics*, Hamburg, 1914, pp. 240–241); also a short Anglo-Saxon text in MS. Laud 482, fol. 28a (printed by Henel, *Studien*, p. 61), and the calendar in MS. Cotton Vitellius E.xviii (printed by K. Wildhagen in *Texte und Forschungen zur englischen Kulturgeschichte*, Halle, 1921, pp. 68–77). For another text (possibly by St. Egbert) in which this usage is ascribed to "the authority of Rome," see J. Johnson, *A Collection of the Laws and Canons of the Church of England* I (Oxford, 1850), 179–180.

[5] As Ælfric does, in his two homilies for Quadragesima Sunday (B. Thorpe, *The Homilies of the Anglo-Saxon Church*, London, 1844ff., I, 178, 4–15; II, 100, 1–11).

For the date of composition of this poem, there is no direct evidence, but the homiletic manner of the entire piece seems to place it with the poetry of the middle or late tenth century rather than with the earlier poetry. The evidence of language and meter also points to a late date.

In this first edition, the text has been handled as conservatively as possible. In general, it seems to be well preserved,[1] but there are a number of passages, especially toward the end, which are obviously corrupt. The emendations in ll. 156, 206–207, and 225 are offered with all proper diffidence; at least they provide the probable meaning in each case. Line 57*b* is likewise meaningless as it stands in the manuscript; but here no suitable emendation has been forthcoming, and the text has therefore been left unaltered. It is to be hoped that further ingenuity will soon be brought to bear on all these passages.[2]

CÆDMON'S HYMN

In striking contrast to the paucity of manuscript sources for most Anglo-Saxon poetical texts, CÆDMON'S HYMN is preserved in no less than seventeen manuscripts, ranging in date from the eighth century to the fifteenth. Four of the seventeen extant copies of the hymn are in the Northumbrian dialect; of the thirteen West Saxon copies, five are preserved as part of the Alfredian translation of Bede's *Ecclesiastical History*, and eight are found in Latin manuscripts of Bede's history. The seventeen texts of CÆDMON'S HYMN may conveniently be listed as follows:[3]

[1] There are two peculiarities of abbreviation, which may have been in the Cotton MS., or may be due to Nowell: (1) the tilde over a vowel is used not only for omitted *m*, but three times for *n*, in *sūnandæge*, l. 59, *þenūga*, l. 96, and *drēg*, l. 227; (2) the abbreviation *ḡ* for *ge*, which is found only three times in the whole of the Exeter Book, appears in this poem no less than fifty-seven times, usually for the prefix *ge-*, but also in *mæniḡ*, l. 25, *anḡþreatiḡ*, l. 84, and *hiḡsynnig*, l. 168.

[2] A separate edition of the poem is announced as in preparation by Dr. Robin Flower of the British Museum.

[3] For a complete study of the MS. sources for the hymn, see Dobbie, *The Manuscripts of Cædmon's Hymn and Bede's Death Song*, pp. 10–48, on which the present discussion is based.

I. The Northumbrian Version.

MS. KK.v.16, UNIVERSITY LIBRARY, CAMBRIDGE (M), the so-called "Moore manuscript" of the *Ecclesiastical History*, in Latin, written about the year 737, probably in some Anglo-Saxon center on the Continent.[1] The text of the hymn is added on fol. 128*b*, the last page of the manuscript, apparently by the same scribe who wrote the text of Bede. The words "Primo cantauit caedmon istud carmen" are added at the end of the hymn.

MS. LAT. Q.v.I.18, PUBLIC LIBRARY, LENINGRAD (L), a copy of Bede's *Ecclesiastical History*, in Latin, of the middle of the eighth century.[2] The place of origin of this manuscript is unknown. The hymn is written in the lower margin of fol. 107*a*, below the relevant passage in the Latin text, and in the same hand.

MS. 574 [334], BIBLIOTHÈQUE MUNICIPALE, DIJON (Di), written at Cîteaux in the twelfth century. The hymn is inserted in the Latin text of Bede's *Ecclesiastical History*, on fol. 59*b*, col. 2.

COD. LAT. 5237, BIBLIOTHÈQUE NATIONALE, PARIS (P), written in or near Cologne about 1425–1430. As in Di, the hymn is inserted in the Latin text of the *Ecclesiastical History*, on fol. 72*b*.

II. The West Saxon Version: In the Alfredian Version of the Ecclesiastical History. These five manuscripts, which are all that remain of the Alfredian translation, all contain CÆDMON'S HYMN as part of the story of Cædmon in Book IV, Chapter 22.

MS. TANNER 10, BODLEIAN LIBRARY (T), page 195 (fol. 100*a*); tenth century.

MS. COTTON OTHO B.XI, BRITISH MUSEUM (C); tenth century. This manuscript was almost entirely destroyed in the Cottonian fire of 1731, and the text of the hymn is not among the scattered

---

[1] The date is indicated by some chronological notes on fol. 128*b*, in a hand contemporary with that of the main text. For descriptions of this MS., see Palaeographical Society, *Facsimiles of Manuscripts and Inscriptions* I (1879), Plates 139 and 140; Plummer, *Bedae opera historica* I, lxxxix-xci.

[2] About 746, judging from some chronological notes in the margins of Book V, Chapter 24. The manuscript is described, with a photograph of the hymn, by O. Dobiache-Rojdestvensky, *Speculum* III, 314–321.

fragments which remain. The readings from this manuscript given in the present edition are taken from the sixteenth-century transcript by Laurence Nowell, now Additional MS. 43,703 in the British Museum.[1]

MS. 279, Corpus Christi College, Oxford (O), fol. 112*b*; late tenth or early eleventh century. Rather carelessly written, with a number of corrections.

MS. Kk.iii.18, University Library, Cambridge (Ca), page 140 (fol. 72*b*); late eleventh century. Apparently a transcript of O.

MS. 41, Corpus Christi College, Cambridge (B), page 322 (fol. 161*b*); eleventh century. The readings *wuldorgodes* and *wundra fela* in l. 3 set this text apart from the other copies of the West Saxon version.

III. The West Saxon Version: In Latin Manuscripts of the Ecclesiastical History. All but Tr₁ are written in the margin of the Latin text of the history.

MS. Hatton 43, Bodleian Library (H), fol. 129*a*; tenth century. The text of the hymn is added in an eleventh-century hand.

MS. of Winchester Cathedral (W), fol. 81*b*; late tenth century. The text of the hymn, written in a hand of the middle eleventh century, has been partly clipped away by a binder, but the important variants are preserved.

MS. Bodley 163, Bodleian Library (Bd₁), fol. 152*b*; beginning of the twelfth century. The text of the hymn has been partly clipped away, as in W, and has also been partly erased by the use of some abrasive. The Latin text of Bede is a transcript of W, but whether the hymn is copied from W is not certain.

MS. Lat. 31, Lincoln College, Oxford (Ln), fol. 70*a*; twelfth century. The spelling of this text of the hymn shows some late forms, as *michte*, l. 2, and *eche*, ll. 4, 8.

---

[1] On this transcript, which also contains the Seasons for Fasting, see above, p. xcii.

MS. 105, MAGDALEN COLLEGE, OXFORD (Mg), fol. 99a; late twelfth century.

MS. R.5.22, TRINITY COLLEGE, CAMBRIDGE (Tr₁), fol. 32b; fourteenth century. The hymn here, unlike the other texts of this group, is inserted in the Latin text of the *Ecclesiastical History* at the proper place in Book IV, Chapter 22. As we might expect at so late a date, this text shows some irregularities, such as the confusion of *f* and *p* in *epter*, l. 8, and *pirum*, l. 9, and the astonishing form *euca* (for *frea*), l. 9.

MS. LAUD MISC. 243, BODLEIAN LIBRARY (Ld₁), fol. 82b; twelfth century.

MS. P.5.I, HEREFORD CATHEDRAL (Hr), fol. 116b; written about 1161–1162.

The last two texts listed, Ld₁ and Hr, belong in a category by themselves, showing several corruptions of the text which do not appear in the other manuscripts. Ld₁ omits l. 4b entirely, reading (ll. 3b–5) *Swa he wundra gehwæs ece drihten þa he ærest sceop eorðe bearnū*, and transfers l. 6b, *halig scyppend* (with the misspelling *scyppeod*), from its proper place to the end of the poem. In Hr, *halig scyppend* again appears at the end (with the same misspelling, *scyppeod*), and a further omission has taken place in ll. 3–5: *weorc wulderfæder swa he ærest sceop eorðe bearnū*, etc. Evidently Hr was copied from Ld₁ by a scribe who did not quite know what to make of his original.

From the variant readings printed below the texts of the hymn,[1] it will be seen that both the Northumbrian and the West Saxon versions show the variants *ælda* (*ylda*) and *eordu* (*eorðan*) in l. 5b. In the Northumbrian version, the two older manuscripts, M and L, read *ælda*, while Di and P, of much later date, read *eordu* (a late spelling of *eorðu*). In the West Saxon version, the manuscripts of the Alfredian Bede, T, C, O, Ca, and B, read *eorðan* (C, *eorþū*); of the Latin manuscripts of Bede's history, Ld₁ and Hr read *eorðe*, while the other six manuscripts, H, W, Bd₁, Ln, Mg, and Tr₁, read *ylda*. It is apparent that from a fairly early period, at least before the Alfredian translation of Bede was made at the end

of the ninth century, two texts of the hymn were in existence, one
with *ælda* (*ylda*), the other with *eorðu* (*eorðan*).[1]

In the thirteen West Saxon texts of the hymn (leaving the
Northumbrian version aside for the moment), we may accordingly
distinguish between a "West Saxon *eorðan*-group" (T, C, O, Ca, B)
and a "West Saxon *ylda*-group" (H, W, Bd₁, Ln, Mg, Tr₁).[2] The
other two West Saxon texts, in Ld₁ and Hr, obviously derive from
the *eorðan*-group[3] but, because of their textual irregularities, must
be placed in a separate category.

There are four half-lines in the text of the hymn, besides l. 5*b*,
in which the West Saxon *eorðan*-group and the *ylda*-group present
different readings:

	(*eorðan*-group)	(*ylda*-group)
l. 3*b*	wundra gehwæs[4]	wundra gehwilc
l. 4*b*	onstealde[5]	astealde
l. 7*a*	þa middangeard	middangearde
l. 8*b*	æfter teode	æfter tida
l. 9*a*	firum foldan	firum on foldum

In l. 3*b*, *gehwæs*, dependent on *or*, l. 4*b*, corresponds to *gihuaes*
in the Northumbrian texts of the hymn and is undoubtedly the
correct reading; the form *gehwilc*, in the *ylda*-group, would have to
be in apposition to *or*, with much less satisfactory sense. In l.
7*a* and l. 8*b* also, the readings of the *eorðan*-group are superior; the
form *middangearde*, in l. 7*a* of the *ylda*-group, as a dative singular
has no conceivable relation to its context, and *tida* (accusative
plural of *tīd*?), in l. 8*b* of the *ylda*-group, evidently rests on a mis-
understanding of *tiadæ*, or a similar form, in the Northumbrian
text of the hymn. In l. 9*a*, the reading *firum on foldum* in the
ylda-group is impossible, since *folde*, "earth," is not used as a

[1] Both *ælda* and *eorðu* are regular Northumbrian forms, *ælda* with *i*-umlaut
of the unbroken *a* before *ld* (Bülbring, *Altenglisches Elementarbuch* I, §§134,
175), and *eorðu* with -*u* in the oblique cases (Sievers, *Angelsächsische Grammatik*, 3d ed., §276, note 5; compare *eorðu*, dat. sing., in LEIDEN RIDDLE 11).

[2] These two groups were first clearly differentiated by Frampton, *Modern
Philology* XXII, 1–15.

[3] As was recognized by Plummer, *Bedae opera historica* II, 252. According
to Frampton, *Modern Philology* XXII, 4, the scribe of Ld₁ wrote from memory;
but for a contrary opinion see Judge, *Harvard Studies and Notes* XVI, 90, note 15.

[4] B, *wundra fela*. [5] B, *astealde*.

plural.[1] The only place where the *ylda*-group has the preferable reading is in l. 4*b*, *astealde*, which corresponds to the forms *astelidæ*, *astalde* in the Northumbrian version. Except for *astealde*, the variant readings of the *ylda*-group are to be taken as scribal errors in the prototype of that group.

Within the West Saxon *eorðan*-group, there are some interesting textual developments, which in part are reflected in the manuscripts of the *ylda*-group. In l. 1*a* the two oldest manuscripts of this group, T and C, omit the pronoun *we*; O has *we* as a corrector's addition, and B has *we* in the original hand.[2] In l. 4*b*, T and C have *or*, O has *oór* corrected to *oórd*, and B reads *ord*. In both cases O (corrected) and B have the same reading as the West Saxon *ylda*-group. But certainly O and B have no special relationship to the *ylda*-group, and therefore the changes from *Nu* to *Nu we*, and from *or* to *ord*, are probably to be taken as intentional modernizations of the language in both groups.[3] In l. 5*a*, on the other hand, B's reading *sceop* agrees with T and C rather than with O and the *ylda*-group.

It is most probable that the original readings of the West Saxon *eorðan*-group (that is, of the Alfredian translation) corresponded closely with those of T, the oldest manuscript of this group, except in l. 4*b*, where *astealde*, found in B, must have been the original form.

For a long time it was uncertain whether the Alfredian copies of the hymn represented an original Anglo-Saxon text or merely a late ninth-century translation from Bede's Latin back into Anglo-Saxon; but Zupitza in 1878[4] argued that the Alfredian text, in spite of its reading *eorðan* in l. 5*b* for M's *ylda*,[5] was a genuine Anglo-Saxon version of the hymn which went back to the original text. The presence of *eorðan* in the Alfredian manuscripts was

---

[1] It is interesting to note the similar addition of *on* in the two later Northumbrian texts: Di, *on foldu*; P, *ol foldu*. Here, however, *foldu* must be singular.

[2] The other MS., Ca, does not need to be considered here, since it is a transcript of O and consequently carries over the corrected readings of O.

[3] See Dobbie, *The Manuscripts of Cædmon's Hymn and Bede's Death Song*, pp. 29–30.

[4] *Zeitschrift für deutsches Altertum* XXII, 210–223.

[5] The other Northumbrian texts, L, Di, and P, being unknown at that time.

finally explained by Wuest's discovery in 1906[1] of the Northumbrian texts Di and P, with their reading *eordu*, and the consequent establishment of an *eorðan*-group in Northumbrian.

At a relatively early stage in the history of the hymn, two separate forms of the text must have arisen, one with *ælda* (as in M and L) in l. 5*b*, the other with *eorðu* or a similar form. The *eorðu* text, which is represented in its Northumbrian form by Di and P, served as the basis for the West Saxon version of the hymn which appears in the Alfredian Bede. The *ælda* text, in a West Saxon form, appears in the tenth century and later, independently of the Alfredian Bede, in Latin manuscripts of the *Ecclesiastical History*. Whether the original Northumbrian text of the hymn had *ælda* or *eorðu* in l. 5*b* is not quite certain, but the appearance of *ælda* in the two oldest manuscripts, together with Bede's rendering *filiis hominum* in his Latin text,[2] makes *ælda* the more probable.

The historicity of Cædmon has been doubted, chiefly because of obvious parallels to the Cædmon story in other literatures;[3] but whether or not we believe in Cædmon's divine inspiration, there is no reason why we should not accept Bede's account, in Book IV, Chapter 22 of the *Ecclesiastical History*, of an unlettered peasant who was suddenly moved to compose religious verse.[4] Assuming the accuracy of Bede's narrative, we can place the composition of the hymn between the years 657 and 680, when Hild, Cædmon's patron, was abbess of Strenaeshalc, or Whitby. The oldest extant text of the hymn, in the Moore manuscript, dates then from some sixty or eighty years after the hymn was composed.

BEDE'S DEATH SONG

The eighth-century poem traditionally known as BEDE'S DEATH SONG is preserved as part of the Latin *Epistola Cuthberti de obitu*

---

[1] *Zeitschrift für deutsches Altertum* XLVIII, 205–226.

[2] Plummer, *Bedae opera historica* I, 259–260.

[3] Especially in the "Prefatio" which is prefixed to most editions of the Old Saxon *Heliand*, and which was first printed by Flacius Illyricus in 1562; for other analogues to the Cædmon story, see the articles by N. S. Aurner, Fr. Klaeber, L. Pound, and L. Whitbread listed in the Bibliography.

[4] On Cædmon's possible authorship of parts of GENESIS, see *Records I, The Junius Manuscript*, p. xxvii.

Bedae, which, judging from the number and distribution of the extant manuscripts, must have had a wide popularity in the Middle Ages. The extant manuscript copies of the song outnumber even the seventeen copies of Cædmon's Hymn. At the present time no less than twenty-nine copies are known to exist,[1] besides a number of texts of the *Epistola Cuthberti* from which the song is omitted. Eleven of these manuscripts, all in continental libraries, give the text of the song in the Northumbrian dialect; seventeen manuscripts, all in libraries of the British Isles, present a West Saxon version of the song which differs in some respects from the Northumbrian version. The classification by dialects of the Anglo-Saxon texts of the song is borne out also by the evidence of the Latin texts of the *Epistola Cuthberti*. All of the eleven manuscripts which contain the song in the Northumbrian dialect present a single recension of the Latin text, which may for convenience be called the Continental Version. All of the seventeen West Saxon texts of the song are found in a recension of the Latin text which differs in many significant details from the Continental Version, and which may be called the Insular Version. The recently discovered Hague MS. 70.H.7 occupies a position intermediate between the two versions. The Latin text of the *Epistola Cuthberti* in this manuscript is best classed with the Continental Version, but it has a number of readings characteristic of the Insular Version. The Anglo-Saxon text agrees in general with the manuscripts of the Northumbrian version, but with some corruptions.[2]

The twenty-nine manuscripts of Bede's Death Song[3] must, therefore, be classified in three separate categories.

I. The Northumbrian Version.

MS. 254, Stiftsbibliothek, St. Gall, Switzerland (Sg), page 253 (fol. 127a), col. 1; ninth century.

[1] Not counting MS. Cotton Titus A.ii or MS. 359 of Corpus Christi College, Cambridge. See p. ciii, note.

[2] See also pp. civ–cv, below.

[3] For a complete study of the MSS. of the song known up to 1936, see Dobbie, *The Manuscripts of Cædmon's Hymn and Bede's Death Song*, pp. 49–92; for the other MSS., see Brotanek, *Anglia* LXIV, 159–190. The text of the *Epistola* in the Hague MS. is printed in full by Ker, *Medium Ævum* VIII, 40–44.

MS. A.I.47 [MS. BIBL. 22], STAATLICHE BIBLIOTHEK, BAMBERG (Ba), fol. 21*a*; eleventh century.

MS. 225, ADMONT, STYRIA (Ad₁), fol. 249*b*; twelfth century.

MS. 787, KLOSTERNEUBURG, LOWER AUSTRIA (Kl₁), fol. 183*a*; early thirteenth century.

COD. LAT. 14603, BAYERISCHE STAATSBIBLIOTHEK, MUNICH (Mu), fol. 138*a*; sixteenth century.

MS. 708, KLOSTERNEUBURG, LOWER AUSTRIA (Kl₂), fol. 372*a*, col. 1; thirteenth or fourteenth century.

MS. 12, HEILIGENKREUZ, LOWER AUSTRIA (Hk), fol. 170*b*, col. 2; late twelfth century.

MS. 336, NATIONALBIBLIOTHEK, VIENNA (V), fol. 235*a*, col. 2; thirteenth century.

MS. 24, ZWETTL, LOWER AUSTRIA (Z), fol. 182*b*, col. 1; early thirteenth century.

MS. 24, ADMONT, STYRIA (Ad₂), fol. 145*a*, col. 2; early thirteenth century.

MS. M.5 [675], MELK, LOWER AUSTRIA (Me), fol. 71*b*, col. 1; fifteenth century.

II. The Hague Manuscript.

MS. 70.H.7, ROYAL LIBRARY, THE HAGUE (Hg), fol. 42*b*–43*a*; early tenth century.

III. The West Saxon Version.

MS. DIGBY 211, BODLEIAN LIBRARY (Dg), fol. 108*a*, col. 2; twelfth century.

MS. 69, STONYHURST COLLEGE, LANCASHIRE (Sh), fol. 15*b*; twelfth century.

MS. E.2.23, TRINITY COLLEGE, DUBLIN (Db), fol. 175*b*; twelfth century.

MS. R.7.3, Trinity College, Cambridge (Tr₂), fol. 167a, col. 2; early fourteenth century.

MS. Arundel 74, British Museum (Ar), fol. 99a, col. 2; fourteenth century.

MS. 99, Christ Church College, Oxford (Chr), fol. 113b; fourteenth century.

MS. Stowe 104, British Museum (St), fol. 112b, early thirteenth century.

MS. B.5, St. John's College, Cambridge (Jc), page 189 (fol. 95a); fourteenth century.

MS. R.5.22, Trinity College, Cambridge (Tr₁), fol. 43b, col. 1; fourteenth century.

MS. V.II.6, Bishop Cosin's Library, Durham (D), pages 56–57 (fol. 29a–29b); early twelfth century.

MS. Cotton Faustina A. v, British Museum (Fa), fol. 42a; twelfth century.

MS. Fairfax 6, Bodleian Library (Fx), fol. 220a, col. 2; late fourteenth century.

MS. Laud Misc. 700, Bodleian Library (Ld₂), fol. 28a; late fourteenth century.

MS. XVI.1.12, Dean and Chapter Library, York (Y), fol. 109a, col. 1; fourteenth century.[1]

MS. Lat. 31, Lincoln College, Oxford (Ln), fol. 99b; twelfth century.

---

[1] Closely related to D, Fa, Fx, Ld₂, and Y are two fourteenth-century MSS. of the *Epistola Cuthberti* which did not originally contain the text of the song, but in each of which the song was added at some time in the sixteenth century: MS. Cotton Titus A.ii, British Museum, fol. 20a (the song, much normalized, is in the hand of John Joscelin, Archbishop Parker's Latin secretary), and MS. 359, Corpus Christi College, Cambridge, fol. 72b. Since these MSS. are of no direct textual value, their variant readings are not given here. See Dobbie, *The Manuscripts of Cædmon's Hymn and Bede's Death Song*, pp. 86–87; Brotanek, *Anglia* LXIV, 174–176.

MS. R.7.28, Trinity College, Cambridge (Tr₃), page 26 (fol. 13*b*); the so-called "Annals of Asser" (or *Chronicon fani sancti Neoti*), written in the twelfth century.

MS. Bodley 297, Bodleian Library (Bd₂), page 281, col. 2; written at Bury St. Edmund's in the third quarter of the twelfth century.

These manuscripts are arranged here not in chronological order, but roughly in the order of their mutual relationships. In the Continental Version of the *Epistola Cuthberti*, Sg and Ba present the most correct copies of the song, all the other manuscripts showing some corruption of the text. Of the later manuscripts, Ad₁ is tolerably accurate, but in l. 5 it has *æster* and *doemud* instead of the proper forms *æfter* and *doemid*. MSS. Kl₁ and Mu, which agree on the spelling *doemnl* in l. 5, must both descend from the same original copy. The last five manuscripts listed under the Continental Version, Hk, V, Z, Ad₂, and Me, are copies of the so-called "Great Austrian Legendary" (*Magnum legendarium Austriacum*), a collection of saints' lives and legends compiled in some Austrian monastery near the end of the twelfth century.[1] As we should expect, they all display very much the same text, with a number of incorrect readings, such as *neidfacre* (*neidfacere* Ad₂), l. 1, *thraf* (*traf* Me), l. 2, *huaex*, l. 4, *godeles* (*godoles* Ad₂), l. 4, *aester*, l. 5, *deohtdaege*, l. 5, and *doemit*, l. 5. MS. Kl₂, though not, strictly speaking, a manuscript of the Austrian Legendary, has a text of the song very similar to that found in the five manuscripts of the Legendary.

The Hague manuscript is difficult to classify. Except for a few easily explained corruptions, its text of the song is not widely different from the earliest Northumbrian copies.[2] Its Latin text of the *Epistola Cuthberti* agrees in the main with the text of the Continental Version, but, as has already been pointed out,[3] there are a number of places in which it follows the readings of the

[1] See the article "De magno legendario Austriaco," *Analecta Bollandiana* XVII (1898), 24–96.

[2] Of the corrupt readings, the form *ester*, l. 5 (for *æfter*, *efter*), may be paralleled in the reading *æster*, found in all of the later Northumbrian copies; *ðono-*, l. 2, and *riae*, l. 2, are obvious scribal errors for *ðonc-* and *siae*.

[3] See p. ci, above.

Insular Version. Unfortunately there are no indications of the place of origin of this manuscript,[1] and it is impossible to tell whether its text of the *Epistola Cuthberti* represents a stage in the transmission of the Continental Version to South Germany[2] or was derived separately from England.

It should be noticed that the Hague text of the song uses the insular ð throughout, where the Northumbrian texts have *th*, and also in other spellings (*wiorðeð*, l. 1, *wiorðe*, l. 5, *deað*-, l. 5, and *ðearf*, l. 2, with the breaking of *a* to *ea*) shows close resemblances to later insular usage.[3] To arrange the readings of the Hague manuscript among the variant readings of the Northumbrian version of the song would be extremely confusing, and a separate text from this manuscript is therefore given.

Within the Insular Version of the *Epistola*, as has been shown elsewhere,[4] we may distinguish three main recensions of the Latin text: a "Digby group," of which MS. Digby 211 is the best extant example, and which includes also MSS. Sh, Db, Tr_2, Ar, Chr, St, Jc, and Tr_1; a "Symeon group," composed of five manuscripts of the *Historia Dunelmensis ecclesiae* of Symeon of Durham, D, Fa, Fx, Ld_2, and Y; and a "Burney group," of which only one manuscript, Ln, contains the text of the song.[5] The last two manuscripts listed under the Insular Version, Tr_3 and Bd_2, do not belong to any of the three groups mentioned and, so far as the Latin text is concerned, must be placed in a special category.[6]

[1] A ten-line salutation addressed to one Albinus (*reuerentissime Albine*) is prefixed to the text of the *Epistola*. This Albinus may be the famous Alcuin, as suggested by Ker, *Medium Ævum* VIII, 40, or it may be Albinus, abbot of St. Augustine's in Canterbury; see Brotanek, *Anglia* LXIV, 162–164.

[2] That is, the Continental Version as represented by Sg, Ba and the later German and Austrian MSS. For the possible lines of transmission see Dobbie, *The Manuscripts of Cædmon's Hymn and Bede's Death Song*, pp. 70–74.

[3] Brotanek, *Anglia* LXIV, 165, suggests that the Hague text is based on a Kentish original.

[4] See Dobbie, *The Manuscripts of Cædmon's Hymn and Bede's Death Song*, pp. 75–105.

[5] This text of the song in Ln is marginal and was apparently copied from a MS. of the Digby group.

[6] The texts of the song in these two MSS. agree completely except in l. 5*a*; according to Brotanek, *Anglia* LXIV, 173–174, Bd_2 may have been copied from Tr_3, or Bd_2 and Tr_3 may go back to the same original.

This division of the manuscripts of the Insular Version into their respective textual groups is of fundamental importance to an editor of the *Epistola Cuthberti*; it is not, however, reflected in the Anglo-Saxon text of BEDE'S DEATH SONG. All the West Saxon texts of the song are substantially alike,[1] with merely orthographical variations. In the Symeon group, for example, we find the spellings *neodfere* (*neofere* Y), l. 1, *nenig*, l. 1, *snottra*, l. 2, *heonen*, l. 5, and *wurðe*, l. 5, where MS. Digby 211 has *nedfere*, *næni*, *snotera*, *heonon*, and *weorþe*. In Tr₃ and Bd₂ there is a systematic substitution of *th* for the letters þ, ð of the other manuscripts, as in *thā*, *tham*, l. 1, and *wyrtheth*, l. 1, and of *e* for *æ*, as in *neni*, l. 1, *ęr*, l. 3, *hwet*, l. 4, and *efter*, l. 5; but most of the latter spellings are also found in the manuscripts of the Digby group, which vary widely among themselves. Such variations of spelling are clearly without significance for the history of the West Saxon version. The evidence of the Latin text of the *Epistola*, however, points to the Digby group as the earliest form of the West Saxon version, and MS. Digby 211 (the oldest complete text of this group) has therefore been selected as the basis for the West Saxon text of the song in this edition.

The principal differences between the Northumbrian and West Saxon versions of the song are:

	Northumbrian (St. Gall MS.)	West Saxon (MS. Digby 211)
l. 2a	thoncsnotturra	þances snotera
l. 3a	ymbhycggannae	gehicgenne
l. 3b	hiniongae	heonengange
l. 5a	aefter deothdaege	æfter deaþe heonon

The reading *þances snotera*, in l. 2a of the West Saxon version, may be due to the simplification of -*snotturra* (as in the Northumbrian text) to -*snotera*, with the addition of the extra syllable after *þanc*- to fill out the shortened half-line;[2] or it may be simply a scribal alteration. The phrase *æfter deaþe heonon*, l. 5a, is almost

[1] Except for Db, Tr₂, Ar, and Chr, of the Digby group, which omit the words *heonengange hwæt his*, ll. 3b-4a. These four MSS. must all go back to a single original.
[2] So Brotanek, *Texte und Untersuchungen*, p. 180.

certainly a scribal error in the West Saxon version, probably an erroneous repetition of *heonen-* in l. 3*b*. The readings of the West Saxon version in l. 3*a* and l. 3*b* are also to be attributed to scribal carelessness; in l. 3*a*, *gehicgenne* provides adequate sense but loses some of the force of *ymbhycggannae*.

The interpretation of the various forms of the pronoun in l. 1*a* of the Northumbrian version presents a more difficult problem, but here the Hague text provides valuable evidence. The diversity of forms in the several Northumbrian texts (*th'e* in Sg, *thae* in Ba, and *the* in the other German and Austrian manuscripts) may derive from an original *thaem* or *them* (corresponding to *þam* in the West Saxon text) or from an original *thaere* or *there*.[1] The paleographical considerations which might favor *thaere*, *there* as the original form in this version[2] now seem insufficient to outweigh the evidence of the form *ðaem* in the Hague manuscript, and at present, therefore, *thaem* or *them* must be regarded as the probable original form of the pronoun in the Northumbrian text.

The text of BEDE'S DEATH SONG has been traditionally regarded as an original composition by Bede, uttered a short time before his death on May 26, 735. This would seem to be the logical conclusion to draw from Cuthbert's account, written, we may presume, shortly after the actual event.[3] Recently, however, Bulst has argued[4] that Bede did not compose the song but merely recited it from memory. He suggests Cædmon as a possible author. But until Bulst's conclusions have been subjected to critical appraisal, it will not be amiss to regard the song as the sole extant composition in English verse by the greatest Anglo-Saxon scholar and churchman, the Venerable Bede.

[1] In the former case the noun would be the masculine *nēdfær*, *nȳdfær*, "sudden peril"; in the latter case the feminine *nēdfaru*, *nȳdfaru*, "forced journey."

[2] Or so it seemed to me in 1937; see Dobbie, *The Manuscripts of Cædmon's Hymn and Bede's Death Song*, pp. 52–54. Professor Förster, in *Archiv* CXXXV, 282–284, and in several letters to me, has consistently upheld the view that Sg's form *th'e* is a contraction of *them*, and now it looks as if he were right. See also Ker, *Medium Ævum* VIII, 78.

[3] Cuthbert was later abbot of Wearmouth and Jarrow. He is perhaps the same Cuthbert to whom Bede's *De arte metrica* was dedicated; but see A. H. Thompson, ed., *Bede, His Life, Times, and Writings* (Oxford, 1935), pp. 34–35.

[4] *Zeitschrift für deutsches Altertum* LXXV, 111–114.

THE LEIDEN RIDDLE

The so-called LEIDEN RIDDLE, in the Northumbrian dialect, is preserved in MS. Voss. Q. 106 of the University Library at Leiden. This is a small manuscript of twenty-five folios, containing the Latin riddles of Symphosius (fol. 2b–8b) and of Aldhelm (fol. 10b–25b). The Anglo-Saxon riddle is written on the lower part of fol. 25b, in the same ninth-century Carolingian minuscule hand in which the Latin riddles are written.

This riddle also appears, in a West Saxon version, as RIDDLE 35 in the Exeter Book, edited in an earlier volume of this series.[1] Both texts are clearly derived from a single translation of Aldhelm's seven-line "Lorica" riddle (Number 33):[2]

> Roscida me genuit gelido de viscere tellus;
> non sum setigero lanarum vellere facta,
> licia nulla trahunt nec garrula fila resultant
> nec crocea Seres texunt lanugine vermes
> nec radiis carpor duro nec pectine pulsor;
> et tamen en vestis vulgi sermone vocabor.
> Spicula non vereor longis exempta faretris.

It will be seen that the Anglo-Saxon versions follow the Latin original very closely, each two lines of the Anglo-Saxon text corresponding to one of the Latin. In one place there is a transposition of material; ll. 7–8 of the Anglo-Saxon text correspond to l. 5 of the Latin text, and ll. 9–10 of the Anglo-Saxon to l. 4 of the Latin. The two Anglo-Saxon texts differ in one important particular, that the Exeter Book text omits the last two lines as found in the LEIDEN RIDDLE (corresponding to the last line of the Latin text), replacing them with a standard riddle formula, *Saga soðcwidum . . . hwæt þis gewæde sy.*[3]

---

[1] See *Records III, The Exeter Book*, p. 198.

[2] The standard edition of Aldhelm's riddles is the one by R. Ehwald, *Aldhelmi opera* (Berlin, 1919), pp. 97–149; Ehwald's text is reprinted, with an English translation, by J. H. Pitman, *The Riddles of Aldhelm* (New Haven, Conn., 1925).

[3] The other differences between the two versions are discussed in the notes, pp. 199–201, below. The more important of them are: l. 6, *ðerih ðreatun giðraec* L, *þurh þreata geþræcu* EB; l. 7, *ne me hrutendu hrisil scelfath* L, *ne æt me hrutende hrisil scripeð* EB.

The history of this riddle in its Anglo-Saxon form presents a difficult problem. The LEIDEN RIDDLE is closer to the original Latin (especially in ll. 13–14) than the version in the Exeter Book, but whether the dialect of the Leiden text represents the original dialect of the translation is hard to say. The language of the LEIDEN RIDDLE, as it stands in the manuscript, is Northumbrian of the middle of the eighth century or slightly later.[1] We know that Aldhelm's collection of riddles made its way to the North of England before the end of the seventh century, being incorporated in the *Epistola ad Acircium*, a treatise on versification addressed to King Aldfrith of Northumbria.[2] There can be little doubt that these riddles circulated widely in Northumbria during the early eighth century and were readily available to a prospective translator. If, on the other hand, the translation of the "Lorica" riddle into Anglo-Saxon was made in the South of England, then this translation (presumably in West Saxon)[3] must have been transmitted to the North and rewritten in the Northumbrian dialect at some time before the middle of the eighth century. It is probable that RIDDLE 40 in the Exeter Book, a translation of Aldhelm's "Creatura" riddle (Number 100), is to be assigned, at least in large part, to the same translator;[4] but, as one might expect, the late West Saxon text of RIDDLE 40 provides no clue to the original dialect. Historical probability, however, favors the conclusion that the translations of both the "Lorica" and "Creatura" riddles were made by a Northumbrian and in the Northumbrian dialect. If so, they were later translated into West Saxon and, in their new West Saxon form, were copied into the Exeter Book. A copy of the Northumbrian version of the "Lorica" riddle was on the Conti-

---

[1] That is, only a little later than the earliest manuscripts of CÆDMON'S HYMN and BEDE'S DEATH SONG. A. H. Smith, *Three Northumbrian Poems*, pp. 26–37, presents a complete grammatical analysis of the three poems.

[2] According to L. Bönhoff, *Aldhelm von Malmesbury* (Dresden, 1894), p. 103, the *Epistola* was written in 695. See also M. Manitius, *Geschichte der lateinischen Literatur des Mittelalters* I (Munich, 1911), 136–138. Aldfrith reigned from 685 to 705.

[3] A. H. Smith, *Three Northumbrian Poems*, p. 18, thinks it possible that Aldhelm himself was the translator. It is true that, according to William of Malmesbury (*Gesta pontificum Anglorum*, Lib. V, §190), Aldhelm was skilled in the composition of vernacular verse.

[4] See Tupper, *The Riddles of the Exeter Book*, pp. 161–164.

nent in the ninth century and was used to fill up a blank space in
the Leiden manuscript, but just when this copy reached the Continent we have no way of knowing.

The text of the LEIDEN RIDDLE, which in places is hopelessly
illegible, has been the subject of repeated examination by various
scholars, with varying results. Dietrich's text of the riddle,
published in 1860, was accompanied by a lithographed facsimile,
which is still helpful to an editor. Four years later Dr. W. G.
Pluygers, the Leiden librarian, was able to produce a somewhat
better text by the application of ammonium sulphide to the manuscript.[1] Further examinations of the manuscript, each of which
has added to our knowledge of the text, have been made by Sweet,
Schlutter, J. H. Kern, and A. H. Smith.[2] Smith's readings, obtained under ultraviolet light, are as good as we are ever likely to
get, considering the state of the text. For this and other reasons,
no attempt has been made to recollate the manuscript for this
edition, but ample use has been made of all the printed editions and
collations, and the important editorial variants have been recorded
in the notes.

LATIN-ENGLISH PROVERBS

Among the lesser literary remains of the late Anglo-Saxon period
are two very brief collections of proverbs in Latin and Anglo-Saxon,
preserved in MS. Cotton Faustina A.x and Royal MS. 2B.v in the
British Museum. Their interest for this edition lies in the fact
that the Anglo-Saxon versions of the two proverbs which are found
in both collections are in metrical form. These amount in all to
only three lines, but they are of some interest as illustrating the
informal use of the alliterative line at this period.

MS. Cotton Faustina A.x (F) is an eleventh-century manuscript
of 151 folios, 8.9 by 5.9 inches (22.5 by 14.8 cm.) in size, containing
Ælfric's Grammar and Glossary, fol. 3a–100b, and the Anglo-Saxon

---

[1] Dr. Pluygers' transcript (dated November, 1864, and inserted by him in
the manuscript) is still preserved. Schlutter's type-facsimile of this transcript,
in *Anglia* XXXII, 387, note 1, is not entirely accurate.

[2] See the references in the bibliography. Schlutter's readings differ in many
particulars from the accepted ones, and a number of them (especially *erðuong*
in l. 1) were soon discredited.

version of the Benedictine Rule, fol. 102a–151b.[1]   At the foot of
fol. 100b, following Ælfric's Glossary, an eleventh-century scribe,
whose work does not appear elsewhere in the manuscript, has written three proverbs in Latin and Anglo-Saxon versions.   The first
of the proverbs, with its Anglo-Saxon version in prose, does not
properly belong in the present edition;[2] the other two proverbs are
edited below.

Royal MS. 2B.v (R) is a volume of 198 folios, about 10.6 by 7.5
inches (27 by 19 cm.) in size.[3]   The so-called "Royal" or "Regius"
interlinear Psalter, together with the usual canticles, occupies fol.
8a–187a; the rest of the volume contains prayers and other short
ecclesiastical texts, written by a number of late tenth- and eleventh-
century scribes.   The Latin and Anglo-Saxon proverbs are on fol.
6a, in an eleventh-century hand.   Here there are four proverbs in
all, the first two of which have their Anglo-Saxon versions in prose.[4]
Neither of these proverbs corresponds to the first proverb in F,
but the last two proverbs, in Latin prose and Anglo-Saxon verse,
are the same as the last two proverbs in F, the only significant variation between the two texts being the form *ealdað*, l. 6, in R for
forealdað in F.

For the date of composition of the Anglo-Saxon verse proverbs
we have no evidence except the later limit provided by the date
of the handwriting, some time in the eleventh century.   The line
Hat acolað, hwit asolað has frequently been compared with Riming
Poem 67, *searohwit solaþ, sumurhat colað*,[5] of which it may be an

---

[1] For fuller descriptions of this MS., see British Museum, *Catalogue of the
Manuscripts in the Cottonian Library* (1802), pp. 604–605; A. Schröer, *Die
angelsächsischen Prosabearbeitungen der Benedictinerregel* (Kassel, 1888), pp.
xxiv–xxv.

[2] It reads: *Pomum licet ab arbore igitur unde reuoluitur tamen prouidit unde
nascitur.   Se æppel næfre þæs feorr ne trenddeð he cyð hwanon he com.*   Both
the Latin and the Anglo-Saxon texts of this proverb are corrupt to some extent;
see Zupitza, *Anglia* I, 285.

[3] On this MS., see H. Wanley, *Catalogus historico-criticus* (Oxford, 1705), p.
182; F. Roeder, *Der altenglische Regius-Psalter* (Halle, 1904), pp. xi–xiii; British
Museum, *Catalogue of Western Manuscripts in the Old Royal and King's Collections* I (London, 1921), 40–41.

[4] These prose proverbs read as follows: *Meliora plura quam grauia honera
fiunt.   Selre byð oft feðre þænne oferfeðre.   Omnis inuocans cupit audiri.   Clipi-
endra gehwylc wolde þæt him man oncwæde.*

[5] See *Records III, The Exeter Book*, p. 168.

imitation; but there are no parallels for the other two lines. The text in this edition is based on F, since a choice was necessary; but the text of F (except perhaps for the one form *forealdað*, l. 6) is not noticeably superior to that of R.

THE METRICAL PREFACE AND EPILOGUE TO THE ALFREDIAN TRANSLATION OF THE PASTORAL CARE

In the notes to his edition of the Alfredian translation of Gregory's *Pastoral Care*, published in 1871, Henry Sweet pointed out that the brief paragraph immediately following Alfred's preface and beginning with the words "Þis ærendgewrit Agustinus ofer sealtne sæ suðan brohte," which he had arranged as prose in his text, was in reality verse, and he appended a metrical arrangement of it. Thirty years later, in 1901, Holthausen became the first to point out that the short epilogue at the very end of the Hatton manuscript was also metrical in form.[1] Whether these poems were composed as an integral part of the Alfredian text it seems unnecessary to decide. There is nothing in the metrical epilogue to connect it inescapably with the *Pastoral Care*, except perhaps the mention of Gregory in l. 23; but the metrical preface, as a brief history of the first bringing of the *Pastoral Care* to England and its translation into English, obviously belongs where it is. The highly difficult and metaphorical style which we find in the metrical epilogue shows many resemblances to the style of the prose preface to Alfred's translation of the *Soliloquies* of St. Augustine,[2] and if Alfred wrote the preface to the *Soliloquies*, then he was probably also the author of the epilogue to the *Pastoral Care*. At any rate, whoever may have been the author or authors of these poems, their presence in the ninth-century Hatton manuscript fixes the date of their composition within the last decade of the ninth century; and they possess, therefore, an extraordinary interest for the student of Anglo-Saxon poetry, as being the only Anglo-

[1] *Archiv* CVI, 346–347.
[2] W. Endter, *König Alfreds des Grossen Bearbeitung der Soliloquien des Augustinus* (Hamburg, 1922), pp. 1–2.

Saxon poems which can be incontestably assigned to the reign of
King Alfred.

There are five manuscripts which must be considered in an
edition of these poems.   They range in date from the ninth century
to the eleventh.

MS. HATTON 20, BODLEIAN LIBRARY (H).[1] This is the ninth-
century copy of the *Pastoral Care* which was sent by Alfred's order
to Wærferth, bishop of Worcester.[2] The manuscript contains 98
folios, 10.75 by 8.6 inches (27.3 by 21.8 cm.) in size. The metrical
preface is at the foot of fol. 2*b*, immediately following the prose
preface. The metrical epilogue covers the last few lines of fol. 98*a*
and the greater part of fol. 98*b*.

MS. JUNIUS 53, BODLEIAN LIBRARY (J).   This is a paper transcript
of the *Pastoral Care* from MS. Cotton Tiberius B.xi, made by
Franciscus Junius in the seventeenth century, with variant readings
from MS. Hatton 20 and MS. Cotton Otho B.ii noted in the
margins.   The Tiberius manuscript, written in the ninth century,
was almost entirely destroyed when the Cottonian Library burned
in 1731, only eight small fragments now remaining.   It is to Junius'
transcript, therefore, that we must look for the text of the *Pastoral
Care* in this manuscript.   The Tiberius text of the metrical preface
is on page 4 of J; the metrical epilogue does not appear in J at all,
since the original manuscript was incomplete at the end.

MS. COTTON OTHO B.II (O).   This early tenth-century manuscript, like MS. Cotton Tiberius B.xi, suffered severely from the
Cottonian fire of 1731, and the only records which we have of the
text of the *Pastoral Care*, beyond the few charred fragments which

[1] For a description of this MS., see New Palaeographical Society, *Facsimiles
of Ancient Manuscripts*, 1st Series, I (1903ff.), Plates 6–8 and the accompanying
letterpress.

[2] As we know not only by the heading, in capitals, at the top of fol. 1*a*, "Ðeos
boc sceal to Wiogoraceastre," but also by the opening sentence of the prose
preface: "Ælfred kyning hateð gretan Wærferð biscep," etc.   A different name
was evidently to be inserted in each copy, but MS. Cotton Tiberius B.xi, the
other ninth-century MS., has no name inserted.   Of the later MSS., O has the
name of Heahstan (bishop of London, 860–898), while MS. Ii.ii.4 has the name
of Wulfsige (bishop of Sherborne).

are preserved, are the scattered variant readings inserted by Junius in the margins of J. For the metrical preface, the only readings preserved are *sealtne*, l. 2, and *læste*, l. 16, in both of which O agrees with H. The manuscript apparently did not contain the metrical epilogue.

MS. 12, CORPUS CHRISTI COLLEGE, CAMBRIDGE (D). The manuscript contains 225 folios, 16.2 by 10.1 inches (41 by 25.5 cm.) in size. The *Pastoral Care*, with the metrical preface and the metrical epilogue, is the only text. It is written in a large and very individual hand, ascribed doubtfully by James to the eleventh century,[1] but perhaps a little earlier. This was once a Worcester manuscript[2] and, according to Turner,[3] is a copy of H. But there is some reason for believing that D may be a copy of MS. Cotton Tiberius B.xi,[4] or of some other manuscript, now lost. It is therefore treated here as an independent source for the text.

MS. R.5.22, TRINITY COLLEGE, CAMBRIDGE (T). This is a composite manuscript of 156 folios, 11.65 by 7.9 inches (29.5 by 20 cm.) in size, made up of three originally separate volumes of different dates, bound together, and once the property of Archbishop Parker. The last of the three volumes is an eleventh-century text of the *Pastoral Care*, perhaps copied from the manuscript sent by Alfred to Wulfsige, bishop of Sherborne.[5] This text of the *Pastoral*

---

[1] *Descriptive Catalogue of the Manuscripts in the Library of Corpus Christi College* I (Cambridge, 1912), 32–33.

[2] As is shown by the presence of the glosses in the "tremulous" hand; see above, p. lxxv.

[3] C. H. Turner, *Early Worcester MSS* (Oxford, 1916), p. lvii.

[4] As is suggested by M. Ångström, *Studies in Old English MSS* (Uppsala, 1937), pp. 37–38. She points out that D often agrees with the Tiberius MS. as against H, and has several passages which are omitted in H. It should be noted that D preserves the metrical epilogue, which was missing from the Tiberius MS. even before the fire of 1731 (see H. Wanley, *Catalogus historico-criticus*, Oxford, 1705, p. 217); but the Tiberius MS. may once have had the epilogue.

[5] According to a note in an early modern hand at the top of fol. 72a, this is the actual MS. sent by Alfred to Wulfsige. Of course, the MS. is much later than that, but it may have come to Archbishop Parker from Sherborne; see M. R. James, *The Western Manuscripts in the Library of Trinity College* II (Cambridge, 1901), 189–192.

Care is numbered fol. 72*a*–158*a* in the present foliation of the manuscript. The metrical preface occupies the first nine lines of fol. 72*a*; the prose preface, "Ælfred cyning hateð gretan," etc., and the metrical epilogue do not appear in this manuscript.

A second eleventh-century copy of Wulfsige's manuscript of the *Pastoral Care*, MS. Ii.ii.4 of the Cambridge University Library, does not contain either of the verse texts.

Leaving O out of consideration because of the scanty record which is preserved, we have four independent manuscript authorities (H, J, D, T) for the text of the metrical preface, and two manuscript texts (H, D) of the metrical epilogue. Of these H, as the oldest of the extant manuscripts, and J, as a modern transcript of the ninth-century Tiberius manuscript, are to be taken as representing most faithfully the readings of the original. The textual differences between H and J are merely variations in orthography, and on purely practical grounds there would seem to be little reason for preferring one or the other of these manuscripts as the basis of the text. But in view of doubts which have been expressed as to the reliability of J as a transcript of MS. Tiberius B.xi,[1] the text of the present edition has been based on H, the readings of the other manuscripts being reported in the footnotes.

THE METRICAL PREFACE TO WÆRFERTH'S TRANSLATION OF GREGORY'S DIALOGUES

The metrical preface which precedes the text of Bishop Wærferth's translation of Gregory's *Dialogues* in MS. Cotton Otho C.i, Part 2, was first arranged as verse by Holthausen in 1900,[2] although its metrical character had already been recognized by Skeat as far back as 1880.[3] None of the other Anglo-Saxon manuscripts of the *Dialogues* contains this poem.

The Cotton manuscript of the *Dialogues* appears to have been

---

[1] See K. Jost, *Anglia* XXXVII (1913), 63–68; also, on the accuracy of Junius' transcripts in general, H. Logeman, *The Rule of S. Benet* (London, 1888), pp. xxxi-xxxii. Sweet, in his edition of the *Pastoral Care*, printed both H and J, in parallel form.

[2] *Archiv* CV, 367–369.

[3] See Krebs, *Anglia* III, 72.

written in the second quarter of the eleventh century.[1] Its place
of origin is unknown, but it contains glosses written by the glossator
with the "tremulous" hand, and must therefore have been at
Worcester in the late twelfth or early thirteenth century.[2] Like
many other Cottonian manuscripts, it was severely damaged in the
fire of 1731. The text of the metrical preface, on fol. 1a of the
Dialogues,[3] is consequently in a rather bad state, a number of
letters being lost along the edges of the parchment, but in most
cases it is not difficult to restore the missing parts of the poem.

According to l. 12 of the metrical preface, "Me awritan het
Wulfstan bisceop," this copy of the *Dialogues* was written by
command of a Bishop Wulfstan—presumably Wulfstan the author
of the homilies, who was bishop of Worcester from 1002 to 1023.
But if the bishop who "received" or "procured" the book (*begeat*,
l. 16) is likewise Wulfstan, then the statement that the "copy"
(*bysene*, l. 23)[4] was given to him by King Alfred is impossible on
chronological grounds. Keller[5] attempted to resolve this difficulty
by assuming that the name *Wulfstan* in the manuscript is a scribal
error for *Wærferð*, in which case l. 23b would refer merely to King
Alfred's having entrusted to Wærferth the task of translating the
Dialogues. The metrical preface, then, would not be the work
of the scribe of the Cotton manuscript, but must have come down
from the original text of the *Dialogues*—a conclusion which is
rendered at least doubtful by the fact that it appears in only one
of the extant manuscripts. Sisam's explanation[6] is somewhat more
plausible, though it depends on a rather long chain of assumptions
which it is not easy to summarize. He points out, first of all, that
the letters *-tan* of *Wulfstan* appear to be written over an erasure,
and he believes that the original form of the name was *Wulfsig*,

[1] Hecht, *Bischofs Wærferth von Worcester Übersetzung der Dialoge Gregors des Grossen*, pp. vii-viii. A description of the MS. is also given in British Museum, *Catalogue of the Manuscripts in the Cottonian Library* (1802), p. 365.

[2] See above, p. lxxv.

[3] The two parts of the manuscript are separately numbered in the official foliation; the Anglo-Saxon gospels, in the first part of the MS., are numbered fol. 1–110, the *Dialogues* fol. 1–155.

[4] For *bysen* in this sense, see the metrical preface to the *Pastoral Care*, l. 14.

[5] *Die litterarischen Bestrebungen von Worcester*, pp. 6–8.

[6] *Modern Language Review* XVIII, 254–256.

that is, Bishop Wulfsige of Sherborne, to whom King Alfred is known to have sent a copy of the *Pastoral Care*.[1] He then advances the hypothesis that the metrical preface was written by Wulfsige for a Sherborne copy of the *Dialogues*, from which the Cotton manuscript was subsequently made; that the Cotton manuscript later found its way to Worcester, where someone substituted the name *Wulfstan* (that is, the Wulfstan who was bishop of Worcester from 1062 to 1095) for the original reading *Wulfsig*. But, leaving out of consideration the speculative basis of this argument, there is no obvious reason why a Worcester monk should have felt impelled to alter Wulfsige's name to someone else's; if the manuscript was written at Worcester, as it may well have been, the scribe might carelessly have substituted a name which was familiar to him for a less familiar name (as Keller thought that the name *Wulfstan* might have been written in error for *Wærferð*), but that anyone should have deliberately altered an older manuscript in this way is hard to believe. Sisam's hypothesis, then, does not help us much, and the true explanation of the reading *Wulfstan* in l. 12 is likely to remain obscure. It seems certain that l. 23*b* refers to Bishop Wærferth and his literary relations with King Alfred; but just when, and by whom, the metrical preface was written cannot be ascertained from internal evidence.

THE METRICAL EPILOGUE TO MS. 41, CORPUS CHRISTI COLLEGE, CAMBRIDGE

At the end of the Anglo-Saxon text of Bede's *Ecclesiastical History* in MS. 41 of Corpus Christi College, Cambridge, one of the scribes has added a short poem of ten lines, beseeching the help and encouragement of his noble readers. The manuscript, which besides the Alfredian Bede also contains a number of marginal texts, has already been discussed in the present volume.[2] The text of the Bede was written about the middle of the eleventh century by three, or possibly four, scribes;[3] the last of these scribes, who began

[1] See above, p. cxiv.
[2] See above, p. lii.
[3] The number of the scribes engaged on this manuscript and the extent of their work have occasioned some diversity of opinion among scholars; M. R.

his work on page 190, is the one who added the metrical epilogue. The text of this epilogue, on pages 483–484 of the manuscript, is written in alternate lines of black and red. The large capital *B* of [*B*]*idde*, l. 1, like most of the large initial capitals in the text of Bede, has never been written in, although a square space four lines deep was left for it.

There are no very serious literary problems to be discussed in connection with this poem. The phrase *bam handum twam*, "with both hands," l. 5, has occasioned some difficulty to editors, especially to Schipper,[1] who suggested the possibility that the scribe was ambidextrous. But Förster, by means of a Latin parallel in a Turin manuscript,[2] has made it clear that no special meaning need be attached to such a phrase as this. The date of writing of the manuscript, that is, about the years 1030–1040,[3] may be taken as indicating also the date of composition of the metrical epilogue, though it is of course possible that the poem, which does not contain the scribe's name, was carried over from an earlier copy.

THE RUTHWELL CROSS AND THE
BRUSSELS CROSS

Among the shorter Anglo-Saxon verse texts are two inscriptions on crosses, the runic inscription on the sides of the stone cross at Ruthwell in Dumfriesshire and the inscription in roman letters on the cross reliquary preserved in the Cathedral of SS. Michel and Gudule at Brussels.

The Ruthwell Cross, now generally assigned to the late seventh or early eighth century, is between seventeen and eighteen feet in

---

James, *Descriptive Catalogue of the Manuscripts in the Library of Corpus Christi College* I (Cambridge, 1912), 81, sees two main hands; Miller, *The Old English Version of Bede's Ecclesiastical History* II, ix, sees three main hands and a number of minor ones. Such a question naturally cannot be settled here.

[1] *König Alfreds Übersetzung von Bedas Kirchengeschichte*, p. xxvii.

[2] *Archiv* CLXII, 230.

[3] Sir G. F. Warner, cited by Miller, *The Old English Version of Bede's Ecclesiastical History* II, x.

height, and has been described as "no doubt the finest stone cross in existence."[1] Its modern history begins in the year 1642, when, in conformity with an act against "idolatrous monuments" passed by the General Assembly at Aberdeen, it was thrown down from its place in the Ruthwell parish church and broken into several pieces. In 1802 the fragments, which for some time had been lying out of doors, were gathered together by the Rev. Henry Duncan, then minister at Ruthwell, and the cross was eventually set up (with restoration of the transverse arms, which have never been found) in the grounds of the manse. Finally, in 1887, to guard against further damage by the weather, the cross was moved back into the church, where it now stands.

The broad faces of the cross (the present north and south faces) are decorated with figure-sculptures in panels, surrounded by Latin inscriptions in roman letters. The figure-sculptures and the Latin inscriptions are of slight importance to an editor of the Anglo-Saxon text, except in determining the date of the cross, and may be disregarded here.[2] The Anglo-Saxon runic inscription is on the east and west faces of the lower shaft, beneath the arms of the cross, on raised borders which enclose vertical panels of vine tracery.

The runes are arranged in horizontal rows, running across the top and down the right edge of each panel, then down the left edge. There are thus four separate passages in the inscription: (1) across the top and down the right edge of the east face, (2) down the left edge of the east face, (3) across the top and down the right edge of the west face, (4) down the left edge of the west face. On the vertical edges, the runes vary from two to four in each row. Naturally, there is no attempt to indicate word division. When the cross was thrown down in 1642, the lower shaft broke in two, and the broken ends were crumbled; a row or two of runes is lost from each of the four rune-passages at this point. The edges of the

---

[1] A. S. Cook, *The Dream of the Rood*, p. ix.

[2] The most complete descriptions of the cross are given by A. S. Cook, *The Date of the Ruthwell and Bewcastle Crosses*, pp. 228–236; by the Royal Commission on Ancient and Historical Monuments and Constructions of Scotland, *Seventh Report, County of Dumfries*, pp. 219–286; and by G. Baldwin Brown, *The Arts in Early England* V, 102–317, *passim*.

shaft were also damaged by the fall, and the fine-grained sandstone of which the shaft is composed weathered considerably during its exposure to the open air; consequently, many of the runes along the edges, especially on the lower part of the shaft, are missing entirely or are no longer legible.

In studying the text of this inscription, we are greatly assisted by the fact that it evidently goes back to the same original as DREAM OF THE ROOD 39–64a, in the Vercelli Book.[1] The first of the rune-passages (*geredæ hinæ*, etc., on the east face of the cross) shows little more than a general resemblance to the text of the DREAM OF THE ROOD, but the other three passages differ from the poem only in minor details.[2] The correspondences between the two texts are:

I. [..]*geredæ hinæ*, etc. = ROOD 39, 40b–41a, 42b
II. [....] *ic riicnæ k̄yniŋc*, etc. = ROOD 44b, 45, 48, 49a
III. *Krist wæs on rodi*, etc. = ROOD 56b–59
IV. *miþ strelum giwundad*, etc. = ROOD 62–64a

It will be seen that there are gaps between the rune-passages as they now stand, but the runes now missing or illegible on the lower part of the shaft must have accounted for most of the intermediate matter in the poem. The relationship between the poem and the cross inscription depends to a large extent on the dating of the cross, which must now be considered.

On the dating of the Ruthwell Cross, as well as of its companion shaft at Bewcastle, there has been considerable difference of opinion.[3] The earliest date which has been suggested for the two crosses is around 670–680, or about the time of Cædmon, the latest date 1150 or thereabouts, in the reign of King David I of Scotland. The twelfth-century dating was vigorously maintained by A. S. Cook,[4] but his arguments from epigraphy and the history of art

[1] See *Records II, The Vercelli Book*, pp. 62–63.
[2] The most noteworthy difference is in *æþþilæ til anum*, corresponding to *to þam æðelinge*, ROOD 58a.
[3] A complete survey of opinion to 1912 is given by A. S. Cook, *The Date of the Ruthwell and Bewcastle Crosses*, pp. 218–228.
[4] "Notes on the Ruthwell Cross," *Publications of the Modern Language Association of America* XVII, 367–391; *The Date of the Ruthwell and Bewcastle*

have been largely disproved, and the linguistic evidence clearly
points to an earlier period. It is hardly credible, in any case, that
so correct an Anglo-Saxon runic inscription could have been
written in the twelfth century; the extant runic inscriptions from
that period (such as the one on the font at Bridekirk in Cumber-
land) are Scandinavian rather than English.[1] The most recent
authorities agree on an early dating for the crosses, between 675
and the end of the eighth century. But even within these limits
of date, we find several widely different views. G. Baldwin Brown,
after an exhaustive study of the Ruthwell Cross, would date the
cross about the year 675.[2] Brøndsted, on the evidence of the
plant and animal ornamentation, would date it "shortly after
A.D. 700."[3] In sharp contrast is the opinion expressed by W. G.
Collingwood, who argues for a date near the end of the eighth
century or, more specifically, around the year 780.[4] All things considered, Brøndsted's conclusions seem the most dependable, and
they are not far out of agreement with the linguistic evidence.
According to Ross,[5] the language of the two cross inscriptions

Crosses, passim. A similar view was expressed by G. T. Rivoira, *Burlington Magazine* XXI (1912), 24, and in his *Lombardic Architecture* II (revised ed., Oxford, 1933), 151.

[1] See M. D. Forbes and B. Dickins, *Burlington Magazine* XXV, 24–29.

[2] *The Arts in Early England* V, 21–22. Other recent writers on medieval art who have favored a date before 700 are A. W. Clapham, *English Romanesque Architecture before the Conquest* (Oxford, 1930), 56–59; F. Henry, *La Sculpture irlandaise pendant les douze premiers siècles de l'ère chrétienne* (Paris, 1933), *passim*; A. K. Porter, *Spanish Romanesque Sculpture* I (Florence, 1928), 2; *The Crosses and Culture of Ireland* (New Haven, Conn., 1931), pp. 99–104. In favor of so early a date for at least the Bewcastle Cross is the fact that this in-scription contains the names of Alcfrith, son of King Oswiu of Northumbria, and his wife Cyniburuh, daughter of King Penda of Mercia. If the Bewcastle Cross was intended as a memorial to Alcfrith, then a date around 670–675 would be very probable.

[3] J. Brøndsted, *Early English Ornament* (London and Copenhagen, 1924), p. 78. He points out especially that the acanthus leaf, one of the principal features of Carolingian plant ornament, appears nowhere on the crosses.

[4] See his article, "A Pedigree of Anglian Crosses," *Antiquity* VI (1932), 35–54, and his *Northumbrian Crosses of the Pre-Norman Age* (London, 1927), pp. 112–119.

[5] *Modern Language Review* XXVIII, 155. A similar opinion is expressed by Bütow, *Das altenglische "Traumgesicht vom Kreuz,"* pp. 117–118.

belongs to "a period very slightly later than that of the early Northumbrian texts," that is, around 740–750. The evidence of both sculpture and language, then, points to some time in the first half of the eighth century as the most probable date for the Ruthwell Cross and its inscription.

It now remains to discuss the historical relationship between the cross inscription and the text of the DREAM OF THE ROOD. That a close relationship exists between the two texts cannot be doubted, but the precise details are naturally unknown. The extant West Saxon text of the DREAM OF THE ROOD is without question a translation from a Northumbrian original, generally assigned to the pre-Cynewulfian period.[1] Brandl suggests further that the poem was inspired by the discovery of a fragment of the True Cross by Pope Sergius I in the year 701;[2] this hypothesis (for it is little more than that) would place the composition of the poem near the beginning of the eighth century. Whether or not we accept Brandl's suggestion, it seems most probable that the DREAM OF THE ROOD antedates the cross inscription, and that the carver who cut the inscription took his text, with some changes, directly from the poem. The alternative possibility[3] is that the extant text of the DREAM OF THE ROOD represents a later revision of the original poem, selections from which were carved on the cross.

The text of the Ruthwell Cross inscription is transliterated in this edition according to the method suggested by Bruce Dickins.[4] This seems to be the simplest and clearest way of representing runic letters in roman type, and is deserving of general adoption. Runes which are no longer visible, or which cannot be identified, are here

---

[1] So, for example, A. J. Barnouw, *Textkritische Untersuchungen nach dem Gebrauch des bestimmten Artikels und des schwachen Adjektivs in der altenglischen Poesie* (Leiden, 1902), pp. 210–211, who argues for a pre-Cynewulfian date on syntactical evidence, and C. Richter, *Chronologische Studien zur angelsächsischen Literatur* (Halle, 1910), p. 101, who assigns the poem to the first half of the eighth century on metrical grounds.

[2] *Sitzungsberichte der kgl. preussischen Akademie der Wissenschaften*, 1905, pp. 716–723; an English version of the same article appears in the *Scottish Historical Review* IX (1912), 139–147.

[3] Suggested by Schücking, in H. Hecht and L. L. Schücking, *Die englische Literatur im Mittelalter* (Wildpark-Potsdam, 1927), p. 28, and later by Dickins and Ross, *The Dream of the Rood*, p. 18.

[4] *Leeds Studies in English* I (1932), 15–19.

represented by points within square brackets; runes which are incomplete, but which can be identified with some confidence, are represented by italic letters. The accompanying drawing will show the position of the runes on the cross, so far as they are discernible at the present time.

The Brussels Cross and its two-line inscription in Anglo-Saxon verse were first brought to the attention of scholars by H. Logeman in 1891.[1] Traditionally reputed to contain the largest extant fragments of the True Cross, it has been preserved at the Cathedral of SS. Michel and Gudule since the middle of the seventeenth century. The cross is 46.5 by 28 cm. (18.3 by 11 inches) in size.[2] The front was once covered by a jeweled gold plate, probably taken away by French soldiers under Dumouriez in 1793; the back is still covered with silver, with the symbols of the four evangelists at the ends of the four arms and the symbol of the *Agnus Dei* in the center. Across the silver plating of the transverse arms the artist has traced his name: +*Drahmal me worhte.*[3] The Anglo-Saxon inscription is contained on a silver strip which runs around the edges of the cross. It is written not in runes, but in roman letters, in a curious mixture of capitals and minuscules. The letters *NE* of *ricne*, *NG* of *cyning*, and *ME* of *bestemed* are written as ligatures.

It is unquestioned that the Brussels Cross was made in England, but the three brothers Ælfric, Æthelmær, and Æthelwold, mentioned in the prose part of the inscription, have never been positively identified. The name of the craftsman, Drahmal, is probably Norse[4] and may indicate that he came from the North of

[1] The metrical form of the two lines was apparently not recognized by Logeman, but was pointed out by Zupitza, *Archiv* LXXXVII, 462.

[2] So D'Ardenne, *English Studies* XXI, 145, and these measurements agree closely with the dimensions (47 by 27 cm.) given by C. Rohault de Fleury, *Mémoire sur les instruments de la passion de Notre-Seigneur Jésus-Christ* (Paris, 1870), p. 151. The dimensions 14 by 7 cm., stated by Dickins and Ross, *The Dream of the Rood*, p. 14, apparently apply not to the entire cross, but to the fragment of the True Cross which it contains.

[3] Complete photographs of the cross are given by Logeman; a more detailed photograph of the Anglo-Saxon inscription (not quite complete) by D'Ardenne.

[4] The place-name Dromonby in the North Riding appears in Domesday Book as *Dragmalebi*; see A. H. Smith, *The Place-Names of the North Riding of Yorkshire* (Cambridge, 1928), pp. 168–169, who suggests that *Dragmal* is an O.N. by-name *Drag-máll*, "drag-speech."

England; nothing more, however, is known about him. Judging
from the language of the inscription as well as from the epigraphy
and the ornamentation, the cross dates from the eleventh century.
The language is a fairly regular Late West Saxon, with one Anglian
form, *bestēmed*, and a few irregular spellings, such as *byfigynde*
(with *y* for *e* in the ending) in the verse, *wyrican* and *beroþor* (both
with an intrusive vowel) in the prose. The form *bestēmed* (for
West Saxon *bestiemed*, *bestȳmed*) does not necessarily indicate a
northern origin for the inscription; it is usually explained as a
traditional spelling taken over from the older poetic vocabulary.[1]

Cook[2] has proposed to identify the three names Ælfric, Æthelmær, and Æthelwold with Alfricus, Agelmarus, and Agelwardus,
three of the six brothers of Eadric Streona mentioned by Florence
of Worcester under the year 1007.[3] Dickins and Ross suggest that
the Æthelmær of the inscription is the well known patron of Ælfric,
who founded the abbey of Eynsham in 1005; but they offer no
identification of the other two names.[4] It is possible, furthermore,[5]
that the holy relic which forms part of the present cross is the same
as the *lignum Domini* sent by Pope Marinus to King Alfred in 883
or 885.[6] None of these possibilities is susceptible of proof. But
D'Ardenne, who favors the identification of the relic with Alfred's
lignum Domini, has studied all the available evidence and presents
a highly plausible account of its later history. According to him,
the relic remained in the hands of the West Saxon royal family
until near the end of the tenth century, when it left the possession
of the direct line. Its new owners had it enclosed in a reliquary

---

[1] See *mid wætan bestemed*, DREAM OF THE ROOD 22; *usses dryhtnes rod ...
blode bistemed*, CHRIST 1084–1085.

[2] *Modern Language Review* X, 157–161.

[3] *Chronicon ex chronicis* (ed. B. Thorpe, London, 1848f.) I, 160. This theory
involves the emendation of Florence's *Agelwardus* to *Agelwaldus*. The equation
of *Æðel-* and *Agel-* offers less difficulty.

[4] *The Dream of the Rood*, p. 15.

[5] As suggested by Logeman, *L'Inscription anglo-saxonne*, p. 15.

[6] This gift is mentioned in the Anglo-Saxon Chronicle, in MS. E under both
years and in MS. A under 885. It is unlikely that two separate cross relics
were sent, and the repetition in E is probably due to an unintended duplication
of the same event.

(the present cross) and presented it to Westminster Abbey. It
later found its way to the Netherlands, probably during the reign
of Stephen, when numbers of Flemish soldiers were in England.
The wanderings of the cross on the Continent form a separate
chapter of its history, which need not be summarized here.[1]

THE FRANKS CASKET

The Franks Casket, probably the best known of the exhibits of
Anglo-Saxon art in the British Museum, is so called because it was
presented to the museum in 1867 by Sir Augustus Wollaston
Franks, the antiquarian. The known history of the casket goes
back to the early years of the nineteenth century, when it was
discovered in the possession of a French family of Auzon (Haute-
Loire). The lid and three of the sides were acquired by a Professor
Mathieu of Clermont-Ferrand,[2] and in 1857, though a Paris dealer
in antiques, came into Franks' hands. The missing right side was
discovered in 1890 in the Carrand Collection at the Museo Na-
zionale in Florence.[3]

The casket, which is made of whalebone, is 9 inches long, 7.5
inches wide, and 5.1 inches high. It has long engaged the attention of scholars, not only for the sake of the five carved panels on
the lid and sides, but also for the inscriptions which surround four
of these panels. Of the lid, only the central strip, extending from
end to end of the casket, still remains, the inscription (if there
was one) being lost; but on the four sides of the casket the inscriptions are well preserved.[4] Two of the inscriptions, on the front

[1] See *English Studies* XXI, 152–160.

[2] Whence the name "Clermont Casket," frequently used by continental
scholars.

[3] A cast of this side has since been fitted into its proper place on the casket at
the British Museum. For further details on the history of the casket, see G.
Stephens, *The Old-Northern Runic Monuments* I, 470–471; A. S. Napier, in *An
English Miscellany*, pp. 362–365; G. B. Brown, *The Arts in Early England*
VI, Part 1, pp. 19–20.

[4] Complete photographs of the casket are available in Napier's article (*An
English Miscellany*, pp. 362–381), and also in E. Wadstein, *The Clermont Runic
Casket*, G. B. Brown, *The Arts in Early England* VI, Part 1, and (somewhat
reduced) in the British Museum's *Guide to Anglo-Saxon Antiquities* (London,
1923), Plate VIII.

and the right side, are in alliterative verse and are edited here. The other three panels do not properly come within the province of this edition.[1]

The carving on the front panel is divided into two parts. On the left is an illustration of an episode from the Weland story.[2] Weland, the captive of King Nithhad, is sitting before his anvil, beneath which is the headless body of one of Nithhad's dead sons. The princess Beaduhild, accompanied by an attendant,[3] is giving

[1] But for completeness of record they may be described briefly, as follows: LID. A man, with bow and arrows, defending a fortified enclosure against armed attackers. A female figure sits behind him. The name *Ægili*, in runic letters, above the man's shoulder, points to the story of Egil, the brother of Weland, but the precise incident has not been identified. There is no inscription. LEFT SIDE. Romulus, Remus, and two wolves being discovered by four men armed with spears. The inscription, in runic letters, reads: *Romulus and Reumwalus, twægen gibroþær. Afœddæ hiæ wylif in Romæcæstri, oplæ unneg.* BACK. Here there are four separate scenes: (1) The capture of Jerusalem by Titus in the year 70 A.D. The inscription, in runic letters, reads: *Her fegtaþ Titus end Giuþeasu.* (2) The flight of the inhabitants from the city. The inscription, except for the last word, is in roman letters: *Hic fugiant Hierusalim afitatores* (= *habitatores*). (3) Apparently a trial scene, with the word *dom*, in runic letters, at the side. (4) A group of men, probably captives, with the word *gisl*, in runic letters. A complete study of the casket is in preparation by P. W. Souers. In the meantime his two articles, "The Top of the Franks Casket" and "The Franks Casket: Left Side," in *Harvard Studies and Notes* XVII (1935), 163–179; XVIII (1935), 199–209, are very helpful. See also Wadstein, *The Clermont Runic Casket*, pp. 6–13, 23–30; Napier, in *An English Miscellany*, pp. 365–367, 369–371.

[2] As was suggested independently by S. Bugge, in Stephens' *The Old-Northern Runic Monuments* I, lxix-lxx, and by Hofmann, *Sitzungsberichte der philos.-philol. und histor. Classe der kgl. bayerischen Akademie der Wissenschaften* I, 665ff.; II, 461f. This episode in the Weland story, briefly referred to in DEOR 1–13, appears in fuller form in the Norwegian *Þiðriks saga*, Chapters 120–135 (H. Bertelsen, *Þiðriks Saga af Bern*, Copenhagen, 1905ff., I, 114–131), and in the *Völundarkviða*, in the Poetic Edda. The relevant part of the *Þiðriks saga* is translated by H. M. Smyser and F. P. Magoun, Jr., *Survivals in Old Norwegian of Medieval English, French, and German Literature, together with the Latin Versions of the Heroic Legend of Walter of Aquitaine* (Baltimore, 1941), pp. 68–74.

[3] According to Schück, *Studier i nordisk litteratur- och religionshistoria* I, 178, this second female figure is independent of those to the left and represents Beaduhild carrying a bag, which perhaps contains the drinking-cup made out of her brother's skull.

him (or receiving from him) some small object, which looks like a
cup.[1] Behind the two women a man's figure (commonly identified
with Egil, Weland's brother) is catching birds, presumably to make
the wings with which Weland later escapes. The carving on the
right-hand side of the front panel (with the word *mægi* in runic
letters) illustrates the Adoration of the Magi. The verse inscription on this side of the casket, beginning at the upper left-hand
corner, runs along the top and down the right-hand edge, then
along the lower edge from right to left and with the runes reversed
(that is, in the form of a vertical mirror-image). This inscription
is the only one on the casket which has nothing to do with the
subjects of the carvings. The waves, it says, have cast up the
fish on the rocky shore—evidently the whale from whose bone the
casket was made. The words *hronæs ban*, in runes along the left-
hand edge, are not part of the two lines of verse, but were probably added by the carver to fill up that edge of the panel.

The interpretation of the runes on the front of the casket is a
simple matter, but the inscription on the right side presents some
unusual difficulties. The most agreeable interpretation of the
carving on this side is that it depicts several scenes from the
Scandinavian story of Sigurd (Sigfrid), but the details are by no
means certain.[2] In the center of the picture we see a man's body
within a tomb, and a horse standing over the tomb in sorrow.

[1] In the Norse sources Beaduhild asks Weland to mend her broken ring, and
this may be the episode illustrated here. But of all the commentators, only
Hofmann has identified the small object as a ring; it certainly looks like a cup.

[2] The connection of this carving with the Sigurd legend was first suggested
by S. Söderberg; see *Academy* XXXVIII (1890), 90. It was later worked out
in detail by Wadstein, *The Clermont Runic Casket*, pp. 34–44, on whose discussion
the present brief description of the carving is chiefly based, and by Miss Clark,
Publications of the Modern Language Association of America XLV, 339–353,
who takes the carving to represent "the Judgment of Sigurd." Less plausible
explanations are offered by Grienberger, *Anglia* XXVII, 443–444, who sees in
the carving a representation of the dead Christ in the tomb; by Boer, *Arkiv
för nordisk filologi* XXVII, 245–259, who suggests that it is based on the story of
Jarl Iron of Brandenburg, found in the *Þiðriks saga*, Chapters 269–274; and by
Imelmann, *Forschungen zur altenglischen Poesie*, pp. 315–341, who (as in his
Zeugnisse zur altenglischen Odoaker-Dichtung, Berlin, 1907) would attach it to
his hypothetical Anglo-Saxon Odoaker cycle.

These figures may represent the dead Sigurd and his horse Grani.[1]
The human figure to the right of the tomb is perhaps the weeping
Gudrun, the widow of Sigurd, and the three persons at the right of
the carving are identified by Wadstein as Brynhild, Gunnar, and
Hogni in conversation.[2] At the extreme left is a figure, apparently
with the head of a horse and the body of a man, sitting on a barrow.
Most scholars have been inclined to see in this figure the *hos*
(*Hos?* or *hors?*) sitting on the *hærmberg*, but what it is intended to
represent, or who the human figure facing it is, we have no way of
knowing.[3]

On this panel, as on the front of the casket, the runic inscription
begins at the upper left-hand corner and runs around the panel
clockwise; the runes along the lower edge run from right to left
and are upside down. Most of the difficulties in the interpretation
of this inscription arise from the fact that the carver used a set of
arbitrary vowel runes which are not elsewhere found. In only two
places[4] does he use the regular vowel runes—the rune ᛗ (= *E*) in
særden, l. 3*a*, and ᚠ (= *A*) in the composite rune *FA* of *sefa*, l.
3*b*.[5] Elsewhere the vowels are represented by the runes h (= *A*),
ᛚ (= *Æ*), ᚷ (= *E*), ᚨ (= *I*), and ᚻ (= *O*).[6] The consonant

---

[1] See, for example, the Poetic Edda, *Guðrúnarkviða II*, str. 5; *Brot af Sigurð-
arkviðu*, str. 7.

[2] We know from the Poetic Edda (*Sigurðarkviða en skamma*, str. 10–12,
17–19), as well as from the *Völsunga saga*, that Brynhild instigated the murder
of Sigurd.

[3] In the upper part of the carving are the words *risci* ("rush"?) and *bita*
("biter"?), and below, the word *wudu*, all in runic letters. Napier, in *An English
Miscellany*, p. 378, suggested doubtfully that we should read *risci-bita* as a
compound, "rush-biter," that is, "horse." Wadstein, *The Clermont Runic
Casket*, p. 37, would take *risci* as for a noun **ricsi*, "darkness." Whatever they
may mean, these words were probably intended as labels for the various parts
of the picture.

[4] Besides the words *risci*, *bita*, *wudu* in the illustration (see the preceding
note), which have the normal vowel runes.

[5] Napier, in *An English Miscellany*, p. 372, points out that *sefu* would be a
more regular form of the genitive singular than *sefa*, and he favors the possibility
that the composite rune stands for *FU*. It is also possible that the rune ᛗ
stands for some other letter than *E*; see the notes on these words, p. 206, below.

[6] G. Hempl, *Transactions of the American Philological Association* XXXII
(1901), 186–195, argues that these vowel runes are not arbitrary creations, but
normally developed variant forms of the regular vowel runes. See also Grienberger, *Zeitschrift für deutsche Philologie* XXXIII, 412–413.

symbols in this inscription are the usual ones. The close similarity of **h** (= *A*) to the usual *C*-rune (as in *fisc, gasric* on the front
of the casket) might have led to difficulties, but the carver has
avoided the *C*-rune in this inscription, using the *G*-rune instead.

Of the various readings of the inscription which have been proposed, Napier's arrangement in three verse lines is the only one
which does justice to both sense and meter, and it has therefore
been adopted for this edition. The reading of l. 2*b*, *swæhirier-
taegisgraf*, causes the greatest perplexity. If we read *swæ hiri
Ertae gisgraf*, with Napier, then the two runes *A* and *E* of *Ertae* must
stand for the equivalent of *Æ*, elsewhere represented by the single
rune ᛨ. For this reason Wadstein and Boer would divide the
words as *erta* and *egisgraf*, taking *egisgraf* as "the grave of awe,"
synonymous with *hærmbergæ*.[1] But *erta egisgraf* raises serious
metrical problems, besides giving double alliteration in a second
half-line.

Two of the inflectional endings deserve notice here; in l. 1*a*,
sitæþ should be *sitiþ* (with *-iþ* as in *drigiþ*), and in l. 2*b* the proper
form of the pronoun would be *hiræ*, not *hiri*. The end of the last
word on the upper edge of the panel, *agl*[.], is lost. The vertical
stroke preserved after *L* may be part of an *A*, and the reading
agl[*ag*] (= *aglac*) is a tempting one; but there does not seem to be
room for two letters after *L*.

Even if all the textual difficulties were resolved, there would still
be little certainty as to what the inscription means. Following
Napier's reading, and omitting the doubtful words *agl*[.] and
særden, we have some such translation as this: "Here *hos* (*Hos?*) sits
on the hill of sorrow, endures . . . , as Erte appointed for her, . . .
of (or with) sorrow and anguish of heart." This may possibly refer
to the legend of Sigurd illustrated on this panel, but since we do not
know what *hos* means or who Erte is, a convincing statement of the
relationship between inscription and illustration seems still to be
beyond our reach.

The date of the casket cannot be later than the first half of the
eighth century. The ending *-u* retained in *flodu*, the *eu* of *greut*,

---

[1] Wadstein, *The Clermont Runic Casket*, p. 42; Boer, *Arkiv för nordisk filologi*
XXVII, 224. The reading *Erta egisgraf* had previously been suggested by
Viëtor. See the notes on this passage, pp. 205–206, below.

and the distinction between -*æ* and -*i* in endings, all point to such a conclusion.   For the letter *G* only the *gifu*-rune is used, and not the later *gār*-rune, which appears together with the *gifu*-rune on the Ruthwell Cross.   The dialect of the inscriptions is Anglian.[1]

THE METRICAL CHARMS

Of the numerous charms and exorcisms preserved in Anglo-Saxon manuscripts, there are only twelve which are in metrical form or which contain verse passages of sufficient regularity to warrant their inclusion in an edition of Anglo-Saxon poetry.[2] These twelve charms are contained in five manuscripts, which may be described briefly as follows:

MS. COTTON CALIGULA A.VII, BRITISH MUSEUM.   This is the famous Cotton manuscript of the Old Saxon *Heliand*.   It contains (or rather contained)[3] 178 folios, approximately 9.3 by 6 inches (23.5 by 15.3 cm.) in size.   On fol. 176*a*-178*a*, following the *Heliand*, is the text of CHARM 1 (For Unfruitful Land), written in a single hand of the early eleventh century.[4]   These last three folios were originally separate from the rest of the manuscript, and were not bound together with the *Heliand* text until the early seventeenth century.[5]

MS. HARLEY 585, BRITISH MUSEUM.   This manuscript, written in a number of hands of the late eleventh century, contains 193 folios, 7.5 by 4.3 inches (19 by 10.9 cm.) in size.   The first part,

---

[1] A complete linguistic analysis of the inscriptions is given by Wadstein, *The Clermont Runic Casket*, pp. 46–54.

[2] To this number Grendon would add a charm for loss of cattle (numbered A15 in his edition), part of which he arranges as verse.   This charm, however, is best regarded as a prose text; see Skemp, *Modern Language Review* VI, 298–299.   The shepherd's charm printed by R. Priebsch, *Academy* XLIX (1896), 428, is Middle English rather than Anglo-Saxon.

[3] Some illuminated folios having been removed and mounted separately in 1931.

[4] The contents of the pages, in terms of the line-numbering of this edition, are: fol. 176*a*, *Her*, l. 1, to *bene-*, l. 13; fol. 176*b*, -*dicti*, l. 13, to *drihten*, l. 27; fol. 177*a*, *bidde*, l. 28, to *eallon*, l. 44; fol. 177*b*, *þam*, l. 44, to *sawen*, l. 63; fol. 178*a*, *Nu*, l. 64, to *þriwa*, l. 82.

[5] See R. Priebsch, *The Heliand Manuscript* (Oxford, 1925), pp. 9–10.

fol. 1*a*-129*b*, contains an Anglo-Saxon translation of the so-called Herbarium of Apuleius; the remainder of the book, fol. 130*a*-193*b*, is taken up by a collection of charms and recipes which, since Cockayne's time, has been known as the "Lacnunga."[1] Five of the charms printed in this edition are contained in the "Lacnunga," as follows: CHARM 2 (the Nine Herbs Charm), fol. 160*a*-163*b*; CHARM 3 (Against a Dwarf), fol. 167*a*-167*b*; CHARM 4 (For a Sudden Stitch), fol. 175*a*-176*a*; CHARM 5 (For Loss of Cattle), fol. 180*b*-181*a*; CHARM 6 (For Delayed Birth), fol. 185*a*-185*b*.[2]

ROYAL MS. 12D. XVII, BRITISH MUSEUM. The oldest extant book of Anglo-Saxon medical recipes, this manuscript is usually called the "Læceboc."[3] It contains 127 folios, approximately 10.2 by 7.2 inches (26 by 18.3 cm.) in size. The entire text is written in a single hand of the tenth century. CHARM 7 (For the Water-Elf Disease), on fol. 125*a*-125*b*,[4] is numbered LXIII in Book III of the manuscript.

MS. 41, CORPUS CHRISTI COLLEGE, CAMBRIDGE. This manuscript, an eleventh-century copy of the Alfredian Bede, is more fully described at an earlier place in this volume.[5] Among the marginal texts are four of the charms printed in this edition: CHARM 8 (For a Swarm of Bees), page 182; CHARM 9 (For Theft of Cattle), page 206; CHARM 10 (For Loss of Cattle), page 206; CHARM 11 (A Journey Charm), pages 350-353.[6] All these charms are written in the same small and rather angular hand which wrote

[1] See Cockayne, *Leechdoms* III, 2ff.
[2] The contents of the pages are: fol. 160*a*, *Gemyne*, 2,1, to *bryo-*, 2,10; fol. 160*b*, *-dedon*, 2,10, to *geond*, 2,20; fol. 161*a*, *lond*, 2,20, to *com*, 2,31; fol. 161*b*, *snican*, 2,31, to *worulde*, 2,39; fol. 162*a*, *earmum*, 2,40, to *grenan*, 2,49; fol. 162*b*, *attre*, 2,49*b*, to *wyrtum*, 2,61; fol. 163*a*, *aspringan*, 2,61, to *sealfe*, 2,69; fol. 163*b*, *on do* (MS. *onde*), 2,69, to *on do*, 2,73; fol. 167*a*, *Wið*, 3,1, to *dagas*, 3,8; fol. 167*b*, *him*, 3,8, to *Fiað*, 3,17; fol. 175*a*, *Wið*, 4,1, to *mægen*, 4,8; fol. 175*b*, *beræddon*, 4,8, to *wære*, 4,23*b*; fol. 176*a*, *ylfa*, 4,23, to *wætan*, 4,29; fol. 180*b*, *þonne*, 5,1, to *cweð*, 5,11; fol. 181*a*, *þriwa*, 5,11, to *Amen*, 5,16; fol. 185*a*, *Se*, 6,1, to *þonne*, 6,18; fol. 185*b*, *Ic*, 6,19, to *metes*, 6,31.
[3] This title appears in a table of contents on fol. 62*a*.
[4] Fol. 125*a* ends at *niþer*, l. 2.
[5] See above, p. lii.
[6] Page 350 ends at *dryhten*, l. 11, page 351 at *sigerofra*, l. 25, page 352 at *eallum*, l. 37.

the text of SOLOMON AND SATURN on pages 196–198 of the manuscript.

ROYAL MS. 4A.XIV, BRITISH MUSEUM. This is a tenth-century manuscript of 108 folios, 10.8 by 7 inches (27.5 by 17.7 cm.) in size. A Latin commentary on Psalms cix-cxlix, fol. 1a-105a, is followed by a Latin homily on Numbers xx.10, fol. 105a-106b; both texts are here attributed to St. Jerome. CHARM 12 (Against a Wen) is written, in a late eleventh-century hand, on the lower half of fol. 106b.

In the present edition the order of the charms is determined not by any classification on the basis of form and content, but simply by the order in which they appear in the manuscripts. It would, in fact, be difficult to work out an arrangement by categories, either of form or of content, into which all the extant Anglo-Saxon charms would fit.[1] And when, as here, twelve of the charms are to be edited separately, selected from the whole body of Anglo-Saxon charm literature because of their metrical form, the problem of classification by content becomes less important. Occasionally, as in the study of other Anglo-Saxon poems, we are tempted to distinguish sharply between heathen and Christian materials, but such distinctions are not easy to justify. CHARM 1, for example, invokes (l. 51) a heathen goddess Erce,[2] but with this exception it is predominantly Christian in spirit. CHARM 2 mentions Woden (l. 32), but also Christ (l. 58). Grendon classifies CHARM 3 among those "distinctly reminiscent of heathendom,"[3] but the Seven Sleepers of Ephesus, whose names appear in the prose part (ll. 3–4), are in the Roman martyrology. Clearly, no division into "heathen" and "Christian" charms is practicable. It is possible to set off CHARM 2 and CHARM 7 as "herbal charms," as Grendon does,[4] but each of these charms contains an incantation (*galdor*) as well

---

[1] The classification given by Grendon, *Journal of American Folk-Lore* XXII, 123 ("A. Exorcisms of diseases or disease-spirits. B. Herbal charms. C. Charms for transferring disease. D. Amulet charms. E. Charm remedies"), is far from satisfactory; see, for example, Skemp, *Modern Language Review* VI, 262.

[2] Or so most scholars have believed; see the note on this line, p. 208, below.

[3] *Journal of American Folk-Lore* XXII, 124.

[4] *Ibid.*, p. 128.

as a recipe, and little would be gained by separating them from the rest. It seems best, then, not to classify, but to take up the twelve charms in order, pointing out their significant features.[1]

The most elaborate of the metrical charms is undoubtedly CHARM 1 (For Unfruitful Land), with its four separate incantations (ll. 26–38, 51–66, 69–71, 75–80) and its detailed ceremonial instructions. According to Skemp,[2] ll. 3–38 are intended for the improvement of pasture land, ll. 39–82 of ploughed land. The sods and the samples of farm produce placed upon them (ll. 3ff.), together with the seeds in the later part of the charm (ll. 45ff.), are symbolic of the desired fertility.

CHARM 2 (the Nine Herbs Charm), for an unspecified malady, has been much commented upon. Of the nine herbs referred to in the metrical part of the charm, seven can be identified with some certainty.[3] The Anglo-Saxon names *mucgwyrt*, l. 1, *wegbrade*, l. 7, *mægðe*, l. 23, *æppel*, l. 34, and *finul*, l. 36, are the same as the modern "mugwort," "waybread" (or plantain), "mayweed" (or camomile, formerly also called "maythe-weed"), "apple," and "fennel." The word *fille*, l. 36, corresponds to the modern "chervil" (which is derived from the fuller Anglo-Saxon form *cerfille*), and *attorlaðe*, l. 21, is the modern "betony." But *stune*, l. 14, and *wergulu*, l. 27, have given considerable difficulty.[4] In the prose recipe at the end of the charm (ll. 64–73),[5] the nine herbs are called *mugcwyrt, wegbrade, lombescyrse, attorlaðe, mageðe, netele, wudusuræppel, fille*, and *finul*. Here *wudusuræppel* ("crab-apple"?) must correspond to

---

[1] It is perhaps unnecessary to point out that little can be said concerning the date of these charms. Many of them undoubtedly contain elements derived from the earliest period of Anglo-Saxon culture, but linguistic and metrical evidence suggest that they were not set down in written form until quite late. CHARM 11 has an early ending in *Biddu*, l. 26, but elsewhere in this charm we find inflectional forms characteristic of the late Anglo-Saxon period.

[2] *Modern Language Review* VI, 264.

[3] There is no standard work on Anglo-Saxon plant names. The best available sources of information are Cockayne, *Leechdoms* III, 309–350, and Hoops, *Über die altenglischen Pflanzennamen*.

[4] Cockayne reads *stime* in l. 14, and so Grendon, but no such word is found elsewhere, and the MS. reading is clearly *stune*; see the note on this line, p. 209, below.

[5] Wülker omits this prose recipe, but it evidently belongs with what precedes; in l. 70, the word *galdor* must refer to the metrical part of the charm.

the simple *æppel* in l. 34, while *lombescyrse* (for *lombescærse*, "lamb's cress") and *netele*, "nettle," seem to correspond to *stune* and *wergulu*. Cockayne[1] identified *wergulu* with the crab-apple, but this can hardly be right, since the apple is mentioned below. Hoops[2] more plausibly translates *wergulu* as "nettle." He suggests further that *stune* and *wergulu* are older names for *lombescyrse* and *netele*.[3] Magoun[4] would relate *stune* to the verb (*wið*)*stunian*, ll. 15–16, and would interpret it as "the fighting herb"; similarly, he would take *stiðe*, l. 16, as meaning "the stiff, strong herb," both words then referring to a single plant (the nettle?), the name of which is not given in the text. This argument from the etymology of the word suggests that *stune* is the nettle; the argument from the order of the herbs favors identifying the nettle with *wergulu*. In either case, the other herb mentioned probably means "lamb's cress."

It is apparent that, from l. 30 on, the text of CHARM 2 is rather confused, and Holthausen[5] rearranges ll. 30–63 in the following order: ll. 41–44, 36–40, 30–35, 45–63. Such an arrangement is in many respects more satisfactory than the one in the manuscript, but that it represents the intention of the Anglo-Saxon compiler may easily be doubted.

The charm "Against a Dwarf" (CHARM 3) is perhaps, as Grendon and Skemp suggest, a remedy for some convulsive disease, or perhaps, as Magoun says, a cure for sleeplessness caused by fever.[6] If we read *spiderwiht* in l. 9*b*, two different explanations of the "spider" are possible. According to Grendon, the spider (*hit*, l. 7) is hung about the neck of the invalid and then rides away, using the "dwarf-demon" as his horse. Skemp prefers to identify the

---

[1] *Leechdoms* III, 35, 348. So also Holthausen, *Englische Studien* LXIX, 180ff., who reads *wergula* in his text.

[2] *Über die altenglischen Pflanzennamen*, p. 59. Bradley, *Archiv* CXIII, 144, also favors "nettle" as the meaning of *wergulu*.

[3] This suggestion is repeated by Grendon, *Journal of American Folk-Lore* XXII, 226, who similarly takes *una*, l. 3, as a by-name of *mucgwyrt*.

[4] *Archiv* CLXXI, 29.

[5] In his text of the charm, *Englische Studien* LXIX, 180ff.

[6] Grendon, *Journal of American Folk-Lore* XXII, 215–216; Skemp, *Modern Language Review* VI, 293–294; Magoun, *Archiv* CLXXI, 20. Grendon points out that the Seven Sleepers are invoked in several prose charms against fever. A fever is also suggested by l. 12*b*.

spiderwiht with the dwarf himself, who in the form of a spider has crept into the victim's body. Grattan, who believes that the charm is a remedy for the nightmare,[1] disposes of the spider entirely by means of a textual emendation.[2] But even if the spider is explained, the relationship of this passage to ll. 13–17, which introduce a new character, is far from clear. In l. 13, the emendation to *dweores sweostar* ("the sister of the dwarf")[3] seems to give the most probable reading; Grattan's theory that we have here the female divinity Eastre (*Eares sweostar*, the goddess of the dawn, who disperses the terrors of the night)[4] introduces a new and unwarranted element into the text.

The metrical portion of CHARM 4 (For a Sudden Stitch) falls logically into two parts: (1) ll. 3–17, an account of an attack by witches (*ða mihtigan wif*), much in the style of epic narrative, but punctuated by the repetition of the exorcismal formula, *Ut, lytel spere*, etc.; (2) ll. 18–28, quite different in style and form and addressed to the patient.

Several commentators have suggested that the two parts of the charm are of different origin. According to Koegel,[5] ll. 20–26 were written at a later time as a substitute for ll. 3–17; according to Horn[6] (who would end the original poem at l. 17), ll. 18–26 were intended as an addition to ll. 3–17 rather than as a substitute for them. But it seems equally possible that the entire charm was written at once, in spite of the differences between the two parts; ll. 3–17 would then be a description of the attack, ll. 18–24 an encouragement or consolation to the victim, and ll. 25–28 the cure.[7]

[1] *Modern Language Review* XXII, 5–6.

[2] See the note on this line, p. 211, below.

[3] Perhaps related to the activity of the *mædenman* in l. 7; see Binz, *Anglia*, Beiblatt XXVII, 163.

[4] An objection to Grattan's interpretation of this text as a "nightmare charm" is found in the fact that in a prose charm against a dwarf (numbered E11 by Grendon), the remedy may be applied either in the daytime or at night.

[5] *Geschichte der deutschen Litteratur bis zum Ausgange des Mittelalters* I, Part 1, p. 93.

[6] *Probleme der englischen Sprache und Kultur*, p. 91.

[7] This explanation is similar to the one advanced by Skemp, *Modern Language Review* VI, 289, who classes this text as a "naming" charm; by defining the malady the exorcist acquires power over it.

Of the three charms for loss or theft of cattle, CHARM 5 and CHARM 10 represent two separate versions of the same original, CHARM 5 being somewhat superior textually.[1] In CHARM 9, as Grendon points out,[2] the metrical incantation, ll. 6–19, is much more heathen in tone than the prose introduction. If we assume separate origins for these two parts, it is likely that l. 6 (*Garmund, godes ðegen*) belongs with the prose introduction rather than with the metrical part of the charm. The identity of Garmund is naturally obscure, and Magoun may be right in suggesting that the alliteration here is quite fortuitous and that the name of any priest could be inserted at this point.[3]

CHARM 6 (For Delayed Birth) consists of a series of five incantatory formulas in verse (ll. 4–6, 9–11, 15, 19–20, 26–28), all only moderately intelligible, and each accompanied by the proper ceremonial directions. The repetition of *Se wifman*, etc. (ll. 1, 16, 21), suggests that we have here three originally separate texts (ll. 1–15, 16–20, 21–31) which were combined into one by the scribe of the Harley manuscript.[4]

Just what the "water-elf disease" may be, for which CHARM 7 is intended, is not clear, and the description of the tearful invalid in ll. 1–2 does not seem quite in harmony with the suggestion of a specific wound in ll. 8–12a.[5] There are two alliterative formulas, neither of which is metrically regular. Lines 8–13 seem intended for recitation over the herbs while the remedy is being compounded; the short formula in ll. 14–15 is presumably to be recited over the wound while the remedy is being applied.

---

[1] Especially in l. 10, where *Charm* 10 omits the words *Crux Christi ab aquilone reducað*. On the readings in l. 3 of the two charms, see note on *Charm* 5,3, on p. 213, below.

[2] *Journal of American Folk-Lore* XXII, 223.

[3] *Archiv* CLXXI, 26. The name Garmund is not found very frequently in Anglo-Saxon; besides the father of the continental Offa, mentioned in BEOWULF 1962, and a reference to a "Garmundi via" near Durham, only three men by this name are listed by Searle, *Onomasticon Anglo-Saxonicum*, p. 254.

[4] The word *Se* has a large capital in each of these places, and there are no other large capitals. The editors, however, treat the text as a single charm rather than as three.

[5] Magoun, *Archiv* CLXXI, 29, suggests that the prose introduction, ll. 1–7, did not originally belong with what follows.

CHARM 8 (For a Swarm of Bees) was explained by Grendon as a charm "to stop bees from swarming."[1] But the admonition to the bees (*sigewif*) in ll. 9–10, together with the words *þonne hi swirman* in l. 7, shows that the charm is for use after the bees have swarmed, to make them stay near the hive and not fly away to the woods.[2] The much-discussed phrase, *wið þa micelan mannes tungan*, l. 6, probably refers to the spell which another man might make to entice the bees away from the desired place of swarming.[3] As Grendon has pointed out,[4] this charm is similar in places to the Old High German *Lorscher Bienensegen*, preserved in a ninth-century manuscript.[5]

CHARM 11 (A Journey Charm) is almost meaningless in several places (especially in the last ten lines), but the general intention of this text—"a kind of lorica," as Magoun calls it[6]—is clear. As protectors of his journey the traveler invokes the Holy Trinity (ll. 10–12), the four evangelists (ll. 26–29), the angels (ll. 19–20), and a number of Old and New Testament worthies (ll. 13–18). Such invocations were quite common in the early Middle Ages, when travel was exceedingly dangerous, and Grendon cites several similar texts from Old High German literature.[7]

CHARM 12 (Against a Wen), in spite of the lateness of its lan-

---

[1] See *Journal of American Folk-Lore* XXII, 169, note 1.

[2] Grendon's translation of *sigewif* as "valkyries" goes back to the earlier commentators, who did not realize that ll. 1–6 and ll. 7–12 were parts of the same charm.

[3] See Skemp, *Modern Language Review* VI, 264; and for the various interpretations of l. 6, see the note on this line, p. 214, below.

[4] *Journal of American Folk-Lore* XXII, 216–217.

[5] Edited by K. Müllenhoff and W. Scherer, *Denkmäler deutscher Poesie und Prosa aus dem VIII.–XII. Jahrhundert* (3d ed., Berlin, 1892) I, 34–35; it is also available in W. Braune, *Althochdeutsches Lesebuch* (8th ed., Halle, 1927) p. 88. Note especially the words *sizi, sizi, bina . . . zi holce ni flûc dû*, in the Old High German text.

[6] *Archiv* CLXXI, 27. The best known example of the lorica in Latin is the Lorica of Gildas, edited with an Anglo-Saxon gloss by Leonhardi, *Kleinere angelsächsische Denkmäler* I, 175ff.

[7] *Journal of American Folk-Lore* XXII, 221. The most elaborate of these German parallels is the *Tobiassegen*, printed by Müllenhoff and Scherer, *Denkmäler* I, 183–192.

guage,[1] is tolerably regular metrically. It lacks the ceremonial directions which accompany the other metrical charm remedies (CHARMS 3, 4, 6, and 7), but in its structure and content it obviously belongs in a single category with them. The six similes in ll. 8–13 are striking; Grendon[2] compares them with the similes in CHARM 9, 16-17 and in CHARM 7,13.

[1] As we have seen (p. cxxxii, above), the extant copy was written down in the late eleventh century. Among the early Middle English characteristics in this text are: (1) inorganic final -e, in *wenne*, l. 1, *wenchichenne*, l. 1, and probably in *scerne*, l. 9; (2) reduction of unstressed vowels, in *timbrien*, l. 2, *habben*, l. 2, and *hauest*, l. 4; (3) the spelling of -*chichenne*, l. 1, and *legge*, l. 5. The fact that in l. 3 the MS. *nort* is corrected to *north* rather than to *norð* is also an evidence of late date.

[2] *Journal of American Folk-Lore* XXII, 120.

ACCENT MARKS IN THE MANUSCRIPTS

WALDERE

dóm I,10, láf II,18, gód II,19 (3 accents).[1]

THE BATTLE OF MALDON

á hof 130, ún weaxen 152, ǽr 290, gód 315 (4 accents).

THE POEMS OF THE ANGLO-SAXON CHRONICLE

THE BATTLE OF BRUNANBURH. MS. A: éac 2, tír 3, écgum 4, hámas 10, sécgas 13, úp 13, morgen tíd 14, éac 19, wíges 20, fórð 20, ón 29, éac 30, ón 36, éac 37, hár 39, ón 41, ón 43, ón 49, ón 51, ón 54, guð hafóc 64, ón 65, ón 66, écgum 68, béc 68 (25 accents).

MS. B: éac 2, tír 3, geslógan 4, bórdweall 5, láfum 6, hórd 10, hámas 10, morgen tíd 14, unrím 31, gebǽded 33, út 35, gewát 35, flód 36, éac 37, fróda 37, cóm 37, constantínus 38, hár 39, þórfte 39, gár mittinge 50, gemótes 50, láf 54, íraland 56, æwisc móde 56, salowig pádan 61, hwít 63, brúcan 63, máre 65, béc 68 (29 accents).

MS. C: tír 3, sáh 17, tó 17, únrím 31, þǽr 32, ón 35, flót 35, út 35, géwat 35, génerode 36, þǽr 37, cóm 37, hár 39, ánlaf 46, þý 46, þá 57, hrá 60, ǽses 63, þǽs 68, ús 68, béc 68, árhwáte 73 (24 accents).

MS. D: éac 2, úp 13, morgen tíd 14, éac 19, éar gebland 26, éac 30, únrim 31, flótan 32, cnéar 35, éac 37, hylde rínc 39, anláf 46, gár mittinge 50, áfaran 52, láf 54, cuð heafóc 64, gitá 66, béc 68, úp 70 (19 accents).

THE CAPTURE OF THE FIVE BOROUGHS. MS. A: éa 4, éac 7, ón 10 (3 accents).

MS. B: dǽdfruma 3, dór 3, éa 4, fífe 5, snotingahám 7, gebǽded 9, hléo 12 (7 accents).

MS. C: þéoden 1, swá 3, éa 4, deorabý 8, hí 11 (5 accents).

MS. D: dór 3, snotinga hám 7, éac 7 (3 accents).

[1] The acute accent mark on *fró* (= *from*) I,30, must have been written in error for the usual horizontal mark of abbreviation.

THE CORONATION OF EDGAR. MS. A: dǽg 8, tó 13, á urnen 16 (3 accents).

MS. B: rímes 11, gebýrd tíde 12, láfe 13, fréan 15, aúrnen 16 (6 accents).

MS. C: baþán[1] 5, þá 10, gebýrdtíde 12, fréan 15, þúsend 16, áurnen 16 (7 accents).

THE DEATH OF EDGAR. MS. A: líf 4, ǽr 6, rím cræfte 7, gewát 8, lífe 9, tó 11, únweaxen 11, ǽr 13, ge wát 14, lóf 17, tó dræfed 18, ón 21, tó bræc 23, ádræfed 24, wís 27, cométa 32 (16 accents).

MS. B: wáce 3, forlét 3, rím cræfte 7, gewát 8, eadgár 9, lífe 9, cyneríce 11, tírfæst 13, ǽr 13, gewát 14, góda 14, wíde 17, móde 21, deormód 24, Oslác 25, wís 27, wíde 31, cométa 32, wíse 33, wíde 34, hrúsan 35 (21 accents).

MS. C: ǽr 6, rím cræfte 7, gewát 8, lífe 9, cyne ríce 11, tír fæst 13, ǽr 13, gewát 14, þá 16, móde 21, tobrǽc 23, þá 24, wíde 31, cométa 32, wíse 33, wíde 34, hrúsan 35 (17 accents).

THE DEATH OF ALFRED. MS. C: Hér 1, sǽt 3, éc 3, þá 6, todráf 7, hí 8, hí 14, þé 15 (8 accents).

MS. D: fordráf 7, dǽd 11, be hét 16 (3 accents).

THE DEATH OF EDWARD. MS. C: tíd 8, á 15, ǽr 16, ofer cóm 18, becóm 22, gód 23, tíd 31 (7 accents).

MS. D: hælo tíd[2] 8, hẹ́leða 8, á 15, ǽr 16, gód 23, bé com 25, sýnum 32, agǽlde 33 (8 accents).

SOLOMON AND SATURN

MS. A: órganes 33, ówiht 33, ána 35, torhte (?)[3] 38, ón | æleð 42, ón | hætan 43, ófer 48, ís 53, órgan 53, óf 55, ásceadan 56, óf 68, tó 69, ór ðancas 72, áhieðeð 73, ón 83, ón 88, á 91, ón 92, á 93a, óf slihð 93b, á 96, ón 98, nó 101, gód 102, wá 104, óf 109, ón 114, átole 129, ón 130, ón gieldað 132, ón 135, cempán 139, ón 139,

---

[1] With *n* added above the line.
[2] With *lo* added above the line.
[3] Apparently an accent over *t*.

órdum 142, bán 144, mán fulra 148, ón foð 151, líc 152, feld góngende 154, ón 155, ón 161, bóc stafas 162, út 164, ón 177, óf 177, ǽr 178, hís 178, férhð 178, áhlog 178, ón 179, mén 180, gewesán 181, wisdóm 181, ánsæceð 182, breost tóga 184, bóca 184, corsías 186, flét 192, nó 203, Wát 204, ón 204, wendel sǽ 204, seccán 205, gilpán 206, fór cumen 207, wát 207, fréond 214, ón 215, óf slog 215, ón 216, óf feoll 216, ón wǽcned 221, ón 225, ón 230, tungán 231, órda 232, órda 233, ánra 234, bringán 234, blicán 236, wín | ród 236, lixán 236, sindón 238, óf 242, ón byregeð 243, bóca 243, ón sendað 245, án 247, ón 247, mónn 252, íc 253, án 255, ón 255, ón 259, ón 262, ón 264, fét 265, ǽr 273, dóm dæges 273, ón 274, ǽr ðon 275, ána 275, híne 276, ófer 276, féor | buende 280, ffuma[1] 281, uása 281, mórtis 281, áweceð 284, ón 287, ðusend ge rímes 291, ón 292, rá | cen teage 294, á breoteð 296, á | styreð 297, ón 297, á filleð 298, ón 298, ófer | wigeð 299, ófer bideð 300, ófer | stigeð 300, stýle 300, ábiteð 301, íren 301, óme 301, déð 301, swá 301, ác 302, fúll 305, ófer bricgeð 306, ón 310, tó 311, ón 315, máne 318, ón 320, flowán 323, mót 323, ófer 324, áwa 324, máne 327, ón 328, lǽnan 328, bróðor 330, ábelgan 330, rapás 333, ác 336, ón 337, dómes 337, óf 338, óf 339, ác 340, óft 349, ór mod 351, á 351, ón medlan 353, áldor 357, scéal 357, ánra 357, ón lutan 358, ón liðigan 358, áre 361, ádreogan 363, ác 364, góde 364, áne 365, ácende 365, gelíc 366, ón 367, ón 370, salomón 371, óft 374, tó 374, áfedeð 374, áfran 377, sórg full | ne 380, ác 386, ón 386, fáran 386, án 387, ón 388, ón 390, ón 392, ón 395, né 398, mót 399, ón 415, ón 416, fýr 417a, ón 417a, ón 417b, tó 418, óft 429, áðreoteð 430, ǽr 430, tó 431, wát 431, ón 432, tó brǽddón 433, ón 433, wís | sefa 440, tó 442, brucán 443, ác 448, tó hwan 448, áðreotan 449, ófer modan 452, ón gan 453, ón 455, [.]éoden 457, óf 458, ón 460, ón fand 462, á weorp 464, óf 464, tó draf 464, á 466, wíc 469, wíntre 469, átol 471, áge 478, ábǽde 479, á banne 481, hís 492, ón 499, ón 500, ón 502, ón 503, wég 503, tó 504, íc 505, áðringan 505, tó middes 506 (236 accents).

MS. B: dóm | dæge 26, írenum 28, ówiht 33, ána 35, fýr 42, on hǽtan 43, fýra 47, gléda 48, fús 58, stána 76 (10 accents).

[1] Accent over r.

Menologium

éce 3, þá 5, ús 7, tír eadige 13, hér 15, túne 16, ǽ gleawe 19, tó 22, aféred 23, óf 24, wícum 24, sé 24, tún 28, wícum 29, hríme 35, hé | riað 42, rím cræftige 44, ús 60, tó 62, þá 63, hé 65, áá 65, ús 72, ben tííd 75, tún 78, lóf 93, hé 98, hér 98, ǽr 102, nú 104, tíída 107, tíd 121, þá 122, ǽr 126, hí[1] 128, un rím 128, ge sýnra 129, líf 146, tíid 154, tún 183, hí 192, úp weg 193, tún 195, ǽr 200, úp engla 210, sǽ grund 212, fús 218, tó 219b (51 accents).

Maxims II

ǽr 12, án haga 19, gár 22, éa 30, tír fæstra 32, rúm 37, hí 45, gód 50, á 54, ǽr 56 (10 accents).

The Judgment Day II

ǽnlicū 7, un hýrlican 11, on héfde 11, mínū 16, éce 17, éac 17, sýnful 29, ge ópeniað 37, mán 37, écū 37, abǽred 41, récene 48, ge scéop 53, þé 65, sǽ 102, embútan 114, Sítt 117, under fó 121, gelíce 144, fýr 147, sýn scýldigra 169, óga 172, wóp 173, nú 176, ondrǽd 182, éagan 194, án syn 203, ínne 205, áht 205, geméted 205, líg 206, fúl 206, nósan 207, hópa 221, geféan 233, gewítað[2] 233, lífe 244, sár 256, éce 272, maría 295, rícu 296, écan 299 (43 accents).

Exhortation to Christian Living

ríce 2, sóð fæstan 14, gýt 20, éce 29, lác 33, ondrǽt 39, héofena 50, hǽl 50, on gýte 58, éþel 60, gedón 61, á 66, líf 68, þú 69a, síðe 74, gesécan 74, glǽdlice 74, úplican 75, éþelríces 75, dǽges 76, drúncen 76, úpplican 78, éard wic 78, éorðan 79, ǽr 79 (26 accents).

Summons to Prayer

Sé 15, onsénded 15, tó 22 (3 accents).

The Lord's Prayer II

éart 1, áre 3, ýþost 3, híg 4, ǽr 4, nú 6, alýse 7, abúgað 10, stǽfne 11, úre 14, héah 18, alýf 28, gehýred 32, éce 36, éce 41, gehýred 46,

[1] With i altered to y.
[2] With w corrected from g.

INTRODUCTION cxliii

þánciað 49, éce 52, á 52, týr eadig 56, héofon rice 60, lǽce 62, réðe
63, hláford 63, éce 74, gebíg 77, þín 78, be tǽcan 82, ús 84*a*, ús
84*b*, úre 85, dóme 85, bán 88, flǽsce 88, béoð 92, búta 92, dýrnan
93, wát 93, áre 98, wé 99, lífe 99, hwíle 100, beswícan 104, brǽcon
109, wé 109, áre 110, héan lice 111, énde dæge 112, éce 118, ánre
119, wé 122, á 123 (52 accents).

THE GLORIA I

MS. J: asýndrod 10, bóca 12, láreow 12, éce 17, éce 22, gód 22,
fǽgere 24, wéorc 24, súnnan dæg 25, sýlf 25, halgó dest 25, gemǽrso-
dest 26, mánegum 26, hélpe 26, héahan 27, dæg 27, fréoðiaþ 27,
cúnnon 28, þéawas 28, héort lufan 29, héhstan 29, gebód 29,
sýmble 31, héo 33, cýðaþ 33, wíde 33, éalle 34, wóruld 34, éce 34,
stándeþ 34, gódes 35, hánd gewéorc 35, héte 35, dréa mas 36, béc
37, wúnað 41, wúldre 42, héah þrýnnesse 43, wlítige 44, énglas 44,
écan 48, mán 54 (44 accents).

MS. C: dóm 4, éart 8, frófre 15, éce 17, ána 17, éce 22, þéawas 28,
híg 33, héte 35, þánc 39, éce 40, þáncung 45, écan 48, ge sýne 50
(14 accents).

THE LORD'S PRAYER III

þín 4, á 13, wóm dǽde 25, écan 26, wíte 27, wéan 27, ús 31, éac 31
(9 accents).

THE CREED

écne 4, gelýfe 5, éart 5, fréa 5, sé 22, frófre 22, fóld buendum 22,
ríces 26, dóma 26, déora 27, fréa 27, þrówade 27, áras 34, fréa 34,
écne 42, þréo 44, gódas 44, án 45, gerýnū 46, síde 47, tíd 56, éce 57,
líf 57 (23 accents).

FRAGMENTS OF PSALMS

mín 5,1,1, gehýr 5,1,2, éce 5,1,2, éac 5,1,5, éce 5,1,5, éce 5,2,1,
gehýr 5,2,2, wát 5,3,2, dǽdum 19,9,1, éac 19,9,2, gehýr 19,9,2,
éac 24,3,2, wíslice 24,5,3, éac 27,10,2, wíge 34,3,2, ánsyne 50,10,1,
á 50,10,1, gód 50,11,2, geníwa 50,11,2, awýrp 50,12,1, wéroda
50,13,3, béaluwe 58,2,3, néode 60,6,2, gedéfe 60,6,4, Gehýr 64,6,1,
sǽ 64,6,3, ús 84,4,2, gebéd 87,13,3, swǽsum 89,18,1, éce 89,18,2,

geréce 89,18,3, móde 89,18,3, gehýr 101,1,2, mándædum 102,3,1, líf 102,4,1, góde 102,4,2, lá 118,176,3, tídum (?) 121,7,2, éce 139,1,2 (39 accents).

THE KENTISH HYMN

án 14, éce 14, mán scilde 23, ón 29, gód fæder 31, ón 40a (6 accents).

PSALM 50

mán 10, ánsende 16, wómdeda 19, doóm 19, hét 21, gód 33, ón 40, ón cwawe 42, án 52, cýnn 59, án 67, óntendes 71, bán 81, ǽr 82, nú 83, ánsione 85, á 103, wán hogan 105, gód 108, múð 117, dún 132, lác 136, ón 138, þín 138, máncynnes 140, ón 142b, móte 145, gód 150, ón 153, ús 154, gód 154, ús 156 (32 accents).

THE GLORIA II
gemǽne 2 (1 accent).

A PRAYER

MS. J: á 18, tír ea dig 22, áre 24, úp 29, wát 52, á 79 (6 accents).

MS. L: geáre 2, síde 7, wíde 7, geswíce 15 (4 accents).

THE SEASONS FOR FASTING

ús 45, árwesan 77, ín 90, ḡwát 144, nán uht 157, íu 176, ælmesdǽde 191, morgen týd 220 (8 accents).

LATIN-ENGLISH PROVERBS
MS. R: hát 3, alápað 4 (2 accents).

CÆDMON'S HYMN
MS. T: éce 8 (1 accent).

MS. O: oórd[1] 4 (1 accent).

MS. Ca: ge scóp 5 (1 accent).

MS. B: éce 4, éce 8 (2 accents).

MS. H: éce 8 (1 accent).

[1] With d added above the line.

The Metrical Preface to the Pastoral Care

MS. H: gindwód 6, má 13 (2 accents).

MS. D: águstinus 1, sǽ 2, geond wód 6, róm wara 9, mín 11, á wende 12, má 13 (7 accents).

The Metrical Epilogue to the Pastoral Care

MS. H: ón 5, béc 11, ón 11, ón 15, ón 16 (5 accents).

MS. D: béc 11, mód 12, ún nyt 15, út 15, díop 17, hlúd 20, undíop 20, nú 22 (8 accents).

The Metrical Epilogue to MS. 41, Corpus Christi College, Cambridge

ríces 2, bóc 2, befó 3, fíra 3, bóc 5, áwrat 5, móte 6, geúnne 8, móte 9 (9 accents).

The Metrical Charms

Charm 1: bót 1, ge dón 2, béaman 8, dǽl 8, mǽl 20, onlút 24, úpheofon 29, áre 37, stór 48, sápan 49, wíf 65, hláf 73 (12 accents).

Charm 3: singán 5 (1 accent).

Charm 7: Gíf 1, ófgeot 6, ác 12, hím 12, món 15, ón 15 (6 accents).

Charm 9: áge 1, ead elénan 2 (2 accents).

Charm 10: mǽre 5, á 9 (2 accents).

Charm 11: síce 2, áre 20, scír ecg 29, láre 32, móte 38 (5 accents).

Charm 12: wenchichénne[1] 1, nihgán 3, á 7, alswǽ 9, scḗsne 9, awagḗ 9, alswǽ 10, linsétcorn 11 (8 accents).

[1] With the second h added above the line.

BIBLIOGRAPHY

BIBLIOGRAPHY

ABBREVIATIONS

Anderson and Williams, *Handbook*. M. Anderson and B. C. Williams, *Old English Handbook* (Boston, 1935).

Bouterwek, *Cædmon*. K. W. Bouterwek, *Cædmon's des Angelsachsen biblische Dichtungen* (Vol. I, Gütersloh, 1854; Vol. II, Elberfeld, 1851).

Bright, *Reader*. J. W. Bright, *An Anglo-Saxon Reader* (New York, 1891; revised ed. by J. R. Hulbert, 1935).

Conybeare, *Illustrations*. J. J. Conybeare, *Illustrations of Anglo-Saxon Poetry* (London, 1826).

Cook and Tinker, *ST*. A. S. Cook and C. B. Tinker, *Select Translations from Old English Poetry* (Boston, 1902).

Dickins, *RHP*. B. Dickins, *Runic and Heroic Poems of the Old Teutonic Peoples* (Cambridge, 1915).

Ettmüller, *Scopas*. L. Ettmüller, *Engla and Seaxna Scopas and Boceras* (Quedlinburg and Leipzig, 1850).

Faust and Thompson, *OEP*. C. Faust and S. Thompson, *Old English Poems, Translated into the Original Meter* (Chicago, 1918).

Flom, *Reader*. G. T. Flom, *Introductory Old English Grammar and Reader* (Boston, 1930).

Gordon, *ASP*. R. K. Gordon, *Anglo-Saxon Poetry* (London and Toronto, 1926).

Grein, *Bibliothek*. C. W. M. Grein, *Bibliothek der angelsächsischen Poesie* (2 vols., Göttingen, 1857–1858).

Hickes, *Thesaurus*. *Linguarum vett. septentrionalium thesaurus grammatico-criticus et archæologicus* (Oxford, 1705).

Klipstein, *Analecta*. L. F. Klipstein, *Analecta Anglo-Saxonica* (2 vols., New York, 1849).

Kluge, *Lesebuch*. F. Kluge, *Angelsächsisches Lesebuch* (Halle, 1888; 2d ed., 1897; 3d ed., 1902; 4th ed., 1915).

Krapp and Kennedy, *Reader.* G. P. Krapp and A. G. Kennedy, *An Anglo-Saxon Reader* (New York, 1929).

MacLean, *Reader.* G. E. MacLean, *An Old and Middle English Reader* (New York, 1893).

Rieger, *Lesebuch.* M. Rieger, *Alt- und angelsächsisches Lesebuch* (Giessen, 1861).

Schücking, *Dichterbuch.* L. L. Schücking, *Kleines angelsächsisches Dichterbuch* (Cöthen, 1919).

Sedgefield, *Verse-Book.* W. J. Sedgefield, *An Anglo-Saxon Verse-Book* (Manchester, 1922).

Spaeth, *OEP.* J. D. Spaeth, *Old English Poetry* (Princeton, 1921).

Sweet, *OET.* H. Sweet, *The Oldest English Texts* (London, 1885).

Sweet, *Reader.* H. Sweet, *An Anglo-Saxon Reader* (Oxford, 1876; 4th ed., 1884; 7th ed., 1894; 9th ed., revised by C. T. Onions, 1922).

Wülker, *Bibliothek.* R. P. Wül(c)ker, *Bibliothek der angelsächsischen Poesie* (Vol. I, Kassel, 1883; Vol. II, Leipzig, 1894; Vol. III, Leipzig, 1898).

Wülker, *KAD.* R. P. Wülcker, *Kleinere angelsächsische Dichtungen* (Halle, 1882).

Wyatt, *Reader.* A. J. Wyatt, *An Anglo-Saxon Reader* (Cambridge, 1919).

Zupitza and Schipper, *Übungsbuch.* J. Zupitza and J. Schipper, *Alt- und mittelenglisches Übungsbuch* (11th ed., Vienna and Leipzig, 1915).

Archiv. Archiv für das Studium der neueren Sprachen und Literaturen.

Beitr. Beiträge zur Geschichte der deutschen Sprache und Literatur.

Eng. Stud. Englische Studien.

JEGPh. Journal of English and Germanic Philology.

MLN. Modern Language Notes.

MLRev. Modern Language Review.

PMLA. Publications of the Modern Language Association of America.

ZfdA. Zeitschrift für deutsches Altertum.

ZfdPh. Zeitschrift für deutsche Philologie.

The items in the bibliographies below are arranged chronologically under each heading. Where there are two or more editions of a work, the page references are to the last edition cited.

THE BATTLE OF FINNSBURH

EDITIONS. Hickes, *Thesaurus*, Part 1, pp. 192–193; N. F. S.
Grundtvig, *Bjowulfs Drape* (Copenhagen, 1820), pp. xl–xlv;
Conybeare, *Illustrations*, pp. 173–182; Klipstein, *Analecta* II,
426–427; Ettmüller, *Scopas*, pp. 130–131; Grein, *Bibliothek* I,
341–343; Rieger, *Lesebuch*, pp. 61–63; Wülker, *KAD.*, pp. 6–7;
Wülker, *Bibliothek* I, 14–17; H. Möller, *Das altenglische Volksepos*
II (Kiel, 1883), vii–ix (in stanzaic form); Kluge, *Lesebuch* (3d ed.),
pp. 127–128; M. Trautmann, *Finn und Hildebrand* (Bonner
Beiträge zur Anglistik, Vol. VII, Bonn, 1903), pp. 36–57; Dickins,
RHP., pp. 64–69; W. S. Mackie, "The Fight at Finnsburg,"
JEGPh. XVI (1917), 250–273; Schücking, *Dichterbuch*, pp. 35–38;
Sedgefield, *Verse-Book*, pp. 25–27; H. Naumann, *Frühgermanisches
Dichterbuch* (Berlin, 1931), pp. 70–72; W. A. Craigie, *Specimens of
Anglo-Saxon Poetry* III (Edinburgh, 1931), 10–11.

The text of the Battle of Finnsburh is also included in the editions of Beowulf by J. M. Kemble (London, 1833; 2d ed., 2 vols.,
1835–1837); F. Schaldemose (Copenhagen, 1847; 2d ed., 1851);
B. Thorpe (Oxford, 1855; 2d ed., 1875; 3d ed., 1889); N. F. S.
Grundtvig (Copenhagen, 1861); M. Heyne (Paderborn, 1863;
5th ed., by A. Socin, 1888; 8th ed., by L. L. Schücking, 1908; 14th
ed., 1931); C. W. M. Grein (Cassel and Göttingen, 1867); J. A.
Harrison and R. Sharp (Boston, 1883); A. J. Wyatt (Cambridge,
1894; 2d ed., 1898); M. Trautmann (Bonner Beiträge zur Anglistik,
Vol. XVI, Bonn, 1904); F. Holthausen (2 vols., Heidelberg, 1905–
1906; Vol. I, 7th ed., 1938; Vol. II, 5th ed., 1929); W. J. Sedgefield
(Manchester, 1910; 2d ed., 1913; 3d ed., 1935); H. Pierquin (Paris,
1912); A. J. Wyatt and R. W. Chambers (Cambridge, 1914; 2d ed.,
1920); F. Klaeber (Boston, 1922; 2d ed., 1928; 3d ed., 1936).

TRANSLATIONS. In English, by Conybeare, *Illustrations*, pp.
173–182 (also in Latin); F. B. Gummere, *The Oldest English Epic*
(New York, 1909), pp. 159–163; Dickins, *RHP.*, pp. 65–69; Faust
and Thompson, *OEP.*, pp. 34–37; Gordon, *ASP.*, pp. 71–72; K.

Malone, *Ten Old English Poems* (Baltimore, 1941), pp. 25–26; in German, by M. Trautmann, *Finn und Hildebrand* (Bonn, 1903), pp. 55–57; H. Naumann, *Frühgermanentum* (Munich, 1926), pp. 59–60; A. Brandl, in *Britannica, Max Förster zum sechzigsten Geburtstage* (Leipzig, 1929), pp. 23–25; in Italian, by F. Olivero, *Traduzioni dalla poesia anglo-sassone* (Bari, 1915), pp. 127–132.

An English translation of the Battle of Finnsburh is to be found in the edition of Beowulf by B. Thorpe (Oxford, 1855; 2d ed., 1875; 3d ed., 1889), a Danish translation in the edition by F. Schaldemose (Copenhagen, 1847; 2d ed., 1851), and a French translation in the edition by H. Pierquin (Paris, 1912). Other translations are contained in the following translations of Beowulf:[1] in English, by J. M. Garnett (Boston, 1882); J. R. C. Hall (London, 1901; 2d ed., 1911); C. G. Child (Boston, 1904), pp. 89–90; W. Huyshe (London, 1907), pp. 201–205; C. S. Moncrieff (London, 1921); R. K. Gordon (London and New York, 1923); W. E. Leonard (New York and London, 1923); H. M. Ayres (Williamsport, Pa., 1933), pp. 45–46; in German, by L. Ettmüller (Zurich, 1840), pp. 36–38; K. Simrock (Stuttgart and Augsburg, 1859); P. Hoffmann (Züllichau, 1893; 2d ed., Hannover, 1900); M. Trautmann (Bonn, 1904); P. Vogt (Halle, 1905), pp. 97–99; H. Gering (Heidelberg, 1906; 2d ed., 1929); in French, by W. Thomas (Paris, 1919); in Danish, by N. F. S. Grundtvig (Copenhagen, 1820); A. Hansen (Copenhagen and Christiania, 1910); in Italian, by C. G. Grion (in Atti della Reale Accademia Lucchese, XXII, Lucca, 1883); in Dutch, by L. Simons (Ghent, 1896); in Norwegian, by H. Rytter (Oslo, 1921).

HISTORICAL AND CRITICAL COMMENT.[2] H. Möller, *Das altenglische Volksepos* I (Kiel, 1883), 46–100, 151–156; H. Schilling, "The Finnsburg-Fragment and the Finn-Episode," *MLN.* II (1887), 291–299; R. Koegel, *Geschichte der deutschen Litteratur bis zum Ausgange des Mittelalters*, Vol. I, Part 1 (Strassburg, 1894), pp.

---

[1] Page numbers are given only where the location of the translation of the Battle of Finnsburh is not readily apparent.

[2] For obvious reasons, this section of the Bibliography has been restricted to titles dealing specifically with the Fragment. Studies of the Episode and of the Finn story in general will be listed in the Bibliography for Beowulf, in Volume IV of this edition.

163–167; R. C. Boer, "Finnsage und Nibelungensage," *ZfdA*. XLVII (1903), 125–160 (notes on the Fragment, pp. 139–147); G. L. Swiggett, "Notes on the Finnsburg Fragment," *MLN*. XX (1905), 169–171; W. W. Lawrence, *PMLA*. XXX (1915), 407–414; N. S. Aurner, *An Analysis of the Interpretations of the Finnsburg Documents* (University of Iowa, Humanistic Studies, Vol. I, Part 6, Iowa City, 1917); R. Imelmann, *Forschungen zur altenglischen Poesie* (Berlin, 1920), pp. 342–381; H. F. Scott-Thomas, "The Fight at Finnsburg: Guthlaf and the Son of Guthlaf," *JEGPh*. XXX (1931), 498–505; F. Klaeber, "Garulf, Guðlafs Sohn, im Finnsburg-Fragment," *Archiv* CLXII (1932), 116–117; J. O. Beaty, "The Echo-Word in Beowulf with a Note on the Finnsburg Fragment," *PMLA*. XLIX (1934), 365–373; F. Klaeber, *Eng. Stud*. LXX (1936), 334–336 (on the problem of Guthere and Garulf); F. P. Magoun, Jr., "Zu Etzeln burc, Finns buruh und Brunan burh," *ZfdA*. LXXVII (1940), 65–66.

TEXTUAL NOTES. A. Holtzmann, *Germania* VIII (1863), 494; C. W. M. Grein, *Germania* X (1865), 422; S. Bugge, *Tidskrift for Philologi og Pædagogik* VIII (1868–1869), 304–305; H. Schilling, *MLN*. I (1886), 231–233; S. Bugge, *Beitr*. XII (1887), 20–28; M. H. Jellinek, *Beitr*. XV (1891), 428–431; F. Holthausen, *Anglia*, Beiblatt X (1900), 270; F. Klaeber, *Anglia* XXVIII (1905), 447, 456; F. Holthausen, *ZfdPh*. XXXVII (1905), 123–124; G. Binz, *ZfdPh*. XXXVII (1905), 531–532; F. Klaeber, *Archiv* CXV (1905), 181–182; M. Rieger, *ZfdA*. XLVIII (1906), 9–12; F. Klaeber, *Eng. Stud*. XXXIX (1908), 307–308; E. A. Kock, *Anglia* XLIV (1920), 97; F. Holthausen, *Anglia*, Beiblatt XXXII (1921), 82; E. A. Kock, *Anglia* XLV (1921), 126; W. J. Sedgefield, *MLRev*. XVI (1921), 59; W. S. Mackie, *MLRev*. XVII (1922), 288; S. J. Crawford, *MLRev*. XIX (1924), 105; F. Klaeber, *Anglia* L (1926), 233; F. Holthausen, *Anglia*, Beiblatt XLIII (1932), 256.

WALDERE

EDITIONS. G. Stephens, *Two Leaves of King Waldere's Lay* (Copenhagen and London, 1860); K. Müllenhoff, *ZfdA*. XII (1860),

264–273; Rieger, *Lesebuch*, pp. xviii-xxii; J. V. Scheffel and A·
Holder, *Waltharius* (Stuttgart, 1874), pp. 168–174; Wülker, *KAD.*,
pp. 8–10; H. Möller, *Das altenglische Volksepos* II (Kiel, 1883),
lxxvi-lxxviii (in stanzaic form); Wülker, *Bibliothek* I, 7–13, 401–403;
Kluge, *Lesebuch*, pp. 119–120; F. Holthausen, *Die altenglischen
Waldere-Bruchstücke* (Göteborg, 1899; with facsimiles of the MS.);
M. Trautmann, "Zur Berichtigung und Erklärung der Waldhere-
Bruchstücke," *Bonner Beiträge zur Anglistik* V (1900), 162–192;
K. Strecker, *Ekkehards Waltharius* (Berlin, 1907; not in 2d ed.,
1924), pp. 94–98; Dickins, *RHP.*, pp. 56–63; Schücking, *Dichter-
buch*, pp. 54–60; Wyatt, *Reader*, pp. 148–149; Sedgefield, *Verse-
Book*, pp. 6–8; H. Naumann, *Frühgermanisches Dichterbuch* (Berlin,
1931), pp. 77–79; F. Norman, *Waldere* (London, 1933).

The text of Waldere is also included in the editions of Beowulf
by C. W. M. Grein (Cassel and Göttingen, 1867); M. Trautmann
(Bonner Beiträge zur Anglistik, Vol. XVI, Bonn, 1904); F. Holthausen (2d ed., Heidelberg, 1909; Vol. I, 7th ed., 1938; Vol. II,
5th ed., 1929; not in 1st ed.); W. J. Sedgefield (Manchester, 1910;
2d ed., 1913; 3d ed., 1935); F. Klaeber (Boston, 1922; 2d ed.,
1928; 3d ed., 1936).

TRANSLATIONS. In English, by G. Stephens, *Two Leaves of King
Waldere's Lay* (Copenhagen and London, 1860), pp. 47–59; F. B.
Gummere, *The Oldest English Epic* (New York, 1909), pp. 164–170;
Dickins, *RHP.*, pp. 57–63; Faust and Thompson, *OEP.*, pp. 29–
33; Gordon, *ASP.*, pp. 73–74; in German, by J. V. Scheffel and A.
Holder, *Waltharius* (Stuttgart, 1874), pp. 171–173; H. Steineck,
Altenglische Dichtungen in wortgetreuer Übersetzung (Leipzig,
1898), pp. 150–151; M. Trautmann, *Bonner Beiträge zur Anglistik*
V (1900), 185–187; K. Strecker, *Ekkehards Waltharius* (Berlin,
1907), pp. 95–99; W. Eckerth, *Das Waltherlied* (2d ed., Halle,
1909), pp. 49–50; H. Naumann, *Frühgermanentum* (Munich, 1926),
p. 61 (Fragment I only).

Translations of Waldere are also to be found in the following
translations of Beowulf: in English, by C. S. Moncrieff (London,
1921); in German, by M. Trautmann (Bonn, 1904); in French, by
W. Thomas (Paris, 1919).

HISTORICAL AND CRITICAL COMMENT. H. Möller, *Das altenglische
Volksepos* I (Kiel, 1883), 156–157; J. Fischer, *Zu den Waldere-*

Fragmenten (Breslau, 1886); F. Dieter, "Die Walderefragmente und die ursprüngliche Gestalt der Walthersage," *Anglia* X (1888), 227–234; XI (1889), 159–170; R. Heinzel, *Über die Walthersage* (Sitzungsberichte der philos.-histor. Classe der k. Akademie der Wissenschaften, Vol. CXVII, Part 2, Vienna, 1889); M. D. Learned, *The Saga of Walther of Aquitaine* (Baltimore, 1892); R. Koegel, *Geschichte der deutschen Litteratur bis zum Ausgange des Mittelalters*, Vol. I, Part 1 (Strassburg, 1894), pp. 235–241; P. J. Cosijn, "De Waldere-Fragmenten," *Verslagen en Mededeelingen der k. Akademie van Wetenschappen, Afd. Letterkunde*, 3d Series, XII (1896), 56–72; C. Kraus, [Review of Koegel, Geschichte der deutschen Litteratur, Vol. I], *Zeitschrift für die österreichischen Gymnasien* XLVII (1896), 328–333; H. Althof, "Über einige Stellen im Waltharius und die angelsächsischen Waldere-Fragmente," *Bericht über das 43. Schuljahr des Realgymnasiums zu Weimar* (1899), pp. 1–11; M. Förster, [Review of Holthausen, Die altenglischen Waldere-Bruchstücke], *Eng. Stud.* XXIX (1901), 107–108; P. Fraatz, *Darstellung der syntaktischen Erscheinungen in den ags. Waldere-Bruchstücken* (Rostock, 1908); J. Seemüller, "Lieder von Walther und Hildegund," in *Mélanges Godefroid Kurth* II (Liège, 1908), 365–371; L. Simons, "Waltharius en de Walthersage: Waldere," *Leuvensche Bijdragen* XII (1914), 5–28; A. Leitzmann, *Walther und Hiltgunt bei den Angelsachsen* (Halle, 1917); G. Neckel, "Das Gedicht von Waltharius manu fortis. II.1. Waltharius und Waldere," *Germanisch-Romanische Monatsschrift* IX (1921), 209–213; A. H. Krappe, "The Legend of Walther and Hildegund," *JEGPh.* XXII (1923), 75–88; L. L. Schücking, "Waldere und Waltharius," *Eng. Stud.* LX (1925), 17–36; L. Wolff, "Zu den Waldere-Bruchstücken," *ZfdA.* LXII (1925), 81–86; F. Klaeber, "Zu den Waldere-Bruchstücken," *Anglia* LI (1927), 121–127.

TEXTUAL NOTES. S. Bugge, *Tidskrift for Philologi og Pædagogik* VIII (1868–1869), 72–78, 305–307; E. Kölbing, *Eng. Stud.* V (1882), 240–241, 292–293 (MS. collations); G. Binz, *Literaturblatt* XXI (1900), 244–245; H. Gering, *ZfdPh.* XXXIII (1901), 139–140; M. Trautmann, "Zum zweiten Waldhere-Bruchstück," *Bonner Beiträge zur Anglistik* XI (1901), 133–138; G. Binz, *ZfdPh.* XXXVI (1904), 507–508; W. Horn, *Anglia* XXIX (1906), 129–130; E. A. Kock, *Jubilee Jaunts and Jottings* (Lund, 1918), pp.

77–78; F. Holthausen, *Anglia*, Beiblatt **XXX** (1919), 4; E. A. Kock, *Anglia* **XLV** (1921), 130; F. Holthausen, *Anglia*, Beiblatt **XXXIV** (1923), 91; F. Klaeber, *Eng. Stud.* **LXX** (1936), 333–334.

THE BATTLE OF MALDON

EDITIONS. T. Hearne, *Johannis confratris et monachi Glastoniensis chronica* (Oxford, 1726), pp. 570–577; B. Thorpe, *Analecta Anglo-Saxonica* (London, 1834; 2d ed., 1846), pp. 131–141; L. C. Müller, *Collectanea Anglo-Saxonica* (Copenhagen, 1835), pp. 52–62; F. W. Ebeling, *Angelsæchsisches Lesebuch* (Leipzig, 1847), pp. 85–93; Klipstein, *Analecta* II, 261–279 (ll. 17–325 only); Ettmüller, *Scopas*, pp. 132–140; Grein, *Bibliothek* I, 343–352; Rieger, *Lesebuch*, pp. 84–94; Sweet, *Reader*, pp. 120–130; K. Körner, *Einleitung in das Studium des Angelsächsischen* II (Heilbronn, 1880), 72–88; Wülker, *KAD.*, pp. 55–65; Wülker, *Bibliothek* I, 358–373; Kluge, *Lesebuch*, pp. 122–129; Bright, *Reader*, pp. 149–159; C. L. Crow, *Maldon and Brunanburh* (Boston, 1897); W. J. Sedgefield, *The Battle of Maldon and Short Poems from the Saxon Chronicle* (Boston, 1908); Zupitza and Schipper, *Übungsbuch*, pp. 76–78 (ll. 1–73 only); Schücking, *Dichterbuch*, pp. 75–86; Wyatt, *Reader*, pp. 188–197; Sedgefield, *Verse-Book*, pp. 70–79; M. H. Turk, *An Anglo-Saxon Reader* (New York, 1927), pp. 159–169; Krapp and Kennedy, *Reader*, pp. 112–122; Flom, *Reader*, pp. 260–270; M. Ashdown, *English and Norse Documents Relating to the Reign of Ethelred the Unready* (Cambridge, 1930), pp. 22–36; Anderson and Williams, *Handbook*, pp. 256–268; E. D. Laborde, *Byrhtnoth and Maldon* (London, 1936); E. V. Gordon, *The Battle of Maldon* (London, 1937).

TRANSLATIONS. In English, by Conybeare, *Illustrations*, pp. xc-xcvi; E. H. Hickey, *Academy* **XXVII** (1885), 365–366; **XXVIII** (1885), 167–168; H. W. Lumsden, "The Song of Maldon," *Macmillan's Magazine* **LV** (1887), 371–379; J. M. Garnett, *Elene; Judith; Athelstan, or the Fight at Brunanburh; and Byrhtnoth, or the Fight at Maldon: Anglo-Saxon Poems* (Boston, 1889), pp. 60–70; W. R. Sims, *MLN.* **VII** (1892), 275–286; J. L. Hall, *Judith, Phoenix, and Other Anglo-Saxon Poems* (New York, 1902), pp.

43–55; Cook and Tinker, *ST.*, pp. 31–43; Faust and Thompson, *OEP.*, pp. 163–175; Spaeth, *OEP.*, pp. 164–174 (ll. 17–319 only); Gordon, *ASP.*, pp. 361–367; M. Ashdown, *English and Norse Documents* (Cambridge, 1930), pp. 23–37; H. J. Rowles, *The Battle and Song of Maldon* (Colchester, n.d.); K. Malone, *Ten Old English Poems* (Baltimore, 1941), pp. 30–40; in German, by K. Körner, *Einleitung in das Studium des Angelsächsischen* II (Heilbronn, 1880), 73–89; U. Zernial, *Das Lied von Byrhtnoths Fall* (Berlin, 1882), pp. 5–9; in Danish, by J. C. H. R. Steenstrup, *Danske og norske Riger paa de brittiske Øer i Danevældens Tidsalder* (Copenhagen, 1882), pp. 230–237; in Italian, by F. Olivero, *Traduzioni dalla poesia anglo-sassone* (Bari, 1915), pp. 145–159 (ll. 2–184, 230–325).

HISTORICAL AND CRITICAL COMMENT.   U. Zernial, *Das Lied von Byrhtnoths Fall* (Berlin, 1882), pp. 9–24; D. Abegg, *Zur Entwicklung der historischen Dichtung bei den Angelsachsen* (Strassburg, 1894), pp. 3–26; F. Liebermann, "Zur Geschichte Byrhtnoths, des Helden von Maldon," *Archiv* CI (1898), 15–28; F. Lange, *Darstellung der syntaktischen Erscheinungen im angelsächsischen Gedichte von Byrhtnoð's Tod* (Rostock, 1906); E. D. Laborde, "The Style of the Battle of Maldon," *MLRev.* XIX (1924), 401–417; E. D. Laborde, "The Site of the Battle of Maldon," *English Historical Review* XL (1925), 161–173; B. S. Phillpotts, "The Battle of Maldon: Some Danish Affinities," *MLRev.* XXIV (1929), 172–190; E. V. Gordon, "The Date of Æthelred's Treaty with the Vikings: Olaf Tryggvason and the Battle of Maldon," *MLRev.* XXXII (1937), 24–32; H. B. Woolf, "The Personal Names in the Battle of Maldon," *MLN.* LIII (1938), 109–112; F. Klaeber, "Zu dem altenglischen Gedicht auf die Schlacht bei Maldon," *Archiv* CLXXIX (1941), 32–33.

TEXTUAL NOTES.   C. W. M. Grein, *Germania* X (1865), 422; H. Kern, *Taalkundige Bijdragen* I (1877), 193ff.; E. Sievers, *Beitr.* X (1885), 517; O. Jespersen, *Nordisk Tidsskrift for Filologi*, 3d Series, I (1893), 126–127; F. Klaeber, *MLN.* XX (1905), 32; F. Holthausen, *Anglia*, Beiblatt XXI (1910), 13–14; F. Holthausen, *Anglia* XXXV (1911), 167; F. Holthausen, *Eng. Stud.* LI (1917),

181; O. F. Emerson, *MLRev.* XIV (1919), 205–207; E. A. Kock, *Anglia* XLIV (1920), 248; F. Holthausen, *Anglia*, Beiblatt XXXI (1920), 254; F. Holthausen, *Anglia*, Beiblatt XXXII (1921), 82; F. Klaeber, *Eng. Stud.* LV (1921), 390–395; E. A. Kock, *Anglia* XLV (1921), 123; F. Klaeber, *JEGPh.* XXIII (1924), 124; C. Brett, *MLRev.* XXII (1927), 260; F. Klaeber, *Anglia* LIII (1929), 227–229.

THE POEMS OF THE ANGLO-SAXON
CHRONICLE

EDITIONS. The Chronicle poems are printed in the editions of the Chronicle by A. Wheloc (Cambridge, 1643; omits DAlf[1] and DEdw) E. Gibson (Oxford, 1692); J. Ingram (London, 1823); H. Petrie and J. Sharp (in *Monumenta historica Britannica* I, London, 1848, 291–466); B. Thorpe (2 vols., Rolls Series, London, 1861); J. Earle (Oxford, 1865); C. Plummer (2 vols., Oxford, 1892–1899); E. Classen and F. E. Harmer (Manchester, 1926; MS. D only, and omits CEdg and DEdg); H. A. Rositzke (Bochum-Langendreer, 1940; MS. C only).

The Chronicle poems are also edited as a group by Grein, *Bibliothek* I, 352–359; Wülker, *KAD.*, pp. 66–69, 70–71, 73–75; Wülker, *Bibliothek* I, 374–388; W. J. Sedgefield, *The Battle of Maldon and Short Poems from the Saxon Chronicle* (Boston and London, 1908); W. A. Craigie, *Specimens of Anglo-Saxon Poetry* III (Edinburgh, 1931), 28–33.

Individual poems are separately edited by Hickes, *Thesaurus*, Part 1, pp. 181–182, 185–186 (Brun, DEdg); C. Michaeler, *Tabulae parallelae antiquissimarum Teutonicae linguae dialectorum* (Innsbruck, 1776), Part 3, pp. 227–240 (Brun); L. C. Müller, *Collectanea Anglo-Saxonica* (Copenhagen, 1835), pp. 49–51 (Brun); F. W. Ebeling, *Angelsæchsisches Lesebuch* (Leipzig, 1847), pp. 93–97, 110–112 (Brun, DEdg); Klipstein, *Analecta* II, 325–331 (Brun, DEdg); Ettmüller, *Scopas*, pp. 204–208 (Brun, FiveB, CEdg, DEdg); Rieger, *Lesebuch*, pp. 94–97 (Brun); K. Körner, *Einleitung in das Studium des Angelsächsischen* II (Heilbronn, 1880), 68–72

---

[1] To save space the names of the poems are here abbreviated; the forms used, in order, are Brun, FiveB, CEdg, DEdg, DAlf, and DEdw.

(Brun); Kluge, *Lesebuch*, pp. 120–122 (Brun); Bright, *Reader*, pp. 146–148 (Brun); MacLean, *Reader*, pp. 20–21 (Brun); C. L. Crow, *Maldon and Brunanburh* (Boston, 1897; Brun); O. T. Williams, *Short Extracts from Old English Poetry* (Bangor, 1909), pp. 71–72 (DEdg); Zupitza and Schipper, *Übungsbuch*, pp. 59–61, 80–82 (Brun, DAlf, DEdw); Schücking, *Dichterbuch*, pp. 71–74 (Brun); Wyatt, *Reader*, pp. 185–187 (Brun); Sedgefield, *Verse-Book*, pp. 68–70, 121–122 (Brun, DEdw); N. Kershaw, *Anglo-Saxon and Norse Poems* (Cambridge, 1922), pp. 59–71 (Brun); W. A. Craigie, *Easy Readings in Anglo-Saxon* (Edinburgh, 1923), pp. 25–27, 34–35 (FiveB, CEdg, DEdg, DEdw); M. H. Turk, *An Anglo-Saxon Reader* (New York, 1927), pp. 170–172 (Brun); Flom, *Reader*, pp. 258–260 (Brun); Anderson and Williams, *Handbook*, pp. 252–255 (Brun); A. Campbell, *The Battle of Brunanburh* (London, 1938; Brun).

TRANSLATIONS. Translations of the Chronicle poems are to be found in the editions of the Chronicle by J. Ingram (London, 1823) and B. Thorpe (2 vols., Rolls Series, London, 1861), and in the translations of the Chronicle by Anna Gurney (Norwich, 1819); J. A. Giles (London, 1847); J. Stephenson (in *Church Historians of England*, Vol. II, Part 1, London, 1853); E. E. C. Gomme (London, 1909). There is also a French translation of MS. A (including Brun, FiveB, CEdg, DEdg) by M. Hoffmann-Hirtz (Strasbourg, 1933).

Numerous translations of the Battle of Brunanburh alone have been published: in English, by Hallam Tennyson, "The Song of Brunanburh," *Contemporary Review* XXVIII (1876), 920–922; Alfred Lord Tennyson, "Battle of Brunanburh," in *Ballads and Other Poems* (London, 1880), pp. 169–178; J. M. Garnett, *Elene; Judith; Athelstan, or the Fight at Brunanburh; and Byrhtnoth, or the Fight at Maldon: Anglo-Saxon Poems* (Boston, 1889), pp. 57–59; Cook and Tinker, *ST.*, pp. 25–30 (Lord Tennyson's version); J. L. Hall, *Judith, Phoenix, and Other Anglo-Saxon Poems* (New York, 1902), pp. 56–59; Faust and Thompson, *OEP.*, pp. 159–162; Spaeth, *OEP.*, pp. 162–164; N. Kershaw, *Anglo-Saxon and Norse Poems* (Cambridge, 1922), pp. 67–71; K. Malone, *Ten Old English Poems* (Baltimore, 1941), pp. 27–29; in German, by K. Körner,

Einleitung in das Studium des Angelsächsischen II (Heilbronn, 1880), 69–73; in Danish, by J. C. H. R. Steenstrup, *Danske og norske Riger paa de brittiske Øer i Danevældens Tidsalder* (Copenhagen, 1882), pp. 76–77; in Italian, by F. Olivero, *Traduzioni dalla poesia anglo-sassone* (Bari, 1915), pp. 161–165.

HISTORICAL AND CRITICAL COMMENT. T. Holderness, *The Battle of Brunanburh: an Attempt to Identify the Site* (Driffield and London, 1888); T. G. Foster, *Judith, Studies in Metre, Language, and Style* (Strassburg, 1892), pp. 100–103; D. Abegg, *Zur Entwicklung der historischen Dichtung bei den Angelsachsen* (Strassburg, 1894), pp. 26–78; G. Neilson, "Brunanburh and Burnswork," *Scottish Historical Review* VII (1910), 37–55, 435–436; J. Wilson, "The Site of the Battle of Brunanburh," *Scottish Historical Review* VII (1910), 212–214; A. Law, "Burnswork and Brunanburh," *Scottish Historical Review* VII (1910), 431–435; C. W. Whistler, "Brunanburh and Vinheith in Ingulf's Chronicle and Egil's Saga," *Saga-Book of the Viking Society* VI (1909), 59–67; A. Mawer, "The Scandinavian Kingdom of Northumbria," *Saga-Book of the Viking Society* VII (1911–1912), 38–64; M. L. R. Beaven, "King Edmund I and the Danes of York," *English Historical Review* XXXIII (1918), 1–9; M. Ashdown, "The Single Combat in Certain Cycles of English and Scandinavian Tradition and Romance," *MLRev.* XVII (1922), 113–130; A. W. Mawer, "The Redemption of the Five Boroughs," *English Historical Review* XXXVIII (1923), 551–557; F. Liebermann, "Das Gedicht von König Eadmund I. a. 942," *Archiv* CXLVIII (1925), 96; F. Klaeber, "A Note on the Battle of Brunanburh," in *Anglica, Untersuchungen zur englischen Philologie* II (Leipzig, 1925), 1–7; K. Malone, "A Note on Brunanburh," *MLN.* XLII (1927), 238–239; J. H. Cockburn, *The Battle of Brunanburh and Its Period* (London and Sheffield, 1931); L. M. Hollander, "The Battle on the Vin-heath and the Battle of the Huns," *JEGPh.* XXXII (1933), 33–43; O. G. S. Crawford, "The Battle of Brunanburh," *Antiquity* VIII (1934), 338–339; F. P. Magoun, Jr., "Territorial, Place-, and River-Names in the Old-English Chronicle, *A*-Text (Parker MS.)," *Harvard Studies and Notes* XVIII (1935), 69–111; A. H. Smith, "The Site of the Battle of Brunanburh," *London Mediæval Studies* I (1937), 56–59; W. E.

Varah, "The Battlefield of Brunan-burh," *Notes and Queries* CLXXIII (1937), 434–436; W. S. Angus, "The Battlefield of Brunanburh," *Antiquity* XI (1937), 283–293; F. P. Magoun, Jr., "Territorial, Place-, and River-Names in the Old-English Annals, *D*-Text (MS. Cotton Tiberius B.iv)," *Harvard Studies and Notes* XX (1938), 147–180; F. P. Magoun, Jr., "Zu Etzeln burc, Finns buruh und Brunan burh," *ZfdA.* LXXVII (1940),,65–66.

TEXTUAL NOTES. E. Sievers, *ZfdA.* XV (1872), 462–464 (collation of the London MSS.); F. Holthausen, *Anglia*, Beiblatt III (1892), 239; J. Heiss, *MLN.* XV (1900), 484–485; F. Klaeber, *MLN.* XX (1905), 31–32; E. Björkman, *Archiv* CXVIII (1907), 384–386; F. Tupper, Jr., *JEGPh.* XI (1912), 91–95; E. A. Kock, *Jubilee Jaunts and Jottings* (Lund, 1918), p. 1; E. A. Kock, *Anglia* XLII (1918), 122; F. Holthausen, *Anglia*, Beiblatt XXXI (1920), 256; E. A. Kock, *Anglia* XLVI (1922), 63–64; O. B. Schlutter, *Anglia* XLVII (1923), 255–257; M. Ashdown, *Review of English Studies* V (1929), 324–326; E. Ekwall, *English Studies* XXI (1939), 219–220; F. Holthausen, *Anglia*, Beiblatt L (1939), 157.

DURHAM

EDITIONS. R. Twysden, *Historiae anglicanae scriptores decem* (London, 1652), col. 76 (and in a corrected text at the end of the glossary); Hickes, *Thesaurus*, Part 1, pp. 178–179; C. Michaeler, *Tabulae parallelae antiquissimarum Teutonicae linguae dialectorum* (Innsbruck, 1776), Part 3, pp. 241–244; J. C. Adelung, *Three Philological Essays*, transl. by A. F. M. Willich (London, 1798), pp. xxii-xxiii; J. Oelrichs, *Angelsächsische Chrestomathie* (Hamburg, 1798), pp. 49–51; T. Wright and J. O. Halliwell, *Reliquiae antiquae* I (London, 1845), 159; J. H. Hinde, *Symeonis Dunelmensis opera* I (Surtees Society, LI, 1867), 153; T. Arnold, *Symeonis monachi opera omnia* I (Rolls Series, London, 1882), 221–222; Wülker, *KAD.*, pp. 76–77 (very incorrectly; see his collation on p. 85); Wülker, *Bibliothek* I, 389–392.

TRANSLATIONS. In English and German, by Adelung; in Latin, by Twysden, Hickes, and Michaeler; in German and Latin, by Oelrichs.

CRITICAL AND TEXTUAL COMMENT. F. Holthausen, *Anglia*, Beiblatt XXXI (1920), 29; M. Schlauch, "An Old English encomium urbis," *JEGPh*. XL (1941), 14–28.

THE RUNE POEM

EDITIONS. Hickes, *Thesaurus*, Part 1, pp. 134–135; W. Grimm, *Ueber deutsche Runen* (Göttingen, 1821), pp. 217–245; J. M. Kemble, *Archaeologia* XXVIII (1840), 339–345; Ettmüller, *Scopas*, pp. 286–289; Grein, *Bibliothek* II, 351–354; Rieger, *Lesebuch*, pp. 136–139; L. Botkine, *La Chanson des runes* (Le Havre, 1879); Wülker, *KAD*., pp. 37–40; Wülker, *Bibliothek* I, 331–337; Kluge, *Lesebuch*, pp. 138–140; Dickins, *RHP*., pp. 6, 12–23; H. Arntz, *Handbuch der Runenkunde* (Halle, 1935), pp. 114–116.

TRANSLATIONS. Translations of the Rune Poem are given in the following editions, cited above: in English, by Kemble and Dickins; in German, by Grimm and Arntz; in French, by Botkine.

CRITICAL AND TEXTUAL COMMENT. C. W. M. Grein, *Germania* X (1865), 428; E. Sievers, *Beitr*. X (1885), 519; T. von Grienberger, "Die angelsächsischen Runenreihen und die s.g. Hrabanischen Alphabete," *Arkiv för nordisk filologi* XV (1899), 1–40; G. Hempl, "Hickes' Additions to the Runic Poem," *Modern Philology* I (1903), 135–141; E. A. Kock, *Anglia* XLIII (1919), 307–308; T. Grienberger, "Das ags. Runengedicht," *Anglia* XLV (1921), 201–220; F. Klaeber, "Die Ing-Verse im angelsächsischen Runengedicht," *Archiv* CXLII (1921), 250–253; A. H. Krappe, "Le Char d'Ing," *Revue germanique* XXIV (1933), 23–25; W. Keller, "Zum altenglischen Runengedicht," *Anglia* LX (1936), 141–149; W. J. Redbond, "Notes on the Word 'eolhx,'" *MLRev*. XXXI (1936), 55–57; W. Keller, "Zur Chronologie der ae. Runen," *Anglia* LXII (1938), 24–32.

SOLOMON AND SATURN

EDITIONS. Complete texts of the poem are given by J. M. Kemble, *The Dialogue of Salomon and Saturnus* (London, 1848); Grein, *Bibliothek* II, 354–368; J. Schipper, "Salomo und Saturn," *Germania* XXII (1877), 50–70; Wülker, *Bibliothek* III, 304–328 (Part

2, pp. 58–82); R. J. Menner, *The Poetical Dialogues of Solomon and Saturn* (New York, 1941).

Partial texts are printed by Conybeare, *Illustrations*, pp. lxxxii-lxxxiv (ll. 1–6a, 314–322); J. M. Kemble, *Archaeologia* XXVIII (1840), 367–370 (ll. 84–139); Ettmüller, *Scopas*, p. 239 (ll. 314–322); Bouterwek, *Cædmon* I, lxv-lxix (ll. 426–506); Rieger, *Lesebuch*, pp. 139–142 (ll. 1–20, 146–169, 282–301); Wyatt, *Reader*, p. 198 (ll. 282–301); W. A. Craigie, *Specimens of Anglo-Saxon Poetry* I (Edinburgh, 1923), pp. 4–5 (ll. 451–476).

TRANSLATIONS. English translations accompany Kemble's complete edition of the poem and the partial text by Conybeare; German translations accompany the partial texts by Ettmüller and Bouterwek.

HISTORICAL AND CRITICAL COMMENT. W. Schaumberg, *Beitr.* II (1876), 29–63; F. Vogt, *Salman und Morolf* (Halle, 1880), pp. xli-lxxviii; A. Ebert, *Allgemeine Geschichte der Literatur des Mittelalters im Abendlande* III (Leipzig, 1887), 91–96; M. Förster, "Das lateinisch-altenglische Fragment der Apokryphe von Jamnes und Mambres," *Archiv* CVIII (1902), 15–28; A. von Vincenti, *Die altenglischen Dialoge von Salomon und Saturn*, Part 1 (Leipzig, 1904; no more published); R. J. Menner, "The vasa mortis Passage in the Old English Salomon and Saturn," in *Studies in English Philology* (Minneapolis, 1929), pp. 240–253; H. Larsen, "Kemble's Salomon and Saturn," *Modern Philology* XXVI (1929), 445–450; R. J. Menner, "Nimrod and the Wolf in the Old English Solomon and Saturn," *JEGPh.* XXXVII (1938), 332–354.

TEXTUAL NOTES. C. W. M. Grein, *Germania* X (1865), 428; H. Sweet, *Anglia* I (1878), 150–154 (collation of MS. A); E. Kölbing, *Eng. Stud.* II (1879), 268–269; J. Zupitza, *Anglia* III (1880), 527–531 (collation of both MSS.); E. Sievers, *Beitr.* X (1885), 519; XII (1887), 480; F. Holthausen, *Anglia* XXIII (1901), 123–125; F. Holthausen, *Eng. Stud.* XXXVII (1907), 205; F. Liebermann, *Archiv* CXX (1908), 156; F. Holthausen, *Anglia*, Beiblatt XXI (1910), 175–176; F. Holthausen, *Anglia* XXXV (1911), 167; F. Holthausen, *Anglia*, Beiblatt XXVII (1916), 351–357; F. Hüttenbrenner, *Anglia*, Beiblatt XXVIII (1917), 52–53; F. Holthausen,

Eng. Stud. LI (1917), 182; E. A. Kock, *Anglia* XLII (1918), 122–123; E. A. Kock, *Jubilee Jaunts and Jottings* (Lund, 1918), pp. 67–69; F. Holthausen, *Anglia*, Beiblatt XXXI (1920), 27, 190–191; E. A. Kock, *Anglia* XLIV (1920), 113, 253.

THE MENOLOGIUM AND MAXIMS II

EDITIONS OF BOTH POEMS. Hickes, *Thesaurus*, Part 1, pp. 203–208; S. Fox, *Menologium seu Calendarium poeticum* (London, 1830); F. W. Ebeling, *Angelsæchsisches Lesebuch* (Leipzig, 1847), pp. 114–121; Grein, *Bibliothek* II, 1–6, 346–347; J. Earle, *Two of the Saxon Chronicles Parallel* (Oxford, 1865), pp. xxix-xxxvi; Wülker, *Bibliothek* I, 338–341; II, 282–293; C. Plummer, *Two of the Saxon Chronicles Parallel* I (Oxford, 1892), 273–282; H. A. Rositzke, *The C-Text of the Old English Chronicles* (Bochum-Langendreer, 1940), pp. 3–11.

SEPARATE EDITIONS OF THE MENOLOGIUM. K. W. Bouterwek, *Calendcwide i.e. Menologium ecclesiae Anglo-Saxonicae poeticum* (Gütersloh, 1857); R. Imelmann, *Das altenglische Menologium* (Berlin, 1902).

SEPARATE EDITIONS OF MAXIMS II. Ettmüller, *Scopas*, pp. 283–284; Sweet, *Reader*, pp. 168–170; Wülker, *KAD.*, pp. 41–43; Kluge, *Lesebuch*, pp. 141–142; B. C. Williams, *Gnomic Poetry in Anglo-Saxon* (New York, 1914), pp. 126–129; Sedgefield, *Verse-Book*, pp. 104–106; A. J. Wyatt, *The Threshold of Anglo-Saxon* (New York, 1926), pp. 33–34 (ll. 5–40a only); Krapp and Kennedy, *Reader*, p. 141 (ll. 21b–36a only); Flom, *Reader*, p. 280 (ll. 38b–57a only); Bright, *Reader* (revised ed.), pp. 177–178 (ll. 1–45a only); Anderson and Williams, *Handbook*, pp. 287–289.

TRANSLATIONS. English translations of both poems are given by Fox in his edition; English translations of Maxims II alone are to be found in Cook and Tinker, *ST.*, pp. 67–68 (ll. 25b–29a, 50–66); Spaeth, *OEP.*, pp. 155–157; Gordon, *ASP.*, pp. 346–347. Latin translations of both poems are given by Hickes, and of the Menologium alone by Bouterwek. A Dutch translation of Maxims II is to be found in J. P. Arend, *Proeve eener Geschiedenis der Dichtkunst* (Amsterdam, 1842), pp. 92–94.

HISTORICAL AND CRITICAL COMMENT. F. Piper, *Die Kalendarien und Martyrologien der Angelsachsen* (Berlin, 1862), pp. 55–57, 71–73; J. Strobl, "Zur Spruchdichtung bei den Angelsachsen," *ZfdA.* XXXI (1887), 54–64; H. Müller, *Über die angelsächsischen Versus gnomici* (Jena, 1893); E. Sokoll, [Review of Imelmann, Das altenglische Menologium], *Anglia*, Beiblatt XIV (1903), 307–315; F. Liebermann, "Zum angelsächsischen Menologium," *Archiv* CX (1903), 98–99; P. Fritsche, *Darstellung der Syntax in dem ae. Menologium* (Berlin, 1907); C. Krüger, *Beiträge zur gnomischen Dichtung der Angelsachsen* (unpublished Ph.D. dissertation, Halle, 1924); H. Henel, *Studien zum altenglischen Computus* (Leipzig, 1934), pp. 71–91.

TEXTUAL NOTES. C. W. M. Grein, *Germania* X (1865), 422, 428; E. Sievers, *ZfdA.* XV (1872), 464–466 (collation of the MS.); E. Sievers, *Beitr.* X (1885), 517; H. Kern, *Taalkundige Bijdragen* I (1877), 193ff.; P. J. Cosijn, *Tijdschrift voor Nederlandsche Taal- en Letterkunde* I (1881), 148–149; F. Holthausen, *Anglia*, Beiblatt III (1893), 239–240; P. J. Cosijn, *Beitr.* XIX (1894), 443–444; F. Holthausen, *Anglia*, Beiblatt V (1895), 225–226; E. A. Kock, *Anglia* XXVII (1904), 229; E. A. Kock, *Jubilee Jaunts and Jottings* (Lund, 1918), pp. 35–37, 55; F. Holthausen, *Anglia*, Beiblatt XXX (1919), 3; E. A. Kock, *Anglia* XLIII (1919), 309–310; F. Holthausen, *Anglia* XLVI (1922), 54; E. A. Kock, *Anglia* XLVII (1923), 267–268; S. J. Crawford, *MLRev.* XIX (1924), 107.

A PROVERB FROM WINFRID'S TIME

EDITIONS OF THE LATIN LETTER (INCLUDING THE POEM). N. Serarius, *Epistolae S. Bonifacii martyris* (Mainz, 1605), p. 73 (no. 61); S. A. Würdtwein, *Epistolae S. Bonifacii* (Mainz, 1789), no. 152; J. A. Giles, *Sancti Bonifacii archiepiscopi et martyris opera quae extant omnia* I (London, 1844), 274 (no. 141); J. P. Migne, *Patrologiae cursus completus: series latina* (Paris, 1844ff.) LXXXIX, col. 798–799 (no. 101); P. Jaffé, *Monumenta Moguntina* (Berlin, 1866), p. 311 (no. 147); E. Dümmler, *S. Bonifatii et Lulli epistolae* (in *Epistolae Merowingici et Karolini aevi* I, Berlin, 1892), pp. 427–428 (no. 146); M. Tangl, *Die Briefe des heiligen Bonifatius und Lullus* (Berlin, 1916), pp. 283–284 (no. 146).

SEPARATE EDITIONS OF THE POEM. G. H. Pertz, *Archiv der Gesellschaft für ältere deutsche Geschichtkunde* III (1821), 171–172; H. F. Massmann, *Die deutschen Abschwörungs-, Glaubens-, Beicht- und Betformeln vom achten bis zum zwölften Jahrhundert* (Quedlinburg and Leipzig, 1839), p. 25 and Plate 1; J. M. Kemble, "Anglo-Saxon Proverb," *Gentleman's Magazine*, New Series, V (1836), 611; T. Wright, *Biographia Britannica literaria* I (London, 1842), 21; Ettmüller, *Scopas*, p. xix; Rieger, *Lesebuch*, p. 129, note; Sweet, *OET.*, pp. 151–152; Wülker, *Bibliothek* II, 315.

HISTORICAL AND CRITICAL COMMENT. F. Holthausen, "Der altenglische Spruch aus Winfrids Zeit," *Archiv* CVI (1901), 347–348; B. C. Williams, *Gnomic Poetry in Anglo-Saxon* (New York, 1914), pp. 69–70.

THE JUDGMENT DAY II, AN EXHORTATION TO CHRISTIAN LIVING, A SUMMONS TO PRAYER, THE LORD'S PRAYER II, THE GLORIA I

EDITIONS OF ALL THE POEMS. J. R. Lumby, *Be Domes Dæge* (London, 1876); Wülker, *Bibliothek* II, 230–244, 250–279.

EDITIONS OF SINGLE POEMS. Hickes, *Thesaurus*, Part 1, pp. 179–180 (Gloria I, 1–50); Klipstein, *Analecta* II, 89–101 (L.P.II, Gloria I); Ettmüller, *Scopas*, pp. 227–229, 231–234 (J.D.II, 1–9; L.P.II, Gloria I); Grein, *Bibliothek* II, 287–292 (L.P.II, Gloria I); Kluge, *Lesebuch* (1st-3d ed.), pp. 120–121 (Summons); H. Löhe, *Be Domes Dæge* (Bonner Beiträge zur Anglistik, Vol. XXII, Bonn, 1907; J.D.II only); Zupitza and Schipper, *Übungsbuch*, p. 79 (Summons). Editions of the Gloria I as part of the Benedictine Office in MS. Junius 121 are listed in the Bibliography for that text, below.

TRANSLATIONS. English translations of all the poems are given by Lumby, and of the Judgment Day II alone by Gordon, *ASP.*, pp. 314–319. A German translation of the Judgment Day II is given by Löhe.

CRITICAL AND TEXTUAL COMMENT. C. W. M. Grein, *Germania* X (1865), 427; A. Brandl, "Be Domes Dæge," *Anglia* IV (1881), 97–104; J. Höser, *Die syntaktischen Erscheinungen in Be Domes Dæge* (Halle, 1888); F. Holthausen, *Beitr.* XVI (1892), 551–552; P. J. Cosijn, *Beitr.* XIX (1894), 443; F. Holthausen, *Anglia*, Beiblatt V (1895), 196–198, 225; F. Holthausen, *Eng. Stud.* XXXVII (1907), 202; F. Holthausen, *Anglia*, Beiblatt XXIII (1912), 87–88; E. A. Kock, *Jubilee Jaunts and Jottings* (Lund, 1918), pp. 9–10; F. Holthausen, *Anglia*, Beiblatt XXXI (1920), 29; F. Holthausen, *Anglia* XLVI (1922), 54.

THE BENEDICTINE OFFICE: THE LORD'S PRAYER III, THE CREED, FRAGMENTS OF PSALMS

EDITIONS OF THE BENEDICTINE OFFICE. G. Hickes, *Several Letters Which Passed between Dr. G. Hickes and a Popish Priest* (London, 1705), Appendix; E. Thomson, *Select Monuments of the Doctrine and Worship of the Catholic Church in England before the Norman Conquest* (London, 1849), pp. 113–211; Bouterwek, *Cædmon* I, clxxix-ccxxiii; E. Feiler, *Das Benediktiner-Offizium* (Heidelberg, 1901).

SEPARATE EDITIONS OF THE POEMS. H. Wanley, *Catalogus historico-criticus* (Oxford, 1705), pp. 48–49 (L.P.III, Creed); Ettmüller, *Scopas*, pp. 229–231 (L.P.III, Creed); Grein, *Bibliothek* II, 147–149, 286, 292–294 (L.P.III, Creed, Psalms); Wülker, *Bibliothek* II, 228–230, 245–249; III, 329–331 (L.P.III, Creed, Psalms). For separate editions of Gloria I, see the preceding Bibliography.

TRANSLATIONS. English translations of the Benedictine Office are given by Hickes and Thomson; a German translation is given by Bouterwek.

CRITICAL AND TEXTUAL COMMENT. C. W. M. Grein, *Germania* X (1865), 427; E. Sievers, *ZfdA.* XV (1872), 465–466 (collation of MS.); P. J. Cosijn, *Beitr.* XIX (1894), 441; F. Holthausen, *Anglia*, Beiblatt V (1895), 196–197; B. Fehr, "Das Benediktiner-Offizium und die Beziehungen zwischen Aelfric und Wulfstan," *Eng. Stud.*

XLVI (1913), 337–346; E. A. Kock, *Jubilee Jaunts and Jottings* (Lund, 1918), p. 52; E. A. Kock, *Anglia* XLII (1918), 114; F. Holthausen, *Anglia*, Beiblatt XXXI (1920), 191.

THE KENTISH HYMN AND PSALM 50

EDITIONS. T. Wright and J. O. Halliwell, *Reliquiae antiquae* I (London, 1845), 34 (Hymn only); F. Dietrich, "Anglosaxonica," in *Indices lectionum . . . quae in Academia Marburgensi per semestre hibernum . . . MDCCCLIV usque ad . . . MDCCCLV habendae proponuntur* (Marburg, 1854), pp. iii-xvi; Grein, *Bibliothek* II, 276–280, 290–291; Kluge, *Lesebuch* (1st-3d ed.), pp. 115–120; A. S. Cook, *A First Book in Old English* (Boston, 1894), pp. 265–267 (Hymn only); Sweet, *Reader* (7th-9th ed.), pp. 196–201 (Psalm only); Wülker, *Bibliothek* II, 224–226; III, 477–482.

TRANSLATIONS. A Latin translation accompanies Dietrich's text of the poem.

CRITICAL AND TEXTUAL COMMENT. C. W. M. Grein, *Germania* X (1865), 427; E. Sievers, *ZfdA.* XV (1872), 465–466 (collation of the MS.); F. Holthausen, *Anglia*, Beiblatt V (1895), 196; A. S. Cook, *Biblical Quotations in Old English Prose Writers* (London, 1898), pp. xx-xxii; F. Holthausen, *Eng. Stud.* XXXVII (1907), 202; LI (1917), 180–181; F. Holthausen, *Anglia*, Beiblatt XXXI (1920), 29.

THE GLORIA II

EDITIONS. E. Sievers, "Bedeutung der Buchstaben," *ZfdA.* XXI (1877), 189–190; W. de G. Birch, *Transactions of the Royal Society of Literature*, 2d Series, XI (1877), 507–509; F. Holthausen, *Anglia* XLI (1917), 401.

A PRAYER

EDITIONS. F. Junius, *Cædmonis monachi paraphrasis poetica Genesios ac præcipuarum sacræ paginæ historiarum* (Amsterdam, 1655), pp. [110–111] (from MS. J); E. Thomson, *Select Monuments of the Doctrine and Worship of the Catholic Church in England before the Norman Conquest* (London, 1849), pp. 212–226 (from MS. J); Bouterwek, *Cædmon* I, 190–192, 328–331 (from MS. J); L. G.

Nilsson, *Några fornengelska andeliga qväden på grundspråket* (Lund, 1857), pp. 4–19 (from MS. J); Grein, *Bibliothek* II, 280–282 (from MS. J); H. Logeman, *Anglia* XI (1889), 103 (from MS. L); Wülker, *Bibliothek* II, 211–217 (from both MSS.); O. T. Williams, *Short Extracts from Old English Poetry* (Bangor, 1909), pp. 72–74 (ll. 21–79 from MS. J).

TRANSLATIONS. An English translation is given by Thomson, a German translation by Bouterwek, and a Swedish translation by Nilsson.

CRITICAL AND TEXTUAL COMMENT. C. W. M. Grein, *Germania* X (1865), 427; E. Sievers, *ZfdA*. XV (1872), 465 (collation of MS. J); R. P. Wülker, *Anglia* XI (1889), 631; A. S. Cook, "New Texts of the Old English Lord's Prayer and Hymns," *MLN*. VII (1892), 21–23; F. Holthausen, *Anglia*, Beiblatt V (1895), 195; M. Förster, *Archiv* CXXXII (1914), 331–332; E. A. Kock, *Jubilee Jaunts and Jottings* (Lund, 1918), p. 52; F. Holthausen, *Anglia*, Beiblatt XXXI (1920), 28.

THURETH

EDITIONS. H. Spelman, *Concilia decreta leges constitutiones in re ecclesiarum orbis Britannici* I (London, 1639), 510–511; H. Wanley, *Catalogus historico-criticus* (Oxford, 1705), pp. 225–226; D. Wilkins, *Leges Anglosaxonum* (London, 1721), p. 119; D. Wilkins, *Concilia Magnae Britanniae* I (London, 1737), 285–286; T. Wright and J. O. Halliwell, *Reliquiae antiquae* II (London, 1845), 195; W. de G. Birch, *Liber vitae: Register and Martyrology of New Minster and Hyde Abbey* (Hampshire Record Society, 1892), pp. xxi-xxii; F. Liebermann, *Die Gesetze der Angelsachsen* I (Halle, 1903), xxxii; A. S. Napier, *Transactions of the Philological Society*, 1903–1906, p. 299; F. Holthausen, *Anglia* XLI (1917), 403–404.

TRANSLATIONS. Latin translations accompany the texts by Spelman and Wilkins.

ALDHELM

EDITIONS. A. S. Napier, *Old English Glosses* (Oxford, 1900), pp. xiv-xv; R. Ehwald, *Aldhelmi opera* (Berlin, 1919), pp. 219–220; F. Holthausen, *Anglia* XLI (1917), 403.

TRANSLATIONS. A Latin translation accompanies Ehwald's text.

THE SEASONS FOR FASTING

CRITICAL COMMENT. R. Flower, "Laurence Nowell and a Recovered Anglo-Saxon Poem," *British Museum Quarterly* VIII (1934), 130–132.

CÆDMON'S HYMN

EDITIONS. A. Wheloc, *Historiæ ecclesiasticæ gentis Anglorum libri V* (Cambridge, 1643), p. 328 (WS);[1] H. Wanley, *Catalogus historico-criticus* (Oxford, 1705), p. 287 (Nthb); J. Smith, *Historiae ecclesiasticae gentis Anglorum libri quinque* (Cambridge, 1722), p. 597 (Nthb); Conybeare, *Illustrations*, pp. 3–7; Ettmüller, *Scopas*, p. 25 (Nthb); Rieger, *Lesebuch*, pp. 154–155; G. Stephens, *The Old-Northern Runic Monuments* I (London and Copenhagen, 1866f.), 433–436; J. E. B. Mayor and J. R. Lumby, *Venerabilis Bedae historiae ecclesiasticae gentis Anglorum libri III IV* (Cambridge, 1879), p. 431* (Nthb); Sweet, *OET.*, pp. 148–149 (Nthb); T. Miller, *The Old English Version of Bede's Ecclesiastical History* (London, 1890ff.) I, 344; II, 408–409 (WS); MacLean, *Reader*, p. 1 (Nthb); A. S. Cook, *A First Book in Old English* (Boston, 1894), pp. 251–253 (Nthb); Wülker, *Bibliothek* II, 316–317; Sweet, *Reader* (7th–9th ed.), p. 175 (Nthb); Kluge, *Lesebuch* (2d-4th ed.), p. 102; C. Plummer, *Baedae opera historica* II (Oxford, 1896), 251–252; J. Schipper, *König Alfreds Übersetzung von Bedas Kirchengeschichte* (Leipzig, 1899), pp. 484, 730–732; P. Wuest, "Zwei neue Handschriften von Cædmons Hymnus," *ZfdA.* XLVIII (1906), 205–226 (Nthb, MSS. Di and P); M. Förster, *Altenglisches Lesebuch* (Heidelberg, 1913), pp. 2–4; Zupitza and Schipper, *Übungsbuch*, pp. 2, 49–50; Sedgefield, *Verse-Book*, pp. 80–81; O. Dobiache-Rojdestvensky, "Un manuscrit de Bède à Léningrad," *Speculum* III (1928), 314–321 (Nthb, MS. L); Flom, *Reader*, p. 287 (Nthb); H. Naumann, *Frühgermanisches Dichterbuch* (Berlin, 1931), p. 127 (Nthb); A. H. Smith, *Three Northumbrian Poems* (London, 1933); C. B. Judge, *Harvard Studies and Notes* XVI (1934), 89–92 (WS, MS. Hr); E. V. K. Dobbie, *The Manuscripts of Cædmon's Hymn and*

---

[1] Editions which contain only the West Saxon version are marked "WS"; those which contain only the Northumbrian version are marked "Nthb." If an edition contains both versions, there is no indication.

Bede's Death Song (New York, 1937). The West Saxon text of the hymn is also included in most Anglo-Saxon readers, as part of the story of Cædmon.

TRANSLATIONS. In English, by Cook and Tinker, *ST.*, pp. 76–77; C. W. Kennedy, *The Cædmon Poems* (London, 1916), p. 3; Faust and Thompson, *OEP.*, pp. 83–84; Gordon, *ASP.*, p. x; in German, by H. Naumann, *Frühgermanentum* (Munich, 1926), p. 77. English and Latin translations also accompany the text by Conybeare; English translations are given by Stephens and Miller.

HISTORICAL AND CRITICAL COMMENT. R. P. Wülcker, "Über den Hymnus Caedmons," *Beitr.* III (1876), 348–357; J. Zupitza, "Über den Hymnus Cädmons," *ZfdA.* XXII (1878), 210–223; A. Schröer, "Über den Hymnus Cædmons," *Archiv* CXV (1905), 67–69; M. Förster, "Paläographisches zu Bedas Sterbespruch und Cædmons Hymnus," *Archiv* CXXXV (1917), 282–284; M. Frampton, "Cadmon's Hymn," *Modern Philology* XXII (1924), 1–15; N. S. Aurner, "Bede and Pausanias," *MLN.* XLI (1926), 535–536; F. Klaeber, "Analogues of the Story of Cædmon," *MLN.* XLII (1927), 390; A. S. Cook, "King Oswy and Cædmon's Hymn," *Speculum* II (1927), 67–72; E. Sievers, "Cædmon und Genesis," in *Britannica, Max Förster zum sechzigsten Geburtstage* (Leipzig, 1929), pp. 57–84 (analysis of the intonation of the hymn, p. 72); L. Pound, "Cædmon's Dream Song," in *Studies in English Philology* (Minneapolis, 1929), pp. 232–239; L. Whitbread, "An Analogue of the Cædmon Story," *Review of English Studies* XV (1939), 333–335.

BEDE'S DEATH SONG

EDITIONS. Conybeare, *Illustrations*, pp. 7–8 (WS);[1] H. Hattemer, *Denkmahle des Mittelalters* I (St. Gall, 1844), 3–4 (Nthb); Ettmüller, *Scopas*, p. 238; Rieger, *Lesebuch*, p. 154 (Nthb); J. E. B. Mayor and J. R. Lumby, *Venerabilis Bedae historiae ecclesiasticae gentis Anglorum libri III IV* (Cambridge, 1879), pp. 177, 403–404; Sweet,

[1] Editions which contain only the West Saxon version are marked "WS"; those which contain only the Northumbrian version are marked "Nthb." If an edition contains both versions, there is no indication.

OET., p. 149 (Nthb); T. Arnold, *Symeonis monachi opera* I (London, 1882), 44; MacLean, *Reader*, pp. 1–2 (Nthb); A. S. Cook, *A First Book in Old English* (Boston, 1894), pp. 253–255 (Nthb); Sweet, *Reader* (7th–9th ed.), p. 175 (Nthb); Kluge, *Lesebuch* (2d–3d ed.), p. 103 (Nthb); C. Plummer, *Baedae opera historica* I (Oxford, 1896), clxi (Nthb); O. Schlutter, *Anglia* XXXVI (1912), 394 (Nthb); R. Brotanek, *Texte und Untersuchungen zur altenglischen Literatur und Kirchengeschichte* (Halle, 1913), pp. 150–194; M. Förster, *Altenglisches Lesebuch* (Heidelberg, 1913), pp. 7–8; Zupitza and Schipper, *Übungsbuch*, pp. 2–3 (Nthb); Sedgefield, *Verse-Book*, p. 81 (Nthb); Flom, *Reader*, p. 287 (Nthb); A. H. Smith, *Three Northumbrian Poems* (London, 1933); E. V. K. Dobbie, *The Manuscripts of Cædmon's Hymn and Bede's Death Song* (New York, 1937); N. R. Ker, "The Hague Manuscript of the Epistola Cuthberti de obitu Bedæ with Bede's Song," *Medium Ævum* VIII (1939), 40–44 (MS. Hg); R. Brotanek, "Nachlese zu den Hss. der Epistola Cuthberti und des Sterbespruches Bedas," *Anglia* LXIV (1940), 159–190.

TRANSLATIONS. In English, by Cook and Tinker, *ST.*, p. 78; Faust and Thompson, *OEP.*, p. 84. There is also the Latin translation by Symeon of Durham; see Arnold, *Symeonis monachi opera* I, 44.

HISTORICAL AND CRITICAL COMMENT. R. Imelmann, *Deutsche Literaturzeitung* XXXIV (1913), 2660–2665; R. Brotanek, *Anglia*, Beiblatt XXV (1914), 51–56; K. Wildhagen, *Archiv* CXXXIV (1916), 173–175; M. Förster, "Paläographisches zu Bedas Sterbespruch und Cædmons Hymnus," *Archiv* CXXXV (1917), 282–284; C. E. Wright, "Bede's Death Song," London *Times Literary Supplement*, March 14, 1936, p. 224; W. Bulst, "Bedas Sterbelied," *ZfdA.* LXXV (1938), 111–114.

THE LEIDEN RIDDLE

EDITIONS. L. C. Bethmann, *ZfdA.* V (1845), 199; F. Dietrich, *Kynewulfi poetae aetas aenigmatum fragmento e codice Lugdunensi edito illustrata* (Marburg, 1860); Rieger, *Lesebuch*, pp. xxii–xxiii; Sweet, *OET.*, pp. 149–151; H. Sweet, *Second Anglo-Saxon Reader*

(Oxford, 1887), p. 90; Kluge, *Lesebuch* (1st-3d ed.), pp. 155–156; Sweet, *Reader* (7th–9th ed.), pp. 175–176; Wülker, *Bibliothek* III, 205–206; O. Schlutter, "Das Leidener Rätsel," *Anglia* XXXII (1909), 384–388, 516; F. Tupper, *The Riddles of the Exeter Book* (Boston, 1910), pp. 27, 153–154; A. J. Wyatt, *Old English Riddles* (Boston, 1912), pp. 92–93; M. Trautmann, *Die altenglischen Rätsel* (Heidelberg, 1915), pp. 20–21; Sedgefield, *Verse-Book*, p. 118; A. H. Smith, *Three Northumbrian Poems* (London, 1933).

CRITICAL AND TEXTUAL COMMENT. J. H. Kern, "Das Leidener Rätsel," *Anglia* XXXIII (1910), 452–456; O. Schlutter, "Zum Leidener Rätsel," *Anglia* XXXIII (1910), 457–466; J. H. Kern, "Noch einmal zum Leidener Rätsel," *Anglia* XXXVIII (1914), 261–265; F. Holthausen, *Anglia*, Beiblatt XXX (1919), 52; M. Trautmann, *Anglia* XLIII (1919), 248; F. Holthausen, "Zu den Leidener Denkmälern," *Eng. Stud.* LV (1921), 312.

LATIN-ENGLISH PROVERBS

EDITIONS. J. Zupitza, "Lateinisch-englische Sprüche," *Anglia* I (1878), 285–286 (from MS. F); R. P. Wülcker, *Anglia* II (1879), 373–374 (from MS. R); F. Holthausen, *Anglia* XLI (1917), 400–401 (from both MSS.); Krapp and Kennedy, *Reader*, p. 138 (from MS. F).

THE METRICAL PREFACE AND EPILOGUE TO THE ALFREDIAN TRANSLATION OF THE PASTORAL CARE

EDITIONS. H. Sweet, *King Alfred's West-Saxon Version of Gregory's Pastoral Care* (London, 1871), pp. 9, 467–469 (arranged as prose), pp. 473–474 (arranged as verse); K. Körner, *Einleitung in das Studium des Angelsächsischen* II (Heilbronn, 1880), 38–39 (metrical preface only); F. Holthausen, "Die Gedichte in Ælfred's Übersetzung der Cura pastoralis," *Archiv* CVI (1901), 346–347.

TRANSLATIONS. An English translation of both texts is given by Sweet, a German translation of the metrical preface by Körner.

THE METRICAL PREFACE TO WÆRFERTH'S
TRANSLATION OF GREGORY'S DIALOGUES

EDITIONS. H. Krebs, "Zur angelsaechsischen Uebersetzung der Dialoge Gregors," *Anglia* III (1880), 70–73 (arranged as prose); H. Hecht, *Bischofs Wærferth von Worcester Übersetzung der Dialoge Gregors des Grossen* (Leipzig, 1900), p. 2 (arranged as prose); F. Holthausen, "Die allitterierende Vorrede zur altenglischen Übersetzung von Gregors Dialogen," *Archiv* CV (1900), 367–369; A. S. Cook, "An Unsuspected Bit of Old English Verse," *MLN.* XVII (1902), 13–20; F. Holthausen, *Anglia* XLI (1917), 402.

CRITICAL COMMENT. W. Keller, *Die litterarischen Bestrebungen von Worcester in angelsächsischer Zeit* (Strassburg, 1900), pp. 6–8, 92–93; K. Sisam, *MLRev.* XVIII (1923), 254–256.

THE METRICAL EPILOGUE TO MS. 41,
CORPUS CHRISTI COLLEGE,
CAMBRIDGE

EDITIONS. T. Miller, *The Old English Version of Bede's Ecclesiastical History* (London, 1890ff.) I, xvi-xvii; II, 596; J. Schipper, *König Alfreds Übersetzung von Bedas Kirchengeschichte* (Leipzig, 1899), pp. xxv-xxvii; F. Holthausen, "Altenglische Schreiberverse," *Anglia*, Beiblatt XXXVIII (1927), 191–192; E. Sievers, "Altenglische Schreiberverse," *Beitr.* LII (1928), 310–311.

CRITICAL COMMENT. M. Förster, "Ae. bam handum twam awritan," *Archiv* CLXII (1933), 230.

THE RUTHWELL CROSS AND THE
BRUSSELS CROSS

THE RUTHWELL CROSS—EARLY REPRODUCTIONS. Hickes, *Thesaurus*, Part 3, Plate 4; A. Gordon, *Itinerarium septentrionale* II (London, 1726), Plates 57–58; Society of Antiquaries of London, *Vetusta monumenta* II (1789), Plates 54–55; H. Duncan, "An Account of the Remarkable Monument in the Shape of a Cross [etc.]," *Archaeologia Scotica* IV (1832), 313–326, Plates 13–15; J.

M. Kemble, *Archaeologia* XXVIII (1840), 349–360, Plates 17–18; G. Stephens, *The Old-Northern Runic Monuments* I (London and Copenhagen, 1866), 405–448 and two plates before p. 405; J. Stuart, *Sculptured Stones of Scotland* II (Edinburgh, 1867), 12–16, Plates 19–20; G. Stephens, *Handbook of the Old-Northern Runic Monuments* (London and Copenhagen, 1884), pp. 130–132.

THE RUTHWELL CROSS—EDITIONS. Sweet, *OET.*, pp. 125–126; H. Sweet, *Second Anglo-Saxon Reader* (Oxford, 1887), p. 87; MacLean, *Reader*, pp. xxviii-xxix, 2–4; Wülker, *Bibliothek* II, 111–116; W. Viëtor, *Die northumbrischen Runensteine* (Marburg, 1895), pp. 2–13; A. S. Cook, *The Dream of the Rood* (Oxford, 1905), pp. ix-xvii, 3–5; Zupitza and Schipper, *Übungsbuch*, pp. 3–7 (text by Viëtor); Royal Commission on Ancient and Historical Monuments and Constructions of Scotland, *Seventh Report, County of Dumfries* (Edinburgh, 1920), pp. 219–286; G. B. Brown, *The Arts in Early England* V (London, 1921), 203–244; Flom, *Reader*, p. 288; B. Dickins and A. S. C. Ross, *The Dream of the Rood* (London, 1934), pp. 1–13, 25–29; H. Bütow, *Das altenglische "Traumgesicht vom Kreuz"* (Heidelberg, 1935), pp. 19–38, 99–144.

THE RUTHWELL CROSS—CRITICAL DISCUSSIONS. J. M. Kemble, "Additional Observations on the Runic Obelisk at Ruthwell [etc.]," *Archaeologia* XXX (1844), 31–39; [J. MacFarlan], *The Ruthwell Cross* (Edinburgh and London, 1885; 2d ed., Dumfries, 1896); G. F. Black, "The Ruthwell-Cross," *Academy* XXXII (1887), 225; H. Bradley, *Academy* XXXIII (1888), 279; A. S. Cook, "The Date of the Ruthwell Cross," *Academy* XXXVII (1890), 153–154; G. F. Browne, "The Date of the Ruthwell Cross," *Academy* XXXVII (1890), 170; A. S. Cook, "Notes on the Ruthwell Cross," *PMLA.* XVII (1902), 367–390; H. Rousseau, "La Ruthwell Cross," *Annales de la Société d'Archéologie de Bruxelles* XVI (1902), 53–71; A. S. Cook, *The Date of the Ruthwell and Bewcastle Crosses* (Transactions of the Connecticut Academy of Arts and Sciences XVII, 213–361, New Haven, Conn., 1912); Sir Martin Conway, "The Bewcastle and Ruthwell Crosses," *Burlington Magazine* XXI (1912), 193–194; W. R. Lethaby, "The Ruthwell Cross," *Burlington Magazine* XXI (1912), 145–146; XXIII (1913), 46–49;

G. B. Brown, *Burlington Magazine* XXIII (1913), 43–46; W. R. Lethaby, "Is Ruthwell Cross an Anglo-Celtic Work?" *Archaeological Journal* LXX (1913), 145–161; J. K. Hewison, *The Runic Roods of Ruthwell and Bewcastle* (Glasgow, 1914); M. D. Forbes and B. Dickins, "The Inscriptions of the Ruthwell and Bewcastle Crosses and the Bridekirk Font," *Burlington Magazine* XXV (1914), 24–29; M. D. Forbes and B. Dickins, "The Ruthwell and Bewcastle Crosses," *MLRev.* X (1915), 28–36; G. F. Browne, *The Ancient Cross Shafts at Bewcastle and Ruthwell* (Cambridge, 1916); A. Brandl, "Zur Zeitbestimmung des Kreuzes von Ruthwell," *Archiv* CXXXVI (1917), 150–151; W. G. Collingwood, "The Ruthwell Cross in Its Relation to Other Monuments of the Early Christian Age," *Transactions . . . of the Dumfriesshire and Galloway Natural History and Antiquarian Society*, Series 3, V (1918), 34–84; J. L. Dinwiddie, *The Ruthwell Cross and Its Story* (Dumfries, 1927); A. S. C. Ross, "The Linguistic Evidence for the Date of the Ruthwell Cross," *MLRev.* XXVIII (1933), 145–155; W. Keller, "Zur Chronologie der ae. Runen," *Anglia* LXII (1938), 24–32.

THE BRUSSELS CROSS.   H. Logeman, *L'Inscription anglo-saxonne du reliquaire de la vraie Croix au trésor de l'église des SS.-Michel-et-Gudule à Bruxelles* (Mémoires couronnés . . . publiés par l'Académie Royale de Belgique, Vol. XLV, Brussels, 1891); J. Zupitza, [Review of Logeman, L'Inscription anglo-saxonne], *Archiv* LXXXVII (1891), 462; Wülker, *Bibliothek* II, 489; A. S. Cook, *The Dream of the Rood* (Oxford, 1905), pp. xlv-xlvii; A. S. Cook, "The Date of the Old English Inscription on the Brussels Cross," *MLRev.* X (1915), 157–161; A. Hensen, "Het Egmonder Kruis," *Het Gildeboek* VIII (1925), 92–97; B. Dickins and A. S. C. Ross, *The Dream of the Rood* (London, 1934), pp. 13–16; F. Norman, *Anglia*, Beiblatt XLVII (1936), 9–10; S. T. R. O. d'Ardenne, "The Old English Inscription on the Brussels Cross," *English Studies* XXI (1939), 145–164, 271–272.

THE FRANKS CASKET[1]

EDITIONS.   G. Stephens, *The Old-Northern Runic Monuments* (London and Copenhagen, 1866ff.) I, 470–476A; III, 200–204;

---

[1] This bibliography is intended to include only studies of the front and the right side of the casket; studies of the other sides of the casket do not fall within the province of this edition.

Wülker, *Bibliothek* I, 281–283 (front of casket only); G. Stephens, *Handbook of the Old-Northern Runic Monuments* (London and Copenhagen, 1884), pp. 142–147; E. Wadstein, *The Clermont Runic Casket* (Skrifter utgifna af K. Humanistiska Vetenskaps-Samfundet i Upsala, Vol. VI, Part 7, Uppsala, 1900); A. S. Napier, "The Franks Casket," in *An English Miscellany* (Oxford, 1901), pp. 362–381; E. Wadstein, "Ett engelskt fornminne från 700-talet och Englands dåtida kultur," *Nordisk Universitetstidskrift* I (1900–1901), 129–153 (also separately, Göteborg, 1901); W. Viëtor, *Das angelsächsische Runenkästchen aus Auzon bei Clermont-Ferrand* (2 parts, Marburg, 1901); F. Holthausen, *Anglia* XLI (1917), 401–402 (right side only).

CRITICAL AND TEXTUAL COMMENT. S. Bugge, *Tidskrift for Philologi og Pædagogik* VIII (1868–1869), 302; K. Hofmann, "Über die Clermonter Runen," in *Sitzungsberichte der philos.-philol. und histor. Classe der kgl. bayerischen Akademie der Wissenschaften* I (1871), 665–672; II (1872), 461–462; H. Sweet, "Gársecg," *Eng. Stud.* II (1879), 314–316; F. Holthausen, [Review of Wadstein, The Clermont Runic Casket], *Literaturblatt* XXI (1900), 208–212; G. Hempl, "The Variant Runes on the Franks Casket," *Transactions of the American Philological Association* XXXII (1901), 186–195; T. von Grienberger, [Review of Wadstein, Napier, Viëtor], *ZfdPh.* XXXIII (1901), 409–421; E. Wadstein, "Zum Clermonter Runenkästchen," *ZfdPh.* XXXIV (1902), 127; H. Schück, *Studier i nordisk litteratur- och religionshistoria* I (Stockholm, 1904), 176–178; O. L. Jiriczek, [Review of Wadstein, Napier, Viëtor], *Anzeiger für deutsches Altertum* XXIX (1904), 192–202; T. von Grienberger, "Zu den Inschriften des Clermonter Runenkästchens," *Anglia* XXVII (1904), 436–449; F. Holthausen, *Anglia*, Beiblatt XVI (1905), 229–231; XVII (1906), 176; XVIII (1907), 205–206; R. C. Boer, "Über die rechte Seite des angelsächsischen Runenkästchens," *Arkiv för nordisk filologi* XXVII (1911), 215–259; F. C. Walker, "Fresh Light on the Franks Casket," *Washington University Studies* II, Part 2 (1915), pp. 165–176; E. A. Kock, *Jubilee Jaunts and Jottings* (Lund, 1918), p. 77; F. Holthausen, *Anglia*, Beiblatt XXX (1919), 4; E. A. Kock, *Anglia* XLIII (1919), 311; R. Imelmann, "Die Hos-Inschrift des Franks Casket," *Forschungen zur altenglischen Poesie* (Berlin, 1920), pp.

315–341; F. Holthausen, *Anglia* XLIV (1920), 354; XLVI (1922), 56–57; E. G. Clark, "The Right Side of the Franks Casket," *PMLA*. XLV (1930), 339–353; G. B. Brown, *The Arts in Early England*, Vol. VI, Part 1 (London, 1930), pp. 18–51; P. W. Souers, "The Magi on the Franks Casket," *Harvard Studies and Notes* XIX (1937), 249–254.

THE METRICAL CHARMS

EDITIONS. B. Thorpe, *Analecta Anglo-Saxonica* (London, 1834; 2d ed., 1846), pp. 116–119 (Charm 1); T. Wright and J. O. Halliwell, *Reliquiae antiquae* II (London, 1845), 237–238 (Charm 4); J. M. Kemble, *The Saxons in England* I (London, 1849; 2d ed., by W. de G. Birch, 1876), 528–535 (Charms 1, 4, 6); Klipstein, *Analecta* I, 251–254 (Charm 1); Ettmüller, *Scopas*, pp. 300–304 (Charms 1, 4, 11); Bouterwek, *Cædmon* I, lxxxv-lxxxvii (Charm 4); Rieger, *Lesebuch*, pp. 142–146 (Charms 1 and 4, entire, and Charm 8, ll. 9–12); O. Cockayne, *Leechdoms, Wortcunning, and Starcraft of Early England* (London, 1864–1866) I, 384–385, 388–393, 398–405; II, 350–353; III, 30–39, 42–43, 52–55, 60–61, 66–69 (Charms 1–11); J. Grimm, *Deutsche Mythologie* (4th ed., by E. H. Meyer, Berlin, 1875) II, 1033–1035, 1039–1040; III, 492–493 (Charms 1, 4, 7–11); W. de G. Birch, *Transactions of the Royal Society of Literature*, 2d Series, XI (1878), 484–486 (Charm 12); J. Zupitza, ' Ein verkannter englischer und zwei bisher ungedruckte lateinische Bienensegen," *Anglia* I (1878), 189–195 (Charm 8); Wülker, *KAD.*, pp. 30–36 (Charms 1, 2, 4, 8); Wülker, *Bibliothek* I, 312–330; II, 202–203 (Charms 1–6, 8–11); Sweet, *Reader* (4th-9th ed.), pp. 104–105 (Charms 4, 8); J. Zupitza, "Ein Zauberspruch," *ZfdA.* XXXI (1887), 45–52 (Charm 12); J. Hoops, *Über die altenglischen Pflanzennamen* (Freiburg i.B., 1889), pp. 55–64 (Charm 2); Kluge, *Lesebuch* (2d-4th ed.), pp. 114–115 (Charms 1, 4, 8; Charm 1 not in 4th ed.); G. Leonhardi, *Kleinere angelsächsische Denkmäler* I (Bibliothek der angels. Prosa, Vol. VI, Hamburg, 1905), 107, 137 (Charm 7, entire, and Charm 2, ll. 64–72); O. Schlutter, *Anglia* XXX (1907), 257–258 (Charm 3, ll. 9–17 only); F. Holthausen, *Anglia*, Beiblatt XIX (1908), 213–215 (Charm 12); O. Schlutter, *Anglia* XXXI (1908), 58–62 (Charm 11, arranged as prose); F.

Grendon, "The Anglo-Saxon Charms," *Journal of American Folk-Lore* XXII (1909), 105–237 (also separately, New York, 1909; repr. 1930); Wyatt, *Reader*, pp. 128–131 (Charms 1, 9); F. Holthausen, "Der altenglische Reisesegen," *Anglia*, Beiblatt XL (1929), 87–90 (Charm 11); Krapp and Kennedy, *Reader*, pp. 139–141 (Charms 3, 5, 8); Flom, *Reader*, pp. 281–282 (Charms 4, 8); F. Holthausen, "Die altenglischen Neunkräutersegen," *Eng. Stud.* LXIX (1934), 180–183 (Charm 2); Bright, *Reader* (revised ed.), pp. 179–182 (Charms 1, 4); Anderson and Williams, *Handbook*, pp. 283–286 (Charms 2, 8).

TRANSLATIONS. In English, by Cook and Tinker, *ST.*, pp. 164–171 (Charms 1, 2, 4, 5, 8); Faust and Thompson, *OEP.*, pp. 38–43 (Charms 1, 4); Spaeth, *OEP.*, pp. 149–151 (Charm 4, entire, and part of Charm 1); Gordon, *ASP.*, pp. 94–104 (Charms 1–4, 8, 9, 11, 12). English translations of all the charms are also given by Grendon in his edition (1909), of Charms 1–11 by Cockayne in his edition (1864–1866), and of Charm 12 by Birch (1878). There are German translations in the following editions of separate charms: of Charm 1, by Bouterwek, *Cædmon* I, lxxxvii; of Charm 2, by Hoops, *Über die altenglischen Pflanzennamen*, pp. 57–61; of Charm 3 (in part), by Schlutter, *Anglia* XXX, 257–258; of Charm 11, by Schlutter, *Anglia* XXXI, 60–62; of Charm 12, by Zupitza, *ZfdA.* XXXI, 47, and Holthausen, *Anglia*, Beiblatt XIX, 214.

CRITICAL AND TEXTUAL COMMENT. R. Koegel, *Geschichte der deutschen Litteratur bis zum Ausgange des Mittelalters*, Vol. I, Part 1 (Strassburg, 1894), pp. 93–95; H. Bradley, "The Song of the Nine Magic Herbs (Neunkräutersegen)," *Archiv* CXIII (1904), 144–145; F. Holthausen, *Anglia*, Beiblatt XVI (1905), 228–229; M. Brie, "Der germanische, insbesondere der englische Zauberspruch," *Mitteilungen der schlesischen Gesellschaft für Volkskunde* XVI (1906), 1–36; O. Schlutter, *Anglia* XXX (1907), 125–128; O. Schlutter, *Anglia* XXXI (1908), 56–58; F. Hälsig, *Der Zauberspruch bei den Germanen* (Leipzig, 1910); A. R. Skemp, [Review of Grendon, The Anglo-Saxon Charms], *MLRev.* VI (1911), 262–266; A. R. Skemp, "The Old English Charms," *MLRev.* VI (1911), 289–301; F. Tupper, Jr., "Notes on Old English Poems, V, Hand ofer Heafod," *JEGPh.* XI (1912), 97–100; R. Meissner, "Die

Zunge des grossen Mannes," *Anglia* XL (1916), 375–393; G. Binz, [Review of Grendon, The Anglo-Saxon Charms], *Anglia*, Beiblatt XXVII (1916), 161–163; F. Holthausen, *Anglia*, Beiblatt XXIX (1918), 283–284; F. Holthausen, *Anglia*, Beiblatt XXXI (1920), 30–32; F. Holthausen, "Zu den altenglischen Zaubersprüchen und Segen," *Anglia*, Beiblatt XXXI (1920), 116–120; F. Klaeber, *Anglia*, Beiblatt XXXII (1921), 37–38; W. Horn, "Der altenglische Zauberspruch gegen Hexenschuss," in *Probleme der englischen Sprache und Kultur, Festschrift Johannes Hoops* (Heidelberg, 1925), pp. 88–104; F. Holthausen, *Anglia*, Beiblatt XXXVI (1925), 219; J. H. G. Grattan, "Three Anglo-Saxon Charms from the Lacnunga," *MLRev.* XXII (1927), 1–6; F. Klaeber, "Belūcan in dem altenglischen Reisesegen," *Anglia*, Beiblatt XL (1929), 283–284; F. Holthausen, "Nochmals der altenglische Reisesegen," *Anglia*, Beiblatt XLI (1930), 255; F. Klaeber, [Review of Grendon, The Anglo-Saxon Charms, repr.], *Anglia*, Beiblatt XLII (1931), 6–7; F. P. Magoun, Jr., "Zu den ae. Zaubersprüchen," *Archiv* CLXXI (1937), 17–35; F. P. Magoun, Jr., "Strophische Überreste in den altenglischen Zaubersprüchen," *Eng. Stud.* LXXII (1937), 1–6; L. K. Shook, "Notes on the Old-English Charms," *MLN.* LV (1940), 139–140.

TEXTS

THE BATTLE OF FINNSBURH

nas byrnaðð?"
Hnæf hleoþrode ða,   heaþogeong cyning:
"Ne ðis ne dagað eastan,   ne her draca ne fleogeð,
ne her ðisse healle   hornas ne byrnað.
5 Ac her forþ berað;   fugelas singað,
gylleð græghama,   guðwudu hlynneð,
scyld scefte oncwyð.   Nu scyneð þes mona
waðol under wolcnum.   Nu arisað weadæda
ðe ðisne folces nið   fremman willað.
10 Ac onwacnigeað nu,   wigend mine,
habbað eowre linda,   hicgeaþ on ellen,
winnað on orde,   wesað onmode!"
    Ða aras mænig goldhladen ðegn,   gyrde hine his swurde.
Ða to dura eodon   drihtlice cempan,
15 Sigeferð and Eaha,   hyra sword getugon,
and æt oþrum durum   Ordlaf and Guþlaf,
and Hengest sylf   hwearf him on laste.
    Ða gyt Garulf   Guðere styrde
ðæt he swa freolic feorh   forman siþe
20 to ðære healle durum   hyrsta ne bære,
nu hyt niþa heard   anyman wolde,
ac he frægn ofer eal   undearninga,
deormod hæleþ,   hwa ða duru heolde.
"Sigeferþ is min nama," cweþ he,   "ic eom Secgena leod,
25 wreccea wide cuð;   fæla ic weana gebad,
heardra hilda.   Ðe is gyt her witod
swæþer ðu sylf to me   secean wylle."
    Ða wæs on healle   wælslihta gehlyn;

Battle of Finnsburh 2 Hnæf] Næfre   heaþogeong] hearo geong   3 eas-
tan] Eastun   11 linda] landa   hicgeaþ] Hie geaþ   12 winnað]
Windað   18 styrde] styrode   20 bære] bæran   25 wreccea] Wrecten
weana] weuna   26 heardra] Heordra

3

sceolde cellod bord   cenum on handa,
30 banhelm berstan   (buruhðelu dynede),
oð æt ðære guðe   Garulf gecrang,
ealra ærest   eorðbuendra,
Guðlafes sunu,   ymbe hyne godra fæla,
hwearflicra hræw.   Hræfen wandrode,
35 sweart and sealobrun.   Swurdleoma stod,
swylce eal Finnsburuh   fyrenu være.
Ne gefrægn ic næfre wurþlicor   æt wera hilde
sixtig sigebeorna   sel gebæran,
ne nefre swetne medo   sel forgyldan
40 ðonne Hnæfe guldan   his hægstealdas.
Hig fuhton fif dagas,   swa hyra nan ne feol
drihtgesiða,   ac hig ða duru heoldon.
Ða gewat him wund hæleð   on wæg gangan,
sæde þæt his byrne   abrocen være,
45 heresceorp unhror,   and eac wæs his helm ðyrel.
Ða hine sona frægn   folces hyrde,
hu ða wigend hyra   wunda genæson,
oððe hwæþer ðæra hyssa

*   *   *

WALDERE

MS. Ny kgl. saml. 167b, Royal Library, Copenhagen

I

hyrde hyne georne:
"Huru Welande[.]   worc ne geswiceð
monna ænigum   ðara ðe Mimming can
heardne gehealdan.   Oft æt hilde gedreas
5 swatfag and sweordwund   secg æfter oðrum.

29 cellod bord] Celæs borð   cenum on] Genumon   34 hwearflicra
hræw] Hwearflacra hrær   38 gebæran] gebærann   39 swetne] swa noc
hwitne   45 heresceorp unhror] Here sceorpum hror   ðyrel] ðyrl
Waldere I, 4 heardne] hearne *with a dot below* n   5 secg] sec

Ætlan ordwyga, ne læt ðin ellen nu gy[.]
gedreosan to dæge, dryhtscipe * * *
[. .] is se dæg cumen
þæt ðu scealt aninga oðer twega,
10 lif forleosan oððe l[. .]gne dom
agan mid eldum, Ælfheres sunu.
Nalles ic ðe, wine min, wordum cide,
ðy ic ðe gesawe æt ðam sweordplegan
ðurh edwitscype æniges monnes
15 wig forbugan oððe on weal fleon,
lice beorgan, ðeah þe laðra fela
ðinne byrnhomon billum heowun,
ac ðu symle furðor feohtan sohtest,
mæl ofer mearce; ðy ic ðe metod ondred,
20 þæt ðu to fyrenlice feohtan sohtest
æt ðam ætstealle oðres monnes,
wigrædenne. Weorða ðe selfne
godum dædum, ðenden ðin god recce.
Ne murn ðu for ði mece; ðe wearð maðma cyst
25 gifeðe to geoce, mid ðy ðu Guðhere scealt
beot forbigan, ðæs ðe he ðas beaduwe ongan
[. .]d unryhte ærest secan.
Forsoc he ðam swurde and ðam syncfatum,
beaga mænigo, nu sceal bega leas
30 hworfan from ðisse hilde, hlafurd secan
ealdne ⋇ oððe her ær swefan,
gif he ða"

* * *

II

"ce bæteran
buton ðam anum ðe ic eac hafa
on stanfate stille gehided.
Ic wat þæt hit ðohte Ðeodric Widian

I,10 l[. .]gne] l[. .]ge   13 sweordplegan] sweord wlegan   25 gifeðe]
gifede   geoce] eoce   29 bega] beaga   30 from] fró   II,4 hit] ic

5 selfum onsendon,   and eac sinc micel
  maðma mid ði mece,   monig oðres mid him
  golde gegirwan   (iulean genam),
  þæs ðe hine of nearwum   Niðhades mæg,
  Welandes bearn,   Widia ut forlet;
10 ðurh fifela gewe[.]ld   forð onette."
    Waldere mað[.]lode,   wiga ellenrof,
  hæfde him on handa   hildefrofre,
  guðbilla gripe,   gyddode wordum:
  "Hwæt! Ðu huru wendest,   wine Burgenda,
15 þæt me Hagenan hand   hilde gefremede
  and getwæmde [..]ðewigges.   Feta, gyf ðu dyrre,
  æt ðus heaðuwerigan   hare byrnan.
  Standeð me her on eaxelum   Ælfheres laf,
  god and geapneb,   golde geweorðod,
20 ealles unscende   æðelinges reaf
  to habbanne,   þonne hand wereð
  feorhhord feondum.   Ne bið fah wið me,
  þonne [..] unmægas   eft ongynnað,
  mecum gemetað,   swa ge me dydon.
25 Ðeah mæg sige syllan   se ðe symle byð
  recon and rædfest   ryh[.]a gehwilces.
  Se ðe him to ðam halgan   helpe gelifeð,
  to gode gioce,   he þær gearo findeð

      *   *   *

  gif ða earnunga   ær geðenceð.
30 Þonne moten wlance   welan britnian,
  æhtum wealdan,   þæt is"

      *   *   *

II,10 gewe[.]ld] ge fe[.]ld   12 hildefrofre] hilde frore   15 Hagenan]
With the e *added above the line*   16 [..]ðewigges] *It is impossible to tell
whether the first letter preserved is* d *or* ð; *see Note*   18 Standeð] standað
19 geweorðod] *With the* ð *added above the line*   21 hand] had   22 Ne] he
30 moten] mtoten

THE BATTLE OF MALDON

MS. Rawlinson B203

                 brocen wurde.
Het þa hyssa hwæne   hors forlætan,
feor afysan,   and forð gangan,
hicgan to handum   and to hige godum.
5 Þa þæt Offan mæg   ærest onfunde,
þæt se eorl nolde   yrhðo geþolian,
he let him þa of handon   leofne fleogan
hafoc wið þæs holtes,   and to þære hilde stop;
be þam man mihte oncnawan   þæt se cniht nolde
10 wacian æt þam wige,   þa he to wæpnum feng.
Eac him wolde Eadric   his ealdre gelæstan,
frean to gefeohte,   ongan þa forð beran
gar to guþe.   He hæfde god geþanc
þa hwile þe he mid handum   healdan mihte
15 bord and bradswurd;   beot he gelæste
þa he ætforan his frean   feohtan sceolde.
    Ða þær Byrhtnoð ongan   beornas trymian,
rad and rædde,   rincum tæhte
hu hi sceoldon standan   and þone stede healdan,
20 and bæd þæt hyra randas   rihte heoldon
fæste mid folman,   and ne forhtedon na.
Þa he hæfde þæt folc   fægere getrymmed,
he lihte þa mid leodon   þær him leofost wæs,
þær he his heorðwerod   holdost wiste.
25 Þa stod on stæðe,   stiðlice clypode
wicinga ar,   wordum mælde,
se on beot abead   brimliþendra
ærænde to þam eorle,   þær he on ofre stod:
"Me sendon to þe   sæmen snelle,
30 heton ðe secgan   þæt þu most sendan raðe
beagas wið gebeorge;   and eow betere is
þæt ge þisne garræs   mid gafole forgyldon,

Battle of Maldon 4 to hige] t hige   5 þa þæt] þ þ   10 þam]þā   wige]
w . . . ge   20 randas] randan

þon we swa hearde   hilde dælon.
Ne þurfe we us spillan,   gif ge spedaþ to þam;
35 we willað wið þam golde   grið fæstnian.
Gyf þu þat gerædest,   þe her ricost eart,
þæt þu þine leoda   lysan wille,
syllan sæmannum   on hyra sylfra dom
feoh wið freode,   and niman frið æt us,
40 we willaþ mid þam sceattum   us to scype gangan,
on flot feran,   and eow friþes healdan."
   Byrhtnoð maþelode,   bord hafenode,
wand wacne æsc,   wordum mælde,
yrre and anræd   ageaf him andsware:
45 "Gehyrst þu, sælida,   hwæt þis folc segeð?
Hi willað eow to gafole   garas syllan,
ættrynne ord   and ealde swurd,
þa heregeatu   þe eow æt hilde ne deah.
Brimmanna boda,   abeod eft ongean,
50 sege þinum leodum   miccle laþre spell,
þæt her stynt unforcuð   eorl mid his werode,
þe wile gealgean   eþel þysne,
Æþelredes eard,   ealdres mines,
folc and foldan.   Feallan sceolon
55 hæþene æt hilde.   To heanlic me þinceð
þæt ge mid urum sceattum   to scype gangon
unbefohtene,   nu ge þus feor hider
on urne eard   in becomon.
Ne sceole ge swa softe   sinc gegangan;
60 us sceal ord and ecg   ær geseman,
grim guðplega,   ær we gofol syllon."
   Het þa bord beran,   beornas gangan,
þæt hi on þam easteðe   ealle stodon.
Ne mihte þær for wætere   werod to þam oðrum;
65 þær com flowende   flod æfter ebban,
lucon lagustreamas.   To lang hit him þuhte,
hwænne hi togædere   garas beron.
Hi þær Pantan stream   mid prasse bestodon,

33 hilde] . . ulde   61 we] þe

Eastseaxena ord   and se æschere.
70 Ne mihte hyra ænig   oþrum derian,
   buton hwa þurh flanes flyht   fyl gename.
   Se flod ut gewat;   þa flotan stodon gearowe,
   wicinga fela,   wiges georne.
   Het þa hæleða hleo   healdan þa bricge
75 wigan wigheardne,   se wæs haten Wulfstan,
   cafne mid his cynne,   þæt wæs Ceolan sunu,
   þe ðone forman man   mid his francan ofsceat
   þe þær baldlicost   on þa bricge stop.
   Þær stodon mid Wulfstane   wigan unforhte,
80 Ælfere and Maccus,   modige twegen,
   þa noldon æt þam forda   fleam gewyrcan,
   ac hi fæstlice   wið ða fynd weredon,
   þa hwile þe hi wæpna   wealdan moston.
   Þa hi þæt ongeaton   and georne gesawon
85 þæt hi þær bricgweardas   bitere fundon,
   ongunnon lytegian þa   laðe gystas,
   bædon þæt hi upgang   agan moston,
   ofer þone ford faran,   feþan lædan.
   Ða se eorl ongan   for his ofermode
90 alyfan landes to fela   laþere ðeode.
   Ongan ceallian þa   ofer cald wæter
   Byrhtelmes bearn   (beornas gehlyston):
   "Nu eow is gerymed,   gað ricene to us,
   guman to guþe;   god ana wat
95 hwa þære wælstowe   wealdan mote."
   Wodon þa wælwulfas   (for wætere ne murnon),
   wicinga werod,   west ofer Pantan,
   ofer scir wæter   scyldas wegon,
   lidmen to lande   linde bæron.
100 Þær ongean gramum   gearowe stodon
   Byrhtnoð mid beornum;   he mid bordum het
   wyrcan þone wihagan,   and þæt werod healdan
   fæste wið feondum.   Þa wæs feohte neh,
   tir æt getohte.   Wæs seo tid cumen

87 upgang] upgangan   97 west] pest? *See Note*   103 feohte] fohte

105 þæt þær fæge men   feallan sceoldon.
Þær wearð hream ahafen,   hremmas wundon,
earn æses georn;   wæs on eorþan cyrm.
Hi leton þa of folman   feolhearde speru,
gegrundene   garas fleogan;
110 bogan wæron bysige,   bord ord onfeng.
Biter wæs se beaduræs,   beornas feollon
on gehwæðere hand,   hyssas lagon.
Wund wearð Wulfmær,   wælræste geceas,
Byrhtnoðes mæg;   he mid billum wearð,
115 his swuster sunu,   swiðe forheawen.
Þær wearð wicingum   wiþerlean agyfen.
Gehyrde ic þæt Eadweard   anne sloge
swiðe mid his swurde,   swenges ne wyrnde,
þæt him æt fotum feoll   fæge cempa;
120 þæs him his ðeoden   þanc gesæde,
þam burþene,   þa he byre hæfde.
Swa stemnetton   stiðhicgende
hysas æt hilde,   hogodon georne
hwa þær mid orde   ærost mihte
125 on fægean men   feorh gewinnan,
wigan mid wæpnum;   wæl feol on eorðan.
Stodon stædefæste;   stihte hi Byrhtnoð,
bæd þæt hyssa gehwylc   hogode to wige
þe on Denon wolde   dom gefeohtan.
130 Wod þa wiges heard,   wæpen up ahof,
bord to gebeorge,   and wið þæs beornes stop.
Eode swa anræd   eorl to þam ceorle,
ægþer hyra oðrum   yfeles hogode.
Sende ða se særinc   suþerne gar,
135 þæt gewundod wearð   wigena hlaford;
he sceaf þa mid ðam scylde,   þæt se sceaft tobærst,
and þæt spere sprengde,   þæt hit sprang ongean.
Gegremod wearð se guðrinc;   he mid gare stang
wlancne wicing,   þe him þa wunde forgeaf.
140 Frod wæs se fyrdrinc;   he let his francan wadan

113 wearð] weard   116 wearð] wærd

þurh ðæs hysses hals,   hand wisode
þæt he on þam færsceaðan   feorh geræhte.
Ða he oþerne   ofstlice sceat,
þæt seo byrne tobærst;   he wæs on breostum wund
145 þurh ða hringlocan,   him æt heortan stod
ætterne ord.   Se eorl wæs þe bliþra,
hloh þa, modi man,   sæde metode þanc
ðæs dægweorces   þe him drihten forgeaf.
    Forlet þa drenga sum   daroð of handa,
150 fleogan of folman,   þæt se to forð gewat
þurh ðone æþelan   Æþelredes þegen.
Him be healfe stod   hyse unweaxen,
cniht on gecampe,   se full caflice
bræd of þam beorne   blodigne gar,
155 Wulfstanes bearn,   Wulfmær se geonga,
forlet forheardne   faran eft ongean;
ord in gewod,   þæt se on eorþan læg
þe his þeoden ær   þearle geræhte.
Eode þa gesyrwed   secg to þam eorle;
160 he wolde þæs beornes   beagas gefecgan,
reaf and hringas   and gerenod swurd.
Þa Byrhtnoð bræd   bill of sceðe,
brad and bruneccg,   and on þa byrnan sloh.
To raþe hine gelette   lidmanna sum,
165 þa he þæs eorles   earm amyrde.
Feoll þa to foldan   fealohilte swurd;
ne mihte he gehealdan   heardne mece,
wæpnes wealdan.   Þa gyt þæt word gecwæð
har hilderinc,   hyssas bylde,
170 bæd gangan forð   gode geferan;
ne mihte þa on fotum leng   fæste gestandan.
He to heofenum wlat:
"Geþancie þe,   ðeoda waldend,
ealra þæra wynna   þe ic on worulde gebad.
175 Nu ic ah, milde metod,   mæste þearfe
þæt þu minum gaste   godes geunne,

171 gestandan] ge stundan   173 Geþancie] ge þance

þæt min sawul to ðe   siðian mote
on þin geweald,   þeoden engla,
mid friþe ferian.   Ic eom frymdi to þe
180 þæt hi helsceaðan   hynan ne moton."
Ða hine heowon   hæðene scealcas
and begen þa beornas   þe him big stodon,
Ælfnoð and Wulmær   begen lagon,
ða onemn hyra frean   feorh gesealdon.
185 Hi bugon þa fram beaduwe   þe þær beon noldon.
Þær wearð Oddan bearn   ærest on fleame,
Godric fram guþe,   and þone godan forlet
þe him mænigne oft   mear gesealde;
he gehleop þone eoh   þe ahte his hlaford,
190 on þam gerædum   þe hit riht ne wæs,
and his broðru mid him   begen ærndon,
Godrine and Godwig,   guþe ne gymdon,
ac wendon fram þam wige   and þone wudu sohton,
flugon on þæt fæsten   and hyra feore burgon,
195 and manna ma   þonne hit ænig mæð wære,
gyf hi þa geearnunga   ealle gemundon
þe he him to duguþe   gedon hæfde.
Swa him Offa on dæg   ær asæde
on þam meþelstede,   þa he gemot hæfde,
200 þæt þær modiglice   manega spræcon
þe eft æt þearfe   þolian noldon.
Þa wearð afeallen   þæs folces ealdor,
Æþelredes eorl;   ealle gesawon
heorðgeneatas   þæt hyra heorra læg.
205 Þa ðær wendon forð   wlance þegenas,
unearge men   efston georne;
hi woldon þa ealle   oðer twega,
lif forlætan   oððe leofne gewrecan.
Swa hi bylde forð   bearn Ælfrices,
210 wiga wintrum geong,   wordum mælde,
Ælfwine þa cwæð,   he on ellen spræc:

186 wearð] wurdon   191 ærndon] ærdon   200 modiglice] modelice
201 þearfe] þære   208 forlætan] for lætun

"Gemunan þa mæla   þe we oft æt meodo spræcon,
þonne we on bence   beot ahofon,
hæleð on healle,   ymbe heard gewinn;
215 nu mæg cunnian   hwa cene sy.
Ic wylle mine æþelo   eallum gecyþan,
þæt ic wæs on Myrcon   miccles cynnes;
wæs min ealda fæder   Ealhelm haten,
wis ealdorman,   woruldgesælig.
220 Ne sceolon me on þære þeode   þegenas ætwitan
þæt ic of ðisse fyrde   feran wille,
eard gesecan,   nu min ealdor ligeð
forheawen æt hilde.   Me is þæt hearma mæst;
he wæs ægðer min mæg   and min hlaford."
225   Þa he forð eode,   fæhðe gemunde,
þæt he mid orde   anne geræhte
flotan on þam folce,   þæt se on foldan læg
forwegen mid his wæpne.   Ongan þa winas manian,
frynd and geferan,   þæt hi forð eodon.
230 Offa gemælde,   æscholt asceoc:
"Hwæt þu, Ælfwine, hafast   ealle gemanode
þegenas to þearfe,   nu ure þeoden lið,
eorl on eorðan.   Us is eallum þearf
þæt ure æghwylc   oþerne bylde
235 wigan to wige,   þa hwile þe he wæpen mæge
habban and healdan,   heardne mece,
gar and godswurd.   Us Godric hæfð,
earh Oddan bearn,   ealle beswicene.
Wende þæs formoni man,   þa he on meare rad,
240 on wlancan þam wicge,   þæt wære hit ure hlaford;
forþan wearð her on felda   folc totwæmed,
scyldburh tobrocen.   Abreoðe his angin,
þæt he her swa manigne   man aflymde!"
Leofsunu gemælde   and his linde ahof,
245 bord to gebeorge;   he þam beorne oncwæð:
"Ic þæt gehate,   þæt ic heonon nelle
fleon fotes trym,   ac wille furðor gan,

212 Gemunan] ge munu   224 ægðer] ægder

wrecan on gewinne   minne winedrihten.
Ne þurfon me embe Sturmere   stedefæste hælæð
250 wordum ætwitan,   nu min wine gecranc,
þæt ic hlafordleas   ham siðie,
wende fram wige,   ac me sceal wæpen niman,
ord and iren."   He ful yrre wod,
feaht fæstlice,   fleam he forhogode.
255 Dunnere þa cwæð,   daroð acwehte,
unorne ceorl,   ofer eall clypode,
bæd þæt beorna gehwylc   Byrhtnoð wræce:
"Ne mæg na wandian   se þe wrecan þenceð
frean on folce,   ne for feore murnan."
260 Þa hi forð eodon,   feores hi ne rohton;
ongunnon þa hiredmen   heardlice feohtan,
grame garberend,   and god bædon
þæt hi moston gewrecan   hyra winedrihten
and on hyra feondum   fyl gewyrcan.
265 Him se gysel ongan   geornlice fylstan;
he wæs on Norðhymbron   heardes cynnes,
Ecglafes bearn,   him wæs Æscferð nama.
He ne wandode na   æt þam wigplegan,
ac he fysde forð   flan genehe;
270 hwilon he on bord sceat,   hwilon beorn tæsde,
æfre embe stunde   he sealde sume wunde,
þa hwile ðe he wæpna   wealdan moste.
   Þa gyt on orde stod   Eadweard se langa,
gearo and geornful,   gylpwordum spræc
275 þæt he nolde fleogan   fotmæl landes,
ofer bæc bugan,   þa his betera leg.
He bræc þone bordweall   and wið þa beornas feaht,
oðþæt he his sincgyfan   on þam sæmannum
wurðlice wrec,   ær he on wæle læge.
280 Swa dyde Æþeric,   æþele gefera,
fus and forðgeorn,   feaht eornoste.
Sibyrhtes broðor   and swiðe mænig oþer
clufon cellod bord,   cene hi weredon;

257 wræce] wręce   279 læge] lęge

bærst bordes lærig,   and seo byrne sang
285 gryreleoða sum. Þa æt guðe sloh
Offa þone sælidan,   þæt he on eorðan feoll,
and ðær Gaddes mæg   grund gesohte.
Raðe wearð æt hilde   Offa forheawen;
he hæfde ðeah geforþod   þæt he his frean gehet,
290 swa he beotode ær   wið his beahgifan
þæt hi sceoldon begen   on burh ridan,
hale to hame,   oððe on here crincgan,
on wælstowe   wundum sweltan;
he læg ðegenlice   ðeodne gehende.
295   Ða wearð borda gebræc. Brimmen wodon,
guðe gegremode;   gar oft þurhwod
fæges feorhhus. Forð þa eode Wistan,
Þurstanes sunu,   wið þas secgas feaht;
he wæs on geþrange   hyra þreora bana,
300 ær him Wigelines bearn   on þam wæle læge.
Þær wæs stið gemot;   stodon fæste
wigan on gewinne,   wigend cruncon,
wundum werige. Wæl feol on eorþan.
Oswold and Eadwold   ealle hwile,
305 begen þa gebroþru,   beornas trymedon,
hyra winemagas   wordon bædon
þæt hi þær æt ðearfe   þolian sceoldon,
unwaclice   wæpna neotan.
Byrhtwold maþelode,   bord hafenode
310 (se wæs eald geneat),   æsc acwehte;
he ful baldlice   beornas lærde:
"Hige sceal þe heardra,   heorte þe cenre,
mod sceal þe mare,   þe ure mægen lytlað.
Her lið ure ealdor   eall forheawen,
315 god on greote. A mæg gnornian
se ðe nu fram þis wigplegan   wendan þenceð.
Ic eom frod feores;   fram ic ne wille,
ac ic me be healfe   minum hlaforde,

292 crincgan] crintgan   297 Forð þa] forða   298 sunu] suna
299 geþrange] geþrang

be swa leofan men,   licgan þence."
320 Swa hi Æþelgares bearn   ealle bylde,
    Godric to guþe.   Oft he gar forlet,
    wælspere windan   on þa wicingas,
    swa he on þam folce   fyrmest eode,
    heow and hynde,   oðþæt he on hilde gecranc.
325 Næs þæt na se Godric   þe ða guðe forbeah

*   *   *

THE POEMS OF THE ANGLO-SAXON CHRONICLE

1. THE BATTLE OF BRUNANBURH (937)

Text from MS. 173, Corpus Christi College, Cambridge (A); variants from MS. Cotton Tiberius A. vi (B), MS. Cotton Tiberius B. i (C), and MS. Cotton Tiberius B. iv (D)

    Her Æþelstan cyning,   eorla dryhten,
    beorna beahgifa,   and his broþor eac,
    Eadmund æþeling,   ealdorlangne tir
    geslogon æt sæcce   sweorda ecgum
5 ymbe Brunanburh.   Bordweal clufan,
    heowan heaþolinde   hamora lafan,
    afaran Eadweardes,   swa him geæþele wæs

324 oðþæt] od þ   325 guðe] gude   Battle of Brunanburh 1 Æþelstan] æþestan *B*   cyning] cing *B C*   dryhten] drihten *B C D*   2 beahgifa] beaggifa *B;* beahgyfa *C*   broþor] broðor *C*   3 ealdorlangne] ealdor lagne *C*   tir] tyr *D*   4 geslogon] geslogan *B*   sæcce] sake *B;* secce *D* sweorda] swurda *C*   ecgum] ecggum *B*   5 ymbe] embe *B C*   Brunanburh] *D;* brunan burh *with a second* n *added above the line after the first* u *in a later hand A;* brun nanburh *C; B's reading is illegible*   Bordweal] bordweall *B C;* heord weal *D*   clufan] clufon *C*   6 heowan] heowon *C* heaþolinde] heaðolina *B;* heaþo linda *C;* heaðolinga *with g dotted beneath for deletion and* d *written above in the same hand D*   hamora] hamera *B D* lafan] lafum *B C D*   7 afaran] eaforan *B;* aforan *C;* eoforan *with the first* o *dotted beneath for deletion and later changed to* a *D*   Eadweardes] eadweardæs *D*   geæþele] ge æðele *D*

from cneomægum,   þæt hi æt campe oft
wiþ laþra gehwæne   land ealgodon,
10 hord and hamas.   Hettend crungun,
   Sceotta leoda   and scipflotan
   fæge feollan,   feld dænnede
   secga swate,   siðþan sunne up
   on morgentid,   mære tungol,
15 glad ofer grundas,   godes condel beorht,
   eces drihtnes,   oð sio æþele gesceaft
   sah to setle.   þær læg secg mænig
   garum ageted,   guma norþerna
   ofer scild scoten,   swilce Scittisc eac,
20 werig, wiges sæd.   Wesseaxe forð
   ondlongne dæg   eorodcistum
   on last legdun   laþum þeodum,
   heowan herefleman   hindan þearle
   mecum mylenscearpan.   Myrce ne wyrndon
25 heardes hondplegan   hæleþa nanum
   þæra þe mid Anlafe   ofer æra gebland
   on lides bosme   land gesohtun,

8 from] fram *B C D*   cneomægum] cneo magum *B*   hi] hie *B*   9 wiþ]
wið *B C D*   laþra] laðra *B*   gehwæne] gehwane *B*   ealgodon]
ealgodan *B;* gealgodon *D*   10 Hettend] heted *D*   crungun] crungon
B C D   11 Sceotta] scotta *B C D*   leoda] leode *B C D*   scipflotan]
scypflotan *C*   12 feollan] feollon *D*   dænnede] *With the second* n *added
above the line A;* dennade *B C;* dennode *D*   13 secga swate] *B C D;* secgas
hwate *A*   siðþan] siþþan *B D;* siððan *C*   up] upp *B C*   15 condel]
candel *B C D*   16 oð sio] þ seo *B;* oþ seo *C;* oð se *D*   17 setle] setle *D*
mænig] manig *B;* monig *C D*   18 ageted] forgrunden *B*   guma] guman
B C D   norþerna] norðerne *B C;* norþærne *D*   19 scild] scyld *B C D*
scoten] sceoten *B D*   swilce] swylce *B D*   Scittisc] scyttisc *B C D*
20 wiges] wigges *B C*   sæd] ræd *D*   Wesseaxe] west sexe *B;* 7 wes sexe *C*
21 ondlongne] andlangne *B C;* 7 langne *D*   eorodcistum] eored cystum
B C D   22 legdun] legdon *B C;* lægdon *D*   laþum] laðum *B*   þeodum]
ðeodon *C;* ðeodum *D*   23 heowan] heowon *C*   herefleman] herefly man
B; here flymon *C;* heora flyman *D*   24 mylenscearpan] mylenscearpum
B C; mycel scearpum *D*   25 heardes] *B C D;* he eardes *A*   hondplegan]
handplegan *B C D*   nanum] namū *with* m *partly corrected to* n *C*
26 þæra þe] *D;* þæ *A;* þara ðe *B C*   æra gebland] eargebland *B C D*
27 lides] liþes *C*   gesohtun] ge sohtan *B;* gesohton *C D*

fæge to gefeohte.   Fife lægun
on þam campstede   cyningas giunge,
30 sweordum aswefede,   swilce seofene eac
eorlas Anlafes,   unrim heriges,
flotan and Sceotta.   þær geflemed wearð
Norðmanna bregu,   nede gebeded,
to lides stefne   litle weorode;
35 cread cnear on flot,   cyning ut gewat
on fealene flod,   feorh generede.
Swilce þær eac se froda   mid fleame com
on his cyþþe norð,   Costontinus,
har hilderinc,   hreman ne þorfte
40 mæca gemanan;   he wæs his mæga sceard,
freonda gefylled   on folcstede,
beslagen æt sæcce,   and his sunu forlet
on wælstowe   wundun forgrunden,
giungne æt guðe.   Gelpan ne þorfte
45 beorn blandenfeax   bilgeslehtes,
eald inwidda,   ne Anlaf þy ma;

28 fæge] fage D   gefeohte] feohte D   lægun] lagon B C D   29 þam]
ðæm B   cyningas] D; cyninges A; ciningas B; cingas C   giunge]
geonge B C; iunga D   30 aswefede] aswefde C   swilce] swylce D
seofene] seofone B; VII C   31 unrim] 7 unrim C   heriges] herges B C D
32 Sceotta] scotta B C D   geflemed] geflymed B C D   33 bregu] brego
B C D   nede] neade C D   gebeded] gebæded B C D   34 stefne]
stæfne D   litle] lytle B C D   weorode] werode C   35 cread] creat D
cnear on] B C D; cnearen A   flot] flod D   cyning] cing B; cining C
35–36 cyning ut gewat on fealene flod] Not in D   36 fealene] fealone B C
feorh] A letter (t?) erased after this word D   generede] generode C D
37 Swilce] Swylce B; swylce D   38 cyþþe] cyððe C D   Costontinus]
consta ntinus B C D   39 har] hal D   hilderinc] B C; hylde rinc D;
hilderᶦng A   hreman] hryman D   þorfte] ðorfte C   40 mæca]
mæcan A; mecea B; meca C; in ecga D   he] her B C   mæga] maga B C
41 on folcstede] on his folcstede C   42 beslagen] forslegen B; besle gen C;
beslægen D   sæcce] sace B; sęcge D   forlet] forlæt D   43 wundun]
wundum B C D   forgrunden] B C D; fer grunden A   44 giungne]
geongne B C D   guðe] guþe B C   Gelpan] gylpan B C D   45 bland-
enfeax] blandenfex B C   bilgeslehtes] bill geslyhtes B; billgeslihtes C D
46 inwidda] inwitta B C; inwuda D   þy] þe B D

mid heora herelafum   hlehhan ne þorftun
þæt heo beaduweorca   beteran wurdun
on campstede   cumbolgehnastes,
50 garmittinge,   gumena gemotes,
wæpengewrixles,   þæs hi on wælfelda
wiþ Eadweardes   afaran plegodan.
Gewitan him þa Norþmen   nægledcnearrum,
dreorig daraða laf,   on Dinges mere
55 ofer deop wæter   Difelin secan,
eft Iraland,   æwiscmode.
Swilce þa gebroþer   begen ætsamne,
cyning and æþeling,   cyþþe sohton,
Wesseaxena land,   wiges hremige.
60 Letan him behindan   hræw bryttian
saluwigpadan,   þone sweartan hræfn,
hyrnednebban,   and þane hasewanpadan,

47 heora] hyra *C D*   herelafum] here leafum *D*   hlehhan] hlihhan *B C;*
hlybban *D*   þorftun] þorftan *B D;* ðorftun *C*   48 heo] hie *B;* hi *C D*
beaduweorca] beadoweorca *B C D*   wurdun] wurdan *B;* wurdon *C D*
49 cumbolgehnastes] *B C D;* cul bod gehnades *with* l cum bel *written above*
cul bod *in a later hand A*   50 garmittinge] gar mittunge *D*   51 þæs]
þæs þe *D*   hi] hie *B*   52 wiþ] wið *C D*   afaran] eafo ran *B;* aforan *C*
plegodan] plegodon *C D*   53 Gewitan] Gewiton *C D*   him] hym *C*
Norþmen] *With the* þ *added above the line A;* norðmenn *B C;* norðmen *D*
nægledcnearrum] *B;* nægled cnearrū *A;* negledcnearrum *C;* dæggled ongarum
D   54 dreorig] dreori *C*   daraða] daroða *B;* dare þa *C;* dareða *D*
Dinges] dynges *B;* dyniges *D*   55 ofer] *With the* r *added above the line in
the same hand D*   deop] deopne *D*   Difelin] dyflen *B;* dyflin *C;* dyflig *D*
secan] secean *B*   56 eft] *With* 7 *added above the line before* eft *A*   Iraland]
B; hira land *A;* yraland *C D*   57 Swilce] swylce *B D*   gebroþer] gebro
ðor *B;* broðor *C;* ge broþor *D*   begen ætsamne] begen ætsomne *B C;*
bege ætrunne *D*   58 cyning] cing *B C*   æþeling] eaðe ling *D*   cyþþe]
cyððe *D*   sohton] sohtan *B*   59 Wesseaxena] west seaxna *B D;* wes-
sexena *C*   wiges] wigges *B C*   hremige] *B C D;* hramige *with a* marked
for deletion and e *written above A*   60 Letan] leton *C;* læton *D*   him] hym
C   behindan] behindon *C*   hræw] *With the* w *added above the line A;*
hraw *B;* hra *C D*   bryttian] bryttigean *B;* brittigan *C;* bryttinga *D*
61 saluwigpadan] salowigpadan *B C D*   hræfn] hrefn *C*   62 hyrnedneb-
ban] hyrnet nebban *D*   þane] þone *B C D*   hasewanpadan] hasopadan
B; hasu padan *C;* hasuwadan *D*

earn æftan hwit,   æses brucan,
grædigne guðhafoc   and þæt græge deor,
65 wulf on wealde.   Ne wearð wæl mare
on þis eiglande   æfre gieta
folces gefylled   beforan þissum
sweordes ecgum,   þæs þe us secgað bec,
ealde uðwitan,   siþþan eastan hider
70 Engle and Seaxe   up becoman,
ofer brad brimu   Brytene sohtan,
wlance wigsmiþas,   Wealas ofercoman,
eorlas arhwate   eard begeatan.

2. THE CAPTURE OF THE FIVE
BOROUGHS (942)

Text from MS. 173, Corpus Christi College, Cambridge (A);
variants from MS. Cotton Tiberius A. vi (B), MS. Cotton
Tiberius B. i (C), and MS. Cotton Tiberius B. iv (D)

Her Eadmund cyning,   Engla þeoden,
mæcgea mundbora,   Myrce geeode,
dyre dædfruma,   swa Dor scadeþ,
Hwitanwyllesgeat   and Humbra ea,
5 brada brimstream.   Burga fife,
Ligoraceaster   and Lincylene

63 æses] æres *with* r *altered to* s *by erasure* D   64 guðhafoc] guþhafoc B;
cuð heafoc D   græge] grege D   66 þis] þys B C; þisne D   eiglande]
eglande B; iglande C D   æfre] B C D; æfer A   gieta] gyta B C; gita D
67 gefylled] afylled B   þissum] þyssum B C D   68 sweordes] swurdes C
þe] ðe C   secgað] secggeaþ B   69 uðwitan] uþwitan B C   siþþan]
syþþan B; siððan C D   70 Seaxe] sexan B; sexe C   up] upp B C
becoman] becomon C D   71 brad] brade B C D   Brytene] bretene C;
britene D   sohtan] sohton C D   72 wigsmiþas] wigsmiðas C D
Wealas] B C D; weealles A   ofercoman] ofercomon C D   73 arhwate]
arhwæte D   begeatan] begeaton B C D   Five Boroughs 1 cyning]
cing B C   2 mæcgea] B; maga A; mecga C; mægþa D   3 scadeþ]
sceadeþ B C; sceadæð D   4 Humbra] humbran B; hunbran C; himbran D
5 brimstream] brym stream D   fife] gife D   6 Ligoraceaster] ligera
ceaster B; ligera cester C; ligere ceaster D   Lincylene] lin cylene *with* d
erased after lin *and* y *on an erasure* A; lind kylne B; lind cylne C; lincolne D

and Snotingaham,   swylce Stanford eac
and Deoraby. Dæne wæran æror
under Norðmannum   nyde gebegde
10 on hæþenra   hæfteclommum
lange þrage,   oþ hie alysde eft
for his weorþscipe   wiggendra hleo,
afera Eadweardes,   Eadmund cyning.

3. THE CORONATION OF EDGAR (973)

Text from MS. 173, Corpus Christi College, Cambridge (A);
variants from MS. Cotton Tiberius A. vi (B) and MS. Cotton Tiberius B. i (C)

Her Eadgar wæs,   Engla waldend,
corðre miclum   to cyninge gehalgod
on ðære ealdan byrig,   Acemannesceastre;
eac hi igbuend   oðre worde
5 beornas Baðan nemnaþ.   þær wæs blis micel
on þam eadgan dæge   eallum geworden,
þone niða bearn   nemnað and cigað
Pentecostenes dæg.   þær wæs preosta heap,
micel muneca ðreat,   mine gefrege,
10 gleawra gegaderod.   And ða agangen wæs
tyn hund wintra   geteled rimes
fram gebyrdtide. bremes cyninges,

7 and] *Not in B C*   swylce] swilce *C*   8 and] *B C D; not in A*   Dæne]
denum *B;* dene *C*   wæran] wæron *B C D*   æror] *B C D;* ær *A*   9 nyde]
nede *B*   gebegde] gebæded *B C D*   10 hæþenra] hæþenum *B;* hæðenra
D   hæfteclommum] hæfte clammum *B*   11 þrage] *B C D;* þraga *A*
oþ hie] oþ hi *C;* oð hy *D*   12 weorþscipe] weorðscipe *B D;* weorðscype *C*
wiggendra] wigendra *D*   13 afera] eafora *B;* afora *C D*   Eadmund]
eadmundes *D*   cyning] cining *B;* cing *C*   Coronation of Edgar 2
corðre] corþre *C*   miclum] micelre *A;* mycclum *B C*   cyninge] kinge
B C   3 ðære] þære *B C*   4 hi] hie *B C*   igbuend] egbuend *B C*
oðre] oþre *B C*   5 Baðan] *B;* baðan *with* o *written above the second* a *A;*
baþan *with the* n *added above the line C*   nemnaþ] nemnað *B;* nemneð *C*
micel] mycel *B*   7 þone] *B C;* þonne *A*   niða] niþa *C*   cigað] cegeað
B; cegeaþ *C*   9 micel] mycel *B C*   ðreat] þreat *B C*   gefrege] gefræge
B C   10 gegaderod] gegadorod *C*   ða] þa *B C*   12 cyninges] cinges
B C

leohta hyrdes,　buton ðær to lafe þa get
wæs wintergeteles,　þæs ðe gewritu secgað,
15 seofon and twentig;　swa neah wæs sigora frean
ðusend aurnen,　ða þa ðis gelamp.
And him Eadmundes　eafora hæfde
nigon and XX,　niðweorca heard,
wintra on worulde,　ða þis geworden wæs,
20 and þa on ðam XXX wæs　ðeoden gehalgod.

4. THE DEATH OF EDGAR (975)

Text from MS. 173, Corpus Christi College, Cambridge (A);
variants from MS. Cotton Tiberius A. vi (B) and MS. Cotton Tiberius B. i (C)

　Her geendode　eorðan dreamas
Eadgar, Engla cyning,　ceas him oðer leoht,
wlitig and wynsum,·　and þis wace forlet,
lif þis læne.　Nemnað leoda bearn,
5 men on moldan,　þæne monað gehwær
in ðisse eðeltyrf,　þa þe ær wæran
on rimcræfte　rihte getogene,
Iulius monoð,　þær se geonga gewat
on þone eahteðan dæg　Eadgar of life,
10 beorna beahgyfa.　Feng his bearn syððan

---

13 hyrdes] hirdes C　buton] butan B C　ðær] þær C　þa get] B;
ðaget C; þa agan A　14 wintergeteles] winter getæles C　ðe] Not in B
15 seofon and twentig] seofan 7 XX B C　16 ðusend] þusend B C　ða þa]
þa ða C　ðis] þis B C　18 nigon] nigen B C　niðweorca] niþweorca B
19 worulde] worlde B; wu rulde C　ða þis] B; þa ðis C; ða not in A
20 and] On B　ðam] þam C　XXX] þrittigæþan B; ðrittigeþan C
ðeoden] þeoden B　Death of Edgar 1 eorðan] eorþan C　2 Engla]
angla C　cyning] cing B C　oðer] oþer B C　3 wlitig] wlytig C
wynsum] winsum C　þis] ðis C　5 men] menn B C　þæne] þone B C
monað] monaþ B　6 in ðisse] on þisse B; on þysse C　eðeltyrf] eþeltyrf
B C　þe] ðe C　wæran] wæron B C　8 monoð] monð B; monþ C
þær] B; ðær C; þ A　gewat] A letter erased after this word A　9 eahteðan]
eahtoðan B; eahtoþan C　beahgyfa] beahgifa B C　Feng] B C; in A
the abbreviation 7 is written before feng in a different hand　syððan] syþþan
B; siððan C

to cynerice,   cild unweaxen,
eorla ealdor,   þam wæs Eadweard nama.
And him tirfæst hæleð   tyn nihtum ær
of Brytene gewat,   bisceop se goda,
15 þurh gecyndne cræft,   ðam wæs Cyneweard nama.
Ða wæs on Myrceon,   mine gefræge,
wide and welhwær   waldendes lof
afylled on foldan.   Fela wearð todræfed
gleawra godes ðeowa;   þæt wæs gnornung micel
20 þam þe on breostum wæg   byrnende lufan
metodes on mode.   Þa wæs mærða fruma
to swiðe forsewen,   sigora waldend,
rodera rædend,   þa man his riht tobræc.
And þa wearð eac adræfed   deormod hæleð,
25 Oslac, of earde   ofer yða gewealc,
ofer ganotes bæð,   gamolfeax hæleð,
wis and wordsnotor,   ofer wætera geðring,
ofer hwæles eðel,   hama bereafod.
And þa wearð ætywed   uppe on roderum
30 steorra on staðole,   þone stiðferhþe,
hæleð higegleawe,   hatað wide
cometa be naman,   cræftgleawe men,
wise woðboran.   Wæs geond werðeode
waldendes wracu   wide gefrege,
35 hungor ofer hrusan;   þæt eft heofona weard

---

11 unweaxen] *A letter* (e?) *erased after this word A;* unwexen B C   12 ealdor]
aldor B C   þam] ðam B   13 hæleð] hæleþ B   tyn] X B C   14 Bry-
tene] britene C   15 ðam] þam B C   16 Ða] þa C   wæs] wearð B C
Myrceon] myrcum B C   17 welhwær] welhrær B   18 Fela] feala B C
wearð] weard B   19 ðeowa] þeowa B C   micel] mycel B   20 þe] ðe C
21 metodes] meotodes B C   þa] ða C   mærða] mærþa C   22 swiðe]
swiþe B   forsewen] forsawen B C   24 And] *Not in* B C   þa] Ða B
hæleð] hæleþ B C   25 yða] yþa B C   gewealc] gewalc B C   26 gamol-
feax] gomolfeax B C   hæleð] hæleþ B C   27 geðring] geþring B C
28 eðel] eþel B C   29 And] *Not in* B C   ætywed] eac ætywed B C
30 staðole] staþole C   þone] ðone B   stiðferhþe] stiþ ferhþe B
31 hæleð] hæleþ B   32 men] menn B C   33 woðboran] B C; soðboran A
werðeode] werþeode B C   34 gefrege] gefræge B C

gebette, brego engla,   geaf eft blisse gehwæm
egbuendra   þurh eorðan westm.

5. THE DEATH OF ALFRED (1036)

Text from MS. Cotton Tiberius B. i (C); variants from MS.
Cotton Tiberius B. iv (D)

Her com Ælfred, se unsceððiga æþeling, Æþelrædes
sunu cinges, hider inn and wolde to his meder, þe on Win-
cestre sæt, ac hit him ne geþafode Godwine eorl, ne ec oþre
men þe mycel mihton wealdan, forðan hit hleoðrode þa
5 swiðe toward Haraldes, þeh hit unriht wære.
  Ac Godwine hine þa gelette   and hine on hæft sette,
  and his geferan he todraf,   and sume mislice ofsloh;
  sume hi man wið feo sealde,   sume hreowlice acwealde,
  sume hi man bende,   sume hi man blende,
10 sume hamelode,   sume hættode.
  Ne wearð dreorlicre dæd   gedon on þison earde,
  syþþan Dene comon   and her frið namon.
  Nu is to gelyfenne   to ðan leofan gode,
  þæt hi blission   bliðe mid Criste
15 þe wæron butan scylde   swa earmlice acwealde.
  Se æþeling lyfode þa gyt;   ælc yfel man him gehet,
  oðþæt man gerædde   þæt man hine lædde
  to Eligbyrig   swa gebundenne.
  Sona swa he lende,   on scype man hine blende,

---

37 westm] wæstm *B C*   Death of Alfred 1 unsceððiga] unsceððia *with* g
inserted after i *D*   Æþelrædes] æþelredes *D*   2 cinges] cynges *D*
meder] modor *D*   3–4 hit him...wealdan] þ ne geþafodon þa þe micel
weoldon on þisan lande *D*   4 forðan] forþan *D*   hleoðrode] hleo þrade *D*
5 toward Haraldes] to harolde *D*   þeh] þeah *D*   6 Ac...sette] Ða let
he hine on hæft settan *D*   7 todraf] eac fordraf *D*   9–10 sume hi man
blende...hættode] 7 eac sume blende 7 heanlice hættode *D*   11 dreorlicre]
dreorilicre *D*   þison] þisan *D*   12 syþþan] siððan *D*   comon] coman *D*
frið] fryð *D*   namon] naman *D*   13 gelyfenne] gelyfanne *D*   ðan]
þan *D*   14 Criste] *D;* xρe *C*   15 swa] *Not in D*   16 lyfode] leofode *D*
gehet] behet *D*   18 Eligbyrig] elibyrig *D*   swa] eal swa *D*

20 and hine swa blindne   brohte to ðam munecon,
   and he þar wunode   ða hwile þe he lyfode.
   Syððan hine man byrigde,   swa him wel gebyrede,
   ful wurðlice,   swa he wyrðe wæs,
   æt þam westende,   þam styple ful gehende,
25 on þam suðportice;   seo saul is mid Criste.

6. THE DEATH OF EDWARD (1065)

Text from MS. Cotton Tiberius B. i (C); variants from MS.
Cotton Tiberius B. iv (D)

   Her Eadward kingc,   Engla hlaford,
   sende soþfæste   sawle to Criste
   on godes wæra,   gast haligne.
   He on worulda her   wunode þrage
5 on kyneþrymme,   cræftig ræda,
   XXIIII,   freolic wealdend,
   wintra gerimes,   weolan britnode,
   and healfe tid,   hæleða wealdend,
   weold wel geþungen   Walum and Scottum
10 and Bryttum eac,   byre Æðelredes,
   Englum and Sexum,   oretmægcum,
   swa ymbclyppað   cealde brymmas,
   þæt eall Eadwarde,   æðelum kinge,

---

20 blindne] blinde *with* n *added above the line after* d *D*   ðam munecon]
þam munecū *D*   21 þar] þær *D*   ða] þa *D*   lyfode] leofode *D*
23 ful wurðlice] þ wæs full weorðlice *D*   24 styple] stypele *D*
25 suðportice] *With* r *corrected from* s? *C*   saul] sawul *D*   Criste] *D;*
xþe *C*   Death of Edward 1 Her] *The capital* H *is lost in* C   kingc] cing
D   Engla] englene *D*   2 soþfæste] *The final* te *is lost in* C; soðfeste *D*
sawle] saule *D*   Criste] kriste *D*   3 wæra] wera *D*   4 worulda]
weorolda *D*   wunode] wunodæ *D*   þrage] þragæ *D*   5 kyneþrymme]
kine þrymme *D*   cræftig] creftig *D*   6 wealdend] wealdand *D*
7 gerimes] rimes *with an erasure before* r *D*   weolan britnode] *D;* weolm
brytnodon *with final* n *added above the line* C   8 and healfe] 7 he hæ *with*
lo *added above the line after* hæ (*i.e.* hælo) *D*   hæleða] hęleða *D*   9
geþungen] ge ðungæn *D*   11 Sexum] sæxum *D*   oretmægcum] orec
mægcum *D*   12 ymbclyppað] ymb clypaþ *with a second* p *added above
the line after* y *D*   cealde] ceald *C;* cealda *D*   13 Eadwarde] eadwardæ *D*
æðelum] æþelum *D*

    hyrdon holdlice   hagestealde menn.
15 Wæs a bliðemod   bealuleas kyng,
    þeah he lange ær,   lande bereafod,
    wunode wræclastum   wide geond eorðan,
    syððan Cnut ofercom   kynn Æðelredes
    and Dena weoldon   deore rice
20 Engla landes   XXVIII
    wintra gerimes,   welan brytnodon.
    Syððan forð becom   freolice in geatwum
    kyningc kystum god,   clæne and milde,
    Eadward se æðela,   eðel bewerode,
25 land and leode,   oðþæt lungre becom
    deað se bitera,   and swa deore genam
    æþelne of eorðan;   englas feredon
    soþfæste sawle   innan swegles leoht.
    And se froda swa þeah   befæste þæt rice
30 heahþungenum menn,   Harolde sylfum,
    æþelum eorle,   se in ealle tid
    hyrde holdlice   hærran sinum
    wordum and dædum,   wihte ne agælde
    þæs þe þearf wæs   þæs þeodkyninges.

14 hyrdon] hyrdan *D*   holdlice] hodelice *with* l *added above the line after* o *D*
hagestealde] hagestalde *D*   15 bealuleas] bealeleas *D*   kyng] king *D*
16 þeah] þah *D*   lange] lang *C;* langa *D*   lande] landes *D*   17 wunode]
wunoda *D*   wræclastum] wreclastum *D*   18 syððan] seoþan *D*   Cnut]
knut *D*   kynn] cynn *D*   19 Dena] deona *D*   21 welan] weolan *D*
brytnodon] *D;* brynodan *C*   22 Syððan] siððan *D*   freolice] freolic *D*
23 kyningc] kinigc *D*   kystum] cystum *D*   clæne] clęne *D*   24 æðela]
æðele *D*   bewerode] bewarede *D*   25 leode] leodan *D*   oðþæt]
oððæt *D*   lungre] lunger *C D*   26 bitera] bytera *with* a *altered from* e *D*
27 æþelne] æðelne *D*   28 soþfæste] soðfeste *D*   innan] inne *D*
29 þeah] ðeah *D*   befæste] befęste *D*   30 heahþungenum] heah ðungna
with e *added above the line after* g *D*   31 æþelum] æðelum *D*   ealle]
ealne *D*   32 hyrde] herdæ *D*   holdlice] hodelice *with* l *added above the
line after* o *D*   hærran] herran *D*   sinum] synum *D*   33 dædum]
dędum *D*   agælde] agęlde *D*   34 þearf] ðearfe *D*   34*b* þæs] ðæs *D*
þeodkyninges] þeodkyngces *D*

DURHAM

Text from MS. Ff. i. 27, University Library, Cambridge (C); variants from Hickes (H)

Is ðeos burch breome   geond Breotenrice,
steppa gestaðolad,   stanas ymbutan
wundrum gewæxen.   Weor ymbeornad,
ea yðum stronge,   and ðer inne wunað
5 feola fisca kyn   on floda gemonge.
And ðær gewexen is   wudafæstern micel;
wuniad in ðem wycum   wilda deor monige,
in deope dalum   deora ungerim.
Is in ðere byri eac   bearnum gecyðed
10 ðe arfesta   eadig Cudberch
and ðes clene   cyninges heafud,
Osuualdes, Engle leo,   and Aidan biscop,
Eadberch and Eadfrið,   æðele geferes.
Is ðer inne midd heom   Æðelwold biscop
15 and breoma bocera Beda,   and Boisil abbot,
ðe clene Cudberte   on gecheðe
lerde lustum,   and he his lara wel genom.
Eardiæð æt ðem eadige   in in ðem minstre
unarimeda   reliquia,
20 ðær monia wundrum gewurðað,   ðes ðe writ seggeð,
midd ðene drihnes wer   domes bideð.

Durham 2 steppa] Steopa *H*   3 ymbeornad] *With* d *altered from* n *C*; ymb
eornað *H*   4 ea] Ean *H*   stronge] strong *H*   5 feola fisca] fcola fisca
with c *of* fcola *added above the line C*; Fisca feola *H*   kyn] kinn *H*
gemonge] gemong *H*   6 ðær] ðere *H*   is] *Not in H*   wudafæstern]
Wuda festern *H*   micel] mycel *H*   7 wuniad] Wuniað *H*   ðem] þem
H   wycum] wicum *H*   8 deope] deopa *H*   in] im *H*   gecyðed]
geciðed *H*   10 Cudberch] Cuðbercht *H*   11 clene] clæne *H*   cyninges]
H; cyniuges *C*   heafud] heofud *H*   12 Osuualdes] Osualdes *H*
Engle] Engla *H*   biscop] bisceop *H*   13 Eadberch] Ædbercht *H*
Eadfrið] Ædfrid *H*   14 midd] mid *H*   Æðelwold] *H*; 7ðelwold *C*
biscop] bisceop *H*   15 Beda] *H*; beba *with the second* b *dotted beneath for
deletion and* d *written above, i.e.* beda *C*   abbot] abbet *H*   16 clene]
clæne *H*   Cudberte] Cuðberchte *H*   gecheðe] gicheðe *H*   17 his]
H; wis *C*   18 Eardiæð] Eardiað *H*   minstre] mynstre *H*   20 ðær]
H; ðe *C*   monia] monige *H*   ðes] *Not in H*   writ] writa *H*
21 midd] Mid *H*   drihnes] drihtnes *H*

27

THE RUNE POEM

   ᚠ (feoh) byþ frofur   fira gehwylcum.
Sceal ðeah manna gehwylc   miclun hyt dælan
gif he wile for drihtne   domes hleotan.
   ᚢ (ur) byþ anmod   and oferhyrned,
5 felafrecne deor,   feohteþ mid hornum,
mære morstapa;   þæt is modig wuht.
   ᚦ (ðorn) byþ ðearle scearp;   ðegna gehwylcum
anfeng ys yfyl,   ungemetun reþe
manna gehwylcun   ðe him mid resteð.
10 ᚩ (os) byþ ordfruma   ælcre spræce,
wisdomes wraþu   and witena frofur,
and eorla gehwam   eadnys and tohiht.
   ᚱ (rad) byþ on recyde   rinca gehwylcum
sefte, and swiþhwæt   ðam ðe sitteþ on ufan
15 meare mægenheardum   ofer milpaþas.
   ᚳ (cen) byþ cwicera gehwam   cuþ on fyre,
blac and beorhtlic,   byrneþ oftust
ðær hi æþelingas   inne restaþ.
   ᚷ (gyfu) gumena byþ   gleng and herenys,
20 wraþu and wyrþscype,   and wræcna gehwam
ar and ætwist   ðe byþ oþra leas.
   ᚹ (wen)ne bruceþ   ðe can weana lyt,
sares and sorge,   and him sylfa hæfþ
blæd and blysse   and eac byrga geniht.
25 ᚻ (hægl) byþ hwitust corna;   hwyrft hit of heofones lyfte,
wealcaþ hit windes scuras,   weorþeþ hit to wætere syððan.
   ᚾ (nyd) byþ nearu on breostan,   weorþeþ hi ðeah oft niþa
                                bearnum
to helpe and to hæle gehwæþre,   gif hi his hlystaþ æror.
   ᛁ (is) byþ oferceald,   ungemetum slidor,
30 glisnaþ glæshluttur,   gimmum gelicust,
flor forste geworuht,   fæger ansyne.
   ᛄ (ger) byþ gumena hiht,   ðon god læteþ,
halig heofones cyning,   hrusan syllan

Rune Poem 23 sorge] forge   26 scuras] scura   31 geworuht] ge worulit

28

beorhte bleda   beornum and ðearfum.
35 Z (eoh) byþ utan   unsmeþe treow,
heard, hrusan fæst,   hyrde fyres,
wyrtrumun underwreþyd,   wyn on eþle.
h (peorð) byþ symble   plega and hlehter
wlancum * * *   ðar wigan sittaþ
40 on beorsele   bliþe ætsomne.
Y (eolhx)secg eard hæfþ   oftust on fenne,
wexeð on wature,   wundaþ grimme,
blode breneð   beorna gehwylcne
ðe him ænigne   onfeng gedeð.
45 ᚻ (sigel) semannum   symble biþ on hihte,
ðonn hi hine feriaþ   ofer fisces beþ,
oþ hi brimhengest   bringeþ to lande.
↑ (Tir) biþ tacna sum,   healdeð trywa wel
wiþ æþelingas,   a biþ on færylde,
50 ofer nihta genipu   næfre swiceþ.
ᛒ (beorc) byþ bleda leas,   bereþ efne swa ðeah
tanas butan tudder,   biþ on telgum wlitig,
heah on helme   hrysted fægere,
geloden leafum,   lyfte getenge.
55 M (eh) byþ for eorlum   æþelinga wyn,
hors hofum wlanc,   ðær him hæleþ ymbe,
welege on wicgum,   wrixlaþ spræce,
and biþ unstyllum   æfre frofur.
ᛗ (man) byþ on myrgþe   his magan leof;
60 sceal þeah anra gehwylc   oðrum swican,
for ðam dryhten wyle   dome sine
þæt earme flæsc   eorþan betæcan.
ᚱ (lagu) byþ leodum   langsum geþuht,
gif hi sculun neþan   on nacan tealtum,
65 and hi sæyþa   swyþe bregaþ,
and se brimhengest   bridles ne gymeð.
ᛝ (Ing) wæs ærest   mid Eastdenum
gesewen secgun,   oþ he siððan eft

37 wyn] wynan   41 secg eard] seccard   53 heah] þeah   56 hæleþ
ymbe] hæleþe ymb   59 man] an   60 oðrum] odrum   64 neþan]
neþun   66 gymeð] gym   68 eft] est

ofer wæg gewat,　wæn æfter ran;
70 ðus heardingas　ðone hæle nemdun.
　ᛟ (eþel) byþ oferleof　æghwylcum men,
　gif he mot ðær rihtes　and gerysena on
　brucan on bolde　bleadum oftast.
　ᛞ (dæg) byþ drihtnes sond,　deore mannum,
75 mære metodes leoht,　myrgþ and tohiht
　eadgum and earmum,　eallum brice.
　ᚪ (ac) byþ on eorþan　elda bearnum
　flæsces fodor,　fereþ gelome
　ofer ganotes bæþ;　garsecg fandaþ
80 hwæþer ac hæbbe　æþele treowe.
　ᚫ (æsc) biþ oferheah,　eldum dyre,
　stiþ on staþule,　stede rihte hylt,
　ðeah him feohtan on　firas monige.
　ᚣ (yr) byþ æþelinga　and eorla gehwæs
85 wyn and wyrþmynd,　byþ on wicge fæger,
　fæstlic on færelde,　fyrdgeatewa sum.
　ᛡ (iar, ior) byþ eafix,　and ðeah a bruceþ
　fodres on foldan,　hafaþ fægerne eard,
　wætre beworpen,　ðær he wynnum leofaþ.
90 ᛠ (ear) byþ egle　eorla gehwylcun,
　ðonn fæstlice　flæsc onginneþ,
　hraw colian,　hrusan ceosan
　blac to gebeddan;　bleda gedreosaþ,
　wynna gewitaþ,　wera geswicaþ.

---

72 rihtes] rihter　73 bolde] blode　86 fyrdgeatewa] fyrd geacewa
87 ior] io　eafix] ea fixa　88 foldan] faldan

SOLOMON AND SATURN

MS. 422 (A) and MS. 41 (B), Corpus Christi College, Cambridge

I

Saturnus cwæð:
"Hwæt! Ic iglanda   eallra hæbbe
boca onbyrged   þurh gebregdstafas,
larcræftas onlocen   Libia and Greca,
swylce eac istoriam   Indea rices.
5 Me þa treahteras   tala wisedon
on þam micelan bec

           *   *   *

        M ces heardum.
Swylce ic næfre on eallum þam fyrngewrytum   findan ne
                                           mihte
soðe samnode.   Ic sohte þa git
10 hwylc wære modes   oððe mægenþrymmes,
elnes oððe æhte   oððe eorlscipes
se gepalmtwigoda   Pater Noster.
Sille ic þe ealle,   sunu Dauides,
þeoden Israela,   XXX punda
15 smætes goldes   and mine suna twelfe,
gif þu mec gebringest   þæt ic si gebyrred
ðurh þæs cantices cwyde   Cristes linan,
gesemesð mec mid soðe,   and ic mec gesund fare,
wende mec on willan   on wæteres hrigc
20 ofer Coferflod   Caldeas secan."
    Salomon cwæð:
"Unlæde bið on eorþan,   unnit lifes,

Solomon and Saturn 1 Hwæt!] *As far as l. 30a, A is only partly legible; the
text of ll. 1–29 is therefore based on B*   6 bec] *After this word space is left in
B for about ten or twelve letters; there is no erasure*   7 heardum] *With the* a
added above the line B   8 fyrngewrytum] *With* u *altered from* e *B*   9 sam-
node] samode *B*   11a æhte] *B*; æh[.]a *A* (*M*)   oððe] *Not in B; supplied
from A*   13 Sille] Wille *B*   14 Israela] iraela *B*   16 gebyrred] ge bryd-
ded *B*   18 fare] fa *at the end of a line, the rest of the word omitted B*
19 hrigc] *B*; [.]ryc[.] *A* (*M*)   21 eorþan] *B*; eorðan *A*   unnit] *A* (*M*);
unit *B*

31

wesðe wisdomes,　　weallað swa nieten,
feldgongende　　feoh butan gewitte,
se þurh ðone cantic ne can　　Crist geherian.
25 Worað he windes full,　　worpað hine deofol
on domdæge,　　draca egeslice,
bismorlice,　　of blacere liðran
irenum aplum;　　ealle beoð aweaxen
of edwittes　　iða heafdum.
30 Þonne him bið leofre　　ðonne eall ðeos leohte gesceaft,
gegoten fram ðam grunde　　goldes and seolfres,
feðersceatum full　　feohgestreona,
gif he æfre ðæs organes　　owiht cuðe.
Fracoð he bið ðonne and fremede　　frean ælmihtigum,
35 englum ungelic　　ana hwearfað."
　　Saturnus cwæð:
"Ac hwa mæg eaðost　　ealra gesceafta
ða halgan duru　　heofona rices
torhte ontynan　　on getælrime?"
　　Salomon cwæð:
"Ðæt gepalmtwigede　　Pater Noster
40 heofonas ontyneð,　　halige geblissað,
metod gemiltsað,　　morðor gefylleð,
adwæsceð deofles fyr,　　dryhtnes onæleð.
Swylce ðu miht mid ðy beorhtan gebede　　blod onhætan,

22 wesðe] B; weste A　　25 Worað] A; warað B　　he] Not in B; supplied
from A　　28 aplum] B; æpplum A? (M)　　30 leofre] Page 2 of A begins
here　　ðeos] A; þeos B　　31 gegoten] geg[.]ten A; gegoten B　　seolfres]
A; silofres B　　32 feðersceatum] A; feðer s cette with an erasure between s
and c B　　feohgestreona] A; fyrn gestreo na B　　33 ðæs] A; þæs B
34 ðonne] A; þanne B　　fremede] A; fremde B　　35 ungelic] A; unge
sibb B　　hwearfað] A; hwarfað B　　36 eaðost] A; eaðusð B　　ealra]
A; eallra B　　gesceafta] gesc[. .]fta A; gesceafta B　　37 halgan] A;
haligan B　　heofona] A; heofna B　　38 getælrime] A (M); ge tales rime B
39 Ðæt] A; þ B　　gepalmtwigede] A; ge palm twigude with l added above
the line B　　40 heofonas] A; heofnas B　　halige] A; ha lie B　　41
gefylleð] gesylleð A; gefilleð B　　42 dryhtnes] A; dryh at the end of a line,
followed by nes at the beginning of the next line B　　43 Swylce] A; Swilce B
mid] In B the d of mid is corrected from some other letter (h?)　　ðy] Not
in B　　beorhtan] be[.]rhtan A; beorhtan B

ðæs deofles dreor,   þæt him dropan stigað,
45 swate geswiðed,   seofan intingum,
egesfullicran   ðonne seo ærene gripu,
ðonne heo for XII fyra   tydernessum
ofer gleda gripe   gifrust wealleð.
Forðon hafað se cantic   ofer ealle Cristes bec
50 widmærost word;   he gewritu læreð,
stefnum steoreð,   and him stede healdeð
heofona rices,   heregeatewa wigeð."
Saturnus cwæð:
"Ac hulic is se organ   ingemyndum
to begonganne   ðam ðe his gast wile
55 meltan wið morðre,   mergan of sorge,
asceadan of scyldum?   Huru him scippend geaf
wuldorlicne wlite.   Mec ðæs on worolde full oft
fyrwit frineð,   fus gewiteð,
mod gemengeð.   Nænig manna wat,
60 hæleða under hefenum,   hu min hige dreoseð,
bysig æfter bocum;   hwilum me bryne stigeð,
hige heortan neah   hædre wealleð."
Salomon cwæð:
"Gylden is se godes cwide,   gimmum astæned,

44 ðæs] *A*; þæs *B*   dreor] dream *A*; dry *B*   þæt] ₍.₎t *A*; ꝥ *B*   45
seofan] *A*; sefan *B*   intingum] *A*; intingan *B*   46 egesfullicran] *A*;
eges fullicra *B*   ðonne] *A*; þane *B*   gripu] *A*; gripo *B*   47 ðonne] *A*;
þoñ *B*   heo] *Not in B*   XII fyra] XII₍.₎yra *A* (*M*); twelf fyra *B*
48 gifrust] *A*; gifrost *B*   wealleð] *A*; weallað *B*   49 Forðon] *A*; forðan
B   51 steoreð] *A*; stereð *B*   him] h₍. ₎ *A*; hī *B*   52 heofona rices] *A*;
heofon rices *B*   heregeatewa] *A*; heregea towe *B*   wigeð] *A*; wegeð
B   53 organ] *A*; organan *B*   54 begonganne] *A*; be gangen ne *B*   ðam
ðe] *A*; þā þe *B*   gast] *A*; gæst *B*   55 meltan] *A*; miltan *B*   mergan]
A; merian *B*   56 asceadan] *A*; Asceaden *B*   scyldum] scyldigū *A*;
scyldū *B*   scippend] *A*; scep pend *B*   57 wuldorlicne wlite] *A* (*M*);
wundor licne wlite *B*   Mec] ₍.₎ec *A*; mec *B*   ðæs] *A*; þæs *B*   worolde]
A; worulde *B*   58 fyrwit] *A*; fyrwet *B*   59 gemengeð] *A*; geond mengeð
B   Nænig] næ₍...₎ *A*; nænig *B*   manna] *A*; monna *B*   60 hefenum]
A; heofnum *B*   dreoseð] *A*; dreogeð *B*   61 bysig] *A*; bisi *B*   hwilum]
A; hwylū *B*   62 neah] *Not in B*   hædre] *A*; hearde *B*   63 gimmum]
A; gym mum *B*   astæned] ₍...₎æned *A*; astæned *B*

hafað sylfren leaf;   sundor mæg æghwylc
65 ðurh gastes gife   godspel secgan.
He bið seofan snytro   and saule hunig
and modes meolc,   mærþa gesælgost.
He mæg ða saule   of siennihte
gefeccan under foldan,   næfre hie se feond to ðæs niðer
70 feterum gefæstnað;   ðeah he hie mid fiftigum
clusum beclemme,   he ðone cræft briceð
and ða orðancas   ealle tosliteð.
Hungor he ahieðeð,   helle gestrudeð,
wylm toweorpeð,   wuldor getimbreð.
75 He is modigra   middangearde,
staðole strengra   ðonne ealra stana gripe.
Lamena he is læce,   leoht wincendra,
swilce he is deafra duru,   dumbra tunge,
scyldigra scyld,   scyppendes seld,
80 flodes ferigend,   folces nerigend,
yða yrfeweard,   earmra fisca
and wyrma welm,   wildeora holt,
on westenne weard,   weorðmynta geard.

---

64 sylfren] *A*; seolofren *B*   leaf] *Not in B*   65 ðurh] *A*; þurh *B*
gastes] *A*; gæstæs *B*   godspel secgan] *A*; god spellian *B*   66 seofan]
A; sefan *B*   snytro] *A*; snytero *B*   saule] *A*; sawle *B*   67] *This
entire line is omitted in A; it is here supplied from B*   68 ða] *A*; þa *B*
saule] *A*; sawle *B*   siennihte] *A*; syn nihte *B*   69 gefeccan] *A*; gefetian
B   hie] *A*; hi *B*   70 gefæstnað] *With the* t *crowded in between* s *and* n
B   ðeah] *A*; þeah *B*   hie] *A*; hi *B*   71 clusum] *A*; clausum *B*
ðone] *A*; þane *B*   72 ða orðancas] *A*; þa orþancas *B*   73 Hungor] *With
the* n *added above the line B*   he ahieðeð] *A*; hege hege hideð with the first*
hege *underlined for deletion B*   74] toweorpeð] *A*; to worpeð *B*
getimbreð] *A*; getym breð *B*   75 is] [.]s *A*; is *B*   middangearde] *A*;
middan geardes *B*   76 staðole strengra] *A*; staðole he is strengra *B*
ðonne] *A*; þone *B*   ealra] *A*; ealle *B*   77 Lamena] *A*; lamana *B*
wincendra] wince[. . .]a *A*; winciendra *with the* e *added above the line B*
78 he is] *A*; he his *B*   dumbra] *A*; deadra *B*   79 scyldigra] *A*; scild
imperfectly altered from swilce *and* ig ra *added B*   scyld] *A*; scild *B*
scyppendes] *A*; scippendes *B*   80 ferigend] *A*; feriend *B*   nerigend] *A*;
ne riend *B*   81 yða] *A*; yþa *B*   earmra fisca] *A*; earma fixa *B*
82 and wyrma welm] 7 wyrma [.]elm *A*; wyrma wlenco *B*   83 on westenne]
A; westenes *B*   weorðmynta] weorðmyn[.]a *A*; weorð myn ta *B*

And se ðe wile geornlice   ðone godes cwide
85 singan soðlice,   and hine siemle wile
lufian butan leahtrum,   he mæg ðone laðan gæst,
feohtende feond,   fleonde gebrengan,
gif ðu him ærest on ufan   ierne gebrengest
prologa prima,   ðam is ◻ P· nama.
90 Hafað guðmæcga   gierde lange,
gyldene gade,   and a ðone grymman feond
swiðmod sweopað,   and him on swaðe fylgeð
·ᚠ·A ofermægene   and hine eac ofslihð.
·ᛏ T· hine teswað   and hine on ða tungan sticað,
95 wræsteð him ðæt woddor   and him ða wongan brieceð.
·ᛗ· E hiene yflað,   swa he a wile
ealra feonda gehwane   fæste gestondan.
Ðonne hiene on unðanc·ᚱ R·   ieorrenga geseceð,
bocstafa brego,   bregdeð sona
100 feond be ðam feaxe,   læteð flint brecan
scines sconcan;   he ne besceawað no
his leomona lið,   ne bið him læce god.
Wendeð he hiene ðonne under wolcnum,   wigsteall seceð,
heolstre behelmed.   Huru him bið æt heartan wa,
105 ðonne [.]e hangiende   helle wisceð,
ðæs ængestan   eðelrices.
Ðonne hine forcinnað   ða cirican getuinnas,
·N· and O s[..]od,   æghwæðer brengeð
sweopan of siðe;   sargiað hwile

---

84 ðone] *A*; þono *B*   85 soðlice] *A*; smealice *B*   siemle] *A*; symle *B*
85*b*–86*a* wile lufian] *A*; luian wile *B*   86 ðone laðan] *A*; þone laþan *B*
gæst] *A*; gesið *B*   87 feohtende] *A*; feohterne *B*   gebrengan] *A*; ge-
bringan *B*   88 gif] *A*; Gyf *B*   ðu] *A*; þu *B*   on] *Not in B*   ierne]
A; yorn *B*   gebrengest] *A*; gebri ngeð *B*   89 prologa prima] *A*; Ᵽlogo
prim. *B*   ðam] *A*; þam *B*   P·] *Here and in the following lines B omits
the runes*   90 guðmæcga] *With* o *written after* guð *in a later hand, at the
end of a line A*; guð maga *B*   gierde] *A*; gyrde *B*   91 a] *Not in B*
ðone] *A*; þone *B*   grymman] g[…]man *A (M)*; grymman *B*   92 sweopað]
A; swapeð *B*   him] *Not in B*   fylgeð] *A*; læteð *dotted beneath for deletion
and* filgið *written above it B*   93 ofslihð] *A*; ofslehð *B*   94 T·] *B ends
here*   106 ængestan] ęngestan *A*   108 and] *Apparently A has the abbreviation* 7, *but the horizontal stroke is not visible*   O] *Not in A*

110 fremdne flæschoman,   feorh ne bemurnað.
    Ðonne ·ᚻ· S· cymeð,   engla geræswa,
    wuldores stæf,   wraðne gegripeð
    feond be ðam fotum,   læteð foreweard hleor
    on strangne stan,   stregdað toðas
115 geond helle heap.   Hydeð hine æghwylc
    æfter sceades sciman;   sceaða bið gebisigod,
    Satanes ðegn   swiðe gestilled.
    Swilce hiene ·ᚱ· Q and ᚾ·V·   cwealme gehnægað,
    frome folctogan,   farað him togegnes,
120 habbað leoht speru,   lange sceaftas,
    swiðmode sweopan,   swenga ne wyrnað,
    deorra dynta;   him bið ðæt deofol lað.
    Ðonne hine I and ·ᚱ·L·   and se yrra ·ᚻ·C·
    guðe begyrdað   (geap stæf wigeð
125 biterne brogan),   bigað sona
    helle hæftling,   ðæt he on hinder gæð.
    Ðonne hiene· ᚱ·F· and ·ᛗ·M·   utan ymbðringað,
    scyldigne sceaðan,   habbað scearp speru,
    atole earhfare,   æled lætað
130 on ðæs feondes feax   flana stregdan,
    biterne brogan;   banan heardlice
    grimme ongieldað,   ðæs hie oft gilp brecað.
    Ðonne hine æt niehstan   nearwe stilleð
    ·ᚷ·G· se geapa,   ðone god sendeð
135 freondum on fultum,   færeð æfter ·ᛞ·D·
    fifmægnum full.   Fyr bið se ðridda
    stæf stræte neah,   stille bideð.
    ·H· onetteð,   engel hine scierpeð,
    Cristes cempan,   on cwicum wædum
140 godes spyrigendes   geonges hrægles.
    Ðonne hine on lyfte   lifgetwinnan
    under tungla getrumum   tuigena ordum,
    sweopum seolfrynum,   swiðe weallað,
    oððæt him ban blicað,   bledað ædran;

---

110 bemurnað] be murneð *A*   114 stregdað] *With* d *added above the line A*
123 I and] *Not in A*   126 hæftling] hæft lig *A*

145 gartorn geotað   gifrum deofle.
    Mæg simle se godes cwide   gumena gehwylcum
    ealra feonda gehwane   fleondne gebrengan
    ðurh mannes muð,   manfulra heap
    sweartne geswencan,   næfre hie ðæs syllice
150 bleoum bregdað.   Æfter bancofan
    feðerhoman onfoð,   hwilum flotan gripað;
    hwilum hie gewendað   in wyrmes lic
    str[.]nges and sticoles,   stingeð nieten,
    feldgongende   feoh gestrudeð.
155 Hwilum he on wætere   wicg gehnægeð,
    hornum geheaweð,   oððæt him heortan blod,
    famig flodes bæð,   foldan geseceð.
    Hwilum he gefeterað   fæges mannes,
    handa gehefegað,   ðonne he æt hilde sceall
160 wið lað werud   lifes tiligan;
    awriteð he on his wæpne   wællnota heap,
    bealwe bocstafas,   bill forscrifeð,
    meces mærðo.   Forðon nænig man scile
    oft orðances   ut abredan
165 wæpnes ecgge,   ðeah ðe him se wlite cweme,
    ac symle he sceal singan,   ðonne he his sweord geteo,
    Pater Noster,   and ðæt palmtreow
    biddan mid blisse,   ðæt him bu gife
    feorh and folme,   ðonne his feond cyme."

              *   *   *

170   "swice,   ær he soð wite,
    ðæt ða sienfullan   saula sticien
    mid hettendum   helle tomiddes.
    Hateð ðonne heahcining   helle betynan,
    fyres fulle,   and ða feondas mid."
175   Hæfde ða se snotra   sunu Dauides
    forcumen and forcyðed   Caldea eorl.
    Hwæðre was on sælum   se ðe of siðe cwom

---

156 hornum] *With* n *added above the line A*   158 gefeterað] *With* ge *added above the line A*

feorran gefered;   næfre ær his ferhð ahlog.

II

Hwæt! Ic flitan gefrægn   on fyrndagum
180 modgleawe men,   middangeardes ræswan,
gewesan ymbe hira wisdom;   wyrs deð se ðe liehð
oððe ðæs soðes ansæceð.   Saloman was bremra,
ðeah ðe S[. . .]rnus   sumra hæfde,
bald breosttoga,   boca c[.]g[.],
185 [. .]ornenga locan;   land eall geondhwearf,
Indea mere,   east Corsias,
Persea rice,   Palestinion,
Niniuen ceastre   and norð Predan,
Meda maððumselas,   Marculfes eard,
190 Saulus rice,   swa he suð ligeð
ymbe Geallboe   and ymb Geador norð,
Filistina flet,   fæsten Creca,
wudu Egipta,   wæter Mathea,
cludas Coreffes,   Caldea rice,
195 Creca cræftas,   cynn Arabia,
lare Libia,   lond Syria,
Pitðinia,   Buðanasan,
Pamhpilia,   Pores gemære,
Macedonia,   Mesopotamie,
200 Cappadocia,   Cristes eðel,
Hieryhco, Galilea,   Hierusalem

*   *   *

"oððe ic swigie,
nyttes hycgge,   ðeah ic no spr[.]c[.].
Wat ic ðonne, gif ðu gewitest   on Wendelsæ
205 ofer Coforflod   cyððe secean,
ðæt ðu wille gilpan   ðæt ðu hæbbe g[. .]ena bearn

180 ræswan] ræswum A   182 ansæceð] So A (M)   183a] So A (M);
see Note   184b] So A (M); see Note   186] See Note   194 cludas]
claudas A   200 eðel] Not in A   201 Hierusalem] hierusa at the end of
page 13 A   203b] So A (M); see Note   205 secean] seccan A   206b]
So A (M); see Note

forcumen and forcyððed.   Wat ic ðæt wæron Caldeas
guðe ðæs gielpne   and ðæs goldwlonce,
mærða ðæs modige,   ðær to ðam moning gelomp
210 suð ymbe Sanere feld.   Sæge me from ðam lande
ðær nænig fyra ne mæg   fotum gestæppan."
    Saturnus cuæð:
"Se mæra was haten   sæliðende
weallende Wulf,   w[.]rðeodum cuð
Filistina,   freond Nebrondes.
215 He on ðam felda ofslog   XXV
dracena on dægred,   and hine ða deað offeoll;
forðan ða foldan ne mæg   fira ænig,
ðone mercstede,   mon gesecan,
fugol gefleogan,   ne ðon ma foldan n[..]t.
220 Ðanon atercynn   ærest gewurdon
wide onwæcned,   ða ðe nu weallende
ðurh attres oroð   ingang rymað.
Git his sweord scineð   swiðe gescæned,
and ofer ða byrgenna   blicað ða hieltas."
    Salomon cwað:
225 "Dol bið se ðe gæð   on deop wæter,
se ðe sund nafað   ne gesegled scip
ne fugles flyht,   ne he mid fotum ne mæg
grund geræcan;   huru se godes cunnað
full dyslice,   dryhtnes meahta."
    Saturnus cuæð:
230 "Ac hwæt is se dumba,   se ðe on sumre dene resteð?
Swiðe snyttrað,   hafað seofon tungan;
hafað tungena gehwylc   XX orda,
hafað orda gehwylc   engles snytro,
ðara ðe wile anra hwylc   uppe bringan,
235 ðæt ðu ðære gyldnan gesiehst   Hierusalem
weallas blican   and hiera winrod lixan,
soðfæstra segn.   Saga hwæt ic mæne."
    Salomon cuæð:
"Bec sindon breme,   bodiað geneahhe

---

212 was] *Or* wæs *A? See Note*   216 deað] of deað *A*   217 ða] *See Note*
223 scineð] scinað *A*   229 full] *See Note*

weotodne willan   ðam ðe wiht hygeð.
240 Gestrangað hie and gestaðeliað   staðolfæstne geðoht,
amyrgað modsefan   manna gehwylces
of ðreamedlan   ðisses lifes."
 Saturnus cwæð:
"Bald bið se ðe onbyregeð   boca cræftes;
symle bið ðe wisra   ðe hira geweald hafað."
 Salomon cuæð:
245 "Sige hie onsendað   soðfæstra gehwam,
hælo hyðe,   ðam ðe hie lufað."
 Saturnus cwæð:
"An wise is   on woroldrice
ymb ða me fyrwet bræc   L wintra
dæges and niehtes   ðurh deop gesceaft;
250 geomrende gast   deð nu gena swa,
ærðon me geunne   ece dryhten
ðæt me geseme   snoterra monn."
 Salomon cwæð:
"Soð is ðæt ðu sagast;   seme ic ðe recene
ymb ða wrætlican wiht.   Wilt ðu ðæt ic ðe secgge?
255 An fugel siteð   on Filistina
middelgemærum;   munt is hine ymbutan,
geap gylden weall.   Georne hine healdað
witan Filistina,   wenað ðæs ðe naht is,
ðæt hiene him scyle eall ðeod   on genæman
260 wæpna ecggum;   hie ðæs wære cunnon,
healdað hine niehta gehwylce   norðan and suðan
on twa healfa   tu hund wearda.
Se fugel hafað   IIII heafdu
medumra manna,   and he is on middan hwælen;
265 geowes he hafað fiðeru   and griffus fet,
ligeð lonnum fæst,   locað unhiere,
swiðe swingeð   and his searo hringeð,
gilleð geomorlice   and his gyrn sefað,
wylleð hine on ðam wite,   wunað unlustum,
270 singgeð syllice;   seldum æfre
his leoma licggað.   Longað hine hearde,

---

255 Filistina] filitina A 261 healdað] healdeð A

ðynceð him ðæt sie ðria XXX   ðusend wintra
ær he domdæges   dynn gehyre.
    Nyste hine on ðære foldan   fira ænig
275 eorðan cynnes,   ærðon ic hine ana onfand
and hine ða gebendan het   ofer brad wæter,
ðæt hine se modega heht   Melotes bearn,
Filistina fruma,   fæste gebindan,
lonnum belucan   wið leodgryre.
280 Ðone fugel hatað   feorbuende,
Filistina fruman,   uasa mortis."
    Saturnus cwæð:
"Ac hwæt is ðæt wundor   ðe geond ðas worold færeð,
styrnenga gæð,   staðolas beateð,
aweceð wopdropan,   winneð oft hider?
285 Ne mæg hit steorra ne stan   ne se steapa gimm,
wæter ne wildeor   wihte beswican,
ac him on hand gæð   heardes and hnesces,
micles and mætes;   him to mose sceall
gegangan geara gehwelce   grundbuendra,
290 lyftfleogendra,   laguswemmendra,
ðria ðreoteno   ðusendgerimes."
    Salomon cuæð:
"Yldo beoð on eorðan   æghwæs cræftig;
mid hiðendre   hildewræsne,
rumre racenteage,   ræceð wide,
295 langre linan,   lisseð eall ðæt heo wile.
Beam heo abreoteð   and bebriceð telgum,
astyreð standendne   stefn on siðe,
afilleð hine on foldan;   friteð æfter ðam
wildne fugol.   Heo oferwigeð wulf,
300 hio oferbideð stanas,   heo oferstigeð style,
hio abiteð iren mid ome,   deð usic swa."
    Saturnus cwæð:
"Ac forhwon fealleð se snaw,   foldan behydeð,
bewrihð wyrta cið,   wæstmas getigeð,

276 gebendan] gebemdan *or* gebeindan *A; see Note*   281 fruman] fruma *A*
288 and] *Not in A*   294 ræceð] ręceð *A*   297 standendne] stan dene *A*
302 behydeð] *With an erasure of one letter after* y *A*

SOLOMON AND SATURN

305 cealde geclungne?   Full oft he gecostað eac
wildeora worn,   wætum he oferbricgeð,
gebryceð burga geat,   baldlice fereð,
reafað"

*   *   *

"swiðor micle   ðonne se swipra nið
310 se hine gelædeð   on ða laðan wic
mid ða fræcnan   feonde to willan."
    Saturnus cwæð:
"Nieht bið wedera ðiestrost,   ned bið wyrda heardost
sorg bið swarost byrðen,   slæp bið deaðe gelicost."
    Salomon cwæð:
"Lytle hwile   leaf beoð grene;
315 ðonne hie eft fealewiað,   feallað on eorðan
and forweorniað,   weorðað to duste.
Swa ðonne gefeallað   ða ðe fyrena ær
lange læstað,   lifiað him in mane,
hydað heahgestreon,   healdað georne
320 on fæstenne   feondum to willan,
and wenað wanhogan   ðæt hie wille wuldorcining,
ælmihtig god,   ece gehiran."
    Saturnus cwæð:
"Sona bið gesiene,   siððan flowan mot
yð ofer eall lond,   ne wile heo awa ðæs
325 siðes geswican,   sioððan hire se sæl cymeð,
ðæt heo domes dæges   dyn gehiere."
    Salomon cwæð:
"Wa bið ðonne ðissum modgum monnum,   ðam ðe her
                              nu mid mane lengest
lifiað on ðisse lænan gesceafte.   Ieo ðæt ðine leode
                              gecyðdon;
wunnon hie wið dryhtnes miehtum,   forðon hie ðæt worc
                              ne gedegdon.

305 he] hie *A*   306 oferbricgeð] *So A (M); see Note*   310 laðan] *With
the letters* an *added above the line A*   327 Wa] swa *A*

330 Ne sceall ic ðe hwæðre, broðor, abelgan; ðu eart swiðe
bittres cynnes,

eorre eormenstrynde.   Ne beyrn ðu in ða inwitgecyndo!"

Saturnus cwæð:

"Saga ðu me, Salomon cyning,   sunu Dauides,

hwæt beoð ða feowere   fægæs rapas?"

Salomon cuæð:

"Gewurdene wyrda,

335 ðæt beoð ða feowere   fæges rapas."

Saturnus cwæð:

"Ac hwa demeð ðonne   dryhtne Criste

on domes dæge,   ðonne he demeð eallum gesceaftum?"

Salomon cwæð:

"Hwa dear ðonne dryhtne deman,   ðe us of duste geworhte,

nergend of niehtes wunde?   Ac sæge me hwæt nærende

wæron."

Saturnus cwæð:

340 "Ac forhwon ne mot seo sunne   side gesceafte

scire geondscinan?   Forhwam besceadeð heo

muntas and moras   and monige ec

weste stowa?   Hu geweorðeð ðæt?"

Salomon cuæð:

"Ac forhwam næron eorð[. .]lan   ealle gedæled

345 leodum gelice?   Sum to lyt hafað,

godes grædig;   hine god seteð

ðurh geearnunga   eadgum to ræste."

Saturnus cwæð:

"Ac forhwan beoð ða gesiðas   somod ætgædre,

wop and hleahtor?   Full oft hie weorðgeornra

350 sælða toslitað;   hu gesæleð ðæt?"

Salomon cuæð:

"Unlæde bið and ormod   se ðe a wile

geomrian on gihðe;   se bið gode fracoðast."

Saturnus cwæð:

"Forhwon ne moton we ðonne ealle   mid onmedlan

---

331 in] *So A (M); see Note*   335 ðæt] *So A (M); see Note*   338 us] *An
erasure of one or two letters after this word A*   344 gedæled] gode led *A*

gegnum gangan   in godes rice?"
Salomon cwæð:
355 "Ne mæg fyres feng   ne forstes cile,
snaw ne sunne   somod eardian,
aldor geæfnan,   ac hira sceal anra gehwylc
onlutan and onliðigan   ðe hafað læsse mægn."
Salurnus cwæð:
"Ac forhwon ðonne leofað   se wyrsa leng?
360 Se wyrsa ne wat   in woroldrice
on his mægwinum   maran are."
Salomon cwæð:
"Ne mæg mon forildan   ænige hwile
ðone deoran sið,   ac he hine adreogan sceall."
Saturnus cwæð:
"Ac hu gegangeð ðæt?   Gode oððe yfle,
365 ðonne hie beoð ðurh ane   idese acende,
twegen getwinnas,   ne bið hira tir gelic.
Oðer bið unlæde on eorðan,   oðer bið eadig,
swiðe leoftæle   mid leoda duguðum;
oðer leofað   lytle hwile,
370 swiceð on ðisse sidan gesceafte,   and ðonne eft mid
sorgum gewiteð.
Fricge ic ðec, hlaford Salomon,   hwæðres bið hira folgoð
betra?"
Salomon cuæð:
"Modor ne rædeð,   ðonne heo magan cenneð,
hu him weorðe geond worold   widsið sceapen.
Oft heo to bealwe   bearn afedeð,
375 seolfre to sorge,   siððan dreogeð
his earfoðu   orlegstunde.
Heo ðæs afran sceall   oft and gelome
grimme greotan,   ðonne he geong færeð,
hafað wilde mod,   werige heortan,
380 sefan sorgfullne,   slideð geneahhe,
werig, wilna leas,   wuldres bedæled,
hwilum higegeomor   healle weardað,

358] mægn] mægnn A   362 forildan] for ildo A   373 widsið] *With
several letters erased before* sið, *at the beginning of a line A*

leofað leodum feor;   locað geneahhe
fram ðam unlædan   agen hlaford.
385 Forðan nah seo modor geweald,   ðonne heo magan cenneð,
bearnes blædes,   ac sceall on gebyrd faran
an æfter anum;   ðæt is eald gesceaft."
    Saturnus cwæð:
"Ac forhwan nele monn him on giogoðe   georne gewyrcan
deores dryhtscipes   and dædfruman,
390 wadan on wisdom,   winnan æfter snytro?"
    Salomon cwæð:
"Hwæt! Him mæg eadig eorl   eaðe geceosan
on his modsefan   mildne hlaford,
anne æðeling.   Ne mæg don unlæde swa."
    Saturnus cwæð:
"Ac forhwam winneð ðis wæter   geond woroldrice,
395 dreogeð deop gesceaft?   Ne mot on dæg restan,
neahtes neðyð,   cræfte tyð,
cristnað and clænsað   cwicra manigo,
wuldre gewlitigað.   Ic wihte ne cann
forhwan se stream ne mot   stillan neahtes."

           *   *   *

400 "his lifes fæðme.   Simle hit bið his lareowum hyrsum;
full oft hit eac ðæs deofles   dugoð gehnægeð,
ðær weotena bið   worn gesamnod.
Ðonne snottrum men   snæd oððglideð,
ða he be leohte gesihð,   luteð æfter,
405 gesegnað and gesyfleð   and him sylf friteð.
Swilc bið seo an snæd   æghwylcum men
selre micle,   gif heo gesegnod bið,
to ðycgganne,   gif he hit geðencan cann,
ðonne him sie seofon daga   symbelgereordu.
410 Leoht hafað heow and had   haliges gastes,
Cristes gecyndo;   hit ðæt gecyðeð full oft.
Gif hit unwitan   ænige hwile
healdað butan hæftum,   hit ðurh hrof wædeð,

384 agen] ængan *A*   387 gesceaft] ge seaft *A*   406 Swilc] *An* e *erased*
after this word A?

bryceð and bærneð   boldgetimbru,
415 seomað steap and geap,   stigeð on lenge,
clymmeð on gecyndo,   cunnað hwænne mote
fyr on his frumsceaft   on fæder geardas,
eft to his eðle,   ðanon hit æror cuom.
Hit bið eallenga   eorl to gesihðe,
420 ðam ðe gedælan can   dryhtnes ðecelan,
forðon nis nænegu gecynd   cuiclifigende,
ne fugel ne fisc   ne foldan stan,
ne wæteres wylm   ne wudutelga,
ne munt ne mor   ne ðes middangeard,
425 ðæt he forð ne sie   fyrenes cynnes."
    Saturnus cwæð:
"Full oft ic frode menn   fyrn gehyrde
secggan and swerian   ymb sume wisan,
hwæðer wære twegra   butan tweon strengra,
wyrd ðe warnung,   ðonne hie winnað oft
430 mid hira ðreamedlan,   hwæðerne aðreoteð ær.
Ic to soðon wat;   sægdon me geara
Filistina witan,   ðonne we on geflitum sæton,
bocum tobræddon   and on bearm legdon,
meðelcwidas mengdon,   moniges fengon,
435 ðæt nære nænig manna   middangeardes
ðæt meahte ðara twega   tuion aspyrian."
    Salomon cwæð:
"Wyrd bið wended hearde,   wealleð swiðe geneahhe;
heo wop weceð,   heo wean hladeð,
heo gast scyð,   heo ger byreð,
440 and hwæðre him mæg wissefa   wyrda gehwylce
gemetigian,   gif he bið modes gleaw
and to his freondum wile   fultum secan,
ðeh hwæðre godcundes   gæstes brucan."
    Saturnus cwæð:
"Ac hwæt witeð us   wyrd seo swiðe,
445 eallra fyrena fruma,   fæhðo modor,
weana wyrtwela,   wopes heafod,

428 strengra] strenra *A*

frumscylda gehwæs   fæder and modor,
deaðes dohtor?   Ac tohwan drohtað heo mid us?
Hwæt! Hie wile lifigende   late aðreotan,
450 ðæt heo ðurh fyrena geflitu   fæhðo ne tydre."
    Salomon cwæð:
"Nolde gæd geador   in godes rice
eadiges engles   and ðæs ofermodan;
oðer his dryhtne hierde,   oðer him ongan wyrcan ðurh
                            dierne cræftas
segn and side byrnan,   cwæð ðæt he mid his gesiðum wolde
455 hiðan eall heofona rice   and him ðonne on healfum sittan,
[.]y[.]ran him mid ðy teoðan dæle,   oððæt he his
                        [..]r[......] cuðe
ende ðurh insceafte.   Ða wearð se æðel[...]eoden
gedrefed ðurh ðæs deofles gehygdo;   forlet hine ða of
                            dune gehreosan,
afielde hine ða   under foldan sceatas,
460 heht hine ðær fæste gebindan.   Ðæt sindon ða usic
                            feohtað on.
    Forðon is witena gehwam   wopes eaca.
    Ða ðæt eadig onfand   engla dryhten,
ðæt heo leng mid hine   lare ne namon,
aweorp hine ða of ðam wuldre   and wide todraf,
465 and him bebead   bearn heofonwara
ðæt hie ec scoldon   a ðenden hie lifdon
wunian in wylme,   wop ðrowian,
heaf under hefonum,   and him helle gescop,
wælcealde wic   wintre beðeahte,
470 wæter in sende   and wyrmgeardas,
atol deor monig   irenum hornum,
blodige earnas   and blace nædran,
ðurst and hungor   and ðearle gewin,
egna egesan,   unrotnesse;
475 and æghwylc him ðissa earfeða   ece stondeð
butan edwende   a ðenden hie lifigað."

Saturnus cwæð:
"Is ðonne on ðisse foldan   fira ænig
eorðan cynnes,   ðara ðe man age,
ðe deað abæde,   ær se dæg cyme
480 ðæt sie his calendcwide   * * *   arunnen
and hine mon annunga   ut abanne?"
    Salomon cwæð:
"Æghwylc[......]   engel onsendeð
dryhten heo[.................]eð;
se sceall behealdan   hu his hyge [.....
485 ...]dig growan   in godes willan,
murnan metodes ðrym,   mid ðy ðe hit dæg bið.
Ðonne hine ymbegangað   gastas twegen;
oðer bið golde glædra,   oðer bið grundum sweartra,
oðer cymeð

        * * *

490   ofer ðære stylenan helle;
oðer hine læreð   ðæt he lufan healde,
metodes miltse,   and his mæga ræd,
oðer hine tyhteð   and on tæso læreð,
yweð him and yppeð   earmra manna
495 misgemynda,   and ðurh ðæt his mod hweteð,
lædeð hine and læceð   and hine geond land spaneð,
oððæt his ege bið,   æfðancum full,
ðurh earmra scyld   yrre geworden.
Swa ðonne feohteð se feond   on feower gecynd,
500 oððæt he gewendeð   on ða wyrsan hand
deofles dædum   dæglongne fyrst,
and ðæs willan wyrcð   ðe hine on woh spaneð.
Gewiteð ðonne wepende   on weg faran
engel to his earde   and ðæt eall sagað:
505 'Ne meahte ic of ðære heortan   heardne aðringan
stylenne stan;   sticað him tomiddes' "

        * * *

478 man] man man *A*   **479** ðe] *Not in A*   **482–485**] *So A (M); see Note*

THE MENOLOGIUM

MS. Cotton Tiberius B. i

Crist wæs acennyd,   cyninga wuldor,
on midne winter,   mære þeoden,
ece ælmihtig,   on þy eahteoðan dæg
Hælend gehaten,   heofonrices weard.
5 Swa þa sylfan tiid   side herigeas,
folc unmæte,   habbað foreweard gear,
for þy se kalend us   cymeð geþincged
on þam ylcan dæge   us to tune,
forma monað;   hine folc mycel
10 Ianuarius   gerum heton.
And þæs embe fif niht   þætte fulwihttiid
eces drihtnes   to us cymeð,
þæne twelfta dæg   tireadige,
hæleð heaðurofe,   hatað on Brytene,
15 in foldan her.   Swylce emb feower wucan
þætte Solmonað   sigeð to tune
butan twam nihtum,   swa hit getealdon geo,
Februarius fær,   frode gesiþas,
ealde ægleawe.   And þæs embe ane niht
20 þæt we Marian   mæssan healdað,
cyninges modor,   forþan heo Crist on þam dæge,
bearn wealdendes,   brohte to temple.
Ðænne þæs emb fif niht   þæt afered byð
winter of wicum,   and se wigend þa
25 æfter seofentynum   swylt þrowade
nihtgerimes,   nergendes þegen,
Mathias mære,   mine gefræge,
þæs þe lencten on tun   geliden hæfde,
werum to wicum.   Swylce eac is wide cuð
30 ymb III and twa   þeodum gewelhwær
his cyme kalend   ceorlum and eorlum
(butan þænne bises   geboden weorðe

Menologium 15 emb] *The letter* e *erased after this word?*   25 swylt] swylc
with c *in a later hand on an erasure*

feorðan geare;   þænne he furðor cymeð
ufor anre niht   us to tune),
35 hrime gehyrsted   hagolscurum færð
geond middangeard   Martius reðe,
Hlyda healic.   Ðænne se halga þæs
emb XI niht   æþele scynde
Gregorius   in godes wære,
40 breme in Brytene.   Swylce Benedictus
embe nigon niht þæs   nergend sohte,
heard and higestrang,   þæne heriað wel
in gewritum wise,   wealdendes þeow
rincas regolfæste.   Swylce eac rimcræftige
45 on þa ylcan tiid   emniht healdað,
forðan wealdend god   worhte æt frymðe
on þy sylfan dæge   sunnan and monan.
    Hwæt, ymb feower niht   fæder onsende,
þæs þe emnihte   eorlas healdað,
50 heahengel his,   se hælo abead
Marian mycle,   þæt heo meotod sceolde
cennan, kyninga betst,   swa hit gecyðed wearð
geond middangeard;   wæs þæt mære wyrd,
folcum gefræge!   Swylce emb feower and þreo
55 nihtgerimes,   þætte nergend sent
Aprelis monað,   on þam oftust cymð
seo mære tiid   mannum to frofre,
drihtnes ærist;   þænne dream gerist
wel wide gehwær,   swa se witega sang:
60 "Þis is se dæg   þæne drihten us
wisfæst worhte,   wera cneorissum,
eallum eorðwarum   eadigum to blisse."
Ne magon we þa tide   be getale healdan
dagena rimes,   ne drihtnes stige
65 on heofenas up,   forþan þe hwearfað aa
wisra gewyrdum,   ac sceal wintrum frod
on circule   cræfte findan
halige dagas.   Sculan we hwæðere gyt
martira gemynd   ma areccan,

65 þe] he

70 wrecan wordum forð,   wisse gesingan,
   þæt embe nihgontyne   niht and fifum,
   þæs þe Eastermonað   to us cymeð,
   þæt man reliquias   ræran onginneð,
   halige gehyrste;   þæt is healic dæg,
75 bentiid bremu.   Swylce in burh raþe
   embe siex niht þæs,   smicere on gearwum,
   wudum and wyrtum   cymeð wlitig scriðan
   þrymilce on tun,   þearfe bringeð
   Maius micle   geond menigeo gehwær.
80 Swa þi ylcan dæge   æþele geferan,
   Philippus and Iacob,   feorh agefan,
   modige magoþegnas   for meotudes lufan.
   And þæs embe twa niht   þætte tæhte god
   Elenan eadigre   æþelust beama,
85 on þam þrowode   þeoden engla
   for manna lufan,   meotud on galgan
   be fæder leafe.   Swylce ymb fyrst wucan
   butan anre niht   þætte yldum bringð
   sigelbeorhte dagas   sumor to tune,
90 wearme gewyderu.   þænne wangas hraðe
   blostmum blowað,   swylce blis astihð
   geond middangeard   manigra hada
   cwicera cynna,   cyninge lof secgað
   mænifealdlice,   mærne bremað,
95 ælmihtigne.   þæs emb eahta and nigon
   dogera rimes   þætte drihten nam
   in oðer leoht   Agustinus,
   bliðne on breostum,   þæs þe he on Brytene her
   eaðmode him   eorlas funde
100 to godes willan,   swa him se gleawa bebead
   Gregorius.   Ne hyrde ic guman a fyrn
   ænigne ær   æfre bringan
   ofer sealtne mere   selran lare,

71 and fifum] *Not in MS.; see Note*   76 embe siex niht þæs] *Not in MS.;*
see Note   78 þrymilce] þrymlice   91 blis] *Followed by a second* s, *in a*
later hand   96 dogera] *With* o *altered to* a *by a later hand*   101 a fyrn]
awyrn

        bisceop bremran.   Nu on Brytene rest
105 on Cantwarum   cynestole neah,
    mynstre mærum.   þænne monað bringð
    ymb twa and feower   tiida lange
    Ærra Liða   us to tune,
    Iunius on geard,   on þam gim astihð
110 on heofenas up   hyhst on geare,
    tungla torhtust,   and of tille agrynt,
    to sete sigeð.   Wyle syððan leng
    grund behealdan   and gangan lator
    ofer foldan wang   fægerust leohta,
115 woruldgesceafta.   þænne wuldres þegn
    ymb þreotyne,   þeodnes dyrling,
    Iohannes in geardagan   wearð acenned,
    tyn nihtum eac;   we þa tiid healdað
    on midne sumor   mycles on æþelum.
120   Wide is geweorðod,   swa þæt wel gerist,
    haligra tid   geond hæleða bearn,
    Petrus and Paulus.   Hwæt, þa apostolas,
    þeodenholde,   þrowedon on Rome
    ofer midne sumor,   miccle gewisse,
125 furðor fif nihtum,   folcbealo þrealic,
    mærne martyrdom;   hæfdon mænige ær
    wundra geworhte   geond wærþeoda,
    swylce hi æfter þam   unrim fremedon
    swutelra and gesynra   þurh sunu meotudes,
130 ealdorþegnas.   þænne ædre cymð
    emb twa niht þæs   tidlice us
    Iulius monað,   on þam Iacobus
    ymb feower niht   feorh gesealde
    ond twentigum,   trum in breostum,
135 frod and fæstræd   folca lareow,
    Zebedes afera.   And þæs symle scriþ
    ymb seofon niht þæs   sumere gebrihted
    Weodmonað on tun,   welhwær bringeð

---

107 feower] þreo; *see Note*   114 leohta] lohta *with* e *added above the line
in a later hand*   128 hi] *With* i *altered to* y *in a later hand*   134 ond] on
138 welhwær] wel hwæt

Agustus   yrmenþeodum
140 hlafmæssan dæg.   Swa þæs hærfest cymð
ymbe oðer swylc   butan anre wanan,
wlitig, wæstmum hladen;   wela byð geywed
fægere on foldan.   Þænne forð gewat
ymb þreo niht þæs   þeodne getrywe
145 þurh martyrdom,   mære diacon,
Laurentius,   hæfð nu lif wiðþan
mid wuldorfæder   weorca to leane.
Swylce þæs ymb fif niht   fægerust mægða,
wifa wuldor,   sohte weroda god
150 for suna sibbe,   sigefæstne ham
on neorxnawange;   hæfde nergend þa
fægere fostorlean   fæmnan forgolden
ece to ealdre.   Þænne ealling byð
ymb tyn niht þæs   tiid geweorðad
155 Bartholomeus   in Brytene her,
wyrd welþungen.   Swylce eac wide byð
eorlum geypped   æþelinges deað
ymb feower niht,   se þe fægere iu
mid wætere oferwearp   wuldres cynebearn,
160 wiga weorðlice.   Be him wealdend cwæð
þæt nan mærra man   geond middangeard
betux wife and were   wurde acenned.
Ond þæs ymbe þreo niht   geond þeoda feala
þætte Haligmonð,   heleþum geþinged,
165 fereð to folce,   swa hit foregleawe,
ealde uþwitan,   æror fundan,
Septembres fær,   and þy seofoþan dæg
þæt acenned wearð   cwena selost,
drihtnes modor.   Þænne dagena worn
170 ymbe þreotyne   þegn unforcuð,
godspelles gleaw,   gast onsende
Matheus his   to metodsceafte,
in ecne gefean.   Þænne ealling cymð
ymb þreo niht þæs   þeodum wide
175 emnihtes dæg,   ylda bearnum.

151 on] *Not in MS.*   156 wyrd] wyrð

Hwæt, we weorðiað   wide ge)nd eorðan
heahengles tiid   on hærfeste,
Michaheles,   swa þæt menigo wat,
fif nihtum ufor   þæs þe folcum byð,
180 eorlum geywed   emnihtes dæg.
And þæs embe twa niht   þæt se teoða monð
on folc fereð,   frode geþeahte,
October on tun   us to genihte,
Winterfylleð,   swa hine wide cigað
185 igbuende   Engle and Seaxe,
weras mid wifum.   Swylce wigena tiid
ymb twentig þæs   twegra healdað
and seofon nihtum   samod ætgædere
on anne dæg.   We þa æþelingas
190 fyrn gefrunan   þæt hy foremære,
Simon and Iudas,   symble wæron,
drihtne dyre;   forþon hi dom hlutan,
eadigne upweg.   And þæs ofstum bringð
embe feower niht,   folce genihtsum,
195 Blotmonað on tun,   beornum to wiste,
Nouembris,   niða bearnum
eadignesse,   swa nan oðer na deð
monað maran   miltse drihtnes.
And þy ylcan dæge   ealra we healdað
200 sancta symbel   þara þe sið oððe ær
worhtan in worulde   willan drihtnes.
Syþþan wintres dæg   wide gangeð
on syx nihtum,   sigelbeortne genimð
hærfest mid herige   hrimes and snawes,
205 forste gefeterad,   be frean hæse,
þæt us wunian ne moton   wangas grene,
foldan frætuwe.   Þæs ymb feower niht
þætte Martinus   mære geleorde,
wer womma leas   wealdend sohte,
210 upengla weard.   Þænne embe eahta niht
and feowerum   þætte fan gode
besenctun on sægrund   sigefæstne wer,

184 cigað] cigð   188 seofon] fif; *see Note*   206 moton] mot

on brime haran,   þe iu beorna fela
Clementes oft   clypiað to þearfe.
215 And þæs embe seofon niht,   sigedrihtne leof,
æþele Andreas   up on roderum
his gast ageaf   on godes wære,
fus on forðweg.   Þænne folcum bringð
morgen to mannum   monað to tune,
220 Decembris   drihta bearnum,
Ærra Iula.   Swylce emb eahta and twelf
nihtgerimes   þætte nergend sylf
þristhydigum   Thomase forgeaf
wið earfeðum   ece rice,
225 bealdum beornwigan   bletsunga his.
Þænne emb feower niht   þætte fæder engla
his sunu sende   on þas sidan gesceaft
folcum to frofre.   Nu ge findan magon
haligra tiida   þe man healdan sceal,
230 swa bebugeð gebod   geond Brytenricu
Sexna kyninges   on þas sylfan tiid.

MAXIMS II

MS. Cotton Tiberius B. i

Cyning sceal rice healdan.   Ceastra beoð feorran gesyne,
orðanc enta geweorc,   þa þe on þysse eorðan syndon,
wrætlic weallstana geweorc.   Wind byð on lyfte swiftust,
þunar byð þragum hludast.   Þrymmas syndan Cristes
myccle,
5 wyrd byð swiðost.   Winter byð cealdost,
lencten hrimigost   (he byð lengest ceald),
sumor sunwlitegost   (swegel byð hatost),
hærfest hreðeadegost,   hæleðum bringeð
geres wæstmas,   þa þe him god sendeð.

213 fela] felda   215 leof] lof   229 tiida] tiid   Maxims II, 9 geres]
A later (modern?) hand has added a *above the line after the first* e   him]
The letter o *has been added above the line after* i *by the same hand which supplied
the* a *above* geres

10 Soð bið switolost,   sinc byð deorost,
   gold gumena gehwam,   and gomol snoterost,
   fyrngearum frod,   se þe ær feala gebideð.
   Weax bið wundrum clibbor.   Wolcnu scriðað.
   Geongne æþeling sceolan   gode gesiðas
15 byldan to beaduwe   and to beahgife.
   Ellen sceal on eorle,   ecg sceal wið hellme
   hilde gebidan.   Hafuc sceal on glofe
   wilde gewunian,   wulf sceal on bearowe,
   earm anhaga,   eofor sceal on holte,
20 toðmægenes trum.   Til sceal on eðle
   domes wyrcean.   Daroð sceal on handa,
   gar golde fah.   Gim sceal on hringe
   standan steap and geap.   Stream sceal on yðum
   mencgan mereflode.   Mæst sceal on ceole,
25 segelgyrd seomian.   Sweord sceal on bearme,
   drihtlic isern.   Draca sceal on hlæwe,
   frod, frætwum wlanc.   Fisc sceal on wætere
   cynren cennan.   Cyning sceal on healle
   beagas dælan.   Bera sceal on hæðe,
30 eald and egesfull.   Ea of dune sceal
   flodgræg feran.   Fyrd sceal ætsomne,
   tirfæstra getrum.   Treow sceal on eorle,
   wisdom on were.   Wudu sceal on foldan
   blædum blowan.   Beorh sceal on eorþan
35 grene standan.   God sceal on heofenum,
   dæda demend.   Duru sceal on healle,
   rum recedes muð.   Rand sceal on scylde,
   fæst fingra gebeorh.   Fugel uppe sceal
   lacan on lyfte.   Leax sceal on wæle
40 mid sceote scriðan.   Scur sceal on heofenum,
   winde geblanden,   in þas woruld cuman.
   Þeof sceal gangan þystrum wederum.   Þyrs sceal on fenne
                                     gewunian
   ana innan lande.   Ides sceal dyrne cræfte,
   fæmne hire freond gesecean,   gif heo nelle on folce geþeon

10 switolost] swicolost   13 Weax] wea   19 earm] earn   24 mencgan]
mecgan   40 scriðan] *With* i *added above the line*

45 þæt hi man beagum gebicge.   Brim sceal sealte weallan,
lyfthelm and laguflod   ymb ealra landa gehwylc,
flowan firgenstreamas.   Feoh sceal on eorðan
tydran and tyman.   Tungol sceal on heofenum
beorhte scinan,   swa him bebead meotud.
50 God sceal wið yfele,   geogoð sceal wið yldo,
lif sceal wið deaþe,   leoht sceal wið þystrum,
fyrd wið fyrde,   feond wið oðrum,
lað wið laþe   ymb land sacan,
synne stælan.   A sceal snotor hycgean
55 ymb þysse worulde gewinn,   wearh hangian,
fægere ongildan   þæt he ær facen dyde
manna cynne.   Meotod ana wat
hwyder seo sawul sceal   syððan hweorfan,
and ealle þa gastas   þe for gode hweorfað
60 æfter deaðdæge,   domes bidað
on fæder fæðme.   Is seo forðgesceaft
digol and dyrne;   drihten ana wat,
nergende fæder.   Næni eft cymeð
hider under hrofas,   þe þæt her for soð
65 mannum secge   hwylc sy meotodes gesceaft,
sigefolca gesetu,   þær he sylfa wunað.

A PROVERB FROM WINFRID'S TIME

MS. 751, Nationalbibliothek, Vienna

Oft daedlata   domę forẹldit,
sigisitha gahuem,   suuyltit thi ana.

THE JUDGMENT DAY II

MS. 201, Corpus Christi College, Cambridge

   Hwæt! Ic ana sæt   innan bearwe,
mid helme beþeht,   holte tomiddes,
þær þa wæterburnan   swegdon and urnon
on middan gehæge,   eal swa ic secge.
5 Eac þær wynwyrta   weoxon and bleowon
innon þam gemonge   on ænlicum wonge,
and þa wudubeamas   wagedon and swegdon
þurh winda gryre;   wolcn wæs gehrered,
and min earme mod   eal wæs gedrefed.
10 Þa ic færinga,   forht and unrot,
þas unhyrlican fers   onhefde mid sange,
eall swylce þu cwæde,   synna gemunde,
lifes leahtra,   and þa langan tid,
þæs dimman cyme   deaðes on eorðan.
15 Ic ondræde me eac   dom þone miclan
for mandædum   minum on eorðan,
and þæt ece ic eac   yrre ondræde me
and synfulra gehwam   æt sylfum gode,
and hu mihtig frea   eall manna cynn
20 todæleð and todemeð   þurh his dihlan miht.
Ic gemunde eac   mærðe drihtnes
and þara haligra   on heofonan rice,
swylce earmsceapenra   yfel and witu.
Ic gemunde þis mid me,   and ic mearn swiðe,
25 and ic murcnigende cwæð,   mode gedrefed:
   "Nu ic eow, æddran,   ealle bidde
þæt ge wylspringas   wel ontynan,
hate of hleorum,   recene to tearum,
þænne ic synful slea   swiðe mid fyste,
30 breost mine beate   on gebedstowe,
and minne lichaman   lecge on eorðan
and geearnade sar   ealle ic gecige.

Judgment Day II, 13 langan tid] *With the letters* gan *added above the line in a different hand*   23 yfel] yfes   28 of] os

Ic bidde eow   benum nu ða
þæt ge ne wandian   wiht for tearum,
35 ac dreorige hleor   dreccað mid wope
and sealtum dropum   sona ofergeotaþ,
and geopeniað man   ecum drihtne.
Ne þær owiht   inne ne belife
on heortscræfe   heanra gylta,
40 þæt hit ne sy dægcuð,   þæt þæt dihle wæs,
openum wordum   eall abæred,
breostes and tungan   and flæsces swa some.
Ðis is an hæl   earmre sauwle
and þam sorgiendum   selest hihta,
45 þæt he wunda her   wope gecyðe
uplicum læce,   se ana mæg
aglidene mod   gode gehælan
and ræplingas   recene onbindan,
ne mid swiðran his   swyþe nele brysan
50 wanhydige mod   wealdend engla,
ne þone wlacan smocan   waces fleaxes
wyle waldend Crist   wætere gedwæscan.
Hu ne gesceop þe se scaþa   scearplice bysne
þe mid Criste wæs   cwylmed on rode,
55 hu micel forstent   and hu mære is
seo soðe hreow   synna and gylta?
Se sceaþa wæs on rode   scyldig and manful,
mid undædum   eall gesymed;
he drihtene swa þeah,   deaðe gehende,
60 his bena bebead   breostgehigdum.
He mid lyt wordum   ac geleaffullum
his hæle begeat   and help recene,
and in gefor   þa ænlican geatu
neorxnawonges   mid nerigende.
65   Ic acsige þe, la,   earme geþanc,
hwi latast þu swa lange,   þæt þu ðe læce ne cyþst,
oððe hwi swigast þu,   synnigu tunge,

45 wope] wopa   47 aglidene mod] Aglidene gyltas. mod god   50
wanhydige mod] wan hydig gemod   51 fleaxes] flæsces   63 and in] 7 n
with i *added above the line before* n   66 cyþst] cysth

nu þu forgifnesse hæfst   gearugne timan,
nu þe ælmihtig   earum atihtum,
70 heofonrices weard,   gehyreð mid lustum?
Ac se dæg cymeð   ðonne demeð god
eorðan ymbhwyrft;   þu ana scealt
gyldan scad wordum   wið scyppend god,
and þam rican frean   riht agyldan.
75 Ic lære þæt þu beo hrædra   mid hreowlicum tearum,
and þæt yrre forfoh   eces deman.
Hwæt ligst þu on horwe   leahtrum afylled,
flæsc, mid synnum?   Hwi ne feormast þu
mid teara gyte   torne synne?
80 Hwi ne bidst þu þe   beþunga and plaster,
lifes læcedomes   æt lifes frean?
Nu þu scealt greotan,   tearas geotan,
þa hwile tima sy   and tid wopes;
nu is halwende   þæt man her wepe
85 and dædbote do   drihtne to willan.
Glæd bið se godes sunu,   gif þu gnorn þrowast
and þe sylfum demst   for synnum on eorðan,
ne heofenes god   henða and gyltas
ofer ænne syþ wrecan wile   ænigum men.
90 Ne scealt þu forhyccan   heaf and wopas
and forgifnesse   gearugne timan.
    Gemyne eac on mode,   hu micel is þæt wite
þe þara earmra byð   for ærdædum,
oþþe hu egeslice   and hu andrysne
95 heahþrymme cyningc   her wile deman
anra gehwylcum   be ærdædum,
oþþe hwylce forebeacn   feran onginnað
and Cristes cyme   cyþað on eorðan.
Eall eorðe bifað,   eac swa þa duna
100 dreosað and hreosað,
and beorga hliðu   bugað and myltað,
and se egeslica sweg   ungerydre sæ
eall manna mod   miclum gedrefeð.
Eal bið eac upheofon

94a hu] hit   egeslice] egeslic   101 hliðu] hlida

105 sweart and gesworcen,   swiðe geþuxsað,
deorc and dimhiw,   and dwolma sweart.
þonne stedelease   steorran hreosað,
and seo sunne forswyrcð   sona on morgen,
ne se mona næfð   nanre mihte wiht,
110 þæt he þære nihte   genipu mæge flecgan.
Eac þonne cumað hider   ufon of heofone
deaðbeacnigende tacn,   bregað þa earman;
þonne cumað upplice   eoredheapas,
stiþmægen astyred,   styllað embutan
115 eal engla werod,   ecne behlænað,
ðone mæran metod   mihte and þrymme.
Sitt þonne sigelbeorht   swegles brytta
on heahsetle,   helme beweorðod.
We beoð færinga   him beforan brohte,
120 æghwanum cumene   to his ansyne,
þæt gehwylc underfo
dom be his dædum   æt drihtne sylfum.
      Ic bidde, man, þæt þu gemune   hu micel bið se broga
beforan domsetle   drihtnes þænne;
125 stent hergea mæst   heortleas and earh,
amasod and amarod,   mihtleas, afæred.
þænne samod becumað   of swegles hleo
eall engla werod,   ecne ymtrymmað.
þænne bið geban micel,   and aboden þider
130 eal Adames cnosl   eorðbuendra
þe on foldan wearð   feded æfre
oððe modar gebær   to manlican,
oþþe þa þe wæron   oððe woldon beon
oþþe towearde   geteald wæron awiht.
135 Ðonne eallum beoð   ealra gesweotolude
digle geþancas   on þære dægtide,
eal þæt seo heorte   hearmes geþohte
oððe seo tunge   to teonan geclypede

---

109 nanre] *The scribe began with* m, *then altered* m *to* na *and added* nre
112 tacn] *Not in MS.*   125 hergea mæst] he *with four or five letters erased
after it*   127 swegles] sweges   129 þænne] Æne   130 eorðbuendra]
eorbuendra   131 feded] fedend

    oþþe mannes hand manes gefremede
140 on þystrum scræfum þinga on eorðan;
    eal þæt hwæne sceamode scylda on worulde,
    þæt he ænigum men ypte oððe cyðde,
    þonne bið eallum open ætsomne,
    gelice alyfed þæt man lange hæl.
145 Ufenan eall þis eac byð gefylled
    eal uplic lyft ættrenum lige.
    Færð fyr ofer eall, ne byð þær nan foresteal,
    ne him man na ne mæg miht forwyrnan;
    eal þæt us þincð æmtig eahgemearces
150 under roderes ryne, readum lige
    bið emnes mid þy eal gefylled.
    Ðonne fyren lig blaweð and braslað,
    read and reaðe, ræsct and efesteð,
    hu he synfullum susle gefremme;
155 ne se wrecenda bryne wile forbugan
    oððe ænigum þær are gefremman,
    buton he horwum sy her afeormad,
    and þonne þider cume, þearle aclænsad.
    þonne fela mægða, folca unrim,
160 heora sinnigan breost swiðlice beatað
    forhte mid fyste for fyrenlustum.
    þær beoð þearfan and þeodcyningas,
    earm and eadig, ealle beoð afæred;
    þær hæfð ane lage earm and se welega,
165 forðon hi habbað ege ealle ætsomne.
    Ðæt reðe flod ræscet fyre
    and biterlice bærnð ða earman saula,
    and heora heortan horxlice wyrmas,
    synscyldigra, ceorfað and slitað.
170 Ne mæg þær æni man be agnum gewyrhtum
    gedyrstig wesan, deman gehende,
    ac ealle þurhyrnð oga ætsomne,

---

140 scræfum] scræfe *with the final* e *dotted beneath for deletion and* ū *written above* 149 eal] Eeal 152 blaweð] blawað 154 gefremme] gefremede 155 wrecenda] *With* n *added above the line* bryne] brynæ *with the* a *dotted beneath for deletion* 157 afeormad] *With* d *altered from* n 170 be agnum] beárnū

breostgehyda   and se bitera wop,
and þær stænt astifad,   stane gelicast,
175 eal arleas heap   yfeles on wenan.
    Hwæt dest þu, la, flæsc?   Hwæt dreogest þu nu?
Hwæt miht þu on þa tid   þearfe gewepan?
Wa þe nu, þu þe þeowast   þissere worulde,
and her glæd leofast   on galnysse
180 and þe mid stiðum astyrest   sticelum þæs gælsan!
Hwi ne forhtas þu   fyrene egsan,
and þe sylfum ondræd   swiðlice witu,
ða deoflum geo   drihten geteode,
awyrgedum gastum,   weana to leane?
185 Þa oferswiðað   sefan and spræce
manna gehwylces   for micelnysse.
Nænig spræc mæg beon,   spellum areccan
ænegum on eorðan   earmlice witu,
fulle stowa   fyres on grunde,
190 þe wæs in grimmum   susle on helle.
Þær synt to sorge   ætsomne gemenged
se þrosma lig   and se þrece gicela,
swiðe hat and ceald   helle tomiddes.
Hwilum þær eagan   ungemetum wepað
195 for þæs ofnes bryne   (eal he is bealuwes full);
hwilum eac þa teþ for miclum cyle   manna þær gryrrað.
Þis atule gewrixl   earmsceapene men
on worulda woruld   wendað þær inne
betwyx forsworcenum   sweartum nihtum
200 and weallendes pices   wean and þrosme.
Þær nan stefn styreð   butan stearcheard
wop and wanung,   nawiht elles;
ne bið þær ansyn gesewen   ænigre wihte,

---

174 astifad] astifed *with the* e *dotted beneath for deletion and* a *written above*
178 Wa þe nu, þu þe] *Second* þe *not in MS.*   þeowast] þeowest *with the
second* e *dotted beneath for deletion and* a *written above*   þissere worulde]
Not in MS.   187 areccan] areccen *with the second* e *dotted beneath for deletion and* a *written above*   189 fulle] fule   197 earmsceapene] earm sceape
200 þrosme] þromes   201 stefn] stef ne

butan þara cwelra   þe cwylmað ða earman.
205 Ne bið þær inne   aht gemeted
butan lig and cyle   and laðlic ful;
hy mid nosan ne magon   naht geswæccan
butan unstences   ormætnesse.
þær beoð þa wanigendan   welras gefylde
210 ligspiwelum bryne   laðlices fyres,
and hy wælgrimme   wyrmas slitað
and heora ban gnagað   brynigum tuxlum.
Ufenon eal þis   bið þæt earme breost
mid bitere care   breged and swenced,
215 for hwi fyrngende flæsc   on þas frecnan tid
hym selfum swa fela   synna geworhte,
þæt hit on cweartern   cwylmed wurde,
þær ða atelan synd   ecan witu;
þær leohtes ne leoht   lytel sperca
220 earmum ænig,   ne þær arfæstnes
ne sib ne hopa   ne swige gegladað
ne þara wependra   worn wihte.
Flyhð frofor aweg;   ne bið þær fultum nan
þæt wið þa biteran þing   gebeorh mæge fremman.
225 Ne bið þær ansyn gemet   ænigre blisse,
ac þær bið angryslic   ege and fyrhtu
and sari mod,   swiðlic gristbigtung;
þær bið unrotnes   æghwær wælhreow,
adl and yrre   and æmelnes,
230 and þær synnge eac   sauwle on lige
on blindum scræfe   byrnað and yrnað.
þonne deriende   gedwinað heonone
þysse worulde gefean,   gewitað mid ealle;
þonne druncennes   gedwineð mid wistum,
235 and hleahter and plega   hleapað ætsomne,

208 unstences] un stence   209 wanigendan] wani gendran *with* r *dotted
beneath for deletion*   215 fyrngende] fyrgende   222 wependra] wera
226 ac þær] þ   227 gristbigtung] grisgbigtung   229 adl] eald   230
synnge] synne   233 gewitað] gegítað *with the second* g *dotted beneath
for deletion and* w *written above*

and wrænnes eac   gewiteð heonone,
and fæsthafolnes   feor gewiteð,
uncyst onweg   and ælc gælsa
scyldig scyndan   on sceade þonne,
240 and se earma flyhð   uncræftiga slæp
sleac mid sluman   slincan on hinder.
Ðonne blindum beseah   biterum ligum
earme on ende   þæt unalyfed is nu;
leofest on life   lað bið þænne,
245 and þæt werige mod   wendað þa gyltas
swiðe mid sorgum   and mid sargunge.
    Eala, se bið gesælig   and ofersælig
and on worulda woruld   wihta gesæligost,
se þe mid gesyntum   swylce cwyldas
250 and witu mæg   wel forbugon,
and samod bliðe   on woruld ealle
his þeodne geþeon,   and þonne mot
habban heofonrice;   þæt is hihta mæst.
Þær niht ne genimð   næfre þeostrum
255 þæs heofenlican   leohtes sciman;
ne cymð þær sorh ne sar   ne geswenced yld,
ne þær ænig geswinc   æfre gelimpeð,
oððe hunger oþþe þurst   oððe heanlic slæp,
ne bið þær fefur ne adl   ne færlic cwyld,
260 nanes liges gebrasl   ne se laðlica cyle.
Nis þær unrotnes   ne þær æmelnys,
ne hryre ne caru   ne hreoh tintrega,
ne bið þær liget   ne laðlic storm,
winter ne þunerrad   ne wiht cealdes,
265 ne þær hagulscuras   hearde mid snawe,
ne bið þær wædl ne lyre   ne deaðes gryre
ne yrmð ne agnes   ne ænigu gnornung,

---

239 scyndan] scyndum *with* u *dotted beneath for deletion and* a *written above,*
i.e. scyndam   þonne] þone   244 leofest] leofes   248 wihta] wiht na
250 witu] witū   252 þonne] *With the second* n *added above the line*
253 heofonrice] *With the first* e *added above the line*   254 genimð] genipð
þeostrum] þeostra   265 snawe] swa se   267 ænigu] nænigu

ac þær samod ricxað   sib mid spede,
and arfæstnes   and ece god,
270 wuldor and wurðmynt,
swylce lof and lif   and leoflic geþwærnes.
Ufenan eal þis   ece drihten
him ealra goda gehwylc   glædlice ðenað,
þær a andweard   ealle weorðaþ
275 and fehþ and geblyssað   fæder ætsomne,
wuldraþ and wel hylt,
fægere frætuað   and freolice lufað
and on heofonsetle   hean geregnað.
His sunu bliðe,   sigores brytta,
280 sylð anra gehwam   ece mede,
heofonlice hyrsta,   þæt is healic gifu,
gemang þam ænlican   engla werode
and þæra haligra   heapum and þreatum.
Þær hy beoð geþeode   þeodscipum on gemang
285 betwyx heahfæderas   and halige witegan,
blissiendum modum,   byrgum tomiddes,
þær þa ærendracan synd   ælmihtiges godes,
and betweoh rosena   reade heapas,
þær symle scinað.
290 Þær þæra hwittra   hwyrfð mædenheap,
blostmum behangen,   beorhtost wereda,
þe ealle læt   ænlicu godes drut,
seo frowe þe us   frean acende,
metod on moldan,   meowle seo clæne.
295 Þæt is Maria,   mædena selast;
heo let þurh þa scenan   scinendan ricu,
gebletsodost ealra,   þæs breman fæder,
betweox fæder and sunu,   freolicum werede,
and betwyx þære ecan   uplicum sibbe
300 rice rædwitan,   rodera weardas.

271 geþwærnes] ge hwærnes *with* þ *crowded in after* h *in a later hand*
275 geblyssað] geblysað   277 lufað] lifað   278 geregnað] gerinnað
283 þreatum] þreapū   288 rosena] rosene   290 þæra] þære *with the*
final e *dotted beneath for deletion and* a *written above*   291 beorhtost]
beortost

Hwæt mæg beon heardes   her on life,
gif þu wille secgan   soð þæm ðe frineð,
wið þam þu mote   gemang þam werode
eardian unbleoh   on ecnesse,
305 and on upcundra   eadegum setlum
brucan bliðnesse   butan ende forð?"

AN EXHORTATION TO CHRISTIAN LIVING

MS. 201, Corpus Christi College, Cambridge

Nu lære ic þe   swa man leofne sceal.
Gif þu wille þæt blowende   rice gestigan,
þænne beo þu eadmod   and ælmesgeorn,
wis on wordum,   and wæccan lufa
5 on hyge halgum   on þas hwilwendan tid,
bliðe mode,   and gebedum filige
oftost symle   þær þu ana sy.
Forðan þæt halige gebed   and seo hluttre lufu
godes and manna   and seo ælmessylen
10 and se miccla hopa   to þinum hælende,
þæt he þine synna   adwæscan wylle,
and eac oþera fela
godra weorca   glengað and bringað
þa soðfæstan   sauwle to reste
15 on þa uplican   eadignesse.
Wyrc þæt þu wyrce,   word oððe dæda,
hafa metodes ege   on gemang symle;
þæt is witodlice   wisdomes ord,
þæt þu þæt ece leoht   eal ne forleose.
20 Þeos woruld is æt ende,   and we synd wædlan gyt
heofena rices;   þæt is hefig byrden.
And þeah þu æfter þinum ende   eall gesylle
þæt þu on eorðan   ær gestryndes
goda gehwylces,   wylle gode cweman,

Exhortation to Christian Living 13 bringað] *With* b *altered from* þ
21 byrden] byr dæn *with* a *dotted beneath for deletion*

25 ne mihtu mid þæm eallum   sauwle þine
   ut alysan,   gif heo inne wyrð
   feondum befangen,   frofre bedæled,
   welena forwyrned;   ac þu wuldres god,
   ece ælmihtigne,   ealninga bidde
30 þæt he þe ne forlæte   laðum to handa,
   feondum to frofre,   ac þu fleoh þanan,
   syle ælmessan   oft and gelome
   digolice;   þæt bið drihtnes lac
   gumena gehwylces   þe on god gelyfð.
35   Ceapa þe mid æhtum   eces leohtes,
   þy læs þu forweorðe,   þænne þu hyra geweald nafast
   to syllanne.   Hit bið swiðe yfel
   manna gehwilcum   þæt he micel age,
   gif he him god ne ondræt
40 swiðor micle   þonne his sylfes gewil.
   Warna þe georne   wið þære wambe fylle,
   forþan heo þa unþeawas   ealle gesomnað
   þe þære saule   swiðost deriað,
   þæt is druncennes   and dyrnegeligere,
45 ungemet wilnung   ætes and slæpes;
   þa man mæg mid fæstenum
   and forhæfdnessum   heonon adrifan,
   and mid cyricsocnum   cealdum wederum
   eadmodlice   ealluncga biddan
50 heofena drihten   þæt he þe hæl gife,
   milde mundbora,   swa him gemet þince.
   And ondræd þu ðe   dihle wisan,
   nearwe geþancas,   þe on niht becumað,
   synlustas foroft   swiðe fremman
55 earfoðlice,   þy þu earhlice scealt
   gyltas þine   swiðe bemurnan,
   har hilderinc;   hefie þe ðincaþ
   synna þine.   Forþam þu sylf ongyte

---

34 gelyfð] belyfð *with* b *dotted beneath for deletion and* g *written above*
47 forhæfdnessum] *With the* d *added above the line*   54 fremman] frēm n
with a *written below in a different hand*   58 ongyte] *With* y *written on an
erasure*

þæt þu alætan scealt   læne staþelas,
60 eard and eþel.   Uncuð bið þe þænne
   tohwan þe þin drihten   gedon wille,
   þænne þu lengc ne most   lifes brucan,
   eardes on eþle,   swa þu ær dydest,
   blissum hremi.   Nu þu ðe beorgan scealt,
65 and wið feonda gehwæne   fæste healdan
   sauwle þine;   a hi winnað
   embe þæt   * * *
   dæges and nihtes   ongean drihtnes lif.
   Þu miht hy gefleman,   gif þu filian wilt
70 larum minum,   swa ic lære þe
   digollice   þæt þu on dægred oft
   ymbe þinre sauwle ræd   swiðe smeage,
   hu þu þæt ece leoht   æfre begytan mæge,
   siðe gesecan;   þu scealt glædlice swiðe swincan
75 wið þæs uplican   eþelrices
   dæges and nihtes,   þu scealt druncen fleon
   and þa oferfylle   ealle forlætan.
   Gif þu wilt þa upplican   eardwic ceosan,
   þænne scealt þu hit on eorðan   ær geþencan,
80 and þu þe sylfne   swiðe gebindan
   and þa unþeawas   ealle forlætan
   þe þu on þis life ær   lufedest and feddest.

A SUMMONS TO PRAYER

MS. 201, Corpus Christi College, Cambridge

   Þænne gemiltsað þe, N.,   mundum qui regit,
   ðeoda þrymcyningc   thronum sedentem
   a butan ende   * * *
   saule þinre   * * *
5 Geunne þe on life   auctor pacis
   sibbe gesælða,   salus mundi,
   metod se mæra   magna uirtute,

80 gebindan] gebinde *with the letters* ge *added above the line*
Summons to Prayer 1 N] ·N̄·   4 þinre] þine; *see Note*

          and se soðfæsta   summi filius
          fo on fultum,   factor cosmi,
10   se of æþelre wæs   uirginis partu
          clæne acenned   Christus in orbem,
          metod þurh Marian,   mundi redemptor,
          and þurh þæne halgan gast.   Uoca frequenter
          bide helpes hine,   clemens deus,
15   se onsended wæs   summo de throno
          and þære clænan   clara uoce
          þa gebyrd bodade   bona uoluntate
          þæt heo scolde cennan   Christum regem,
          ealra cyninga cyningc,   casta uiuendo;
20   and þu þa soðfæstan   supplex rogo,
          fultumes bidde friclo   uirginem almum,
          and þær æfter to   omnes sancti
          bliðmod bidde,   beatus et iustus,
          þæt hi ealle þe   unica uoce
25   þingian to þeodne   thronum regentem,
          æcum drihtne,   alta polorum,
          þæt he þine saule,   summus iudex,
          onfo freolice,   factor aeternus,
          and he gelæde   luce perhennem,
30   þær eadige   animæ sanctæ
          rice restað   regna caelorum.

          THE LORD'S PRAYER II

          MS. 201, Corpus Christi College, Cambridge

          Pater noster.
          Þu eart ure fæder,   ealles wealdend,
          cyninc on wuldre.   Forðam we clypiað to þe,
          are biddað,   nu þu yþost miht
          sawle alysan.   Þu hig sændest ær

17 þa] þe   bodade] boda   21 bidde] *Added above the line in the same hand*
friclo] fricolo *with the first* o *dotted beneath for deletion*   26 æcum]
Ęcum   30 animæ sanctæ] Animę scę   31 restað] restat

5 þurh þine æþelan hand   in to þam flæsce;
  ac hwar cymð heo nu,
  buton þu, engla god,   eft hig alyse,
  sawle of synnum   þurh þine soðan miht?
      Qui es in celis.
  Ðu eart on heofonum   hiht and frofor,
10 blissa beorhtost;   ealle abugað to þe,
  þinra gasta þrym,   anre stæfne
  clypiað to Criste,   cweþað ealle þus:
  "Halig eart þu, halig,   heofonengla cyningc,
  drihten ure,   and þine domas synd
15 rihte and rume,   ræcað efne gehwam,
  æghwilcum men   agen gewyrhta.
  Wel bið ðam þe wyrcð   willan þinne!"
      Sanctificetur nomen tuum.
  Swa is gehalgod   þin heah nama
  swiðe mærlice   manegum gereordum,
20 twa and hundseofontig,   þæs þe secgað bec,
  þæt þu, engla god,   ealle gesettest
  ælcere þeode   þeaw and wisan.
  Þa wurþiað þin weorc   wordum and dædum,
  þurh gecynd clypiað   and Crist heriað
25 and þin lof lædað,   lifigenda god,
  swa þu eart geæþelod   geond ealle world.
      Adueniat regnum tuum.
  Cum nu and mildsa,   mihta waldend,
  and us þin rice alyf,   rihtwis dema,
  earda selost   and ece lif,
30 þar we sibbe and lufe   samod gemetað,
  eagena beorhtnysse   and ealle mirhðe,
  þar bið gehyred   þin halige lof
  and þin micele miht,   mannum to frofre,
  swa þu, engla god,   eallum blissast.
      Fiat uoluntas tua.
35 Gewurðe þin willa,   swa þu, waldend, eart
  ece geopenod   geond ealle world,

Lord's Prayer II, 15 ræcað] ræcð   30 sibbe and lufe] sib 7 lufu
31 beorhtnysse] beorhtnys

and þu þe silf eart   soðfæst dema,
rice rædbora,   geond rumne grund.
Swa þin heahsetl is   heah and mære,
40 fæger and wurðlic,   swa þin fæder worhte,
æþele and ece,   þar ðu on sittest
on sinre swiðran healf.   þu eart sunu and fæder,
ana ægþer;   swa is þin æþele gecynd
micclum gemærsod,   and þu monegum helpst,
45 ealra cyninga þrym,   clypast ofer ealle.
Bið þin wuldorword   wide gehyred,
þonne þu þine fyrde   fægere geblissast,
sylest miht and mund   micclum herige,
and þe þanciað   þusenda fela,
50 eal engla þrym,   anre stæfne.
   Sicut in celo.
Swa þe on heofonum   heahþrymnesse
æþele and ece   a þanciað,
clæne and gecorene   Cristes þegnas,
singað and biddað   soðfæstne god
55 are and gifnesse   ealre þeode;
þonne þu him tiðast,   tyreadig cyningc,
swa þu eadmod eart   ealre worlde.
Sy þe þanc and lof   þinre mildse,
wuldor and willa;   þu gewurðod eart
60 on heofonrice,   heah casere,
   Et in terra.
and on eorðan,   ealra cyninga
help and heafod,   halig læce,
reðe and rihtwis,   rumheort hlaford.
þu geæþelodest þe   ealle gesceafta,
65 and tosyndrodest hig   siððan on manega,
sealdest ælcre gecynde   agene wisan
and a þine mildse   ofer manna bearn.
   Panem nostrum cotidianum.
Swa mid sibbe   sænst urne hlaf
dæghwamlice   duguðe þinre,
70 rihtlice dælest

42 sinre] þinre   43 æþele] æþela   66 ælcre gecynde] ælcege cynd

mete þinum mannum   and him mare gehætst
æfter forðsiðe,   þines fæder rice,
þæt wæs on fruman   fægere gegearwod,
earda selost   and ece lif,
75 gif we soð and riht   symle gelæstað.
Da nobis hodie.
Syle us to dæg,   drihten, þine
mildse and mihta   and ure mod gebig,
þanc and þeawas,   on þin gewil.
Bewyrc us on heortan   haligne gast
80 fæste on innan,   and us fultum sile,
þæt we moton wyrcan   willan þinne
and þe betæcan,   tyreadig cyningc,
sawle ure   on þines silfes hand.
Et dimitte nobis debita nostra.
Forgif us ure synna,   þæt us ne scamige eft,
85 drihten ure,   þonne þu on dome sitst
and ealle men   up arisað
þe fram wife and fram were   wurdon acænned.
Beoð þa gebrosnodon   ban mid þam flæsce
ealle ansunde   eft geworden;
90 þar we swutollice   siððan oncnawað
eal þæt we geworhton   on worldrice,
betere and wyrse,   þar beoð buta geara.
Ne magon we hit na dyrnan,   for ðam þe hit drihten wat,
and þar gewitnesse beoð   wuldormicele,
95 heofonwaru and eorðwaru,   helwaru þridde.
Þonne bið egsa   geond ealle world,
þar man us tyhhað on dæg   twegen eardas,
drihtenes are   oððe deofles þeowet,
swa hwaðer we geearniað   her on life,
100 þa hwile þe ure mihta   mæste wæron.
Sicut et nos dimittimus debitoribus nostris.
Ac þonne us alyseð   lifigende god
sawle ure,   swa we her forgifað
earmon mannum   þe wið us agilt.

86 arisað] ariseð   88 gebrosnodon] gebrosnodon eft   96 bið] beoð
101 alyseð] alysað   102 forgifað] gifað

Et ne nos inducas in temtationem.

And na us þu ne læt   laðe beswican
105 on costunga,   cwellan and bærnan
sawla ure,   þeah we sinna fela
didon for ure disige   dæges and nihtes,
idele spræce   and unrihte weorc,
þine bodu bræcon.   We þe biddað nu,
110 ælmihtig god,   are and gifnesse;
ne læt swa heanlice   þin handgeweorc
on endedæge   eal forwurðan,
Set libera nos a malo.
ac alys us of yfele.   Ealle we beþurfon
godes gifnesse;   we agylt habbað
115 and swiðe gesingod.   We ðe, soðfæstan god,
heriað and lofiað,   swa þu, hælend, eart
cynebearn gecydd   cwycum and deadum,
æþele and ece   ofer ealle þingc.
Þu miht on anre hand   eaðe befealdan
120 ealne middaneard.   Swilc is mære cyningc.
Amen.
Sy swa þu silf wilt,   soðfæst dema;
we þe, engla god,   ealle heriað,
swa þu eart gewurðod   a on worlda forð.

THE GLORIA I

Text from MS. Junius 121 (J); variants from MS. 201, Corpus
Christi College, Cambridge (C)

Gloria.
Sy þe wuldor and lof   wide geopenod
geond ealle þeoda,   þanc and wylla,
mægen and mildse   and ealles modes lufu,
soðfæstra sib,   and ðines sylfes dom

110 gifnesse] gifnes   Gloria I, 1 *Gloria*] Gloria patri *J*; la *C*   geopenod]
geopnod *C*   2 wylla] willa *C*   4 ðines] þines *C*   sylfes] silfes *C*

5 worulde gewlitegod,   swa ðu wealdan miht
eall eorðan mægen   and uplyfte,
wind and wolcna.   Wealdest eall on riht.
  Patri et filio et spiritui sancto.
þu eart frofra fæder   and feorhhyrde,
lifes latteow,   leohtes wealdend,
10 asyndrod fram synnum,   swa ðin sunu mære
þurh clæne gecynd,   cyning ofer ealle,
beald gebletsod,   boca lareow,
heah higefrofer   and halig gast.
  Sicut erat in principio.
Swa wæs on fruman   frea mancynnes
15 ealre worulde   wlite and frofer,
clæne and cræftig.   þu gecyddest þæt
þa ðu, ece god,   ana gewrohtest
þurh halige miht   heofonas and eorðan,
eardas and uplyft   and ealle þing.
20 þu settest on foldan   swyðe feala cynna
and tosyndrodost hig   syððon on mænego;
þu gewrohtest, ece god,   ealle gesceafta
on syx dagum,   and on þone seofoðan þu gerestest.
þa wæs geforðad   þin fægere weorc,
25 and ðu sunnandæg   sylf halgodest
and gemærsodest hine   manegum to helpe.
þone heahan dæg   healdað and freoðiaþ
ealle þa ðe cunnon   cristene þeawas,
halige heortlufan   and ðæs hehstan gebod;

---

5 worulde] world C   ðu] þu C   6 uplyfte] up lifte C   7 eall] ealle C
8 þu] Ðu C   feorhhyrde] feorh hyrda C   9 latteow] laððeow C
10 asyndrod] asundrod C   synnum] sinnū C   ðin] þin C   11 cyning]
cyninc C   13 higefrofer] hige frofre J C   and halig gast] *Not in* C
15 worulde] worlde C   frofer] frofre J C   17 gewrohtest] geworhtest C
19 þing] þinc C   20 swyðe] swiðe C   feala] fela C   21 tosyndrodost]
tosyndrodest C   syððon] siððan C   mænego] manega C
22 gewrohtest] geworhtest C   23 syx] six C   and on þone] *Not in* C
24 geforðad] geforðod C   25 ðu] þu C   sylf] silf C   26 gemærsodest]
þu mærsodest C   27 heahan] hea an C   freoðiaþ] friðiað C
29 halige] haligne J C   ðæs] þæs C   hehstan] hihstan C

30 on drihtnes namon   se dæg is gewurðod.
    Et nunc et semper.
    And nu and symble   þine soðan weorc
    and ðin mycele miht   manegum swytelað,
    swa þine cræftas heo   cyðaþ wide
    ofer ealle woruld;   ece standeþ
35 godes handgeweorc,   groweð swa ðu hete.
    Ealle þe heriað   halige dreamas
    clænre stefne   and cristene bec,
    eall middaneard,   and we men cweþað
    on grunde her: "Gode lof and ðanc,
40 ece willa,   and ðin agen dom!"
    Et in secula seculorum.
    And on worulda woruld   wunað and rixað
    cyning innan wuldre   and his þa gecorenan,
    heahþrymnesse   haliges gastes,
    wlitige englas   and wuldorgyfe,
45 soðe sibbe,   sawla þancung,
    modes miltse.   Þær is seo mæste lufu;
    haligdomes   heofonas syndon
    þurh þine ecan word   æghwær fulle,
    swa syndon þine mihta   ofer middangeard
50 swutele and gesyne,   þæt ðu hy sylf worhtest.
    Amen.
    We þæt soðlice   secgað ealle:
    Þurh clæne gecynd   þu eart cyning on riht,

---

30 drihtnes] drihtenes *C*   namon] naman *C*   31 And nu and] *Second
and not in C*   symble] symle *C*   32 ðin] þin *C*   mycele] micele *C*
swytelað] swutelað *C*   33 heo] hig *C*   cyðaþ] cyðað *C*   34 woruld]
world *C*   standeþ] standað *C*   35 ðu] þu *C*   36 heriað] heriað
heriað *C*   37 stefne] stæfne *C*   38 eall] eal *C*   cweþað] cweðað *C*
39 ðanc] þanc *C*   40 ðin] þin *C*   41 worulda woruld] worlda world *C*
42 cyning] cyninc *C*   43 heahþrymnesse] *C*; heah þrynnesse *J*   haliges
gastes] halige gastas *C*   44 wuldorgyfe] wuldorgife *C*   45 þancung]
C; þangung *J*   46 miltse] mildse *C*   þær] þar *C*   47 haligdomes] *C*;
halig domas *J*   48 word] *C; not in J*   æghwær] æghwar *C*   49
syndon] synd *C*   middangeard] middan eard *C*   50 swutele] swutole *C*
þæt] þat *C*   ðu] þu *C*   hy] hig *C*   sylf] silf *C*   52 cyning] cyninc *C*

clæne and cræftig.　Þu gecyddest þæt
þa ðu, mihtig god,　man geworhtest
55 and him on dydest　oruð and sawul,
sealdest word and gewitt　and wæstma gecynd,
cyddest þine cræftas.　Swylc is Cristes miht!

THE LORD'S PRAYER III

MS. Junius 121

Pater noster qui es in cęlis.
Fæder manncynnes,　frofres ic þe bidde,
halig drihten,　þu ðe on heofonum eart.
Sanctificetur nomen tuum.
Þæt sy gehalgod,　hygecræftum fæst,
þin nama nu ða,　neriende Crist,
5 in urum ferhðlocan　fæste gestaðelod.
Adueniat regnum tuum.
Cume nu to mannum,　mihta wealdend,
þin rice to us,　rihtwis dema,
and ðin geleafa　in lifdæge
on urum mode　mære þurhwunige.
Fiat uoluntas tua sicut in cęlo et in terra.
10 And þin willa mid us　weorðe gelæsted
on eardunge　eorðan rices,
swa hluttor is　in heofonwuldre,
wynnum gewlitegod　a to worulde forð.
Panem nostrum cotidianum da nobis hodie.
Syle us nu to dæge,　drihten gumena,
15 heofena heahcyning,　hlaf urne,
þone ðu onsendest　sawlum to hæle
on middaneard　manna cynnes;
þæt is se clæna　Crist, drihten god.
Et dimitte nobis debita nostra.
Forgyf us, gumena weard,　gyltas and synna,
20 and ure leahtras alet,　lices wunda

55 oruð] orð *C*　　sawul] sawle *C*　　57 Swylc] swilc *C*

and mandæda,   swa we mildum wið ðe,
ælmihtigum gode,   oft abylgeað,
   Sicut et nos dimittimus debitoribus nostris.
swa swa we forlætað   leahtras on eorþan
þam þe wið us   oft agyltað,
25 and him womdæde   witan ne þencað
for earnunge   ecan lifes.
   Et ne nos inducas in temptationem.
Ne læd þu us to wite   in wean sorge
ne in costunge,   Crist nerigende,
þy læs we arlease   ealra þinra mildsa
30 þurh feondscipe   fremde weorðan.
   Sed libera nos a malo.
And wið yfele gefreo   us eac nu ða
feonda gehwylces;   we in ferðlocan,
þeoden engla,   ðanc and wuldor,
soð sigedrihten,   secgað georne,
35 þæs ðe þu us milde   mihtum alysdest
fram hæftnyde   hellewites.
   Amen.
Weorðe þæt.

THE CREED

MS. Junius 121

   Credo in deum patrem omnipotentem.
Ælmihtig fæder   up on rodore,
þe ða sciran gesceaft   sceope and worhtest
and eorðan wang   ealne gesettest,
ic þe ecne god   ænne gecenne,
5 lustum gelyfe.   þu eart lifes frea,
engla ordfruma,   eorðan wealdend,
and ðu garsecges   grundas geworhtest,
and þu ða menegu canst   mærra tungla.

Lord's Prayer III, 22 abylgeað] abylgeat   25 þencað] þenceð   35 þu|
Added above the line   Creed 8 þu ða] ða þu   menegu] manega

*Et in Iesum Christum filium eius unicum, dominum
nostrum.*

Ic on sunu þinne soðne gelyfe,
10 hælendne cyning, hider asendne
of ðam uplican engla rice,
þone Gabriel, godes ærendraca,
sanctan Marian sylfre gebodode.

Ides unmæne, heo þæt ærende
15 onfeng freolice, and ðe fæder sylfne
under breostcofan bearn acende.

Næs ðær gefremmed firen æt giftum,
ac þær halig gast handgyft sealde,
þære fæmnan bosm fylde mid blisse,
20 and heo cuðlice cende swa mærne
eorðbuendum engla scyppend,
se to frofre gewearð foldbuendum,
and ymbe Bethleem bodedan englas
þæt acenned wæs Crist on eorðan.

  Passus sub Pontio Pilato.

25 Ða se pontisca Pilatus weold
under Romwarum rices and doma,
þa se deora frea deað þrowade,
on gealgan stah, gumena drihten,
þone geomormod Iosep byrigde,
30 and he of helle huðe gefette,
of þam suslhofe, sawla manega,
het ða uplicne eþel secan.

  Tertia die resurrexit a mortuis.

Þæs þy ðriddan dæge þeoda wealdend
aras, rices frea, recene of moldan,
35 and he XL daga folgeras sine
runum arette, and ða his rice began,
þone uplican eðel secan,
cwæð þæt he nolde nænne forlætan
þe him forð ofer þæt fylian wolde
40 and mid fæstum sefan freode gelæstan.

---

13 sanctan] Sc̄a 34 recene] recen

Credo in spiritum sanctum.

Ic haligne gast   hihte beluce,
emne swa ecne   swa is aðor gecweden,
fæder oððe freobearn,   folca gereordum.
Ne synd þæt þreo godas,   þriwa genemned,
45 ac is an god,   se ðe ealle hafað
þa þry naman   þinga gerynum,
soð and sigefæst   ofer side gesceaft,
wereda wuldorgyfa,   wlanc and ece.
Sanctam ęcclesiam catholicam.
Eac ic gelyfe   þæt syn leofe gode
50 þe þurh ænne geþanc   ealdor heriað,
heofona heahcyning   her for life,
Sanctorum communionem.
and ic gemænscipe   mærne getreowe
þinra haligra   her for life.
Remissionem peccatorum.
Lisse ic gelyfe   leahtra gehwylces,
Carnis resurrectionem.
55 and ic þone ærest   ealra getreowe,
flæsces on foldan   on þa forhtan tid,
Et uitam ęternam.
þær ðu ece lif   eallum dælest,
swa her manna gehwylc   metode gecwemað.

FRAGMENTS OF PSALMS

MS. Junius 121

(5,1) *Verba mea auribus percipe, domine; intellege cla-*
    morem meum.
Word þu min onfoh,   wuldres ealdor,
and mid earum gehyr,   ece drihten.
[*I*]*ntende uoci orationis męę, rex meus et deus meus.*
Ongyt mine clypunga   cuðum gereorde,
beheald min gebed   holdum mode;

---

57 þær] ær *with the colored capital omitted*   dælest] dældest

þu eart min cyning   and eac ece god.

(5,2) *Quoniam ad te orabo: Domine, mane exaudies uocem meam.*

Forðon ic to ðe,   ece drihten,
soðum gebidde,   and ðu symble gehyr
morgena gehwylce   mine stefne.

(5,3) *Mane adstabo tibi et uidebo, quoniam non deus uolens iniquitatem tu es.*

Ic þe æt stande   ær on morgen
and ðe sylfne geseo;   forðon ic to soðe wat
þæt ðu unriht ne wilt   ænig, drihten.

(19,9) *Domine, saluum fac regem, et exaudi nos in die qua inuocauerimus te.*

Do, drihten, cyng   dædum halne,
and us eac gehyr   holdum mode,
swylce we ðe daga,   drihten, cigen.

(24,3) *Uias tuas, domine, notas fac mihi, et semitas tuas edoce me.*

Do me wegas þine   wise, drihten,
and me ðinra stiga   stapas eac gelær.

(24,4) *Dirige me in ueritate tua, et doce me, quia tu es deus salutaris meus et te sustinui tota die.*

Gerece me on ræde   and me ricene gelær,
þæt ic on þinre soðfæstnysse   simble lyfige.

(24,5) *Reminiscere miserationum tuarum, domine, et misericordię tuę, quę a seculo sunt.*

Wes ðu gemyndig   miltsa þinra,
þe ðu, drihten, dydest   syððan dagas wæron,
and ðu wislice   þas woruld gesettest.

(24,6) *Delicta iuuentutis meę et ignorantias meas ne memineris, domine; secundum magnam misericordiam tuam memor esto mei, deus.*

Ne gemynega þu me   minra fyrena
gramra to georne,   þe ic geong dyde
and me uncuðe   æghwær wæron;

Psalm 19,9,1 cyng] god *with* cyng *written above in another but similar hand*
24,3,2 stapas] stapa

for ðinre þære myclan   mildheortnysse
weorð gemyndig min,   mihtig drihten.

(27,10) *Saluum fac populum tuum, domine, et benedic*
hereditati tuę, et rege eos et extolle illos usque in aeternum.

Hal do þin folc,   halig drihten,
and ðin yrfe eac   eal gebletsa;
rece þu heo swylce   and on riht ahefe,
þæt hi on worulde   wynnum lifigen.

(32,18) *Fiat misericordia tua, domine, super nos, quem-*
admodum sperauimus in te.

Wese þin mildheortnys,   mihtig drihten,
wel ofer us,   swa we wenað on ðe.

(34,1) *Iudica, domine, nocentes me; expugna inpugnantes*
me.

Dem, drihten, nu   þa me deredon ær,
afeoht swylce   þa me fuhtan to.

(34,2) *Adprehende arma et scutum, et exsurge in adiu-*
torium michi.

Gegrip gar and scyld,   and me georne gestand
on fultume   wið feonda gryre.

(34,3) *Effunde framea[m] et conclude aduersus eos qui me*
persecuntur; dic anime meę, Salus tua ego sum.

Heald me herewæpnum   wið unholdum
and wige beluc   wraðum feondum
þe min ehtend   ealle syndon;
sæge þonne syððan   sawle minre
þæt ðu hire on hæle   hold gestode.

(40,4) *Ego dixi, Domine, miserere mei; sana animam*
meam, quia peccaui tibi.

Ic nu mægene cweðe: "Miltsa me, drihten,
hæl mine sawle,   forðon me hreoweð nu
þæt ic firene on ðe   fremede geneahhige."

(43,27) *Exsurge, domine, adiuua nos, et libera nos propter*
nomen tuum.

Aris, drihten, nu   and us ricene do
fælne fultum,   and us æt feondum ahrede,

27,10,2 yrfe] yrre   27,10,4 wynnum] synnum

forðon we naman þinne   nyde lufiað.

(50,1) *Miserere mei, deus, secundum magnam misericordiam tuam.*

Mildsa me, mihtig drihten,   swa ðu manegum dydest,
æfter ðinre þære mycelan   mildheortnysse.

(50,10) *Auerte faciem tuam a peccatis meis, et omnes
iniquitates meas dele.*

Awend þine ansyne   a fram minum
fræcnum fyrenum,   and nu forð heonon
eall min unriht adwæsc   æghwær symle.

(50,11) *Cor mundum crea in me, deus, et spiritum rectum
innoua in uisceribus meis.*

Syle me, halig god,   heortan clæne,
and rihtne gast,   god, geniwa
on minre gehigde   huru, min drihten.

(50,12) *Ne proicias me a facie tua, et spiritum sanctum
tuum ne auferas a me.*

Ne awyrp þu me,   wuldres ealdor,
fram ðinre ansyne   æfre to feore,
ne huru on weg aber   þone halgan gast,
þæt he me færinga   fremde wyrðe.

(50,13) *Redde michi lętitiam salutaris tui, et spiritu
principali confirma me.*

Syle me þinre hælu   holde blisse,
and me ealdorlice   æþele gaste
on ðinne willan getryme,   weroda drihten.

(53,1) *Deus, in nomine tuo saluum me fac, et in uirtute
tua libera me.*

On þinum þam halgan naman,   gedo me halne, god;
alys me fram laðum   þurh þin leofe mægen.

(58,1) *Eripe me de inimicis meis, deus meus, et ab in-
surgentibus in me libera me.*

Ahrede me, halig god,   hefiges niðes
feonda minra,   þe me feohtað to;
alys me fram laðum   þe me lungre on
risan willað,   nymþe þu me ræd gife.

50,11,3 min] mi   50,13,3 ðinne] ðinre   58,1,3 lungre] luge

(58,2) *Eripe me de operantibus iniquitatem, et de uiri[s] sanguinum salua me.*

Genere me fram niðe   nahtfremmendra
þe her unrihtes   ealle wyrceað,
and me wið blodhreowes weres   bealuwe gehæle.

(60,6,2–4) *Sic psalmum dicam nomini tuo, deus, in seculum seculi, ut reddam uota mea de die in diem.*

Swa ic naman þinum   neode singe,
þæt ic min gehat   her agylde
of dæge on dæg,   swa hit gedefe wese.

(64,6) *Exaudi nos, deus salutaris noster, spes omnium finium terre et in mari longe.*

Gehyr us, hælend god,   þu eart hiht ealra
þe on ðisse eorðan   utan syndon
oððe feor on sæ   foldum wuniað.

(69,1) *Deus, in adiutorium meum intende; domine, ad adiuuandum me festina.*

Wes, drihten god,   deore fultum;
beheald, drihten, me,   and me hraðe syððan
gefultuma   æt feorhþearfe.

(70,7) *Repleatur os meum laude tua, ut possim cantare gloriam tuam, tota die magnificentiam tuam.*

Sy min muð and min mod   mægne gefylled,
þæt ic þin lof mæge   lustum singan
and wuldor ðin   wide mærsian
and ðe ealne dæg   æghwær herian.

(79,18) *Domine deus uirtutum, conuerte nos et ostende faciem tuam, et salui erimus.*

Gehweorf us, mægna god,   and us milde æteow
þinne andwlitan;   ealle we beoð hale.

(84,4,1–2) *Conuerte nos, deus salutaris noster, et auerte iram tuam a nobis.*

Gehweorf us hraðe,   hælend drihten,
and ðin yrre fram us   eac oncyrre.

(87,13) *Et ego ad te, domine, clamaui, et mane oratio mea preueniet te.*

60,6,3 ic] *Not in MS.*   69,1,2 beaheald, drihten, me] *The text of this verse on fol. 51a has* beheald me drihten; *see Note*

Ic me to ðe,   ece drihten,
mid modgehygde   mægne clypode,
and min gebed   morgena gehwylce
fore sylfne ðe   soðfæst becume.

(89,15) *Conuertere, domine, aliquantulum, et deprecabilis
esto super seruos tuos.*

Gehweorf us hwæthwygu,   halig drihten;
wes ðinum scealcum   wel eaðbene.

(89,18) *Respice in seruos tuos et in opera tua, domine, et
dirige filios eorum.*

Geseoh þine scealcas   swæsum eagum,
and on þin agen weorc,   ece drihten,
and heora bearn gerece   bliðum mode.

(89,19) *Et si[t] splendor domini dei nostri super nos, et
opera manuum nostrarum dirige super nos, et opus
manuum nostrarum dirige.*

Wese us beorhtnys ofer   bliðan drihtnes,
ures þæs godan godes   georne ofer ealle;
gerece ure handgeweorc   heah ofer usic.

(101,1) *Domine, exaudi orationem meam, et clamor
meus ad te perueniat.*

Þu min gebed,   mære drihten,
gehyr, heofones weard,   and gehlyde min
to ðe becume,   þeoda reccend.

(102,1) *Benedic, anima mea, domino, et omnia interiora
mea nomen sanctum eius.*

Bletsa, mine sawle,   bliðe drihten,
and eall min inneran   his þone ecan naman.

(102,2) *Benedic, anima mea, domino, et noli obliuisci
omnes retributiones eius.*

Bletsige, mine sawle,   bealde drihten,
ne wilt ðu ofergeotul   æfre weorðan
ealra goda   þe he ðe ær dyde.

(102,3) *Qui propitiatur omnibus iniquitatibus tuis, qui
sanat omnes languores tuos.*

He þinum mandædum   miltsade eallum

101,1,2 heofones] heofonas

and ðine adle   ealle gehælde.

(102,4) *Qui redemit de interitu uitam tuam, qui sanat in*
bonis desiderium tuum.

Se alysde þin lif   leof of forwyrde,
fylde þinne willan   fægere mid gode.

(102,5) *Qui coronat te in miseratione et misericordia;*
renouabitur sicut aquile iuuentus tua.

He ðe gesigefæste   soðre mildse
and ðe mildheorte   mode getrymede;
eart ðu edniwe   earne gelicost
on geoguðe nu   gleaw geworden.

(118,175) *Uiuet anima mea et laudabit te, et iudicia tua*
adiuuabunt me.

Leofað sawul min   and ðe lustum hereð,
and me þine domas   dædum fultumiað.

(118,176) *Erraui sicut ouis que perierat; require seruum*
tuum, domine, quia mandata tua non sum oblitus.

Ic gedwelede   swa þæt dysige sceap,
þæt ðe forwurðan   wolde huru;
la, sec þinne esne   elne, drihten,
forðon ic ðinra beboda ne forgeat   beorhtra æfre.

(121,7) *Fiat pax in uirtute tua, et abundantia in turribus*
tuis.

Sy ðe on ðinum mægne sib   mæst and fyrmest,
and on þinum torrum wese   tidum genihtsum.

(139,1,1–2) *Eripe me, domine, ab homine malo; a uiro*
iniquo libera me.

Genere me wið niþe   on naman þinum,
fram yfelum men,   ece drihten.

(140,2) *Dirigatur, domine, ad te oratio mea sicut incensum*
in conspectu tuo.

Sy on ðinre gesihðe   mines sylfes gebed
full ricene gereht,   swa recels bið,
þonne hit gifre   gleda bærnað.

THE KENTISH HYMN

MS. Cotton Vespasian D.vi

Wuton wuldrian weorada dryhten
halgan hlioðorcwidum, hiofenrices weard,
lufian liofwendum, lifęs agend,
and him simle sio sigefęst wuldor
5 uppe mid ænglum, and on eorðan sibb
gumena gehwilcum goodes willan.
We ðe heriað halgum stefnum
and þe blætsiað, bilewit fęder,
and ðe þanciað, þioda walden,
10 ðines weorðlican wuldordreames
and ðinra miclan mægena gerena,
ðe ðu, god dryhten, gastes mæhtum
hafest on gewealdum hiofen and eorðan,
an ece fęder, ælmehtig god.
15 Ðu eart cyninga cyningc cwicera gehwilces,
ðu eart sigefest sunu and soð hęlend
ofer ealle gescęft angla and manna.
Ðu, dryhten god, on dreamum wunast
on ðære upplican æðelan ceastre,
20 frea folca gehwæs, swa ðu æt fruman wære
efeneadig bearn agenum fæder.
Ðu eart heofenlic lioht and ðæt halige lamb,
ðe ðu manscilde middangeardes
for þinre arfęstnesse ealle towurpe,
25 fiond geflæmdest, follc generedes,
blode gebohtest bearn Israela,

Kentish Hymn 5 ænglum] ænlum 6 gehwilcum] *With the* h *added above the line* goodes] *With the second* o *added above the line* 8 bilewit] bilewitne 10 weorðlican] *Added above the line in the same hand* 11 ðinra] ðare 15 cynincg] *With the second* n *added above the line* 17 angla] *With the* g *added above the line* 23 ðu] ðy 25 follc] *With the* c *added above the line* 26 Israela] isla *with* rae *added above the line in the same hand*

ða ðu ahofe   ðurh ðæt halige triow
ðinre ðrowunga   ðriostre senna,
þæt ðu on hæahsetle   heafena rices
30 sitest sigehræmig   on ða swiðran hand
ðinum godfæder,   gasta gemyndig.
Mildsa nu, meahtig,   manna cynne,
and of leahtrum ales   ðine ða liofan gescęft,
and us hale gedo,   heleða sceppend,
35 niða nergend,   for ðines naman are.
Ðu eart soðlice   simle halig,
and ðu eart ana   æce dryhten,
and ðu ana bist   eallra dema
cwucra ge deadra,   Crist nergende,
40 forðan ðu on ðrymme ricsast   and on ðrinesse
and on annesse,   ealles waldend,
hiofena heahcyninc,   haliges gastes
fegere gefelled   in fæder wuldre.

PSALM 50

MS. Cotton Vespasian D.vi

Dauid wæs haten   diormod hæleð,
Israela bręga,   æðelæ and rice,
cyninga cynost,   Criste liofost.
Wæs he under hiofenum   hearpera mærost
5 ðara we an folcum   gefrigen hæbben.
Sangere he wæs soðfæstest,   swiðe geðancol
to ðingienne   þiodum sinum
wið þane mildostan   manna sceppend.
Wæs se dryhtnes ðiowa   Dauid æt wige
10 soð sigecempa,   searocyne man,

28 ðrowunga] *With the* n *added above the line*   34 sceppend] *With the* n
added above the line   37 ana] *Added above the line in the same hand*
39 nergende] nergend   42 heahcyninc] *With second* n *added above the line*
Psalm 50, 7 þiodum] *With the* o *added above the line*

casere creaftig,   þonne cumbulgebrec
on gewinndagum   weorðan scoldan.
Hwęðere him geiode,   swa ful oft gedeð
þætte godferhte   gylt gefræmmað
15 þurh lichaman   lene geðohtas.
Gelamp þæt him mon ansende   saula neriend,
witgan mid wordum,   weorada dominus,
and secgan het,   selfum gecyðan
ymb his womdeda   waldendes doom,
20 þæt se fruma wære   his feores sceldig,
for ðam þe he Uriam het   aldre beneman,
fromne ferdrinc   fere beserode,
and him Bezabe   brohte to wife
for gitsunga,   þe he godes eorre
25 þurh his selfes weorc   sona anfunde.
Him ða ðingode   þioda aldor,
Dauid georne,   and to dryhtne gebæd,
and his synna hord   selfa ontende,
gyltas georne   gode andhette,
30 weoruda dryhtne,   and ðus wordum spæc:
    Miserere mei deus secundum magnam misericordiam tuam.
"Miltsa ðu me, meahta walden,   nu ðu wast manna
                                    geðohtas,
help ðu, hælend min,   handgeweorces
þines anes,   ælmehtig god,
efter þinre ðære miclan   mildhiortnesse.
    *Et secundum multitudinem miserationem tuarum dele
    iniquitatem meam.*
35 Ond eac efter menio   miltsa ðinra,
dryhten weoruda,   adilga min unriht
to forgefenesse   gaste minum.
    *Amplius laua me ab iniustitia mea et a delicta mea munda
    mæ.*

---

11 cumbulgebrec] cū bur gebrec *with the first* r *dotted beneath for deletion and*
l *written above*   17 dominus] dñs   31 Miltsa] *With the* t *added above the*
line   34 ðære] ðara   mildhiortnesse] mildhior *at the end of a line,*
followed by nesse *at the beginning of the next line*   35 miltsa] *With the* t
added above the line

Aðweah me of sennum, saule fram wammum,
gasta sceppend, geltas geclansa,
40 þa ðe ic on aldre æfre gefremede
ðurh lichaman leðre geðohtas.

Quoniam iniquitatem meam ego agnosco et delictum meum
coram me est semper.

Forðan ic unriht min eal oncnawe,
and eac synna gehwær selfum æt eagan,
firendeda geðrec beforan standeð,
45 scelda scinað; forgef me, sceppen min,
lifes liohtfruma, ðinre lufan blisse.

Tibi soli peccaui et malum coram te feci ut iustificeris in
sermonibus tuis et uincas dum iudicaris.

Nu ic anum ðe oft syngode,
and yfela feola eac gefræmede,
gelta gramhegdig, ic ðe, gasta breogo,
50 helende Crist, helpe bidde,
ðæt me forgefene gastes wunde
an forðgesceaft feran mote,
þy ðine wordcwidas weorðan gefelde,
ðæt ðu ne wilnast weora æniges deað;
55 ac ðu synfulle simle lærdes
ðæt hio cerrende Criste herdon
and hiom lif mid ðe langsum begęton,
swilce ðu æt dome, dryhten, oferswiðdest
ealra synna cynn, saula neriend.

Ecce enim iniquitatibus.

60 Ic on unrihtum eac ðan in synnum
geeacnod wæs. Ðu ðæt ana wast,
mæhtig dryhten, hu me modor gebær
in scame and in sceldum; forgef me, sceppend min,
ðæt ic fram ðæm synnum selfa gecerre,
65 þa ðe mine ældran ær geworhtan
and ic selfa eac sioððan beeode.

---

38 sennum] sennū *with the first* n *added above the line*   42 oncnawe] ón
cwawe   57 langsum] *With the* g *added above the line*   58 oferswiðdest]
ofer swiddest *with the* t *added above the line*   65 ðe] ðy

Ecce enim ueritatem.
Ac ðu, selua god,   soð an lufast;
þy ic ðe mid benum   biddan wille
lifes and lisse,   liohtes aldor,
70 forðan ðu me uncuðe   eac ðan derne
þinre snetera hord   selfa ontendes.
Asperies me ysopo et mundabor.
Ðu me, meahtig god,   milde and bliðe
þurh ysopon   ealne ahluttra,
þonne ic geclænsod   Criste hero,
75 and eac ofer snawe   self scinende
þinre sibbe lufan   sona gemete.
Auditui meo dabis gaudium.
Ontyn nu, elmehtig,   earna hleoðor,
þæt min gehernes   hehtful weorðe
on gefean bliðse   forðweard to ðe;
80 ðanne bioð on wenne,   waldend, simle
þa gebrocenan ban,   bilwit dominus,
ða þe on hænðum ær   hwile wæron.
Auerte faciem tuam a peccatis meis et omnes.
Ahwerf nu fram synnum,   saula neriend,
and fram misdedum   minra gylta
85 þine ansione,   ælmeahtig god,
and ðurh miltsunga   meahta þinra
ðu unriht min   eall adilga.
Cor mundum crea in me deus et spiritum rectum.
Æc ðu, dryhten Crist,   clęne hiortan
in me, mehtig god,   modswiðne geðanc
90 to ðolienne   ðinne willan
and to healdenne   halige domas,
and ðu rihtne gast,   rodera waldend,
in ferðe minum   feste geniowa.
Ne proicias me a facie tuae et spiritum sanctum tuum.
Ne aweorp ðu me,   weoruda dryhten,
95 fram ansione   ealra þinra miltsa,
ne ðane godan fram me   gast haligne

81 dominus] dñs   91 to healdenne] to ðolienn healdenne *with* ðolienn
marked beneath for deletion

aferre, domine,   frea ælmeahtig,
þinra arna me   eal ne bescerwe.
Redde mihi letitiam.
Sæle nu bliðse me,   bilewit dominus,
100 þinre hælo heht,   helm alwihta,
and me, lifgende   liohtes hiorde,
gaste ðine,   god selfa, getreme,
ðæt ic aldorlice   a forð sioððan
to ðinum willan   weorðan mote.
Doceam iniquos uias tuas et impii ad te.
105 Simle ic ðine weogas   wanhogan lærde,
ðæt hio arlease   eft gecerdan
to hiora selfra   saula hiorde,
god selfa, to ðe   gastes mundberd
ðurh sibbe lufan   seocan scoldan.
Libera me de sanguinibus.
110 Befreo me an ferðe,   fæder mancynnes,
fram blodgete   and bealaniðum,
god lifigende,   gylta geclansa,
helo and helpend,   hiofenrices weard;
ðanne tunge min   triowfest blissað
115 for ðines selfes   soðfestnesse.
Domine labia mea aperies et os meum adnuntiauit.
Ontyn nu, waldend god,   weoloras mine;
swa min muð sioððan   mæhte ðine
and lof georne   liodum to bliðse,
soð sigedryhten,   secgende wæs.
Quoniam si uoluisses.
120 Ic ðe onsegednesse   sona brohte,
weoruda dryhtne,   ðer ðu wolde swa,
ða ðu þæt ne lufedest,   lifes bretta,
ðæt ic ðe bernelac   brengan moste
deadra neata,   dryhtne to willan.
Sacrificium deo spiritus contribulatus.
125 Ac ðe micle ma,   mehtig dryhten,

97 aferre, domine] aferredne   98 þinra] þinre   99 dominus] dñs
109 scoldan] *With the* l *added above the line*   119 secgende] seccende
123 brengan] bregan

lifiende Crist,   liicwerðe bið
se gehnysta gast,   hiorte geclansod
and geeadmeded   ingeþancum;
ða ðu, ælmæhtig,   æfre ne æwest.
    Benigne fac domine in bona uoluntate.
130 Gedoo nu fræmsume   frofre ðine
    to ðinum godan   gastes willan,
    ðætte Sione dun   sigefest weorðe,
    and weallas Sion   wynfęste getremed,
    Hierusolimę,   god lifiende.
    Tunc acceptabis sacrificium.
135 Swa þu, frea meahtig,   anfehst siþðan
    liofwende lac   lioda þinra,
    hælend manna;   hio ðæt halige cealf
    on wigbed þin   willum asettað,
    liohtes aldor.   Forgef me, lifigende
140 meotod mancynnes,   mæhtig dominus,
    ðæt ða sorhfullan   saule wunde,
    þa ðe ic on ælde   uel on giogeðe
    in flæschaman   gefręmed hæbbe
    leahtra hegeleasra,   mid lufan þinre
145 gastæ forgeofene   glidan mote."
        Swæ þingode   þiode aldor,
    Dauid to dryhtne,   deda gemyndig,
    þæt hine męhtig god   mannum to frofre
    ðæs cynedomes,   Crist neriende,
150 waldende god,   weorðne munde.
    Forðon he gebette   balaniða hord
    mid eaðmede   ingeþance,
    ða ðe he on ferðe   gefręmed hæfde,
    gastes wunde.   Forgef us, god mæahtig,
155 þæt we synna hord   simle oferwinnan

126 liicwerðe] *With the* r *added above the line*   136 þinra] þinre *with the* r *added above the line*   140 dominus] dñs   142 uel] ł   143 flæschaman] *With the* s *added above the line*   144 þinre] þinra   145 glidan mote] glid *at the end of a line, followed by* mote *at the beginning of the next line*   153 hæfde] *Preceded by* hebbe *marked for deletion and partly erased*

and us geearnian   æce dreamas
an lifigendra   landes wenne. Amen.

THE GLORIA II

MS. Cotton Titus D.xxvii

Wuldor sy ðe and wurðmynt,   wereda drihten,
fæder on foldan,   fægere gemæne,
mid sylfan sunu   and soðum gaste.   Amen.

A PRAYER

Text from MS. Cotton Julius A.ii (J); variants from MS. 427,
Lambeth Palace (L)

    Æla, drihten leof!   Æla, dema god!
Geara me,   ece waldend.
Ic wat mine saule   synnum forwundod;
    gehæl þu hy,   heofena drihten,
5 and gelacna þu hy,   lifes ealdor,
    forþan ðu eðest miht   ealra læca
ðæra þe gewurde   side oððe wyde.
    Æla, frea beorhta,   folkes scippend!
Gemilsa þyn mod   me to gode,
10 sile þyne are   þynum earminge.
    Se byð earming   þe on eorðan her
dæiges and nihtes   deofle campað
and hys willan wyrcð;   wa him þære mirigðe,

Prayer 1a Æla] Eala L   1b Æla] eala L   2 Geara] geáre L   3 saule]
sauwle L   4 heofena] heofona L   5 hy] heo L   ealdor] al dor L
6 forþan] for þon L   eðest] eþest L   læca] læc a *with a letter* (e?) *erased
after* c L   7 ðæra] ðara L   wyde] wide L   8 Æla] Eala L   beorhta]
brihta L   folkes] folces L   scippend] scyppend L   9 Gemilsa]
gemilda L   þyn] þin L   10a sile] Syle L   þyne] ðine L   10b þynum]
þyne J; þinum L   11 byð] bið L   þe] L; þeo J   12 dæiges] dæges L
deofle] deoflon J; deoflū L   campað] compað L   13 hys] his L
mirigðe] myrigðe L

þonne he ða handlean   hafað and sceawað,
15 bute he þæs yfeles   ær geswyce.
Se byð eadig,   se þe on eorðan her
dæiges and nyhtes   drihtne hyræð
and a hys willan wyrcð;   wel hym þæs geweorkes,
ðonne he ða handlean   hafað and sceawað,
20 gyf he ealteawne   ende gedreogeð.
Æla, leohtes leoht!   Æla, lyfes wynn!
Getiþa me,   tireadig kyning,
þonne ic minre sawle   swegles bydde,
ece are.   Þu eart eaðe, god,
25 hæfst and waldest
ana ofer ealle   eorðan and heofonas
syddra gesceafta.   Ðu eart soð meotod,
ana ofer ealle   eorðbugende,
swilce on heofonum up   þu eart hælend god.
30 Ne mæg þe aherian   hæleða ænig;
þeh us gesomnie   geond sidne grund,
men ofer moldan,   geond ealne middaneard,
ne mage we næfre asæcgan,   ne þæt soðe witan,
hu þu æðele eart,   ece drihten.
35 Ne þeah engla werod   up on heofenum
snotra tosomne   sæcgan ongunnon,
ne magon hy næfre areccean,   ne þæt gerim wytan,
hu þu mære eart,   mihtig drihten.
Ac is wunder mycel,   wealdend engla,
40 gif þu hit sylfa wast,   sigores ealdor,
hu þu mære eart,   mihtig and mægenstrang,
ealra kyninga kyning,   Crist lifiende,
ealra worulda scippend,   wealdend engla,
ealra dugeþa duguð,   drihten hælend.
45   Ðu eart se æðela   þe on ærdagum
ealra femnena wyn   fægere akende
on Bethleem ðære byrig   beornum to frofre,
eallum to are   ylda bearnum,
þam þe gelyfað   on lyfiendne god

14 he ða] *Not in L*   15 bute] butan *L*   yfeles] yfles *L*   geswyce] ge
swíce *L; MS. L ends with this word*   42 lifiende] lifiend *J*

50 and on þæt ece leoht   uppe on roderum.
   Ðyn mægen ys swa mære,   mihtig drihten,
   swa þæt ænig ne wat   eorðbuende
   þa deopnesse   drihtnes mihta,
   ne þæt ænig ne wat   engla hades
55 þa heahnisse   heofena kyninges.
   Ic þe andette,   ælmihtig god,
   þæt ic gelyfe on þe,   leofa hælend,
   þæt þu eart se miccla   and se mægenstranga
   and se eadmoda   ealra goda
60 and se ece kyning   ealra gesceafta,
   and ic eom se litla for þe   and se lyðra man,
   se her syngige   swiðe genehhe,
   dæges and nihtes   do, swa ic ne sceolde,
   hwile mid weorce,   hwile mid worde,
65 hwile mid geþohte,   þearle scyldi,
   inwitniðas   oft and gelome.
   Ac ic þe halsige nu,   heofena drihten,
   and gebidde me to þe,   bearna selost,
   þæt ðu gemilsige me,   mihtig drihten,
70 heofena heahkyning   and se halga gast,
   and gefylste me,   fæder ælmihtig,
   þæt ic þinne willan   gewyrcean mæge,
   ær ic of þysum lænan   lyfe gehweorfe.
   Ne forweorn þu me,   wuldres drihten,
75 ac getyþa me,   tyreadig kyning,
   læt me mid englum   up siðian,
   sittan on swegle,
   herian heofonas god   haligum reorde
   a butan ende.   Amen.

51 Ðyn] yn *with the initial capital torn away J*   73 lænan] hlænan *J*

THURETH

MS. Cotton Claudius A. iii

Ic eom halgungboc;   healde hine dryhten
þe me fægere þus   frætewum belegde.
Þureð to þance   þus het me wyrcean,
to loue and to wurðe,   þam þe leoht gesceop.
5 Gemyndi is he   mihta gehwylcre
þæs þe he on foldan   gefremian mæg,
and him geþancie   þeoda waldend
þæs þe he on gemynde   madma manega
wyle gemearcian   metode to lace;
10 and he sceal æce lean   ealle findan
þæs þe he on foldan   fremaþ to ryhte.

ALDHELM

MS. 326, Corpus Christi College, Cambridge

Þus me gesette   sanctus et iustus
beorn boca gleaw,   bonus auctor,
Ealdelm, æþele sceop,   etiam fuit
ipselos on æðele   Angolsexna,
5 byscop on Bretene.   Biblos ic nu sceal,
ponus et pondus   pleno cum sensu,
geonges geanoðe   geomres iamiamque,
secgan soð, nalles leas,   þæt him symle wæs
euthenia   oftor on fylste,
10 æne on eðle   ec ðon ðe se is
yfel on gesæd.   Etiam nusquam
ne sceal ladigan   labor quem tenet
encratea,   ac he ealneg sceal
boethia   biddan georne
15 þurh his modes gemind   micro in cosmo,

Thureth 10 æce] ęce   Aldhelm 4 æðele] æðel   Angolsexna] angel sexna
with o *written above the first* e   12 sceal] seal   13 ealneg] *With the final*
g *almost entirely erased*

97

þæt him drihten gyfe   dinams on eorðan,
fortis factor,   þæt he forð simle

* * *

THE SEASONS FOR FASTING

Additional MS. 43,703

Wæs on ealddagum   Israheala folc
þurh Moysen,   mærne lareow,
anlyht and gelared,   swa hine lifes frea,
heofna heahcyning,   her on life
5 þurh his sylfes word   sette for leodum,
rincum to ræde,   and him runa gescead
sylfum asæde,   hu he þone soþan weg
leofum leodscipe   læran sceolde.
    Þa se leoda fruma   larum fyligde
10 heofena heahcyninges,   and þa hæleþ samod,
swa hie on leodscipe   lærede wæron;
gyf hie wancule   weorc ongunnon,
heom þæs of heofonum   hearm to leane
asende sigora god,   and hie sona to him
15 fryþa wilnodan   and þær fundon raþe,
gif hie leohtras heora   letan gewyrpan.
    Feala is mægena   þe sio mære þeod
on þam herescype   heold and worhte,
þendan hie lifes frean   lufian woldon;
20 ac him se ende wearð   earm and þrealic,
þa hie besyredon   sylfne dryhten,
on beam setton   and to byrgenne
* * * gedemdon;   he þær bedigled wæs,
and þy þryddan dæge   þeodum ætywed.
25   We þæt gehyrdon   hæleþa mænige
on bocstafum   breman and writan,

Seasons for Fasting 5 þurh] þurh þurh   8 sceolde] sceold   12 weorc]
weorce   14 sigora] sigona   16 gewyrpan] ḡ wyrþan   20 þrealic]
þreoring

þæt hie fæstenu   feower heoldon
and þonne offredan   unmæne neat,
þæt is lamb oþþe styrc,   leofum to tacne
30 þe for worulde wæs   womma bedæled.
   Ac arisan ongan   rices ealdor
of byrgenne,   blæda gefylled,
and mid heofenwarum   ham gesohte,
eard mid englum,   and us eallum þone
35 hyht and gehateð,   gyf we his willaþ
þurh rihtne sefan   rædum fyligan.
Na þær in cumeð   atele gefylled,
womme gewesed,   ac scal on wyrd sceacan.
   Nu we herian sceolan   her for life
40 deorne dædfruman,   and him geara gerim
ælmesdædum   ure gefyllan,
and on fæstenum,   swa se froda iu
Moyses mælde,   and we þa mearce sceolan
heoldan higefæste   * * *   mid Anglum,
45 swa hie gebrefde us   beorn on Rome,
Gregorius,   gumena papa.
   We þæt forme sceolan   fæsten heowan
on þære ærestan   wucan lengtenes,
on þam monþe   þe man Martius
50 geond Romwara   rice nemneð,
and þær twelfe sceolan   torhtum dihte
runa gerædan   in þæs rican hofe,
heofona heahcyninges,   herian mid sange,
wlancne weorþian   wuldres bryttan.
55   Ofer þa Eastertid   oþer fæsten
ys to bremenne   Brytena leodum
mid gelicum lofe,   þe gelesen hafað
on þære wucan   þe æfter cumeð
þam sunnandæge   þe geond sidne wang
60 Pentecostenes dæg   preostas nemnað,
on þam monþe,   þæs þe me þinceð,

---

30 worulde] woruld   38 womme] wōmo   40 him] him do   47 Wel þe
48 wucan] wircan   50 nemneð] nemnað   51 dihte] dyh te *with* i *written*
above y   58 þære] þær   cumeð] cumað

þe man Iunius   gearum nemde.
   Ðonne is þæt þrydde   þinga gehwelces
fæsten on foldan   fyra bearnum
65 dihte gelicum   on þam deoran hofe
to brymenne   beorhtum sange
on þære wucan   þe ærur byð
emnihtes dæge   ælda beornum,
on þam monþe,   mine gefræge,
70 þe man September   * * *   genemneð.
   We þæt feorþe sceolen   fæsten gelæstan
on þære wucan   þe bið ærur full
dryhtnes gebyrde,   and we mid deornum scylan
wordum and weorcum   wuldres cyninge
75 in þa ylcan tid   eallum gemynde
þeodne deman   þinga gehwylces,
efne swa swa ærran,   and þone arwesan
leofne leoda frean   lifes biddan.
   On þissum fæstenum   is se feorþa dæg
80 and sixta samod   seofoþa getinge
to gelæstanne   lifes ealdre
and to bremenne   boca gerynum
emb þa nigoþan tyd;   nan is on eorþan,
butan hine unhæl   an geþreatige,
85 þe mot, hæt, oþþe wæt   ærur þingan,
þæs þe us boca dom   þeodlic demeð.
   Gif þe þonne secgan   suþan cymene
bryttan Franca,   þæt þu gebann sceole
her on eorþan   ænig healdan,
90 þæs þe Moyses iu   mælde to leodum,
na þu þæs andfeng   æfre gewyrþe,
ac þu þæt sylfe heald   þæt þe suþan com
from Romana   rices hyrde,
Gregoriæ,   gumena papa.

---

71 fæsten] fæste   gelæstan] ḡ læsten   72 þære] þær   80 seofoþa]
feoroþa   82 gerynum] ḡ rinū *with* i *dotted beneath for deletion and* y *written
above*   84 butan] *At the end of a page, and repeated at the head of the next page*
88 bryttan] brytt *at the end of a line*   90 iu] ín   92 sylfe] sylf
93 rices] rice

95 Þus he gesette   sylf ond dyhte
   þa þenunga,   þeodlareow,
   fæstendtida;   we þam forþ nu gyt
   geond Engla land   estum filiað.
   Swa he æt þæm setle   sylfa gedemde,
100 sancte Petres   preostas syþþan
   lange lifes tyd   leordun þæt sylfe,
   þæt þu oþrum ne scealt   æfre filian.
   Eac we feowertig daga   fæsten healden
   ær þæm æriste   ures dryhtnes,
105 þæt nu lengtentid   leoda nemnað,
   and hit ærest ongan   eorl se goda,
   mære Moyses,   ær he on munt styge;
   he þæt fæsten heold   feowertig daga
   and nyhta samod,   swa he nahtes anbat
110 ær he þa deoran æ   dryhtnes anfenge.
   Him þær gesealde   sylfe dryhten
   bremne boca cræft,   bæle behlæned,
   of his haligan   handa gescrifene,
   het hine leodum þone   leoran and tæcan
115 elda orþancum   eallum to tacne,
   þæt we mid fæstene magon   freode gewinnan
   and þa deopan   dryhtnes gerynu,
   þa þe leoran sceolan   leoda gehwylce,
   gif us þære duguþe hwæt   dryhten sylleð.
120 Eft Helias,   eorl se mæra,
   him on westene   wiste geþigede,
   þær him symbelbread   somod mid wætere
   dryhtnes engla sum   dihte togeanes,
   and se gestrangud wearð   styþum gyfle
125 to gefæstenne   feowertig daga
   and nihta samod,   swa he nahtes anbat
   ær he on Horeb dun   hali ferde.
   Uton þæt gerine   rihte gehicgan,
   þæt se mæra þegen   mihta ne hæfde

98 geond] ḡeond   filiað] fihað   99 gedemde] ḡdēda   109 anbat]
anbate   111 gesealde] ḡ scealde   115 orþancum] on þancū   118 leoran]
leora   124 se gestrangud] ge se strangud   129 þegen] hegen

130 to astigenne   stæppon on ypplen
       ær him þæt symbel wearþ   seald fram engle.
       We sint on westene   wuldres blisse
       on þæm ænete   ealra gefeana;
       nu is helpes tid,   halig dryhten,
135 hu we munt þinne   mærne gestygan.
          Sint for englas geteald   eorþbugendum
       þa þe dryhtnes word   dædum lærað.
       We þa andlifene   ofstum þycgen
       and þone deoran wist,   dryhtnes lare;
140 uton fæstan swa   fyrene dædum
       on forhæfenesse   her for life,
       þæt we þæs muntes mægen   mærþa gestigan
       swa se ealda dyde   Elias iu.
          Is to hicganne   hu se halga gewat
145 of þissum wangstede   wuldres neosian;
       hine fyren scryd   feower mærum
       wlangum wicgum   on weg ferede
       on neorxnawong,   þær us nergend Crist
       gehaten hafað   ham mid blisse,
150 gif we þæt fæsten her   fyrena gelæstað
       and þone uplican   æþel secað.
          Nu wæs æt nehstan   þæt us nergend Crist,
       halig heofenes weord,   heolp and lærde.
       He hine dyppan let   deorum þweale,
155 fulwihtes bæðe,   fyrena bedæled,
       and he feowertig daga   firsude mettas,
       eac nihta swa feala   nanuht gyltig,
       leodum to lare,   þæt hie on lengten sceolan
       efen feowertig daga   fæsten hewan.
160   Hine costude þær   Cristes gewinna
       on þæm ænete   eald and fræte,
       geseah mærne frean   mannum gelicne
       and þa wenan ongann,   wommes gemyndig,
       þæt he stræla his   stellan mihte

136 eorþbugendum] eorþ burgendū   140 fæstan] sæstan   143 dyde]
dyda   155 bæðe] bað   156 firsude mettas] firude metta

165 on þam lichoman;   næs þæs leahtra nan,
    ac on hinder gewat   hearmes brytta,
    and þær englas hyra   ealdor sohtan.
      Higesynnig man,   gyf þe susla weard
    costian durre,   þonne he Crist dyde,
170 wereda wulderfrean,   womma leasne,
    ne mæg he þæs inne   ahwæt scotian
    gif he myrcels næfþ   manes æt egum,
    ac he on hinder scriþ,   and þe halig * * *
    englas ærfæste   æghwær helpað,
175 gif þu dryhtnes her   dædum fylgest.
      Hæbbe we nu gemearcod   hu þa mæran iu
    feowertig daga   fæsten hewdon,
    and we bebeodað   þurh beorn godes
    þæt manna gehwilc   þe for moldan wunað
180 ær þam æreste   ures dryhtnes
    efen feowertig daga   fæsten hewe
    oþ þa nigoþan tid,   and he na bruce
    flæsces oþþe fyrna,   þæ læs þe he fah wese.
      Sceolan sacerdas   singan mæssan,
185 dæghwamlice   dryhten biddan
    on þam fæstenne   þæt he freond wese
    folce gynd foldan,   and þa fyrna sceolan
    þam sacerdan   secgan gehwilce
    and þa dymnissa   dædum betan
190 wordes and weorces,   wuldres ealdor
    þurh ælmesdæde   eall gegladian.
      Þonne is þearf micel   þeoda mænium
    þæt þa sacerdos   sylfe ne gyltan,
    ne on leahtrum hiora   ligegen to fæste.
195 Hwa mæg þyngian   þreale hwilcum
    wiþ his arwesan,   gyf he him ærur hæfð
    bitere onbolgen,   and þæs bote ne deð,
    ac þa æbyligþe   ealdere wrohte,
    dæghwamlice   dædum niwað?

165 lichoman] lichoman an   172 myrcels] myrcelrs   177 feowertig]
þ feowertig   183 wese] were   189 dymnissa] dȳ nisca   193 sylfe]
sylfne   199 dæghwamlice] dæg ghamlice

200   Gyf se sacerd hine   sylfne ne cunne
    þurh dryhtnes ege   dugeþum healdan,
    nu þa, folces mann,   fyrna ne gyme
    þe gehalgod mann   her gefremme,
    ac þu lare scealt   lustum fremman
205 ryhthicgennde   þe he to ræde tæchð,
    drince he him þæt drofe   oððe þæt dæghluttre
    wæter of wege,   þæt is wuldres lare.
      Ac ic secgan mæg,   sorgum hremig,
    hu þa sacerdas   sace niwiað,
210 dæghwamlice   dryhten gremiað
    and mid æfeste   ælcne forlædað
    þe him fylian wyle   folces manna;
    sona hie on mergan   mæssan syngað
    and forþegide,   þurste gebæded,
215 æfter tæppere   teoþ geond stræta.
      Hwæt! Hi leaslice   leogan ongynnað
    and þone tæppere   tyhtaþ gelome,
    secgaþ þæt he synleas   syllan mote
    ostran to æte   and æþele wyn
220 emb morgentyd,   þæs þe me þingeð
    þæt hund and wulf   healdað þa ilcan
    wisan on worulde   and ne wigliað
    hwæne hie to mose fon,   mæða bedæled.
      Hi þonne sittende   sadian aginnað,
225 sinne semað,   syllað gelome,
    cweðað goddlife   gumena gehwilcum
    þæt wines dreng   welhwa mote,
    siþþan he mæssan hafað,   meþig þicgan,
    etan ostran eac   and oþerne
230 fisc of flode

*   *   *

200 sylfne] sylne   202 ne] ni   203 gehalgod] ḡ halgode   204 fremman]
frēnan   205 ræde] rædi   206–207 drofe . . . wæter] drofe duge hluttre
þe wæter   211 æfeste] æleste   220 þæs] þæ   me þingeð] þingað me
with marks for inversion   223 hwæne] hwænne   225 sinne] win
226 cweðað] cwedað   227 welhwa] wel wel hwa

CÆDMON'S HYMN

NORTHUMBRIAN VERSION

Text from MS. Kk. v. 16, University Library, Cambridge (M), with variants from the other MSS. (for the sigla, see Introd., p. xcv)

Nu scylun hergan   hefaenricaes uard,
metudæs maecti   end his modgidanc,
uerc uuldurfadur,   sue he uundra gihuaes,
eci dryctin,   or astelidæ.
5 He aerist scop   aelda barnum
heben til hrofe,   haleg scepen;
tha middungeard   moncynnæs uard,
eci dryctin,   æfter tiadæ
firum foldu,   frea allmectig.

Cædmon's Hymn 1 Nu] Nu *pue Di P* scylun] scilun *L;* sciulun *Di;* sciulin *P* hergan] hergen *with the second* e *dotted beneath for deletion and* a *written above it M;* herga *L Di P* hefaenricaes] hefenricæs *L;* hefunricaes *with* n *added above the line Di;* hefunrincaes *P* uard] pueard *Di P* 2 metudæs] metudaes *Di;* metuudaes *P* maecti] mehti *L;* mechti *Di P* end] and *L Di P* modgidanc] modgithanc *L;* modgedeanc *Di;* modgedanc *P* 3 uerc] puerc *Di;* puere *P* uuldurfadur] puldurfudur *Di;* fadur *P* sue] suae *Di P* he] hae *Di* uundra] pundra *Di P* gihuaes] gihuæs *L* 4 dryctin] *With* yc *altered from* in *M;* drichtin *Di;* drochtin *with* o *cancelled and* i *written above it P* astelidæ] astalde *Di P* 5 aerist] ærist *L;* uerst *with* a *written above* u *Di;* raeirst *P* scop] scoop *Di P* aelda] ældu *L;* eordu *Di P* barnum] bearnum *Di;* pearnum *P* 6 heben] hefen *L;* efen *Di* til] to *L Di P* hrofe] hrofæ *L* haleg] halig *L Di P* scepen] sceppend *L Di P* 7 tha] da *Di;* dā *P* middungeard] *With the first* d *altered from* n *M;* middingard *L;* middumgeard *Di P* moncynnæs] moncinnes *Di P* uard] peard *Di P* 8 dryctin] drintinc *Di;* drichtim *P* æfter] efter *Di;* aefter *P* tiadæ] tiade *Di P* foldu] fold^v *M;* foldu *L;* on foldu *Di;* ol foldu *P* allmectig] allmehtig *L;* allmechtig *Di P*

105

CÆDMON'S HYMN

WEST SAXON VERSION

Text from MS. Tanner 10 (T), with variants from the other
MSS. (for the sigla, see Introd., pp. xcv–xcvii)

> Nu sculon herigean   heofonrices weard,
> meotodes meahte   and his modgeþanc,
> weorc wuldorfæder,   swa he wundra gehwæs,
> ece drihten,   or onstealde.
> 5 He ærest sceop   eorðan bearnum
> heofon to hrofe,   halig scyppend;
> þa middangeard   moncynnes weard,
> ece drihten,   æfter teode
> firum foldan,   frea ælmihtig.

Cædmon's Hymn 1 Nu] Ne *C;* Nu we *with* we *added above the line O;* Nu we
Ca B H W Bd₁ Ln Mg Tr₁ Ld₁ Hr   sculon herigean] herigan sculon *B*
sculon] sculan *O;* sceolan *Ca Ld₁ Hr;* sculun *Ln;* sceolon *Tr₁*   herigean]
hergean *C;* herian *O H Bd₁ Ln Mg Hr;* herian heri *with* heri *underlined for
deletion W;* herian herian *with second* herian *underlined for deletion Ld₁;*
herion *Tr₁*   heofonrices] heofenrices *Tr₁*   2 meotodes] metodes *C O
Ca B;* metoddes *with first* d *dotted beneath for deletion W;* metudes *H Bd₁
Ln Mg Tr₁ Ld₁ Hr*   meahte] mihte *C O Ca B W Mg Tr₁ Ld₁ Hr;* myhte
H Bd₁; michte *Ln*   and] Ond *C*   modgeþanc] modgeþonc *C O*   3
weorc] weoroda *C;* wera *with* a *altered from* o *O;* wera *Ca;* wurc *H Bd₁ Mg*
wuldorfæder] wuldorgodes *B;* wuldorfeder *Tr₁;* wuldorfæder *with* o *altered
from* u *H;* wulder fæder *Ld₁ Hr*   wundra gehwæs] wuldres gehwæs *Ca;*
wundra fela *B;* wundra gehwilc *H W Mg;* wundra gehwylc *Ln Tr₁;* wundra
[. . . .]ylc *with* y *altered from* i *Bd₁*   3b–5a wundra . . . He] *Not in Hr*
4 ece] eche *Ln*   drihten] dryhten *O*   or onstealde] *Not in Ld₁, which adds*
þa *before* he, *l. 5*   or] oórd *with* d *added above the line O;* ord *Ca B H
Bd₁ Ln Mg Tr₁;* word *W*   onstealde] astealde *B H W Bd₁ Ln Tr₁;*
astalde *Mg*   5 He] Hu (*or* Nu?) *Tr₁*   ærest] æres *Ca;* ærust *Ln;* erust
Tr₁; [.]ræst *W*   sceop] scop *C;* gesceop *O H Bd₁;* gescop *Ca W Mg Ln Tr₁*
eorðan] *With* e *crowded in after the rest had been written Ca;* eorþū *C;* eorðe
Ld₁ Hr; ylda *H W Bd₁ Ln Mg Tr₁*   bearnum] *An erasure of two or
three letters after this word O*   6 heofon] heofen *with the second* e *dotted
beneath for deletion and* o *written above it W*   hrofe] rofe *Ca W Mg*
halig scyppend] *Ld₁ and Hr omit this half-line here but insert* halig scyppeod
at the end of the poem after frea ælmihtig   scyppend] scypend *C;*

(Continued at foot of p. 107.)

BEDE'S DEATH SONG

NORTHUMBRIAN VERSION

Text from MS. 254, St. Gall (Sg), with variants from the other
MSS. (for the sigla, see Introd., pp. ci–cii)

Fore thaem neidfaerae   naenig uuiurthit
thoncsnotturra,   than him tharf sie
to ymbhycggannae   aer his hiniongae
huaet his gastae   godaes aeththa yflaes
5 aefter deothdaege   doemid uueorthae.

Bede's Death Song 1 Fore] fere Z thaem] th'e Sg; thae Ba; the Ad_1
$Kl_1 Mu Kl_2 Hk V Z Ad_2 Me$; *see Note*   neidfaerae] neidfare Ad_1; neidfaere
Kl_1; neydfaere Mu; neidfacre $Kl_2 Hk V Z Me$; neidfacere Ad_2 uuiurthit
vüiürthit Mu 2 thoncsnotturra] toncsnotturra Kl_1; thonesnotturra
Kl_2; thonscnothturra Ad_2 tharf] *With* f *added above the line* Sg; thars
Mu; chraf Kl_2; thraf $Hk V Z Ad_2$; traf Me sie] sie̜ $Hk Ad_2$ 3 to] tho
Kl_2 ymbhycggannae] ymbhycgganne̜ Ba; ymbicggannae Kl_1; ymhicg-
gannae $Kl_2 V$; ymhycgannae $Hk Z Ad_2 Me$ hiniongae] *With* a *added
above the line* Sg; hyniongae Kl_2 4 huaet] huaex $Kl_2 Hk V Z Ad_2 Me$
gastae] gaste $Ad_1 Kl_1 Mu Kl_2 Hk V Z Ad_2 Me$ godaes] godeles $Kl_2 Hk$
$V Z Me$; godoles Ad_2 aeththa] a&htha $Sg Ba$ 5 aefter] aester Ad_1
$Kl_1 Mu Kl_2 Hk V Z Ad_2 Me$ deothdaege] deohtdaege $Kl_2 Hk V Z Ad_2 Me$
doemid] doemud Ad_1; doemnl $Kl_1 Mu$; doemit $Kl_2 Hk V Z Ad_2 Me$
uueorthae] *With* a *added above the line* Sg; uueorthe $Ad_1 Kl_1 Kl_2 Hk V Z$
$Ad_2 Me$; vueorthe Mu

(Continued from p. 106.)
scippend W 7 þa middangeard] ða middongeard O; þe middangeard
B;   middangearde $H Ln Mg Tr_1$;   middanear$_{[..]}$ W; $_{[...]}$ danea$_{[.]}$de
Bd_1 moncynnes] manncynnes $B W$; mancynnes $H Bd_1 Mg$; mankynnes
$Ln Tr_1$ weard] *The letter* e *erased after this word* Ln 8 ece] eche Ln
drıhten] dryhten O; drihī Ca; drihtent Hr æfter] æfī Ca; epter Tr_1;
efter Hr teode] *An erasure of one letter* (d?) *after* o O; eode C; tida $H W$
$Bd_1 Ln Mg Tr_1$ 9 firum] finū C; fyrum $B W Ld_1$; fyrū Hr; pirum Tr_1
foldan] *With* n *added above the line* O; on foldum $H W Bd_1 Ln Mg Tr_1$; on
folden $Ld_1 Hr$ frea] euca Tr_1 ælmihtig] ælmyhtig H; ealmihti W;
elmihtig Tr_1; Ld_1 *and* Hr *add* halig scyppeod (*for l.* 6b) *after* ælmihtig

BEDE'S DEATH SONG

WEST SAXON VERSION

Text from MS. Digby 211 (Dg), with variants from the other MSS. (for the sigla, see Introd.. pp. cii–civ)

> For þam nedfere næni wyrþeþ
> þances snotera, þonne him þearf sy
> to gehicgenne ær his heonengange
> hwæt his gaste godes oþþe yfeles
> 5 æfter deaþe heonon demed weorþe.

Bede's Death Song 1 For] ffor *Ar* þam] þan *St Tr₁;* thā *Tr₃;* tham *Bd₂* nedfere] nedfare *Tr₁;* neodfere *D Fa Fx Ld₂;* neofere *Y* næni] næm *Sh;* neni *Db Tr₂ Ar Chr Tr₃ Bd₂;* nam *Jc;* nani *Tr₁;* næne *Ln;* nenig *D Fa Fx Ld₂ Y* wyrþeþ] wyrþeh *Db;* wirþeh *Tr₂ Ar;* þyrþeh *Chr;* wyrþaw *St;* wurþeþ *Jc;* wyrdeð *Tr₁;* wirþeþ *Ln;* wyrþeð *D Fa Fx Ld₂ Y;* wyrtheth *Tr₃ Bd₂* 2 þances] þankes *Tr₁;* thances *Tr₃ Bd₂* snotera] suotena *Jc;* snottra *D Fa Fx Ld₂ Y* þonne] þone *Db Tr₂ Ar Chr;* thonne *Tr₃ Bd₂* him] hym *Ar;* lū *Jc* þearf] thearf *Tr₃ Bd₂* sy] si *St Jc Ln* 3 gehicgenne] gehiggenne *D Fx Ld₂;* gehiggene *Fa;* gehisgenne (?) *Y* ær] ar *Tr₁;* ęr *Tr₃ Bd₂* his] *With is written over an erasure Ln* heonengange] heonengage *St;* heonangange *Tr₁* 3–4 heonengange hwæt his] *Not in Db Tr₂ Ar Chr* 4 hwæt] hwet *St Fa Ln Tr₃ Bd₂;* hyet *Jc;* hwat *Tr₁* gaste] staft *Jc* godes] sodes *St Jc* oþþe] oðöe *Tr₁;* öðe *D Fa Fx Ld₂ Y;* othe *Tr₃ Bd₂* yfeles] yuolys *Db Tr₂ Ar Chr;* yueles *Fa Tr₃ Bd₂* 5 æfter] æfī *Dg Sh St;* efter *Tr₁ Tr₃ Bd₂;* æften *Ld₂;* æsc̄ (*with c partially altered to* t?) *Ln* deaþe] cleaye *Tr₂;* deþe *St;* deaðe *Tr₁ Ld₂ Y;* deaðe with ð̄e on an erasure D;* daðe *Fx;* deathe *Tr₃ Bd₂* heonon] henon *Db Tr₂ Ar Chr;* heonen *Jc D Fa Fx Ld₂ Y Bd₂* demed] demeþ *St* weorþe] wurþe *Jc;* weorðe *Tr₁;* þeorþe *Chr;* wurðe *D Fa Fx Ld₂ Y;* weorthe *Tr₃ Bd₂*

BEDE'S DEATH SONG

MS. 70.H.7, Royal Library, The Hague

> Fore ðaem nedfere nenig wiorðeð
> ðonosnottorra ðon him ðearf riae
> to ymbhycgenne aer his hinionge
> hwet his gastę godes oððe yfles
> 5 ester deaðdege doemed wiorðe.

Bede's Death Song 3 ymbhycgenne] *With the second y altered from* i

THE LEIDEN RIDDLE

MS. Voss. Q. 106, University Library, Leiden

Mec se ueta uong,   uundrum freorig,
ob his innaðae   aerest cæn[.]æ.
Ni uaat ic mec biuorthæ   uullan fliusum,
herum ðerh hehcraeft,   hygiðonc[.....].
5 Uundnae me ni biað ueflæ,   ni ic uarp hafæ,
ni ðerih ðreatun giðraec   ðret me hlimmith,
ne me hrutendu   hrisil scelfath,
ni mec ouana   aam sceal cnyssa.
Uyrmas mec ni auefun   uyrdi craeftum,
10 ða ði geolu godueb   geatum fraetuath.
Uil mec huethrae suae ðeh   uidæ ofaer eorðu
hatan mith hęliðum   hyhtlic giuæde;
ni anoegun ic me aerigfaerae   egsan brogum,
ðeh ði n[...]n siæ   niudlicae ob cocrum.

LATIN-ENGLISH PROVERBS

Text from MS. Cotton Faustina A.x (F); variants from Royal
MS. 2B. v (R)

Ardor frigesscit,   nitor squalescit,
amor abolescit,   lux obtenebrescit.
Hat acolað,   hwit asolað,
leof alaðaþ,   leoht aðystrað.
5 Senescunt omnia   que ęterna non sunt.
Æghwæt forealdað   þæs þe ece ne byð.

Leiden Riddle 1 ueta] *Two letters erased after this word*   3 Ni] *Not in MS.*
uaat] *See Note*   4 hygiðonc-] *With* c *written above the line and* h *altered
from* b   6 ðret] ðr&   7 hrutendu] *See Note*   10 geolu] *See Note*
11 huethrae] huethrae *or* hucthrae *with the second* h *added above the line*
14a] *See Note*   Latin-English Proverbs 1 Ardor] *With* e *erased after this
word* F   frigesscit] refriescit R   squalescit] quualescit *with the first
* u *cancelled* R   4 alaðaþ] alaþað R   leoht] *A letter erased between* h
and t R   aðystrað] aþeostrað R   5 omnia] *Not in R*   que] quę R
ęterna] eterna R   6 forealdað] ealdað R

THE METRICAL PREFACE TO THE PASTORAL CARE

Text from MS. Hatton 20 (H); variants from MS. Junius 53 (J), MS. 12, Corpus Christi College, Cambridge (D), and MS. R. 5.22, Trinity College, Cambridge (T)

þis ærendgewrit   Agustinus
ofer sealtne sæ   suðan brohte
iegbuendum,   swa hit ær fore
adihtode   dryhtnes cempa,
5 Rome papa.   Ryhtspell monig
Gregorius   gleawmod gindwod
ðurh sefan snyttro,   searoðonca hord.
Forðæm he monncynnes   mæst gestriende
rodra wearde,   Romwara betest,
10 monna modwelegost,   mærðum gefrægost.
Siððan min on englisc   Ælfred kyning
awende worda gehwelc,   and me his writerum
sende suð and norð,   heht him swelcra ma
brengan bi ðære bisene,   ðæt he his biscepum
15 sendan meahte,   forðæm hi his sume ðorfton,
ða ðe lædenspræce   læste cuðon.

Metrical Preface to the Pastoral Care 1 þis] Ðis *J D*   ærendgewrit] ærent ge wryt *T*   Agustinus] augustinus *T*   2 sealtne] saltne *J* suðan] suþan *T*   3 iegbuendum] eorðbugendū *T*   swa] swæ *J*   4 adihtode] adihtnode *T*   5 Ryhtspell] ryht spel *D;* riht spel *T*   6 gindwod] geond wód *D T*   7 ðurh] þurh *T*   snyttro] snytro *T* searoðonca] searo þanca *T*   8 Forðæm] forðon *J D;* for þæm þe *T* monncynnes] moncynnes *J D;* mann cynnes *T*   gestriende] gestrynde *J* 9 rodra] rodera *D T*   Romwara] rom warena *T*   betest] betst *D T* 10 monna] manna *T*   modwelegost] mod weligost *T*   mærðum] merþum *T*   11 Siððan] Seððan *T*   min] me *T*   englisc] englesc *T*   Ælfred] ælf fred *D;* ælfræd *T*   kyning] cyning *D;* cynincg *T* 12 awende] awęnde *T*   gehwelc] gehwilc *T*   13 suð] suþ *T*   norð] norþ *T*   heht] het *T*   swelcra] swylcra *T*   14 brengan] bringan *T* bi] be *J D T*   ðære] þære *T*   bisene] bysene *J T*   ðæt] þæt *J T* biscepum] bisceopum *T*   15 meahte] myahte *T*   forðæm] for þæm *T*   hi] hie *J D*   sume] sūme *(the mark over* u *in a later hand?) D* ðorfton] beþorftan *T*   16 ða] þa *T*   ðe] þe *J T*   lædenspræce] leden spræce *T*   læste] læsðe *J*   cuðon] cuþon *T*

THE METRICAL EPILOGUE TO THE PASTORAL CARE

Text from MS. Hatton 20 (H); variants from MS. 12, Corpus
Christi College, Cambridge (D)

Ðis is nu se wæterscipe   ðe us wereda god
to frofre gehet   foldbuendum.
He cwæð ðæt he wolde   ðæt on worulde forð
of ðæm innoðum   a libbendu
5 wætru fleowen,   ðe wel on hine
gelifden under lyfte.   Is hit lytel tweo
ðæt ðæs wæterscipes   welsprynge is
on hefonrice,   ðæt is halig gæst.
Ðonan hine hlodan   halge and gecorene,
10 siððan hine gierdon   ða ðe gode herdon
ðurh halga bec   hider on eorðan
geond manna mod   missenlice.
Sume hine weriað   on gewitlocan,
wisdomes stream,   welerum gehæftað,
15 ðæt he on unnyt   ut ne tofloweð.
Ac se wæl wunað   on weres breostum
ðurh dryhtnes giefe   diop and stille.
Sume hine lætað   ofer landscare
riðum torinnan;   nis ðæt rædlic ðing,
20 gif swa hlutor wæter,   hlud and undiop,
tofloweð æfter feldum   oð hit to fenne werð.
Ac hladað iow nu drincan,   nu iow dryhten geaf
ðæt iow Gregorius   gegiered hafað

Metrical Epilogue to the Pastoral Care 1 Ðis] *With the* i *written inside the
initial capital* ð H; *the capital is omitted in* D   wereda] weroda D
3 worulde] weorulde D   5 fleowen] fliowen D   hine] hiene D
6 gelifden] geliefden D   7 wæterscipes] wæter sciepes D   8 hefonrice]
heofonrice D   ðæt] þæt D   gæst] gast D   9 Ðonan] ðonon D
hine] hiene D   hlodan] hlodon D   halge] halige D   10 siððan]
sieððan D   hine] hiene D   gierdon] gieredon D   herdon] hierdon D
11 hider] hieder D   12 manna] monna D   13 hine] hiene D   16 wæl]
wel D   18 hine] hie ne D   21 werð] wyrð D

111

to durum iowrum   dryhtnes welle.
25 Fylle nu his fætels,   se ðe fæstne hider
kylle brohte,   cume eft hræðe.
Gif her ðegna hwelc   ðyrelne kylle
brohte to ðys burnan,   bete hine georne,
ðy læs he forsceade   scirost wætra,
30 oððe him lifes drync   forloren weorðe.

THE METRICAL PREFACE TO
WÆRFERTH'S TRANSLATION OF
GREGORY'S DIALOGUES

MS. Cotton Otho C. i

[.]e ðe me rædan ðance,
he in me findan mæ[.],   gif hine feola lysteð
gastlices lifes   godre biesene,
þæt he ful eaþe mæg   upp gestigan
5 to ðam heofonlican hame,   þar byð a hyht and wyn,
bl[.]s on burgum,   þam þe bearn godes
sielfes hiora eagum   geseon motan.
Þæt mæg se mon begytan,   se þe his modgeðanc
æltowe byþ,   and þonne þurh his ingehygd
10 to þissa haligra   helpe geliefeð,
ond hiora bisene fulgað,   swa þeos boc sagað.
Me awritan het   Wulfstan bisceop,
þeow and þearfa   þæs þ[.] alne þrym aof,
and eac walden is   wihta gehwelcre,
15 an ece god   eallra gesc[...]ta.
Bideþ þe se bisceop,   se þe ðas boc begeat
þe þu on þinum handum nu   hafast and sceawast,
þæt þu him to þeossum halgum   helpe bidde,

---

24 iowrum] eowrum *D*   dryhtnes] driht nes *D*   welle] wille *D*
28 hine] hiene *D*   30 lifes] liefes *D*   Metrical Preface to Gregory's
Dialogues 1*b*] *See Note*   12 Wulfstan] *With* tan *on an* erasure?
14 wihta] wiht   16*a* þe] *An erasure of about two letters after this word*

þe heo[..] gemynd her on   gemearcude siendon,
20 and þæt him god ællmihtig
forgyu[.] þa gyltas   þe he geo worhte,
and eac resðe mid him,   se ðe ah ealles rices gewe[...],
and eac swa his beahgifan,   þe him ðas bysene forgeaf,
þæt is se selesða   sinc[..] brytta,
25 Ælfryd mid Englum,   ealra cyninga
þara þe he sið oððe ær fore   secgan hyrde,
oððe he iorðcyninga ær   ænigne gefrugne.

THE METRICAL EPILOGUE TO MS. 41, CORPUS CHRISTI COLLEGE, CAMBRIDGE

Bidde ic eac   æghwylcne mann,
brego, rices weard,   þe þas boc ræde
and þa bredu befo,   fira aldor,
þæt gefyrðrige þone writre   wynsum cræfte
5 þe ðas boc awrat   bam handum twam,
þæt he mote manega gyt   mundum synum
geendigan,   his aldre to willan,
and him þæs geunne   se ðe ah ealles geweald,
rodera waldend,   þæt he on riht mote
10 oð his daga ende   drihten herigan. Amen. Geweorþe þæt.

21 geo worhte] geworhte   27 iorðcyninga] hiorð cyninga   Metrical
Epilogue to MS. 41, 1 Bidde] idde *with space before the word for a large
capital*

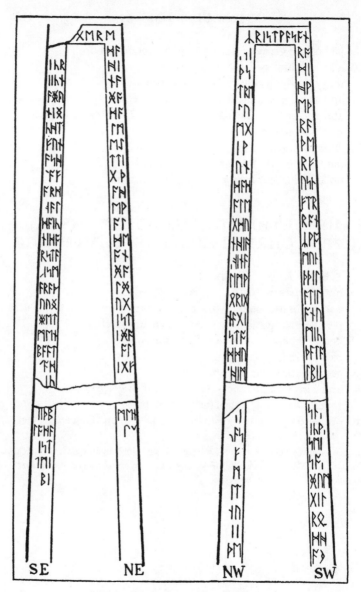

THE RUTHWELL CROSS

(From *The Dream of the Rood*, by B. Dickins and A. S. C. Ross.
Reproduced by permission of the publishers,
Messrs. Methuen and Co., Ltd.)

THE RUTHWELL CROSS

I

[..]geredæ hinæ ḡod almeȝttig,
þa he walde on ḡalḡu gistiḡa,
[.]odig f[.......] men.
[.]ug[.............................]

II

[....] ic riicnæ k̄yniŋc,
hêafunæs hlafard, hælda ic ni dorstæ.
Bismærædu uŋk̄et men ba ætgad[..];
ic [...] miþ blodæ [.]istemi[.],
bi[.......................................]

III

Krist wæs on rodi.
Hweþræ þer fusæ fêarran kwomu
æþþilæ til anum.   Ic þæt al bi[....].
S[...] ic w[.]s mi[.] so[.]ḡum gidrœ[..]d,
h[.]aḡ [..................]

IV

miþ strelum giwundad.
Alegdun hiæ hinæ limwœrignæ,
gistoddu[.] him [......]icæs [..]f[..]m;
[...]êa[.]du[..]i[.] þe[..........
..........................]

THE BRUSSELS CROSS

Rod is min nama.   Geo ic ricne cyning
bær byfigynde,   blode bestemed.
Þas rode het Æþlmær wyrican and Aðelwold hys beroþor
Criste to lofe for Ælfrices saule hyra beroþor.

Brussels Cross 3 beroþor] beroþo

115

THE FRANKS CASKET

1. Front

Fisc flodu ahof   on fergenberig;
warþ gasric grorn,   þær he on greut giswom.
Hronæs ban.

2. Right Side

Her Hos sitæþ   on hærmbergæ,
agl[.] drigiþ,   swæ hiri Ertae gisgraf
særden sorgæ   and sefa tornæ.

THE METRICAL CHARMS

1. FOR UNFRUITFUL LAND

MS. Cotton Caligula A. vii

Her ys seo bot, hu ðu meaht þine æceras betan gif hi
nellaþ wel wexan oþþe þær hwilc ungedefe þing on gedon bið
on dry oððe on lyblace. Genim þonne on niht, ær hyt
dagige, feower tyrf on feower healfa þæs landes, and gemearca
5 hu hy ær stodon. Nim þonne ele and hunig and beorman,
and ælces feos meolc þe on þæm lande sy, and ælces treow-
cynnes dæl þe on þæm lande sy gewexen, butan heardan
beaman, and ælcre namcuþre wyrte dæl, butan glappan anon,
and do þonne haligwæter ðær on, and drype þonne þriwa on
10 þone staðol þara turfa, and cweþe ðonne ðas word: Crescite,
wexe, et multiplicamini, and gemænigfealda, et replete, and
gefylle, terre, þas eorðan. In nomine patris et filii et spiritus
sancti sit benedicti. And Pater noster swa oft swa þæt oðer.
And bere siþþan ða turf to circean, and mæssepreost asinge
15 feower mæssan ofer þan turfon, and wende man þæt grene to
ðan weofode, and siþþan gebringe man þa turf þær hi ær
wæron ær sunnan setlgange. And hæbbe him gæworht of

Charms 1, 6 ælces] *Added above the line*   1,7 heardan] *With the letters* dan
added above the line

THE FRANKS CASKET: FRONT

THE FRANKS CASKET: RIGHT SIDE

cwicbeame feower Cristes mælo and awrite on ælcon ende:
Matheus and Marcus, Lucas and Iohannes. Lege þæt
20 Cristes mæl on þone pyt neoþeweardne, cweðe ðonne: Crux
Matheus, crux Marcus, crux Lucas, crux sanctus Iohannes.
Nim ðonne þa turf and sete ðær ufon on and cweþe ðonne
nigon siþon þas word, Crescite, and swa oft Pater noster,
and wende þe þonne eastweard, and onlut nigon siðon
25 eadmodlice, and cweð þonne þas word:
    Eastweard ic stande,   arena ic me bidde,
    bidde ic þone mæran domine,   bidde ðone miclan drihten,
    bidde ic ðone haligan   heofonrices weard,
    eorðan ic bidde   and upheofon
30   and ða soþan   sancta Marian
    and heofones meaht   and heahreced,
    þæt ic mote þis gealdor   mid gife drihtnes
    toðum ontynan   þurh trumne geþanc,
    aweccan þas wæstmas   us to woruldnytte,
35   gefyllan þas foldan   mid fæste geleafan,
    wlitigigan þas wancgturf,   swa se witega cwæð
    þæt se hæfde are on eorþrice,   se þe ælmyssan
    dælde domlice   drihtnes þances.
Wende þe þonne III sunganges, astrece þonne on andlang
40 and arim þær letanias and cweð þonne: Sanctus, sanctus,
sanctus oþ ende. Sing þonne Benedicite aþenedon earmon
and Magnificat and Pater noster III, and bebeod hit Criste
and sancta Marian and þære halgan rode to lofe and to
weorþinga and to are þam þe þæt land age and eallon þam þe
45 him underðeodde synt. Ðonne þæt eall sie gedon, þonne
nime man uncuþ sæd æt ælmesmannum and selle him twa
swylc, swylce man æt him nime, and gegaderie ealle his
sulhgeteogo togædere; borige þonne on þam beame stor and
finol and gehalgode sapan and gehalgod sealt. Nim þonne
50 þæt sæd, sete on þæs sules bodig, cweð þonne:
    Erce, Erce, Erce,   eorþan modor,
    geunne þe se alwalda,   ece drihten,

1,19 Marcus] mr̄cs   Iohannes] Ioħes   1,21 Marcus] mr̄c   1,35
gefyllan] gefylle   1,37 eorþrice] *With* r *corrected from* l   1,44 to are þam]
þā are *with three letters erased after* are

 æcera wexendra   and wridendra,
eacniendra   and elniendra,
55   sceafta hehra,   scirra wæstma,
and þæra bradan   berewæstma,
and þæra hwitan   hwætewæstma,
and ealra   eorþan wæstma.
Geunne him   ece drihten
60   and his halige,   þe on heofonum synt,
þæt hys yrþ si gefriþod   wið ealra feonda gehwæne,
and heo si geborgen   wið ealra bealwa gehwylc,
þara lyblaca   geond land sawen.
Nu ic bidde ðone waldend,   se ðe ðas woruld gesceop,
65   þæt ne sy nan to þæs cwidol wif   ne to þæs cræftig man
þæt awendan ne mæge   word þus gecwedene.
Þonne man þa sulh forð drife and þa forman furh onsceote,
cweð þonne:
Hal wes þu, folde,   fira modor!
70   Beo þu growende   on godes fæþme,
fodre gefylled   firum to nytte.
Nim þonne ælces cynnes melo and abacæ man innewerdre
handa bradnæ hlaf and gecned hine mid meolce and mid
haligwætere and lecge under þa forman furh. Cweþe þonne:
75   Ful æcer fodres   fira cinne,
beorhtblowende,   þu gebletsod weorþ
þæs haligan noman   þe ðas heofon gesceop
and ðas eorþan   þe we on lifiaþ;
se god, se þas grundas geworhte,   geunne us growende
gife,
80   þæt us corna gehwylc   cume to nytte.
Cweð þonne III Crescite in nomine patris, sit benedicti.
Amen and Pater noster þriwa.

1,55 hehra] hen se   scirra] scire   1,56 þæra] þære   1,57 þæra] þære
1,60 heofonum] eofonum   1,66 ne mæge] *Added above the line*   word]
woru d *with* l *erased after* u   1,72 innewerdre] Innewerdne

2. THE NINE HERBS CHARM

MS. Harley 585

Gemyne ðu, mucgwyrt,   hwæt þu ameldodest,
hwæt þu renadest   æt Regenmelde.
Una þu hattest,   yldost wyrta.
Ðu miht wið III   and wið XXX,
5   þu miht wiþ attre   and wið onflyge,
þu miht wiþ þam laþan   ðe geond lond færð.
Ond þu, wegbrade,   wyrta modor,
eastan openo,   innan mihtigu;
ofer ðe crætu curran,   ofer ðe cwene reodan,
10   ofer ðe bryde bryodedon,   ofer þe fearras fnærdon.
Eallum þu þon wiðstode   and wiðstunedest;
swa ðu wiðstonde   attre and onflyge
and þæm laðan   þe geond lond fereð.
Stune hætte þeos wyrt,   heo on stane geweox;
15   stond heo wið attre,   stunað heo wærce.
Stiðe heo hatte,   wiðstunað heo attre,
wreceð heo wraðan,   weorpeð ut attor.
Þis is seo wyrt   seo wiþ wyrm gefeaht,
þeos mæg wið attre,   heo mæg wið onflyge,
20   heo mæg wið ðam laþan   ðe geond lond fereþ.
Fleoh þu nu, attorlaðe,   seo læsse ða maran,
seo mare þa læssan,   oððæt him beigra bot sy.
Gemyne þu, mægðe,   hwæt þu ameldodest,
hwæt ðu geændadest   æt Alorforda;
25   þæt næfre for gefloge   feorh ne gesealde
syþðan him mon mægðan   to mete gegyrede.
Þis is seo wyrt   ðe wergulu hatte;
ðas onsænde seolh   ofer sæs hrygc
ondan attres   oþres to bote.
30   Ðas VIIII magon   wið nygon attrum.
Wyrm com snican,   toslat he man;

2,6 þam] þa   2,8 openo] opone   2,9a ðe] ðy   crætu] cræte
2,9b ðe] ðy   2,10a ðe] ðy   2,10b þe] þy   2,20 ðam] ða   2,30 magon]
ongan   2,31 he man] henan

  ða genam Woden VIIII wuldortanas,
  sloh ða þa næddran, þæt heo on VIIII tofleah.
  þær geændade æppel and attor,
35 þæt heo næfre ne wolde on hus bugan.
  Fille and finule, felamihtigu twa,
  þa wyrte gesceop witig drihten,
  halig on heofonum, þa he hongode;
  sette and sænde on VII worulde
40 earmum and eadigum eallum to bote.
  Stond heo wið wærce, stunað heo wið attre,
  seo mæg wið III and wið XXX,
  wið feondes hond and wið færbregde,
  wið malscrunge manra wihta.
45 Nu magon þas VIIII wyrta wið nygon wuldorgeflo-
                    genum,
  wið VIIII attrum and wið nygon onflygnum,
  wið ðy readan attre, wið ðy runlan attre,
  wið ðy hwitan attre, wið ðy wedenan attre,
  wið ðy geolwan attre, wið ðy grenan attre,
50 wið ðy wonnan attre, wið ðy wedenan attre,
  wið ðy brunan attre, wið ðy basewan attre,
  wið wyrmgeblæd, wið wætergeblæd,
  wið þorngeblæd, wið þystelgeblæd,
  wið ysgeblæd, wið attorgeblæd,
55 gif ænig attor cume eastan fleogan
  oððe ænig norðan * * * cume
  oððe ænig westan ofer werðeode.
    Crist stod ofer adle ængan cundes.
  Ic ana wat ea rinnende
60 þær þa nygon nædran nean behealdað;
  motan ealle weoda nu wyrtum aspringan,
  sæs toslupan, eal sealt wæter,

2,33 on] *With* n *added above the line* 2,43 and wið færbregde] 7 wið
þæs hond wið frea begde 2,44 manra] minra 2,46 onflygnum] *With*
1 *added above the line* 2,47b ðy] ða 2,53 þystelgeblæd] þysgeblæd
2,54 ysgeblæd] *With* þ *erased before* y 2,55 cume] *Added above the line*
2,58 adle] alde 2,60 þær] 7 nean] *Not in MS.*

ðonne ic þis attor   of ðe geblawe.

Mugcwyrt, wegbrade þe eastan open sy, lombescyrse,
65 attorlaðan, mageðan, netelan, wudusuræppel, fille and finul,
ealde sapan.   Gewyrc ða wyrta to duste, mængc wiþ þa
sapan and wiþ þæs æpples gor.   Wyrc slypan of wætere
and of axsan, genim finol, wyl on þære slyppan and beþe mid
æggemongc, þonne he þa sealfe on do, ge ær ge æfter.   Sing
70 þæt galdor on ælcre þara wyrta, III ær he hy wyrce and
on þone æppel ealswa; ond singe þon men in þone muð and
in þa earan buta and on ða wunde þæt ilce gealdor, ær he
þa sealfe on do.

3. AGAINST A DWARF

MS. Harley 585

Wið dweorh man sceal niman VII lytle oflætan, swylce
man mid ofrað, and writan þas naman on ælcre oflætan:
Maximianus, Malchus, Iohannes, Martimianus, Dioni-
sius, Constantinus, Serafion.   Þænne eft þæt galdor, þæt
5 her æfter cweð, man sceal singan, ærest on þæt wynstre
eare, þænne on þæt swiðre eare, þænne bufan þæs mannes
moldan.   And ga þænne an mædenman to and ho hit on
his sweoran, and do man swa þry dagas; him bið sona sel.

Her com in gangan,   in spiderwiht,
10   hæfde him his haman on handa,   cwæð þæt þu his
                                     hæncgest wære,
legde þe his teage an sweoran.   Ongunnan him of þæm
                                     lande liþan;
sona swa hy of þæm lande coman,   þa ongunnan him
                                     ða liþu colian.

Þa com in gangan   dweores sweostar;
þa geændade heo   and aðas swor

2,69 æggemongc] aagemogc   on do] onde   2,73 on do] onde   3,2
writan] writ at the end of a line, followed by tan in the next line   3,6
bufan] hufan   3,9 spiderwiht] spiden wiht with n altered from some other
letter   3,10 hæncgest] With c added above the line   3,11 legde þe]
legeþe   3,12 ða liþu] þa with ðali written above the line before þ and u
above a, i.e. ða liþu   3,13 dweores] deores

15   ðæt næfre þis ðæm adlegan   derian ne moste,
      ne þæm þe þis galdor   begytan mihte,
      oððe þe þis galdor   ongalan cuþe. Amen. Fiað.

4. FOR A SUDDEN STITCH

MS. Harley 585

Wið færstice feferfuige and seo reade netele, ðe þurh
ærn inwyxð, and wegbrade; wyll in buteran.
      Hlude wæran hy, la, hlude,   ða hy ofer þone hlæw ridan,
      wæran anmode,   ða hy ofer land ridan.
5   Scyld ðu ðe nu, þu ðysne nið   genesan mote.
      Ut, lytel spere,   gif her inne sie!
      Stod under linde,   under leohtum scylde,
      þær ða mihtigan wif   hyra mægen beræddon
      and hy gyllende   garas sændan;
10   ic him oðerne   eft wille sændan,
      fleogende flane   forane togeanes.
      Ut, lytel spere,   gif hit her inne sy!
      Sæt smið,   sloh seax lytel,
      * * * iserna,   wundrum swiðe.
15   Ut, lytel spere,   gif her inne sy!
      Syx smiðas sætan,   wælspera worhtan.
      Ut, spere,   næs in, spere!
      Gif her inne sy   isernes dæl,
      hægtessan geweorc,   hit sceal gemyltan.
20   Gif ðu wære on fell scoten   oððe wære on flæsc scoten
      oððe wære on blod scoten
      oððe wære on lið scoten,   næfre ne sy ðin lif atæsed;
      gif hit wære esa gescot   oððe hit wære ylfa gescot
      oððe hit wære hægtessan gescot,   nu ic wille ðin helpan.
25   þis ðe to bote esa gescotes,   ðis ðe to bote ylfa gescotes,
      ðis ðe to bote hægtessan gescotes;   ic ðin wille helpan.

3,15 ðæm] ðǣ *added above the line*   adlegan] *With the second* a *altered from
some other letter and* n *added above the line*   3,16 ne] *Added above the line*
4,5 nu] *An erasure of one letter after this word*   4,11 flane] flañ   4,12
lytel] lyte *at the end of a line*   4,14 wundrum] wund   4,18 isernes]
isenes

Fleoh þær * * *   on fyrgenheafde.
Hal westu,   helpe ðin drihten!
Nim þonne þæt seax, ado on wætan.

5. FOR LOSS OF CATTLE

MS. Harley 585

Þonne þe mon ærest secge þæt þin ceap sy losod, þonne
cweð þu ærest, ær þu elles hwæt cweþe:
 Bæðleem hatte seo buruh   þe Crist on acænned wæs,
 seo is gemærsod   geond ealne middangeard;
5 swa þyos dæd for monnum   mære gewurþe
 þurh þa haligan Cristes rode! Amen. Gebide þe þonne
þriwa east and cweþ þonne þriwa: Crux Christi ab oriente
reducað. Gebide þe þonne þriwa west and cweð þonne
þriwa: Crux Christi ab occidente reducat. Gebide þe
10 þonne þriwa suð and cweþ þriwa: Crux Christi ab austro
reducat. Gebide þonne þriwa norð and cweð þriwa: Crux
Christi ab aquilone reducað, crux Christi abscondita est et
inuenta est. Iudeas Crist ahengon, dydon dæda þa
wyrrestan, hælon þæt hy forhelan ne mihtan. Swa þeos
15 dæd nænige þinga forholen ne wurþe þurh þa haligan
Cristes rode. Amen.

6. FOR DELAYED BIRTH

MS. Harley 585

Se wifman, se hire cild afedan ne mæg, gange to gewitenes
mannes birgenne and stæppe þonne þriwa ofer þa byrgenne
and cweþe þonne þriwa þas word:
 Þis me to bote   þære laþan lætbyrde,
5 þis me to bote   þære swæran swærbyrde,
 þis me to bote   þære laðan lambyrde.
And þonne þæt wif seo mid bearne and heo to hyre hlaforde

4,27 Fleoh] fled   þær] þr̄   fyrgenheafde] fyrgen hæfde   5,4
gemærsod] ge mærsad *with a dotted beneath for deletion and* o *written
above*   5,5 þyos] *With* y *altered from* u?   5,15 forholen] fer ho len
haligan] *With* i *added above the line*   6,5 swærbyrde] swært byr de

on reste ga, þonne cweþe heo:
    Up ic gonge,   ofer þe stæppe
10   mid cwican cilde,   nalæs mid cwellendum,
    mid fulborenum,   nalæs mid fægan.
And þonne seo modor gefele þæt þæt bearn si cwic, ga
þonne to cyrican, and þonne heo toforan þan weofode cume,
cweþe þonne:
15   Criste, ic sæde,   þis gecyþed!
Se wifmon, se hyre bearn afedan ne mæge, genime heo
sylf hyre agenes cildes gebyrgenne dæl, wry æfter þonne on
blace wulle and bebicge to cepemannum and cweþe þonne:
    Ic hit bebicge,   ge hit bebicgan,
20   þas sweartan wulle   and þysse sorge corn.
Se wifman, se ne mæge bearn afedan, nime þonne anes
bleos cu meoluc on hyre handæ and gesupe þonne mid hyre
muþe and gange þonne to yrnendum wætere and spiwe þær
in þa meolc and hlade þonne mid þære ylcan hand þæs
25 wæteres muð fulne and forswelge. Cweþe þonne þas word:
    Gehwer ferde ic me þone mæran   maga þihtan,
    mid þysse mæran   mete þihtan;
    þonne ic me wille habban   and ham gan.
Þonne heo to þan broce ga, þonne ne beseo heo, no ne eft
30 þonne heo þanan ga, and þonne ga heo in oþer hus oþer heo
ut ofeode and þær gebyrge metes.

7. FOR THE WATER-ELF DISEASE

Royal MS. 12D.xvii

Gif mon biþ on wæterælfadle, þonne beoþ him þa hand-
næglas wonne and þa eagan tearige and wile locian niþer.
Do him þis to læcedome: eoforþrote, cassuc, fone nioþo-
weard, eowberge, elehtre, eolone, merscmealwan crop,
5 fenminte, dile, lilie, attorlaþe, polleie, marubie, docce, ellen,
felterre, wermod, streawbergean leaf, consolde; ofgeot mid
ealaþ, do hæligwæter to, sing þis gealdor ofer þriwa:
    Ic benne awrat   betest beadowræda,

6,17 wry] þry   6,21 Se wifman, se ne mæge] Seman seþemæge
7,8 benne] binne

swa benne ne burnon,   ne burston,
10   ne fundian,   ne feologan,
ne hoppettan,   ne wund waxsian,
ne dolh diopian;   ac him self healde halewæge,
ne ace þe þon ma,   þe eorþan on eare ace.
Sing þis manegum siþum: Eorþe þe onbere eallum hire
15 mihtum and mægenum. Þas galdor mon mæg singan on
wunde.

8. FOR A SWARM OF BEES

MS. 41, Corpus Christi College, Cambridge

Wið ymbe nim eorþan, oferweorp mid þinre swiþran
handa under þinum swiþran fet, and cwet:
Fo ic under fot,   funde ic hit.
Hwæt, eorðe mæg   wið ealra wihta gehwilce
5   and wið andan   and wið æminde
and wið þa micelan   mannes tungan.
And wiððon forweorp ofer greot, þonne hi swirman, and
cweð:
Sitte ge, sigewif,   sigað to eorþan!
10   Næfre ge wilde   to wuda fleogan.
Beo ge swa gemindige   mines godes,
swa bið manna gehwilc   metes and eþeles.

9. FOR THEFT OF CATTLE

MS. 41, Corpus Christi College, Cambridge

Ne forstolen ne forholen nanuht, þæs ðe ic age, þe ma ðe
mihte Herod urne drihten. Ic geþohte sancte Eadelenan
and ic geþohte Crist on rode ahangen; swa ic þence þis feoh
to findanne, næs to oðfeorrganne, and to witanne, næs to
5 oðwyrceanne, and to lufianne, næs to oðlædanne.
Garmund,   godes ðegen,
find þæt feoh   and fere þæt feoh
and hafa þæt feoh   and heald þæt feoh
and fere ham þæt feoh.

10   Þæt he næfre næbbe landes,   Þæt he hit oðlæde,
     ne foldan,   Þæt hit oðferie,
     ne husa,   Þæt he hit oðhealde.
     Gif hyt hwa gedo,   ne gedige hit him næfre!
     Binnan Þrym nihtum   cunne ic his mihta,
15   his mægen and his mihta   and his mundcræftas.
     Eall he weornige,   swa syre wudu weornie,
     swa breðel seo swa Þystel,
     se ðe ðis feoh   oðfergean Þence
     oððe ðis orf   oðehtian ðence. Amen.

10. FOR LOSS OF CATTLE

MS. 41, Corpus Christi College, Cambridge

Ðis man sceal cweðan ðonne his ceapa hwilcne man for-
stolenne.   Cwyð ær he ænyg oÞer word cweðe:
     Bethlem hattæ seo burh   ðe Crist on geboren wes,
     seo is gemærsod   ofer ealne middangeard;
5   swa ðeos dæd wyrÞe   for monnum mære,
per crucem Christi!   And gebide Þe ðonne Þriwa east and
cweð Þriwa: Crux Christi ab oriente reducat.   And III
west and cweð: Crux Christi ab occidente reducat.   And
III suð and cweð: Crux Christi a meridie reducant.   And
10 III norð and cweð: Crux Christi abscondita sunt et inuenta
est.   Iudeas Crist ahengon, gedidon him dæda Þa wyrstan;
hælon Þæt hi forhelan ne mihton.   Swa næfre ðeos dæd
forholen ne wyrðe per crucem Christi.

11. A JOURNEY CHARM

MS. 41, Corpus Christi College, Cambridge

Ic me on Þisse gyrde beluce   and on godes helde bebeode
wið Þane sara stice,   wið Þane sara slege,

9,12 he hit oðhealde] hehit oðhit healde   9,13 hyt] *With a letter erased
between* h *and* y   9,16 syre] syer   9,17 seo] Þeo   10,1 hwilcne] *With*
c *added above the line*   forstolenne] forstelenne *with* o *written above the
first* e   10,2 Cwyð] cyð   10,7 Crux] ✠   III] in   10,9 III] in
10,10 III] in   11,2 stice] síce

wið þane grymma gryre,
wið ðane micela egsa   þe bið eghwam lað,
5 and wið eal þæt lað   þe in to land fare.
Sygegealdor ic begale,   sigegyrd ic me wege,
wordsige and worcsige.   Se me dege;
ne me mere ne gemyrre,   ne me maga ne geswence,
ne me næfre minum feore   forht ne gewurþe,
10 ac gehæle me ælmihtig and sunu   and frofre gast,
ealles wuldres   wyrðig dryhten,
swa swa ic gehyrde   heofna scyppende.
Abrame and Isace
and swilce men,   Moyses and Iacob,
15 and Dauit and Iosep
and Evan and Annan   and Elizabet,
Saharie and ec Marie,   modur Cristes,
and eac þæ gebroþru,   Petrus and Paulus,
and eac þusend   þinra engla
20 clipige ic me to are   wið eallum feondum.
Hi me ferion and friþion   and mine fore nerion,
eal me gehealdon,   me gewealdon,
worces stirende;   si me wuldres hyht,
hand ofer heafod,   haligra rof,
25 sigerofra sceolu,   soðfæstra engla.
Biddu ealle   bliðu mode
þæt me beo Matheus helm,   Marcus byrne,
leoht, lifes rof,   Lucos min swurd,
scearp and scirecg,   scyld Iohannes,
30 wuldre gewlitegod   wælgar Serafhin.
    Forð ic gefare,   frind ic gemete,
eall engla blæd,   eadiges lare.
Bidde ic nu sigeres god   godes miltse,
siðfæt godne,   smylte and lihte

11,8 mere] mer   11,10a ælmihtig] ælmihti gi   11,10b and] *Not in MS.*
11,11 wyrðig] wyrdig   11,19 þinra] þira   11,22b me] men
11,25 sceolu] sceote   11,27a þæt me beo Matheus] þ me beo hand ofer
heafod mathe us   11,29 scearp] scerp *with* a *added above the line between*
r *and* p, *i.e.* scerap   11,30 wælgar] wega   11,33] bidde ic nu god *with*
sigere *and* godes miltse *added above the line; see Note*

35 windas on waroþum.   Windas gefran,
  circinde wæter   simble gehælede
  wið eallum feondum.   Freond ic gemete wið,
  þæt ic on þæs ælmihtgian frið   wunian mote,
  belocun wið þam laþan,   se me lyfes eht,
40 on engla blæd   gestaþelod,
  and inna halre hand   heofna rices,
  þa hwile þe ic on þis life   wunian mote.   Amen.

12. AGAINST A WEN

Royal MS. 4A.xiv

  Wenne, wenne,   wenchichenne,
  her ne scealt þu timbrien,   ne nenne tun habben,
  ac þu scealt north eonene   to þan nihgan berhge,
  þer þu hauest, ermig,   enne broþer.
5   He þe sceal legge   leaf et heafde.
  Under fot wolues,   under ueþer earnes,
  under earnes clea,   a þu geweornie.
  Clinge þu   alswa col on heorþe,
  scring þu   alswa scerne awage,
10   and weorne   alswa weter on anbre.
  Swa litel þu gewurþe   alswa linsetcorn,
  and miccli lesse alswa anes handwurmes hupeban, and
  alswa litel þu gewurþe þet þu nawiht gewurþe.

11,35 windas on waroþum] wind wereþum   11,36 simble gehælede]
simbli gehaleþe   11,38 þæs ælmihtgian frið] þis ælmih gian on his frið
11,39 þam] þa   11,40 blæd] bla blæd   11,41 heofna] hofna   rices]
rices blæd   12,1 wenchichenne] *With the second* h *added above the line*
12,2 timbrien] *With* r *added above the line*   12,3 north] *With* h *added above*
the line   12,6 wolues] uolmes   12,9 scerne] scesne

NOTES

ABBREVIATIONS IN THE NOTES

Names cited without further particulars are the names of editors, listed under "Editions" in the several bibliographies. The titles of poems are not abbreviated in this volume.

Special lists of abbreviations are given at the head of the notes on Waldere and on Solomon and Saturn.

Anglia Beibl. Beiblatt zur Anglia.
Anz.fdA. Anzeiger für deutsches Altertum.
Archiv. Archiv für das Studium der neueren Sprachen und Literaturen.
Beitr. Beiträge zur Geschichte der deutschen Sprache und Literatur.
Bonner Beitr. Bonner Beiträge zur Anglistik.
Bos.-Tol. Bosworth-Toller, Anglo-Saxon Dictionary.
Eng. Stud. Englische Studien.
Grein, Spr. Sprachschatz der angelsächsischen Dichter.
Grein-Köhler. Sprachschatz der angelsächsischen Dichter, revised ed. by Köhler.
Indog. Forsch. Indogermanische Forschungen.
JEGPh. Journal of English and Germanic Philology.
Kock, JJJ. Jubilee Jaunts and Jottings.
MLN. Modern Language Notes.
MLRev. Modern Language Review.
N.E.D. New English Dictionary.
PMLA. Publications of the Modern Language Association of America.
Sievers, Angels. Gram. Angelsächsische Grammatik, 3d ed., 1898.
ZfdA. Zeitschrift für deutsches Altertum.
ZfdPh. Zeitschrift für deutsche Philologie.

NOTES ON THE BATTLE OF FINNSBURH

The Battle of Finnsburh] For a discussion of the literary and historical problems connected with this poem, see Introd., pp. xiii ff.   1–2] Hickes' text reads ... *nas byrnað. Næfre hleoþrode ða*, etc.   Thorpe and most later edd. take *Næfre* as the last word of l. 1, beginning a new line and a new sentence with *hleoþrode*, thus:

> ...nas   byrnað næfre."
> Hleoþrode ða, etc.

Holthausen, with this arrangement, reads *Ða hleoþrode*, l. 2a, for metrical reasons.   But Trautmann (Finn, p. 37) emends *Næfre* to *Hnæf*, placing it at the beginning of l. 2a; he also transposes to read *Hnæf þa hleoþrode*.   Klaeber (3 ed.) adopts the emendation to *Hnæf*, but retains Hickes' word order, *Hnæf hleoþrode ða*.   Klaeber's reading seems highly probable, and has been adopted in the text.   Hickes' *Næfre* makes no sense at all in l. 2a, and *byrnað næfre* in l. 1, at the end of a sentence, would be very unlikely.   But *Hnæf*, with *heaþogeong cyning* parallel to it, is unobjectionable.   Since Hickes was probably not expecting a personal name here, his error is easily explained.   Most edd. complete -*nas* to read [*hor*]*nas*; see l. 4b.   The punctuation in the text, with a question mark after *byrnað*, follows Chambers (who, however, reads *byrnað næfre*); ll. 3–4 are best taken as Hnæf's answer to a question asked by one of his companions.   See Introd., p. xvi.   2b heaþogeong] So Grundtvig (1820) and most later edd., for Hickes' *hearo geong*.   Trautmann (Finn, p. 38) reads *heaþogeorn cyning*, "the king eager for battle."   Dickins follows Hickes, taking *hearo*- as a variant of *heoru*-.   Kemble (Beowulf, 1835) and Ettmüller had previously read *heorogeong*.   Neither *heorugeong* nor *heaþogeong* is recorded elsewhere.   3 eastan] So most edd., for Hickes' *Eastun*.   The appearance of a similar -*u*- spelling in *weuna*, l. 25, might argue for the retention of -*u*- here; but it seems more probable that Hickes misread an *a* in the MS. as *u* in both places.   On the question of Hickes' accuracy, see Introd., p. xiii.   5 Ac her forþ berað] With Hickes' reading *Ac her forþberað*.   *Fugelas singað*, there is no object for *forþberað* (or *forþ berað*, as most edd. read).   Most of the edd. assume the loss of two half-lines after *berað* and supply the gap in various ways: Rieger suggests *fyrdsearu rincas, fynd ofer foldan;* Grein (Beowulf) and Holthausen (1 ed.) supply *feorhgeniðlan, fyrdsearu fuslicu;* Bugge, Beitr. XII, 22f., *fyrdsearu rincas, flacre flanbogan;* Rieger, ZfdA. XLVIII, 9, accepts Bugge's *fyrdsearu rincas* for l. 5b, but would then begin a new sentence: [*Nalles her on flyhte*] *fugelas singað*, etc.   Kluge, Sedgefield, Chambers indicate the loss of two half-lines after *berað*, but supply nothing.   Other edd., without assuming a loss in the MS., emend l. 5a in various ways.   Grundtvig (1820) suggested

131

Ac hēr forþ fērað, with the subject (the enemy warriors) unexpressed; so also Holthausen (3 ed.) and Mackie. Grein (Bibliothek) and Schücking read *ac fēr* (= *fǣr*, "sudden attack") *forð berað;* Holthausen (4 ed.) reads *ac her forþ brecað*, again with the subject unexpressed. Klaeber follows the MS. reading, in spite of the lack of subject and object, and in the absence of a convincing emendation this seems as good a course as any; perhaps translate, "but here they are bearing forth [weapons, etc.]." An intransitive use of *beran* ("they are hurrying forth"), as proposed by Dickins, seems less probable. **5-6 fugelas ...grǣghama]** Bugge, Tidskrift for Philologi og Pædagogik VIII, 304, would translate *fugelas*, l. 5, not as "birds," but as "arrows"; in Beitr. XII, 22f., he supplies *flacre flanbogan* before *fugelas* (see the preceding note), "the birds of the arrow." Similarly Boer, ZfdA. XLVII, 140ff., takes *grǣghama*, l. 6, as referring to a coat of mail. With this interpretation, ll. 5*b*-7*a* all refer to the noise made by weapons of war, by arrows, a coat of mail, a spear, and a shield. But since the cries of birds and beasts of prey before a battle (as in Elene 27ff., Genesis 1983ff., Exodus 162ff., etc.) are a well defined convention in Anglo-Saxon poetry, it seems more natural to follow the literal interpretation here: *fugelas*, "birds," and *grǣghama*, "wolf." **5b singað]** Trautmann emends to *swinsað*, as a noun, "cry, noise," object of *berað*, l. 5*a*. Such a noun is not elsewhere recorded; it would, however, be similar in formation to *huntað*, *fiscað*, etc. But if *swinsað* can be a noun, so presumably can *singað*. **7 Nu scyneð þes mona]** Trautmann (Finn, p. 54) and Holthausen (1 ed.) read *þēr* (= *þǣr*) for *þes*, and Boer, ZfdA. XLVII, 143, would omit *þes* entirely. But for a defence of *þēs* in this context, see Klaeber, Archiv CXV, 181f. Trautmann also omits *Nu* in l. 7*b*, for metrical reasons, and so Holthausen (1 ed.). In later editions Holthausen follows Hickes. **8b-9]** As they stand in Hickes' text, these lines seem sufficiently clear, "Now arise deeds of woe which will carry out (i.e. bring to fruition) this hostility of the people." But Boer, ZfdA. XLVII, 143f., would read *þisses* for *ðisne*, l. 9*a*, and *wille* for *willað*, l. 9*b*, "Now arise deeds of woe which the hostility of this people [the Frisians] will carry out." Rieger, ZfdA. XLVIII, 10, retaining Hickes' reading, would take *weadǣda* as an instrumental gen. plur., with *ðe*, l. 9*a*, standing by itself as subject (as in Rune Poem 22). He would evidently translate: "Now they arise by means of deeds of woe, who wish to carry out this hostility of the people." Ten Brink, in Paul's Grundriss der germ. Philologie (1 ed.), Vol. II, Part 1, p. 545, would supply *þam* before *þe*, "Now arise deeds of woe for those who wish," etc. **10 onwacnigeað]** Trautmann (Beowulf) and Holthausen (4-7 ed?) read *onwæcnað*, apparently for metrical reasons. **11 habbað eowre linda]** Hickes' reading *landa* is obviously an error, and various emendations have been proposed. Bugge, Tidskrift for Philologi og Pædagogik VIII, 305, proposed *linda*, and so most later edd. Trautmann (Finn, pp. 40f.) emends to *hlencan*, and so Holthausen (1-3 ed.), Chambers, Dickins; see Exodus 218. Rieger, ZfdA. XLVIII, 10, would read *randas*, citing Maldon 20. Grein, Heyne, Wülker, Sedgefield read *handa;* this reading requires the further emendation of *habbað* to *hebbað*, and Grein, Heyne, Trautmann, and Sedgefield (2-3 ed.) read *hebbað*. Wülker's reading, *habbað eowre handa*, is meaningless unless some such adjective as *gearwe* is supplied in sense. The reading adopted in the present text, *habbað eowre linda*, has been objected to from the point of view of alliteration, but it gives good sense and is close to the text reported by Hickes.   **12** winnað] There has been some doubt whether Hickes' reading is *Windað* or *þindað*. The initial letter was undoubtedly intended for *W;* though it is different in shape from Hickes' usual runic capital *W* (the *wyn*-rune) and is somewhat like *þ*, the same form of the letter reappears in *Wrecten*, l. 25; see Dickins, note. Rieger, ZfdA. XLVIII, 10, and Mackie, reading *þindað* in Hickes' text, take it as meaning "swell (with courage)"; Trautmann, also reading *þindað* in Hickes, emends to *standað*. If we read *windað*, interpretation is very difficult (Dickins, "dash to the van"), and most edd. have preferred to emend to *winnað*, "fight."   onmode] So Trautmann, Holthausen, Schücking, Chambers, Mackie. See Genesis 1650, Exodus 203, etc. Other edd. read *on mode* as two words. If we read *on mode*, the alliteration is on the two verbs (both half-lines being A-type); if we read *onmode*, we have vocalic alliteration on *orde* and *onmode* (A3- and C-type half-lines). **13]** Line 13*a* is unusually long for a half-line, and Rieger, Grein (Beowulf) and Wülker make two half-lines out of it. They take *Ða aras mænig* as l. 13*b*, indicating the loss of a half-line before it; then *goldhladen ðegn* follows as the first half of the next line. Trautmann reads *Ða aras [of reste rondwigend] mænig* as l. 13, taking *goldhladen...swurde* as l. 14. Holthausen (1–3 ed.) reads *Ða aras [of ræste rumheort] mænig* for l. 13; in his 4th ed. he reads *Ða aras [hraðe]* for l. 13*a*, but in the later editions he returns to his original reading. In his l. 14*a*, he reads *goldhladen [gum]ðegn* for metrical reasons; see his note in ZfdPh. XXXVII, 123. All these arrangements of the text add an extra line to the poem. The other edd. retain Hickes' reading, as in the present text, in spite of the unusual length of l. 13*a*.   **15** Eaha] Möller, Das altengl. Volksepos, p. 86, calls the intervocalic *h* impossible, and would emend to *Eawa* as a more correct form; so also Trautmann, Holthausen. But on *Eaha* as a possible form of the name, see Bugge, Beitr. XII, 25, and especially Dickins, note, who cites similar forms with -*ch*-.   **17]** The punctuation in the text, with *Hengest* subject of *hwearf*, follows the practice of most recent edd. Jellinek, Beitr. XV, 428, would end the sentence with *sylf*, with no punctuation after *laste*, thus making *Garulf*, l. 18, the subject of *hwearf*. Holthausen (3–7 ed.) puts a colon after *sylf* and a period after *laste;* but just what the subject of *hwearf* would be in that case is not evident.   **18** Garulf] Trautmann, Chambers, Klaeber emend to *Garulfe*, as dative of person after *styrde*. See note on *styrde*, below. Most edd. assume that *Guðere* is nominative and *Garulf* (or *Garulfe*) dative, that is, that Guthere is restraining Garulf, though the reverse might be equally true, judging from the forms in Hickes' text. It is at least apparent that both Guthere and Garulf are Frisians. For the probable situation at this point in the poem, see Introd., p. xvi.   Guðere] So nearly all edd., as a proper noun; see the preceding note. But Grein (Bibliothek) and Boer, ZfdA. XLVII, 144ff., read *guðhere* as a common noun, "troop of warriors," taking *Garulf* as the subject of the sentence; i.e. Garulf warns the Frisian warriors not to expose themselves. Bugge, Beitr. XII, 25, would emend to *Guðdene* (a tribal name, like *Guð-Geatas*, etc.), as referring either to Sigeferth or to the Danes in general.

So also Jellinek, Beitr. XV, 428f., who thinks the *Guð̄dene* is Hengest.   styrde]
Hickes' reading *styrode*, from *styrian*, "to stir up, excite," gives just the opposite
meaning from the one required here.   Trautmann and most later edd., following a suggestion by Ettmüller, emend to *stȳrde*, from *stēoran*, *stȳran*, "to restrain"; see Bos.-Tol., p. 917, under *stēoran* II.   Mackie defends *styrode* as
meaning "exhorted."   **19** feorh] Holthausen, ZfdPh. XXXVII, 123, suggests
feoh.   See Beowulf 1210, where Sievers, Beitr. IX, 139, proposed a similar
emendation.   **20** bære] Proposed by Kemble (Beowulf, 1835) for Hickes'
bæran, and adopted by most modern edd.   The subject of *bære* is *he*, l. 19.
Grein (Bibliothek), retaining *bæran*, emends *he* to *hi;* Schücking also emends
he to *hie*, as referring to both Guthere and Garulf.   **22** he] Either Guthere or
Garulf, depending on the interpretation of l. 18; see the notes on that line.
eal] Trautmann, Holthausen emend to *ealle*, for metrical reasons.   But see
Maldon 256, *ofer eall clypode*.   **24** cweþ he] Omitted by Rieger, Trautmann,
Holthausen, Sedgefield.   The words are certainly extrametrical, and are without parallel in Anglo-Saxon poetry, although such indications of speaker are
frequently found in the Old Saxon Heliand (ll. 141, 222, 226, 259, etc.).   **25**
weana] See l. 3, note.   **26** heardra] So Kemble (Beowulf) and most later edd.,
for Hickes' form *heordra*.   **27** swæþer] "Whichever (of two things)," i.e. good
or evil (Chambers), victory or death (Klaeber).   **28** healle] Ettmüller suggested *wealle*, to alliterate with *wælslihta*, and so most later edd.; but Dickins,
Mackie, Klaeber, Sedgefield (Beowulf, 3 ed.) retain *healle*, in spite of the ab-
normal alliteration with *gehlyn*.   There is no mention of a wall or stockade here;
the fight is around the doors of the hall itself.   See l. 20.   **29** sceolde... handa]
Hickes' reading *Sceolde Celæs borð*.   *Genumon handa* makes no sense at all, and
various efforts have been made to restore the original text.   Line 29*b* offers
little difficulty, and all edd. since Grein read *cenum on handa* for this half-line.
In l. 29*a* the most usual emendation is Rieger's *cellod bord*, based on the half-line
clufon cellod bord in Maldon 283; but since the meaning of *cellod* in the latter
passage is not precisely known, mere emendation does not help us much.   Grein
(Bibliothek) reads *cēlod* ("keel-shaped"? Spr. I, 157); Jellinek, Beitr. XV, 431,
suggests *cēled*, "cooled," as referring to a shield covered with the dew of night.
Holthausen (1 ed.) reads *ceorlæs* (= *ceorles*), following his note in ZfdPh.
XXXVII, 123; in his 3d ed. he reads *clǣne*, in his 6th ed. *celced*, "chalked,"
whitened."   Sedgefield reads *celod*, but does not translate.   All other edd.
follow Rieger in reading *cellod*.   Trautmann (Finn, p. 46) explains *cellod* as a
Kentish form for *cyllod*, from *cyll*, "leather bag or bottle"; the meaning of
cellod bord would then be "shield covered with leather."   **30***a* banhelm]
Bugge, Beitr. XII, 26, would read *bārhelm*, "boar-helmet."   Reading *banhelm*
with Hickes, we can translate as "bone-protection," i.e. shield, or, as Dickins
takes it, "helmet decorated with bones (or horns)."   **30***b*] The treatment of
buruhðelu dynede as a parenthesis follows Schücking and Mackie.   **32**
eorðbuendra] To be translated not "of earth-dwellers" (the usual meaning of
eorð̄buend), but "of the dwellers of that country," i.e. of the Frisians.   Trautmann (Finn, p. 47) cites *eorð̄cyninges*, Beowulf 1155.   **34***a* hwearflicra hræw]
Hickes' impossible reading, *Hwearflacra hrær*, has undergone more varied

emendation than any other passage in the Fragment. The emendation to *hwearflicra hræw*, as in the text, was first made by Grundtvig (1820) and Grein (Beowulf), and has been more recently adopted by Kluge, Sedgefield, Mackie, and Klaeber. Mackie translates, "the corpses of the fleeting," i.e. the mortal ones. Klaeber suggests that *hwearflic* may mean either "agile" or "obedient." Holthausen (1 ed.) reads *Hwearflicra hræw*, but begins a new sentence with *Hwearflicra*, and reads *weardode* (with *hræfen* subject, *hræw* object) in l. 34*b*. See his note in ZfdPh. XXXVII, 124. Crawford, MLRev. XIX, 105, suggests *hwearflicra hræs* (= *hrēas*, "fell"), with *hwearflicra* (for *hweorflicra*, "transient, short-lived") parallel to *godra*, l. 33*b*. Jellinek, Beitr. XV, 431, would read *hwearf laðra hreas*, "caterva hostium cecidit"; similarly, Holthausen (2 ed.) reads *Hwearf blacra hreas*, "the troop of pale ones fell." Sedgefield, MLRev. XVI, 59, would read *hreas wlancra hræw*. Trautmann reads *hreaw-* (= *hræw-*) *blacra hwearf*, "die menge der totenbleichen," parallel to *godra fæla*, l. 33*b*. Kock, Anglia XLV, 126, suggests *hwearf flacra earn*, "the flickering eagle moved about"; similarly Holthausen, Anglia Beibl. XLIII, 256, *hwearf hlacra earn* (assuming an adjective **hlacor*, "screaming"), and so Holthausen (7 ed.). Bugge, Beitr. XII, 26ff., had proposed the reading *Hwearf flacra hræw hræfen fram oðrum*, i.e. the raven flew from one body to another. Chambers follows Bugge in l. 34*a*, but is more conservative in the second half-line, *Hwearf flacra hræw hræfen, wandrode*, "the quickly moving raven hovered over the corpses." Schücking (Dichterbuch and Beowulf, 12 ed.) reads *Hwearf flacra hræfn, [hungrig] wandrode*. In this embarrassment of critical riches a choice is difficult, but *hwearflicra hræw*, parallel to *godra fæla*, offers good sense with perhaps the least violence to Hickes' text.   **34b** wandrode] Trautmann emends to *wundrode*, i.e. the raven was amazed at the number of dead! See also the preceding note.   **36** Finnsburuh] Trautmann, Holthausen (1 ed.), Sedgefield read *Finnes buruh*, and similarly Magoun, ZfdA. LXXVII, 65f. (*Finns buruh*); Dickins reads *Finnesburuh* as one word.   **39** swetne] Hickes' text reads *Ne nefre swa noc hwitne medo. Sel forgyldan*. Most modern edd. follow Grein's emendation to *ne nefre swanas swetne medo sel forgyldan*. The emendation of *hwitne* to *swetne* had previously been made by Ettmüller, who, however, altered the text unnecessarily in other respects. Dickins, Mackie, Klaeber emend to *swanas*, with Grein, but retain *hwitne*. The chief objection to *swanas* is the fact that *swān* elsewhere in Anglo-Saxon means "herdsman"; nor does O.N. *sveinn* (influence of which has been suspected) usually mean "warrior," the sense required here. Rieger omits *swa noc* entirely and emends *hwitne* to *swetne*, thus reading *ne nefre swetne medo sel forgyldan*, the subject of *forgyldan* being carried over from *sixtig sigebeorna*, l. 38*a*. So also Trautmann, Holthausen (1 ed.), and Sedgefield (Beowulf, 3 ed., and Verse-Book). This seems to be the most satisfactory solution; Trautmann (Finn, p. 50) plausibly explains *swa noc* and *hwitne* as two separate attempts by a scribe to reproduce a partly legible *swetne* in his original. Holthausen (4 ed.) makes two lines:

> ne næfre swanas swetne medo[drinc]
> sel forgyldan [hira sincgifan],
> ðonne...

but such additions to the text are unnecessary.   **41**] As this line stands in Hickes, the alliteration is irregular, with *feol*, the alliterating word in l. 41*b*, coming on the second stress.   Line 28 may, however, serve as a parallel; see the note on this line.   If an emendation is to be made here, Holthausen's transposition (3–6 ed.) to *swa ne feol hyra nan* is the simplest possible change. So also Kock, Anglia XLIV, 97.   Holthausen (7 ed.) retains Hickes' reading in l. 41*b*, but emends *fif*, l. 41*a*, to *nigon!*   In ZfdPh. XXXVII, 124, Holthausen had suggested *niht fife*, l. 41*a*, for *fif dagas*.   Trautmann emends to read *Hig fuhton fif dagas,* [*ferhðgrimme hæleð, and niht eal-*]*swa: hyra nan oðfeol*.   Rieger and Holthausen (1 ed.) indicate the loss of two half-lines after *dagas*, but supply nothing.   **45** heresceorp unhror] Hickes' reading *Here sceorpum hror*, i.e. *heresceorpum hror*, "strong with war equipments," must refer back to *wund hæleð*, l. 43.   But Thorpe's emendation *heresceorp unhror*, "the weak war-gear," referring to the *byrne*, l. 44, seems to give somewhat better sense.   Holthausen (2–5 ed.), Sedgefield, Dickins, Mackie follow Hickes; Holthausen (1, 6, 7 ed.), Schücking, Chambers, Klaeber follow Thorpe.   Trautmann would read *heresceorp ahroren*, "(sein) heerkleid beschädigt."   ðyrel] So Trautmann, Holthausen, Sedgefield (2–3 ed.), Klaeber, for Hickes' *ðyrl*.   **46** Ða hine sona frægn] Holthausen (1 ed.) transposes to *Ða hine frægn sona*, but in later editions to *Ða frægn hine sona*, to regularize the alliteration.

NOTES ON WALDERE

Special abbreviations:

Bugge.   Tidskrift for Philologi og Pædagogik VIII, 72ff., 305ff.

Cosijn.   Verslagen en Mededeelingen der k. Akademie van Wetenschappen, Afd. Letterkunde, 3d Ser., XII, 56ff.

Heinzel.   Über die Walthersage (Vienna Sitzungsberichte, 1889).

Holthausen (1899).   Die altenglischen Waldere-Bruchstücke.

I

Waldere] For a description of the MS. and a discussion of the literary problems connected with the poem, see Introd., pp. xix ff.   In the text the separate line-numbering of the two fragments is retained, since the proper order of the fragments is not yet finally settled.   **I,1b** hyrde hyne georne] Generally taken as introducing the speech in ll. 2ff., "[Hildegyth] encouraged him eagerly." Cosijn, p. 68, suggests that the lost first half of the line contained the heroine's name.   Bugge, pp. 72f., would take l. 1*b* as part of Hildegyth's speech, describing the making of the sword Mimming, "[Weland] hardened it diligently." For the form of the name *Hildegyð*, see Introd., p. xxiv.   **I,2**] The *-s* of *Welande*[*s*], required by the sense, is no longer visible in the MS.   The letters *welande* come at the end of the first line of the MS. text, followed by a rubbed place in the parchment; *worc* is the first word of the next line.   This "handiwork of Weland" is the sword Mimming, mentioned in the next line.   For the form *worc*, see *hworfan*, l. 30.   **I,4** heardne] The MS. *hearne* (with a dot below *n*)

has been variously interpreted. Bugge, p. 73, takes *hearne* as a spelling variant
of *heardne*, citing *Heaðobearna*, Beowulf 2067; see also *Heaðabearna*, Beowulf
2037. Cosijn, p. 68, also takes the word as for *heardne*, but regards the MS.
hearne as a scribal error rather than as a spelling variant. Förster, Eng. Stud.
XXIX, 107f., suggests that the dot under *n* was intended as a mark of deletion,
and would read *hear[d]e;* this reading involves the assumption that the scribe,
after deleting *n*, meant to add *d* above the line but did not do so. Rieger had
previously taken *hearne* as for *hārne*. Recent edd., except Dickins and Norman,
emend to *heardne*. **I,6a** Ætlan ordwyga] "Champion of Attila" (Dickins),
"vorkämpfer im streite" (Trautmann, Bonner Beitr. V, 170f.), but perhaps
simply "leader, chief," like *ordfruma*, Beowulf 263. Heinzel, p. 5, would
translate *ordwyga* as "warrior," citing *æscwiga*, Beowulf 2042, *garwiga*, Beowulf
2674, 2811, etc. **I,6b**] All edd. restore *gy[t]*. **I,7**] The MS. reading *gedreosan
to dæge dryhtscipe* is evidently defective. Stephens supplied *feallan* after
dryhtscipe, to complete l. 7b, and so the earlier edd.; Dickins and Sedgefield also
adopt this reading. For the first half of l. 8, Grein (Beowulf) supplies *deor and
domgeorn;* Sedgefield (Verse-Book, p. 138) suggests *dom alicgan*, citing Beowulf
1528. But *to dæge*, l. 7, followed so closely by *se dæg*, l. 8, looks suspicious, and
Holthausen (1899), Kluge (3–4 ed.), Schücking, and Kock, JJJ., p. 77f., omit
to dæge, following a suggestion by Cosijn, p. 68; in this arrangement *gedreosan*,
dryhtscipe (with *dryhtscipe* parallel to *ellen*, l. 6) forms l. 7a, with *Nu* (or *Ac*)
is se dæg cumen taken as l. 7b. Cosijn suggests, as an alternative, that *gedreosan
to dæge dryhtscipe* may be taken as an expanded (three-stress) half-line. Trautmann, Bonner Beitr. V, 171, reading *ðus* for *ðin*, l. 6b, would emend to *gedreosan
to ðæs dryhtscipe*, translating, p. 185, "lass entfallen dir nicht so den tapfren
sinn." Trautmann (Beowulf) has the MS. *ðin* in l. 6b, but reads *gedreosan*,
þinne dryhtscipe for l. 7a. In both cases he takes *Nu is se dæg cumen* as l. 7b.
Holthausen (Beowulf, 4–7 ed.) reads

> gedreosan to dæge, [þinne] dryhtscipe,
> [deormod hæle!] Nu is se dæg cumen, etc.

Certainly something is wrong with the text here, and the omission of *to dæge*
gives the smoothest reading. On the other hand, it seems more likely that a
scribe has omitted something (after *dryhtscipe*) than that he has added a phrase
(*to dæge*) which was not in his copy. In view of the numerous possibilities,
the passage has been left unemended in the text. **I,8a**] Most recent edd.
restore *[nu]* before *is*, following Bugge, p. 73. Stephens' reading *ac* is less
probable; see Holthausen (1899), p. 5. **I,9** aninga] Trautmann would emend
to *earnigan* (Northumbrian *earniga*), as infinitive: "you must merit one of two
things." oðer twega] See Maldon 207. **I,10b**] The damaged word is
certainly to be restored to *l[an]ge*, and most edd. emend to *langne*, acc. sing.
masc., modifying *dom*. **I,12ff.**] The meaning is, "I cannot say that I have
ever seen you flee in battle." **I,15** on weal fleon] "Flee to the wall," i.e. to
shelter. See Beowulf 2956f., *beah...under eorðweall*. **I,18** feohtan] Here
and in l. 20 the edd. take *feohtan* as acc. sing. of the fem. *feohte*, "fight," rather
than as an infinitive. **I,19** mæl ofer mearce] The interpretation of this half-

line presents difficulties. Rieger took *mæl* as a figurative synonym for *feohte*, citing O.H.G. *mahal*, O.N. *mál*, "speech, meeting." Similarly Dickins, who cites O.N. *sœkja mál*, "to prosecute, press a suit." The corresponding Anglo-Saxon form is *mæðel* (see *meðelstede*, "battle-ground," Beowulf 1082), and Cosijn, p. 68, takes the MS. *mæl* as for *mæðel*. Bugge, p. 74, suggests *mæles ofer mearce*, with *mæl* = "time"; i.e. "beyond the proper time, too long." So also Kluge. The word *mæl* seems to be parallel to *feohtan*, regardless how we translate it. The phrase *ofer mearce* is probably best rendered "beyond the line" (Cosijn), i.e. "further and further," perhaps "without limit" (Sedgefield, Verse-Book, p. 139). Norman's interpretation of *mæl ofer mearce*, "a place over the boundary," that is, outside the fortification, seems less plausible. metod] "Fate" (Grein, Spr. II, 240) or "God" (Bugge, p. 74)? Bugge compares *ic ondræde me god* (as in the Anglo-Saxon translation of *deum...timeo*, Genesis xlii. 18), and would take *ic ðe metod ondred* as "I feared God for thee," or "I feared lest God be angry with thee." The meaning "God" here is perhaps established by the similar idea in l. 23b, "as long as God takes care of you"; see the note on that line.   **I,20** fyrenlice] "Vehemently, rashly" (Bos.-Tol., p. 352)? Or, less probably, from *fyren*, "fiery," i.e. in a fiery manner. Trautmann, Bonner Beitr. V, 173f., would emend unnecessarily to *fromlice*.   **I,21** æt ðam ætstealle] The meaning of *ætsteall*, found also in Guthlac 179, is not quite clear; in the Guthlac passage, *him to ætstælle...arærde Cristes rode*, it seems to mean "station, camp," and Gollancz, The Exeter Book, Part 1, p 115, translates *to ætstælle*, "to mark his station." The same meaning may be applied to the present passage; then *æt ðam ætstealle* means "at the battle-station" of the other man, that is, she fears that Waldere will give his opponent the choice of position. Trautmann, Bonner Beitr. V, 174, translates *ætsteall* simply as "battle-place." Sedgefield (Verse-Book) emends to *æscstealle*, citing (p. 139) *æscstede*, "battle-place."   **I,22** wigrædenne] Acc. sing., parallel to *feohtan*, l. 20. The meaning is probably the same as that of the uncompounded *wíg*, "warfare"; see Bos.-Tol., p. 1222. But Norman would take *wigrædenne* as an instrumental, "according to his plan of battle."   **I,23** ðenden ðin god recce] "As long as God cares for you," i.e. takes care of you. The suggestion by Trautmann, Bonner Beitr. V, 175, of *þæt* for *ðenden*, "so that God may receive you," does not improve the sense.   **I,24** Ne murn ðu, etc.] "Do not be concerned about your sword" (Cosijn, p. 69), i.e. trust your sword to do you good service.   **I,25** mid] According to Holthausen (1899), the final letter of this word in the MS. is *d*. The first two letters, as they appear in his facsimile, can be either *mi-* or *un-*. Dickins, Sedgefield, Norman read *unc*, placing it at the end of l. 25a, *gifeðe to geoce unc*. Other edd. read *mid*, at the beginning of l. 25b, as in the text.   **I,26** beot forbigan] "Humble [Guthhere's] boast," with *Guðhere*, l. 25, taken as dat. sing. Trautmann, Bonner Beitr. V, 175, reads *bælc*, "pride, arrogance," for the MS. *beot*, citing Genesis 54, Judith 267.   **I,27a**] The first word of this half-line is undoubtedly to be restored as [*mi*]*d*, though only the *d* is clear in the MS. Of the *u* of *unryhte*, only the second stroke is now clear, but there can be no doubt what the letter was.   **I,29** bega] The MS. reading, with *beaga* alliterating with itself, is highly questionable, and Dietrich (in

WALDERE   139

Müllenhoff, ZfdA. XII, 268) suggested *bega,* "of both," in l. 29*b.* Bugge, p. 75,
rejects *bega* as referring to three things, but, p. 306, points out other instances
in which "both" can refer to three. But in any case, since *beaga mænigo,* l. 29*a,*
and *syncfatum* probably refer to the same treasure, there are only two separate
things, the sword and the treasure, to which *bega* can refer; see Cosijn, p. 70.
Most recent edd. emend to *bega.* The emendation is perhaps unnecessary, as
Dickins and Norman say, but it improves the sense.   **I,30** hlafurd] Subject
of *sceal,* l. 29, and its dependent infinitives. Cosijn, p. 70, cites Beowulf 520f.
as a parallel. Trautmann unnecessarily emends to *hleoburg,* acc. sing.   **I,31**
ᛟ] For *eþel,* the usual meaning of this rune. See Rune Poem 71, and note.

II

II,1b -ce bæteran] Stephens' restoration, [*beadome*]*ce bæteran,* is impossible
metrically, but most edd. have restored [*me*]*ce.* See l. 6. Bugge, pp. 75f.,
pointing out that l. 2*a* presupposes a negative in l. 1, would restore the entire
line to read [*ne seah* (or *nat*) *ic mid mannum me*]*ce bæteran.* Norman restores
[*swil*]*ce,* taking the letters *swil-,* at the end of the narrow fragment of text
attached to fol. 1*a,* as the beginning of this word; see Introd., p. xx. So also
Leitzmann, Walther und Hiltgunt bei den Angelsachsen, p. 7. Such an arrangement is quite possible, but it gives a somewhat difficult meaning; see Holthausen
(1899), pp. 2–3. Klaeber, Eng. Stud. LXX, 334, suggests the further restoration to [*ne geseah ic æfre swil*]*ce bæteran.*   **II,2** hafa] Rieger, Sedgefield emend
to *hafu,* a more normal form.   **II,3** stanfate] Most of the earlier edd. interpreted as "stone-vessel," perhaps a jeweled casket in which the sword was
kept. But, as Dietrich first suggested (in Müllenhoff, ZfdA. XII, 269f.), the
word probably means "jeweled sheath," especially since M.H.G. *vaz* is found
in the sense of "sheath." See Dickins, note, and Koegel, Geschichte der
deutschen Litteratur, Vol. I, Part 1, p. 239. On the identity of the speaker of
these lines, see Introd., p. xxiv.   **II,4** hit] So most edd., following Rieger, for
the MS. *ic.* Trautmann, Bonner Beitr. V, 177, says that *hit* is impossible as
referring to the masculine *mece;* he suggests *hine,* but prefers to read *Ic wat
þæt geðohte* in l. 4*a* and to emend *selfum,* l. 5*a,* to *selfne,* object of *onsendon.* In
his Beowulf he reads *Ic wat, þone ðohte* in l. 4*a,* returning to the MS. *selfum* in
l. 5*a.* Dickins adopts Trautmann's suggestion of *hine* for *ic.* But in a new
sentence *hit* can refer to "sword" in general, without necessarily agreeing with
mece. Norman, reading [*swil*]*ce* in l. 1*b* (see note on that line), suggests that
swilce alliterated with *sweord* in l. 1 and that the neuter *hit* refers back to *sweord.*
II,5 onsendon] For *onsendan,* infinitive.   **II,6** mid him] That is, *mid ði mece,*
l. 6*a.*   **II,7** golde gegirwan] Cosijn, p. 70, suggests *gegirwed,* and so Kluge
(3–4 ed.) and Holthausen (Beowulf, 4–7 ed.). Trautmann, Bonner Beitr. V,
177f., proposed *wolde gegildan, iulean sellan,* but in his Beowulf he restores the
MS. *golde,* taking his emendations *gegildan* and *sellan* as dependent on *onsendon,*
l. 5. Binz, ZfdPh. XXXVI, 507, suggests *golde gegirwad gimma iulean,* "a
reward of gems, adorned with gold." But, as Norman points out, Binz's
reading is unlikely if only because of the double alliteration in the second half-

line.   The MS. reading makes satisfactory sense if we take *iulean genam* (the subject of which must be Widia) as a parenthesis.   Then *gegirwan* is parallel to *onsendon*, l. 5*a*.   Dickins takes all of ll. 7*b*–9*b* as a parenthesis, with difficulties of interpretation.   **II,10*a***] The reading of the MS. seems to be *gefe*[.]*ld*, the lost letter evidently being *a*.   Since a noun *gefeald* is not elsewhere recorded, any attempt to assign a meaning must rest upon conjecture, and most edd. emend to *geweald*.   Sedgefield retains *gefeald* as "dwelling place?"   According to Binz, Literaturblatt XXI, 244, the MS. really has *geweald*.   Trautmann, Bonner Beitr. XI, 133ff., would emend to *ðurh fiþera geweald*, as possibly referring to a pair of wings made by Widia for Theodric; but he admits there is nothing in heroic legend to substantiate his reading.   **II,11*a***] The restoration to *maðe*[*e*]*lode* is obvious.   **II,12**] The MS. has *hilde frore*, with no sign of a loss.   Bugge, p. 77, suggested *hildefromre*, "battle-bold," dat. sing., modifying *handa*.   But all edd. adopt Müllenhoff's emendation, ZfdA. XII, 270, to *hildefrofre*, "battle-comfort," object of *hæfde*.   **II,13** guðbilla gripe] The meaning of this phrase is somewhat obscure.   Dietrich (in Müllenhoff, ZdfA. XII, 270) suggested "the thing gripped by swords," i.e. a shield, in which case *hildefrofre*, l. 12, would mean "shield" instead of "sword," as it is usually translated.   Heinzel, p. 10, suggested that *gripe* is the same word as O.N. *gripr*, "jewel"; then *guðbilla gripe* would be similar in meaning to *irena cyst*, Beowulf 673, etc.   Cosijn, p. 71, suggests that the phrase means "sword-cut," and by extension of meaning "a cutting sword."   Dickins accepts Cosijn's explanation and translates, "his trenchant blade."   Trautmann reads *guðbill on gripe*, which gives excellent sense at the cost of a rather simple emendation. Sedgefield's explanation, "the grasp of a sword," or perhaps "handle of a sword," requires us to take the plural *guðbilla* as a singular, or to emend, with Wyatt, to *guðbillas* (i.e. *guðbilles*) *gripe*.   The Mod. Eng. word *grip*, in the sense of "handle," is not recorded by the N.E.D. before the nineteenth century, but it may have existed earlier.   None of the proposed explanations of *guðbilla gripe* is entirely satisfactory.   **II,14ff.**] That is, "You expected that Hagena would do battle with me and would separate me from foot-battle," or, as we would say, "put me hors de combat."   In the MS., it is not quite clear whether the first letter preserved in [. .]*ðewigges* is *d* or *ð*.   According to Holthausen (1899), there are no traces of a cross-stroke, but Norman gives . . *ðe wigges* as the MS. reading.   In any case, the alliteration points the way to the proper restoration, [*fe*]*ðewigges*.   Trautmann thinks that *and getwæmde feðewigges* is too long for a half-line; he would omit *gefremede and*, thus reading:

> þæt me Hagenan hand   hilde getwæmde,
> feðewigges,

with *hilde* and *feðewigges* both genitives after *getwæman*.   So also Kluge (3–4 ed.), Schücking.   **II,18** Standeð] So Müllenhoff, ZfdA. XII, 269, and all later edd. except Norman, who retains the MS. *standað* and explains it, p. 6, as a Northumbrian form of the 3d pers. sing.   **II,19** geapneb] For possible interpretations of this word, see Dickins, note ("broad-bossed"), and Hoops, Eng. Stud. LXIV, 204 ("mit strotzendem Antlitz," or "breitgestirnt").   Grein,

Spr. I, 496, suggested *geaþueb* (= *geaþweb*). Trautmann, Bonner Beitr. V, 180, emends *geaþneb* to *gegerwed* (for *gegyrwed*), citing Riddle 20,2. In Bonner Beitr. XI, 137, and in his Beowulf he emends to *gearwod*. **II,20** ealles unscende] "Noble in every way." **II,22** Ne bið fah wið me] "It will never prove false to me," referring to the corselet. So Dickins, Sedgefield (Verse-Book) interpret the passage, and Cosijn, p. 72, indicates a similar rendering, "it shall never be an enemy to me." Stephens' emendation of the MS. *he* to *ne* has been followed by most later edd., since a negative seems necessary here. Holthausen (1899) emends *fah* to *flāh*, "treacherous." No such word as *flāh* is recorded elsewhere in Anglo-Saxon, but O.N. *flár* has a metaphorical sense of "false, treacherous"; see Cleasby-Vigfusson, Icelandic-English Dict., p. 159. Wyatt accepts *flah*. Trautmann emends to *ne bioð fea wið me*, "not a few (enemies, referring back to *feondum*, l. 22) are against me," though the immediate relevance of such a remark is not evident. **II,23a**] The MS. has *þoñ* (for *þonne*), followed by not more than two illegible letters at the end of the line; the first letters in the following line are *un mægas*. Various attempts have been made to read the illegible letters. Bugge, p. 306, would read *oŋ*, as for *ong*, taking these letters with the letters *un* in the next line as *ongun* = *ongum*, dat. plur. of *onga*, "arrow"; see Riddle 23,4. But the symbol *ŋ* for *ng* is not Anglo-Saxon, though it is found in Old Norse MSS. According to Holthausen (1899), there is an *m*, or the remains of *nu*, at the end of the line; according to Norman, the last letter in the line looks like *s*. Editorial practice seems, however, to be based on conjecture rather than on attempts to read the MS.: Holthausen (1899), Trautmann (Bonner Beitr. V, 186), Wyatt, Schücking read *þonne* [*nu*] *unmægas;* Trautmann (Beowulf) reads *þon* [*me*] *unmægas;* Holthausen (Beowulf, 6–7 ed.) reads *þonne* [*mec*] *unmægas.* The restoration of *mec* (or *me*) would supply a needed object for *ongynnað*, if there were any warrant for it in the MS. Kluge, Dickins, Sedgefield (Verse-Book) omit the doubtful letters entirely, reading *þonne unmægas;* Norman indicates an omission in his text, but does not attempt to supply it. It is of course also possible that the illegible letters were actually erased by the scribe. **II,23b** ongynnað] Apparently without either a direct object or a dependent infinitive. The reading *þonne* [*mec*] *unmægas* in l. 23a (see the preceding note) would supply a direct object, and for *onginnan*, "attack" see Psalms 85,13,2; 123,2,1. But *mec* (or *me*) does not seem to be the MS. reading in l. 23a. Trautmann emends *gemetað*, l. 24a, to *gemetan*, dependent on *ongynnað*, and so Kluge (3–4 ed.); but according to Horn, Anglia XXIX, 129, *onginnan* is found only with simple verbs, as a device for indicating perfective meaning. If *ongynnað* is to be taken by itself, in an intransitive meaning, Sedgefield's translation (Verse-Book, p. 139) of *eft ongynnað* as "renew their tricks" seems a possible way out of the difficulty. **II,26a** recon] Dietrich (in Müllenhoff, ZfdA. XII, 272f.), Grein, Kluge (3–4 ed.) read *reccend*, "ruler"; Trautmann reads *rēcend*, "protector." But *recon*, as for *recen*, "swift, prompt," parallel to *rædfest*, gives unexceptionable sense. **II,26b**] The restoration to *ryh*[*t*]*a* is obvious. **II,27ff.**] In these concluding lines of the poem, both meaning and sentence-division are very obscure. With the MS. reading of l. 28b, *he þær gearo findeð*, there is no object for *findeð*.

Rieger and Trautmann (Bonner Beitr. V, 186) assume the loss of a line after l. 28; Trautmann, Bonner Beitr. XI, 137f., would either supply *hie* after *he* in l. 28*b* or emend *he* to *hie*. Sedgefield (Verse-Book, p. 140) would take *þonne*, l. 30, as meaning "more than"; he describes such an omission of *ma* as frequent, but does not cite any parallels. Sedgefield's interpretation calls for a comma instead of a semicolon after *geðenceð*, l. 29*b*. Other edd. leave l. 28*b* unaltered, with either a semicolon or a period after *geðenceð*, in spite of the difficulty of construction. But *findeð* must once have had an object, and the assumption of a line lost from the text after l. 28 seems the simplest solution. Trautmann, Bonner Beitr. XI, 137f., reading *hie* in l. 28*b*, begins a new sentence with *Gif*, l. 29*a*, supplies *he* after *Gif*, and emends *ær*, l. 29*b*, to *are*, "favors," parallel to *earnunga*. But l. 29 seems to go with what precedes; that is, a man finds help ready there if he has given thought to his deserts. The reference of ll. 30–31 would perhaps be clearer if more of the text were preserved.

NOTES ON THE BATTLE OF MALDON
1–100

The Battle of Maldon] For a discussion of the literary and historical problems raised by this poem, see Introd., pp. xxvi ff. The references to "MS." in the following notes are to MS. Rawlinson B203, not to Hearne's printed text. **1 brocen wurde**] For the probable extent of the lost matter at the beginning of the poem, see Introd., p. xxviii. Klaeber, Anglia LIII, 228, suggests a tentative reconstruction of l. 1 to [*ær se burhstede a*]*brocen wurde*, the *burhstede* then being the town of Maldon. **2 Het**] The subject is Byrhtnoth, the *eorl* of ll. 6, 28. **hwæne**] Rieger reads *gehwæne*, "each one." But the pronoun *hwæne*, "some one," evidently refers to the *Offan mæg*, l. 5. **3 afysan**] Transitive, and parallel to *forlætan*, l. 2; see *fysde*, l. 269, and Klaeber, Eng. Stud. LV, 393. **4 hicgan to handum, etc.**] "To put his mind on his hands (i.e. the use of his hands in battle) and on high courage"; see Klaeber, Eng. Stud. LV, 393. Compare l. 128, and also Exodus 218, Finnsburg 11. **5 þa**] So most edd., for the *þ* in Hearne's text. Grein, Körner omit the word, beginning the line with *þæt*. **7 handon**] The late ending *-on* for *-um* is especially frequent in this text; see *leodon*, l. 23, *Denon*, l. 129, *Myrcon*, l. 217, *Norðhymbron*, l. 266, *hwilon*, l. 270, *wordon*, l. 306. **leofne**] So the MS., not *leofre* as in Hearne's text; see Introd., p. xxvii. **10 wige**] The MS. indicates only two or three letters lost between *w* and *ge*, not four as in Hearne's text. Most edd. restore to *wige*, but Gordon to *wigge*. **11 Eac him**] "Besides him." See *eac þissum idesum*, Genesis 2502, *eac gode sylfum*, Guthlac 206. **15 bradswurd**] The alliteration favors a compound here, and so Holthausen, Anglia Beibl. XXI, 13. The edd. read *brad swurd* as two words. **20 randas**] So all edd., except Wülker and Laborde, who retain the MS. *randan*. **22 hæfde þæt folc**] Holthausen, Anglia Beibl. XXXII, 82, would read *þæt folc hæfde*, for metrical reasons. **29**] Rieger reads *me sendon sæmen snelle to þe*, and in l. 32 *þæt ge mid gafole forgyldon garræs þisne*, to regularize the alliteration. **31 beagas wið gebeorge**] "Rings (i.e. treasure)

in exchange for protection"; for this meaning of *wið*, see ll. 35, 39.   **33 þon]**
The edd. all emend to *þonne*, but *þon* is a permissible variant of *þonne;* see Riddle
54,9, note, in Records III, The Exeter Book, p. 349.   hilde] The edd. all
restore . . *ulde* to *hilde*, as required by the alliteration. The *u* of the MS.
evidently represents the second vertical stroke of *h* followed by *i*.   dælon]
See Beowulf 2534.   **34b]** "If you are rich to that extent"; see Klaeber, MLN.
XX, 32.   **45a** Gehyrst] So the MS. and Hearne, not *gehyrt* as reported by
Wülker.   **45b]** Rieger transposes to *hwæt segeð þis folc*, to regularize the
alliteration, and so also Holthausen, Anglia Beibl. XXXII, 82.   **48** heregeatu]
That *heregeatu* is "an ironic use of the legal term 'heriot' " is suggested by
Brett, MLRev. XXII, 260, who cites the similar use of irony in Beowulf 154ff.
But even without any reference to heriot, the ironical effect of the litotes is
unmistakable, "the war-equipment which will not help you any in battle."
See Klaeber, Anglia LIII, 228. We should however expect the acc. sing. form
heregeatwe, and so Kluge (3–4 ed.). The other edd. retain *heregeatu*.   **52**
gealgean] For *ge-ealgian*, "to defend." See *gealgodon*, Brunanburh 9 (MS. D).
54 Feallan sceolon] Holthausen, Anglia Beibl. XXI, 13, would supply *nu* after
sceolon, for metrical reasons.   **55–58]** On the irony in these lines, see Klaeber,
Anglia LIII, 227.   **68** Pantan] The proper form of the nom. sing. of this name
is *Pante* (weak feminine), and not *Panta*, as most edd. give it. See E. Ekwall,
English River-Names (Oxford, 1928), pp. 319–320; P. H. Reaney, Place-Names
of Essex (Cambridge, 1935), pp. 9–10.   prasse] The exact meaning of the
word *prass* is uncertain, but in the four other instances of its occurrence in
Anglo-Saxon (Wulfstan, ed. Napier, 148, 32; Ælfric's Lives of Saints, ed. Skeat,
I, 488, 26; II, 86, 302; II, 182, 208), it appears to mean "pomp, display,"
but in a disparaging sense, "wicked pomp." Here the word is applied both to
the East Saxons and to the invading Norsemen, and may mean nothing more
than "battle-array," as Sedgefield glosses it. Gordon, p. 76, glosses the word
as "proud array."   **75b]** Ettmüller, Rieger transpose to *se wæs Wulfstan haten*,
and Holthausen, Anglia Beibl. XXI, 13, to *Wulfstan wæs haten* (omitting *se*),
to regularize the alliteration.   **84** hi] Referring here to the Norsemen. In
l. 84b, the word *georne*, "eagerly," is not what we should expect, and it may be
that we should emend to *geare*, "certainly, clearly."   **86** laðe] So the MS.,
not *luðe* as in Hearne's text; see Introd., p. xxvii.   **87]** upgang] So Rieger and
most later edd. But Körner, Kluge, Wülker, Wyatt, Schücking, Laborde
retain the MS. *upgangan*. There is, however, no evidence, outside of this
single instance, for a weak noun *up(p)gange*, "ascent."   **97** west] The reading
of the MS. is ambiguous, either *west* or *pest;* but certainly *west* was intended.

101–200

103 feohte] So Ettmüller, Grein, and later edd., except Wülker, for the MS.
fohte. In writing *fohte*, the scribe may have been misled by the form *getohte*
in the next line.   **106** Þær] The early edd. read *þa* for *þær;* but see l. 116.
hremmas] The MS. and Hearne's text have *hremmas*, not *bremmas* as reported
by Wülker and Sedgefield.   **109** gegrundene] Holthausen, Anglia Beibl. XXI,

13, would supply the adverb *grimme* before *gegrundene;* see Ruin 14. Ettmüller had previously supplied *golde*. But for other half-lines of this type, see Riddles 25,6*a*; 27,7*a*. **122** stemnetton] "Stood fast." See Gordon, note. Sedgefield's suggestion, "fought in their turn," seems less probable. stiðhicgende] So the MS., not *stið hugende* as in Hearne's text; see Introd., p. xxvii. **123** hysas] The form *hyssas* would be more regular; see ll. 112, 169. **126** wigan] Kock, Anglia XLIV, 248, suggests taking this word as dat. sing., parallel to *men*. But the usual interpretation, as nom. plur., parallel to *hysas*, seems more natural. Grein-Köhler, p. 794, takes *wigan* as infinitive, parallel to *gewinnan*. **134** superne gar] A spear thrown from the south? But the Norsemen were presumably to the north of the English; see Introd., p. xxxi. Perhaps a spear imported from the South of Europe, and therefore superior to the native weapons? See Gordon, note. **137** sprengde] Transitive, "caused the spear to spring"; see Klaeber, Eng. Stud. LV, 394. **147** modi] For the spelling without final *g*, see *frymdi*, l. 179, *formoni*, l. 239. **149** drenga] The word *dreng*, not elsewhere recorded in Anglo-Saxon, is a loan-word from O.N. *drengr*, "young man," and is therefore appropriately used to designate the Norse invaders. **160** gefecgan] For *gefeccan, gefetian,* "fetch." **172**] The transcript does not indicate any loss in the MS. at this point. Ettmüller and Grein, taking *He to heofonum wlat* as the second half of l. 172, supply *heard heaðurinc* before it, as the first half-line, continuing the sense of l. 171. Laborde supplies *wigendra hleo* as the first half-line. Körner, Wülker supply *hleoðrode eorl* after *wlat*. Holthausen, Anglia Beibl. XXI, 13, suggests *hæleð gemælde*, apparently as the first half of the line, citing l. 230, *Offa gemælde*. Whether a half-line is missing here at all is at least doubtful; and in any case it is impossible to be sure whether a first half-line or a second half-line is to be supplied. **173** Geþancie] So Kluge, Bright, Sedgefield, Gordon, for the MS. *geþance*. Ettmüller, Rieger, Sweet, Kluge, Bright, Sedgefield, Gordon supply *Ic* before the verb; Grein also supplies *Ic*, but reads *þance* for the MS. *geþance*. Sweet (4 ed.) reads *Ic þe þancige*. **179** ferian] For this intransitive use of *ferian*, as the equivalent of *fēran*, see Genesis 2100, Riddle 52,1 *(fergan)*. **183** Apparently the Wulfmær of l. 155. Another warrior of the same name has been mentioned in l. 113. begen] To provide the missing alliteration in this line, Grein and most later edd. read *bewegen*, "slain," for the MS. *begen*. Unfortunately such a meaning is not recorded for the verb *bewegan*, which elsewhere means "surround"; see Fortunes of Men 42. See, however, the phrase *forwegen mid his wæpne*, Maldon 228. It may well be that *begen* is a scribal reminiscence of the word *begen* in the preceding line; but in that case *forwegen* (or the inflected form *forwegene*) would be a more satisfactory emendation than *bewegen*. Gordon, note, also suggests *on (þam) wæle*, citing ll. 279, 300. As the line stands in the MS., it makes good sense if not good verse. **186** þær wearð Oddan bearn] The plural verb *wurdon* in the MS. here, followed by *Godric* and the singular verbs in the next line, is difficult to explain, unless the names *Godric*, l. 187, and *Godrine* and *Godwig*, l. 192, be taken as forming together (in sense, if not grammatically) a plural subject of *wurdon*. It seems much more natural to emend to the singular *wearð* (taking *bearn* as singular), and so Kock, JJJ., p. 9, and Holthausen,

Anglia Beibl. XXXII, 82.   See ll. 237f., *Godric...*, *earh Oddan bearn*.   Sedgefield, p. 37, suggests *wurde* for the MS. *wurdon*, though how a subjunctive would
be suitable here is not apparent.   **189** þe ahte his hlaford] Rieger transposes
to *þe his hlaford ahte*, to regularize the alliteration, and so also Holthausen,
Anglia Beibl. XXXII, 82.   But there are other cases of irregular alliteration in
this poem (see the notes on ll. 29, 45*b*, 75*b*).   It is also possible that the poet
intended the alliteration of *eoh* and *ahte;* for a similar alliterative pattern, see l.
22.   **192** Godrine] No such personal name as *Godrine* is recorded in Anglo-
Saxon, and unless we read *Godrȳne* with Ettmüller, it seems extremely unlikely
that such a name ever existed.   On the proper form of the name here, the edd.
divide: Sweet, Körner, Bright emend to *Godrinc* (assuming that a final *c* was
miscopied as *e* in Elphinston's transcript); Rieger and the other edd. read
Godwine (assuming a *w* misread as *r*).   That *Godwine* was a very frequent name
in Anglo-Saxon England is attested by the number of persons by that name
listed in Searle, Onomasticon Anglo-Saxonicum, pp. 264–266.   No other
instance of *Godrinc* is reported by Searle, but it is a possible name, and except
for its similarity to *Godric*, there is no reason why it should not be the name
intended here.   In view of the double possibility, no alteration has been made
in the text.   **198** on dæg ær] "Early on the same day"; see Kock, JJJ., p. 9,
who cites Riming Poem 45.   **200** modiglice] So Bright and Sweet (4 ed.)
for the MS. *modelice*, an impossible form.   Thorpe, Ettmüller, and Sweet (1 ed.)
had read *modlice*, and so Holthausen, Anglia Beibl. XXI, 13, for metrical
reasons.   manega] The form *manege* (nom. plur. masc.) would be more
regular, and so Ettmüller.

201–325

201 æt þearfe] The MS. has *þe eft æt þære*, the noun being omitted.   Rieger,
Wülker, Kluge, Sedgefield, Schücking supply *þearfe* after *þære*, which satisfies
all the requirements of sense and meter.   But the article form *þære* does not
seem to belong here, and nowhere else do we find *þearf* used with the article in
this way.   See l. 307, below, and Beowulf 1477, 2694.   It seems better, therefore, to take the MS. *þære* as a corruption of *þearfe*, reading *þe eft æt þearfe*, as
in the text.   So Grein, Laborde, Gordon.   **212** Gemunan þa mæla] The MS.
has *ge munu þa mæla*.   Grein and most later edd. emend *ge munu* to the imperative *gemunað*.   But the 1st pers. plur. imperative form *gemunan*, as in
Christ and Satan 201, 206, makes equally good sense; and from the paleographical point of view it is less difficult to explain the loss of a final *-n* than of
a final *-ð*.   Jespersen, Nordisk Tidsskrift for Filologi, 3d Ser., I, 126f., objects
to the article *þa*, and would read *gemunaþ a mæla* (gen. plur.).   Sweet (4 ed.),
Wyatt, Gordon read *Gemunað þara mæla*.   But *þa mæla* is the correct acc.
plur. form of the feminine *mæl*, "speech," for which see Holthausen, Altengl.
etymol. Wörterbuch, p. 211 (under *mæl* 4).   **224**] Holthausen, Eng. Stud. LI,
181, would rearrange this line to read *he wæs min ægðer mæg and hlaford*, to
regularize the alliteration.   Ettmüller had suggested *mandryhten* for the MS.
hlaford.   **228–230**] Rieger and Sedgefield place only a comma after *eodon*,

l. 229, taking *Offa*, l. 230, as the subject of *Ongan*, l. 228. The traditional
punctuation, with a full stop after l. 229, has been preferred in the text. The
words *Ongan ... manian*, l. 228, must refer to Ælfwine; see *þu, Ælfwine, hafast ...
gemanode*, l. 231.   **237** godswurd] Best taken as a compound; see l. 15, note.
239 formoni] "Very many (a man)," with the intensifying prefix *for-* (also found
in *foreaðe*, "very easily," *foroft*, "very often)." So Körner, Wülker, Kluge,
Laborde, Gordon. Other edd. read *for moni* as two words. But the sense
requires the compound, although the alliteration should be on *m*.   **242**
scyldburh tobrocen] Holthausen, Anglia Beibl. XXXII, 82, would transpose to
tobrocen scyldburh, to regularize the alliteration.   **249** embe] Grein reads *on*,
without comment.   **257** wræce] The MS. has *wręce*, not *wræce* as in Hearne's
text; see Introd., p. xxvii.   **270** on bord] M. Deutschbein, Zur Entwicklung
des engl. Alliterationsverses (Halle, 1902), p. 46, would read *to borde*, for metrical
reasons, and so Holthausen, Anglia Beibl. XXI, 13.   **271**] Unless we allow
the alliteration of *st* with *s*, it is doubtful whether this line ever had any alliteration. The use of end-rime here may be an anticipation of the rimed poetry
of the 11th century; see Kluge, Beitr. IX, 445ff. In l. 282 we find end-rime
(*broðor : oþer*) with alliteration.   **274** gearo] So the MS., not *gearc* as in
Hearne's text; see Introd., p. xxvii.   **276** leg] For *læg*, and the older edd. and
Sedgefield emend to *læg;* but for the *e*, see *wrec*, l. 279.   **279** læge] The MS.
has *lęge*, not *læge* as in Hearne's text; see Introd., p. xxvii.   **287–288**] The
transposition of these two lines by Zernial in his translation is uncalled for.
The *Gaddes mæg* is evidently Offa; see Klaeber, Eng. Stud. LV, 390.   **288**
Offa forheawen] Rieger reads *forheawen Offa*, to regularize the alliteration.
292 crincgan] Whether the MS. *crintgan* is to be emended to *cringan* or to
crincgan is not a question of great importance; but *crincgan* is more likely on
paleographical grounds (with the *t* of the MS. form taken as an error for *c*)
and has been preferred by most edd.   **300** Wigelines] Laborde, Gordon emend
to *Wigelmes* (= *Wighelmes*), following the suggestion by Sedgefield, p. 38.
But Eckhardt, Eng. Stud. XXXII (1903), 348, explains *Wigelin* as a diminutive
form in *-lin* of some compound with *Wīg-* (such as *Wigbeald* or *Wīghelm*).
He cites also the names *Bēslin, Cēawlin, Hugelin,* and *Tidlin* (Searle, Onomasticon Anglo-Saxonicum, pp. 105, 127, 304, 453). There is some difficulty about
the identity of the son of Wigelin, since Wistan (who might logically be so
identified) is described in l. 298 as the son of Thurstan.   **315** A mæg gnornian]
Rieger reads *mæg gnornian a*.

NOTES ON THE POEMS OF THE
ANGLO-SAXON CHRONICLE

1. The Battle of Brunanburh (937)

The Battle of Brunanburh] For a description of the MSS. and a discussion of
the literary and historical problems raised by the Chronicle poems, see Introd.,
pp. xxxii ff.   **1** Her] The regular formula for the beginning of an entry in the
Chronicle. The word *Her* is not necessary for the meter here, but in Corona-

tion of Edgar 1 it is required by the meter.   5 ymbe] For the use of *ymbe* here, Campbell compares Chronicle 777 A: *Her Cynewulf and Offa gefuhton ymb Benesingtun.*   Brunanburh] For the proper form of this name, see Introd., p. xxxviii.   B's reading is impossible to make out in the MS., but there seems to be room for two *n*'s in the middle of the word.   6 lafan] A's reading *lafan* is a late variant form, with weakened ending, of the dat. plur. *lafum* found in B, C, and D.   In view of the late and generally nonliterary character of this part of the Chronicle, it seems advisable to let such forms stand.   See below, ll. 24 (*mylenscearpan*), 43 (*wundun*).   7–8 swa him...cneomægum] "As it was natural to them from their [royal] lineage."   11 leoda] Nom. plur. of the feminine *lēod*, "people, nation."   Both *leoda* (as in A) or *leode* (as in the other MSS.) are permissible forms.   12 dænnede] The interpretation of this word has caused much controversy.   The second *n* of A's reading *dænnede*, added above the line, seems to be in the same or a contemporary hand.   The spelling of *dænnede* with two *n*'s is also supported by the readings *dennade, dennode,* in the other MSS.   The verb *dennian,* "to become slippery," given by Bos.-Tol., p. 200, Grein-Köhler, p. 115, is unsupported by other evidence, but is favored by Ekwall, English Studies XXI, 219f., and Holthausen, Altengl. etymol. Wörterbuch, p. 72.   The early edd. read *dæniede* in MS. A, and Rieger explained it as for *dengede, dengode,* "manured," from a verb *dengan, dengian,* a variant of *dyngan.*   So also Ten Brink, Geschichte der engl. Lit. I (2d ed., Strassburg, 1899), 108, "das Feld wurde mit dem Blute der Männer gedüngt."   Heiss, MLN, XV, 484f., suggested *dēanian, dīenan,* "to steam," citing Gothic *dauns,* "odor."   Björkman, Archiv CXVIII, 384ff., read *dyn(n)ede,* "das Feld brauste von dem Blute der Männer."   Ashdown, Review of Eng. Studies V, 324ff., would also read *dynede,* but takes l. 12*b* as a parenthesis; see the next note.   But Beowulf 2558, *hruse dynede,* cited by Björkman, is hardly a close parallel in meaning.   The form *dynede* would also make the half-line too short, and Klaeber, in Anglica II (Leipzig, 1925), 1, note 2, would assume the formation, beside *dynnan* and *dynian,* of a new verb *dynnian, dennian.*   Sedgefield (1908), p. 39, would emend to *ðānode,* "became wet," from the adjective *ðān,* "moist."   So also Schlutter, Anglia XLVII, 255ff., *ðēnode, ðǣnode,* from *ðēnian, ðǣnian,* with the same meaning as Sedgefield's *ðānode.*   The form *ðāniaþ,* "madescunt," cited by Bos.-Tol., p. 1037 (under *þānian*), supports Sedgefield's reading, but *þǣnie,* also cited, is an error; see Campbell, p. 102.   Körner, translating "klatschte," i.e. "resounded" (*dynede*), also suggested *dunnode,* "became dark," and so also Holthausen, Anglia Beibl. III, 239, Anglia Beibl. XXXI, 256, and Campbell in his text.   For *dunnian,* apparently intransitive, see Boethius (ed. Sedgefield), 10,6.   Either *dunnode* or Sedgefield's *ðanode* is defensible, but in view of other possibilities the text has not been emended.   An excellent survey of critical opinion on this passage up to 1911 is given by Tupper, JEGPh. XI, 91–95.   13 secga swate] A's reading, *secgas hwate,* is evidently an error, and the reading of the other MSS. has been adopted in the text.   So also most edd.   Ashdown, Review of Eng. Studies V, 324ff., retains *secgas hwate,* parallel to *Hettend, leoda,* and *scipflotan,* with l. 12*b* taken as a parenthesis.   16 oð sio] B's reading *þ seo* suggests the possibility that the original text had *oðþæt* *sio* or *oðþæt seo.* Ettmüller, Grein, Wülker, and Sedgefield (1908) read *oðþæt* for *oð.*   18 ageted] B's reading *forgrunden*, though admirable in sense, is inexplicable except as an intentional emendation of *ageted*, which the scribe may not have known. See Campbell, p. 103. For *agetan*, "pierce," see Kock, JJJ., p. 1.   guma norþerna] The singular form in A agrees better with l. 17 than the plurals in the other MSS.   20 sæd] "Weary, sated." Grein reads *sæd*, "seed," but in Spr. II, 394, glosses under *sæd*. Sedgefield (1908) reads *sæd*, evidently "the seed of battle." But see Klaeber, MLN. XX, 31. Compare also *hilde* (gen.) *sædne*, Beowulf 2723, *beadoweorca sæd*, Riddle 5,2.   22 on last legdun] This construction, with intransitive *lecgan*, is not found elsewhere in Anglo-Saxon, but the meaning obviously is "followed in the tracks of the hostile peoples." The phrase *lastas lecgan* (as in the modern colloquial expression "to make tracks") is found four times in Genesis A; see Bos.-Tol., p. 622. Campbell, p. 104f., suggests that the syntax of the present passage is telescoped from *on last legdun lastas laþum þeodum.*   24 mylenscearpan] For *mylenscearpum*, as in B and C. See l. 6, note.   26 þæra þe] This reading, following D, seems most satisfactory, in that it explains A's form *þæ* as the result of the omission of *-ra þe* through confusion of *þæ-* and *þe.* See Campbell, p. 106. The idiom *þæra þe*, or *þara þe*, is more natural than the simple relative after the genitive *hæleþa* in l. 25.   æra gebland] The compound *eargebland*, as in B, C, and D, would be more normal. But since *ear*, "sea," is found as a simple noun (see Riddle 3,22 and the emended reading in Daniel 323), it is possible to retain A's *æra gebland* as a variant of *eara gebland.* See also *aryða geblond*, Andreas 532.   32 flotan and Sceotta] Although the four MSS. agree on *flotan*, Ettmüller, Kluge (3–4 ed.), Campbell emend to *flotena.* But for *flota* in the collective sense, "a fleet, crews of ships," see Bos.-Tol., Supplement, p. 227, and Ekwall, English Studies XXI, 220.   35 cread] As Campbell, p. 108, points out, *crūdan*, "to crowd, press," can be either transitive or intransitive. In Riddle 3,28 it is intransitive, but here a transitive meaning is quite possible, with *cnear* acc. sing. and *cyning*, l. 35*b*, subject of both *cread* and *gewat.*   cnear on] A's form *cnearen* is an obvious error for *cnear on*, the reading of the other MSS.   38 Costontinus] The reading *constantinus*, in B, C, and D, is the more literary form of the name, but A's form *costontinus* can be justified as a Vulgar Latin spelling with regular loss of *n* before *s.* See Campbell, p. 109f., who points out the form *Cosstantin* in Chronicle 926D. The M.E. *Custance* (for *Constance*), as in Chaucer's Man of Law's Tale, is also from the Vulgar Latin form of the name.   40 mæca gemanan] "(He might not rejoice at) the meeting of swords." Campbell emends to *mecga* (= *mæcga*), "of men," which he gives as the reading of D. But D clearly has *in ecga.* The readings *mecea, meca*, in B and C are evidently correct, A's form *mæcan* being perhaps influenced by the final *-n* in *gemanan.* The etymologically proper root vowel of this word is *æ*, as in A; see Holthausen, Altengl. etymol. Wörterbuch, p. 210. D's reading *in ecga* is evidently due to the scribe's having expected a form of *ecg*, "sword," here.   40–41 sceard...gefylled] The MSS. all agree on *gefylled* in l. 41*a*, although the verb *(ge)fyllan* does not properly mean "to deprive (of)," but "to cast down, destroy." Grein-Köhler, p. 234, suggests reading *befylled*, as in

Genesis 2124, and so Campbell. It is also possible that *gefylled* is an uninflected form for *gefylledra*, modifying *freonda;* see Klaeber, JEGPh. XIX, 411. Kock, Anglia XLVI, 63, cites O.N. *fella* in support of *gefylled* in the meaning "deprived." **42 beslagen]** "Deprived, bereft," parallel to *sceard*, l. 40. The word *gefylled*, l. 41, may also be part of the parallelism; see the preceding note. **43 wundun]** For *wundum*, as in B, C, and D. See l. 6, note. **forgrunden]** Uninflected, though logically referring to the acc. sing. *sunu*, l. 42. **46 inwidda]** A has *inwidda*, B and C have *inwitta*, and most authorities take these two spellings as equivalent, "malicious, deceitful (one)." But Holthausen, Altengl. etymol. Wörterbuch, p. 189, recognizes two separate words, a noun *inwidda*, "Gegner, Feind," and an adjective *inwitt*, "böse, schlecht, listig." The noun *inwit*, "malice, deceit," also has the two forms *inwit* and *inwid;* see Bos.-Tol., p. 597. For *inwidda*, see also Judith 28. **48 heo]** A's form *heo* may be retained, though *hie, hi* in the other MSS. would be more regular for the nom. plur. masc. **48ff.]** The genitives *beaduweorca, cumbolgehnastes, garmittinge, gemotes*, and *wæpengewrixles* are all genitives of specification after *beteran*. This construction is rather frequent in Anglo-Saxon poetry; see Riddle 33,6 (*biter beadoweorca*), and also Beowulf 269 (*larena god*), 318 (*siða gesunde*), 1220 (*lara liðe*); Andreas 329 (*sigora selost*), 482f. (*larna... este*), etc. **49 cumbolge-hnastes]** A's *culbodgehnades* (partly corrected by a later hand) is an impossible form. **51 þæs]** For adverbial *þæs*, "because" (*þæs þe*, D), see *Waa me ðæs ic swigode*, "vae mihi quia tacui," Pastoral Care (ed. Sweet), 379,24. **56 eft Iraland]** The abbreviation 7 (= *and*) added above the line in A seems to be in a contemporary hand; but the omission of *and* in all the other MSS. suggests that the conjunction was not an original part of the text. A's reading *hira land* is shown to be corrupt by the alliteration. **63 æses brucan]** Parallel to *hræw bryttian*, l. 60, the subjects of the infinitives being the four animals (the raven, the eagle, the war-hawk, and the wolf) enumerated in ll. 61-65. The distribution of the adjectives in ll. 61ff. is open to some question, but *saluwigpadan* and *hyrnednebban* seem to refer to the raven, *hasewanpadan* to the eagle. **66 þis]** For *þȳs*, instr. sing. **68 þæs þe]** "According to what, as"; see Bos.-Tol., p. 850, under *se* V.2c.

2. THE CAPTURE OF THE FIVE BOROUGHS (942)

2 mæcgea] A's reading, *maga* (gen. plur. of *mæg*, "kinsman"?), seems less appropriate here than *mæcgea, mecga*, "(protector) of men," in B and C. B's reading *mæcgea* has accordingly been adopted in the text. **3-5]** Sedgefield emends *brada*, l. 5, to *bradan*, taking *ea* and *brimstream* as accusatives, objects of *scadeþ*. But *Dor, Hwitanwyllesgeat*, and *Humbra ea* are all parts of the boundary of Mercia and subjects of *scadeþ*. Although a singular form, *scadeþ* can be taken collectively with the three parallel subjects. See Klaeber, MLN. XX, 32, who properly supplies "them" (i.e. the Mercians, the territory of the Mercians) in sense from *Myrce*, l. 2. That is, "as Dor, Hwitanwyllesgeat, and the River Humber, the broad estuary, bound [them]." On the place-names *Dor* and *Hwitanwyllesgeat*, see Introd., p. xlii, note 2. **8 and]** Though not in

A, the conjunction is required by sense and meter.   Dæne] The reading *denum*, in B, would have to be construed as parallel to *under Norðmannum*, l. 9a, omitting the period after *Deoraby;* that is, the Five Boroughs were "subject by force to the Danes, the Northmen." So Sedgefield, who bases his text on B. But *Norðmannum* must refer not to the Danes of the Five Boroughs, but to the Norwegians under Anlaf; see Introd., p. xli. The distinction between *Dene* and *Norðmen* is well illustrated in Chronicle 924 A, where the people of the North submit to Edward: *ealle þa þe in Norþhymbrum bugeaþ, ægþer ge Englisce, ge Denisce, ge Norþmen, ge oþre.*   æror] A's reading *ær* is less satisfactory metrically.   In any case, the word belongs in this line, rather than in l. 9, where Wülker and Sedgefield print it.   9 nyde gebegde] The reading *nyde* (*nede*) *gebæded*, in B, C, and D, is supported by Brunanburh 33, *nede gebeded*. But A's *gebegde* (from *gebīegan*, "subdue") gives an acceptable meaning and is retained in the text.

3. THE CORONATION OF EDGAR (973)

2 miclum] A has *corðre micelre*, fem., B and C have *corðre mycclum*. The noun *corðor*, "troop, band," is found elsewhere only as a neuter, and O.H.G. *kortar* is also neuter.   Since there is no evidence for a feminine variant, the text has been emended to *miclum*, preserving the usual *i*-spelling of A (ll. 5, 9, etc.). 10ff.] That is, it was a thousand years after the birth of Christ (ll. 11–12), minus twenty-seven (ll. 13b–15a).   13 þa get] A's reading, *þa agan* ("then passed"?) does not fit into the meaning here, and we must read *þa get*, with B and C. 15b–16a] "So nearly was a thousand [winters] passed for the Lord of victories." The turn of phrase is rather awkward, but the meaning must be, "So nearly were a thousand years of the Christian era passed."   20 XXX] For *þrittigeþan*, as in the other MSS.   That is, Edgar was in his thirtieth year.

4. THE DEATH OF EDGAR (975)

8 þær] The reading *þær*, *ðær*, "when," in B and C is required by the sense in place of A's *þ* (= *þæt*).   10b] Since the abbreviation 7 (= *and*) in A was added in a quite different, probably later, hand and does not appear in B and C, the word was presumably not a part of the original text.   14 of Brytene gewat] That is, "died...in a natural manner" (*þurh gecyndne cræft*). So Klaeber, MLN. XX, 32, who cites *fæder ellor hwearf*, Beowulf 55. Plummer, on the other hand (Two of the Saxon Chronicles Parallel II, 163), thinks the phrase need merely mean "departed from Britain," perhaps on a journey to Rome.   16 Myrceon] For *Myrcum*, as in B and C. See Brunanburh 6, note. 29 And...ætywed] Here A has *And þa wearð ætywed*, B and C have *þa wearð eac ætywed*. Which of these was the original reading it is impossible to say, but since the alliteration (*ætywed : uppe*) does not require *eac*, A's reading has been followed.   33 woðboran] A reads *soðboran*, B and C *woðboran*. A noun *soðbora* ("truth-bearer"?) does not appear elsewhere in Anglo-Saxon, whereas *woðbora*, "orator, prophet," is well authenticated. See Christ 302, Gifts of Men 35, etc. The text accordingly follows B and C.

5. The Death of Alfred (1036)

4 hit hleoðrode, etc.] That is, the popular opinion was in Harold's favor.   5
toward Haraldes] D reads *to harolde.* Sedgefield emends C's reading to *toward
Harolde,* dat. sing. But *toweard,* "toward, in the direction of," can also take
the genitive; see Bos.-Tol., p. 1010.   7 todraf] Holthausen, Anglia Beibl. L,
157, would read *tōdroh,* to provide a rime. He also suggests the following
changes, elsewhere in the poem, to provide rime or assonance: the addition of
ær after *earde,* l. 11, and of *ðenne* after *gode,* l. 13; the addition of *swiðe* after
blission, l. 14a, and the emendation of l. 14b to *mid Jesu Criste bliðe;* the emendation of *gyt* to *get,* l. 16; the addition of *on fenne* after *Eligbyrig,* l. 18, and of *softe*
after *munecon,* l. 20 (putting *brohte* in the first half-line); and the emendation of
l. 23 to read *þæt wæs ful wurðlice* [*gedon*] *swa he wyrðe wæs* [*to fon*].   11 þison]
For *þissum,* dat. sing. Other instances of the reduction of *-m* to *-n* are to be
found in *ðan,* l. 13, and *munecon,* l. 20.

6. The Death of Edward (1065)

3 wæra] For *wære,* dat. sing. The words *worulda,* l. 4, and *Dena,* l. 19, are also
spelled with final *-a* where we should expect *-e.* The readings of D (*wera,* l. 3,
weorolda, l. 4, and *deona,* l. 19) differ in spelling from those of C, but the MSS.
agree in each case on final *-a.* In so late a text it seems inadvisable to follow
traditional spelling too rigorously, and the *-a* forms have therefore been retained
in the text. In two places, l. 12b and l. 16a, where we should expect *cealde*
and *lange,* C has the metrically impossible forms *ceald* and *lang,* whereas D
has *cealda* and *langa.* In these two half-lines it has seemed wise to emend to
the usual forms *cealde* and *lange.*   4 worulda] For *worulde;* see l. 3, note.
6–8 XXIIII...wintra gerimes...and healfe tid] That is, twenty-four and a half
years. But Edward ruled only twenty-three and a half years, from June, 1042,
to January, 1066; see Plummer, Two of the Saxon Chronicles Parallel II, 253,
who prefers D's reading *and he hælotid* in l. 8, though he does not say how he
would construe it. Earle (cited by Plummer) suggested *and he ealle tid.*   7
weolan britnode] C's *weolm brytnodon* is impossible, and the reading of D has
been adopted.   12 cealde] So Sedgefield, for C's *ceald* and D's *cealda.* See
l. 3, note.   16 lange] See l. 3, note.   19 Dena] For *Dene,* nom. plur. See
l. 3, note.   weoldon] According to Kock, Anglia XLII, 122, *weoldon* governs
two cases, instr. sing. (*deore rice*) and gen. sing. (*Engla landes*), in which case
Engla landes should be set off by commas. But the other construction, taking
Engla landes as dependent on *rice,* is also possible.   25 lungre] C and D both
read *lunger,* but the adverbial form, *lungre,* is required.

NOTES ON DURHAM

Durham] For a description of the MS. sources, and a discussion of the literary
and historical problems raised by this poem, see Introd., pp. xliii ff. The text
follows MS. C, except where C is obviously in error.   2 steppa] For *steape,*
and Arnold translates l. 2a, "firmly built on high." Wülker normalizes to

steape.   3 ymbeornad] Arnold reads *ymbeornað*, with H. Wülker emends to *ymbeorneð*, as a singular form.   The spelling with *eo* (-*eornan* for -*irnan*, -*yrnan*) occurs frequently in late Anglian texts; see Surtees Psalter (ed. J. Stevenson), Psalms lvii. 8, cxlvii. 4; Rushworth Gospels (ed. Skeat), Matthew xxviii. 8, etc.   4 stronge] Holthausen, Anglia Beibl. XXXI, 29, would read *strong* (H's form), for metrical reasons.   5 feola] The form *fcola*, produced by the corrector of C, is naturally to be emended to *feola*.   So Arnold, Wülker. 6] Holthausen, Anglia Beibl. XXXI, 29, reading *wuda fæstern* as two words, and placing *wuda* in the first half-line, suggests *westen* for *fæstern*, to provide alliteration.   This emendation had been previously suggested by Arnold.   But it seems better to read *wudafæstern* as a compound (= *wudufæsten*), in which case the alliteration is satisfactory without any emendation.   7 wuniad] Wülker reads *wuniað*, with H.   See l. 3, note.   wilda deor] Holthausen, Anglia Beibl. XXXI, 29, would read *wildeor*.   8 deope] Wülker corrects to *deopum*. 10–11] Wülker prints ll. 10–11 as one line.   Holthausen, Anglia Beibl. XXXI, 29, arranges them properly as two lines, but adds *eac* in l. 11*a* and makes some further alterations for the sake of inflectional regularity:

> ðe arfesta   eadiga Cuðbercht
> and ðes clenan eac   cyninges heafud.

Wülker had previously read *eadiga*, l. 10*b*, and *clenen*, l. 11*a*.   12 leo] For *hleo*, with the regular Middle English loss of initial *h* before a liquid.   13 geferes] The word *geferes*, instead of the regular weak form *geferan*, is perhaps to be explained as a Northumbrian plural in -*s* (Sievers, Angels. Gram., §276, Anm. 5), but more probably as a Middle English analogical plural.   14 Æðelwold] The form 7*ðelwold* in C is perhaps due to a previous copy in which &*ðelwold* was erroneously written for the proper form *æðelwold*.   15*a*] Wülker supplies the article *ðe* before *breoma*, and so Holthausen, Anglia Beibl. XXXI, 29; but Holthausen would omit either *breoma* or *bocera*, for metrical reasons. 16] Holthausen, Anglia Beibl. XXXI, 29, supplies *ðone* before *clene*, l. 16*a*, and would emend *clene* to the weak form *clenan*.   In l. 16*b*, he would emend *gecheðe* (evidently a late spelling of *geogoðe*) to *cildhade*, for metrical reasons. 17] C's form *wis* is evidently an error for *his* (as in H) and has been emended accordingly.   Holthausen, Anglia Beibl. XXXI, 29, would omit *wel*.   18 eadige in in] The appearance of two *in*'s in l. 18*b* suggests the likelihood of an unconscious scribal repetition, and Wülker omits one *in*.   So also Holthausen, Anglia Beibl. XXXI, 29.   In l. 18*a*, Wülker emends *eadige* (referring to Cuthbert) to the dative *eadigen;* Holthausen normalizes further to *eadigan*.   In l. 18*b*, Holthausen supplies *æðelan* before *minstre*, for the alliteration.   But if we retain the MS. *in in ðem minstre*, with the first *in* taken as the adverb *in* (as in the usual Anglo-Saxon combination *in on*) and therefore stressed, all the requirements of alliteration are satisfied.   It is of course possible (though not likely) that the first *in* is the noun *in*, "dwelling."   In this text the omission of the dat. sing. ending would not be significant.   19–21] As they stand in C, these lines are difficult to interpret.   C's reading is *unarimeda reliquia ðe monia wundrum gewurðað ðes ðe writ seggeð midd ðene drihnes wer domes bideð.*

Wülker emends gewurðað, l. 20, to gewurðad, and transfers ðe, l. 20a, to the beginning of l. 21. Holthausen, Anglia Beibl. XXXI, 29, follows Wülker's arrangement of these lines, except that he puts monia (which he emends to H's reading monige) in l. 19b, after reliquia. Holthausen also emends seggeð to segeð, and bideð to bidað, to regularize the grammar. This treatment of ll. 19–21 would suggest the following translation: "many uncounted relics, celebrated with wonders (i.e. miracles), as writ says, which with the man of God await the Judgment." But a simpler and more convincing reading can be obtained by emending ðe, l. 20, to H's reading ðær, and taking gewurðað as a form of geworðan, "happen," rather than of geweorðian. Then bideð, l. 21, taken as a plural, continues the construction of Eardixð, l. 18. Translating from the beginning of the sentence: "Uncounted relics dwell with the blessed one inside the minster, where many things come to pass by means of miracles, as writ says (or, as writings say), [and] with the man of God await the Judgment."

NOTES ON THE RUNE POEM

The Rune Poem] For a discussion of this poem and the similar rune poems in Old Icelandic and Old Norwegian, see Introd., pp. xlviff. In the following notes no attempt is made to give a complete treatment of the Anglo-Saxon runic alphabet, but the name and significance of each of the runes is briefly stated. The rune names in the other Anglo-Saxon runic alphabets (the chief of which are in MS. Cotton Domitian A.ix, MS. Cotton Galba A.ii, and Vienna MS. 795) show for the most part unimportant variations, and since they have been printed in full by Grienberger, Arkiv för nordisk filologi XV, 1–8, they are not cited here except where the proper form of the Anglo-Saxon rune name is doubtful. But the Scandinavian rune names are noted, together with the Gothic rune names in Vienna MS. 795, fol. 20b. The forms labeled "Gothic" are those of the Vienna MS.; the hypothetical (starred) Wulfilan forms are based primarily on Holthausen, Gotisches etymologisches Wörterbuch (Heidelburg, 1934).   1 ᚠ] The rune for feoh, "money, property" (O.N. fé; Gothic fe, Wulfilan *faihu), with the sound value of f. This rune is also found in the four Cynewulfian runic signatures; in Fates of the Apostles 98, Elene 1269, and Christ 807 it stands for the word feoh, as here, but in Juliana 708 its significance is not quite certain (see Records III, The Exeter Book, p. 287).   2 miclun] For miclum, "largely, freely." Other instances of -un for -um, dat.-instr. plur., are to be found in ungemetun, l. 8, gehwylcun, ll. 9, 90, wyrtrumun, l. 37, and secgun, l. 68. In view of the frequency of the -un ending in this poem, these words have not been emended.   4 ᚢ] The rune for ūr, "wild ox, buffalo" (O. Norw. úr, "slag"; O. Icel. úr, "drizzling rain"; Gothic uraz, Wulfilan *ūrs), with the sound value of u. The rune name is cognate with the first element of German Auerochs. This rune is also found in the four Cynewulfian signatures, with various interpretations by the editors; see Fates of the Apostles 101, Elene 1265, Christ 805, Juliana 706, and notes.   oferhyrned] "Having horns above," Bos.-Tol., p. 735. Dickins, however, takes ofer- as an intensifying prefix (as in

oferceald, l. 29, *oferleof*, l. 71, *oferheah*, l. 81), "having great horns."   **7 ▶**]
Hickes gives ðorn as the name of this rune, though, as Wülker points out, þorn
(as in MS. Galba A.ii) would be a better spelling. The meaning is "thorn,"
and the sound value is þ. The O.N. and Gothic names of this rune are quite
different: O.N. þurs, "giant," Gothic *thyth*, of uncertain meaning.   **8 anfeng**
ys yfylj So Kluge, Wülker, Dickins, as suggested by Grein, Germania X, 428.
Hickes' text has *anfen-gys yfyl*, and the older edd. and Grienberger,
Anglia XLV, 206, read *anfengys* (gen. sing.) *yfyl*, "bad to take hold of" (Bos.-
Tol., p. 1292).   The y for an unstressed e, as in *yfyl*, is common in this text;
see *eadnys*, l. 12, *recyde*, l. 13, *herenys*, l. 19, *underwreþyd*, l. 37, etc.   **10 ᚠ**]
The name *os*, given for this rune by Hickes, is perhaps the Anglo-Saxon word
*ōs, "(heathen) god" (O.N. *áss*; Germanic **ansuz*; see also the form *Ansis*,
acc. plur., in Jordanes, De origine actibusque Getarum, chap. 13).   This word
does not occur elsewhere in Anglo-Saxon in its simple form, but is frequently
found as the first element in personal names (Oswald, Oswine, etc.; see Searle,
Onomasticon Anglo-Saxonicum, pp. 370–381).   The gen. plur. *esa*, in Charm
4,23, is a related form.   According to the generally accepted view, following
Hempl, MLN. XI (1896), 350–351, and Grienberger, Arkiv för nordisk filologi
XV, 19–20, the rune itself is a ligature of ᚠ and ᛉ, used originally to represent
the Anglo-Saxon ō which developed from -an- followed by a voiceless continuant.
The Gothic rune name *aza* is unexplained, and is probably unrelated.   In the
Icelandic rune poem the rune (in a somewhat different form) stands for *óss*
(or *áss*), "god," but in the Norwegian rune poem it stands for *óss*, "river-
mouth, estuary."   An alternative translation of the Anglo-Saxon rune name,
by Kemble, Archaeologia XXVIII, 340, favored by Dickins and accepted by
Keller, Anglia LX, 142, takes *os* as the Latin noun, "mouth."   This meaning
fits better with the rest of l. 10, "source of every language," but no other foreign
words are found in the poem as the names of runes.   **13 ᚱ**] The rune for *rād*,
"riding, a raid" (O.Norw. *ræið*, O.Icel. *reið;* Gothic *reda*, Wulfilan **raida*),
with the sound value of *r*.   In this stanza most edd. have detected an antithesis
between *sefte* and *swiðhwæt*, "Riding is (or, seems) easy to every warrior in the
hall, but very strenuous to one who sits on a powerful horse over the roads."
So, for example, Dickins, and so also Grienberger, Anglia XLV, 207f.   Grein-
Köhler, p. 540, would assume a double meaning for *rād*, "music" (the movement
or modulation of musical tones) and "riding"; i.e. music is very pleasant to a
man indoors, but riding is very hard for a man on a horse.   Bos.-Tol., p. 781,
records a noun *rād* in the double meaning of "furniture (of a house), harness
(of a horse)," i.e. the furniture of a house is soft, and the harness of a horse very
strong.   A similar suggestion is made by Chadwick, in Dickins, p. 14.   Kemble,
Archaeologia XXVIII, 340, had previously translated *rād* as "saddle."   But
except for the O.N. word *reiði*, "tackle, rigging, harness," there is nothing to
show the existence of an Anglo-Saxon word *rād* with these meanings.   The
antithesis between riding as imagined at home and as experienced on the road
was probably the poet's intention.   In any case, the syntax seems to require a
comma after *sefte*, l. 14*a*.   **16 h**] The rune for *cēn*, "pine torch" (O.N. *kaun*,
"boil, ulcer"; Gothic *chozma*, of uncertain derivation), with the sound value of

k, c. This rune is found also in the Cynewulfian signatures, Fates of the Apostles 103, Elene 1257, Christ 797, Juliana 704, with various possible meanings. 19 X] The rune for *gyfu,* "gift" (Gothic *geuua,* Wulfilan *giba*), with the sound value of palatal *g.* The word *gyfu* here probably means "generosity," in its double effect on the bestower (*gleng, herenys, wyrþscype*) and on the receiver (*wraþu, ar, ætwist*). 21 oþra] Referring to *ar* and *ætwist,* "help and sustenance," l. 21a. Kock, Anglia XLIII, 307f., would translate *ar* and *ætwist* as "shelter and residence," citing Beowulf 2606f. 22 ᚹ] The proper form of the name of this rune, *wyn,* "joy" (see Sievers, Anglia XIII, 3–4), is found in MS. Galba A.ii and, as *uyn,* in the Vienna MS. The Gothic rune name is *uuinne* (Wulfilan *winja,* "pasture"?); the *W*-rune does not occur in the O.N. alphabet. The rune *wyn* is also found in the four Cynewulfian rune passages; in Fates of the Apostles 100, Elene 1263, and Christ 804 it stands for *wyn,* as here, but in Juliana 706 it seems to have only its letter value, *W.* The name *wen* recorded by Hickes is probably a Kentish form, as in the Kentish text of Psalm 50, ll. 80, 157. Elsewhere in the Rune Poem the West Saxon form *wyn* is regularly used (ll. 55, 85, 89, 94). Hickes' reading ᚹ *ne* must be taken as for *wenne,* gen. sing. (not dat. sing., as Dickins says), object of *bruceþ.* 24 byrga geniht] Not "a sufficiency of cities," but "the abundance (characteristic) of cities"; see Grienberger, Anglia XLV, 208f. 25 ᚺ] The rune for *hægl,* "hail" (O.N. *hagall;* Gothic *haal,* Wulfilan **hagl*), with the sound value of *h.* 26 scuras] The noun *scūr,* "shower," is regularly masc. in Anglo-Saxon (although Gothic *skūra* and O.N. *skúr* are fem.), and Grimm, Ueber deutsche Runen, p. 219, and Ettmüller emend Hickes' form *scura* to *scuras* as nom. plur. So also Bos.-Tol., p. 846. The other edd. retain *scura* as nom. plur. fem. 27 ᚾ] The rune for *nȳd,* "affliction, trouble" (O.N. *nauð(r);* Gothic *noicz,* Wulfilan *nauþs*), with the sound value of *n.* This rune appears also in the Cynewulfian signatures, standing for *nȳd* in Fates of the Apostles 104, Elene 1260, Christ 800, but having only its letter value, *N,* in Juliana 704. breostan] For *breostum,* dat. plur. See also *magan* for *magum,* l. 59. 28b] The meaning evidently is, "if they anticipate it." Dickins translates, "to everyone who heeds it betimes." 29 ᛁ] The rune for *īs,* "ice" (O.N. *íss;* Gothic *iiz,* Wulfilan **eis*), with the sound value of *i.* 31 fæger ansyne] "Fair in aspect," Bos.-Tol., p. 45. 32 ᛄ] The rune for *gēr, gēar,* "year" (O.N. *ár;* Gothic *gaar,* Wulfilan *jēr*), originally with the sound value of *j,* later of palatal *g.* According to Dickins, the word *gēr* here refers specifically to summer; see Beowulf 1134. Grein-Köhler, p. 250, glosses as "annona," i.e. "produce, means of subsistence," a meaning also recorded for O.N. *ár.* ðon] The edd. emend to *ðonne,* but for *ðon* as a variant of *ðonne,* see Riddle 54,9, note, in Records III, The Exeter Book, p. 349. 35 Z] The name *eoh,* given here by Hickes, appears to be a variant of the word *iw,* "yew"; see Dickins, p. 16, and Grienberger, Arkiv för nordisk filologi XV, 9–12. The Vienna MS. gives *ih* as the name of this rune; there are no corresponding O.N. or Gothic rune names. The original sound value of the rune in Anglo-Saxon is not clear, but in reversed form it appears once on the Ruthwell Cross, representing ʒ of *almeʒttig.* The name *eoh* survives in Middle English as *yogh, yok,* the name of the letter ʒ; see Paues, MLRev. VI (1911), 441–454. 36 hyrde

fyres] "The guardian of the fire," referring to a yew log on the hearth?   37
wyn] For Hickes' form *wynan*, most edd. read *wyn*, nom. sing., parallel to
treow, l. 35.   Grienberger, Anglia XLV, 211, takes *wynan* as a variant spelling
of *wynnum*, adverbial dative.   See *breostan*, l. 27, and note.   38 ƕ] One of
the forms of the rune for *peorð*, with the sound value of *p*.   The meaning of the
word *peorð* is uncertain.   W. Grimm, Ueber deutsche Runen, pp. 239f., suggests
that it is related to O.N. *peð*, "pawn (in chess)"; see also J. Grimm, Deutsche
Grammatik I (2d ed., Göttingen, 1822), 126.   Dickins translates doubtfully as
"chessman."   Grienberger, Beitr. XXI (1896), 212, suggests "throat, gullet,"
but does not make clear his evidence for this meaning.   The text of the poem
unfortunately does not help us much.   The Gothic rune name is *pertra* (Wulfilan
*pairþra), which Brate, Arkiv för nordisk filologi XXXVI (1920), 201, would
derive from Low Lat. *paraverēdus*, "horse."   But such a meaning does not fit
here in the Rune Poem.   A more recent interpretation of *peorð*, by Marstrander,
Norsk tidsskrift för sprogvidenskab I (1928), 138ff., would derive it and the
Gothic *pertra* from a Gaulish *p*-form corresponding to the Irish ogom name for
Q, quert (O.Irish *ceirt*, "apple-tree"); the Anglo-Saxon rune name *cweorð* (not
found in the Rune Poem) would be similarly derived from the Goidelic form
with *q*-.   Other suggested explanations of *peorð* are briefly noted by Philippson,
PMLA. LIII (1938), 331, note 49.   The form of this rune, ƕ, differs from the
more common *P*-rune, found in Riddle 64,6 and Solomon and Saturn 89, and
also in the other Anglo-Saxon runic alphabets, as, for example, in MS. Domitian
A.ix and in the Vienna MS.   39 wlancum] A word or two must have dropped
out of the text here, although Hickes does not note any loss in the MS.   Ettmüller supplies *willgesiðum* after *wlancum;* Rieger, note, suggests *wlancum on
wingedrince*.   Grein's reading *wlancum on middum* has been adopted by Kluge
(2–4 ed.) and Dickins.   Kluge (1 ed.) had read *wlancum on middan*.   Grienberger, Anglia XLV, 211, thinks a noun has been lost and suggests *wlancum
werum*, but this would give too short a half-line.   It seems more probable that
wlancum was followed by *and* and another adjective; for example, *wlancum and
wisum*.   But since there are numerous possibilities for the second adjective,
nothing has been supplied in the text.   41 ᛦ] The name of this rune, as given
by Hickes, is *eolhx*, standing for the letter *X*, and corresponding to the form
ilcs in the Vienna MS.   The original sound value of the rune was *z*, corresponding to the Gothic rune name *ezec*, of uncertain meaning.   The O.N. name of the
z- (ʀ-)rune is *ȳr*, "yew tree, bow," which is related etymologically to Anglo-
Saxon *eoh* (see the note on l. 35, above) but not to Anglo-Saxon *eolhx* or to
Gothic *ezec*.   The word *eolhx* is taken by all commentators as the first element
of a compound noun *eolhxsecg*, denoting some kind of water-reed.   After the
rune, Hickes reads *seccard hæfþ*, which Grimm, Ueber deutsche Runen, p. 221,
and later edd. emend to *secg eard hæfþ*.   Bos.-Tol., p. 253, following the older
edd., takes *eolhx*- as gen. sing. of *eolh*, "elk," but the gen. sing. of *eolh* would be
eol(h)es, and Bos.-Tol., Supplement, p. 191, gives *eolhsecg* as the proper form of
the compound.   The meaning of *eolhxsecg* (or *eolhsecg*) is indicated by several
glosses in which the forms *eolxsecg, eolugsecg, ilugsegg, ilugseg* are glossed "pa-
piluus" (for "papyrus"?); see Wright-Wülker, Anglo-Saxon and Old English

Vocabularies I, 271, 21; 468, 11; Sweet, Oldest English Texts, p. 86. Cockayne, Leechdoms III, 324f., proposing a connection with *holeg*, would translate "sea-holly, eryngium maritimum." Wimmer, Die Runenschrift (Berlin, 1887), pp. 132ff., suggests that the rune name *eolhx* had no meaning of its own, but was merely a mechanical abstraction from the full form of the compound *eolhxsecg*. The most recent interpretation of *eolhx* is that by W. J. Redbond, MLRev. XXXI, 55ff., who would derive it from Latin *helix;* the word *helix*, however, usually refers to some kind of twisted plant, such as ivy, though the meaning "willow" is also recorded. 43 breneð] As a form of *bærnan* (Bos.-Tol., Supplement, p. 105), this verb does not fit the context. Dickins suggests that it is a form of *beirnan*, "to cover," citing the passage *ures drihtnes rod bið blode beurnen* in Wulfstan (ed. Napier, pp. 182–183, variant reading of MS. B). The word is more plausibly interpreted by Grein (see Grein-Köhler, p. 70) as for *brēneð*, a (Kentish?) form of a verb *brȳnan*, otherwise unrecorded but to be taken as a causative verb from *brūn*, i.e. "makes brown with blood." So also Grienberger, Anglia XLV, 212. The meter requires a long *e* in this word. 45 ᚻ] The rune for *sigel*, "the sun," with the sound value of *s*. See Riddle 6, note, in Records III, The Exeter Book, p. 325. The Gothic name of the rune is *sugil;* the O.N. name *sól*, "sun," is perhaps related. 46 ðonn] Possibly to be emended to *ðonne*, with the edd., but see *ðon*, l. 32, and note. hine] Dickins takes *hine* as a variant of *heonon*, "hence, away," but Grienberger, Anglia XLV, 212, more plausibly as the pronoun, referring to *brimhengest* in the next line. With Dickins' interpretation, *feriaþ* must be intransitive, as in Psalm 67,8,2 and Maldon 179. 48 ↑] The rune for *tīr*, which, according to Grienberger, Arkiv för nordisk filologi XV, 15, is a late substitution for *Tī*, *Tīw*, the name of a Germanic god (O.N. *Týr*, the one-handed god), found as *ti* in the Vienna MS. and as *Tīw*- in the word *Tīwesdæg*, "Tuesday." For other occurrences of the word, see R. Jente, Die mythologischen Ausdrücke im altengl. Wortschatz (Heidelberg, 1921), pp. 86–89. It is not related etymologically to the Anglo-Saxon common noun *tīr*, "glory, honor" (O.N. *tírr*), but may have been influenced by it. The Gothic name of the rune is *tyz* (Wulfilan *Teius or *Teiwis). Jente, p. 88, note 2, suggests that the Anglo-Saxon rune name with *-r* is a borrowing from the O.N. name of the rune, *Týr*. So also Keller, Anglia LX, 147f. Here in the Rune Poem the word evidently refers to some star or constellation. The planet Mars (suggested by the gloss *tiig*, "mars, martis," in the Epinal, Erfurt, and Corpus glossaries, in Sweet, Oldest English Texts, pp. 77–78) is ruled out by ll. 49b-50, and it is probable that Ursa Minor or some other circumpolar constellation is referred to; see Botkine, La Chanson des runes, p. 19. 51 ᛒ] The rune for *beorc*, "birch," with the sound value of *b*. The O.N. name of the rune is *bjarkan;* the Gothic name is *bercna* (possibly an error for *bercha*, and thus corresponding to Wulfilan *bairka). According to Dickins, however, the birch is not the tree described here. Dickins cites several glosses in which the forms *birce, birciae, byrc, byric* are glossed "populus," i.e. the poplar, and he believes that this is the tree meant. Grienberger, Anglia XLV, 214, sees in l. 51a (the *beorc* without fruit) a play on the word *gebeorc*, "bark (of a dog)"—but surely such a suggestion need not be taken seriously. 52 butan

tudder] "Without seed," Dickins.   53 hrysted] For *hyrsted*, "decorated,
adorned."   55 M] The rune for *eh*, "horse" (more usually spelled *eoh*), with
the sound value of *e*. There is no corresponding rune name in O.N. (though
O.N. *jór*, "steed," is a cognate); the Gothic rune name is *eyz* (Wulfilan
*aihws?). This rune appears also in two of the Cynewulfian rune passages, in
Elene 1261, where it stands for the word *eoh*, and in Juliana 706, where it has
its usual letter value, *E*.   56 hæleþ ymbe] Hickes' text has *hæleþe ymb*, but a
nom. plur. *hæleþe* is not elsewhere recorded, the regular forms being *hæleþ* and
hæleþas. Ettmüller, Grein, Wülker read *hæleþ ymb;* Sievers, Beitr. X, 519,
would read *hæleþ ymbe* for metrical reasons, and so Kluge (2–4 ed.), Dickins,
and Grienberger, Anglia XLV, 214. The usual postpositive form of the preposition is *ymbe*, as in Genesis 371, 669, Beowulf 2597, and the emendation to *ymbe*
here can be justified on other than metrical grounds. The phrase *him . . . ymbe*
= "about him (the horse)."   59 M] The rune for *man*, *mon*, "man" (O.N.
maðr; Gothic *manna*), with the sound value of *m*. The form *an* given by
Hickes is an obvious error. This rune is also found in Ruin 23, where it stands
for *mon-*, the first element of the compound *mondreamum*.   magan] For *magum;* see *breostan*, l. 27, and note.   60 oðrum swican] "Depart from, give
way to another"? Dickins, however, translates, "yet every man is doomed to
fail his fellow."   63 ſ] The rune for *lagu*, "sea, water" (O.N. *lögr;* Gothic
laaz, Wulfilan **lagus*), with the sound value of *l*. This rune also occurs in the
four Cynewulfian rune signatures, in Fates of the Apostles 102, Elene 1268, and
Christ 806, where it stands for *lagu*, and in Juliana 708, where its meaning is
disputed (see Records III, The Exeter Book, p. 287).   67 ᛝ] The rune for
Ing, the eponymous hero of the Ingwine, a name applied to the Danes in Beowulf 1044, 1319, and generally equated with the Ingaevones (more correctly
*Inguaeones) mentioned by Tacitus, Germania, chap. 2. The Gothic rune
name *enguz* (Wulfilan **iggws*?) must be related, though the phonology of the
Gothic word is not clear; there is no corresponding O.N. rune name. The sound
value of the rune in Anglo-Saxon is *ng* (η). For the relationship of Ing to the
gods Njörðr and Ingwi-Freyr of the Norse mythology and to the Nerthus
mentioned by Tacitus, see H. M. Chadwick, The Origin of the English Nation
(Cambridge, 1907), pp. 230ff., 287ff.; Dickins, p. 20; Klaeber, Archiv CXLII,
250ff.; Krappe, Revue germanique XXIV, 23–25.   68 eft] Most edd., including Wülker and Dickins, retain Hickes' reading *est*, as for *ēast*, "to the east."
But Grein emends to *eft;* and for a justification of this reading see Klaeber,
Archiv CXLII, 251. Kluge (2–4 ed.) also reads *eft*.   70 heardingas] Grein,
Wülker, Dickins take this word as a proper noun, corresponding to the O.N.
tribal name *Haddingjar*. But Grein, Germania X, 428, reads *heardingas* as a
common noun, "brave ones, warriors," and this seems a more likely meaning;
see *heardingas*, Elene 25, 130, and Klaeber, Archiv CXLII, 251.   71 ᛟ] The
rune for *ēþel*, "native country, home," with the sound value of *œ* (later *ē*).
Originally the Germanic *O*-rune, ᛟ is called *utal* (Wulfilan **ōþal*) in Gothic;
there is no corresponding O.N. rune name. This rune is also used three times
in Beowulf (twice for the word *eþel*, ll. 520, 913, and once for the first element
of the noun *eþelweard*, l. 1702) and in Waldere I, 31.   72 on] Taken by Ett-

müller and Bos.-Tol., p. 432 (under *gerisene*, n.) as the first element of a compound *onbrucan*, l. 73*a*. But the meter requires *on* in l. 72*b*, and it is best to regard *on* as an adverb, reinforcing the meaning of *ðær*. For *ðær...on*, see also Psalms 56,8,2; 103,24,2, etc.   73 bleadum] For *blædum*, "with prosperity." Kluge (3–4 ed.) emends to *bleaðum*, dat. plur. of *blēað*, "gentle, timid."   74 ᛗ] The rune for *dæg*, "day," with the sound value of *d*. The corresponding Gothic rune name is *daaz* (Wulfilan *dags*); the *D*-rune does not occur in the O.N. alphabet.   77 ᚠ] The rune for *āc*, "oak," with double reference, to acorns as the food of swine (ll. 77–78*a*) and to the wood of the oak as a material for building ships (ll. 78*b*-80).   For a similar riddle theme, see Tupper's note on Riddle 55,9 (56,9 in his numbering), The Riddles of the Exeter Book, p. 191.   According to Hempl, MLN. XI (1896), 348ff., this rune is a ligature of ᚠ and ᛁ, originally representing the Germanic diphthong *ai* which developed into Anglo-Saxon *ā*; see also Grienberger, Arkiv för nordisk filologi XV, 19f. 81 ᚠ] The rune for *æsc*, "ash," originally the Germanic *A*-rune, but used for the sound *æ* after the early Anglo-Saxon sound change *a* > *æ*. Dickins apparently takes l. 83, *ðeah...monige*, as a reference to the difficulty of chopping down an ash tree.   But it is quite possible that here, as in the preceding stanza, we have a double reference, to the ash as tree (ll. 81-82*a*) and as spear (ll. 82*b*-83).   See Grienberger, Anglia XLV, 218; Tupper, The Riddles of the Exeter Book, pp. 211–212.   84 ᛡ] The rune for *ȳr*, the meaning of which is disputed. Grein-Köhler, p. 853, defines doubtfully as "horn," Grienberger, Anglia XLV, 219, as "saddle" or "(wooden) saddle-bow," both apparently on the evidence of the context.   Dickins suggests a connection with the word *æxe-ȳr*, recorded in the Anglo-Saxon Chronicle, 1012 E, where it seems to mean "axe-iron, axe-head."   The most generally accepted interpretation of *ȳr* is "bow," the meaning which O.N. *ȳr* has in the Icelandic rune poem.   In the Norwegian rune poem *ȳr* means "yew-tree," the meaning of Anglo-Saxon *eoh*, l. 35, above.   But assuming a possible connection between O.N. *ȳr*, "bow," and the Anglo-Saxon rune name *ȳr*, the mutual relationships of the two words are difficult to explain. It is probable that the rune ᛡ is a ligature of ᚾ and ᛁ, formed to represent the new sound *y* which resulted from the *i*-umlaut of *u*.   Keller, Anglia LX, 145ff., believes that the rune name *ȳr* was borrowed from the Old Norse word (in spite of the previous existence in Anglo-Saxon of the cognate rune name *eoh*) and that the meaning "bow," as found in the Icelandic rune poem, was applied to it. This seems as satisfactory an explanation as any.   The rune also appears in the four Cynewulfian rune passages, with various interpretations by the edd.; see Fates of the Apostles 103, Elene 1259, Christ 800, Juliana 704, and notes.   87 *] The rune for *īar*, *īor*, of uncertain meaning and origin, but evidently with the sound value of *io*.   Hickes gives the name *iar* with *io* written above it, probably to indicate two variant forms of the rune name, *īar* and *īor*.   MS. Domitian A.ix and MS. Galba A.ii give *ior* as the name of the rune.   No such word as *īar*, *īor* is recorded elsewhere, but the meaning required here is obviously "eel" (suggested by Grimm, Ueber deutsche Runen, p. 244, and doubtfully accepted by Kemble, Archaeologia XXVIII, 344) or some other river fish.   The rune * appears four times in the O.H.G. Wessobrunner Gebet as an abbrevia-

tion for the syllable *ga* (as in * *fregin*, l. 1).   The fundamental sound value of
the rune in Anglo-Saxon appears to have been *j;* see Dickins, pp. 22–23.   Keller,
Anglia LX, 148f., explains the name *īar, īor* as a modification of O.N. *ár* (<
*jār), the name of the *gēr*-rune (see l. 32, above, and note) in the older Norse
alphabet.   The Anglo-Saxon * has nothing to do with the O.N. rune *, which
has the sound value of *h*.   eafix] So Rieger, Dickins, for Hickes' reading *ea
fixa*.   Grimm, Ueber deutsche Runen, p. 224, Ettmüller, Kluge (2–4 ed.) read
eafisc.   Grein, Wülker read *eafixa sum*, retaining the genitive at the cost of an
unusual metrical type.   Grienberger, Anglia XLV, 219, would retain *eafixa*
without any addition, explaining *Iar biδ eafixa* as a construction similar to
Higelac Geata, Beowulf 1202, etc., and translates, "Ior gehört zu den Fluss-
fischen."   But the genitive construction in the predicate is at least unusual,
and it seems better to emend to the nom. sing. *eafix*.   90 ᛉ] The rune for
ēar, to be explained, with Grein, as a form cognate with O.N. *aurr*, "clay, loam."
Then *ear* in the present context would mean "ground, earth," with special
reference to a grave.   93 blac] Nom. sing., "pallid," modifying *flæsc* and
hraw, not acc. sing., as Dickins' translation would indicate.   94 wera] For
wǣra, "covenants"?   So Grein-Köhler, p. 755, and most edd.

NOTES ON SOLOMON AND SATURN

Special abbreviations:
   Assmann.   Volume III of Wülker, Bibliothek der angelsächsischen Poesie.
   Schipper.   His edition of the poem in Germania XXII, 50–70.
   Vincenti.   Die altenglischen Dialoge von Salomon und Saturn, Part 1.

1–100

Solomon and Saturn] For a discussion of the manuscripts and of the literary
problems raised by this poem, see Introd., pp. 1ff.   Readings of MS. A
which are ascribed to "A (M)" in the footnotes to the text are from Menner's
new edition of the poems; all other readings of MS. A are from my own collations.   2 gebregdstafas] "Literary arts"?   See Bos.-Tol., p. 376.   Or, more
literally, "letters of cunning," and for *gebregd*, "cunning," see Fortunes of Men
71.   6–7] Here the scribe of B wrote the words *on þam micelan bec* and then
left blank sufficient space for ten or twelve letters, in the middle of a line, before
writing the next words *M ces heardum*.   What *M ces* may mean is not evident
from the context, and it is undoubtedly corrupt; l. 6 is also probably corrupt,
since *boc* is regularly feminine.   From the fact that the scribe left so large a
space in the MS., it may reasonably be conjectured that his original was only
partly legible at this point, and that ll. 6–7 are attempted restorations of the
parts of the text which he thought he could read.   Vincenti, p. 53, note 3,
would take *M ces* as a reference to Moses, "In den erhabenen, schwierigen
Büchern Mosis?"   Holthausen, Anglia Beibl. XXVII, 351, would not assume a
gap in the text here but, emending *M ces* to *modes,* would read *on þa miclan bec
modes heardum* as a single line, with *heardum* in apposition to *Me*, l. 5.   8a]
Holthausen, Anglia Beibl. XXVII, 351, would supply *neode* after *ic,* printing

næfre on eallum as the second half of l. 8, with *þam fyrngewrytum findan ne mihte* then forming his l. 9. Menner, assuming the loss of only a half-line after *on þam micelan bec*, l. 6, then reads *M.ces heardum* as a first half-line, with a comma after it, and *swylce ic næfre on eallum* as the second half of the same line. But there seems to be no reason why *Swylce...fyrngewrytum* cannot be taken as a single half-line, and it is so printed in the text. See l. 43*a*.   9 samnode] B's reading *samode* can hardly be taken as a variant of *samod*, "together," which would give too short a half-line, but is more probably an error for *samnode*, "collected," from *samnian*, and so Holthausen, Anglia Beibl. XXVII, 351, and Menner. This emendation had previously been suggested in Grein-Köhler, p. 566. The word *soðe* is most naturally taken as the adverb, "truly." But Grein-Köhler, p. 621, takes it as acc. plur. masc. of the adjective *soð*, to provide an object for *findan*.   10ff.] "What the palm-twigged Pater Noster might be with respect to pride or majesty, power or possessions or nobility." The word *oððe*, l. 11*b*, required by the meter, is omitted in B but is one of the few words which can be made out on the first page of A.   16 gebryrded] B has *gebrydded* here, and Bos.-Tol., p. 377, and Grein-Köhler, p. 75, gloss *gebryddan*, "to frighten, terrify"; but such a meaning does not fit the passage, and Grein suggested *gebryrded*, "incited, inspired." So also Vincenti, p. 54, "angeregt." But the edd. retain *gebrydded*. Rieger emends *si gebrydded* to *gebrydded si* for metrical reasons, and so Holthausen, Anglia XXIII, 124.   17 cantices] *Cantic*, "the Lord's Prayer," as also in ll. 24, 49.   linan] A form of *līne*, "line for guidance, rule"; see Bos.-Tol., p. 642. It is probably instr. sing. after *gebryrded*, but may be gen. sing., parallel to *cantices* (Grein-Köhler, p. 428), or acc. sing., parallel to *cwyde*, in both of which cases a comma belongs after *cwyde*.   18 fare] The edd. restore the MS. *fa* to *fare*, but Grein, Germania X, 428, and Holthausen, Anglia Beibl. XXVII, 352, point out that with *fare* we should expect the dative *me* instead of *mec;* see Genesis 543. Holthausen suggests *fadie*, "dispose, guide," though *fadian* is not elsewhere recorded in the poetry.   20 Coferflod] Identified by Vincenti, p. 54, with the River Chabur (Habor in the English Bible, 2 Kings xvii.6), a tributary of the Euphrates, but by Menner, p. 107, with the Chobar (Chebar in the English Bible, Ezekiel i.3).   25 worpað] From *worpian*, "cast, throw (stones at)"; i.e. "the devil stones him... with iron balls from a black sling," etc. See Elene 492, 824.   28 aplum] So B, not *aflum*, as reported by Schipper.   31 gegoten] It is impossible to be sure whether A had *gegoten* or *gegeoten*, but it is probable that only a single letter is lost between *g* and *t*. In any case, we have B's authority for *gegoten*, as in the text.   32 feðersceatum] "In its four quarters"; see Bos.-Tol., p. 285. For *feðer-* = *fiðer-*, "four," see Holthausen, Altengl. etymol. Wörterbuch, p. 103, and the compounds of *fiðer-* listed by Bos.-Tol., Supplement, p. 222.   33 organes] Referring to the *cantic* of ll. 17, 24, 49; see also l. 53. That is, "it would be better for him (l. 30*a*)...if he had ever known anything of the Pater Noster."   40 ontyneð] B reads *ontyneð*, as in A, not *untyneð*, reported by Zupitza, Anglia III, 528, and Assmann.   42*b* dryhtnes] With *fyr* to be supplied in sense from l. 42*a*.   43–48] This passage is extremely difficult, but as it stands in the text it seems to mean: "Likewise with this bright prayer thou mayest heat the blood

of the devil, so that drops arise on him, made strong with blood, in the affairs
of his mind, more terrible than the brazen cauldron when it wells most eagerly
over the grip of coals through the twelve infirmities of men." Why the Pater
Noster should heat the blood of the devil is not clear.   **43** Swylce...on-
hætan] Kemble prints this as two lines, assuming a loss in the text after *miht*,
thus:

> Swylce ðu miht   ....
> mid ðy beorhtan gebede   blod onhætan.

So also Holthausen, Anglia Beibl. XXVII, 352.   But see l. 8*a*, note.   **44**
dreor] Neither A's *dream*, "joy," nor B's *dry*, "magician," is appropriate here.
Grein suggested *dreor*, as a synonym of *blod*, l. 43, and so Menner.   This emendation is adopted in the text.   **69–70*a*]** For the punctuation here, see ll. 149–
150*a*, and Kock, JJJ., pp. 67f.   **72** orðancas] Kemble translates as "devices,"
i.e. cunningly wrought bonds.   **74** wylm] The fire of hell; see l. 467.   **88**
ierne] For *georne*, "eagerly"; compare the variant form *yorn* (= *iorn*?) in B.
89 prologa prima] Neither A's reading *prologa prima* nor B's *prologo prim[o]* is
what we should expect here, and Schipper, Grein, Assmann emend to *prologum
primum*.   **89ff.]** On the runes in this passage, which were first correctly interpreted by Kemble, Archaeologia XXVIII, 370, see Introd., p. liv.   **98**
ieorrenga geseceð] Holthausen, Anglia Beibl. XXVII, 352, would read *geseceð
ieorrenga* (type C) for metrical reasons.   **99** bocstafa brego] "The prince of
letters," perhaps because of the use of the Greek letter P (the Latin *R*) in the
monogram of Christ; see Ebert, Allgemeine Geschichte der Literatur des Mittelalters III, 93, note 2.

101–200

101 scines] Holthausen, Anglia Beibl. XXVII, 352, would emend to *scinnes*, for
metrical reasons, and so Menner in his text; but surely *scines* is a possible variant.   **105]** Although the *h* of *he* is lost in a hole in the parchment, the proper
reading is obvious. For *hangiende*, Holthausen, Anglia Beibl. XXVII, 352,
would read *hangende* (an Anglian form; see Sievers, Angels. Gram., §412, Anm.
11), for metrical reasons.   **106]** The MS. seems to have *ęngestan*, not *engestan*
as reported by Menner.   **107** forcinnað] For this verb, which is not recorded
elsewhere in Anglo-Saxon and the meaning of which is disputed ("repudiate,"
Bos.-Tol., p. 303; "zerstören, vernichten?" Holthausen, Altengl. etymol.
Wörterbuch, p. 49), Grein in his edition suggested *forcirrað* ("avoid?"), but in
Germania X, 428, *forcumað*, "overcome." Holthausen, Anglia Beibl. XXVII,
352, doubtfully suggests *forcrimmað*, "rend in pieces," but the compound
forcrimman is not elsewhere recorded. It seems possible, however, to retain
forcinnað, and so Menner, who glosses doubtfully as "destroy."   ðа cirican
getuinnas] Holthausen proposed two emendations for *cirican*: in Anglia XXIII,
123, *cinlican* (= *cynlican*); in Anglia Beibl. XXXI, 190, *cirlican* (= *cierllican*,
ceorllican).   But *cirican* is perfectly in place here; the phrase means "the twins
(i.e. twin letters, since they are together in the order of the alphabet) of the
church," "die Zwillinge der Kirche" (Vincenti, p. 57).   **108*a*]** The MS.

apparently has ·n·7 s[..]od for this half-line. The letters s[..]od are evidently to be restored to *samod;* but both sense and meter indicate that something has been lost after *and.* The addition of the letter *O,* with Grein, making the half-line read ·N· *and O samod,* seems to be the best reading, since it brings *O* into its proper place among the letters of the Pater Noster; see Introd., p. liv. According to Menner, there is no 7 in the MS., but only a straight vertical line after ·n·; accordingly, he reads *N, O* s(am)od in his text. The alliteration of this half-line falls on both *N* and *O,* since *N* was pronounced "en"; see Holthausen, Anglia Beibl. XXVII, 352, who cites Ælfric's Grammar (ed. Zupitza), 6, 1–4.   109 sargiað] Menner emends to the singular *sargað,* parallel to *brengeð,* and retains *bemurneð* in l. 110*b.*   111] Holthausen, Anglia Beibl. XXVII, 353, note, suggests that the letter *S* is called *engla geræswa,* "the prince of angels," with reference to the words Σωτήρ and *Salvator* as designations of Christ.   112 wuldores stæf] Holthausen, Anglia Beibl. XXVII, 353, would read [weorð] *wuldres stæf,* for metrical reasons.   114*b*] Assmann and Menner report 7 (= *and*) before *stregdað,* but in spite of repeated search I was unable to see 7 in the MS., and there does not seem to be room for it between *stan* and *stregdað.*   123*a* I and] Supplied by Grein, Assmann, and Menner. In the order of the letters of the Pater Noster, the letter *I* is to be expected at this point, but the proper order of *C* and *L* has not been observed by the poet. See Introd., p. liv. Whether the alliteration requires the addition of *I and* is questionable, since *L* (pronounced "el"; see l. 108*a,* note) can alliterate with *yrre;* but without this addition, the half-line is too short.   132 brecað] For this word, which seems to contradict the context, Grein suggested *sprecað,* and Holthausen, Anglia Beibl. XXVII, 353, *wrecað.* Either of these emendations is possible, but in any case the precise reference of the half-line is not clear. Bos.-Tol., Supplement, p. 104, explains *brecað* as "fail to perform."   133 Ðonne...æt niehstan] "Soon after, demnächst"; see Kock, Anglia XLIV, 253.   136 fifmægnum] Holthausen, Anglia Beibl. XXVII, 353, would read *fiflmægnum,* "filled with giant-powers." But for a defence of the MS. reading, see Menner, p. 115.   Fyr bið se ðridda] Holthausen, Anglia Beibl. XXVII, 353 (taking the half-line as meaning "Further, there is the third letter"; see Grein-Köhler, p. 235), would emend *ðridda* to *oðer,* since we expect the letter *B* here, not *C,* which has appeared in l. 123. See Introd., p. liv.   140 godes spyrigendes] "Of an enquirer after God"? So Bos.-Tol., p. 906. The words *godes spyrigendes* are here taken as dependent on *geonges hrægles;* see G. Shipley, The Genitive Case in Anglo-Saxon Poetry (Baltimore, 1903), p. 90. Kock, JJJ., p. 67, would read *spyrigende,* acc. sing., parallel to *cempan,* and would take *godes* as *gōdes,* "of good." Apparently he would take *geonges hrægles* as parallel to *on cwicum wædum,* both with instrumental force after *scierpeð.* Menner reads *Godes spyrigende,* "a seeker of God," in his text, but also suggests, p. 116, *on cwicum wædum Godes spyrigendes, geongum hrægle.*   143 weallað] The verb *weallan,* "to well, flow," is not elsewhere found in a transitive use; the form in the text is perhaps to be taken as a variant of *willað, wiellað,* from the causative verb *willan* (Bos.-Tol., p. 1228), and in a figurative sense; see *wylleð,* l. 269. Menner emends to *wælað,* "scourge, torment."   149–150*a*] See ll. 69–70*a,* note.   151 flotan gripað] Kock, JJJ., pp. 67f., reads *flot angripað*, "take to swimming" (with *angripan* = *onfon*). It is at least clear that ll. 150*b* ff. represent the evil spirits as taking successively the forms of birds, fish, and serpents.   153*a*] The restoration to *str[o]nges* is obvious.   155 he] With change of subject from plural to singular, but still referring to the *manfulra heap*, l. 148.   158*a*] The addition of *folme* after *he*, by Grein, Rieger, and Assmann, is unnecessary, since *handa* is to be taken as object of both *gefeterað* and *gehefegað;* see Holthausen, Anglia Beibl. XXVII, 353, and Kock, JJJ., p. 30.   164 orðances] "Without thought" (with the negative prefix *or-*, as in *orsorg, orwena,* etc.). Bos.-Tol., p. 767, translates as "heedlessly."   167 palmtreow] Holthausen, Anglia XXIII, 124, would read *gepalmtwigede* instead of *palmtreow,* for both sense and meter.   181 liehð] Holthausen, Anglia Beibl. XXVII, 353, would take *liehð* as a form of *lēan,* "to blame," rather than of *lēogan,* "to lie."   183*a*] To be restored to *ðeah ðe S[atu]rnus.* The initial *s-* of *S[atu]rnus,* reported by Menner, was not visible to me in the MS.   184*b*] To be restored to *boca c[æ]g[a]*, with *[le]ornenga locan* in l. 185*a*. The *g* of *c[æ]g[a]*, reported by Menner, was not visible to me.   186ff.] On this extraordinary list of names, see especially Vincenti, pp. 66–67, Holthausen, Anglia Beibl. XXVII, 354, and Menner, pp. 118–120.   A number of rather vague names of regions of the Orient (such as *Indea mere*, l. 186, *Persea rice*, l. 187, *Meda maððumselas*, l. 189, *Filistina flet*, l. 192, *wudu Egipta*, l. 193, etc.) are intermingled with more specific geographical designations from Asia, Asia Minor and Greece (Palestine, l. 187, Bithynia, l. 197, Pamphilia, l. 198, Macedonia and Mesopotamia, l. 199, and Cappadocia, l. 200), a few place-names of Palestine (Jericho, Galilee, and Jerusalem, l. 201), and a number of other names which are unknown or which can be identified only by conjecture (*Corsias*, l. 186, *Predan*, l. 188, *Geallboe* and *Geador*, l. 191, *Buðanasan*, l. 197, etc.).   The phrase *Pores gemære*, l. 198, must refer to the territory of the Indian king Porus, Alexander's opponent at the battle of the Hydaspes.   Tantalizing as this list is to us at the present time, perhaps it was intended to do no more than suggest Saturn's wide academic experience.   186] The letters *ea* of *Indea* and *ea* of *east* are now illegible in the MS., but the line is printed on the authority of Zupitza, Anglia III, 529.   Menner reads *East-Corsias* as a compound, and also *Norð-Predan* in l. 188*b*, following Holthausen, Anglia Beibl. XXVII, 354.   192*b* Creca] Grein suggests *Creta*, since the *Creca cræftas* are mentioned below in l. 195.   193*b* Mathea] Menner emends to *Mathean*, taking the word as a reference to the Vulgate Madian, the land of the Midianites.   Holthausen, Anglia Beibl. XXVII, 354, had previously suggested *Matheanes*.   194 cludas] The emendation was suggested by Holthausen, Anglia Beibl. XXVII, 354, and so Menner, who translates, "the rocky cliffs of Horeb"; see his note, pp. 119–120.   For the spelling *au* for *ū*, see B's reading *clausum* for *clūsum*, l. 71.   197*a*] Menner emends to *Bitðinia* here, and to *Pamphilia* in l. 198*a*.   200 eðel] A word must be added here to complete the half-line, and Grein's *eðel* is accepted by Assmann and Menner.

201-300

202–203] The MS. clearly has *swigie*, l. 202 (not *stigie* as reported by Schipper), and *hycgge*, l. 203*a* (not *bycgge*). In l. 203*b*, the restoration to ð*eah ic no spr*[*e*]*c*[*e*] is obvious. The *o* of *no* and the *c* of *spr*[*e*]*c*[*e*], reported by Menner, were not visible to me in the MS. 206*b*] With *g*[*um*]*ena* to be restored; the final *a*, reported by Menner, was not visible to me. 209–210] "Where a warning (*moning*, for *manung*) came to them in the south on the field of Saner," that is, the Sennaar of Genesis x. 10 (Shinar in the English Bible). Menner, JEGPh. XXXVII, 333, reads ð*æt* for ð*ær* in l. 209*b*, but in his edition returns to the MS. reading. 212*a*] Menner reports *was* in the MS; my collation has *wæs*, but see ll. 177, 182. 212*b* sæliðende] The line does not alliterate, and Grein, note, suggested *mereliðende*. So Menner in his text. 213*b*] To be restored to *w*[*e*]*rðeodum cuð*. 214 freond Nebrondes] "The friend of Nimrod." Holthausen, Anglia XXIII, 124, would emend to *Nembrodes*, as closer to the proper form of the name. See the emended reading *fæder Nebroðes* in Genesis 1628; it may be that we should read *Nebrodes* here. In l. 214*a*, *Fīlistīna* is too short for a half-line, and Hüttenbrenner, Anglia Beibl. XXVIII, 52f., would read *Filistina* [*fruma*], *freond Nebrondes*, citing ll. 278, 281. Menner, JEGPh. XXXVII, 343, suggests as an alternative *Filistina freond*, [*fæder*] *Nebrondes;* in his edition, p. 124, he suggests that the original reading was *Filistina fruma*, [*fæder*] *Nebrondes*. All these emendations require the insertion of a comma at the end of l. 213*b*. 216*b*] As it stands in the MS., *and hine ða of deað offeoll*, this half-line cannot be construed. Menner omits *of*, following Grein (who, however, emends *offeoll* to *onfeoll*). Assmann retains *of*, but does not explain how he would translate. 217 ða] This word comes at the end of a line in the MS. The edd., except Menner, read ð*as*, but there does not seem to be any letter, certainly no *s*, after ð*a*. 219] The letters *n* and *t* of *neat* are all that is visible in the MS. 221 onwæcned] The edd. read *onwæcned*, but the penultimate letter of this word may be *a*. Either form is possible (from *onwæcnan* or from *onwæcnian*), but *onwæcned* seems more likely; see Phoenix 648, Azarias 83. 229 full] The MS. apparently has *full*, although the second *l* is not very clear. 230ff.] This description of a book (see Solomon's reply, ll. 238ff.) with seven tongues is taken by Vincenti, p. 69, to refer to the book with seven seals in Revelation v. 1, each of the *XX orda*, l. 232, being a page or leaf of the volume. 236 winrod] The meaning of this word is uncertain. Bos.-Tol., p. 1286, and Grein-Köhler, p. 841, gloss *wyn-rōd*, "a joy-giving cross," "crux lætifica"; but *rōd* is feminine, and the proper form of the acc. sing. would be *winrōde*. Holthausen, Anglia XXIII, 124, would emend to *wuldor*, or, Anglia Beibl. XXVII, 355, to *wundor*. 242 ðreamedlan] So the MS., here and in l. 430. The existence of a noun *þreamedla* (glossed "Drohmittel" by Schipper, Germania XIX, 331) is at least uncertain. Besides the two occurrences in the present poem, it appears in Guthlac 696 in the dat.-instr. plur., *þrea medlum*, but is there usually emended to *þreaniedlum*, "with harsh restraints." Menner emends to ðrea-

niedlan here and in l. 430. **246** hælo hyðe] Apparently meaning simply "a refuge." See Psalm 106,29, *he hi on hælo hyþe gelædde*, "deduxit eos in portum." **247** wise] The MS. has *wise*, not *wisa* as reported by Schipper and Assmann. For this use of *wise*, see l. 427. **250** nu] The MS. has *nu*, not *iu* as reported by Schipper and Assmann. **258** wenað ðæs ðe naht is] "They expect without reason"? So Vincenti, p. 70. At least, *naht* appears to be for *nawiht*, "they expect that which is nothing, that," etc., with ðæs to be taken as gen. sing. after *wenað*. **259** genæman] "To take away (by force)"; see Bos.-Tol., Supplement, p. 377. **264** hwælen] Kock, JJJ., p. 68, would take *hwælen* as a corruption of *swæ leon*. The word *geowes*, l. 265, is gen. sing. of *giw*, "griphus" (Bos.-Tol., p. 479, and Supplement, p. 473), and the occurrence of *griffus* in the second half of the line raises doubts of the genuineness of *geowes*. Kock would take it as a corruption of *geoþes*, "of an eagle" (from a noun *geoð, "eagle," not elsewhere recorded in Anglo-Saxon, but cognate with O.N. *gjóðr*). **269** wylleð hine] "Torments himself"? See Bos.-Tol., p. 1228. Holthausen, Anglia Beibl. XXVII, 355, would emend to *wylteð*, from *wiltan*, "to roll," Bos.-Tol., p. 1230. **271** leoma] For *leomu*, nom. plur. Longað] The edd., except Menner, read *lengað* here, but the MS. seems to have *longað*, from *langian*, "it distresses him severely"; see Soul and Body I, 152f. **272** ðria] For *þriwa*, "thrice," here and in l. 291. That is, "thrice thirty thousand years" in the present passage, "thrice thirteen thousand" in l. 291. **276** gebendan] There is one stroke too many in the MS., which must be read either as *gebemdan* or as *gebeindan*. The text here looks as if an alteration had been attempted, perhaps from *gebunden*. Either *gebendan* or *gebindan* must be the proper reading, probably the former. **287** heardes and hnesces] With ellipsis of the governing word, "but to it submits [everything] hard and soft." See Shipley, The Genitive Case in Anglo-Saxon Poetry, p. 94. **288** micles and mætes] The reading of A, *micles mætes*, is difficult to construe as it stands. Grein-Köhler, p. 465, takes *mætes* as for *metes*, gen. sing. of *mete*, "meat, food." So previously Kemble. But we expect a pair of opposites, like *heardes and hnesces*, l. 287, and the most satisfactory sense is obtained by the addition of *and* in l. 288a, as in the text. Wyatt, Menner read *micles, mætes*, with the same interpretation. See the preceding note. **291** ðria] See l. 272, note. **299**] Holthausen, Eng. Stud. XXXVII, 205, would rearrange this line to read *Heo wulf oferwigeð [ond] wildne fugol*, to improve the alliteration. Rieger had previously read *wulf heo oferwigeð, wildne fugol*, and so Menner in his text. Such a rearrangement of l. 299 involves placing a period after ðam, l. 298, and taking *friteð* with the verbs in ll. 296–298a. **300**] Rieger emends *oferstigeð* to *ofersticeð*, and rearranges the line to read *heo ofersticeð style, stanas heo oferbideð*. See the preceding note.

301–400

306b] The last word of this half-line is clearly *óferbricgeð* or *óferbricgað;* the penultimate letter is not clear in the MS. In the text *oferbricgeð* is printed, on Menner's authority, although we should rather expect the form *oferbricgað*.

For *oferbrycgian*, "to bridge over," see Bos.-Tol., p. 731. The earlier edd. had read *oferhrægeð*. **307** geat] So the MS. Kemble and Grein read *geatu*, and it is true that we should expect a plural here. **308**] There is a gap in the text after *reafað*, the last word on page 18 of A; it is likely that a leaf is lost from the MS. at this point. See Introd., p. lv. **311a**] Holthausen, Anglia XXIII, 124, calls this half-line incomplete and would supply *fyrd* after *fræcnan*, citing Genesis 689. So also Menner in his text. **323ff.**] A reference to the flooding of the earth at the Last Judgment? Accounts of the final destruction of the earth usually emphasize fire rather than flood (for example, Christ 930ff., Judgment Day II, 145ff.); but see Judgment Day I, 1–2, in the Exeter Book. **324** ðæs] Schipper puts *ðæs* at the beginning of l. 325. But the meter requires *ðæs* in l. 324, and the word is used not as the definite article, but adverbially, "with respect to this." **327** Wa] So the edd., except Schipper, for the MS. *swa*. **329** forðon] "Therefore," rather than "because." A reference to the tower of Babel? See Introd., p. lviii. **331b** in] The vowel is obscure in the MS., but *in* is printed in the text on Menner's authority. The earlier edd. had read *on*. **334** Gewurdene] This form of the past participle of *weorðan* is unusual, but is paralleled in the prose dialogue (see Menner's note, p. 132). Grein, Germania X, 428, suggested *gewundene*, "entwined, twisted fates." So also Grein-Köhler, p. 802, "verschlungene Geschicke." According to Vincenti, p. 73, the four fates are the ones mentioned in ll. 312–313 (*nieht*, *ned*, *sorg*, *slæp*). **335** ðæt] The older edd. read *ðæ*, but according to Menner the *t* is concealed by a fold in the parchment. **339** niehtes] This form is noteworthy here, since the gen. sing. *nihtes* (on the analogy of *dæges*) is elsewhere found only in adverbial use, "noctu," as in ll. 396, 399, below. Just what "from the wounds of night" would mean, is not clear. Holthausen, Anglia Beibl. XXVII, 355, suggests *niðes*. nærende] This form is also puzzling. Grein's suggestion that *nærende* is a present participial form of *neom*, "non sum," is hardly tenable. The form may possibly be a corruption of *neriende*, present participle of *nerian*, and Vincenti, p. 73, translates: "Wer waren die Retter?" Holthausen, Anglia XXIII, 124, and Anglia Beibl. XXVII, 355, suggests as possible emendations *nearwende*, *neosende*, *nætende*, *nægende*. Menner emends plausibly to *hwæt næren ðe wæron*, "what (sort of things) might not exist that (yet) would exist"; see his note, pp. 133–134. But since Saturn does not answer this question put to him by Solomon, it is impossible to tell from the context just what the proper form or meaning is, and the MS. *nærende* is therefore retained in the text. **341** besceadeð] Holthausen, Anglia XXIII, 125, would read *bescĕadweð* for metrical reasons. **344a**] The proper restoration is obviously *eorð[we]lan*. **347** eadgum] The older edd. read *endgum* (Grein suggesting *eadgum* as an emendation), but the MS. clearly has *eadgum*. Is *eadgum* adverbial? **360** woroldrice] So the MS., not *woruldrice* as reported by Menner. **362** forildan] Schipper, Assmann follow the MS. reading *for ildo*. As it stands in the MS., the sentence is without a verb, and Schipper suggests that a verb has fallen out after *sið*, l. 363. But the addition of a verb to l. 363a would cause metrical difficulties, and the emendation of *for ildo* to *forildan* seems the best way out of the difficulty. So also Menner. Kemble, Grein read *foryldan*, without noting the MS. reading.   **363** deoran] Grein suggested *deopan* and, in Germania X, 428, *deorcan*. But *deoran*, from *dēor*, "severe, dire," gives the desired meaning. See l. 122.   **364** Gode oð̃ðe yfle] Apparently nom. plur., referring to the *twegen getwinnas*, l. 366. The stressed position of *ðæt*, l. 364a, in the verse requires us to take it as a pronoun rather than as a conjunction, and the punctuation in the text, with a question mark after *ðæt*, seems to do justice to the poet's intention. Translate: "But how does this happen? Twins, good or bad, [even] when they are born of the same mother do not have the same honor."   **367–369**] Menner, putting *swiðe* at the end of l. 367, arranges *leoftæle...hwile* as a single expanded (three-stress) line. In the older arrangement (as in the present text), l. 369a is unusually short, and Holthausen, Anglia XXXV, 167, would add *her* after *leofað*. In Eng. Stud. XXXVII, 205, he had proposed a more extensive change, transferring *on eorðan* from l. 367 to l. 369, and transposing l. 367b:

> oð̃er bið unlæde,   oð̃er eadig bið,
> swiðe leoftæle   mid leoda duguð̃um,
> oð̃er lytle hwile   leofað on eorð̃an, etc.

384 agen hlaford] The earlier edd., retaining the MS. *ængan*, took *fram ðam unlædan ængan hlaford* together, and so Bos.-Tol., p. 16, and Grein-Köhler, p. 26, who read *hlaforde* for *hlaford*. Bos.-Tol. translates, "from the sole lord." Holthausen, Anglia Beibl. XXVII, 355, objects to the half-line *ængan hlaforde* on metrical grounds, and would read *fregan* (the old uncontracted form of *frean*) for *hlaforde*. But the adjective *unlædan* must refer to the unfortunate man rather than to his lord, and the emendation of *ængan* to *agen*, as in the text, brings out this meaning. Translate, "his own lord looks away frequently from the miserable man." Menner emends *ængan* to *ænga*, nom. sing., "his only lord."   **388** gewyrcan] So the MS., not *gewyrcean* as reported by Menner. **389** and dædfruman] Kemble, Grein read *and dæd fremman* (*dæda* would be more regular), but Menner, p. 136, explains this line as meaning "illustrious renown for courage and an heroic prince (as his lord)."   **396** neð̃yð̃] Assmann reads *ne ð̃yð̃* as two words, but the MS. has *neð̃yð̃*. The negative *ne ð̃yð̃*, "does not thrive" (with *ð̃ȳð̃* from *ð̃eon*), would be inconsistent with ll. 398b–399, and it seems that we must read *neð̃yð̃* (= *nēð̃eð̃*, from *nēð̃an*). Kock, JJJ., p. 69, translates, "at night it boldly flows." Menner emends to *nēð̃eð̃* in his text. Holthausen, Anglia Beibl. XXVII, 356, takes *neð̃yð̃* as a corruption of *nȳdeð̃*, "strives, hastens," but *nȳdan, nīdan*, "to compel, urge," is not elsewhere found in intransitive use. As it stands in the MS., l. 396b has no alliteration, and Kock, JJJ., p. 69, would emend *cræfte* to *[neod]cræfte;* similarly Holthausen, Anglia XXIII, 125, suggests *[nearo]cræfte*, and so Menner in his text.   **399** stillan neahtes] There is a gap in the text at this point, the end of page 22 of A, where a leaf has probably been lost from the MS.; see Introd., **p.** lv.

<h1 style="text-align:center">401–505</h1>

404 æfter] So the MS., not *æftær* as reported by Assmann.   **419** eorl to gesihð̃e] So the MS. Kemble, Schipper read *eorlum gesihð̃e* without comment, Grein *eorlum on gesihðe,* Assmann and Menner *eorle to gesihðe.* Grein's reading makes the best sense, but it is possible that something is lost here, or that the text is otherwise corrupt.   **430** ðreamedlan] See l. 242, note.   hwæðerne aðreoteð ær] "Which one will become weary first," with *aðreotan* used impersonally with the accusative. See Bos.-Tol., Supplement, p. 55. **434** moniges fengon] "Obtained many a thing." The transitive use of *fōn* with genitive object is not unparalleled; see *heaþoglemma feng, deopra dolga,* Riddle 56, 3–4.   **436** tuion] For *twēon,* acc. sing. of *twēo,* "doubt," here used in the sense of "difference."   **439** scyð] Menner expands to *scyðeð.* Regardless of the form, the verb must be *sceððan,* "to injure."   **448** tohwan] The MS. seems to have *to hwan,* not *to hwon* as reported by Menner.   **449–450**] The impersonal use of *aðreotan,* as in l. 430: "Lo! it (*hie,* acc. sing., i.e. fate), living, will be wearied at last, so that it will not propagate enmity through the conflicts of crimes."   **451** Nolde gæd geador] "There would not [be] any fellowship together." The use of *Nolde* is unusual, but the sense is clear.   **453–454**] Line 453*b* seems overlong, and Holthausen, Anglia Beibl. XXVII, 356, would arrange ll. 453–454 to read:

> oðer his dryhtne hierde,   oðer him ðurh dierne cræftas
> ongan wyrcan ....
> segn ond side byrnan, etc.

455–457] A good deal of these three lines is now illegible in the MS. The letters *-an* of *sittan,* l. 455*b,* were not visible to me, but are printed on the authority of Zupitza, Anglia III, 530, and Menner. In ll. 456–457 only those letters are printed which Menner reports as clear in the MS. He restores with some certainty to [*t*]*y*[*d*]*ran* in l. 456*a, his* [*to*]*r*[*nes ne*] *cuðe* in l. 456*b,* and *se æðel*[*a ð*]*eoden* in l. 457*b.* Zupitza had previously read *cuðe* in l. 456*b,* but *cyrran* at the beginning of l. 456*a.* Menner translates ll. 456*b*–457*a,* "until he should know no end of his spite (?) through internal generation."   **459–460**] Menner, following Holthausen, Anglia Beibl. XXI, 175, arranges ll. 459–460*a* as one line and reads *Þæt sindon* [*ða feondas*] *ða usic feohtað on* as the following line. But the reading of the text, without any addition to l. 460*b,* seems adequate: "Those are the ones who fight against us."   **465*a***] This half-line is unusually short, and Holthausen, Anglia Beibl. XXVII, 356, would supply *beorhta* after *him.* Earlier, in Anglia XXIII, 125, he had suggested *bealu* (acc. plur. neuter of the adjective, modifying *bearn*) after *him.* But *bearn,* l. 465*b,* may be singular, "the child of the inhabitants of heaven," referring to Christ or to an angel, and subject of *bebead;* see Vincenti, p. 79. Holthausen, Anglia Beibl. XXVII, 356, suggests *brego heofonwara.*   **469** wælcealde] The weak adjective forms, here and in *ðearle,* l. 473, are worthy of notice.   **478** ðara ðe man age] The MS. *ðara ðe man man age* is evidently a corruption, and a vocalic alliteration is required. Holthausen, Anglia XXIII, 125, would read *ðara ðe æðm age,* "of those who have breath," following Bouterwek's suggestion. Later suggestions by Holthausen are *ðara ðe mægn age,* Anglia Beibl. XXVII, 357, and *ðara ðe age naman,* Anglia Beibl. XXXI, 27. For the latter reading, he compares Genesis 719. Kock, Anglia XLIV, 113, would read *ðara ðe endeman age,* with *endemān* meaning "final pain." Menner emends to *ðara ðe a manige* *deað abæde*, "who may ever claim death, compel it." None of these emendations is wholly convincing. Except for the alliteration, *ðara ðe man age*, "of those who have crime," i.e. "of those who are sinful," does reasonably well. This reading requires the insertion of a relative in l. 479a.   **479a**] Supplying the relative *ðe*, with Holthausen, Anglia Beibl. XXVII, 357, translate, "Is there any of men on this earth...who may compel death," etc.   In Anglia Beibl. XXXI, 191, Holthausen supplies *ðone* for the relative, taking *deað* as the subject of *abæde*.   **480**] Unless *cwide* is corrupt, we must read *calendcwide* as a compound, "tale of days," with a word to be supplied to fill out the second half-line.   Holthausen, Anglia XXIII, 125, suggests the addition of *clæne*, "completely," before *arunnen*, and so Menner in his text.   **482–485**] The letters printed in the text are those which Menner reports as clear in the MS. The letters *en-* of *engel*, l. 482b, and *-an* of *willan*, l. 485b, were not visible to me when I examined the MS.   In l. 482a Menner restores *Æghwylc*[*um men*] (as also previously Schipper and Assmann); in l. 483, *dryhten heo*[*fona ðonne dæg styr*]*eð;* in ll. 484b–485a, *hu his hyge* [*wille græ*]*dig growan*, etc.   **489–490**] There is no indication of a loss in the MS. here.   We need, however, an antithesis between the good angel and the bad angel, as in the preceding and following lines.   Grein assumed the loss of a full line, *oðer cymeð of heahþrymme heofona rices*, before l. 489; he then reads *oðer cymeð of steame þære stylenan helle.*   Assmann also assumes the loss of a line before l. 489, but supplies nothing. Holthausen, Anglia Beibl. XXVII, 357, assumes only the loss of *of steame* after *oðer cymeð*.   The arrangement in the text follows Menner.

NOTES ON THE MENOLOGIUM
1–100

The Menologium] For a discussion of this poem, see Introd., pp. lx ff.   **4** Hælend] Probably intended as a translation of the name Jesus, as assumed by Fox, p. 59, and Wülker.   See Ormulum (ed. Holt), ll. 4266ff., 4302ff.   That is, the baptism of the Lord took place on the eighth day after his birth (Luke ii.21), or January 1st.   The phrase *on midne winter*, l. 2, is taken by the edd. to refer to the specific date of the birth of Christ, December 25th, rather than to "midwinter" in general.   But December 24th, the vigil of the Nativity, may be intended; see Introd., p. lxiii.   **5** þa sylfan tiid] Accusative of time, "eodem tempore," Grein-Köhler, p. 674.   That is, "At this same time [people] have the early [part of the] year."   The construction with a preposition is found in l. 45, *on þa ylcan tiid.*   **8** to tune] Here and in ll. 16, 34, 89, 108, 219; the alternative form *on tun* appears in ll. 28, 78, 138, 183.   These seem to be the earliest examples in English of the popular locution, "to town," as in the Middle English "Lenten ys come wiþ love to toune" and the modern "when summer comes to town."   **10** gerum] For *gēarum*, "formerly."   The usual form is *gēara*.   Wülker suggests a doubt whether the MS. has *gerum* or *geriim*, but the reading seems quite clearly to be *gerum*.   **11** embe...þætte] An elliptical construction used frequently in this text, ll. 15–16, 19–20, 23, 54–55, etc.   See

Fritsche, Darstellung der Syntax in dem altengl. Menologium, p. 26.   13
twelfta dæg] "Twelfth-night." Holthausen, Anglia Beibl. III, 239, would read
twelftan, acc. sing., agreeing with *þæne*. Holthausen's reading is perhaps
more in accord with ideal syntax, but see Grein-Köhler, p. 303 (under *hātan*,
4), and Cosijn, Beitr. XIX, 443. Wülker puts *twelfta dæg* within quotation
marks.   18 fær] The neuter noun *fǽr*, "journey," here and in l. 167, with
Februarius and *Septembres* genitive. So Cosijn, Beitr. XIX, 443f. Grein-
Köhler, p. 174, suggests that *fær* is for *fǽr*, a variant spelling of *fæger*, "fair,"
and so Wülker.   31 cyme] Instr. sing.?   That is, "the month (*kalend*) is
known by its coming"?   The construction here is rather obscure, but this
seems to be the only possible interpretation.   32 bises] "Bissextile, leap
year."   The form *bisses*, proposed by Holthausen, Anglia XLVI, 54, would be
preferable on both metrical and etymological grounds.   33 he] Referring
back to *kalend*, l. 31.   43 þeow] Holthausen, Anglia Beibl. V, 226, would
emend to *þeos* (= *þēowas*) as a plural, parallel to *rincas*. But *þeow* is acc.
sing., parallel to *þæne*, l. 42.   54 folcum gefrǽge] Parallel to *mǽre*, l. 53;
see Kock, Anglia XLVII, 267. Translate, "that was a famous event, well known
to peoples." Grein, Wülker omit the comma after *wyrd*.   60 Þis is, etc.]
A translation of Psalm cxvii.24 (Psalm cxviii.24 in the English Bible). The
corresponding passage, Psalm 117,22, in the Paris Psalter is similar,

> Þis ys se dæg   þe hine drihten us
> wisfæst geworhte   wera cneorissum,
> eallum eorðtudrum   eadgum to blisse,

and the quotation here is perhaps derived from it. For the bearing of this
on the date of the Menologium, see Introd., p. lxv.   66 wisra gewyrdum]
"By the rules of wise men," Bos.-Tol., p. 473.   ac sceal, etc.] "But a man
wise with years will skillfully find the holy days in the cycle."   70 wisse]
If the MS. *wisse* is retained, we must take it as the adverbial form of *wis(s)*,
"certain, sure"; but *wis(s)* is not elsewhere found in the poetry, the usual word
being the compound *gewis(s)*. Bouterwek emends to *wise*, and so Grein,
Germania X, 422 ("cantu," Grein-Köhler, p. 806). Or we might read *wise*
as the adverb, "wisely."   71a þæt] Holthausen, Anglia Beibl. III, 239,
would read *þæs*, citing ll. 11, 19, 23, etc.; but the adverbial *þæs* (corresponding
to *þæs* in the other passages) is already present in l. 72. The word *þæt*, l. 71,
is the conjunction in the dependent clause, *areccan...þæt...man reliquias rǽran
onginneð*, etc. The pleonastic *þæt* in l. 73 is not unparalleled.   71b niht
and fifum] For l. 71 the MS. has only *þ embe nihgontyne niht*. To fill out the
verse, Grein and Imelmann read *niht[gerimes]*. But nineteen days after April
1st would give only April 20th, and the Greater Litany, to which reference is
evidently made here, falls on April 25th. Henel, Studien zum altenglischen
Computus, pp. 79f., would therefore read *niht [and fifum]*, i.e. nineteen and five,
or twenty-four, nights after April 1st. Henel's reading has been adopted in the
text.   76] There is no sign of a loss in the MS., but most edd. assume that
a half-line is missing here. Grein, taking *smicere on gearwum* as the second
half-line, supplies *smylte and smeðe* for the first half of the line. In Germania

X, 422, he would supply *þæs embe siex nieht* for l. 76*a*. Imelmann supplies *ymb syx niht þæs*, and this reading satisfies both sense and meter. We expect a number in this line, connecting April 25th, the last date referred to (see l. 71*b*, note), with May 1st, and six is the correct number of days.   **78 þrymilce]** Suggested by Plummer and adopted by Imelmann in his text, for the MS. *þrymlice*. Except for January and July, all the other Anglo-Saxon month-names are mentioned in the text (ll. 16, 37, 72, 108, 138, 164, 184, 195, 221), and it is probable that the name of May was intended here, a simple error of transposition having been made by the scribe.   **þearfe]** "Benefit"; see Bos.-Tol., p. 1040, under *þearf*, V.

<h1 style="text-align:center">101–200</h1>

101 guman a fyrn] The MS. *guman awyrn* does not make sense, and Grein, Germania X, 422, and Wülker read *guman a fyrn*, with *a fyrn*, "ever before," parallel to *ær*, l. 102. This emendation, also approved by Holthausen, Anglia Beibl. III, 240, is not entirely satisfactory on stylistic grounds, but it may stand in default of a better reading. Another possibility is Grein's earlier reading, *gumena fyrn*, with *gumena* gen. plur. dependent on *ænigne*. Imelmann reads *guman awern* but does not tell how he would interpret it.   **106*b*–109]** Bouterwek, Wülker take *monaÐ*, l. 106, and *Ærra LiÐa*, l. 108, as parallel nominatives, with *Iunius*, l. 109, accusative. But Kock, JJJ., p. 55, rightly takes *Ærra LiÐa* as parallel to *Iunius*, both accusative in spite of the nominative endings. **107 twa and feower]** So Imelmann, following Piper, Die Kalendarien und Martyrologien der Angelsachsen, p. 56. The other edd. retain the MS. *twa and þreo*. The count here is from St. Augustine's Day (May 26th, according to the traditional English reckoning) to June 1st, or six days. A similar error occurs in l. 188, where the proper reading is indicated by the alliteration; see the note on that line.   **117 Iohannes]** That is, John the Baptist (June 24th), not John the Apostle, in spite of the phrase *þeodnes dyrling*, l. 116*b*, and such biblical passages as John xiii.23, xix.26, etc. John the Baptist is mentioned again in ll. 156*b*–162, under August 29th, the day of his death.   **wearÐ acenned]** There is no alliteration in this half-line. Holthausen, Anglia Beibl. III, 240, would move *wearÐ* to l. 115, before *wuldres*, and transpose l. 117 to read *Iohannes acenned | in geardagum*. In Anglia Beibl. V, 226, he takes *acenned* as the first word of a line otherwise lost, and rearranges to read:

Iohannes wearÐ   in geardagum
acenned . . . .

Kock, JJJ., p. 55, keeping the MS. arrangement of this line, would provide the alliteration by adding *iu* before *wearÐ*, thus: *Iohannes in geardagum [iu] wearÐ acenned*.   **119]** Bouterwek and Grein end the sentence with *sumor*, reading *Mycles on æþelum wide is geweorÐod*, etc., as the beginning of the new sentence. So also Kock, Anglia XLIII, 309, who interprets *on æþelum* as "amongst men, here on earth," parallel to *geond hæleÐa bearn*, l. 121. The MS. has a large colored capital *W* in *Wide*, but the evidence of capital letters is not necessarily conclusive.   **134 ond]** The MS. has *on*, emended by Bouterwek and Wülker to *ond.* Imelmann reads *eac twentigum.* 136–137 þæs...þæs] Grein, Germania X, 422, would omit *þæs* in one of these two places; Holthausen, Anglia Beibl. III, 240, points out that the meter does not permit the omission of *þæs* in l. 137. Imelmann omits *þæs* in l. 136. This is, naturally, the easiest recourse for an editor. But the word *symle* in the same half-line also falls under suspicion, since *symle...ymb seofon niht* should mean "every seven days"; see Soul and Body, I, 10, Andreas 157. It is quite possible that a deeper corruption underlies the MS. reading here, and the text has therefore not been emended. 137 sumere] For the MS. *sumere,* Bouterwek reads *smicere,* "finely, elegantly," and so Grein, Germania X, 422, and Imelmann. Much can be said for *smicere* on palaeographical grounds, and l. 76, above, provides a possible parallel. But it is not true that *sumere* is meaningless, as Imelmann says; the expression "made bright with summer" is certainly not unintelligible, though perhaps somewhat poetic. If an emendation is to be made, *sunnan* (instr.) *gebrihted* is also a possibility. 138 welhwær] The MS. *welhwæt,* "everything," might be object of *bringeð* (as Bos.-Tol., p. 1186, and Grein-Köhler, p. 770, seem to take it), but it can hardly be parallel to *hlafmæssan dæg,* l. 140. The emendation to *welhwær,* "everywhere," gives good sense with little violence to the MS. 139 Agustus] The word *Agustus* is hardly long enough for a half-line, and Holthausen, Anglia Beibl. V, 226, would supply *fær* (as in ll. 18, 167) or *monð* (for *monað,* as in ll. 56, 132) after *Agustus.* He would also add *fær* or *monð* to fill out l. 196a, *Nouembris,* and l. 220a, *Decembris.* There are other words besides *fær* and *mon(a)ð* which might be supplied here; but since we have to do not with a single short half-line but with three half-lines of similar form (ll. 139a, 196a, 220a), and since the Anglo-Saxon treatment of foreign proper names seems to have been guided by variable factors (see Genesis 1240, 1241, 1736, etc.), it is perhaps better not to emend. 141 ymbe...wanan] "After the same number of days except one wanting," i.e. after six days. 151 on neorxnawange] The MS. *neorxnawange,* if taken as dat. sing., has no apparent syntactical relationship to the rest of the sentence. Wülker reads *neornawang,* acc. sing., parallel to *ham,* but the half-line is then too short. Bouterwek, Grein emend to the gen. sing. *neorxnawanges,* dependent on *ham,* and so also Holthausen, Anglia Beibl. V, 226. A further possibility is *on neorxnawange,* as in the text. 155 Bartholomeus] Gen. sing. 156 wyrd] The MS. *wyrð,* retained by Wülker and Plummer, does not mean anything unless it is an error for *wyrðe,* "worthy," parallel to *welþungen.* Grein, Imelmann read *wyrd,* as in the text, "an excellent event." See *mære wyrd,* l. 53. 167 fær] See l. 18, note. 170 ymbe] Apparently *ymbe* goes with both *dagena worn* and *þreotyne,* "after a number of days, thirteen," etc. 172 his] Modifying *gast,* l. 171, not *metodsceafte.* 184 cigað] So Bouterwek, Grein, Wülker, as plural verb with *igbuende.* Holthausen, Anglia Beibl. V, 226, condemns *cigað* on metrical grounds and assumes a singular verb *cigð* with plural subject. 187 healdað] With an indefinite "they" to be supplied in sense? Or perhaps *igbuende,* l. 185, is to be carried over as subject. 188 seofon] The feast of St. Simon and St. Jude, October 28th, is twenty-seven days after the first of the month, not twenty-five as indicated by the MS. reading *ymb twentig...and fif nihtum.*

Here the alliteration confirms the emendation to *seofon*. See l. 107, note.
193 ofstum] Bouterwek emends to *ofetum*, "fructibus."   bringð] At first
sight there seems to be no subject for this verb, but *Blotmonað*, l. 195, and
Nouembris, l. 196, are subjects, with *eadignesse*, l. 197, object. The sequence
of ideas here is somewhat complex.   **196** Nouembris] See l. 139, note.

201–231

206 moton] So Grein, for the MS. *mot*, to agree with the plural subjects in ll.
206*b*–207*a*. Sievers, Beitr. X, 517, condemns *moton* on metrical grounds and
would retain *mot* as singular verb with plural subject. See the note on *cigað*,
l. 184. Wülker retains *mot* here, but emends to *cigað*, l. 184. If we read
cigað in l. 184, consistency requires *moton* here.   wangas grene] Parallel to
foldan frætuwe, l. 207*a*, both being subjects of *wunian ne moton*. Translate,
"so that to us may not remain the green plains, the ornaments of the earth."
Grein-Köhler, p. 836, takes *wangas grene* as accusative, object of *wunian*,
"that the ornaments of the earth may not inhabit the green fields."   **211**
fan gode] The early edd. made heavy work of the MS. *fangode*. The reading
fan gode, "[men] hostile to God," was proposed by Grein, Germania X, 422, and
adopted by Wülker and Imelmann.   **214** Clementes] Acc. sing.   **219**
morgen . . . monað] Is *morgen* acc. sing. and *monað* nom. sing., or *morgen* nom.
sing. and *monað* acc. sing.? The former construction is perhaps preferable
(and so Grein-Köhler, pp. 479–480), but there is no way of being sure. The
forms *Decembris* and *Ærra Iula*, ll. 220–221, do not help, since they are not
necessarily nominatives; see ll. 106*b*–109, note.   **220** Decembris] See l. 139,
note.   **229** tiida] The meaning requires a plural here, and Cosijn, Beitr.
XIX, 444, suggests that the MS. *tiid* may be a neuter plural. But the noun
tid is not elsewhere found as a neuter, and the emendation to *tiida*, acc. plur.
feminine, is not unnecessarily violent.   **231** on þas sylfan tiid] "At this same
time"? Liebermann, Archiv CX, 99, would take this half-line to mean "concerning these same feast days," in which case *tiid* must be emended to *tiida*,
as in l. 229. Liebermann, in support of his interpretation, argues that the
compiler of this calendar can hardly be comparing it with earlier works of the
same sort, and that therefore *on þas sylfan tiid* cannot mean "at this time."
But "at this time," even if it does not refer to the *haligra tiida þe man healdan
sceal*, l. 229, can certainly refer to the *gebod Sexna kyninges*, ll. 230–231, and
Imelmann, p. 39, so takes it. Sokoll, Anglia Beibl. XIV, 315, would interpret
the phrase to mean "at the same time in the year," as referring only to the
fixed feasts in the church calendar, since the author of the poem does not attempt to indicate (except in the reference to Easter, ll. 56ff.) the possible dates
for the moveable feasts.

NOTES ON MAXIMS II

Maxims II] For a discussion of this text, and a comparison with Maxims I
in the Exeter Book, see Introd., pp. lxvi f.   **6***b*] The edd. place commas before
and after l. 6*b*, without parentheses; but the words *he bið lengest ceald* are clearly

parenthetical, interrupting the parallel structure of ll. 5*b*–6*a*, 7*a*, etc. Line 7*b* is a similar interruption of syntax. These two half-lines, l. 6*b* and l. 7*b*, are accordingly placed within parentheses in the text. Lines 8*b*–9 are, however, not to be taken as a parenthesis, since *hærfest* is the subject not only of *byð*, carried over in sense from l. 5*b*, but also of *bringeð*.   9 geres, him] Kluge, Wülker, Sweet (4–9 ed.), Sedgefield read *geares* in l. 9*a*, though Sievers, ZfdA. XV, 466, and Plummer note that the *a* is in a later hand. The *o* above *him*, l. 9*b*, reported by Sievers and Plummer as written by a later hand, is rejected by Wülker, who calls it merely a round spot on the MS. But both the *a* and the *o* are clearly visible as such, in a somewhat reddish ink, and were perhaps added as late as the sixteenth century. In the text the uncorrected readings *geres* and *him* are preferred.   10 switolost] The MS. reading *soð bið swicolost*, "truth is most treacherous," gives a rather difficult interpretation. Sweet emends to *swutolost*, "truth is most evident," and so also Sedgefield. Williams reads *switolost*, as a variant of Sweet's *swutolost;* this form is closer palaeographically to the MS. reading, and has been adopted in the text. Kock, JJJ., p. 35, would read *swæð bið swicolost*, "slippery ground is most treacherous," citing O.N. *svað*, "slippery place"; but no such meaning of *swæð* is known in Anglo-Saxon. Holthausen, Anglia Beibl. XXX, 3, suggests *sēað* for *soð*, perhaps as referring to a pit used as a trap.   13 Weax] The reading in the text, "Wax is wonderfully sticky," with *weax* for the MS. *wea*, follows the suggestion of *wex* (= *weax*) made by Cosijn, Tijdschrift voor Nederlandsche Taal- en Letterkunde I, 148. Cosijn's note, written as far back as 1881, has been unaccountably overlooked by the edd. The MS. *wea*, "grief," is hardly defensible.   19 earm] So Ettmüller, Grein, and later edd., except Earle, Kluge, and Plummer, for the MS. *earn*. The phrase *earm anhaga* is parallel to *wulf*, l. 18*b*.   24 mencgan] The MS. *mecgan* is retained by most of the early edd. and by Williams, in the sense "to stir, mix." There are two probable examples of *mecgan* in Anglo-Saxon medical recipes (see Bos.-Tol., p. 675), but in any case the verb requires a direct object which is lacking here. The emendation *mengan, mencgan*, first proposed by Ettmüller and adopted by Sweet, Kluge, Wülker, and Sedgefield, is partly open to the same objection, since *mengan* is regularly transitive. There is, however, one clear example of intransitive *mengan, mencgan* in Christ and Satan 131, *hat and ceald hwilum mencgað*, and Middle English examples of the intransitive use are given in the N.E.D. under *meng*. The emendation to *mencgan* is therefore adopted in the text, with *mereflode* taken as instrumental, "mingle with the sea-flood." Kock, JJJ., p. 36, takes *mereflode* as for *on mereflode*, a variation of *on yðum*.   31 flodgræg] "Flood-gray," appropriate enough as applied to a river. Kock, JJJ., p. 36, would read as two words, *flod græg*, "the torrent gray." The earlier edd. read the MS. incorrectly as *fold græg*, and Sweet retains *foldgræg* as an emendation. H. Kern, Taalkundige Bijdragen I, 193ff., would read *foldgæg*, "earth-swift." No adjective *gæg* is recorded in Anglo-Saxon, but Kern cites O.H.G. *gâhi*, Dutch *gauw*, "swift." The MS. reading seems adequate without emendation.   34 beorh] Perhaps for *beorc*, "birch-tree"? 40 mid sceote] Evidently "with rapid movement," though *scēot*, "quick, ready"

176 NOTES

176 NOTES

176 NOTES
176   NOTES

(O.N. *skjótr*), is not elsewhere used as a noun. But the form here may be *scĕote*, for *scote;* see Bos.-Tol., p. 839 (under *scot* III). Compare also *mid swiftum gesceote*, "with swift movement," Old English Version of the Heptateuch (ed. S. J. Crawford), 415, 42. For *scĕot* as an adjective, see Benedictine Rule (ed. A. Schröer), 97, 16. on heofenum] Sweet's emendation *of heofenum* gives somewhat better sense. 43*b*–45*a*] "A woman must visit her friend with hidden craft (i.e. secretly), if she does not wish to bring it about among the people that she is bought with rings." For this use of *gepĕon*, see Maxims I, 49. The passage is somewhat complicated in phraseology, and the meaning is not entirely clear. Perhaps the intention is: "A woman must conduct secret intrigues if she does not wish to be sought in marriage," with reference to marriage by purchase, and intended ironically, "A woman will not be married if she has had secret intrigues with a lover." Crawford, MLRev. XIX, 107, follows this interpretation. Williams, p. 150, suggests *wille* for *nelle*, "The woman shall by secret craft seek her friend, if she would . . . be bought with rings," evidently taking *dyrne cræfte* as meaning "by sorcery." Mawer's suggestion (quoted by Crawford), "A woman will find a lover by sorcery, if she does not succeed in getting married," does too much violence to the text, especially to the verb *nelle*. 45 sealte] Sweet, note, suggests *sealt*, as an adjective. 46 lyfthelm and laguflod] "Air and water," taken by Williams, pp. 150–151, as applying to fresh water in contrast with the salt water in l. 45*b*. The punctuation here is difficult; are *lyfthelm* and *laguflod* subjects of *weallan* or of *flowan*? 50ff.] With *sacan*, l. 53, to be understood throughout the sentence. 54 synne stælan] "Impute crime (or, hostility)," perhaps, as suggested by Kock, Anglia XXVII, 229, with the meaning of *stælan* extended to "avenge." See Beowulf 1340, 2485, and Klaeber, Modern Philology III, 261. Sweet's suggested translations (in his note), "institute sin" or "wage hostility," are now generally discredited. The meaning of *stælan* (though ambiguous in some passages) is certainly "impute, blame," rather than "institute," whether or not we accept Kock's translation "avenge" in the present passage. 56 fægere] "Justly," Bos.-Tol., Supplement, p. 198; or perhaps "fittingly," as in Maldon 22. Grein suggests the emendations *fĕore* and *fǽge*. 59 for] Probably for *fore*, "before," i.e. "who go before God," for judgment. The phrase is then parallel in sense to *domes bidað*, l. 60. The interpretation given by Williams, p. 151, "who for God depart," etc., is less convincing. 60 bidað] Sweet (4–9 ed.), note, suggests *bidan*, infinitive parallel to *hweorfan*, l. 58.

NOTES ON A PROVERB FROM WINFRID'S TIME

A Proverb from Winfrid's Time] For a discussion of this text, see Introd., pp. lxviiff. The interpretation of the two lines offers some difficulties, and no satisfactory translation exists. It is evident that *foręldit* is for *foryldeð*, *forieldeð*, "defers, delays," and that *domę* is dat. sing. There is therefore no direct object for *foręldit*. It seems best to take *domę* as parallel to *sigisitha gahuem,* and to translate, "Often a sluggard delays in his [pursuit of] glory, in each of victorious undertakings; therefore he dies alone." Williams, Gnomic Poetry in Anglo-Saxon, p. 70, note 3, translates *domę foręldit* as "loses by his delay."

NOTES ON THE JUDGMENT DAY II

1-100

The Judgment Day II] For a description of the MS. and a discussion of the literary problems connected with this poem, see Introd., pp. lxix ff.   3] As this line stands in the MS., there is no alliteration. Ettmüller suggested reading *swete burnan* (*swetan* would be more correct) for *wæterburnan*, or, as an alternative, *wægdon* (= *wagedon?*) for *swegdon* in the second half-line. Wülker, note, would read *wagedon* for the MS. *swegdon*. But, as Cosijn, Beitr. XIX, 443, pointed out, *wagedon* would properly refer to trees, as in l. 7, rather than to running brooks, as here. The MS. *swegdon*, on the other hand, makes excellent sense (compare the association of *swegan* and *forðyrnan* in Ælfric's Catholic Homilies (ed. Thorpe), I, 562, 14: *swegde ut ormæte wyll-spring, and mid micclum streame forð-yrnende wæs*), and the lack of alliteration in this line is paralleled in a number of other lines of the poem (such as ll. 4, 28, 42, 190, 251) for which plausible emendations are not available.   4] To supply the missing alliteration, Ettmüller reads *swa ic mægðum* (or *monnum* or *hæleðum*) *secge* for the second half-line. But see the preceding note.   8 gryre] Löhe emends to *styre*, "durch den antrieb der winde."   wolcn] Löhe reads *wop* for the MS. *wolcn*, "Weinen ward erregt"; but the half-line refers to the blowing of the wind described in ll. 7–8a. There is no corresponding matter in the Latin text.   11 unhyrlican] The word *unhyrlic* usually means "fierce, savage," Bos.-Tol., p. 1118; but here it must mean "mournful." The Latin text (see Introd., p. lxxi) has *carmina. . .lugubria.*   onhefde] A weak preterite of *onhebban,* elsewhere inflected as a strong verb.   12 eall swylce þu cwæde] Neither the Latin poem nor the English translation is addressed to any specific person, and there is nothing in the Latin text which sheds any light on the reference of this half-line. Löhe, p. 72, suggests that it was intended as a translation of *utpote* in the Latin.   12–13 synna, leahtra] Genitive objects of *gemunde;* see the other examples in Grein-Köhler, p. 484. Löhe unnecessarily emends *leahtra* to the accusative *leahtras.* The objects of *gemunde* in ll. 13b–14a are accusative, but such a shift of case is by no means unparalleled.   13 langan] Löhe emends to *laðan,* corresponding to the *inamabile tempus* of the Latin text, l. 7.   34 þæt ge. . .tearum] The Latin (l. 16) has *effusis lacrymis non parcite statim.*   41 abæred] This verb is not elsewhere recorded, but *abæred* evidently means "brought to light"; see the adjective *æ-bære,* Bos.-Tol., Supplement, p. 9. Trautmann (see Löhe, p. 73) suggested *abræded,* "spread out." For the Latin text of this passage, see the next note.   42] The Latin text here (ll. 20–21) has:

> omnia quin luci verbis reddantur apertis
> pectoris et linguae, carnis vel crimina saeva.

The words *crimina saeva* are not represented in the Anglo-Saxon text. Löhe therefore rearranges the passage as follows:

> openum wordum,
> eall abæred   breostes and tungan
> and flæsces swa some   [fyrena hreowe].

See also his note, p. 73.   This rearrangement of the text is possible but unnecessary.   The genitives in l. 42 may depend on *gylt* carried over from l. 39 (as Lumby suggested, p. 58); and for the lack of alliteration in this line, see l. 3, note.   **43 an]** Löhe emends to the weak form *ane*, for metrical reasons. **45 wope]** So all edd., for the MS. *wopa*.   The Latin text has *cum lacrymis*. **47]** For this line, the MS. has the unintelligible *Aglidene gyltas. mod god gode gehælan.*   Lumby doubtfully emended to *agiltende gyltas* ("the offenders in guilt") *mid gode gehælan*, omitting *god* as a scribal repetition and taking *mod* as an error for *mid*.   But Brandl, Anglia IV, 102, defends *aglidene* as meaning "slipped off, away" (see Bos.-Tol., Supplement, p. 29) and reads *aglidene mod* as the first half-line, taking *gyltas* as a gloss on these words which has crept into the text.   Brandl also omits *god*, reading *gode gehælan* as the second half-line.   Grein (see Wülker, note) retains *aglidene gyltas*, "past sins," omitting *mod god*.   Wülker follows Brandl in omitting *gyltas*, but reads *aglidene modgod*, with *modgod*, "good of mind," referring to *læce* in l. 46.   Holthausen, Anglia Beibl. V, 197, accepts Brandl's reading, which seems to give the most satisfactory sense.   The Latin text here has *qui solet allisos sanare*, and *aglidene mod* evidently represents the Latin *allisos*.   Compare also *wanhydige mod*, l. 50.   Löhe, following Trautmann (see his note, p. 75), emends to *agnidene gystas* (= *gāstas*) *mid gode gehælan*.   The verb *āgnīdan* is not recorded in the sense "to cast down," but for *forgnīdan*, "allidere," see Bos.-Tol., p. 311.   **51 waces fleaxes]** "Of pliant flax."   So Brandl, Anglia IV, 103, and Löhe, for the MS. *waces flæsces*.   The Latin (l. 26) has *nec lini tepidos undis exstinguere fumos*.   **57 on]** Löhe, following Trautmann (see his note, p. 75), reads *oþ* for the MS. *on*, citing the corresponding words *usque crucem* in l. 29 of the Latin text.   **66 cyþst]** So Lumby and Löhe, for the MS. *cystþ*.   Grein (see Wülker, note) and Wülker retain the MS. *cystþ* (= *cyst*) as a variant form. **81 lifes læcedomes]** Löhe reads *læcedomas* as accusative object of *bidst*, omitting *lifes*.   Wülker explains the MS. *læcedomes* as acc. plur., with weakened ending. Holthausen, Anglia Beibl. V, 197, would read *lifes læcedom*, for metrical reasons. The objects of *bidst* in l. 80b are accusative, and an accusative object would perhaps be preferable here; but for a similar shift of case, see ll. 12–13 and note. The Latin text (ll. 40–41) has *Cur. . .tibi non oras placidae fomenta medelae?* **94 egeslice]** So Löhe, for the MS. *egeslic*.   An adverb is required by the sense. **95 heahþrymme]** Instrumental, as in l. 116b; see Brandl, Anglia IV, 103.   The Latin text (ll. 48–49) has *celsithronus. . .judex.*

101–200

101 hliðu] The MS. has *hlida*, interpreted by Lumby and Wülker as "lids," i.e. the lids of graves.   But the Latin text (l. 51) corresponding to ll. 99–101 is *Terra tremet, montesque ruent, collesque liquescent,* with no reference to graves or tombs. Löhe reads *hliðu,* "und der berge abhänge weichen und zerschmelzen," the meaning indicated by the Latin text. The phrase *beorga hliðu,* "slopes of mountains," is perhaps unusual, but for the compound *beorhhliþ,* see Bos.-Tol., p. 86.   **102 sæ]** Gen. sing. fem.; see Sievers, Angels. Gram., §266, Anm. 2. Lumby unnecessarily emends to *sæs.*   **105 geþuxsað]** Löhe emends to *geþuxsad* as a past participle, following the reading *geþuhsod* in the homily (Wulfstan, ed. Napier, 137, 9). The verb *þuhsian, þuxian* ("to become dark, make dark"?) is not elsewhere recorded, but for possible etymologies of the word, see Holthausen, Anglia Beibl. V, 197, and Altengl. etymol. Wörterbuch, p. 373.   **110 flecgan]** This verb is not elsewhere found in Anglo-Saxon, and is unexplained unless we can take it as causative and related in some way to *fléogan.* Lumby, Wülker consider it an error for *flēgan, flȳgan,* "to put to flight"; Wülker suggests emending to *fleogan* or *flegan,* but *fléogan* is not authenticated as a transitive verb. Löhe, following Trautmann (see his note, p. 77), emends to *flēman.* The Latin text (l. 55) has merely *pallida nocturnam nec praestat luna lucernam,* and the reading of the homily (Napier, 137, 11–12), *and se mona næfð nane lihtincge,* offers no help.   **112 deaðbeacnigende tacn]** The MS. here has only *deað beacnigende,* which is incomplete in sense unless we accept *beacnigende* as a substantive, as Lumby does ("death-tokenings"). But the Latin text (l. 56) has *signa minantia mortem,* and the homily (Napier, 137, 13) accordingly reads *deað beacnigende tacn.* The word *tacn,* nom. plur., is evidently to be supplied here in the poem, and so Wülker (*tacen*). And *deaðbeacnigende* is best read as a compound, in spite of the loss of alliteration; see Bos.-Tol., Supplement, p. 147.   **114 styllað]** Intransitive, corresponding to *superum. . .veniet. . .potestas* in l. 57 of the Latin text. See Christ 745, 747. The homily (Napier, 137, 14) has *standað.*   **120 æghwanum]** For *æghwanan,* "on every side."   **121 .gehwylc]** So the MS., not *gewhylc,* as reported by Wülker and Löhe.   **125]** Not only is the MS. *stent he heortleas and earh* too short for a full line, but the pronoun *he* has no antecedent nearer than *gehwylc* in l. 121. The proper form of the line, *stent hergea mæst,* etc., is indicated by the corresponding text in the homily (Napier, 137, 22), *þonne ðær stent ealra hergea mæst heortleas and earh.* The letters erased from the MS. after *he* cannot be deciphered; it may be that the scribe found the text in a corrupt state and was unable to resolve the difficulty.   **126 amarod]** This word is not elsewhere recorded in Anglo-Saxon, but Holthausen, Anglia Beibl. V, 197, suggests that it is connected with *mearu,* "tender."   **129 þænne]** The edd., except Löhe, retain the very unlikely MS. reading *Æne,* translated by Lumby, "at once." But the homily (Napier, 137, 23–24) has *þonne bið gebann mycel þyder aboden,* and Löhe's emendation of *Æne* to *þænne* seems necessary. For the form *þænne* (= *þonne*), see ll. 29, 124, 244.   **131 feded]** The homily (Napier, 137, 25) reads *þe on foldan wearð æfre gefeded.*   **140 þinga on eorðan]** Löhe emends to *þissere eorðan,* following the reading of the homily (Napier, 137, 31–138, 1), *on þystrum healum þissere worulde.*   **149 eahgemearces]** "As far as the eye can reach," Bos.-Tol., Supplement, p. 165.   **153 reaðe]** For *reðe,* "fierce." The scribe repeated mechanically the *ea* of the preceding adjective *read.* See l. 166, below. Lumby compares also Fortunes of Men 46, *read reþe gled*.   ræsct] Löhe reads *ræst*, from *ræ̆san*, "rush," as a synonym of *efesteð*, and corresponding to *festinans* in the Latin text (l. 76). But there is no objection to the MS. *ræsct*, from *ræscettan*, "to crackle," repeating the sense of *braslað* in l. 152.   154 gefremme] The preterite *gefremede* is out of place here after the present forms in ll. 152–153, and Löhe emends to *gefremme*, following the reading of the homily (Napier, 138, 8–9), *hu he synfullum susle gefremme*.   170 be agnum gewyrhtum] So Grein (see Wülker, note) and later edd., for the MS. *bearnū gewyrhtum*. Trautmann (in Löhe, note) proposed *be earnung-gewyrhtum*.   178] As it stands in the MS., *Wa þe nu þu þeowast*, this line is incomplete in sense. But, as Wülker, note, points out, the text of the homily (Napier, 138, 19–20) furnishes the correct reading, *wa ðe nu, ðu þe þeowast ðissere worulde*, and the text has been emended accordingly. Löhe supplies *þissere worulde*, but not the relative *þe* before *þeowast;* he puts the comma before *nu*, and translates, "Wehe dir, nun dienst du dieser welt."   182 ondræd] An imperative? The homily (Napier, 138, 21) has *ondrætst*, and perhaps we should so emend here. Löhe reads *ondrætst* in his text.   184 weana] Löhe emends to *womma*, following the reading of the homily (Napier, 138, 23), *womma to leanes*.   185–186] The Latin text (l. 92) has *Quae superant sensus cunctorum et dicta virorum*.   187 beon] Trautmann (in Löhe, p. 80) suggests *geo* for the MS. *beon*. The Latin text (l. 93) has *Nec vox ulla valet miseras edicere poenas*.   189 fulle] So Brandl, Anglia IV, 103, and Löhe, following the Latin text (l. 94), *ignibus. . .loca plena*. The reading of the homily (Napier, 138, 24) is also incorrect, *and ða fulan stowa*.   190] There is no alliteration in this line, but see l. 3, note. Grein (see Wülker, note) would read *singrimmum* for the MS. *grimmum*.   192 þrosma] Gen. plur.? The homily (Napier, 138, 26) has *se þrosmiga lig*, and so Löhe in his text. In the second half-line, *þrece* is probably for *þræce*, gen. sing. of *þracu*; see Wülker, note.   195 he] The oven, in l. 195*a*. Löhe would omit all of l. 195*b*, which has no counterpart in the homily and which he would explain as a late addition to the text.   197ff.] Löhe reads *þæt is atul gewrixl!* for l. 197*a*, and then takes *wendað* in the intransitive sense, "Die armen geschöpfe gehen. . .darin," etc. But *wendað* is more probably transitive, with *gewrixl* as subject: "This dire vicissitude turns miserable men therein for ever," etc. This agrees with the sense of the Latin text (l. 98), *His miseris vicibus miseri volvuntur in aevum obscuras inter. . .noctes*. Wülker, note, explains *gewrixl* as object of *wendað*, but how he would construe the rest of the sentence he does not say. In l. 197*b*, the MS. *earm sceape* is an obvious error for *earmsceapene;* the homily (Napier, 138, 29–30) has *Ðuss atelic gewrixl þa earmsceapenan men*, etc.

201–306

201 stefn] So Löhe, for the MS. *stef ne*. The MS. reading may, however, be a corruption of *stefn ne*, repeating the negative.   stearcheard] Löhe reads *stearc and heard*, for metrical reasons, following Holthausen, Anglia Beibl. V, 197.   202 nawiht elles] Löhe emends to *for wohdædum*, the reading of the

homily at this point (Napier, 139, 4).   **208** unstences] So Lumby and Wülker, for the MS. *un stence.* Löhe emends to *unstenca,* following the plural form in the homily, *buton unstenca ormætnessa* (Napier, 139, 7–8). But since our poem has the singular *ormætnesse,* the correct emendation here is probably *unstences.* **215ff.**] Löhe begins a new sentence with *For hwi,* l. 215, with a question mark after *witu,* l. 218. But the Latin text (ll. 107–108) has an indirect question here, *cur caro. . .atro perpetuas meruisset carcere poenas.*   **215** fyrngende] The Latin text (l. 107) has *caro luxurians.* There is no Anglo-Saxon verb *fyrgan, fyrian* which can be forced into this meaning, and Wülker, Löhe emend the MS. *fyrgende* to *fyrngende,* from *fyrenian,* "to sin."   **219** leoht] For *leohteþ,* "gives light."   **222**] This line as it stands in the MS., *ne þara wera worn wihte,* is much too short metrically, and the reference of *wihte* is not apparent. Holthausen, Anglia Beibl. V, 197, citing the Latin *flentibus* (l. 111), emends to *þara we[þend]ra worn* for l. 222a, and transfers *ne* to the second half-line, *ne wiht e[lles].* Löhe accepts Holthausen's *wependra,* but reads *ne wependra worn wiht gefrefreð.* The emendation to *wependra* seems highly probable, and it has been adopted in the text; but the suggested emendations of l. 222b are more speculative.   **226** ac þær] For the MS. *þ bið,* Lumby and Wülker read *þær bið.* But we expect an adversative conjunction here, corresponding to *sed* in the Latin text (l. 114). Brandl, Anglia IV, 103, reads *ac bið,* Löhe *ac þær bið.* Löhe's reading has been adopted in the text.   **229** adl] The MS. *eald* as an adjective is impossible here, and the reading of the homily, *adl and yrre and æmelnys* (Napier, 139, 17–18), indicates the proper emendation. So Wülker, note, and Löhe.   **230** synnge] So Holthausen, Anglia Beibl. V, 197, for the MS. *synne;* he cites *errantesque animae* in the Latin text (l. 116) and *synnige. . .sawla* in the homily (Napier, 139, 18).   **239** scyndan] Löhe emends to *scyndaþ,* but the infinitive *scyndan,* dependent on *gewiteð,* l. 237, is quite in place here, and so Lumby, Wülker. See *flyhð. . . slincan,* ll. 240–241.   þonne] The noun *sceadu* is feminine, and the MS. *þone* cannot be taken as an article. Löhe reads *þonne,* following Höser, Die syntaktischen Erscheinungen in Be Domes Dæge, pp. 18–19, and this seems to be the correct reading; *þonan,* "thence," would also be possible.   **242** beseah] To take the MS. *beseah* in the sense of "saw" is clearly impossible, but Grein (see Wülker, note) very plausibly explains it as from a verb *beseon* (from **besihan*), "drench," see Christ 1087. Line 243b, *þæt unalyfed is nu,* is the subject of *beseah.* Grein translates, "Dann hat die elenden mit blindem feuer übergossen, was hier (in dieser welt) unerlaubt war." The Latin text (l. 123) has *tunc caecis merget flammis sine fine misellos.* Löhe unnecessarily emends *beseah* to *besencþ.*   **243** on ende] Löhe emends to *buton ende,* corresponding to *sine fine* in the Latin (l. 123).   **250** witu] So Löhe, following the reading of the homily (Napier, 139, 23). The words *cwyldas* and *witu* are objects of *forbugon.*   forbugon] For *forbugan,* infinitive.   **251**] Alliteration is lacking here, and Löhe assumes the loss of two half-lines between l. 251a and l. 251b. But the sense is complete, and although the passage does not quite agree verbally with the Latin (l. 126), *cum sanctisque simul laetatur in omnia saecla,* there is no need to assume that any of the text is missing.   **252** geþeon]

Löhe, following Trautmann (see his note, p. 82), emends to *geþeod*, from *geþēodan*, "to join, unite," in accordance with the reading of the Latin text (l. 127), *conjunctus Christo*. But an infinitive, parallel to *forbugon*, l. 250, seems preferable here, and the MS. *geþeon* is best taken, with Wülker, as meaning "thrive," i.e. "thrive to his Lord"; see Resignation 13, Homiletic Fragment II, 1, also Ælfric's Homilies (ed. Thorpe), I, 130, 33; I, 444, 16; II, 22, 15; II, 280, 32, etc. 254] The MS. has *þær niht ne geniþð næfre þeostra*. The text of the homily has *þær niht ne genimð næfre þurh þystru þæs heofonlican leohtes sciman* (Napier, 139, 25–26), and Löhe accordingly emends *geniþð* to *genimð*, and *þeostra* to the instrumental *þeostrum*, "durch ihr dunkel." The verb *genīpan*, "grow dark," is nowhere recorded in a causative sense, and the reference of *þeostra* as a genitive plural is not evident; Löhe's emendations have therefore been adopted in the text. The scribal error *geniþð* for *genimð* may easily have been suggested by the word *niht* which precedes it.   265 snawe] So all edd., for the MS. *swa se*.   267 ne ænigu] So Wülker and Löhe, to regularize the alliteration. See Seafarer 25 and note. The homily (Napier, 139, 32–140, 1) has *ne ænig gnornung*.   270] Löhe, pp. 61, 83, suggests *and wynsumnes* for the second half-line. But there may never have been a second half-line; see l. 276.   273 ðenað] Apparently transitive, with *ealra goda gehwylc* as object; compare the Latin (l. 138), *Insuper omne bonum cunctis Deus ipse ministrat*. For this use of the verb, see Bos.-Tol., p. 1045 (under *þegnian*, II).   274 þær a] So Löhe, for the MS. *þæra*; compare the Latin *semper adest praesens* (l. 139).   275 geblyssað] So Holthausen, Anglia Beibl. V, 197, and Löhe, for the MS. *geblysað*.   276] Löhe, pp. 61–62, suggests that a second half-line has been lost here; see l. 270, note.   278 geregnað] The MS. *gerinnað* here is certainly corrupt, for we expect a verb meaning "put, set, arrange," corresponding to the Latin *collocat altithrono. . .in sede polorum* (l. 141). Brandl, Anglia IV, 104, proposed *gerimeð* (from *gerȳman*, "locum dare") in place of *gerinnað*. Löhe, following a suggestion by Trautmann, emends to *geregnað* (from *geregnian*, *gerēnian*), which provides the required meaning. The past participial form *girinad*, "ornatum," appears in the Rushworth Gospels (Luke xxi.5), and a number of forms of *gehrīnan*, "ornare," are cited by Bos.-Tol., Supplement, p. 394 (under *geregnian*); it may be that *gerinað* was the original form in our text.   284 þeodscipum on gemang] "Among the peoples." The usual form is *on* (*in*) *gemange;* see Phoenix 265, Juliana 528, Riddles 31, 4; 31, 11.   289] Taking *hy*, l. 284, as subject of *scinað*, the sense is complete without the second half of l. 289. But Löhe supplies *scire ceastra*, as subject of *scinað*, for l. 289b, citing the words *splendentia castra* in the Latin (l. 146). Grein (see Wülker, note) had previously suggested *swegltorhtan wic* for l. 289b. There is nothing in the Latin which corresponds to *scinað*.   290 mædenheap] Löhe emends to *mædena heap*, to provide a reference for the genitives *þæra hwittra* in l. 290a. Grein (see Wülker, note) had previously proposed *heap mædena*.   292 læt] For *lædeð*, "leads." See *let*, l. 296.   292–293 drut, frowe] Neither *drut* nor *frowe* is elsewhere recorded in Anglo-Saxon. The noun *drūt*, "friend," cognate with O.H.G. *trût*, appears in Middle English, but as a borrowing from Old French; see N.E.D. (under *drut*) and Zupitza, Archiv

LXXXVI, 408. Likewise *frowe*, "lady," is not an English word and is difficult to explain except as a borrowing from one of the continental dialects. 300 weardas] Lumby emends to *weardes*, gen. sing. But *rædwitan* and the MS. *weardas* are better taken as acc. plur., objects of *let*, l. 296a, which otherwise would have no object; see Brandl, Anglia IV, 104. 303 wið þam þu mote] "In consideration [of the fact] that thou mayst." See Pastoral Care (ed. Sweet), 255, 3, *wið ðæm ðe we mægen geearnian ðone hefonlican eðel*, etc. 304 unbleoh] Löhe, p. 83, following Trautmann, emends to *anwealh*, "whole, entire," corresponding to *incolumem* in the Latin text (l. 155). But *unbleoh* as a synonym of *foremære*, "illustrious," is found in the West Saxon prose Psalter, Psalm xv.6 (J. W. Bright and R. L. Ramsay, The West-Saxon Psalms, p. 28): *for þam is min land nu foremære and me swyðe unbleo* = *etenim hereditas mea praeclara est mihi*. Such a meaning fits very well here, and there is no need to emend the text.

NOTES ON AN EXHORTATION TO CHRISTIAN LIVING

An Exhortation to Christian Living] For a discussion of this poem, see Introd., pp. lxxii f. 2] There is no alliteration in this line, and Grein (see Wülker, note) suggested the addition of *bliðe* after *rice*, presumably putting *rice* at the end of the first half-line. Holthausen, Anglia Beibl. XXIII, 87, would read *rodera* for the MS. *þæt blowende*. But for the lack of alliteration, see ll. 9, 11, 25, etc., and Judgment Day II, 3, note. 4 lufa] Imperative of *lufian*, "love watchfulness." 9 ælmessylen] Holthausen, Anglia Beibl. XXIII, 87, would emend to *gōda sylen*, to provide alliteration. But for *ælmesselen*, *-sylen*, see Bos.-Tol., Supplement, p. 16. In l. 10a, Holthausen would read *se hopa miccla*, for the alliteration. 11–12] To restore alliteration here, Holthausen, Anglia Beibl. XXIII, 87, would read

> þæt he þine synna [samod] adwæsce,
> [and seo eadmedu] and eac oþra fela, etc.

16 Wyrc...wyrce] According to Grein (see Wülker, note), the protasis of a conditional sentence (ll. 16–17). Translate: "Whatever you do, ...have ..." 17 on gemang] This phrase does not seem especially appropriate here, and *on gemynde* would give better sense. 25] To provide the missing alliteration, Holthausen, Anglia Beibl. XXIII, 87, would emend *eallum* to *sincum*, referring back to *goda gehwylces*, l. 24. The MS. *eallum* refers back to *eall*, l. 22. 29 ece] Wülker takes *ece* as an adverb, in which case the emendation to *ecne* is unnecessary. 39] Holthausen, Anglia Beibl. XXIII, 87, would read *gif he him [on geogoðe] god ne ondrædeð*, to complete the line. But it may be that this line and l. 46 were left in an incomplete state by the poet. 44 dyrnegeligere] The edd. print as two words, and it may be so intended here; but for other examples of the compound, see Bos.-Tol., Supplement, p. 153. 46] Holthausen, Anglia Beibl. XXIII, 87, would read *þa man [fæste] mæg mid fæstenum*, to complete the line. See l. 39, note. 56 gyltas] Holthausen,

Anglia Beibl. XXIII, 88, suggests *synna*, as in l. 58, to provide the missing alliteration.   58 ongyte] The regular imperative singular form would be *ongyt, ongit*, as in Beowulf 1723, Daniel 420, etc., and Holthausen, Anglia Beibl. XXIII, 88, would so emend.   66–67] Wülker prints ll. 66–67 as one, with *a hi winnað embe þæt* as the second half-line. But the reference of *þæt* is obscure, unless we take *sauwle* as the antecedent, and in that case we should expect the feminine *þa* instead of *þæt*; see Holthausen, Anglia Beibl. V, 197. Lumby omits *þæt*, "Ever they labour around." The arrangement in the text, with the assumption of a loss after *þæt*, follows Holthausen. In any case, l. 66 has no alliteration, and Holthausen suggests *simle* for *a* in l. 66*b*.   74 glædlice] As it stands in the MS., l. 74*b* seems too long, and Holthausen, Anglia Beibl. V, 198, would omit *glædlice*. But this reading leaves the double alliteration in the second half-line, and it may be that the text is otherwise corrupt at this point. 80] Holthausen, Anglia Beibl. XXIII, 88, would add *scealt* after *sylfne*, but the sense is complete without any addition, the verb *scealt* being carried over in sense from l. 79.

NOTES ON A SUMMONS TO PRAYER

A Summons to Prayer] For a discussion of this poem, see Introd., p. lxxiii. Grammatical errors in the Latin half-lines are not corrected in the text, but the suggested emendations are recorded in the notes, below.   2 thronum sedentem] Lumby, Kluge, Wülker correct *sedentem* to the nom. sing. *sedens*. Holthausen, Anglia Beibl. V, 225, would also emend the MS. *thronum* to the dat. sing. *throno*.   4 saule þinre] The edd. give *saule wine* as the MS. reading, and Holthausen, Anglia Beibl. V, 225, would supply *-dryhten* after *wine*. But the MS. seems to have *þine* rather than *wine*, the vertical stroke of *þ* being purposely left short by the scribe, so as not to interfere with the initial large capital *Þ* of *Þænne*, l. 1, which is written directly above. The Latin parts of ll. 3–4 are omitted in the MS., but if we emend to *saule þinre* for l. 4*a*, parallel to *þe*, l. 1, the sense of the passage is complete as it stands.   9 fo on fultum] Holthausen, Anglia Beibl. V, 225, would supply *þe* after *fo*, and *þe* must at least be supplied in sense from l. 5. Lumby translates, "receive (thee) into favour." 10] There is no alliteration in this line. Holthausen, Beitr. XVI, 551, would read *freore*, dat. sing. of *frēo*, "noble," for the MS. *æþelre*, with alliteration of *f* and *v*, as in l. 21.   13 and þurh þæne halgan gast] Holthausen, Beitr. XVI, 551, would read *frofre gast*, to alliterate with *uoca* in the second half-line; see l. 10, note. For *frofre gast*, "Holy Ghost," see especially Andreas 1684. Grein (see Wülker, note) had previously conjectured *wuldres gast*. Except for the lack of alliteration, there would be no objection to the MS. reading. 14 clemens deus] The edd. emend to the acc. sing. *clementem dominum*, though *deum* would be closer to the MS. abbreviation *dš* (= *deus*).   15ff.] The poet here confuses the Annunciation by the angel Gabriel (ll. 15–19) and the Conception by the Holy Ghost (ll. 10–13*a*). Holthausen, Anglia Beibl. V, 225, suggests that part of the text has fallen out before l. 15.   17 þa gebyrd bodade] The MS. has *þe gebyrd boda*. Lumby made a compound *gebyrd-boda*, "the messenger of (Christ's) birth," with consequent difficulties due to the lack of a verb. The reading in the text follows Wülker.   20 rogo] The imperative *roga* is correct here, and so the edd.   21 bidde] Holthausen, Anglia Beibl. V, 225, would delete this word for metrical reasons, calling it superfluous after *rogo* (for *roga*) in the preceding line.   friclo] This word also appears in the Læceboc (ed. G. Leonhardi, Bibl. der angels. Prosa, VI), p. 59, with the meaning "appetite." Here it seems to mean "eager desire" (Bos.-Tol., Supplement, p. 267), "ask (thy) eager desire for help." For *biddan* with accusative of the thing asked, see *hwæne he byddan mihte lifes fultum*, Apollonius of Tyre (ed. J. Zupitza, Archiv XCVII, 24), l. 35.   almum] The edd. emend to the feminine *almam*.   22 sancti] The edd. emend this word, and *beatus* and *iustus* in l. 23, to the acc. plur. forms *sanctos, beatos, iustos*.   25 regentem] Wülker emends to the dat. sing. *regenti*.   26 alta polorum] Parallel to *thronum*, l. 25, and object of *regentem* (for *regenti*).   29 gelæde] With *þe*, as object, to be supplied in sense, or *þine saule* to be carried over from l. 27. luce perhennem] The edd. emend to *in lucem perhennem* (or *perennem*).   31 regna] Lumby, Kluge emend to *regnis*, Wülker to *regno*, parallel to *rice* in l. 31a. Grein (see Wülker, note) conjectured *in regna caelorum*.

NOTES ON THE LORD'S PRAYER II

The Lord's Prayer II] For a discussion of this poem, see Introd., pp. lxxiiif. 6] There is no indication of a loss in the MS., and the sense of the passage is complete. Ettmüller, Grein supply *cyning wuldres* for the second half-line. See l. 2a.   11 gasta] Ettmüller, Grein, Wülker emend to *engla* to provide the proper alliteration. Metrically, this poem is better than either the Judgment Day II or the Exhortation to Christian Living, and such an emendation would be more justified here than in the other two poems.   15 ræcað] The MS. *ræcð*, as a singular, has no apparent subject. The edd. emend to the plural *ræcað*, parallel to *synd*, with *domas* as subject. Another alternative, suggested by Wülker, would be *ræcst*, with *þu*, l. 13, carried over as subject. 16 gewyrhta] For *gewyrhtu*, acc. plur., object of *ræcað*.   20 twa and hundseofontig] Seventy-two as the number of nations and languages resulting from the confusion of tongues (Genesis xi.6–9) is nonscriptural but is attested by rabbinical and patristic sources; see F. Kaulen, Die Sprachverwirrung zu Babel (Mainz, 1861), p. 228. Other Anglo-Saxon references are to be found in the Alfredian Boethius (ed. W. J. Sedgefield), 42, 27; 99, 16–17; in Ælfric, On the Old and New Testament (ed. S. J. Crawford, The Old English Version of the Heptateuch), 24, 212ff.; 69, 1176 ff.; and in Ælfric's Sigewulfi interrogationes (ed. G. E. MacLean, Anglia VII, 40), l. 376. A probable source for these Anglo-Saxon passages is Bede's commentary In principium Genesis, Book III (F. A. Giles, Venerabilis Bedæ opera VII, 140).   30 sibbe and lufe] The emendation of the MS. *sib* 7 *lufu* to the acc. sing. forms in the text seems necessary. Ettmüller inconsistently reads *sibbe and lufu*, Lumby *sib and lufe;* Grein and Wülker retain the MS. reading.   31 beorhtnysse] The MS. has *beorhtnys*, but see the preceding note.   37 silf] Holthausen, Anglia XLVI, 54 would read *silfa* for metrical reasons.   **42** sinre] The MS. *þinre* is evidently wrong, and Ettmüller, Grein, Wülker emend to *sinre*. Lumby retains *þinre*, as implying the identity of the Son with the Father (see his note, p. 70).   But the passage is a reminiscence of the Apostles' Creed, *sedet ad dexteram Dei patris omnipotentis*.   **43** æþele] The MS. has *æþela*, but *gecynd*, which appears to be either feminine or neuter, is not recorded as a masculine.   **47** fyrde] "Host," Lumby.   This is the only occurrence of the word *fyrd* as referring to the host of angels in Heaven.   **56** tiðast] Used here in the absolute sense, "fulfil their wishes." For other examples, see Bos.-Tol., p. 989, under *tīþian* (d).   **63** reðe] An unusual adjective to apply to God, but probably best translated as "austere"; see Christ 825 (*reðe ond ryhtwis*), Descent into Hell 36 (*reþust ealra cyninga*).   **64** þe] "For thyself" (Lumby).   **66** ælcre gecynde] The MS. has *ælcege cynd* (for *ælce gecynd*).   But *ælce gecynd* and *agene wisan* cannot both be accusative objects, and Ettmüller, Grein emend to *ælcre gecynde*, as a dative indirect object.   Grein, Germania X, 427, and Wülker retain the MS. reading, taking *ælce gecynd* as the direct object of *sealdest*, and *agene wisan* as an "instrumental accusative." Holthausen, Anglia Beibl. XXXI, 29, would read [*on*] *ælce gecynd*, with *agene wisan* as accusative object.   Neither of these attempts to save the MS. reading is convincing, and the emendation to *ælcre gecynde* has been adopted in the text.   **68** Swa mid sibbe] Ettmüller, Grein supply *þu* before *mid*.   The pronoun must at least be supplied in sense, unless we punctuate with a comma at the end of l. 67 and carry *þu* over in meaning from l. 64.   See Gloria I, 7.   sænst] For *sendest*; a similar spelling with *æ* appears in l. 4, above.   **70**] Ettmüller, Grein supply *rumheort hlaford* as the second half of this line, with commas before and after.   See l. 63*b*.   There is no indication of any loss in the MS.   **76** Syle us to dæg] Holthausen, Anglia Beibl. XXXI, 29, would read *Syle to dæg us*, for metrical reasons.   The form *to dæg*, instead of the usual *to dæge*, is suspicious, but see Psalm ii.7 in the West Saxon prose Psalter (J. W. Bright and R. L. Ramsay, The West-Saxon Psalms, p. 3).   **82–83** þe...on þines silfes hand] For this construction, with both the dative of the pronoun and a prepositional phrase, see Joshua x.32, *Drihten him sealde...ða buruh on his handa* (S. J. Crawford, The Old English Version of the Heptateuch, p. 395).   **84** synna] The Latin *debita*, as well as the alliteration with *scamige*, suggest that we should read *scylda* here; see Holthausen, Anglia Beibl. XXXI, 29.   But *synna* makes satisfactory sense.   **88**] The word *eft*, after *gebrosnodon* in the MS., is unusual as coming between the adjective and the noun; furthermore, we have *eft* in l. 89.   The *eft* in l. 88 is therefore probably due to a scribal misconception, and Ettmüller, Grein rightly omit it. Lumby and Wülker follow the MS. reading.   **92** buta geara] For *buta*, a weakened form of *bu tu*, see Riddle 54, 6.   But *geara* is also noteworthy, as a late variant of *gearu*, nom. plur. neuter. Ettmüller, Grein, Lumby read *butu geara*.   But if *buta* is emended, consistency requires the emendation of *geara*.   The present text follows the MS. reading in both cases.   **96** bið] The edd. retain *beoð*, but *egsa* is singular.   See l. 101, note.   **97** on dæg] "On that day"; see Maldon 198, and Kock, JJJ., pp. 9f.   **101** alyseð] So Grein, Lumby for the MS. *alysað*.   See l. 96, note.   **102–103**]

The necessity of emending *gifaŏ* to *forgifaŏ* (= *dimittimus*) is at once apparent·
So Ettmüller and Wülker, who, however, do nothing to provide alliteration.
Grein, retaining the MS. *gifaŏ*, supplies *some* after *her*; for *sōm*, "reconciliation,"
see Grein-Köhler, p. 623. But in Germania X, 427, Grein reads *her [sylfe for-]
gifaŏ*, and so Holthausen, Eng. Stud. XXXVII, 202. In l. 103, the form *agilt*
gives trouble, and Holthausen would read *earmon mannon* (with *mannon* as
dat. sing. of *manna*, "man") to secure a singular subject for *agilt*. But the
MS. *earmon mannum* is most probably dat. plur., and Ettmüller, Wülker read
agylton, agilton as preterite plural, Grein, Lumby *agiltaŏ* as present plural.
A further possibility is to retain *agilt*, as in the text, with ellipsis of the auxiliary
habbaŏ; see l. 114. Holthausen, Anglia Beibl. V, 196, rearranges the text
rather violently, with emendations, to read:

<blockquote>swa we [sellaŏ] her
earmon [are], þe wiŏ us agilt,</blockquote>

with *earmon* taken as dat. sing. 104 laŏe] I.e. devils; see Christ 776, Psalm
56, 3, 2, etc. 110 gifnesse] Lumby, Grein, Wülker retain the MS. *gifnes*,
but Ettmüller emends to *gifnesse*, the proper form (genitive of the thing asked)
after *biddan*. This emendation is also suggested by Grein, note. See l. 55,
above. 115 soŏfæstan] Apparently a weak dat. sing., in apposition with
ŏe. Holthausen, Anglia Beibl. V, 196, prescribes the vocative *soŏfæst*, for
metrical reasons. See l. 121*b*. A vocative, either *soŏfæst* or the weak *soŏfæsta*,
would seem more normal here. 117 gecydd] For *gecyŏed*, "manifested."

NOTES ON THE GLORIA I

The Gloria I] For a discussion of this poem, see Introd., p. lxxiv. 2 wylla
"Love," here and in l. 40, as also in Lord's Prayer II, 59. See Ælfric's Catholic
Homilies (ed. Thorpe), I, 282, 3–4, *soŏlice willa and lufu getacniaŏ an ŏing.*
5 worulde] Grein, note, suggests *wuldre*. 7 wolcna] So both MSS. Ettmüller,
Grein emend to the more normal form *wolcnu*, but the MS. *wolcna* may perhaps
be retained as a late variant; see Lord's Prayer II, 92, note. Wealdest]
See Lord's Prayer II, 68, note. 13 higefrofer] Both MSS. have the oblique
form *higefrofre*, and *frofre* in l. 15. Thomson, Bouterwek, Grein emend to
frofer in l. 15, but retain *higefrofre* here. Ettmüller and Wülker retain (-)*frofre*
in both places. Lumby emends in both passages, and so the present text.
14 Swa wæs on fruman] Holthausen, Anglia XLVI, 54, would read *Swa on
fruman wæs*, for metrical reasons. 15 frofer] See l. 13, note. 23*b*] This
half-line is abnormally long, and Holthausen, Eng. Stud. XXXVII, 202, assuming a loss after *gerestest*, would arrange the text to read:

<blockquote>on syx dagum, ond on þone seofoŏan þu
gerestest. . . . .</blockquote>

29 halige] So Thomson, Bouterwek, Grein for the *haligne* of both MSS. Wülker,
retaining *haligne*, cites *for minum lufan*, Wulfstan (ed. Napier), 231, 17, as
possible evidence for a masculine noun *lufa*. 33 heo] Plural subject of

188 NOTES

cyðað, with *þine cræftas* object.   36 Ealle] Holthausen, Eng. Stud. XXXVII, 202, would emend to *Hlude* or *Hædre*, to regularize the alliteration.   42*b*] Holthausen, Anglia Beibl. V, 196, would read *and his þa gecorenan folc*, or, Eng. Stud. XXXVII, 202, *and þa gecorenan his*, for metrical reasons.   43 heahþrymnesse] The reading of J, *heahþrynnesse* ("the high Trinity of the Holy Ghost"?), has little to commend it, and all edd. except Ettmüller follow C's reading *heahþrymnesse*.   47 haligdomes] So Holthausen, Anglia Beibl. V, 196, following the reading of C. Holthausen points out that ll. 47–48 are a reminiscence of the Te Deum: *Pleni sunt coeli et terra majestatis gloriae tuae.* Wülker follows J in reading *haligdomas*, parallel to *lufu*. This reading requires a semicolon after *haligdomas*, and only a comma after *lufu*.   51 soðlice] Intended as a translation of *Amen*? Wülker puts *soðlice* within quotation marks. But the word can be taken merely as a qualifying adverb.

NOTES ON THE LORD'S PRAYER III

The Lord's Prayer III] For a brief comment on this text, see Introd., p˙ lxxvii.   3 Þæt sy gehalgod] Optative subjunctive, "May thy name be hallowed," corresponding to the Latin *Sanctificetur.*   15 urne] Holthausen, Anglia Beibl. V, 196, would read *userne*, for metrical reasons. See Lord's Prayer I, 7, in the Exeter Book.   22 abylgeað] Cosijn, Beitr. XIX, 441, suggests *agyltað*, as in l. 24. But *abylgeað*, "offend, vex," makes good sense here, although the construction *wið ðe* after this verb is unusual. If there is an error in the text, it may lie in *wið ðe* rather than in the verb.   23 forlætað] "Forgive." For this meaning of *forlætan*, see Psalm 84,2,1, in the Paris Psalter.   24 us] Holthausen, Anglia Beibl. V, 196, would read *usic*, for metrical reasons.

NOTES ON THE CREED

The Creed] For a brief comment on this poem, see Introd., p. lxxvii.   8 menegu] The MS. form *manega* is probably due to a scribe who took the word to be a form of the adjective *manig*. Wülker retains *manega;* Thomson, Bouterwek emend to *manego*, Grein to *manegu*.   13 sanctan] The MS. has *Sĉa*, i.e. *Sancta*. Ettmüller, Grein, Wülker read *sanctan*, and this was probably the form intended. Feiler reads *sanctam*. Another possibility would be the Latin dat. sing., *sanctae* or *sancte*.   14 Ides unmæne] Kock, JJJ., p. 52, takes these words as in apposition to *Marian*, l. 13, and places a semicolon after *unmæne*. He suggests that *ides unmæne* may be either an uninflected appositive or a scribal error for *ides'* (for *idese*) *unmænre*. The present text follows the traditional punctuation.   34 recene] So the edd., except Wülker and Feiler, for the MS. *recen*.   40 freode] Ettmüller, Grein. Wülker emend to *freoðe*, but the MS. *freode* is the proper reading here. See Beowulf 2476, Andreas 390, etc. In Beowulf 1706ff., *gelæstan freode*, the reading of the MS. (*freode* or *freoðe*?) is disputed.   41 hihte beluce] Line 41 evidently translates the Latin *Credo in spiritum sanctum*, though the precise meaning of *beluce* is obscure. Thomson translates, "I with hope embrace the Holy Ghost," and Bouterwek, "Ich umfasse [den] heiligen Geist in Hoffnung." Or it may be that *beluce* here means "mention," i.e. "I mention the Holy Ghost with hope," though no exact parallels for such a meaning of *belūcan* are available. See, however, Bos.-Tol., Supplement, p. 77, under *belūcan*, Va. There is no plausible emendation; if, for example, *beluce* is an error for *belife* (present indicative of *belīfan*, "believe"), we should expect the preposition *on* before *haligne gast*. Bos.-Tol., p. 580 (under *hyht*), omits the comma at the end of this line, translating, "I believe the Holy Ghost to be just as eternal," etc. **55** ærest] For *ærist*, "resurrection." **57** dælest] So all edd. except Wülker and Feiler.

NOTES ON FRAGMENTS OF PSALMS

Fragments of Psalms] For the relationship of these Psalm fragments to the Paris Psalter, see Introd., pp. lxxvii f. **19,9,1** cyng] The MS. has *god*, with *cyng* written above it by a contemporary corrector. The correction *cyng* provides the proper reading here, corresponding to the Latin *Domine, saluum fac regem*. The scribe seems to have been misled by the frequent use of the formula *drihten god* as a vocative, as in Psalm 69,1,1; see also the Paris Psalter, Psalms 73, 20,1; 85,14,1; 87,1,1; etc. **19,9,3** swylce...daga] "On whichever of days." Holthausen, Anglia Beibl. XXXI, 191, would read *dagena*, for metrical reasons. **24,3,1** wise] This meaning of *wīs*, "known, evident," is frequent in the Paris Psalter; see Psalms 102,7,1; 118,151,2; 118,168,3. The West Saxon prose Psalter has *gedo me þine wegas cuðe* (J. W. Bright and R. L. Ramsay, The West-Saxon Psalms, p. 50). **27,10,3** on riht] So the MS., not *owiht* as reported by Wülker. **32,18,2** us] Holthausen, Anglia Beibl. XXXI, 191, would read *usic*, for metrical reasons. See Lord's Prayer III, 24, note. **34,3,1** wið unholdum] Holthausen, Anglia Beibl. XXXI, 191, would read *wið unholdum werum*, to regularize the alliteration. **34,3,2** wige] "By fighting," according to Kock, Anglia XLII, 114, who takes this and the preceding line as structurally parallel. The usual interpretation of *wige belucan* is "to protect against fighting," here and in Beowulf 1770. **50,11,2** rihtne gast] Holthausen, Anglia Beibl. XXXI, 191, would read *gast rihtne*, to regularize the alliteration. **53,1**] This and the following verses are also preserved in the Paris Psalter. Additional textual and critical comment may be found in the notes to that text (Records V, The Paris Psalter and the Meters of Boethius, pp. 207 ff.). **60,6,3** ic] Supplied from the text of this verse in the Paris Psalter. **69, 1, 1–3**] This verse appears twice in the Benedictine Office, on fol. 43b and on fol. 51a. The only variant is *beheald me drihten*, l. 2, on fol. 51a; otherwise these two fragments agree with each other and with the Paris Psalter. **89,18,1** Geseoh þine scealcas] The Paris Psalter has *Beseoh on þine scealcas*, and the presence of *on* in l. 2 of this verse suggests that *Beseoh on* was the original reading here also. Compare the Latin *Respice in seruos tuos*. **101,1,2** heofones] So the Paris Psalter, as required by the sense. **102,4,1** Se] The Paris Psalter has *He*, corresponding to the pronoun in the other verses of Psalm 102.

NOTES ON THE KENTISH HYMN

The Kentish Hymn] For a description of the MS. and a discussion of the literary problems raised by this poem, see Introd., pp. lxxviii ff.   **2** hiofenrices] So the MS., not *hiofonrices* as reported by Wülker.   **3** lifęs] The MS. spellings with ę, as here and elsewhere in the present poem (*sigefęst*, l. 4, *fęder*, ll. 8, 14, *hęlend*, l. 16, etc.) and in Psalm 50 (*bręga*, l. 2, *hwęðere*, l. 13, etc.) have not been normalized in the text; see Introd., p. lxxxii.   **8a** þe] So the MS., not *we* as reported by Wülker.   **8b** bilewit] The MS. form *bilewitne*, if retained, must be taken as acc. sing., parallel to *þe*. We should expect the vocative here, as in Daniel 362, Azarias 73, 139, and the text has been so emended.   **9** walden] The form with -*en* is unusual, but such forms occur elsewhere in the work of this scribe, *walden*, Psalm 50,31, *sceppen*, Psalm 50,45, and several times in the glosses in the earlier part of the MS.   The form *walden* also appears in the metrical preface to Wærferth's translation of Gregory's Dialogues (pp. 112f. of this volume), l. 14.   Bülbring's attempt, Indog. Forsch. VI (1896), 140, to explain such participial forms in -*en* as vocatives corresponding to the Indo-European vocative in -*nt* was questioned by Kluge, Indog. Forsch. VI, 341. On this problem see Dobbie, The Manuscripts of Cædmon's Hymn and Bede's Death Song (New York, 1937), pp. 13–15.   **11** ðinra...gerena] A genitive, parallel to *wuldordreames* in l. 10, is required here after *þanciað*, and *gerena* is best taken as gen. plur. of the neuter *gerýne*.   For the MS. *ðare*, Dietrich, Grein read *ðinre*, *þinre*, but Grein-Köhler, p. 466 (under *micel*), emends to *þinra*, without comment.   Kluge, Wülker, Cook retain the MS. *ðare*, which Wülker explains as gen. sing., with *gerena* also taken as gen. sing. of a feminine noun *gerýnu*, *gerýn*, not elsewhere recorded.   In the present text the emendation to *ðinra*, gen. plur., has been adopted; *ðara* would also be possible, but in view of *ðines* in the preceding line it seems less likely.   **12** ðe ðu] Apparently for *ðu ðe*, "thou who," and corresponding to the Modern German *der du* construction ("Der du von dem Himmel bist," etc.).   mæhtum] The MS. seems to have *mæhtum*, not *miehtum* as reported by Wülker.]   **13** gewealdum] Holthausen, Eng. Stud. XXXVII, 202, would emend to *gehealdum*, to improve the alliteration in the first half-line.   **17** ,angla] For *engla*, "of angels"; this form is not likely to be a scribal error, and is perhaps a learned affectation on the part of the poet.   **23** ðe ðu] The MS. reading *ðe ðy* is difficult to explain. Grein suggested *ðe ðu*, as in !. 12, and so Cook.   Dietrich had previously translated, "qui [tu] scelerum culpam mundi...disjecisti," although he retained *ðy* in his text.   The reading *ðe ðu* is evidently correct.   **27–28**] The meaning of ll. 27–28a is fairly apparent, "when thou didst raise, through the holy tree of thy suffering," but the phrase *ðriostre senna*, l. 28b, presents difficulties.   The word *ðriostre* must be intended as a form of *ðeostru*, "darkness," but its case is uncertain.   Is it acc. sing., object of *ahofe*, with *senna* (for *synna*) gen. plur., "the darkness of sins," or is it gen. sing., with *senna* acc. plur., "the sins of darkness"?   The former seems more probable, but in any case *ðriostre* as gen. or acc. sing. is highly unusual, *ðeostru*, -*o* being the regular forms.   The word has, however, not been emended, in view of its dubious interpretation.   The form *ðrowunga*, l. 28*a*, as a gen. sing. is not unusual; see Sievers, Angels. Gram., §255, 1.   35 niða] A variant of *niðða*, "of men," and Holthausen, Eng. Stud. XXXVII, 202, would so emend.   But see Daniel 312, Andreas 1377, Elene 503, 1085, etc.   39 nergende] So Holthausen, Anglia Beibl. V, 196, for the MS. *nergend*. The emendation can be justified on other than metrical grounds; see Christ 157, Lord's Prayer III, 28, Psalm 50,149.

NOTES ON PSALM 50

Psalm 50] For a discussion of this poem and its relationship to other Anglo-Saxon Psalm versions, see Introd., pp. lxxx f.   2 brega] See Kentish Hymn 3, note.   3 cynost] For *cēnost*, "bravest." See *searocyne*, l. 10. Grein-Köhler, p. 105, assumes an adjective *cyne*, *cȳne* ("regius, nobilis? oder audax?"), for which no authority is available, but also lists this form under *cēne*.   11 cumbulgebrec] Apparently a plural, in view of the plural form *scoldan*, l. 12. The regular nom. plur. would be *-gebrecu;* see Riddle 3,44.   16 mon] Kluge (3 ed.) and Sweet read *Gelamp þæt him ansende* for l. 16*a*, omitting *mon*, and with no comma after *neriend*. It is true that *mon* overweights the line somewhat, but it does not interfere with the alliteration (taking the half-line as an A3-type), and there is no other serious objection to it. Retaining *mon*, we have *witgan*, l. 17*a*, in apposition.   17 dominus] The Latin abbreviation *dñs*, for *dominus*, appears four times in this poem, here and in ll. 81, 99, and 140; the abbreviation *l*, for *uel*, appears in l. 142. In l. 97, also, the MS. *aferredne* is best explained as an error for *aferre dñe* (= *aferre, domine*). Elsewhere, as in ll. 62, 94, 125, etc., the form *dryhten* is used, with no attempt to abbreviate. The edd. regularly emend *dñs* and *l* to their Anglo-Saxon equivalents *dryhten* and *oððe*, except Kluge, who retains *dñs* without expansion wherever it occurs, but reads *oððe*, l. 142, with the other edd. But if the scribe had wanted to say *dryhten* and *oððe* in these places, he would undoubtedly have written *dryhten* and *oððe*, or for *dryhten* he might have used the abbreviations *drih*, *dryh* found in other MSS. The Latin abbreviations have therefore been expanded in the text to the Latin forms *dominus* and *uel*. See also Azarias 100, where the abbreviation 7 in the Latin context is properly expanded to *et* rather than to *ond*.   22 beserode] For *besyrode*, preterite of *besyrian*, "to deprive," Grein-Köhler, p. 665 (under *besyrwan*).   31] Dietrich arranges l. 31 as two lines, the second line, beginning with *nu ðu*, then being too short. So also Kluge and Sweet, who indicate a loss after *wast*.   34 ðære] The MS. *ðara* does not make sense, and Sweet omits it entirely. But the emendation to *ðære* is supported by Psalms 108,25,4; 113,10,1, in the Paris Psalter.   42 oncnawe] So all edd., for the MS. *ón cwawe*, except Kluge and Wülker, who retain *oncwawe*. Kluge in his glossary lists *oncwāwan* as a Kenticism for *oncnāwan*. But no such verb as *oncwāwan* is recorded elsewhere, and if it existed its etymology would be extremely problematic.   43 gehwær] "Everywhere," with *synna* gen. plur., parallel to *firendeda*, l. 44. But *scelda*, l. 45, is nom. plur.   51 me forgefene gastes wunde] Apparently an accusative absolute, with *ic* to be supplied in sense in l. 52: "the wounds (i.e. sins; see ll. 141, 154, below) of the spirit being forgiven me, I may travel into the future life." **71** snetera] For *snyt(t)ro, snyt(t)ru,* gen. sing. The words *uncuðe* and *derne* may be taken either as adverbs, "in an unknown and hidden manner," or as adjectives, acc. plur. neuter (Sievers, Angels. Gram., §293, Anm. 3), modifying *hord.* The evidence of the Latin *incerta et occulta sapientiæ tuæ manifestasti mihi* favors the latter alternative. Translate, "because thou thyself hast revealed to me unknown and hidden treasures of thy wisdom." **75** ofer snawe] "More than snow"; see *ofer Offan,* Widsith 37. **79** bliðse] Taken by Dietrich as a form of the verb *bliðsian, blissian,* "ut obedientia mea...laetitiâ exhilaretur," in which case a comma is required after *weorðe,* l. 78. Or *bliðse* may be dat. sing. of the noun *bliðs, bliss,* "joy" (also found in l. 99), with *gefean* gen. sing. Sweet in his glossary takes *bliðse* as a noun, and Kluge and Wülker, with no comma after *weorðe,* seem to favor this interpretation. **88** clẹne hiortan] Object of *geniowa,* l. 93, and parallel to *modswiðne geðanc,* l. 89, and *rihtne gast,* l. 92. **97** aferre, domine] The MS. *aferredne,* taken as a past participial form of *afyrran,* is very difficult to construe, and it seems probable that it is an error for *aferre dñe* (= *domine*); see Holthausen, Eng. Stud. LI, 180, who would read *aferre, dryhten.* But the Latin form *domine* has been preferred in the text; see l. 17, note. **98** þinra] Grein, Wülker, Sweet emend the MS. *þinre* to *þinra,* required by the sense. See l. 136, note. **119** secgende] The MS. *seccende* is obviously an error for *secgende,* as conjectured by Grein. Sweet emends to *secgende,* but the other edd. retain the MS. reading. There are sporadic instances of *c, cc* for *cg* in other MSS., as *sec* for *secg,* Beowulf 2863, *sæcc* for *secg,* Elene 1256, but such spellings are probably to be regarded as scribal errors. **120** brohte] Subjunctive, "I would bring," together with *ðer ðu wolde swa,* "if thou didst so wish," corresponding to the Latin *si voluisses sacrificium, dedissem utique.* **130** fræmsume] An adverb, "benignly," according to Bos.-Tol., Supplement, p. 264; or an adjective, acc. sing. feminine, modifying *frofre,* according to Grein-Köhler, p. 221. Either construction is possible as a free rendering of the Latin *Benigne fac, domine, in bona voluntate tua Sion.* **136** lioda þinra] The MS. reading *lioda þinre* must be emended either to *liode þinre,* gen. sing., or to *lioda þinra,* gen. plur. The plural usage is much the more common in Anglo-Saxon poetry (see Grein-Köhler, p. 413) and is shown to be correct here by the plural form *hio...asettað,* ll. 137–138. Sweet emends to *lioda þinra;* the other edd. retain the MS. reading in spite of the lack of grammatical concord. The scribe seems to have had difficulty with the forms of *þin;* in l. 98 he has made the same error, *þinre* for *þinra,* and in l. 144 he has written *þinra* for *þinre.* **144** þinre] See l. 136, note. **154** gastes wunde] Dietrich, Grein, Wülker begin a new sentence with *gastes wunde,* as object of *forgef,* l. 154*b*; Kluge and Sweet arrange as in the text, with *gastes wunde* parallel to *balaniða hord,* l. 151, and *ða,* l. 153. The latter arrangement is to be preferred stylistically.

NOTES ON THE GLORIA II

The Gloria II] For a discussion of this poem, see Introd., pp. lxxxiii ff. **2** gemæne] Perhaps meaning no more than "together," i.e. "Glory and honor be to thee...joyously together." 3 sylfan] The strong form *sylfum* would be more regular here; see *soðum* in the second half-line.

NOTES ON A PRAYER

A Prayer] For a description of the MSS. and a discussion of the literary problems raised by this poem, see Introd., pp. lxxxv ff. 7 ðæra þe gewurde] For the subjunctive singular after *þara þe*, see Christ 276f., *seo clæneste cwen...þara þe gewurde to widan feore*. side oððe wyde] So both MSS. Grein emends to *wide oððe side*, to improve the alliteration. 10b þynum] The form *þyne* in J is evidently a scribal reminiscence of *þyne* in the first half-line. 12 deofle campað] "Fights for the devil"; see *gode campode*, Guthlac 643. Both MSS. here have plural forms (*deoflon, deoflum*), but *hys*, l. 13a, clearly points to a dat. sing. *deofle*, and Bouterwek, Grein, Wülker so emend. See also the parallel construction in ll. 17–18. 13 þære mirigðe] Gen. sing.; see l. 18b, below, and also *Wa him þæs þeawes*, Riddle 11,8. 15 bute] The form *butan* in L is more regular, but *bute* is an acceptable variant; see Meters of Boethius 18,10. 24 ece are] Acc. sing., object of *Getiþa*, l. 22. A genitive object would be more regular after this verb. eaðe] "Easy to be entreated, gentle," Bos.-Tol., Supplement, p. 176. See also *eadmoda* (for *ēaþmōda*), l. 59. 26 ana... heofonas] Best taken as an adverbial clause; see Holthausen, Anglia Beibl. V, 195. Wülker, note, seems to take *eorðan* and *heofonas* as gen. sing., dependent on *syddra gesceafta*, l. 27a. But the two words are more probably accusative objects of the preposition *ofer;* see the similar construction in l. 28. 31 us gesomnie] Kock, JJJ., p. 52, translates as "we assemble," with the subject to be found in *men ofer moldan*, l. 32: "even if we men on earth assemble." For the reflexive use of this verb, see Bos.-Tol., Supplement, p. 400 (under *gesamnian*, VI). 40 sylfa wast] The MS. has *sylf* at the end of one line, and *awast* at the beginning of the next line. Wülker accordingly reads *sylf awast*. But no verb *āwitan* is recorded in Anglo-Saxon, and the proper word division is *sylfa wast*, as the older edd. read. For the weak form *sylfa*, see Genesis 570, 2919, etc. 41b] To avoid the double alliteration in the second half-line, Holthausen, Anglia Beibl. XXXI, 28, would emend to *mihtig on strengo*. 42 lifiende] So Holthausen, Anglia Beibl. V, 195, for the MS. *lifiend*. See Kentish Hymn 39, note, and also *god lifigende*, Christ and Satan 573, Andreas 1409, etc. 52 eorðbuende] Holthausen, Anglia Beibl. V, 195, would read *eorðbuendra*, citing the genitive *hades* in l. 54b. 64–65 hwile...hwile...hwile] The plurals *hwilum...hwilum...hwilum* would be more regular. 66 inwitniðas] Object of *do*, l. 63. The comma after *do* in the text is intended to set off *swa ic ne sceolde* as a parenthetic clause. 78 heofonas] A genitive singular in -*as;* see Sievers, Angels. Gram., §237, Anm. 1. Holthausen, Anglia Beibl. V, 195, would emend to the plural *heofona*, citing ll. 4, 55, 67, etc.

NOTES ON THURETH

Thureth] For a description of the MS. and a discussion of this poem, see Introd., pp. lxxxviii ff. 1 halgungboc] For the meaning and reference of this word, which

is not elsewhere recorded, see Introd., p. lxxxix.   4 loue] For *lofe*, dat. sing.;
scattered examples of *u* for medial *f*, in such words as *selua* for *selfa*, *yuel* for
yfel, etc., are found in late Anglo-Saxon texts; see also *seolua*, Christ and
Satan 13.

NOTES ON ALDHELM

Aldhelm] For a description of the MS. and a discussion of the literary problems
raised by this poem, see Introd., pp. xc ff.   The text is frequently very difficult of comprehension; the following notes are based principally on Napier,
Old English Glosses, pp. xiv–xv.   1 me] The book is represented as the
speaker; see *Biblos*, l. 5.   2 beorn boca gleaw] The same formula is applied
to Boethius in Meters 1,52.   4 ipselos] Greek ὑψηλός, "high, eminent."
æðele] Holthausen, Anglia XLI, 403, reads *ēðle*, without comment.   But for
æðel as a variant spelling of *ēðel*, "country," see *æþel*, "patria," Wright-Wülker,
Anglo-Saxon and Old English Vocabularies I, 325, 16; also Christ and Satan 107,
Seasons for Fasting 151.   5 Biblos] Greek βίβλος, "book," in apposition
to *ic*.   6 ponus] Greek πόνος, "work, toil."   7 geanoðe] This word is not
recorded elsewhere in Anglo-Saxon, but Napier assumes a noun *gēanoþ*, "mourn-
ing, lamentation," citing Gothic *gaunōþus*.   Even then, the reference of *geanoðe*
as a dat. sing. is not quite clear.   Perhaps translate, "with the lamentation of
recent sorrow."   9 euthenia] Greek εὐθηνία, "abundance,"   10 æne] This
could be the adverb *æne*, "once," but Napier suggests that it is Greek αἴνη,
"fame."   se] We should expect the dative *him* here, "fame (*æne*) likewise
(*ec ðon*) in the land to him concerning whom evil has been spoken" (?).   Ehwald,
p. 220, translates ll. 10b–11a, "etiamsi de eo mala sunt dicta."   13 encratea]
Greek ἐγκράτεια, "self-control."   The case of *encreatea* is uncertain; Ehwald,
p. 220, translates, "Etiam nusquam is...excuset se oportet patientiâ (i.e....
nunquam se satis laborasse dicat)."   This seems reasonably close to the desired
meaning, but the details of syntax are obscure.   14 boethia] Greek βοήθεια,
"help, support."   15 micro in cosmo] Greek μικρῷ ἐν κόσμῳ, "in the little
world."   16 dinams] Greek δύναμις, "strength, power," and Holthausen,
Anglia XLI, 403, emends to *dinamis*.   17 simle] The text of the poem ends
here in an incomplete state, though no loss is indicated in the MS., the prologue
to the De virginitate following immediately.   Ehwald, p. 220, suggests that the
passage meant "ut iam semper [in opere perseveret]"; but on metrical grounds
we must assume that at least a full line is missing, and it may be that a fairly
extensive piece of the text has been lost here.

NOTES ON THE SEASONS FOR FASTING
1–100

The Seasons for Fasting] For a discussion of this poem, see Introd., pp. xcii ff.
2 Moysen] The Latin acc. sing. form.   In Anglo-Saxon the usual acc. sing. is
Moyses, like the nom. sing.; see Elene 785, Psalms 104,22,1; 105,14,2, etc.   But

the phrase *þurh Moysen* occurs in Exodus ix.35, Leviticus viii.36 (S. J. Crawford, *The Old English Version of the Heptateuch*, pp. 238, 293), etc.   3 anlyht] For *anlyhted*, past participle of *onlihtan*, "to enlighten."   hine] I.e. Moses, object of *sette*, l. 5.   6 runa gescead] "Discrimination of mysteries"; see *Æghwæþres...gescad*, Beowulf 287f.   13 þæs...to leane] "As a retribution for that," with *hearm* object of *asende*.   15 fryþa] For *friþu*, peace," the indeclinable feminine noun? If so, it can be either gen. sing. or acc. sing. after *wilnodan*. The other alternative would be to take *fryþa* as gen. plur. of *friþ* "peace, truce"; but this noun is not recorded in the plural, and a plural would be very unlikely.   16 leohtras] For *leahtras*, "sins." The spelling *eo* for *ĕa* is common in this text (see *heoldan*, l. 44, *beornum*, l. 68, *weord*, l. 153, *heolp*, l. 153, etc.) and is therefore not emended.   gewyrpan] The MS. *ḡ wyrþan* cannot be explained as from *geweorðan* or from *gewyrðan*, "to estimate, value," and it is probably an error for *gewyrpan*, "to recover, get better"; i.e. "if they let their sins change for the better."   20 earm and þrealic] The MS. *þreoring* is quite unintelligible, and it is difficult to find a wholly satisfactory emendation. The change to *þrealic*, "miserable, calamitous," at least provides a plausible adjective; the word *freorig*, "sad, mournful," would give a less probable meaning, though it would be just as likely from the paleographical point of view.   23*a*] An adjective (or adverb) alliterating in *d*- is missing here, perhaps *deadne, deoþne, dierne*, or some other word.   35 hyht] For *hyhteð*, "hopes"? That is, "hopes for it for us and promises it to us." The verb *hyhtan* is usually followed by a prepositional phrase with *to* or *on*, but for the transitive use see *hyhtan hidercyme*, Christ 142.   40*b*] It seems necessary to omit the MS. *do*. Translate, "and fulfil for him our count of years with alms-giving and in fasting," etc.   44 mid Anglum] "Among the English people"; see *Brytena leodum*, l. 56. But in l. 98, *Engla land*, we have the more usual form.   45 gebrefde] See Bos.-Tol., Supplement, p. 298.   47 heowan] This verb also appears in ll. 159 (*hewan*), 177 (*hewdon*), and 181 (*hewe*). It evidently means "to hold, perform (a fast)," and corresponds to *gelæstan*, ll. 71, 150, and *healdan*, l. 103. No such verb as *hewan* is recorded in Anglo-Saxon, but these forms are perhaps for *hēgan*, "to do, perform, hold." The compound *gehēgan* is found in Beowulf 425, Andreas 930, Phoenix 493, etc. The alternation of intervocalic *g* and *w* is not unparalleled; see *hīwan, hīgan*, "companions, members of a household."   51–52 twelfe...runa] A reference to the lessons for Saturday of Ember week, which in the Middle Ages was called "Sabbatum duodecim lectionum." On this term, the exact significance of which is disputed, see L. Eisenhofer, Handbuch der katholischen Liturgik I (Freiburg i.B., 1932), 485.   51*b* dihte] Past participle of *dihtan*, "to set, appoint." The meaning of this half-line is then "brightly appointed," referring to the *twelfe...runa*. The verb *dihtan*, not elsewhere found in the poetry, is a favorite of this poet; see ll. 65, 95, 123.   52*b* hofe] For *hof* in the sense of "temple" (here and in l. 65), see Bos.-Tol., Supplement, p. 556.   57 þe gelesen hafað] There is no apparent meaning for this half-line as it stands in the MS. The text is probably corrupt here, but no plausible emendation suggests itself.   58 cumeð] The MS. *cumað* must be so emended;

for the form, see l. 37.   **65 dihte gelicum]** "Likewise appointed"? See
torhtum dihte, l. 51.   But it should be noted that here we have the weak (neuter
singular) form of the past participle.   The form *gelicum* (adverbial instrumental,
like *torhtum* above, instead of the usual adverb *gelice*?) is not elsewhere recorded
in this use.   **67 ærur]** For the analogical comparative *ærur* as a preposition,
"before" (here and in l. 72), see Meters 20,41, *æror ðe.*   **68 ælda beornum]**
The Anglian *ælda* (as in Cædmon's Hymn 5, MSS. M and L) is surprising in the
present context.   For the form, see Bülbring, Altengl. Elementarbuch I (Heidelberg, 1902), §175.   **71 fæsten]** The MS. *fæste* might perhaps be taken as the
adverb, "firmly," but we expect the noun *fæsten* here, as in ll. 47, 55, 64.   The
awkward internal rime, *fæsten gelæstan,* may have confused the scribe of the
Cotton MS. and caused him to write *gelæsten* instead of the proper form *gelæstan,*
besides omitting the final *n* of *fæsten.*   **72–73 ærur...dryhtnes gebyrde]**
"Before the Lord's birth"; see l. 67, note.   **75 eallum gemynde]** "With all
our mind."   The phrase *wuldres cyninge,* l. 74, is parallel to *þeodne,* l. 76, both
being dative objects of *deman,* "celebrate."   **77 arwesan]** See also l. 196.
The adjective *ārwesa,* "honored," is elsewhere recorded only once, in the Benedictine Rule (ed. Schröer), 115,20; see Bos.-Tol., Supplement, p. 48.   **80
seofoþa]** In the MS. reading of ll. 79–80, the fourth and sixth days (Wednesday
and Friday) of the Ember weeks are mentioned, but there is no allusion to
Saturday of Ember week.   Since *feoroþa* does not alliterate and gives no
satisfactory meaning, it is probably an error for *seofoþa,* nom. sing., parallel
to *sixta.*   The words *feoroþa* and *seofoþa* would be very similar in Anglo-Saxon
script, and the corruption is therefore easy to explain.   Here *samod* has the
force of "and" or "likewise"; see Christ 91, *sunu Solimæ somod his dohtor.*
getinge] Possibly for *getenge,* "near, adjacent to" (that is, the sixth day and the
seventh day adjacent to it), but more probably for *getynge,* "eloquent" (see
Bos.-Tol., p. 459, under *ge-tinge,* and Supplement, p. 441).   In the latter case
we may translate, "During these feasts the fourth day and the sixth together
with the seventh are eloquent to serve and to celebrate the prince of life," etc.
The verb *gelæstan* normally takes an accusative object, as does *breman,* but for
gelæstan with the dative, see Bos.-Tol., Supplement, p. 353 (under *ge-læstan*
V 1 a).   **83b–86]** As they stand in the MS., these lines are not entirely clear;
but there is no reason for believing them to be corrupt.   The meaning obviously
is that on Ember days no one, unless he is ill, is to break his fast before the
service at the hour of none (*emb þa nigoþan tyd,* l. 83a).   On the Anglo-Saxon
custom of fasting until none of fast days, see F. Tupper, PMLA. X (1895),
174–175.   **91 na þu...gewyrþe]** "Never value the reception of it."   The
form *gewyrþe* is probably from *gewyrþan,* "to estimate, value" (Bos.-Tol., p.
473), but may be for *geweorða,* imperative singular of *geweorðian.*   **92 sylfe]**
Both meter and grammar indicate *sylfe* as the proper form here.   **97 fæstend-
tida]** The form *fæstentida,* without the *d,* would be more regular.   **þam]**
Dative object of *filiað,* l. 98.   **99 gedemde]** The MS. *ḡdēda* (= *gedemda*),
with the *-a* ending in the preterite singular, is paralleled by the MS. *dyda* in
l. 143.   Both forms have been emended in the text.   Translate l. 99, "As he
himself ordained at his [papal] throne."

101–230

101 leordun] Apparently for *lǣrdon*, "taught." See *leoran and tǣcan*, l. 114.
103 we...healden] Hortatory subjunctive, "let us observe." Or perhaps we should emend *healden* to the indicative *healdað*. **109** anbat] For the emendation to *anbat*, see l. 126. **112** bæle behlæned] "Encompassed with fire," modifying *dryhten*—an allusion to Exodus xix.18. For *behlænan*, see Bos.-Tol., Supplement, p. 74. **114** þone] That is, the *bremne boca cræft*. leoran] See l. 101, note. **118** leoran] The MS. *leora* is apparently to be emended to *leoran*, as in l. 114. Translate, "those which are to teach to each of peoples whether the Lord gives us anything of benefit." **124ff.**] An allusion to 1 Kings xix.4–8 (3 Kings xix.4–8 in the Vulgate). **129** þegen] Appropriate as designating a minister or messenger of God. The MS. *hegen* is meaningless. **130** stæppon] For *stæppan*, acc. plur., "to ascend the steps to the summit." **133** ænete] For *anæde*, dat. sing. of *ānað, ānæd*, "desert." **139** wist] Usually feminine, but some of the compounds seem to have masculine forms; see *biwist, dægwist*, Bos.-Tol., Supplement, pp. 95, 145. **140** fæstan...fyrene dædum] "Abstain from deeds of sin." See *fyrene fæstan*, Daniel 591. **143** dyde] See l. 99, note. **150** fæsten...fyrena] "Abstinence from sins"; see l. 140 and note. **151** æþel] For *ēþel*, "country"; see Aldhelm 4, note. **155** bæðe] The dat. sing., parallel to *þweale*, is required by the sense. **156** firsude mettas] The MS. *firude metta* is obviously wrong. The simplest way of securing the required sense, "did without food," seems to be the emendation to *firsude mettas*, as in the text. For *fyrsian, firsian*, "to remove to a distance," see Bos.-Tol., p. 354, and Supplement, p. 221. The plural forms of *mete*, "food," have two *t*'s; see Sievers, Angels. Gram., §263, Anm. 3. **159** hewan] See l. 47, note. **161** fræte] For this word, see Bos.-Tol., Supplement, p. 261. **169** þonne] For *þonne*, "sicut," see Psalm 122,2,1–2a, *mine eagan synt...þonne esne bið* (translating the Latin *sicut oculi servorum*). **172** egum] For *ēagum*. Translate, "if he does not have any target of evil in sight." **175** dryhtnes] The dat. sing. *dryhtne* would be preferable here, "if you follow the Lord here with your deeds." **176** Hæbbe] Present indicative plural; see Sievers, Angels. Gram., §360, 2. **177** hewdon] For this form and for *hewe*, l. 181, see l. 47, note. **187b–190a** "And they (the *folc*, l. 187a) should tell to the priests each of sins (*fyrna...gehwilce*) and remedy with [their] deeds the darknesses of word and of work." The form *sacerdan*, l. 188, is a variant form, with reduced ending, of the dat. plur. *sacerdum*. **191** eall] Adverbial, as in Beowulf 1708, Christ 366, etc. **194** ligegen] For *licgen*, "lie," present subjunctive plural? **196** arwesan] See l. 77, note. Here the word is best translated by a noun, "Lord." **198** wrohte] For *worhte*, "performed." **200–201** hine sylfne...healdan] See Bos.-Tol., p. 518, under *healdan*, IV. **206–207**] The MS. *drince he him þæt drofe duge hlutter þe wæter of wege*, etc., is meaningless, and the somewhat extensive emendation in the text seems to be the only way of producing any sense at all. The whole passage is rather figurative; it seems to mean that we should follow the priest's teaching, whether he drinks from muddy streams or from the limpid streams of spiritual wisdom. **211** æfeste] The emendation

gives good sense, "and with malice leads astray each of the race of men who will follow him." **214** forþegide] This may be for *forþigede*, weak past participle of a verb *forþicgan;* for *þicgan* as a weak verb, see Sievers, Angels. Gram., §400, Anm. 1b. A verb *forþicgan* is not recorded elsewhere, but *forþegide* may perhaps be explained as meaning "having overeaten," on the analogy of *fordruncen*, "drunken, having drunk to excess." Otherwise the word is obscure. **215** teoþ] Intransitive, "impelled by thirst, they go after the tavern-keeper through the streets." **220** þæs þe me þingeð] See l. 61*b*. The emendation of the MS. þingað to þingeð is necessary; see l. 58, note. **222** wigliað] "Divine, foresee," from *wiglian*, Bos.-Tol., p. 1221? **223**] With emendation of the MS. *hwænne* to *hwæne*, "whom they may capture for food." For *mæða bedæled*, see Wulfstan (ed. Napier), 157, 19. **225** sinne semað] This emendation leaves much to be desired, but it seems to be the best one available for the meaningless *win semað* of the MS. Translate, "pacify enmity," and for *syn*, "enmity," see Beowulf 2472, Phoenix 54, and especially Maxims II, 54.

NOTES ON CÆDMON'S HYMN

Cædmon's Hymn] For a list of the MSS. and a discussion of the literary problems raised by Cædmon's Hymn, see Introd., pp. xciv ff. The head-words in the notes below are the readings of MS. M, but the notes are to be taken as applying also to the West Saxon version. **1** Nu] The omission of the pronoun subject *we* (in M and L of the Northumbrian version, and T and C of the West Saxon *eorðan*-group) is not unparalleled in early Northumbrian (see Genesis 1098, where *ic* is omitted in the MS., and also Genesis 828, 885, where *ic* has been added above the line) but may well have seemed, to the later scribes, to require emendation. scylun] For the forms *sciulun, sciulin* in Di and P, see Dobbie, The Manuscripts of Cædmon's Hymn and Bede's Death Song, p. 20. **3** gihuaes] Dependent on *or*, l. 4, "the beginning of each of wonders." The West Saxon *ylda*-group erroneously reads *gehwilc, gehwylc*. **4** astelidæ] This reading, in M and L, is evidently an analogical form for the proper *astalde* (in Di and P), *astealde* (in most of the West Saxon MSS.). **5** ælda] On the significance of the readings *ælda* (*ylda*) and *eordu* (*eorðan*) for the history of the text, see Introd., pp. xcvii f. **6** scepen] M's reading *scepen* has been variously interpreted. It may be a scribal error for *sceppend, scyppend* in the other MSS., or it may be a different word (from a Germanic *skapinaz?) with a similar meaning. For a survey of the suggested explanations, see Dobbie, The Manuscripts of Cædmon's Hymn and Bede's Death Song, pp. 13–15. **7** moncynnæs uard] A. H. Smith puts a semicolon after this half-line, but a comma is more usual; the half-lines *moncynnæs uard, eci dryctin*, and *frea allmectig* are parallel subjects of *tiadæ*, with *middungeard* and *foldu* as parallel objects. Translate: "then (*tha*) the Guardian of mankind, the eternal Lord, afterwards created the world, the earth for men, the almighty Lord." **9** foldu] Here M reads *fold*ᵛ, the small mark after *d* being very much like a flattened *v*. The other Northumbrian MSS. read *foldu* (*on foldu* Di, *ol foldu* P), and most edd. assume *foldu* in M. But Förster, Archiv CXXXV, 282ff., would take the mark after *d* in M as a general mark of abbreviation and would read *foldun*, citing *scylun*, l. 1, and *middun-*, l. 7. Whatever the proper form (and in view of *foldu* in L, *foldu* seems more probable in M also), the word is certainly accusative (not genitive, as Wuest, ZfdA. XLVIII, 225, suggests), parallel to *middungeard*, l. 7. For the acc. sing. in *-o*, *-u* in Northumbrian, see Sievers, Angels. Gram., §276, Anm. 5. The West Saxon copies of the hymn have the proper West Saxon form *foldan*.

NOTES ON BEDE'S DEATH SONG

Bede's Death Song] For a list of the MSS. and a discussion of the literary problems raised by this poem, see Introd., pp. c ff. The head-words in the notes below are based on the Northumbrian version, but the notes are to be taken as applying also to the West Saxon text. **1 thaem**] For *thaem*, *them* as the probable reading in the original of the Northumbrian version, see Introd., p. cvii. The use of *ae* for Anglo-Saxon *æ* elsewhere in the text (*-faerae, naenig, aer*) suggests *thaem* as the proper form here. uuiurthit] The diphthong *iu* has been interpreted in various ways; see Bülbring, Anglia Beibl. IX (1898), 69; Luick, Historische Grammatik der englischen Sprache I (Leipzig, 1921), §155, note 2; Brotanek, Texte und Untersuchungen, pp. 166–170. It may be, as Brotanek suggests, that the *iu* is an attempt by a German scribe to indicate the Northumbrian *y* which we should expect here (original Northumbrian **wiur-* becomes **wur-*, and the *u*, by *i*-umlaut, becomes *y*); see also Dobbie, The Manuscripts of Cædmon's Hymn and Bede's Death Song, pp. 108–110. But the reading *wiorðeð* of the Hague MS. may preserve a genuine Anglo-Saxon diphthong, however such a diphthongal form is to be explained. The final *-t* of *uuiurthit* is due to German scribal custom, like the final *t*'s (in *foręldit, suuyltit*) in the Proverb from Winfrid's Time. **2 than**] "Than that..." That is, "Before his death no one becomes wiser than that he needs to consider," etc. **4–5**] "What of good or evil may be adjudged to his spirit after his death-day." **5 aefter deothdaege**] The form *æfter deaþe heonon* in the West Saxon version is evidently a scribal error in the prototype of that version; see Introd., p. cvi.

NOTES ON THE LEIDEN RIDDLE

The Leiden Riddle] For a discussion of this riddle and its relationship to Riddle 35 in the Exeter Book, see Introd., pp. cviii ff. **1 se ueta uong**] There seems to be little doubt about the reading of the MS. at this point. Schlutter, Anglia XXXII, 387, reads *se ueta erðuong* in the MS., but Kern, Anglia XXXIII, 453, and other scholars who have examined the MS. have failed to find the letters *erð-*. In any case, there is room for only two letters betwen *ueta* and *uong*. Pluygers (see Introd., p. cx) read the erased letters as *ne* or *nae*, Kern as *ue* or *uo*, A. J. Smith as *na*. According to Holthausen, Eng. Stud. LV, 312, the first of the two erased letters seems to be *u*. **2b**] Schlutter, Anglia XXXII, 387, reads *ærist*, and so Sweet (Oldest Eng. Texts, p. 150), doubtfully. Other edd. read *ærest*. According to A. H. Smith, only *cæn[.]æ* is visible of the last word in this line, but the restoration to *cændæ* (*cende* in the Exeter Book) needs no comment. **3 Ni uaat**] All edd. read *Uuat* in the MS. except A. H. Smith, who reads *Uaat* by ultraviolet light. The form *Uaat* is normal for this text, with a single *u* to represent the *w*-sound (as in *ueta*, l. 1, *uarþ*, l. 5), and with *aa* for the long vowel (as in *aam*, l. 8). For this half-line, then, the MS. appears to have *Uaat ic mec biuorthæ*. Schlutter, Anglia XXXII, 387, reads *NI* in the left-hand margin before *Uaat* (which he reads as *Uuat*), but other commentators deny the existence of these letters in the MS. See especially Kern, Anglia XXXIII, 454; Holthausen, Eng. Stud. LV, 312. However, the negative (which appears in the Exeter Book version, *Ne wat ic mec beworhtne*) is necessary to the sense and is supplied in the text. Translate, "I know that I am not made of the fleeces of wool," etc.   biuorthæ] For *biuorhtæ*. The Exeter Book version has *beworhtne*, masculine, but the feminine form would more readily apply to *byrne*, "coat of mail," the subject of the riddle.   uullan] The usual form of this word is *wull*, strong feminine, as in the Exeter Book reading *wulle*. See also Psalm 147,5,2, *wulle flys*.   4 hygiðonc-] So A. H. Smith, by ultra-violet light. The proper restoration, *hygiðonc[um min]*, is provided by the reading of the Exeter Book, *hygeþoncum min*. The meaning seems to be "in my thoughts," taking *min*, with Wyatt, as the gen. sing. of the personal pronoun. See note on Riddle 35,4, in Records III, The Exeter Book, p. 340. 5 hafæ] The early edd. read *hefæ*, but Schlutter, Anglia XXXII, 387, reads *hafæ*, and so Trautmann and A. H. Smith.   6 ðreatun] Pluygers' transcript reads *ðrea.un*, with an illegible letter between *a* and *u*; Sweet (Oldest Eng. Texts, p. 151) supplied the *t* on the evidence of *þreata* in the Exeter Book text, and so most later edd. According to A. H. Smith, the *t* is actually visible in the MS. Schlutter's reading *þreavun-*, Anglia XXXII, 516, is hardly possible. The Exeter Book here reads *þurh þreata geþræcu*, "through the crowdings of multitudes," or (with Tupper) "through the force of many strokes," apparently referring to the action of the loom. The form *ðreatun* in the Leiden text is difficult to explain; we should expect a gen. plur.   ðret] For *þræd*, "thread," as in the Exeter Book. The abbreviation *&* (for -*et*) is not uncommon in continental MSS.; see Bede's Death Song 4 (MSS. Sg and Ba).   hlimmith] So Sweet (Oldest Eng. Texts, p. 151) and most later edd.   7 hrutendu] The edd. have read this word variously. Pluygers read *hrutendū* (i.e. *hrutendum*); Dietrich read *hrutendi*, Schlutter, Anglia XXXII, 387, *hrutende* (and so Kern, Anglia XXXIII, 455); Bethman, ZfdA. V, 199, and A. H. Smith read *hrutendu*. The last is the most likely reading, taking *hrisil* as nom. plur. neuter, with *hrutendu* dependent on it, "roaring shuttles." See the next note. scelfath] So A. H. Smith, by ultraviolet light; earlier edd. had read *scelfæð*. Taking *hrutendu hrisil* as nom. plur. (see the preceding note), *scelfath* would be the proper form; see *fraetuath*, l. 10. The verb *scelfan* is not normally transitive, but apparently must be so taken here; the Latin riddle has *nec radiis carpor*. The Exeter Book text has *ne æt me hrutende hrisil scriþeð* for this line.   8 ni mec] Schlutter, Anglia XXXII, 387, reads *ne mec;* other edd. agree on *ni mec*. ouana] For *ohwonan*, "from anywhere," as in the Exeter Book text. Pluygers read *ou...ia*, Sweet *ou[ua]n[a]*, Schlutter, Anglia XXXII, 387, *oua[n]a*. According to A. H. Smith, all the letters come out clearly by ultraviolet light. aam] The slay of a weaver's loom. The Exeter Book text incorrectly reads *amas*. See note on this line, Records III, The Exeter Book, pp. 340–341.   9 uyrdi] Gen. sing. fem.; the Exeter Book has *wyrda*, gen. plur. Schlutter, Anglia XXXII, 387f., read *uyndicraeftum*, "polymitaria arte," and so Sweet (A. S. Reader), who glosses *wyndecræft*, "art of embroidery." 10 geolu] A. H. Smith reads *geolu* without comment, but all other edd. give *goelu* as the MS. reading. Dietrich's facsimile also has *goelu*. geatum] For *geatuum* (= *geatwum* in the Exeter Book), "with (splendid) ornaments." 11 Uil mec] Holthausen, Anglia Beibl. XXX, 52, would supply *mon* after *mec*, as in the Exeter Book version, to secure a subject for *hatan*, l. 12. huethrae] Schlutter, Anglia XXXII, 387, reads the MS. as *huethrae*, A. H. Smith as *hucthrae* (with *c* perhaps a faded *e*); both report the second *h* as written above the line. 12 mith heliðum] The Exeter Book text has *for hælebum*. giuæde] So Sweet (Oldest Eng. Texts, p. 151) and Schlutter, Anglia XXXII, 387. According to A. H. Smith, the final *e* is no longer visible. 13 ni anoegun ic] Like the *-un* of *ðreatun*, l. 6, the ending of *anoegun* is difficult to explain. All edd. agree on the spelling of the word in the MS. If the verb is *onēgan*, "to fear," a normal Northumbrian form would be *anoegu* (as suggested by Trautmann, p. 97); if *onēgnan*, then *anoegnu* would be possible, and so Schlutter, Anglia XXXIII, 466. Bos.-Tol., p. 750, suggests *Ni anoegu na ic*, and so Tupper, Sedgefield. In view of the several possibilities, no emendation has been made in the text. aerig-faerae] West Saxon *earhfære*, dat. sing. of *earhfaru*, "flight of arrows." 14] Parts of this line are very obscure in the MS., and restoration is difficult, especially since it is impossible to tell exactly how many letters are lost. In Dietrich's facsimile and in Pluygers' transcript, the letters *ðehði ni* are reported at the end of one line, with some space after them, and *adlicae* (Pluygers, *inadlicae* or *madlicae*) in the next line, with space for a few letters before them. Sweet (Oldest Eng. Texts, p. 151) restored to *ðeh ði ni[man flanas frac]adlicae ob cocrum*, and most edd. have followed his reading, with slight modifications. The letters in the text are those reported by A. H. Smith as visible to him in the MS. He restores to read *ðeh ði n[ume]n siæ niudlicae ob cocrum*, that is, "though it [the flight of arrows, l. 13] be eagerly taken from quivers."

NOTES ON LATIN-ENGLISH PROVERBS

Latin-English Proverbs] For a description of the MSS. and a discussion of these two proverbs, see Introd., pp. cx ff. 4 leof alaðaþ] "That which is dear becomes hostile," a very free rendering of the Latin *amor abolescit*. In the other three parts of this proverb the Anglo-Saxon conforms closely to the Latin in phraseology as well as in meaning. 6 þæs þe] "With respect to that which is not eternal." The sense would be complete, and closer to the Latin, without *þæs*.

NOTES ON THE METRICAL PREFACE
TO THE PASTORAL CARE

The Metrical Preface to the Pastoral Care] For a description of the MSS. of the Pastoral Care and a discussion of the metrical preface and epilogue, see

Introd., pp. cxii ff.   1 Agustinus] The usual Anglo-Saxon spelling of the name (following the Vulgar Latin form), as also in Menologium 97 and in the manuscripts of the Alfredian Bede.   3–4 fore adihtode] Sweet, in his prose arrangement of the text, reads *foreadihtode* as one word, and so Bos.-Tol., Supplement, p. 237, but the meter indicates the correct word division.   6 gindwod] For *geondwod* (as in D and T), "went through [a subject], made himself acquainted with"; see Bos.-Tol., Supplement, p. 386. The object is *Ryhtspell monig,* l. 5.   8 gestriende] "Acquired, won over." Sweet translates, "For he gained over most of mankind to the Guardian of heaven."   14 bi ðære bisene] "According to the (original) copy."

NOTES ON THE METRICAL EPILOGUE
TO THE PASTORAL CARE

The Metrical Epilogue to the Pastoral Care] See Introd., pp. cxii ff.   1 Ðis is nu se wæterscipe] "These are now the waters" (Sweet), that is, the spring of wisdom, l. 14.   4–5 of ðæm innoðum...ðe wel on hine, etc.] "From the hearts [of those] who believed in him well under the sky."   26] Holthausen, Archiv CVI, 347, begins a new sentence with *cume* and places a comma after *hræðe.* But the half-line *cume eft hræðe* seems rather to belong to the same sentence with *Fylle,* l. 25.

NOTES ON THE METRICAL PREFACE TO
BISHOP WÆRFERTH'S TRANSLATION
OF GREGORY'S DIALOGUES

The Metrical Preface to Bishop Wærferth's Translation of Gregory's Dialogues] For a description of the MS. and a discussion of this preface, see Introd., pp. cxv ff. In the following notes, the name "Holthausen," without any further indication, refers to both his critical editions of the poem, in Archiv CV, 367–369, and Anglia XLI, 402. References to one or the other of these editions are given in the usual form.   1] The poem begins at the top of fol. 1*a*, with EÐEMERÆDAN in large capitals; then there is a long and fairly wide hole extending from side to side of the parchment, then a second line of large capitals, ÐANCE·HEINMEFINDANMÆ, followed by the remainder of the poem in ordinary small letters. In Hecht's edition, there are three asterisks between RÆDAN and ÐANCE, evidently indicating the loss of a full line of large capitals after RÆDAN. But a study of the text at the top of fol. 1*b* shows that nothing has been lost from fol. 1*a* at this point, except the initial *S* of the word *Se,* l. 1, and that the apparent width of the hole in the leaf is due to the shrinking of the parchment. But the meter indicates a loss here, and Holthausen restores [*Rinca æghwylc s*]*e* ðe, etc. Holthausen also reads ðænce for the MS. ðance, without comment. Directly above the first line of large capitals is the rubric *Incipit Liber* þ[..]*mus dialogorum* in smaller capitals, which seem to be contemporary with the text of the poem.   2] The *g* of *mæg,* l. 2*a*, at the end of the second line of large capitals, has been burned away.   3 godre biesene]

Holthausen, Archiv CV, 367, reads *gode bysne* as accusative object of *lysteð*. But *lystan* usually takes a genitive of the thing desired; see Whale 52, Meters 10,14; 26,71, etc. The words *gastlices lifes* are dependent on *godre biesene*. 5 hame] Holthausen reads *ham*, for metrical reasons.   6] The word *bl*[.]*s* comes at the end of a line in the MS. The letters *b, l,* and *s* are plainly visible, but the *i* is now lost.   10 þissa haligra] The construction evidently is *geliefeð to helpe þissa haligra.* Compare Waldere II, 27, *Se ðe him to ðam halgan helpe gelifeð,* where *helpe* is accusative.   13*b*] The restoration of *þ*[*e*] causes no difficulty. The form *aof,* for *ahof,* is unusual, and Holthausen normalizes. 14 walden] See Kentish Hymn 9, note.   15*b*] The letters following *gesc,* at the end of a line, have been burned away; the next line of the MS. begins with *ta.* The proper restoration is obviously *gesc*[*eaf*]*ta,* and so Krebs, Holthausen. 19*a*] The restoration to *heo*[*ra*] is made by Krebs and Holthausen (*hiora* in Archiv CV, 368).   20–21] There is no indication of a loss in the MS. (except of the *e* of *forgyu*[*e*]), and the sense of ll. 20–21 is complete, although a half-line is lacking to the meter in l. 20. In l. 21, also, the MS. reading is without alliteration. Holthausen, Archiv CV, 368, reads *and þæt him God ællmihtig forgiefe þa gyltas* for l. 20, and then restores l. 21 to read *þe he* [*on eorðan her ær*] *geworhte.* In Anglia XLI, 402, Holthausen reads *and þæt him* [*gearolice*] *god ællmihtig* for l. 20, and arranges l. 21 as in the text, with the emendation of *geworhte* to *ge*[*o*] *worhte.* Either of these readings gives good sense and meter. The emendation *geo worhte* has been adopted in the text, but l. 20 has been left unaltered.   22*a* resðe] For *reste,* "rest." See *selesða,* l. 24.   22*b*] Krebs, Holthausen read *geweald.*   24*b*] Krebs reads *sincbrytta* as a compound, but the letters *sinc* come at the burned edge of the parchment, with one letter (*a* or *e*?) partly preserved after them. Holthausen's restoration to *sinc*[*es*] *brytta* is undoubtedly right.   26 fore] Holthausen, Anglia XLI, 402, omits for metrical reasons.   27 ænigne] Holthausen, Anglia XLI, 402, omits this word, placing *ær* in the second half-line.

NOTES ON THE METRICAL EPILOGUE TO MS. 41, CORPUS CHRISTI COLLEGE, CAMBRIDGE

The Metrical Epilogue to MS. 41, Corpus Christi College] For a discussion of this poem, see Introd., pp. cxviif. References to "Holthausen" in the following notes are to his article in Anglia Beibl. XXXVIII, 191–192.   1 Bidde ic eac] This half-line is too short, and Holthausen reads *to eacan* for the MS. *eac.* 3–4] In l. 3*a* the alliteration falls not on the noun (as in the older poetry) but on the verb (as frequently in the Battle of Maldon and other late texts). Holthausen accordingly rearranges ll. 3–4 as three lines, in order to make *bredu* alliterate:

> and þa bredu befo [burgum on innan],
> fira aldor,   þæt gefyrðrige
> þone writ[e]re,   wynsum cræfte, etc.

This gives almost too good a metrical form for a poem of the eleventh century.
7 his] Holthausen omits, for metrical reasons. 8 and] Holthausen reads
þæt for the MS. and, without comment, apparently through oversight.

NOTES ON THE RUTHWELL CROSS

The Ruthwell Cross] For a discussion of the cross and its runic inscription, see
Introd., pp. cxviii ff. References to "Rood" in the following notes are to
the Dream of the Rood, in the Vercelli Book. I,1] The first word is probably
to be restored as [on]geredæ. See Rood 39a, Ongyrede hine. I,3] Most edd.
restore [m]odig [fore allæ] men. There is no corresponding phrase in the Vercelli
Book text. I,4] According to Dickins-Ross, about thirty runes are missing
after the letters ug. Part of the lost matter is probably to be restored as
[b]ug[a ic ni dorstæ]; see II,2, below, and Rood 42b. Sweet reads buga ic ni
darste. II,1] With [Ahof] to be restored at the beginning, and so Sweet.
See Rood 44b. II,3–4] The second æ of Bismærædu cannot be justified
historically, and Ross, MLRev. XXVIII, 149ff., suggests Bismæradu as the
most likely form. Ross also suggests blodi for blodæ. Wülker had reported
blodi as the reading on the cross. The text of Rood 48 provides the proper
restoration of the gaps in ll. 3–4: ætgad[re]; ic [wæs] miþ blodæ [b]istemi[d].
II,5] According to Dickins-Ross, about forty runes are missing after the letters
bi. Most edd. restore bi[goten of], as in Rood 49a, but make no effort to restore
the rest of the passage. III,3–5] The proper restoration here is Ic þæt al
bi[heald]. S[are] ic w[æ]s mi[þ] so[r]gum gidræ[fi]d, h[n]ag [ic hweþræ], etc.
According to Dickins-Ross, there is room for about eighteen runes after h[.]ag,
or not quite enough to accommodate the whole of Rood 59b. IV,1] The last
word of this line is giwundad (not giwundæd, as Wülker reports); see Ross,
MLRev. XXVIII, 145, note 1. IV,3–4] To be restored as gistoddu[n] him
[æt his l]icæs [hea]f[du]m; [bih]ea[l]du[n h]i[æ] þe[r heafunæs], etc., following Rood
63b–64a. Dickins-Ross estimate that about forty runes are missing after þe,
but a more complete restoration is naturally impossible.

NOTES ON THE BRUSSELS CROSS

The Brussels Cross] For a discussion of this inscription, see Introd., pp. cxxiii ff.
2 byfigynde] For bifigende, present participle. On this form, see especially
D'Ardenne, English Studies XXI, 149–150. bestemed] An Anglian form;
see Introd., p. cxxiv. 3 beroþor] On the intrusive vowel e, see D'Ardenne,
English Studies XXI, 150–152, 271–272.

NOTES ON THE FRANKS CASKET

Franks Casket] For a discussion of the Franks Casket and its inscriptions, see
Introd., pp. cxxv ff. 1,1–3] Stephens, The Old-Northern Runic Monuments
I, 475, took hronæs ban, on the left-hand edge of the front side, together with fisc
flodu ahof, etc. So also Sweet, Eng. Stud. II, 314ff., and Wülker, reading
fiscflodu as a compound and taking hronæs ban as the object of ahof, "the fish-

flood cast the whale's bone," etc. But Hofmann, in Sitzungsberichte...der kgl. bayerischen Akademie I, 670, properly separated *hronæs ban* from the rest of the inscription and read *fisc flodu* as two words. So most later edd. **1,1** flodu ahof] If *flodu* is taken as a plural, we should expect the plural verb *ahofon*, and Kock, Anglia XLIII, 311, would read *ahofon*, taking the runes *ON* as representing both the verb-ending and the following preposition. Besides several Norse examples of this double use of runes, he cites Riddle, 19,5–6, where *WEGAR* (i.e. *rad* plus the four runes in l. 6, read backward) is sometimes taken as for *wīg-gār;* see the note on this passage, in Records III, The Exeter Book, pp. 331–332. A half-line *fisc flodu ahofon* would be abnormally long. But *flodu* is perhaps singular, and Sievers, Angels. Gram., §273, Anm. 4, explains it as a very old *u*-stem nom. sing., with the ending still preserved after a long vowel. So also Wadstein, The Clermont Runic Casket, p. 15.   on fergenberig] "On to the mainland" (Sweet, Eng. Stud. II, 315), or "on to the cliff-bank" (Wadstein, The Clermont Runic Casket, p. 16).   **1,2** warþ gasric grorn] Sweet, Eng. Stud. II, 315, Grienberger, Anglia XXVII, 445, and Kock, JJJ., p. 77, take *gasric* as referring to the ocean. According to Sweet, *gāsrīc* ("rager"? he compares O.N. *geisa*, "to rage") is the original form of *gārsecg*, "ocean." He would also translate *grorn* as "turbid," citing a similar transference of meaning in the verb *gedrēfed*, "turbid, sad." On the other hand, Wadstein, The Clermont Runic Casket, p. 17, believes that *gasric* refers to the whale. So also Holthausen, Anglia Beibl. XVI, 229f., Anglia Beibl. XXX, 4, and Bos.-Tol., Supplement, p. 283. Wadstein would take *gasric* as a metathesis of *gār-sīc* (= West Saxon *gārsēoc*), "spear-wounded." Whether or not we accept Wadstein's explanation of the word *gasric*, it is probably the whale, rather than the ocean, which is referred to here. Translate, "The whale became sad, where he swam on the shingle"—a normal reaction for a whale.   **2,1–3]** Some of the difficulties raised by this inscription are discussed in the Introd., pp. cxxviii f. Most commentators accept Napier's arrangement in three verse lines, which is followed in the text. But Wadstein, The Clermont Runic Casket, pp. 31ff., divides the inscription into three separate parts: (1) *Hēr hos sitæð on hærm-bergæ; āg-l[āc] drīgið swī(ð)*, "Here the horse sits on the sorrow-hill, suffers strong torment." (2) *Hiri erta*, "Her incitation" (apparently referring to the female figure in the right-hand group in the picture). (3) *Egis-graf, sǣr-den sorgæ and sefa-tornæ*, "The grave of awe, the grievous cave of sorrows and afflictions of mind." Wadstein's reading *swī(ð)*, at the end of his first passage, is based on a misreading (*i* for *æ*) of the incomplete photograph which he used. Viëtor reads: *Hēr ho[r]s sitæþ | on hærm-bergæ || āglā[c] drīgiþ swæ || h[ē]r is Ertaegis graf (? Erta egisgraf?) || sǣrdun sorgæ | and sefa-tornæ.* He translates: "Here the horse (Hors?) is sitting on the harm-hill. Woe he is suffering so. Here is Ertaegi's grave (? Erta's terror-grave?). They mourned in sorrow and heart-grief." See the notes on *Hos, hiri*, below, for the details of Viëtor's explanation.   **2,1** Hos] This may be a proper name, as suggested by Napier, p. 376. Wadstein, The Clermont Runic Casket, p. 33, takes it as for *ho[r]s*, "horse," and so Holthausen, Anglia Beibl. XVI, 230f. Grienberger, Anglia XXVII, 442, reads *hōs*, "cohors," translating, "hic cohors sedet ad tumulum

sepulcralem." Similarly Imelmann, Forschungen, p. 319. Viëtor, p. 7, takes
the eighth rune of the inscription (*I* with six strokes instead of the usual four)
as a ligature, *SI*, and then interprets the resulting *hosssîtæþ* as an error by the
carver for *hors sitæþ*.   sitæþ] The proper form of the verb would be *sitiþ;* see
drigiþ, l. 2.   **2,2a**] It is evident that something is lost after the letters *A G L*,
and the vertical stroke after *L* is probably part of a following letter; but there
does not seem to be enough room for *agl[ac]*, the most generally accepted restoration.   Besides, we might rather expect *agl[ag]*, on the evidence of *gisgraf* in
l. 2*b*.   Boer, Arkiv för nordisk filologi XXVII, 221, would restore to read
agl[a], as the Northumbrian acc. sing. (without -*n*; see Sievers, Angels. Gram.,
§ 276, Anm. 5) of a weak noun **agla* (**agle*), "affliction," cognate with Gothic
aglo.   Napier, p. 375, suggests *agl[æ]*, acc. sing. of a strong feminine **ægl*,
related to the adjective *egle*.   Whatever the proper reading, it is likely that the
carver made an error here and cut away everything after the vertical stroke.
2,2b hiri] For *hiræ*, "to her, upon her"?   Or an error for *him* (referring to the
masculine *hors*), as suggested by Jiriczek, Anz.fdA. XXIX, 200, note 2, and
Holthausen, Anglia Beibl. XVI, 230f.?   Viëtor would take the second *I* (with
five strokes, instead of the usual four) as a ligature, *IS*, and then, emending
hir to *her*, read *her îs Ertaegis graf*.   Boer, Arkiv för nordisk filologi XXVII,
224, would read *swæ hir is Erta* (gen. sing.) *egisgraf*, "da hier das traurige grab
Erta's ist."   This is similar to Viëtor's alternative reading.   Ertae] Evidently a feminine proper name.   Stephenson (in Napier, p. 375, note 5) suggests that *Ertae* is an error for *Erce*, the *eorðan modor* of Charm 1,51, and so
Holthausen, Anglia Beibl. XVI, 230f.   Grienberger, Anglia XXVII, 441,
reads *ertae = eorþe*, "terra," and translates, "quam ei terra imposuit."   Imelmann, Forschungen, pp. 321f., would read *ertan = ærtān*, "vorher bestimmtes
los."   Neither of these two suggestions is likely.   But if the proper form of the
word is *ertae*, it is not apparent why the carver used two runes instead of one
to represent the letters *A E*; see Introd., p. cxxix.   For Boer's reading *Erta
egisgraf*, see the preceding note.   gisgraf] If we read *gisgraf* here (and the
meter and alliteration favor it), it must be taken as for *gescráf*, preterite of
gescrīfan.   So Napier, pp. 374–375, and Grienberger, Anglia XXVII, 436ff.
Napier suggests that the carver was forced to cut *gisgraf* instead of *giscraf*
because he was using the *C*-rune for *A*.   **2,3** særden] The interpretation of
this word is complicated by the fifth rune, M, apparently used for *E* instead
of the usual *E*-rune of this inscription.   Reading *særden*, is this form to be
taken as a verb or as a noun?   Viëtor emends to *særdun*, "they mourned in
sorrow and heart-grief."   Napier, p. 375, suggests *sær dœn*, as the equivalent
of *sār (gi)dœ̄n*, "rendered miserable."   Grienberger, Anglia XXVII, 447, takes
særden as for *særde [i]n*, "exagitata illa in sollicitudine et cordis tribulatione."
Wadstein, The Clermont Runic Casket, pp. 42–43, reads *særden* as a noun,
"grievous cave."   So also Boer, Arkiv för nordisk filologi XXVII, 225.   Holthausen, Anglia Beibl. XVI, 230f., would emend to *særned* (= *sārnēd*).   In
Anglia XLI, 401f., he would read *sær end sorgæ*, "sorrow and care," and so also
Imelmann, Forschungen, pp. 323ff.   sorgæ and sefa tornæ] If *sorgæ* and *tornæ*
are gen. sing. (so Holthausen, Literaturblatt XXI, 212), we should expect

tornæs instead of *tornæ*. They may, however, be gen. plur. (and so Wadstein, The Clermont Runic Casket, pp. 42–43), or dat.-instr. sing. In *sefa*, the ligature *FA* has ᚠ instead of the rune ᚺ, which represents *A* elsewhere in this inscription. Napier, p. 372, suggests reading *sefu;* see Introd., p. cxxviii, note 5. But reading *sefa*, we have the weak gen. sing., with loss of final *-n*.

NOTES ON THE METRICAL CHARMS

Metrical Charms] For a discussion of these charms, see Introd., pp. cxxx ff. For convenience of reference, I list here the numerical correspondences between the present edition and the editions by Wülker and Grendon. (Charms 7 and 12 are omitted by Wülker.)

This edition	Wülker	Grendon
1	I	A13
2	IV	B4
3	VI	A2
4	II	A1
5	V.A	A22
6	VII	E1
7		B5
8	III	A4
9	V.C	A16
10	V.B	A21
11	VIII	A14
12		A3

1,2 on gedon] Grendon erroneously reads *ungedon*.   **1,8** anon] For *ānan,* "except the burdock alone." The ending in *-on* is frequent in the prose parts of this charm, but usually for *-um;* see *turfon*, l. 15, *ælcon*, l. 18, *siþon* (*siðon*), ll. 23, 24, etc.   **1,10** staðol] The under side of a sod; see Bos.-Tol., p. 912. **1,11** et ... and] Here and elsewhere in this charm the abbreviation & (usually in a Latin context) has been expanded as *et*, and 7 as *and*.   **1,12** terre] The proper form here would be *terram*, acc. sing., and so most edd. But in the present volume errors in the Latin are generally left uncorrected.   **1,13** sit] Here and in l. 81, *sit* is an error for *sitis*, 2d person plural, present subjunctive, or for *sint*, 3d person plural. Thorpe, Ettmüller, Rieger omit *sit* entirely, in both places; Grendon emends to *sitis*.   **1,15** and wende ... to ðan weofode] "And have the green part turned towards the altar," Grendon.   **1,27** domine] We should expect *dominum*. Grimm reads *dryhten* (see Deutsche Mythologie, 4th ed., II, 1034), and so Ettmüller; Rieger similarly reads *drihten*. But *drihten* occurs in the second half-line, and may not have been intended here. **1,30**] Holthausen, Anglia Beibl. XXXI, 116, would read *and ða soþan* [*mægð*] *sancta*[*m*] *Marian*. But in view of the popular nature of these charms it seems unnecessary to emend on metrical grounds.   **1,32–33**] Grendon's translation, "that I ... this spell may with my teeth dissolve," is highly questionable, and Skemp, MLRev. VI, 264, would translate simply as "that I may utter this charm" (that is, the charm which is being spoken). Similarly Klaeber, Anglia Beibl. XLII, 7. **1,35** gefyllan] So Grimm (see Deutsche Mythologie, 4th ed., II, 1034) and most edd., as parallel to *ontynan, aweccan,* etc. **1,36** se witega] The psalmist; see Shook, MLN. LV, 139. According to Shook, the reference here is to Psalm cxii (cxi in the numbering of the Vulgate). **1,37**] Holthausen, Anglia Beibl. XXXI, 30, would make a full line of l. 37*a*, taking *se þe ælmyssan* as the first half of another line, the rest of which is lost. But the arrangement in the text seems preferable. **1,38** drihtnes þances] "By the grace of the Lord." See *godes þonces,* Chronicle 883 E, 897 A, and the other examples cited by Bos.-Tol., p. 1036. **1,39** III] For *þriwa,* "thrice," as also in ll. 42, 81. **1,40–42**] On the significance of the Tersanctus, the Bene-dicite, the Magnificat, and the Pater Noster in a fertility charm, see Shook, MLN. LV, 140. **1,41** aþenedon earmon] "With outstretched arms." **1,42** hit] The prayer (ll. 26–38)? So Grendon takes it. **1,44** to are þam] For the MS. *þā are,* most edd. read *þam to are;* Wülker reads *are þam.* But the reading in the text, *to are þam,* gives a smoother reading and was most probably the scribe's intention. **1,48–49** borige þonne...finol] That is, "place in a hole bored in the plough-tail incense and fennel," etc. This meaning of *borian,* not elsewhere found, is recognized by Bos.-Tol., Supplement, p. 102. According to Magoun, Archiv CLXXI, 24, *beam* is for *sulhbeam.* **1,51** Erce, Erce, Erce] In accordance with Grimm's suggestion (see Deutsche Mythologie, 4th ed., I, 210) the word *Erce* has been generally taken as the name of a Germanic goddess of fertility, "mother of earth." See especially R. Jente, Die mytholo-gischen Ausdrücke im altengl. Wortschatz (Heidelberg, 1921), p. 110, and E. A. Philippson, Germanisches Heidentum bei den Angelsachsen (Leipzig, 1929), pp. 126–128. W. Seelmann, Jahrbuch des Vereins für niederdeutsche Sprach-forschung XLIX (1923), 55ff., following Grimm, would equate *Erce* with Frau Herke, a Low German goddess of fertility. A more cautious stand, however, is favored by J. de Vries, Altgermanische Religionsgeschichte I (Berlin, 1935), 250, and Grendon, p. 220, would see in this half-line only an incantatory phrase, "the meaning of which, if it ever had any, has been lost." **1,55** sceafta hehra] For the inexplicable *hen se* of the MS., Wülker reads *heries* (or *herges*), gen. sing. after *geunne,* that is, "a multitude of blades (of grain)." Schlutter, Anglia XXX, 125–128, would emend *hen se* to *herse,* "millet," a noun which is not elsewhere recorded in Anglo-Saxon but which would be cognate with O.H.G. *hirsi.* Schlutter would then read either *sceafta herses, scire wæstma,* or *sceafta scira hersewæstma,* with transposition of *scira* (for the MS. *scire*) and *herse.* Grendon also reads *sceafta scira hersewæstma,* "abundance of bright millet-harvests," but this transposition does violence to the alliteration. Holthausen. Anglia Beibl. XXXI, 116, would take *hen se* as a corruption of *hehra* (= *hēahra*), "of high blades." For the final *-e* of the MS. *hen se,* he compares the MS. *scire* (for *scirra*), l. 55*b*, and *þære* (for *þæra*), ll. 56, 57. In the absence of other evidence for an Anglo-Saxon noun *herse,* Holthausen's reading seems the best way out of the difficulty. **1,56** berewæstma] For metrical reasons, Holthausen, Anglia Beibl. XXXI, 116, would read *bærlicwæstma.* **1,58–59**] These two lines are rather short. In l. 58, Rieger suggests *arena* after *eorþan,* thus putting *eorþan* in the first half-line; in l. 59 he reads *Geunne him se alwalda, ece drihten*, as in l. 52. **1,60** and his halige] Holthausen, Anglia Beibl. XXXI, 116, would add *eac* after *halige*, for metrical reasons. **1,63** þara lyblaca] Rieger supplies *þe* after *þara*, and so also Cockayne, note, and Holthausen, Anglia Beibl. XXXI, 116, "[each] of those who sow witchcrafts throughout the land." But then *þara þe* would logically have to be parallel to *feonda*, l. 61, rather than to *bealwa*, l. 62. For this reason the MS. reading, with *þara lyblaca* parallel to *bealwa*, seems preferable. Translate ll. 62–63, "and [that] it be protected against each of all evils, [against] witchcrafts sown throughout the land." **1,72** innewerdre] So Grimm (see Deutsche Mythologie, 4th ed., II, 1035) and later edd., except Cockayne, for the MS. *Innewerdne*. Translate, "a loaf as broad as the inside of the hand." **1,80** corna gehwylc] "Every kind of grain." See Skemp, MLRev. VI, 264, who cites *ælces cynnes melo*, l. 72. **1,81** sit] See l. 13, note. **2,2** Regenmelde] This word is here taken as a place-name, following Bradley, Archiv CXIII, 144, and Magoun, Archiv CLXXI, 28–29. See *Alorforda*, more obviously a place-name, in l. 24. **2,4**] Apparently meaning, "Thou mayest avail against thirty-three evil spirits." The same thing is said of another herb (it is not clear which one) in l. 42. In both places, Holthausen, Eng. Stud. LXIX, 180f., reads *wið III[um] ond wið XXX[um]*, dat. plur., for metrical reasons. **2,6** þam laþan] So Hoops, p. 56, and Holthausen, Eng. Stud. LXIX, 180, here and in l. 20. See *þæm laðan*, l. 13. færð] Grattan, MLRev. XXII, 2, would read *færeð*, for metrical reasons. **2,8** openo] So Wülker and Grendon, for the MS. *opone*. **2,9a** ðe] Although it appears four times in ll. 9–10, the MS. *ðy, þy* cannot be instrumental and must be for *ðe, þe*, dat. sing. It is here emended in all four places, following Wülker and Grendon. crætu] The word *cræt*, "cart," is neuter, and Wülker, Grendon read *crætu, cræto*, for the MS. *cræte*. curran] Taken by Hoops, p. 56, note 3, and Grendon as preterite plural of *ceorran*, "to creak," rather than for *curdan, cyrdan* (from *cyrran*), as Wülker took it. See also Sievers, Angels. Gram., §388, Anm. 1. **2,9b** reodan] For *ridon*, "rode." **2,10** bryodedon] From *breodian*, "to cry out"; see Vainglory 28. **2,11b**] Holthausen, Eng. Stud. LXIX, 180, supplies *a*, "always," after *wiðstunedest*, for metrical reasons. In l. 13a, he supplies *eac* after *laðan*, likewise for metrical reasons. **2,14–16**] The interpretation of the MS. *stune*, l. 14, and *stiðe*, l. 16, has given the edd. some difficulty. For *stune*, which is perfectly clear in the MS., Cockayne and Grendon read *stime*, as the name of an herb; Cockayne III, 345, glosses *stime* as "nettle." Wülker suggests that *stune* (or *stime*) and *stiðe* are the names of two different plants; but as Bradley, Archiv CXIII, 145, points out, *heo* in l. 16 must refer to the herb which has been mentioned previously. Holthausen, Eng. Stud. LXIX, 180, emends *stune* to *stūrne*, but does not gloss the word. For other explanations of *stune*, see Introd., p. cxxxiv. **2,21–22**] If we take *fleoh* as intransitive, "fly (from)," with Grendon, these two lines are quite unintelligible. But the passage is brilliantly cleared up by Skemp, MLRev. VI, 300, who takes *fleoh* as transitive, "put to flight," citing Bos.-Tol., p. 292 (under *fleon* II). Then *seo læsse* and *seo mare* are nom. sing. feminine, agreeing with *attorlaðe*, while *ða maran* and *þa læssan* are acc.

plur. neuter, with *attru*, "poisons," understood. Skemp translates, "Thou Attorlade, conquer now the greater poisons, (though thou be) the lesser; thou, the mightier, conquer the lesser poisons; until the patient is cured of both (greater and lesser)." Holthausen, Eng. Stud. LXIX, 180, omits *beigra*. **2,24** geændadest] Grendon translates, "brought about." Klaeber, Anglia Beibl. XLII, 7, suggests that *geændadest* is an error for *geǣrendadest*, parallel to *ameldodest*, l. 23. But some such meaning as "prepared, arranged," seems preferable; see *renadest*, l. 2. **2,25** for gefloge] "On account of an infectious disease"; see Bos.-Tol., Supplement, p. 327. Holthausen, Eng. Stud. LXIX, 180, emends to *þæt for gefloge nænig feorh ne gesealde*. **2,29** ondan...to bote] "To heal the horror of other poison," Grendon. Holthausen, Eng. Stud. LXIX, 181, emends *ondan* to *ondgan*, from *andig*, "envious." **2,30**] This line has given rise to much conjecture. Wülker suggested that it was prematurely inserted here instead of after l. 44. Holthausen, Eng. Stud. LXIX, 181, rearranges ll. 30ff. considerably; see Introd., p. cxxxiv. But even so, the MS. *ongan* in l. 30 causes difficulties. Bradley, Archiv CXIII, 145, suggested a noun *onge* or *onga*, equivalent to O.N. *angi*, "sprout, shoot," but this interpretation still leaves the line with no verb. Grendon translates *ongan* as "fought," but in this case, as Holthausen, Anglia Beibl. XXXI, 117, points out, we should at least expect *ongunnon*. Holthausen would emend *ongan* to *magon*, citing ll. 19–20, 42, 45. This seems to be the best reading and is adopted in the text. **2,31** he man] So Wülker and Grendon, following Cockayne's suggestion. Grattan, MLRev. XXII, 2, thinks that the MS. *henan* needs no emendation, but merely respacing to *he nan*, "nought did he destroy." **2,33** on VIIII] "In nine pieces." **2,34–35**] Since *heo*, taken as feminine singular, cannot refer to either *æppel* (masc.) or *attor* (neut.), Wülker assumes the loss of a line after l. 34. But Bradley, Archiv CXIII, 145, would translate *geændade* as "brought about" (see l. 24, above), that is, "apple and poison brought about that she (the adder) nevermore would enter house." Similarly Grattan, MLRev. XXII, 3. Skemp, MLRev. VI, 300f., would take *and*, l. 34b, as a preposition, "against" (see Bos.-Tol., p. 39), i.e. "there Apple accomplished [this] against poison, that," etc., with *heo*, as in Bradley's interpretation, referring to the adder. Holthausen, Anglia Beibl. XXXI, 117, would emend l. 34 to read *þær geændade æppel wið nædran*, apparently taking *geændade* as meaning "spoke" (see Klaeber's comment on l. 24, above); in l. 35 Holthausen would read *nest* for the MS. *hus*, to provide alliteration. In Eng. Stud. LXIX, 181, Holthausen emends l. 35 (l. 44 in his numbering) to read *þæt heo næfre ne wolden nan hus bugan*, with *heo* evidently referring to the two nouns in l. 34b. But Bradley's interpretation still seems the best. **2,38** þa he hongode] That is, while he was hanging on the cross. See Hoops, p. 58, note 3, and Grendon, p. 228. **2,42**] See l. 4, note. **2,43b**] The MS. *and wið þæs hond wið frea begde* is meaningless, and the reading in the text follows Bradley, Archiv CXIII, 145. So also Grendon, who translates, "and against sudden guile." Grattan, MLRev. XXII, 3, reads *and wið freabregde* (translating, "against hand of fiend, and against mighty devices"), and so Holthausen, Anglia Beibl. XXIX, 284. No such compound as *frēabregd* is elsewhere found, but Bradley points out that there are synonymous compounds of *fær* (e.g. *færsearo*). **2,44** manra] So Bradley, Archiv CXIII, 145, and Holthausen, Eng. Stud. LXIX, 181, for the MS. *minra;* in Anglia Beibl. XVI, 228, Holthausen had proposed *mircra*, which is also acceptable. **2,45ff.**] Cockayne, Wülker print ll. 45–63 as prose, but Grendon properly as verse. See Grattan, MLRev. XXII, 3. **2,48** wedenan] Holthausen, Anglia Beibl. XXXI, 118, would read *hæwenan*, "blue," for the alliteration, and so also Gratton, MLRev. XXII, 3. The word *wedenan* ("bluish," see Holthausen, Anglia Beibl. XVI, 229) also appears in l. 50*b* and may well be an error here. **2,53** þystelgeblæd] So Cockayne and Grattan, MLRev. XXII, 3, for the MS. *þysgeblæd.* Holthausen, Eng. Stud. LXIX, 181, emends to *þyrsgeblæd.* In l. 54, Holthausen emends the MS. *ysgeblæd* to *ȳstgeblæd*, but he does not say what this word would mean. **2,55–56**] Grendon arranges ll. 55–56 as a single line, and Grattan, MLRev. XXII, 3, would omit *cume* at the end of l. 56*b*, describing it as "scribes' editing." Holthausen, Anglia Beibl. XXXI, 118, arranges as two lines, as in the text, adding *neahwian* after *norðan.* In Eng. Stud. LXIX, 181, he arranges the text similarly, but omits *attor.* Grattan suggests *genægan* in l. 56*b*. **2,58**] Cockayne suggested *adle*, for the MS. *alde*, and so Wülker, Grendon. In l. 58*b*, Wülker and Grendon read *ængan cundes* as two words. Bos.-Tol., Supplement, p. 17, taking *ængancundes* as a single word, glosses doubtfully as "in a way that is unique." Reading *adle* and *ængan cundes*, Grendon translates, "Christ stood over poison of every kind." But Grattan, MLRev. XXII, 4, would retain *alde*, and in l. 57*b* would emend to *ængancunde*, acc. plur. of an adjective. He translates, "Christ stood above the ancient ones, the malignant ones," i.e. the powers of Evil. **2,59–60**] Grendon prints ll. 59–60 as one line, but the arrangement in the text seems preferable. The addition of *nean* in l. 60*b* follows Holthausen, Anglia Beibl. XXXI, 118, and Eng. Stud. LXIX, 181; Grattan, MLRev. XXII, 3, suggests *nu.* In l. 60*a* Holthausen, Eng. Stud. LXIX, 181, reads *þa þa* for the MS. 7 *þa*, but *þær þa*, as in the text, gives a more satisfactory meaning. **2,64ff.**] Omitted by Wülker, but see Introd., p. cxxxiii, note 5. **3,3** Martimianus] So the MS., not *Martinianus* as reported by the edd. The scribe was undoubtedly confused by the name *Maximianus* which precedes. **3,5** cweð] Magoun, Archiv CLXXI, 21, suggests that *cweð* is an error for *cymð* or for *cweden is.* **3,6** bufan] Cockayne, Grendon read *ufan* for the MS. *hufan.* The emendation in the text, *bufan*, was suggested by Binz, Anglia Beibl. XXVII, 163. **3,9** spiderwiht] For the MS. *spiden wiht*, Wülker and Grendon read *spider wiht;* but we should perhaps expect Anglo-Saxon **spīþre* (from **spin-bre*), rather than *spīder.* In any case, the word is best taken as a compound. Holthausen, Anglia Beibl. XXXVI, 219, taking *in* as part of the compound, would read *inspiderwiht*, referring to the house spider. Grattan, MLRev. XXII, 4f., would emend to *inwriðen wiht*, "a creature all swathed," taking the spider out of the picture altogether. **3,10** haman] Grendon translates as "harness," and Grattan, MLRev. XXII, 4, as "bridle," both on the evidence of the context. Skemp, MLRev. VI, 294f., would take *haman* as referring to "a disguising covering." **3,11a**] The reading *legde þe*, as in the text, was proposed by Skemp, MLRev.

VI, 294, and is accepted by Holthausen, Anglia Beibl. XXXI, 118, and Grattan, MLRev. XXII, 4. Schlutter, Anglia XXX, 257, reads *Legeþ he*, beginning a new sentence, and so Grendon, who translates, "He puts his traces on thy neck." **3,11b]** Holthausen, Anglia Beibl. XXXI, 118, would arrange this as a full line, supplying *þa laþan* after *him*. But even with this change, we have double alliteration in the second half-line. **3,13 dweores]** Suggested by Binz, Anglia Beibl. XXVII, 163, as gen. sing. of *dweorh*. Holthausen, Anglia Beibl. XXXI, 118, makes a similar suggestion. Grattan, MLRev. XXII, 5f., would emend the MS. *deores* to *Eares*, as the name of a god (*Er*, preserved in the Bavarian *Ertag*, "Tuesday"). Grendon retains *deores*, translating, "the sister of the beast." Skemp, MLRev. VI, 295, would place l. 13 immediately after l. 10a, to avoid the awkward change of number at that point. The lack of alliteration in l. 13 and l. 15 suggests that something is wrong here (if indeed these lines ever had any alliteration), but the arrangement in the text seems to be the most satisfactory one. **3,14 geændade]** For *geærendade*, "spoke"? This suggestion was made by Klaeber, Anglia Beibl. XLII, 7; see the note on Charm 2, 24. **3,15 derian]** To provide alliteration, Holthausen, Anglia Beibl. XXXI, 118, suggests *eglan* (or, as an alternative, *dreorgan* for *adligan* in the first half-line). Grattan, MLRev. XXII, 6, reads *eglian* for *derian*. **4,1-2 þurh ærn]** "Through the house"? So most commentators. Skemp, MLRev. VI, 290f., would translate, "through the wall into the house." But Magoun, Archiv CLXXI, 19, is probably right in identifying *ærn* with the second element of *Rugern*, "rye-harvest, August" (see Holthausen, Altengl. etymol. Wörterbuch, under *ern* 2); he would translate it as "grain," that is, the red nettle "which grows through the grain." **4,4 land]** Ettmüller, Rieger emend to *eard*, to provide alliteration; Holthausen, Anglia Beibl. XXXI, 30, suggests as an alternative the emendation of *anmode*, l. 4a, to *leohtmode*. **4,5]** This line is very difficult to construe. Grendon, punctuating as in the text, translates, "Now shield thyself, that thou this onslaught mayst survive!" Sweet, evidently with a similar translation in mind, supplies *þæt* between *nu* and *þu*. Horn, in Probleme der englischen Sprache und Kultur, p. 89, suggests that we have here a conditional clause without an introductory conjunction, "if you wish to escape this enmity." But Grattan, MLRev. XXII, 1-2, would see only an implied condition in paratactic form: "Shield thou thee now; then mayest thou survive this onset." Holthausen, Anglia Beibl. XXXI, 30, would read *nið ðysne*, for metrical reasons. **4,7 Stod]** With *ic* to be supplied in sense. **under linde]** Not "under the linden (tree)," as Grendon seems to take it (see his remarks on p. 117), but "under the linden (shield)," parallel to *under ... scylde* in the second half-line. **4,11 fleogende flane]** The MS. has *fleo gende flañ*. Cockayne resolves the abbreviation *flañ* as *flane*, Rieger, Wülker, Grendon as *flanne*. The noun is usually masculine, but undoubted examples of its use as a feminine are given by Bos.-Tol., p. 291, and Supplement, p. 223. The word is therefore printed in the text as *flane*, acc. sing. fem., with *fleogende* as modifier. The masculine *oðerne*, l. 10, must refer to *gar* understood; see *garas*, l. 9. **4,13 Sæt smið]** There are several short half-lines in this passage, but it is very doubtful whether we should emend them in the interests of metrical regularity. Here Holthausen, Anglia Beibl. XXXI, 30, would supply *ana* after *smiδ*. **4,14**] The MS. reading *iserna wund swiδe* is obviously corrupt, but Rieger's emendation of *wund* to *wundrum* gives a plausible reading for the second half-line. Rieger would read *iserna [wraδost]* or *iserna [wrætlicost]* for l. 14a; Holthausen, Anglia Beibl. XXXI, 30, would read *[weard] iserna*, but does not explain what this would mean. Sweet emends *iserna* to *iserne*, explaining *iserne wund swiδe* as referring to the knife, "wounded with iron"; but he does nothing to fill out the line. **4,17a**] Grattan, MLRev. XXII, 2, would supply a second *ut*, for metrical reasons. Holthausen, Anglia Beibl. XXXI, 30, would read *ut, [lytel] spere*, as in l. 15a. **4,19** hit] Holthausen, Anglia Beibl. XXXI, 30, would emend to *hāt*, presumably as a noun, "heat shall melt it." But *hyt* in Beowulf 2649 is now generally regarded as a noun, "heat," and this may be what is intended here. The alternative is, of course, to take *hit* as the neuter pronoun, with *gemyltan* intransitive. **4,21**] Grimm supplied *oδδe wære on ban scoten* for the second half of this line; see Deutsche Mythologie, 4th ed., II, 1040. So also most edd. **4,22** næfre... atæsed] "May thy life never be injured." Here, as in l. 24b, we have a mixture of constructions, with the present instead of the preterite subjunctive which we should expect after *wære* in the hypothetical condition. **4,24** δin helpan] Holthausen, Anglia Beibl. XXXI, 117, would read *helpan δin*, for metrical reasons. **4,27–28a** Fleoh...Hal westu] The MS. has *fled þr̄ on fyrgen hæfde halwestu*. Rieger, Wülker read *hæfde hal westu* as l. 28a; Grimm (see Deutsche Mythologie, 4th ed., II, 1039f.), Ettmüller, Grendon read *heafde* for *hæfde*, and Grendon translates, "Be hale in head!" In l. 27, Grimm reads *fleo þær on fyrgen* as the first half-line and suggests *seo þone flan sceat* (or *sende*) for the second half-line; Ettmüller also reads *seo þone flan sende* for l. 27b, Bouterwek (Cædmon I, lxxxvii) and Grendon, *seo þa flane sende*. But *hæfde* (or *heafde*) more properly belongs in l. 27b; the resulting l. 28a, *hal westu*, is short, but not as short as *Ut, spere*, l. 17. Sweet, reading *hal wes-tu!* for l. 28a, prints *Fleo on fyrgenheafde* as his l. 27; this gives a short line here, as does also the proposal by Skemp, MLRev. VI, 292f., who would restore *Fleoh þær [flan] on fyrgen-heafde*, "fly there, arrow, to the mountain-headland." Holthausen, Anglia Beibl. XXXI, 117, would read *fleoh on fyrgen[stream]* for l. 27a, and for l. 27b suggests *þær þu friδu hæfdest*. Grattan, MLRev. XXII, 2, retaining the MS. *hæfde*, would read *fleah þær on fyrgen[holt; fyrst ne] hæfde*, "it hath fled there to the mountains; no respite it hath had." In l. 28a he would read *hal westu [nu]!* But Grattan's preterites *fleah* and *hæfde* interrupt the direct address in the other lines, and it seems probable that *fleoh* (for the MS. *fled*) and *heafde* (for the MS. *hæfde*) are the proper readings. In the text *fyrgenheafde* is taken as a compound (as in Sweet's reading), since uncompounded *fyrgen* does not occur elsewhere in Anglo-Saxon. **5,1** secge] Wülker suggests *sege, sæge*, from *sēon*, "to see." But the intended meaning here is "tell," i.e. "as soon as someone tells you that," etc. **5,3**] The metrical arrangement of this line is somewhat doubtful. Grendon prints it as two lines, the first ending in *buruh;* but he arranges Charm 10,3 as one line. In Charm 10,3 *geboren* might possibly be taken (ignoring *Crist* earlier in the same half-line) as alliterating with *Bethlem* and *burh,* but here in Charm 5 there is no alliterative link between the two half-lines. Magoun, Archiv CLXXI, 27, taking *acenned* as alliterating with *Crīst*, prefers the reading of Charm 5 to that of Charm 10. **5,15** nænige þinga] "In no way, by no means." **6,1** gewitenes mannes] Not "of a wise man," as Grendon translates, but "of a dead man" (from *gewītan*). **6,5** swærbyrde] The edd. follow the MS. *swært byr de,* and Grendon translates as "swart-birth," taking *swært-* as for *sweart,* "black." Bos.-Tol., Supplement, p. 716, glosses under *sweart-byrd,* but translates as "a dismal, hapless birth." The simple emendation to *swær-byrde,* "difficult birth," gives much better sense. **6,15** Crīste…gecyþed] "By Christ, I said, this has been made known!" **6,26** þihtan] This word, here and in l. 27, is unexplained. Grendon translates, "this great strong hero," apparently taking *maga* as an error for *magan,* from the adjective *maga,* "strong." Holthausen, Anglia Beibl. XXXI, 119, suggests that *þihtan* is for *þihtgan,* from *þȳhtig,* "strong." He also suggests reading *maguþihtgan* as a compound. But since we have *þihtan* twice here, the form may be genuine and the corruption may lie somewhere else. Under these circumstances, the text is left unaltered. **7,1** on] The text of this charm shows two abbreviations which are not generally used by Anglo-Saxon scribes: *ō* for *on,* here and in ll. 13, 14 (*ō bere* for *onbere*), and *ꝺ solde* for *consolde,* l. 6. **7,10–12a**] Magoun, Archiv CLXXI, 29, explains the verbs in these lines as subjunctive forms with late *-an* for *-en,* in a hortatory use. **7,11** waxsian] The MS. has *wa∞ sian.* The letter following *wa* is read by Leonhardi and Grendon as *co,* i.e. *waco sian* (and Grendon translates, "nor be filthy wounds"); but it may equally well be a rounded form of *x,* although no other *x* of such a shape occurs in this part of the MS. The word *waxsian* makes excellent sense here and is adopted in the text. Grimm (see Deutsche Mythologie, 4th ed., II, 1040) reads *waxian.* **7,12** halewæge] "Holy, or hallowed, cup," as referring to the vessel in which the remedy is brought? On this word see especially Magoun, Archiv CLXXI, 29. **7,13** on eare] Magoun, Archiv CLXXI, 29, would translate "in the ear," and take *eorþan* as referring to a warm poultice of mud applied to the ear. Grendon's translation, "Then it will pain you no more than it pains the land by the sea," is much less likely. **7,14–15** Eorþe:…mægenum] "May the earth diminish thee (the wound?) with all her powers." **8,3**] According to Wülker, *funde* is optative, but he does not say how he would translate. Zupitza, Anglia I, 192, more properly takes it as a variant form of the indicative *fand.* See *onfunde,* Beowulf 750, 809, 1497. **8,5** æminde] "Forgetfulness"? So Grendon, following Zupitza, Anglia I, 193. Bos-Tol., Supplement, p. 16, glosses *æmynde,* "want of care (?), neglect." But Magoun, Archiv CLXXI, 22f., explains the word as meaning "malevolence." So previously Cockayne, "malice." J. R. Clark Hall, Concise Anglo-Saxon Dictionary (3d ed.), p. 8, glosses *æmynd,* "jealousy." **8,6**] The meaning of this line is rather uncertain. Grendon translates, "and against the mighty spell of man," taking *tungan* as referring to a spoken incantation. But Meissner, Anglia XL, 375ff., questions the interpretation of *micel* as "mighty, powerful." Wülker construes as "*þa tungan micelan mannes* (= *domini*?)." Meissner, p. 379, also takes *micelan mannes* together, "the tongue of the great man," explaining "the great man" as a taboo-designation for a bear. But we should then expect the pronoun form *þæs* rather than *þa* in l. 6*a*. Magoun, Archiv CLXXI, 22f., reverts to the older interpretation, "gegen die grosse (kräftige, zauberredende) Menschen-zunge." 8,7 wiðöon] The MS. has *wið on*. Cockayne would place *and wið on* in the preceding sentence, translating *on* as "displeasure"! Zupitza, Anglia I, 193, suggests reading *wiððon*, "on the contrary." Wülker would transpose to read *Wið ðon þonne* (or *þæt*) *hi swirman, forweorþ ofer greot and cweð*. Sweet, Grendon omit *And wið on* altogether. Zupitza's *wiððon* gives good sense and is adopted in the text. See Menologium 146. 8,10 wilde] Taken by most edd. as the adjective, "wild." Grendon translates, "Never fly wild to the woodland!" 9,1–2] The MS. has *ma* and *drihten*, not *na* and *drihen* as re-ported by Wülker. 9,1 Ne forstolen...nanuht] With *sy, sie* to be supplied in sense, "May nothing be stolen or concealed." Magoun, Archiv CLXXI, 26, would supply *sy* in the text. 9,2 mihte] With "hide" to be supplied in sense. Grendon translates, "any more than Herod could [steal or hide] our Lord." Eadelenan] That is, apparently, *Ēad-Elenan*, referring to St. Helena, the mother of Constantine. As Magoun, Archiv CLXXI, 26, points out, the use of *Ēad-* as a prefix in a non-English personal name is highly unusual. 9,4 oðfeorrganne] For *oðferianne*. 9,10] The punctuation in the text, with a new sentence in l. 10, follows Magoun, Archiv CLXXI, 26. Translate, "May he (that is, the thief) never have any land, because he leads it away." Compare l. 13*b*. 9,14 cunne ic his mihta] "May I know his powers"; see Magoun, Archiv CLXXI, 26. 9,16–18] For the arrangement of ll. 16–18, see Magoun, Archiv CLXXI, 26. In l. 16*b*, Cockayne suggested *fyer* (= *fyr*) for the MS. *syer*, and Grendon translates, "as fire destroyeth wood"; but *weornian* is not generally transitive. Magoun's reading *syre* (= *siere*, "sere") gives the re-quired sense. In l. 17*a*, the edd. have had trouble with the MS. *þeo* (as in Grendon's translation, "as bramble or as thistle injures thigh"); but the emenda-tion to *seo* (= *sie*, present subjunctive) removes the difficulty. This emendation was suggested in Bos.-Tol., Supplement, p. 759 (under *briþel*, "fragile, weak, perishable"). Translate, "May he wither away entirely, as dry wood withers away, may [he] be as perishable as thistle [wool], he who," etc. 10,1 man forstolenne] With *hæfð* or *hafað* to be supplied in sense. 10,3] On the metrical arrangement of this line, see Charm 5,3, note. 10,6 per crucem Christi] Here and in l. 13, corresponding to *þurh þa haligan Cristes rode* in Charm 5. 10,7–10] In these lines the scribe has written *in* instead of the proper *.iii.* (= *þriwa*); this is evident not only from *þriwa* in l. 6 but also from the corresponding text in Charm 5. Grendon emends to *III* in all three places; the earlier edd. retain *in*. 10,10] After *cweð*, Magoun, Archiv CLXXI, 27, would supply *Crux Christi ab aquilone reducat* from Charm 5. 11,1 gyrde] Schlutter, Anglia XXXI, 60, interprets as "cross," and so Grendon, doubtfully. The suggestion by Stopford Brooke, History of Early English Literature I (London, 1892), p. 341, that *gyrd* here refers to an "ancient rune-stick," is hardly tenable. It seems best to translate the word simply as "staff" (and *sigegyrd*, l. 6, as "protecting staff"), though exactly what kind of staff is re-ferred to here is not certain. Holthausen, Anglia Beibl. XL, 89, and Anglia

Beibl. XLI, 255, would interpret as "walking-stick"; Klaeber, Anglia Beibl. XL, 283f., suggests a ceremonial staff of some kind.   beluce] To be taken with *wið*, ll. 2ff.: "By means of this staff I protect myself...against," etc. See l. 39, below, and Psalm 34,3,2 in the Benedictine Office.   helde] Dat. sing. of *hyld*, "protection." Translate, "and commend myself to the protection of God."   **11,2a** sara] Grammatical correctness would require *saran* here, and also *saran*, l. 2*b*, *grymman*, l. 3, and *micelan egsan*, l. 4. Holthausen, Anglia Beibl. XL, 88, emends accordingly; Wülker and Grendon emend in ll. 3–4, but retain *sara* in both halves of l. 2. But the inflectional endings are so carelessly handled in this poem that it seems advisable not to emend for grammatical reasons. See also *inna* for *innan*, l. 41.   **11,5** lað] Holthausen, Anglia Beibl. XL, 88, emends to *laðe*, but in Anglia Beibl. XLI, 255, would retain *lað* as a noun.   land] We should expect *lande*, and so Ettmüller, followed by Schlutter, Anglia XXXI, 59, and Holthausen, Anglia Beibl. XL, 88.   **11,7** Se me dege] "May it avail me"?   Grendon translates, "May they potent be." The form *dege* may perhaps be taken as for *dēage*, an analogical present subjunctive form of *dugan*, used instead of the proper form *duge*. Holthausen, Anglia Beibl. XL, 88, emends to *duge*. For metrical reasons, Holthausen supplies *wel* before *duge*, following Ettmüller. Schlutter, Anglia XXXI, 59, supplies *þæt* at the beginning of l. 8.   **11,8** mere ne gemyrre] So Holthausen, Anglia Beibl. XXXI, 30, taking *mere* as for *mǣre*, "nightmare"—evidently the proper meaning. Ettmüller, Wülker, Grendon emend to *mērra gemyrre*, but Grendon translates *mērra* as "nightmare demon."   maga] Probably the Anglo-Saxon noun *maga*, "maw, belly" (and so Grendon, "belly fiend," and Schlutter, Anglia XXXI, 61), but Holthausen, Anglia Beibl. XL, 88f., takes it as the Latin noun *maga*, "enchantress." Earlier, Holthausen, Anglia Beibl. XXXI, 119, had taken it as the adjective *maga*, "the strong one," but this seems very improbable.   **11,9a** The two datives, *me* and *minum feore*, are open to suspicion, and Holthausen, Anglia Beibl. XL, 88f., supplies *on* before *minum feore*, "that [it], dreadful, may never come to me in my life." As an alternative, he suggests the omission of *me*.   **11,10** ælmihtig] Holthausen, Anglia Beibl. XXXI, 31, suggests emending to *fæder*, to provide alliteration, and so also in his text, Anglia Beibl. XL, 88.   **11,12ff.**] Holthausen, Anglia Beibl. XXXI, 119, omitting the punctuation after *scyppende*, would insert *gedon* in l. 13, emending the names to read *Abram* [*gedon*] *and Isaac*. His interpretation, then, is (ll. 10ff.): "but may [God] guard me...just as I have heard that [he] has guarded Abraham and Isaac," etc. For a further justification of this arrangement, see Anglia Beibl. XLI, 255. The traditional punctuation, with a period after *scyppende*, l. 12, is followed in the text. See also Klaeber, Anglia Beibl. XL, 284. Properly, we should have the acc. sing. forms *Abram* and *Isaac* in l. 13*a*, parallel to the other objects of *clipige* in ll. 14ff., but apparently the MS. readings are only another instance of the poet's carelessness in grammatical matters; see *Saharie* and *Marie*, l. 17, and l. 2*a*, note, above.   **11,14** swilce men] Holthausen, Anglia Beibl. XXXI, 119, emends to *men swilce*, with no punctuation after *swilce*, "and men such as Moses and Jacob."   **11,15**] Holthausen, Anglia Beibl. XXXI, 119, omits

and before *Dauit*, and for l. 15*b* would supply *and Daniel.* **11,17** Saharie]
Cockayne, Grendon translate as "Sarah," and Holthausen, Anglia Beibl.
XXXI, 31, explains the form *Saharie* as influenced by the name *Marie* which
follows; but in Anglia Beibl. XL, 89, Holthausen identifies *Saharie* (which he
emends to *Sacharie*) with Zacharias, the father of St. John the Baptist. **11,18**
gebroþru] Holthausen, Anglia Beibl. XL, 88f., emends to *apostolas*, pointing
out that Peter and Paul were not brothers and that *gebroþru* disturbs the
alliteration. But for a defence of the MS. reading, see Magoun, Archiv CLXXXI,
25. **11,19** þusend] Holthausen, Anglia Beibl. XXXI, 119, would read
þusendu, for metrical reasons. þinra] Grendon translates the MS. *þira
engla* as "of the angels," but the form *þira* is questionable, and it seems better
to emend to *þinra.* Holthausen, Anglia Beibl. XXXI, 119, would retain
þira as a variant of *þinra*, citing Sievers, Anglia XIV (1892), 144. **11,21a**]
Holthausen, Anglia Beibl. XXXI, 31, would read *Hi me friþion and ferion*
for this half-line. Ettmüller had previously transposed the two verbs. The
verbs in ll. 21–22 are of course subjunctive, "May they convey me and protect
me," etc. **11,22b** me gewealdon] So most edd., for the MS. *men gewealdon.*
Holthausen, Anglia Beibl. XXXI, 31, would supply *eal* before *me*, as in l. 22*a*,
for the alliteration. **11,23** worces] For *weorces*? Or, as Holthausen, Anglia
Beibl. XL, 89, takes it, for *wærces*, gen. sing. of *wærc*, "pain"? The verb
stirende is from *stēoran*, "to restrain" (with genitive of the thing); here it probably means "protecting from (pain)." **11,24** hand ofer heafod] "A protecting
hand." So Schlutter, Anglia XXXI, 59, and Skemp, MLRev. VI, 296. Tupper, JEGPh. XI, 97ff., would see here a reference to the Germanic rite of com-
mendation; he cites Wanderer 41ff. and Maxims I, 67, and translates: "May
mine be hope of glory,...Sovereign protection, and the shelter of saints..."
A closer parallel, Psalm 138,3,3–4, is pointed out by Holthausen, Anglia Beibl.
XL, 89. rof] This word, as it stands in the MS., is difficult to explain.
Skemp, MLRev. VI, 296, suggests that it is an error for *hrof*, translating,
"a protecting cloud of saints." Schlutter, Anglia XXXI, 59, assumes a noun
rōf, "number," cognate with O.H.G. *ruoba.* Grendon translates as "choir."
Holthausen, Anglia Beibl. XXXI, 120, emends to *werod*, which gives excellent
sense. But in Anglia Beibl. XL, 88f., Holthausen retains *rof*, explaining it
either as the adjective, modifying *sceolu* in the next line, or as a noun, with
Schlutter. In his Altengl. etymol. Wörterbuch, p. 263, Holthausen accepts
a noun *rōf*, "number, series." **11,25** sceolu] For the MS. *sceote*, Schlutter,
Anglia XXXI, 60, reads *sceole*, Holthausen, Anglia Beibl. XXXI, 31, *sceolu*,
"troop." See Christ 928. **11,26** bliðu] For *bliðe*, instr. sing.? Most edd.
emend to *bliðum*, dat. sing. See l. 2*a*, note. **11,27a**] The MS. reading,
þ me beo hand ofer heafod mathe us helm, etc., is probably due to a reminiscence
of l. 24*a*, and Ettmüller, note, and Grendon omit *hand ofer heafod.* So also
Holthausen, Anglia Beibl. XXXI, 120, and Anglia Beibl. XL, 88. **11,28**
leoht, lifes rof] Grendon reads *leoht-lifes rof* and translates, "a bright life's
covering," taking *rof* as for *hrof.* Holthausen, Anglia Beibl. XXXI, 31, 120,
and Anglia Beibl. XL, 88, emends *rof* to *hrof.* In the present text *rof* is taken
as an adjective. **11,30** wælgar] Following the identification of the four

evangelists with weapons of defence, we expect the *Serafhin* (taken by the poet as a singular) to represent a weapon also. Holthausen, Anglia Beibl. XXXI, 31, therefore emends the MS. *wega* to *wælgar;* in Anglia Beibl. XL, 88ff., he would read *wegar*, as for *wēggār* (compare *wægsweord*), citing the runes *WEGAR* in Riddle 19,5–6; see the note on this passage in Records III, The Exeter Book, pp. 331–332. If an emendation is to be made, *wælgar* seems preferable. The attempts to preserve the MS. *wega* are very unsatisfactory; Grendon translates, "the Seraph of journeys," as referring to St. John. **11,31 gefare]** Holthausen, Anglia Beibl. XXXI, 31, reads *gefēre*, for metrical reasons. **11,32 eall]** We should expect *eallne*, acc. sing. masc., and so Holthausen, Anglia Beibl. XL, 89. **11,33–34]** The MS. has *bidde ic nu god sið fæt godne*, with *sigere* and *godes miltse* written above in the same hand. The comma-shaped mark, which serves the purpose of the modern caret, is inserted after *nu*, but whether this mark applies to all three of the added words, or only to *sigere*, is not clear. The edd. read the MS. as *bidde ic nu sigere godes miltse god*. Ettmüller, emending *sigere* to *sigores*, reads *bidde ic nu god sigores, godes miltse*, apparently taking *miltse* as gen. sing., parallel to *sigores*. Wülker reads *Bidde ic nu god, sigeres godes miltse* ("I ask the compassion of the god of victories"?). Holthausen, Anglia Beibl. XXXI, 120, and Anglia Beibl. XL, 89, emends to read *Bidde ic nu sigeres god sinre miltse*, with *sinre miltse* gen. sing., object of *Bidde*. The reading in the text is Grendon's; it assumes that the scribe meant to add *sigere* after *nu* and *godes miltse* after *god;* with the emendation of *sigere* to *sigeres*, it gives an adequate but not wholly satisfactory meaning. **11,34ff.]** Holthausen, Anglia Beibl. XXXI, 120, emends to *siðfætes godes, smyltes and leohtes* in l. 34, as genitive objects of *Bidde*, l. 33; see the preceding note. In ll. 35–36*a* he emends more extensively to read *windes on wederum, wēgas* (gen. sing.) *geferan, sincendes wætres*. Wülker had previously read *wind wederum* in l. 35*a*. Binz, Anglia Beibl. XXVII, 163, emends the MS. *werepum* doubtfully to *werodum*, but does not explain what his reading would mean. Holthausen's reading in Anglia Beibl. XL, 89, is similar to his earlier one, but has *windes on warepum*, l. 35*a*, and *circindes wæteres*, l. 36*a*. The verb *biddan* usually takes a genitive of the thing asked, but for the accusative in this construction see Bos.-Tol., Supplement, p. 90 (under *biddan* III a 2); we should, however, expect *æt* or *to* in l. 33*a*. Wülker, Grendon retain *siðfæt godne* in l. 34*a*, and emend to *smyltne and lihtne* in l. 34*b*. The reading in the text, with *windas on waropum* in l. 35*a*, parallel to *siðfæt godne*, seems to give a plausible meaning without excessive emendation. The repetition of *windas* in l. 35 is open to question, but it is not impossible in such a text as this; it is at least not much worse than *wind...windas* in the MS. **11,36 circinde]** Schlutter, Anglia XXXI, 56ff., would assume a verb *circian*, "to turn," a derivative of *cierran*. As an alternative, Skemp, MLRev. VI, 296, suggests *cercinde*, from *cearcian*, "to crash, gnash," i.e. "the crashing water." Holthausen, Anglia Beibl. XL, 89–90, reads *circindes wæteres*, citing Mod. Eng. *chirk* (N.E.D.). But there is no alliteration in this line, and Holthausen, Anglia Beibl. XXXI, 31, suggests emending to *swiðrendes wæteres* (gen. sing.; see the preceding note). In Anglia Beibl. XXXI, 120, he would emend to *sincendes* *wæteres.* simble gehælede] So Wülker, note, and Grendon, for the MS *simbli gehalepe.* Holthausen, Anglia Beibl. XXXI, 31, would read *simble me gehealde,* apparently with *sigeres god,* l. 33, as subject, "may he always guard me." In Anglia Beibl. XL, 89, he reads *cwicne gehealde,* to alliterate with *circindes* in the first half-line; see the preceding note.   **11,37** gemete] Subjunctive, as in l. 31.   Grendon translates, "may I meet with friends."   **11,38**] As it stands in the MS., *þ ic on þis ælmih gian on his friö wunian mote,* this line is hopeless metrically.   Wülker suggested the addition of *wære* after *ælmihtgian,* for alliteration, but this does nothing to cure the metrical difficulties.   Schlutter's reading, Anglia XXXI, 60, with the transfer of *halre hand* from l. 41a to l. 38a, after *ælmihtgian,* also ignores metrical considerations.   Grendon emends *þis* to *þæs,* but otherwise preserves the MS. reading; his translation, "That I may dwell in the Almighty's sheltering care," is obviously what we expect here. The reading in the text, with *þæs* for *þis* and with *on his* omitted, seems quite satisfactory except for the lack of alliteration.   The emendation by Holthausen, Anglia Beibl. XXXI, 32, and Anglia Beibl. XL, 89, *þæt ic on wære godes wunian mote,* gives the desired alliteration but is rather violent.   **11,39** þam] So Wülker, Grendon, and Holthausen, Anglia Beibl. XL, 89, for the MS. *þa,* following Cockayne's suggestion. See Charm 2,6 and note.   eht] For *ēhteö,* with genitive object, "who pursues my life."   **11,40** blæd] Holthausen, Anglia Beibl. XL, 89, reads *blæde,* the proper form of the dat. sing.   gestaþelod] Skemp, MLRev. VI, 297, supplies *bliöe,* Holthausen, Anglia Beibl. XL, 89, supplies *æfre* before *gestaþelod,* to fill out the line.   **11,41** inna] For *innan;* see l. 2a, note.   halre hand] "(In) the secure protection"?   As possible emendations of *halre,* Holthausen suggests *hælres,* "of the Saviour" (Anglia Beibl. XXXI, 32), *halgan* (Anglia Beibl. XL, 90), or *hea(h)re* (Anglia Beibl. XLI, 255).   heofna rices] The word *ölæd,* in the MS. after *rices,* is probably an unconscious repetition of *blæd* in l. 40a, and is omitted by Skemp, MLRev. VI, 297, and Holthausen, Anglia Beibl. XL, 89, following Cockayne's suggestion. **12,1** wenchichenne] Undoubtedly to be translated as "little wen," with Birch and Grendon.   The second element is explained by Zupitza, ZfdA. XXXI, 47f., as for Anglo-Saxon *cīecen,* "chicken."   The palatalization of the second *c,* though it would appear to be the normal development, is not found elsewhere. The nouns in this line are nom.-voc. sing., with the Middle English inorganic final *e.*   Magoun, Archiv CLXXI, 21, regards *wenchichenne* as corrupt, and doubtfully suggests the emendation *wende ic heone[ne],* "Wen, wen, I send (you?) away."   **12,3** eonene] For *heonan,* "hence."   to þan nihgan berhge] "To the near-by hill" (Grendon), with *berhge* for Anglo-Saxon *beorge.*   Birch's translation, "to the nearest town," with *berhge* for the feminine *byrig,* seems less probable; see Zupitza, ZfdA. XXXI, 48.   **12,4** ermig] For *erming,* "poor wretch."   Zupitza, ZfdA. XXXI, 48, compares the development of *pening,* "penny," to *penig.*   **12,6** wolues] So Grendon, for the MS. *uolmes.*   The spelling *uolues* would be less probable, since *u* is used for initial *f* in *ueþer,* l. 6b, but not for initial *w* anywhere in this charm.   **12,9** alswa scerne awage] The MS. *scesne* is obviously corrupt, and Grendon reads *scearn,* "muck, filth." The form in the text, *scerne* (with Middle English inorganic final *e;* see l. 1, note), is, however, closer to the MS. reading. Magoun, Archiv CLXXI, 22, reads *scern* without the *e*. Zupitza, ZfdA. XXXI, 48f., explains *awage* as for *on wāge* ("on the wall"?). So also Binz, Anglia Beibl. XXVII, 163, and Magoun, Archiv CLXXI, 22. Grendon's translation, "in the stream," presupposes Anglo-Saxon *on wæge*, but *æ* appears uniformly as *e* in this charm; see *nenne*, l. 2, *þer*, l. 4, *enne*, l. 4, etc.   **12,10** anbre] For *ambre*, dat. sing. of *amber*, "pail, pitcher."   **12,11** linsetcorn] For *linsædcorn*, "a grain of linseed." **12,12** hupeban] Explained by Magoun, Archiv CLXXI, 21, as a Norman spelling of *hypebān*, with *u* for *y*; or alternatively as from the unumlauted form *hupbān*. For *hupbān* beside *hypebān*, see Bos.-Tol., p. 582.